# European Politics

# European Politics

Edited by Hay and Menon

OXFORD
UNIVERSITY PRESS

# OXFORD

UNIVERSITY PRESS

Great Clarendon Street, Oxford OX2 6DP

Oxford University Press is a department of the University of Oxford.
It furthers the University's objective of excellence in research, scholarship,
and education by publishing worldwide in

Oxford New York

Auckland Cape Town Dar es Salaam Hong Kong Karachi
Kuala Lumpur Madrid Melbourne Mexico City Nairobi
New Delhi Shanghai Taipei Toronto

With offices in

Argentina Austria Brazil Chile Czech Republic France Greece
Guatemala Hungary Italy Japan Poland Portugal Singapore
South Korea Switzerland Thailand Turkey Ukraine Vietnam

Oxford is a registered trade mark of Oxford University Press
in the UK and in certain other countries

Published in the United States
by Oxford University Press Inc., New York

British Library Cataloguing in Publication Data
Data available

Library of Congress Cataloging in Publication Data
Data available

Typeset by Laserwords Private Limited, Chennai, India
Printed in Great Britain
on acid-free paper by
CPI Bath Ltd, Bath

ISBN 978-0-199284-28-3

10 9 8 7 6 5 4 3 2 1

# Table of Contents

# Detailed Contents

## Part One  Politics in European States                1

### 1  Germany                                          3
*John Bendix*

### 2  France                                           17
*Robert Elgie*

### 3  Italy                                            31
*David Hine*

# Introduction

COLIN HAY AND ANAND MENON

## Politics in Europe

Whether it be the latest crisis confronting the European Union (EU), or events within other European states, or attempts by those states to work together to secure their broader international objectives, 'Europe' has become a political reality for its citizens. The central purpose of this book is to enable those with little or no knowledge of the politics of the 'old continent' to begin to understand them. It is designed for students, and is intended to provide basic knowledge about not only the individual European states, but also the broader themes and issues that characterise and shape contemporary European politics.

From some perspectives, such an undertaking may seem curious. According to its more extreme proponents, globalisation—the impact of trade, of technological change, of massive international capital flows, of the erosion of borders in the construction of a 'global' village, in short, of the 'end of geography' (O'Brian 1992)—has served to render largely irrelevant studies of national or even regional politics.

Yet, for all these far-reaching claims, more nuanced analyses of the reality of 'globalisation' cast doubt upon such sweeping generalisations. In particular, they point to the strong economic effects exerted by geography; a distance of 2,500 miles reduces trade by 82 per cent, equity flows by 69 per cent and foreign direct investment by 44 per cent (Hirst and Thompson 2002: 258). Moreover,

analysis reveals a strong regional concentration of trade of the individual EU states (Tsoukalis 1997: 227–8).

So Europe is a reality in economic terms. Equally importantly, it represents an idea that is taken seriously by political actors. Talk of a 'European model', or of the notion of a 'return to Europe' in those countries on the eastern side of the Iron Curtain, along with the increasing tendency on the part of national governments to work together with their neighbours and look for 'European' solutions to common problems helps to make a reality of the notion of 'European politics'.

More broadly, in intellectual terms, the study of politics in a region provides a middle ground between two extremes commonly found in the political science literature. On the one hand, there are proponents of universalist social science, anxious to apply general concepts to politics the world over, and relatively insensitive to national or regional differences. On the other, there are those who emphasise uniqueness over commonalities, whose focus on politics in specific countries or regions blinds them to common responses to common pressures, or to evidence of convergence between different political systems. An emphasis on the politics of a region allows us to both appreciate the global and regional level dynamics that affect politics, while nevertheless remaining conscious of the different natures and trajectories of politics within the individual states.

None of this is, of course, to suggest that Europe is an easy or a stable concept. Indeed, the end of the Cold War and the liberation of the states of Central and Eastern Europe altered 'world politics from centrally organised, rigidly bounded environments that are hysterically concerned with impenetrable boundaries, to ones in which territorial, ideological, and issue boundaries are attenuated, unclear and confusing' (Katzenstein 2005: 11). This fluidity has been exemplified by the debates surrounding, and the progress of, EU enlargement (and indeed one of the confusing things about 'Europe' is the way in which it tends to be—wrongly—conflated with the borders of the European Union). If, as Tim Haughton (Chapter 9) claims, those wanting to understand contemporary Europe need to adjust their mental maps to take account of the emergence of Central and Eastern Europe, they equally need to ensure those maps are flexible enough to deal with forthcoming debates about the possible EU membership not only of Turkey and the western Balkans but also Ukraine and Georgia. Europe, therefore, may be a reality, but it is one whose precise nature and borders are changing and hotly contested.

# The Book

The book is intended to provide a detailed and comprehensive introduction to politics in contemporary Europe. It blends an analysis of individual nation states, and groups of states, with an examination of the critical substantive issues that confront them all, and which are addressed comparatively. It is structured in such a way as to take account of both the national and transnational/international factors that affect and are affected by politics in Europe—notably, though not exclusively, European integration and globalisation.

All the chapters in the volume are organised in a similar way: each begins with a reader's guide, laying out the basic structure to follow. Each highlights key terms useful to understand and explain the subject at hand as well as identifying useful websites and further reading. A list of key points summarises each substantive section and each chapter ends with a list of questions the reader should be able to address having digested its contents.

The book has deliberately been structured very much like an introductory course on European politics. Part 1 provides basic information about, and the essential debates concerning, the states of Europe and the European Union. Familiarity with the basics of the individual states is necessary in order that students be able more easily to discuss and reflect on the comparative themes that follow. Each chapter provides a self-contained summary of each political system or group of systems, which can be used as reference points and revision guides for the student reader. These chapters provide the crucial background knowledge of the systems they describe. After initially describing the political institutions and practices of each polity (or group of polities) and locating these in their appropriate historical context (and one of the lessons of the book is the degree to which history has shaped political institutions and practice in the various European states), they identify key episodes and themes in the post-war development of each case, pointing in particular to their changing position with respect to the EU and Europe more broadly. They also identify key contemporary controversies which animate the polity, indicating, in so doing, something of the character of political debate in each national setting. Each chapter also contains basic background data.

These chapters are supported by the OUP website that accompanies the volume with a whole series of useful statistics and data. This provides information on population size, capital city, principal cities, principal political parties, political structure, system of representation, current government, nature of the electoral system, outcomes of recent elections, turnout levels, scale of representation in the European Parliament, gross domestic product (GDP) per capita along with average rates of unemployment, inflation and union density over the last ten years, system of wage-bargaining, and a series of key historical dates (key elections, extensions of the franchise, membership of the European Community (EC)/EU, European Monetary Union (EMU), key referenda dates and so forth).

Part 2 explores political dynamics in Europe, investigating the nature and development of the European Union before proceeding to an analysis of political parties, social change, executives and courts. The latter chapters are comparative, drawing on the country-specific information presented in Part 1 to illustrate these dynamics in Europe as a whole.

Part 3 is also comparative, outlining developments in specific policy sectors at the national level and locating them in terms of the developing EU/European context. The chapters in this section seek to identify common trends and tendencies, where these exist, and also to explore the impact of European-level initiatives and processes on such trends and tendencies. Each chapter outlines the key features of European politics, providing a sense of the major areas of continuity and change across Europe as a whole.

Finally, Part 4 outlines the nature of the external relations of Europe. These chapters examine both EU and individual member states in their attempt to provide an overall impression of Europe's dealings with, and influence upon, the global context.

## Overarching Themes

Above and beyond the specific countries, issues and themes covered in the individual chapters, the book will equip students to consider broader issues shaping and characterising European politics more generally. Three of these are flagged throughout the volume and are considered in text boxes in each substantive chapter. The impact of globalisation and of European integration and the question of the democratic legitimacy of the processes and institutions described in each chapter are given special prominence throughout the volume. Some initial thoughts on the overall lessons to be learnt from the various chapters are presented in the conclusion.

A final issue worthy of consideration takes us back to the earlier discussion of universalism versus national specificity. Confronted with often similar pressures upon them—whether international (such as globalisation) or regional (the European Union)—it is interesting to consider the degree (if any) to which European states—their political institutions and processes as well as their public policies—are converging. Convergence, if it is occurring, is doing so from highly divergent starting points—the chapters on the Netherlands and Belgium and on Turkey, Greece and Cyprus illustrate that even close neighbours can be very different from each other. And different structures, of course, can shape very different attitudes towards politics which, themselves, can shape political practice. Revealing in this respect is the statement by the Danish prime minister, quoted by Eric Einhorn and John Logue (Chapter 5), that major reforms by narrow majorities are cause for misgivings. A cursory comparison with attitudes in Britain serves to reveal how differently politics is viewed by governing elites on that island.

Convergence in the face of common pressures and constraints is, therefore, far from inevitable, not least because the impact of these pressures is mediated through very different national institutions and national 'mental maps' of how politics should work. Given the highly fluid nature of politics in Europe, moreover, any preliminary responses suggested in the pages that follow will be, at best, tentative. It would, from our perspective, be an achievement if the chapters that follow serve to provide students with sufficient information and sufficient exposure to the major themes and debates to allow the start thinking knowledgeably about these issues.

# About the Contributors

**John_Bendix** is Professor of Sociology, Universität Göttingen, Germany, and a translator/editor.

**Ingrid_van_Biezen** is Senior Lecturer in Comparative Politics in the Department of Political Science and International Studies at the University of Birmingham, UK.

**Lisa_Conant** is Associate Professor in the Department of Political Science at the University of Denver, USA.

**Colin_Crouch** is Professor of Governance and Public Management and Chair of the Institute of Governance and Public Management at the Warwick Business School, UK.

**Desmond_Dinan** is the Jean Monnet Professor of Public Policy at George Mason University, Virginia, USA.

**Eric_S._Einhorn** is Professor of Political Science at the University of Massachusetts, Amherst, USA.

**Robert_Elgie** is Paddy Moriarty Professor of Government and International Studies at Dublin City University, Ireland.

**Jane_Feehan** is a project manager in the European Environment Agency, Copenhagen, Denmark, and a research fellow in the School of Geography, Planning and Environmental Policy at University College Dublin, Ireland.

**Wyn_Grant** is Professor of Politics at the University of Warwick, UK.

**Randall_Hansen** is Professor of Political Science and Canada Research Chair in Immigration and Governance at the University of Toronto, Canada.

**Linda_Hantrais** is Professor of European Social Policy at Loughborough University, UK; and Research Fellow in the Centre for International Studies at the London School of Economics, UK.

**Tim_Haughton** is Senior Lecturer in the Politics of Central and Eastern Europe at the University of Birmingham, UK.

**Colin_Hay** is Professor of Political Analysis at the University of Birmingham, UK.

**David_Hine** is University Lecturer in Politics at Christ Church and Director of the Centre for the Study of Democratic Government in the Department of Politics and International Relations at the University of Oxford, UK.

**Jonathan_Hopkin** is Senior Lecturer in Comparative Politics at the London School of Economics and Political Science, and Research Associate of the Johns Hopkins Bologna Center, Bologna, Italy.

**Jolyon_Howorth** is Jean Monnet Professor ad personam of European Politics at the University of Bath, UK and Visiting Professor of Political Science at Yale University, US.

**Hussein_Kassim** is Senior Lecturer in Politics at Birkbeck, University of London, UK.

**Ania_Krok-Paszkowska** is Visiting Lecturer on Central and Eastern European Countries at Cyprus College, Greece.

**Robert_Ladrech** is Senior Lecturer in Politics at Keele University, UK.

**John_Logue** is Professor of Political Science at Kent State University, Ohio, USA.

**Lee_McGowan** is Senior Lecturer in European Politics in the School of Politics, International Studies and Philosophy at Queen's University, Belfast.

**Anand_Menon** is Professor of European Politics at the University of Birmingham, UK.

**B._Guy_Peters** is Maurice Falk Professor of American Government at the University of Pittsburgh, USA.

**Ben_Rosamond** is Professor of Politics and International Studies at the University of Warwick, UK.

**Grahame_F._Thompson** is Professor of Political Economy at the Open University, UK.

**Nathalie_Tocci** is a Marie Curie Fellow at the Robert Schuman Centre for Advanced Studies of the European University Institute, Florence, Italy.

**Steven_B._Wolinetz** is Professor of Political Science at Memorial University of Newfoundland, Canada.

**Alasdair_R._Young** is a senior lecturer in the Department of Politics, University of Glasgow, UK.

**Jan_Zielonka** is Professor of European Politics at the University of Oxford, UK and Ralf Dahrendorf Fellow at St Antony's College.

# Acknowledgements

Volumes like this do not grow on trees. Indeed, putting together a text as large and as wide-ranging as this was never going to be a simple task. We have been fortunate, however, in those with whom we have worked. We would like to express our gratitude to the contributors, all of whom responded promptly and with remarkable good humour to the persistent and sometimes somewhat pernickety requests for amendments from the editors. Special thanks also go to David Bailey who has been responsible for creating the superb Online Resource Centre that supports the book. This would, quite simply, not have been possible without him and the credit for it should be his alone. Finally, we are immensely grateful to our editor, Ruth Anderson, for her unique blend of optimism, encouragement and occasional kind cajoling. Ruth took this project over when it was already underway. But she instantly became an integral part of it. That it now sees the light of day and is as well integrated as it is, is due, more than anything else, to her considerable efforts on our behalf. Thanks, Ruth!

# Guided tour of Learning Features

This text is enriched with a range of learning tools to help you navigate the text material and reinforce your knowledge of European politics. This guided tour shows you how to get the most out of your textbook package and do better in your studies.

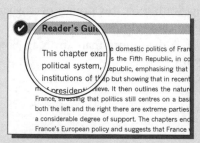

## Reader's Guides

Reader's Guides at the beginning of every chapter set the scene for upcoming themes and issues to be discussed, and indicate the scope of coverage within each chapter topic.

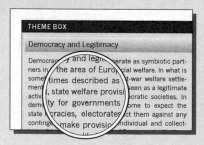

## Boxes

A number of topics benefit from further explanation or exploration in a manner that does not disrupt the flow of the main text. Throughout the book, boxes provide you with extra information on particular topics that complement your understanding of the main chapter text. Most chapters contain boxes on the impact of the European Union, globalization, and democracy and legitimacy.

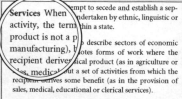

## Glossary terms

Key terms are bold-faced in the text the first time they are used in a chapter and defined in a glossary at the end of the text, to aid you in exam revision.

**KEY POINTS**

- The rise of the services sectors is of increased productivity in man of the globalisation of producti growing demands for certain kin

- The services sectors can be div tributive, business, social, and

## Key Points

Each main chapter section ends with a set of Key Points that summarise the most important arguments developed within each chapter topic.

**? QUESTIONS**

1. ... give the relative advantages of parliame
2. How do ... sus forms of parliamentary go political co...
3. What form ... administrative structure are ... linking citi... to government?
4. Does bu... cratic recruitment on the basis o ... rms of governing?
5. What elements are most important for definir

## Questions

A set of carefully devised questions has been provided to help you assess your comprehension of core themes, and may also be used as the basis of seminar discussion and coursework.

**≋ FURTHER READING**

- McCormick, J. (2...01), *Envi... e overview of EU ... n the a comprehensive ... l po
- Grant, W., Matt ... atthews, D. and New ... toke, Palgrave. Exam ... ), *T... Policy,* Basingstoke ... ective
- Barnes, P. M. and ... and Barnes, I. G ... vironm Edward Elgar. A very tho ... thorough ... matic trea
- Weale, A. (1992), *The New Politics of Pollution.* Ma ... ful and thought-provoking extended essay that tac

## Further Reading

To take your learning further, reading lists have been provided as a guide to find out more about the issues raised within each chapter topic and to help you locate the key academic literature in the field.

**⊕ IMPORTANT WEBSITES**

- ... niversity of Min ... du/dupolitics.html Mai ... with links to Dutch and E (departments), cons ... laws, parties and elect

**BELGIUM:**

- ... w.usem... elgium/belgovern.htm this site ... overview of the Belgian feder

## Web Links

At the end of every chapter you will find an annotated summary of useful web sites that are central to European politics and that will be instrumental in further research.

# Guided tour of the Online Resource Centre

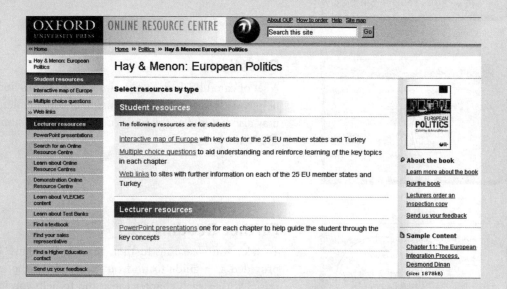

 **www.oxfordtextbooks.co.uk/orc/hay_menon/**

The Online Resource Centre that accompanies this book provides students and instructors with ready-to-use teaching and learning materials. These resources are free of charge and designed to maximise the learning experience.

## Interactive map of Europe

An interactive map of Europe with 'hot-spots' for 26 countries. Simply click on each country for vital social and political facts, key historical dates and annotated web links.

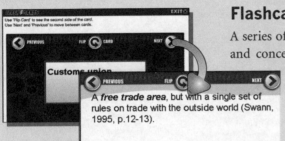

## Flashcard glossary

A series of interactive flashcards containing key terms and concepts has been provided to test your understanding of European politics terminology.

## Multiple-choice questions

The best way to reinforce your understanding of European politics is through frequent and cumulative revision. As such, a bank of self-marking multiple-choice questions have been provided for each chapter of the text, and include instant feedback on your answers and cross-references back to the main textbook.

## PowerPoint slides (instructors only)

These complement each chapter of the book and are a useful resource for preparing lectures and handouts. They allow lecturers to guide students through the key concepts and can be fully customised to meet the needs of the course.

# PART 1

# Politics in European States

# 1

# Germany

JOHN BENDIX

## Chapter Contents

- Introduction: The Difficult Path to Democracy
- Political Institutions, Elections and Parties
- *Land der Mitte*: Germany in Europe
- Germany in the World
- Conclusion: Key Contemporary Issues

## Reader's Guide

This chapter first briefly discusses political history to 1945, when Germany unconditionally surrendered to the Allies, ending the Second World War in Europe. These four
powers occupied and divided it into two states by 1949; separation ended in 1990
when East Germany formally acceded to West Germany. Political institutions originally developed in West Germany now apply to the entire country, but also reflect the
country's difficult path to democracy. Germany has long seen itself as geo-politically
'in the middle', an inward-looking view that shapes its interactions with the EU and
its responses to globalisation. Key issues facing Germany—its reluctance to take the
initiative internationally, the integration of East and West Germany, whether the social
compact can hold—close out the chapter.

# Introduction: The Difficult Path to Democracy

'What is wrong with Germany', the British historian A. J. P. Taylor wrote at the height of the Cold War in 1967, 'is that there is too much of it.' Yet, only a generation later, Czech President Vaclav Havel said 'Germany can be as large as she wants to, as long as she stays democratic' (in Hyde-Price 1996: 175–6). Taylor reflected the lingering fear that if Germany could launch two world wars (1914–18 and 1939–45), it might do so again, and in the immediate post-1945 period this desire to bind and control Germany was part of neighbouring France's motivation to support the transnational economic and political structures that now have become the EU. Since 1945, Europe's democracies have not waged war on one another and have prospered economically; Havel reminds us that it is the political form a country takes that matters, not its size.

Germany's path to democracy was long and rocky. After the end of the Napoleonic Wars in 1815, the future Germany was fragmented into 39 competing states. Efforts to unify them into a single country, to introduce liberal constitutional reforms permitting more political self-determination, or to ensure individual rights, failed during the 1848 revolution. Instead, under the influence of Otto von Bismarck, named **Prussia's** Prime Minister and Foreign Minister in 1862, aristocratic and monarchical rule from this northern state was reinforced through customs unions between various German states and by brief wars with various neighbouring countries. National unification in 1871 came from above, with the *Reich* ruled by the Prussian kings Wilhelm I and Wilhelm II. This 'Wilhelmine era' ended in 1918 with Germany's defeat in the First World War.

A brief and chaotic attempt to establish parliamentary democracy under the Weimar Republic then ensued. It collapsed by early 1933 with the appointment of Adolf Hitler as German Chancellor: he rapidly consolidated his political power though an emergency decree that suspended civil liberties and by use of an 'Enabling Act' that permitted him to rule by decree. By mid-July of 1933, his Nazi Party was the only political party left, and its doctrine was that of a centralised state in which all German institutions were forced into line under a *Führer*, with the message that a single, superior, pure 'Aryan' race needed more territory for its natural development. That served as justification for Germany to invade Austria and Czechoslovakia in 1938, and then Poland in 1939, triggering the Second World War.

Hitler's toxic brew of populism, inhumanity and militarism launched a ruinous war that cost the lives of millions across Europe. (See Background box 1.1.) It would take the combined military efforts of the Allies to defeat him, and the war in Europe finally ended with Germany's unconditional surrender. Germans, more than 75 per cent of whom were born *after* Hitler's 1945 suicide, often refer

---

**BACKGROUND BOX 1.1**

### Genocide

Jews, first in Germany but later throughout continental Europe and most especially in Poland, were the scapegoats and the major (though not the only) victims of Nazi rule. Passage of the Nuremberg Laws racially defined and discriminated against Jews in Germany already in 1935, and similar laws would be adopted in countries Germany occupied or conquered. Under them, Jews were dismissed from professions, forced to pay punitive taxes, driven out of their homes, and saw their possessions plundered. Those unable to flee abroad were concentrated together in labour camps and city ghettos, ruthlessly exploited for their labour, starved to death, and finally murdered by the millions. The Auschwitz extermination camp in southern Poland has become the symbol for Nazi rule as well as of genocide (a word first used in 1944)—the deliberate, systematic, mass murder of a specified group of people.

to the 12 years of Hitler's 'Third Reich' as the *Schreckensherrschaft*, the rule of terror and horror.

The victorious Allied armies controlled all of Germany, and soon divided it into zones of occupation. By 1949, American, British and French zones had joined economically and politically to form West Germany, while the USSR-controlled zone became East Germany; both would formally become sovereign nations in 1955. The Union of Soviet Socialist Republics (USSR) also controlled Eastern Europe militarily, politically and economically, and relinquished this control only by the late 1980s. (See Background box 1.2.) In 1990, East Germany was formally incorporated into West Germany, but 40 years of separation and diametrically opposed political and economic developments has made it difficult for the two to fuse.

From 1862 to 1945, Germany defined itself by asserting itself internationally, often through war. From 1949 to 1989, Germany was defined instead by the foreign powers that occupied and divided it; liberal democratic West Germany looking to the USA, socialist East Germany looking to the USSR.

### BACKGROUND BOX 1.2

#### The Sinatra Doctrine

German unification was only possible once the USSR officially renounced its control over Eastern Europe. When Soviet Communist Party Secretary-General Mikhail Gorbachev had his spokesman Genady Gerasimov announce that Eastern Europe was being released from Soviet **tutelage** under the 'Sinatra doctrine'—from Frank Sinatra's hit song 'I Did It My Way'—no one quite believed their ears. Was the 'Iron Curtain' that Winston Churchill in 1946 had said the USSR had drawn across Eastern Europe being ripped away by a joking reference to a popular singer? Indeed it was. After 1989, all Eastern European countries were free to go their own way, including East Germany.

Since 1990, Germany has more explicitly acknowledged its many internal contrasts (Protestant north v. Catholic south, differing political heritages and societies in West and East, resident foreigners living among native Germans) while defining itself externally relative to its place in Europe and in the world.

### KEY POINTS

- German territory was fragmented into 39 separate states after 1815, but by 1871, Bismarck finally united Germany under the leadership of the hereditary King of Prussia.

- After 1890, the German Empire pursued an aggressive foreign policy that helped trigger the First World War. This Second Reich ended in 1918, succeeded by the Weimar Republic, Germany's first, though unsuccessful, attempt at parliamentary democracy.

- The Weimar Republic, 'a republic without republicans', ended in early 1933 with the appointment of Adolf Hitler, head of the fascist Nazi Party, as German Chancellor. By 1939, Hitler had led Germany into the Second World War. His rule, and his Third Reich, ended in 1945 with Germany's defeat and unconditional surrender to the Allies.

- American, British and French forces occupied what became West Germany; Soviet forces occupied what became East Germany. Both West and East Germany were founded formally in 1949, and both became sovereign in 1955.

- Russian control of Eastern Europe collapsed by the late 1980s, allowing East and West Germany to unify in 1990.

# Political Institutions, Elections and Parties

Since all East German political structures vanished after 1990, this section addresses only institutions developed in and for West Germany. In fact, the West German *Grundgesetz* of 1949 was explicitly formulated as a substitute for a constitution until such time as the country reunified. After 1989, and with relatively minor modifications, that *Grundgesetz* became the constitution for all of Germany. (See Theme box: Democracy and Legitimacy.)

The *Grundgesetz* defines Germany as a democratic, federal and social state, operating under the rule of law, whose authority derives from the people. It is the state's responsibility to ensure that every member of the community is free from want, can live in circumstances worthy of human dignity, and has a fair share of the nation's general prosperity. The protection of human dignity and of individual freedoms are the highest principles of law, and a long list of basic rights is enumerated in the first 19 articles.

Supreme legislative authority is vested in the *Bundestag*, whose members are elected in general,

---

**THEME BOX**

### Democracy and Legitimacy

Germany's current political institutions are the result of a combination of external pressure, particularly from the USA and the UK (1946–9), and the desires of German politicians to create a stable democratic structure that could not lead to a collapse of the political system in a manner that could usher in a system like that of the Third Reich. Because politicians writing the *Grundgesetz* had themselves been exiled or persecuted, they were particularly concerned to ensure that no one ever need suffer that fate again, and therefore included many individual rights and institutional safeguards. Thus, the *Grundgesetz* stipulates that the lower house can express its lack of confidence in the leader of government it has elected only if it simultaneously musters a majority willing to elect a successor (Art. 67). This 'constructive vote of no confidence' was intended to preclude the unstable transitions between governments that plagued the Weimar Republic. During Weimar, minuscule political parties also regularly brought coalition cabinets to fall by quitting government, so German political parties must obtain at least 5 per cent of the national vote to win seats in parliament. The Weimar Republic had also barely been formed before both extreme left (in 1919, 1921 and 1923) and extreme right (in 1920 and 1923) parties tried to overthrow it. That experience, along with the rise of the Nazi Party, prompted a blunt and pre-emptive clause:

> " Parties which, by reason of their aims or the behaviour of their adherents, seek to impair or abolish the free democratic basic order or to endanger the existence of the Federal Republic of Germany, shall be unconstitutional. (Art. 21(2)) "

In still another nod to history, the *Grundgesetz* also contains a stark anti-war provision:

> " Acts tending to and undertaken with the intent to disturb the peaceful relations between nations, especially to prepare for aggressive war, shall be unconstitutional. They shall be made a punishable offence. (Art. 26) "

In 1994 and again in 1999, this article was amended to permit the deployment of German troops on UN missions and international operations (e.g. as in Kosovo), but Germany was not willing to join the USA in invading Iraq. In early 2006, the German Chancellor also openly criticised the USA for continuing to hold suspected terrorists at Guantanamo Bay, which one can interpret as a defence of the highest principles of law inscribed in the first articles of the *Grundgesetz*.

direct, free, equal and secret elections for four-year terms. By the constitution, members of parliament are answerable only to their consciences but, in practice, representatives have little power if they flout the instructions of the parliamentary parties they belong to. This house represents the German people, exercises oversight functions over the government, and also elects the German Federal Chancellor as the head of government.

The Chancellor recommends a Cabinet that must be approved by the German Federal President, the formal head of state whose powers are largely ceremonial (signing bills into law), symbolic (representing the country abroad) or held in reserve (dissolving the lower house and calling new elections). Chancellors alone are responsible for federal policies, and these are binding upon the Cabinet. However, Cabinet ministers have autonomy over the internal workings of their departments, and disputes between ministers over competencies must be resolved in the Cabinet.

Germany is divided into 16 sovereign states, each with its own elected parliament, executive and independent judiciary. This federal structure is mirrored by the *Bundesrat*, a body specifically responsible for ensuring the national government does not violate the legitimate interests of the states laid out in the *Grundgesetz*. Its major, negative, power is to initiate compromise proceedings when it objects to legislation proposed by the *Bundestag*. The upper house can be overruled, but it can also independently introduce legislation, though it has done so rarely since 1949. *Bundesrat* members are appointed (not directly elected to the upper houses in the USA or Switzerland) and are typically the senior ministers from each state. State elections have increasingly become critical evaluations of the performance of the seated national government, so the *Bundesrat* has tended to be less a body that represents state interests than a forum for party political opposition.

Finally, there are specialised higher courts, the most important of which politically is the Federal Constitutional Court. Created at US insistence and modelled on the US Supreme Court, it has the power of judicial review. This court has the power to judge whether a governmental action taken or a bill passed is in conformity with the constitution. As in the USA, key political issues are increasingly decided by this court, not in the legislature.

## Elections and parties

Germany's electoral system is 'mixed member proportional', unusual for allowing two votes to be cast for the legislature. In a proportional representation system, parties nominate lists of candidates in multi-member districts, and voters select a party list. Seats in the legislature are distributed, following prescribed calculation formulae, depending on how many votes a given party list receives.

But, in Germany, this applies only to half the legislators elected; the other half are selected by plurality from single-member districts. Thus, on the left side of a German ballot paper, one finds a list of names of individual candidates offered as district representatives by various parties, to be selected by plurality in single-member districts (the 'first' vote). On the right side, one finds the names of the parties, to be selected by proportional representation in multi-member districts (the 'second' vote). The first vote deliberately personalises the election, while the second is assumed to more accurately reflect party preferences, and is often decisive in determining whether a small party will receive parliamentary seats and thus representation (e.g. the 5 per cent rule). By 2000, nearly one in five Germans gave their first vote to a district representative from one party, their second vote to a different party.

West Germany long had a stable 'two-and-a-half' party system. The conservative Christian Democrats (the CDU, along with its smaller, exclusively Bavarian, CSU sister party) and the left-wing Social Democrats (SPD) have dominated, accounting for a combined average of 88 per cent of the party vote in the six *Bundestag* elections from 1965 to 1983. Across the 11 *Bundestag* elections from 1953 to 1990, the CDU/CSU averaged 46 per cent of the vote (range: 44–50 per cent), and the SPD averaged 38 per cent (range: 29–45 per cent). The liberal Free Democrats (FDP), averaging 8 per cent (range: 6–13 per cent), were the crucial 'half-party' needed to form a majority, more often in coalition with the CDU/CSU (21 years) than with the SPD (13 years). The FDP was excluded only once, when CDU/CSU and SPD ruled in 'grand coalition' during 1966–9.

In the five *Bundestag* elections since 1990, however, the combined CDU/CSU and SPD average has dropped to 76 per cent of the party vote. (See Table 1.1.) Both SPD and FDP have remained at their previous averages and ranges, but the CDU/CSU has slipped badly (average: 39 per cent, range: 35–44 per cent), with results since 1998 their worst ever. In the weeks following the 2005 elections, after exhaustively considering all possible party coalitions, the CDU/CSU and SPD agreed for the first time since 1969 to form a 'grand coalition' government, excluding the FDP in the process, and electing Angela Merkel (CDU) as Germany's first female Federal Chancellor to lead it. While the raw tone of German political discourse in the *Bundestag* is sometimes criticised, this choice to form a 'grand coalition' government can be read to say either that the two large parties have moved closer to one another over time (or closer than they would sometimes like their voters to believe during election campaigns), or that voters are tired of the politics of antagonism and ultimately prefer a politics of cooperation.

Still, it is important to have a strong opposition in a democracy. Some political scientists argue that the ability to transfer power from a party in power to a party previously in opposition, and do so peacefully, is one of the hallmarks of a democracy. This presupposes that a party, or a coalition of parties, in opposition can viably exercise leadership. In the post-2005 configuration, this is not possible since the opposition is divided among three equally weak parties—FDP, Greens, Left—that lack a history of willingness to cooperate with one another.

The major change in recent decades has been the emergence of the Green Party out of the mass environmental and anti-nuclear campaigns of the 1970s and 1980s to challenge the FDP. By 1983, the Greens had 27 representatives to the *Bundestag* and, by 1987, held only four fewer seats than the FDP. In 1994, the Greens edged past the FDP, and from 1998 to 2005 were strong enough to be part of the SPD–Green governing coalition. However, fresh Green ideas appeal only as long as they are not co-opted by other parties; the party itself has never received more than 8.6 per cent of the second vote.

Eastern voters have added volatility to German elections, voting for the CDU that brought them reunification in the early 1990s, but later rewarding the SPD for its socio-economic efforts. Disillusionment with both has set in: nearly half the Eastern voters asked in a 2004 poll answered 'none' when asked which major party they trusted most to resolve their economic problems. Such frustration has led some voters to turn to the Party of Democratic Socialism (PDS), the successor to the Socialist Unity Party (SED) that ran East Germany with an iron fist from 1949 to 1989. The PDS has distanced itself from the more unsavoury, authoritarian aspects of the SED, and in the 1990s was elected into several state governments in the East. In 2005, bolstered by a fusion with a small party of renegade ex-SPD members, it refashioned itself as the Left Party and did surprisingly well in the national elections.

Last but not least, there has been weak support for smaller, extremist parties, including those on the far right (SRP) and far left (KPD), both of which were declared unconstitutional under Art. 21(2) in West

**Table 1.1** German *Bundestag* Elections since 1990 (in percentage of second votes obtained)

|            | 1990 | 1994 | 1998 | 2002 | 2005 |
|------------|------|------|------|------|------|
| CDU/CSU    | 43.8 | 41.4 | 35.1 | 38.5 | 35.2 |
| SPD        | 33.5 | 36.4 | 40.9 | 38.5 | 34.2 |
| FDP        | 11.0 | 6.9  | 6.2  | 7.4  | 9.8  |
| Greens     | 3.8  | 7.3  | 6.7  | 8.6  | 8.1  |
| PDS        | 2.4  | 4.4  | 5.1  | 4.0  | 8.7* |
| Other      | 5.5  | 3.6  | 5.9  | 3.0  | 4.0  |

* Left Party (a fusion of the PDS with a small party comprised of former SPD members and leaders)

Germany during the 1950s, and dissolved. Some far right parties have formed since (NPD in 1964; DVU in 1971; REP in 1983), though the media attention devoted to them far outstrips their meagre, brief and local or regional political successes.

### KEY POINTS (Political Institutions)

- Current German political institutions resulted partly from pressure exerted by occupying Allies and partly from the desires of post-war German politicians.

- The West German *Grundgesetz* of 1949 was a temporary constitution until such time as Germany unified; slightly modified in 1989, it has become the constitution for all of Germany. A number of its provisions are explicit efforts to avoid past mistakes.

- The German Chancellor is the head of government, with considerable power over national policy as well as over the Cabinet. The German President is the head of state, with powers in reserve and largely symbolic functions.

- The lower house (*Bundestag*) is the legislative body that oversees government functions. The upper house (*Bundesrat*), which exercises legislative oversight in the interest of Germany's 16 states, has tended to be an institutionalised forum for party political opposition.

- The Federal Constitutional Court, with its power of judicial review, has become an increasingly important locus for resolving political disputes.

### KEY POINTS (Elections and Parties)

- Germany's mixed member proportional electoral system combines a first, personalised vote for a representative (plurality) and a second vote for a party (proportional representation); each vote selects half the representatives to the *Bundestag*, though the second ultimately determines how many representatives each party will send to parliament.

- Germany long had a stable 'two-and-a-half' party system comprised of the Christian conservative CDU, the social democratic SPD and the small, liberal FDP. From 1953 to 1990, German governments were more frequently CDU/FDP coalitions than SPD/FDP coalitions.

- Since 1998, the CDU has performed worse than at any time since 1949, while both the SPD and FDP have stagnated. Germany appears to be moving towards a 'multi-party' system: the two largest parties, CDU and SPD, each received only about one-third of the vote in 2005.

- Recent major changes have been the rise of the Green Party to levels that challenge the FDP, and the growing influence of the PDS (now Left Party), particularly at the state level in the east.

- West Germany has banned parties deemed a threat to its democratic order, and efforts by far right parties to secure national representation have failed, though they have had some local or regional successes.

# *Land der Mitte*: Germany in Europe

Germany has long seen itself as the *Land der Mitte*, a country in and of the middle, both geographically and politically. Located between Poland to the east, France to the west, Switzerland to the south and Denmark to the north, each major direction represents a type of political system Germany has tried: socialist one-party rule (East Germany), representative multi-party democracy with federalism (West Germany) and monarchy (Wilhelmine era).

Historically, being in the middle meant lurching between political models. The failure in 1848–9 left a deep suspicion of constitutions, liberalism and democracy, so 1871 national unification under a Prussian king, supported by an interlinked army, aristocracy and bureaucracy, lacked all three. Authoritarian imperialism was idealised, with old German culture exalted as superior to modern, decadent Anglo-Saxon civilization. Defeat in the First World War did not end this idealisation or exaltation, though German industrialisation during the Second Reich as well as the 1917 Russian Revolution added new elements. One result was to find Weimar politicians and intellectuals alike arguing that Germany should pursue a unique cultural and economic path, a *Sonderweg* that would steer it between socialism and capitalism (Faulenbach 1980: 279–303), if not between political left and right. One could even argue that by naming his party the National Socialist German Workers' Party, Hitler did something similar rhetorically by trying to appeal to both left wing (socialist, worker) and right wing (national, German) at once. But tradition may have weighed more heavily: throughout the Second World War, the German army officer corps remained dominated by aristocrats, much as the Prussian Army had been.

The forced unity of the Third Reich was succeeded by physical division between a socialist East Germany (it had little choice) and a capitalist, but ambivalent, West Germany. In principle and in practice, the latter was bound to the democratic West, but some of its SPD politicians continued to look East. In a crucial 1959 party congress, the SPD renounced revolution, ceased calling itself a worker's party, and vowed to work for reforms within the constitutional democratic order. By the early 1970s, Chancellor Brandt (SPD) was making overtures eastwards, particularly to Poland, though without forgetting his western commitments and, by the mid-1980s, even conservative Chancellor Kohl (CDU) was practising rapprochement with East Germany. Germany's capital is once again in Berlin, near Poland (replacing Bonn, the former West German capital near France); as East Berlin was East Germany's capital, this move merges long-separated seats of power. (See Background box 1.3.)

West Germany also pursued a middle course in the 1950s and 1960s by adopting a 'social market economy' orientation in which the state set general frameworks for the economy, including acting as a mediator between labour and capital. Industrial relations were regulated through a state-encouraged system of 'co-determination' that regularly brought employer and employee representatives together at all levels to engage in (it was hoped) mutually beneficial cooperative bargaining. At the same time, the German state acted to protect and secure citizen well-being through its social policies, under the notion that 'social peace in the long term can only be secured when economic rationality and societal solidarity enhance one another' (Schröder 2005). The 1960s were also the era of the 'economic miracle', with rapid, export-driven growth that came to focus on high-quality, high-technology goods particularly in the automotive, chemical, electrical and pharmaceutical sectors, manufactured by a highly educated and well paid workforce. The balance of state oversight and market forces was symbolised by the tight control maintained on the value of the currency, the German mark, with an eye to avoiding the hyperinflation that plagued the Weimar economy. One can summarise this complex interaction by saying that public, semi-public and private regulatory institutions have orchestrated and negotiated between economic actors (Padgett 2003: 122), or one can just say that Germany prospered by being cautious and by pursuing policies of cooperation and compromise.

Germany behaved no differently towards Europe. It was a charter member of the Coal and Steel Community, and the founding of the European Economic Community, whose goal was to create a single, common market to ensure the free movement of goods, people, capital and services between the member nations, opened up just the kind of trade and export opportunities Germany's booming economy needed at the time.

**BACKGROUND BOX 1.3**

## A Chronology of Germany in Europe since 1945

| | |
|---|---|
| 1945 | Unconditional surrender of German forces; Allied occupation begins |
| 1948 | USA, UK and French zones of occupation fused into a single economic area |
| 1949 | Basic Law passed, establishing West Germany; East Germany also established. North Atlantic Treaty Organisation (NATO) created to defend Western Europe from Soviet aggression |
| 1951 | European Coal and Steel Community Treaty signed in Paris |
| 1954 | Paris Treaty formally ends the occupation of Germany by the USA, UK and France (though troops remained stationed on German soil) |
| 1955 | West Germany formally regains sovereignty, re-establishes army, joins NATO. East Germany formally regains sovereignty; joins Warsaw Pact, formed this year partly as a response to NATO |
| 1957 | European Economic Community Treaty signed in Rome |
| 1961 | Berlin Wall built |
| 1970 | German–Soviet and German–Polish Treaties signed. Meeting between leaders of West and East Germany, leading first to a Transit Agreement (1971), then to a Basic Treaty (1972), between the two Germanies |
| 1971 | West and East Germany become UN members |
| 1986 | Reagan–Gorbachev meeting in Reykjavik; beginning of USA and USSR nuclear disarmament |
| 1987 | First visit by the East German head of government to West Germany |
| 1989 | Berlin Wall and inter-German borders fall, paving the way to reunification |
| 1989/90 | USSR supremacy over Eastern European ends |
| 1992 | Maastricht Treaty creates the European Union |
| 1999 | The euro, the EU's common currency, introduced |

In French eyes, binding Germany into European cooperative economic structures would lead it to share so many interests with its neighbours that it would have no reason to wage war on them again. German politicians themselves were only too happy to seek prosperity through economic cooperation, and remained cautious about being overbearing. 'Owing to Germany's political and economic clout,' former Chancellor Schröder wrote, 'we have a particular responsibility in Europe, but we have never staked a claim to leadership' (Schröder 2005). Instead, there has been close cooperation 'with our friends and partners in the EU', particularly with France, the two countries often serving as Europe's engine, whether by deepening ties between, or widening the circle of, members. Germany has become by far the biggest net contributor to the EU, in 2005 providing twice the amount of funding to the EU as France, and both the EU and Germany have benefited mutually. (See Theme box: The Impact of the European Union.)

**THEME BOX**

## The Impact of the European Union

Because Germany has been involved in the closer integration of Europe since the early 1950s, the impact of the EU is a two-way street. On the one hand, Germany has successfully 'uploaded' a number of policies, including environmental and competition policies, and the framework for the free movement of persons across European borders (Schengen Agreement). On the other hand, Germany has 'downloaded' principles of EU law that have led it to liberalise its energy and telecommunication markets, and change its fiscal and monetary policies (Dyson 2003: 163–4). The relatively easy, bi-directional flow might be due to similarities between the EU's multi-level governance structure and how policy-making has evolved in Germany's federalised, cooperative decision-making structure, but it may also be because Germany has deliberately Europeanised its policy-making.

Cooperation with France has not been easy, as the two countries have different ideas about the proper mix of state, market and society, and have disagreed over foreign policy *vis-à-vis* the USA, Russia and the Middle East. German Chancellors and French Presidents often do not even belong to the same party families. Yet that Germany has learned to cooperate with its long-standing enemy is excellent preparation for its new geo-political role as *Land der Mitte* between existing Western European EU members and the ten new members from Eastern Europe that have joined in 2004.

**KEY POINTS**

- Germany's self-image is of being in, and of, the middle, both geographically and politically, now underscored by the recent expansion of the EU into Eastern Europe (2004).

- That role long meant lurching from one political model to the next: attempted liberal reform (1848), authoritarian monarchy (1871), a republic trying to forge a path between capitalism and socialism (Weimar) and then fascism (Hitler); the failure of the *Sonderweg* was underscored by the post-1945 division of the country. West German Chancellors looked West (1950s–1960s), then East (1970s), then in both directions (1980s). Reunification ended efforts to unify socialist and capitalist

ideas politically—though one can argue West Germany tried to do so in its socio-economic policies especially from the 1950s to the 1970s.

- German socio-economic policies have been cautious, orientated to cooperation and compromise, and mediated by the government. That carries over to Germany's approach to the EU (and its precursors); Germany is the EU's biggest net contributor.

- Germany's ability to cooperate with France since the 1960s, in particular to drive the European project forward, stands it in good stead in its new role 'in the middle' between the older, democratic members of the EU and the new, ex-socialist members from Eastern Europe.

# Germany in the World

In international politics, Germany has continued to play a cautious and modest role. Its interest in obtaining a permanent seat on the UN Security Council can be seen in this light, as its fundamental orientation—among politicians and voters alike—is to strongly favour mediation or dispute resolution, and to see military solutions as an absolute last resort. In international crises, Germany has earned praise for its efforts and spirit of cooperation with other nations (it played an important mediator role in brokering a peace agreement for Afghanistan), though also criticism that it has 'punched below its weight' and not used its considerable resources, or even the reservoir of political goodwill

it has accumulated, to intervene more forcefully when it should have, as in ex-Yugoslavia or in Rwanda.

The international economic integration implied by 'globalisation' has proven a far more difficult challenge. Globalisation is a buzzword for disparate phenomena related to flows and networks, from the rapid increase of capital movements around the globe to the rise of the internet, or from the internationalisation of manufacturing and production practices to the ease with which one can now fly (nearly) anywhere. By and large, globalisation is rooted in technological and economic changes, with the expectation, at least among journalists, that these necessarily will bring large-scale political, social or cultural changes in their wake. Academics remain sceptical on this score, and point to global winners and losers: some (few?) individuals, companies and nations are simply better able to take full advantage of the opportunities while many others will bear the consequences and costs such networks and flows engender.

**THEME BOX**

**The Impact of Globalisation**

Economic and technological dimensions are far easier to grasp than the political, social or cultural meaning of globalisation, but even so, it is unclear whether (or what) globalisation homogenises and standardises. Such pressures might instead act to hybridise or encourage differentiation at national, regional and local levels (e.g. an emphasis on 'Made in Germany' as a means to differentiate products or as a sign of high-quality goods). The global marketplace has brought intense competition to reduce costs, whether by finding cheaper labour (e.g. the 'race to the bottom') or in manufacturing methods (e.g. computerisation, just-in-time, outsourcing). Because Germany is 'heavily dependent on the capacity of domestic institutions to balance the demands of high performance economy with high-wage labour markets and high levels of social protection in the welfare state' (Padgett 2003: 127), it is ill equipped to respond to this challenge.

Germany has found global challenges difficult. (See Themebox: The Impact of Globalisation.) The largest export-oriented firms (VW, Bayer, Siemens) could more readily respond by internationalising production and distribution networks, thereby remaining globally competitive, but middle-sized firms have been slow to move production to cheaper sites in Eastern Europe or China even when it was to their advantage (Fischermann *et al.* 2005). The cooperative, collaborative structures by which the state has protected market actors and highly paid workers ill-prepares firms or workers for cut-throat competition from low-cost producers abroad. Welfare state costs now also account for almost half of all federal outlays—pensions alone have increased from 13 per cent in 1964 to 31 per cent in 2004, owing to an ageing population—which sharply reduces the government's ability to provide relief through targeted subsidies as in the past. Globalisation coincides with a general shift away from the manufacturing and into the service sector (e.g. telecommunication, computers, financial services), a disadvantage if the mainstays of the economy are capital- and technology-intensive and relatively immobile (e.g. chemicals, pharmaceuticals, automotive). Globalisation demands lean and flexible production, rapid adaptation to technological change, low-cost manufacturing and low-wage labour, and ready access to capital—all of which the German economy is either unable or slow to provide.

# Conclusion: Key Contemporary Issues

Domestically, the major issue since 1990 has been how to integrate the former East Germany states and population into the former West German way of life. Most state-supported, but ultimately uncompetitive and unprofitable, East German enterprises were closed, creating high

unemployment rates. Though large sums of public money—the figure often cited is 1.4 billion euros—have been invested in the East since 1990, particularly in infrastructure, the statistics show a steady population drain from east to west. Easterners continue to resent what they feel is a devaluation by Westerners even of non-political aspects of their lives under socialist rule (close social ties, professional qualifications), and that some of the best-paid, high-status jobs in the eastern states are held by *Wessis* has not helped. Many think it will take a generation at least for these differences and resentments to dissipate.

Germans are not only concerned over such weighty matters as political and cultural integration, but also increasingly worry about the impact they are having on the natural environment around them. Of equal import, particularly

to those affected, is the impact the denizens of that environment are having on humans (see **Background Box 1.4**:). This small story is included to help dissipate the lingering image that Germans, including its lawyers and journalists, are incapable of a sense of humour.

Internationally, German politicians have spent much time cultivating economic ties with EU neighbours and other wealthy nations, as well as with important new players such as China. It can remain unclear what the direct results of such contacts are, other than in such prestige projects as the German-built maglev train that now runs from

---

### BACKGROUND BOX 1.4

#### A Different Sort of Contemporary Issue

In the wintertime, Germans are fond of dining on wild boar, and with their heft (35–50 kg when adult), bristly pelt and rooting snouts, boar seem to symbolise the uncultivated and savage, not doubt one reason why they can often be admired safely inside fenced enclosures in forests throughout Germany. Yet wild boar have also become a major animal pest since the 1980s. The many warm and mild winters (food available all year-round—boar are omnivores), combined with large fields edged with woods to retreat into (forests cover 30 per cent of Germany), together with an absence of predators like lynx, wolves or bears, have made reproduction rates soar. For every 68 Germans there is now one boar in the country, and they are getting more and more like us—living longer (to age 20, up from an average age of 7–8 years) and getting heavier (up to as much as 200 kg).

Human–boar encounters are becoming increasingly common, as the animals wander not just through the forests and fields but across busy roads. Every year sees about 30,000 traffic accidents due to wild boar, leading to 50 deaths and 2,500 injuries among humans. Wild boar are increasingly also finding their way into urbanised areas, to root around in gardens and public parks, in cemeteries and most especially near those lovely homes that have such irresistible smelling refuse standing in bins just outside. In Berlin—a city where 62 per cent of the land is boar-unfriendly as it is covered by houses, roads or water—1,341 boar were bagged in 2001 alone, a number twice as high as a decade before. That was

just a minuscule part of the national hunting tally: 531,887 wild boar officially reported killed in 2001, a 67 per cent increase over 2000, and a 430 per cent increase since 1980.

Boar are also becoming more and more intimate with humans. A court in Lüneburg was recently faced with a claim brought by Frau Günther, of Wathlingen, against a hunter who had conducted a game drive, the result of which, she claimed, was to have a wild boar sow crash through the glass door from the terrace of her house and land in her 66-year-old arms as she was sitting on the sofa. The sow then jumped off her and raced into the kitchen, where Herr Günther, with the help of a neighbour, who happened to be a hunter, shot it dead. News reports did not reveal the subsequent fate of the sow (see wintertime, above?), but the claim against the hunter was for 20,000 euros for damage to the living room, dining room and kitchen, as well as for the destruction of the sofa, chairs, carpet and orchids—and a further 6,000 euros for a broken tooth, bruises, continuing back pain and nightmares. Judge Karin Faulhaber turned down the claim, arguing that it was not conceivable that the hunter conducting the game drive could have prevented this incident, let alone the fact that no proof had been established that the sow had actually run from the field where the battue was being conducted. Perhaps the judge also had the words of the hunter's lawyer in her ears: 'Maybe the sow was a little crazy. Why should it be just humans who are mentally ill?'

the airport into booming Shanghai, though German politicians do try to profit domestically from the image of being active—even when they know their actions may have little impact on the global marketplace. In economics, too, Germany may be 'punching below its weight' and could become more assertive in the future.

Domestically, the key issue for a rapidly ageing population goes back to the social compact implied in the *Grundgesetz*. Will the German state continue to be able to provide benefits and security as before, to ensure that all are free from want and can share in the nation's general prosperity? And will it be able to defend the European humanistic tradition that respects the dignity of the individual, that values social justice and tolerance, that prizes freedom and democracy, in a global order that seems willing to sacrifice everything, including differing worldviews, on the altar of capitalism (Jessen 2005)?

## QUESTIONS

1. Why didn't (or couldn't) Germany become democratic earlier?

2. What is the major difference between the 1860–1945 and 1946–89 eras?

3. What are some examples of *Grundgesetz* provisions meant to avoid past mistakes?

4. What do each of the two votes Germans cast for parliament do?

5. What does it mean to say Germany had a stable 'two-and-a-half' party system?

6. What is a *non*-geographic example of Germany seeing itself as *Land der Mitte*?

7. How does 'co-determination' show the German state's desire for compromise?

8. What was the key objective of the European Economic Community?

9. What has Germany 'uploaded to' or 'downloaded from' the EU?

10. Why has globalisation been a difficult challenge for Germany?

## FURTHER READING

■ Brady, J., Crawford, B. and Wiliarty, S. (1999) (eds), *The Postwar Transformation of Germany: Democracy, Prosperity, and Nationhood*, Ann Arbor, University of Michigan Press. A worthy successor to Baker, Dalton and Hildebrandt, *Germany Transformed* (Harvard, 1981), this volume's four sections address Germany's place in the world, the German economy, the evolution of national identity, and the political culture and institutions that have helped Germany build its democracy.

■ Craig, G. (1982), *The Germans*, New York, Meridian. Written by one of the most erudite and eloquent historians of Germany, this work is a contextually rich, entertaining and highly informative view of various characteristics of German life, past and present.

■ Fritsch-Bournazel, R. (1992), *Europe and German Reunification*, Oxford, Berg. With admirable brevity and written soon after the events, this book provides all the historical and political details needed for understanding German reunification.

■ Padgett, S., Paterson, W. and Smith, G. (2003) (eds), *Developments in German Politics 3*, Houndmills, Palgrave. The authoritative and comprehensive collection for the serious student of the subject, it covers politics, polity, policy, political economy and the role of Germany in Europe and the wider world.

■ **Umbach, M. (2002) (ed.),** *German Federalism: Past, Present, Future*, **Houndmills, Palgrave.** A multidisciplinary collection providing interesting historical, linguistic and cultural perspectives to explain modern Germany's political form.

■ **Yoder, J. (1999),** *From East Germans to Germans? The New Postcommunist Elites*, **London, Duke University Press.** One of the few studies to examine how those in leadership positions in the former East Germany have responded to their country being absorbed into the West German state.

 ## IMPORTANT WEBSITES

● **www.bund.de** Portal of the Federal Republic of Germany; numerous links.

● **www.embassyworld.com/embassy/Germany/Germany1.html** Information from German embassies abroad.

● **www.dw-world.de** International radio (and television) broadcasts from Deutsche Welle; the website has considerable information about current affairs in Germany.

 **Visit the Online Resource Centre that accompanies this book for lots of useful additional material, including an interactive map of Europe. www.oxfordtextbooks.co.uk/orc/hay_menon/**

# 2

# France

**ROBERT ELGIE**

 **Chapter Contents**

- Introduction
- The Fifth Republic in Context
- The Political Institutions of the Fifth Republic
- Political Parties in France
- France's European Policy
- Conclusion

 **Reader's Guide**

This chapter examines the domestic politics of France. It begins by placing the current political system, known as the Fifth Republic, in context. It outlines the main political institutions of the Fifth Republic, emphasising that the system creates the expectation of presidential leadership but showing that in recent years such leadership has become more difficult to achieve. It then outlines the nature of party politics in contemporary France, stressing that politics still centres on a basic left–right division but that within both the left and the right there are extreme parties that have the potential to win a considerable degree of support. The chapter ends by identifying the key features of France's European policy and suggests that France will have difficulty in maintaining its traditional position at the forefront of the process of European integration.

# Introduction

The current French political system is known as the Fifth Republic. It was established in 1958. Since the Revolution in 1789 there have been no fewer than 13 different constitutions in France, an average of one every generation. More than that, on occasions the move from one regime to another has been marked by violent and bloody conflict. For example, the 1789 Revolution, which was founded on recognisably democratic principles, was soon transformed into the Terror in which thousands of people were killed. In 1870 the collapse of the Second Empire led to the Paris Commune, which was crushed by the army. In 1940 politicians of the Third Republic ceded power to Marshal Pétain who established the Nazi-style so-called **Vichy regime** in which political opponents were summarily killed. In short, the last 200 years of French politics have been marked by frequent periods of political instability and often swift and sometimes brutal shifts from one regime type to another.

# The Fifth Republic in Context

The transition to the Fifth Republic from its predecessor, the Fourth Republic, was swift and peaceful. However, it occurred in the context of an ongoing crisis caused by the struggle for independence in Algeria. At that time, Algeria was an integral part of France. In 1954 the Algerian independence movement began a campaign of violence. By 1958 successive governments in France had been unable to resolve the situation and there were fears that generals opposed to Algerian independence would seize power and impose martial law. In May of that year, another government fell and the President of the Fourth Republic, René Coty, requested that Charles de Gaulle serve as Prime Minister.

General Charles de Gaulle was a Second World War veteran who had led the French forces in exile in London in their resistance against the Nazi occupation of France and the Vichy regime. General de Gaulle was acceptable to the dissident elements of the army because at that time it was felt that he would support their desire for Algeria to remain French. In addition to being an army man, de Gaulle was also a politician and a democrat. He had led the first post-Liberation government in 1944, but he had retreated into political exile in 1946. He opposed the political structure of the Fourth Republic and argued that France needed a completely different type of political system if the country was going to succeed, a system that provided strong political leadership. Against this background, de Gaulle agreed to President Coty's request on condition that the Fourth Republic be dissolved and that a constitution for a new republic be drawn up. On 4 October 1958 the Fifth Republic was officially established and, in December 1958, de Gaulle was elected as the first President of the new Republic.

Even from such a brief historical overview, a number of key factors emerge that help to put the Fifth Republic in context. For example, in France political institutions have often been highly contested. There have been frequent and often sweeping reforms of the political system in order to try to improve the quality of political life. In this way, the instability of French political institutions stands in stark contrast to the stability of equivalent institutions in, say, Britain or the USA. Also, French politics has not been based on consensus, unlike the situation in, for example, post-war Germany.

Often, the divisions in France have been so bitter that compromise has been impossible. In this case, those excluded from power have often felt hostility towards the political system as a whole and have worked actively to bring down the regime and to impose their own preferred system. A further point concerns France's international standing. France has suffered a number of humiliating military defeats and foreign forces have occupied French territory, most recently during the period 1940–4. Thus, the idea that France needed to regain its status as a major international actor was very prevalent during the time of the creation of the Fifth Republic. Finally, Charles de Gaulle's impact on the Fifth Republic can scarcely be overestimated. He helped to establish a system with strong political leadership in which the President was main political actor.

In many respects, the creation of the Fifth Republic marked a watershed in French political history. There is now little appetite for a major overhaul of the political system. There is a lobby for the creation of a Sixth Republic, but most people and parties are satisfied with the status quo. The creation of the Fifth Republic also marked the beginning of the end of the Algerian crisis. As President, de Gaulle took the decision to initiate independence negotiations with the Algerian forces. Elements within the army were opposed to this decision and tried on more than one occasion to assassinate the President. However, the public supported de Gaulle's policy and in 1962 Algeria gained full independence. In more general terms, the creation of the Fifth Republic marked the point when France stopped looking towards its colonies and started to look towards Europe as a way of exercising influence internationally. Overall, France remains a country in which institutional change is always on the agenda, where multiple and often incompatible political ideas compete with each other, and where the European and international arena is used to promote France's national self-interest and international prestige. (See Theme box: Democracy and Legitimacy.)

---

**KEY POINTS**

- The last 200 years of French history have been marked by frequent periods of political instability.

- There is no consensus politics in France.

- French political leaders and the French public believe that France should be a major international actor.

- President Charles de Gaulle had a major impact on the development of the Fifth Republic.

---

**THEME BOX**

!

### Democracy and Legitimacy

After nearly 200 years of political instability, the Fifth Republic, which was founded in 1958, seems to have been accepted by the French people. There are calls for the creation of a Sixth Republic, but there is little appetite for the sweeping reforms that this would entail. One of the reasons for the popularity of the Fifth Republic is the direct election of the President. The French like being led by a strong leader. However, this system has its discontents and, in part, these feelings are fed by what has made the Fifth Republic relatively popular. Presidential elections create a mood for change. However, change is difficult to achieve. Many matters are decided at the European level now and the French government cannot go it alone in an increasingly globalised world. Also, there are more checks and balances at the domestic level, even if Parliament remains very weak. As a result, popular demands for change are often disappointed. Even in 1981, when a socialist government that included four Communist Party ministers was elected after 25 years of unbroken right-wing rule, there was soon a sense of disappointment and/or powerlessness. So, the political system is stable, especially when compared with previous regimes. However, people who feel frustrated by the lack of change and/or who feel threatened by the direction of change often take it into their own hands to try to force events along. There is a long tradition of direct action, notably strikes by public-sector workers that shut down transport services and protests by French farmers that affect agricultural distribution across Europe widely. There is also long-standing support for extreme and/or anti-system parties, particularly the extreme right-wing National Front. These aspects of the political process are unlikely to disappear very soon.

# The Political Institutions of the Fifth Republic

## A presidentialised system of government

The Constitution of the Fifth Republic establishes a semi-presidential system. Semi-presidentialism is where the people directly elect the President, as in the USA, but where there is also a Prime Minister who can be dismissed by Parliament, as in Britain. In the French system, this means that there are two key political actors: the head of state (the President) and the head of government (the Prime Minister).

In France, both the President and the Prime Minister have constitutional powers. For instance, the President appoints the Prime Minister, but the Prime Minister proposes the names of government ministers to the President. The President chairs the meetings of the Council of Ministers, the French equivalent of the British Cabinet, but the Prime Minister is in general charge of the government's work and is responsible for the government's business in Parliament. The President is responsible for negotiating and ratifying international treaties and is the head of the armed forces, but the Prime Minister is responsible for national defence. In short, both people have important powers, but the President would appear to have greater responsibility for the high matters of state, while the Prime Minister would appear to be responsible for matters relating to domestic policy.

In fact, for the vast majority of the Fifth Republic's political history, the President has been the dominant political actor in all regards. This trend was set by Charles de Gaulle in 1958. In addition

to taking personal responsibility for resolving the Algerian situation, de Gaulle set the general direction for the country. He was particularly active in foreign affairs and defence policy. For example, he tried to steer a third way between the Americans, on the one hand, and the Soviet Union, on the other. In so doing, he often annoyed the Americans, who felt that he was not a loyal ally. Crucially, France developed nuclear weapons during de Gaulle's presidency. As commander-in-chief, de Gaulle assumed responsibility for these weapons. This meant that, henceforth, whatever the constitution might say, the President was the person who dictated France's defence policy. For de Gaulle, the pursuit of an independent foreign policy and the acquisition of military hardware with which the country's territory could be defended were essential not just for France's international self-esteem, but also as a real deterrent to any country that might threaten France in the future.

In domestic policy too, de Gaulle was influential. He let the Prime Minister manage the policy process and the Prime Minister had particular responsibility for ensuring that the government's legislation passed through Parliament. (Constitutionally, the President is not even allowed to set foot in Parliament.) All the same, de Gaulle made sure that the Prime Minister was putting forward policies with which he agreed. Indeed, at times, de Gaulle felt the need to intervene directly. For example, it is said that in 1968 the Finance Minister learned that the currency was not going to be devalued only when he watched the President announce the decision on television!

The precedent set by de Gaulle has been followed by all of his successors. (See Background box 2.1.). What this means is that Fifth Republic France has established a tradition of presidential leadership. The President is the dominant actor within the political system. The Prime Minister is also important, but generally speaking the Prime Minister is subordinate to the President and is charged with implementing the programme set out by the President.

The key to understanding why the system usually operates in this way is the direct election of the President. As in the USA, presidential elections are the defining moments of the political process. In France, the direct election of the President was introduced in 1962 and the first election was in 1965. De Gaulle knew that he had the support of the people generally. However, he also knew that his successors would not be able to rely on the same sort of charismatic authority that he enjoyed. Therefore, de Gaulle wanted to give future presidents the ability to claim that they were speaking on behalf of France as a whole. He believed that only the direct election of the President would

enable them to do so. He was correct. The electoral system is such that the successful candidate will have won more than 50 per cent of the votes cast. (In 1995, when he was first elected, Chirac won nearly 53 per cent.) Moreover, at the election candidates put forward their vision of France. This vision always includes some very lofty ideals, but it also includes some very concrete policy proposals. The public expects the successful candidate to stick to their ideals and implement the policies they outlined. This is why the Prime Minister is subordinate to the President. The President appoints the Prime Minister and the Prime Minister takes office with an agenda that has been set by the President. Thus, the President and Prime Minister are both important actors but usually the President is better placed than the Prime Minister to exercise leadership.

The exception to this rule is **cohabitation**— where there is a President from one party and a Prime Minister from an opposing party. Even though the President appoints the Prime Minister, the Prime Minister has to be acceptable to the lower house of Parliament, the National Assembly.

---

**BACKGROUND BOX 2.1**

Presidents and Prime Ministers in the Fifth Republic, 1959–2005

| President | Prime Minister |
| --- | --- |
| Charles de Gaulle, 1959–69 (Gaullist) | Michel Debré, 1959–62 (Gaullist); Georges Pompidou, 1962–8 (Gaullist); Maurice Couve de Murville, 1968–9 (Gaullist) |
| Georges Pompidou, 1969–74 (Gaullist) | Jacques Chaban-Delmas, 1969–72 (Gaullist); Pierre Messmer, 1972–4 (Gaullist) |
| Valéry Giscard d'Estaing, 1974–81 (centre-right liberal) | Jacques Chirac, 1974–6 (Gaullist); Raymond Barre, 1976–81 (centre-right, but no official party affiliation) |
| François Mitterrand, 1981–95 (socialist) | Pierre Mauroy, 1981–4 (socialist); Laurent Fabius, 1984–6 (socialist); Jacques Chirac, 1986–8 (Gaullist); Michel Rocard, 1988–91 (socialist); Edith Cresson, 1991–2 (socialist); Pierre Bérégovoy, 1992–3 (socialist); Édouard Balladur, 1993–5 (Gaullist) |
| Jacques Chirac, 1995—(Gaullist/centre-right) | Alain Juppé, 1995–7 (Gaullist/centre-right); Lionel Jospin, 1997–2002 (socialist); Jean-Pierre Raffarin 2002–5 (centre-right); Dominique de Villepin, 2005—(centre-right) |

Therefore, the President can appoint a loyal Prime Minister only when the parliamentary majority is also loyal to the President. At times, this has not been the case. Most recently, in 1997 the parliamentary elections returned a left-wing majority. This meant that President Chirac, a centre-right politician, had to appoint a left-wing Prime Minister. He appointed the leader of the socialists, Lionel Jospin. Without the support of a loyal Prime Minister, the President's influence was greatly reduced. Chirac maintained a high-profile presence in foreign affairs, but in other areas the only policies passed were the ones the Prime Minister wanted. The President had little or no opportunity even to veto the left-wing government's legislation and the Prime Minister set the policy agenda. This can only happen during cohabitation. There have been three periods of cohabitation to date: 1986–8, 1993–5, and 1997–2002. In 2000 the constitution was amended to make cohabitation less likely by reducing the length of the President's term of office to five years—the same as the parliamentary term—and by holding presidential and legislative elections at pretty much the same time. Given that voters who support the President at the presidential election are likely to support the President's party at the parliamentary election just a few weeks later, cohabitation is discouraged. So, in 2002 Chirac's presidential election victory was followed by a victory for his party at the parliamentary election that was held soon afterwards. However, the constitutional reform does not completely eliminate the possibility of cohabitation and if it does occur again the leadership dynamic of the Fifth Republic will change.

## The wider French state

The direct election of the President creates great expectations among the public. In order to win the election, candidates make great promises. After the election, there is the expectation that the successful candidate will keep these promises. Increasingly, though, presidents have found it hard to do so.

This is partly because France operates within an increasingly European and global system and partly because of the nature of the French party system. Partly, it is because of the changing nature of the French state. The traditional view of the French system was that it was highly state-centred. Public sector institutions were very strong. This view is no longer accurate. Certainly, the French public sector is still very important. However, it no longer occupies the dominant position that it used to. This may or may not be a good thing. Whatever the verdict, the President faces more countervailing powers now than was ever the case before. This means that it is increasingly difficult for the President to meet the public's expectations.

The French state is large and influential. The public sector consumes around 45 per cent of the country's total gross domestic product; in 1992–3 an official report estimated that a total of 6,460,000 people were employed by the state (Picq 1995: 147). The country's most senior civil servants attend specialist training schools that prepare them for a life in the higher levels of the public administration. Over the years, France has followed a state-centred dirigiste model of economic and social development. The state has been the vehicle through which the country's economic and social problems have been addressed. In the post-war period, there was a series of five-year state-directed economic plans that were highly successful in rebuilding the war-torn economy. The state has also been used to place France at the cutting-edge of technology. The country's high-speed train network would not have been built without the involvement of the state. The state is also a partner with private enterprise in the development of infrastructure projects, perhaps the most notable of which is the Channel Tunnel. There is a strong model of public service in France. The public sector delivers, and is expected to deliver, a wide variety of services, including transport, post, health and social security.

In the past, when political leaders wanted reform, they would usually try to bring about such reform by way of the public sector. For example, state-owned banks would lend money at low rates of interest, state-owned investment agencies would provide subsidies for industrial projects, and the government would use taxpayers' money to bail out ailing public-sector companies. This situation has changed. The European Union now enforces strict rules that limit the extent to which governments can subsidise companies. This has made life difficult for political leaders. At election campaigns, they may win votes by saying that they will tackle unemployment. However, in office, they find that they have to acknowledge that they can no longer use government cash to keep insolvent companies afloat and jobs are lost. Moreover, the European Union has insisted that public-sector monopolies be subject to private competition and independent regulation. This has meant that public companies, like the state-owned electricity and gas companies, no longer enjoy the same protection from market forces as before and independent regulators make decisions that affect how they operate. This development has challenged the traditional model of public-service delivery in France and has reduced the power of ministers to regulate policy sectors. Also, French companies now compete with foreign companies across the globe. To survive, they need to invest in product development and new technologies. The cost of such investment has become prohibitive for the state. Thus, companies that at one time personified the French state-centred model, such as Air France, Renault and France Telecom, have been fully or partly privatised. All of these changes have meant that political leaders face a much more difficult situation than before. At elections, they continue to make grand claims about what they intend to do. In office, though, they are often unable to deliver these promises.

This situation can be seen more broadly still. In the past, France was a highly centralised state in which the executive branch of government was dominant. This is no longer the case. For example, since 1982 there has been a series of decentralisation reforms. These reforms have shifted the responsibility for the delivery of certain policies from central government to regional, departmental and municipal government. At the 2002 presidential election Jacques Chirac promised to extend the process of decentralisation even further, and under the premiership of Jean-Pierre Raffarin reforms to this end were passed. While the decentralisation of the Republic may be popular, it has reduced the power of political leaders at the centre. This may be a good thing, but, again, it means that such leaders often find it more difficult to keep their election promises than was previously the case. A similar point applies to the development of the judicial system over the years. In France, the judiciary was usually seen as a tool of the government. However, this situation has started to change. Since the early 1980s, the Constitutional Council has developed into a powerful institution. At times, it has struck down government bills in a way that was unheard of during the first 25 years of the Fifth Republic. Again, the power of political leaders has been reduced as a consequence. The net result of all these changes is that political leaders find it increasingly difficult to keep the promises they make at elections. Their inability to do so has led to a sense of public distrust of the political class and has fuelled support for extreme political parties.

---

**KEY POINTS**

- The Fifth Republic established a tradition of presidential leadership.

- The President's powers have been reduced during periods of cohabitation with an opposing Prime Minister.

- The political system now has more checks and balances than in the early years of the Fifth Republic.

# Political Parties in France

France has a two-block, multi-party system. That is to say, political competition takes places between two blocks—the left and the right. However, within each block there are several parties, hence a multi-party system. Moreover, within both the left and the right blocks there are extreme views. In recent times, support for such views has increased.

The largest group within the left block is the Socialist Party. The socialists are the French equivalent of the British Labour Party. However, the French socialists have not adopted third-way style policies with which, for example, the UK Prime Minister, Tony Blair, is associated. They accept the need for the state and the market to work together. However, they believe that the state should play a key role in solving the country's problems. For example, during the Jospin administration (1997–2002), the government created a large number of public-sector jobs for young unemployed people and for the long-term unemployed. Similarly, the government obliged employers to introduce a 35-hour working week in the hope that they would take on more workers to make up for the loss of production. There is a debate as to whether the unemployment rate fell because of these initiatives or whether it would have fallen even without them. Whatever the case, they represented a very different way of tackling the problem of unemployment from the one followed by the Blair government in the UK. So, while the policies of the French Socialist Party have become less state-centric over the years, they are still more oriented towards the public sector than policies put forward by equivalent parties in other European countries.

Most of the other parties on the French left promote an even greater role for the state. As recently as the late 1970s, France had the second largest Communist Party in Western Europe. (The largest was in Italy.) At the 1978 election, the communists won 21.4 per cent of the vote. Since this time, they have declined and at the 2002 parliamentary election they won less than 5 per cent of the vote. Even so, they remain important politically. This is because the socialists usually need their support in order to win elections. Given their current level of support, the socialists are unlikely to win enough seats in Parliament to form a majority government on their own. Moreover, presidential candidates need to win support from outside their party faithful if they want to stand a chance of being elected. This is true even for a big party like the Socialist Party. What this means is that the socialists rely on the support of other parties, notably the communists and the greens. As a reward for supporting the socialists at the 1997 parliamentary election, there were communist ministers in the 1997–2002 government. In policy terms, the French Communist Party has shifted considerably following the collapse of the Soviet Union. However, it has not changed its name and it continues to champion the role of the state in its support of the working class. The same is true for the dissident communist parties in France. At the 2002 presidential election, the candidate of the Communist Party won 3.4 per cent of the vote. However, there were three other communist candidates and between them they won over 10 per cent of the vote. These parties do not wish to enter government. They do not consider joining an electoral alliance with the Socialist Party. They brand themselves as anti-capitalist parties. They compete with the Communist Party for votes. In one sense, they are marginal. However, in a European context it is remarkable that in the early twenty-first century extreme left-wing parties still won the support of nearly one voter in every 12 at the country's most important election. This is an indication that political preferences in France remain highly polarised. The other main party on the left is the Green Party. In terms of their policies, the greens closely resemble their counterparts in countries such as Germany.

However, the French greens have been more reluctant to join an alliance with the socialists. They did enter the Jospin government, but elements within the party were very dissatisfied with the outcome. The socialists need the support of the greens to win elections, but it is not always clear that the greens are willing to support the socialists, even if it means that their chances of exercising power are minimal as a result.

The main party on the right is now the Union for a Popular Majority (UMP). The UMP was formed in 2002 when representatives of a number of right-wing parties merged. The dominant members within the UMP are former supporters of General de Gaulle. Although de Gaulle left office in 1969, his legacy was so great that a Gaullist party continued to exist even afterwards. In terms of economic policy, the **Gaullists** were on the right in the sense that they promoted the market. All the same, they also supported the French model of state-centred public service delivery and believed that the state should play a major role in economic development. The former Gaullists in the UMP continue to believe that the state has a role to play in the development of the economy and society. Indeed, Jacques Chirac emphasised the importance of the state in both his successful presidential campaigns, 1995 and 2002. That said, up and coming UMP figures, such as Nicholas Sarkozy, emphasise more than ever before the role of the market and the need for the state to be reformed. Thus, there are some profound ideological divisions within the UMP.

The other significant party on the right is the National Front (FN). The FN is an extreme right-wing party. Its leader, Jean-Marie Le Pen, believes that the gas chambers were a 'minor detail' in the history of the Second World War. He believes that the country's unemployment problems could be solved by sending immigrants 'home'. He believes that French people should have preference over immigrants when it comes to receiving public-sector services and state benefits. By any right-thinking person's standards, Le Pen is an extreme political figure. He has complete control over his party. He believes the other political parties are corrupt. He reserves a special hatred for former Gaullists within the UMP because he still considers that de Gaulle betrayed France when he allowed Algerian independence in the early 1960s. Le Pen does not want the FN to form a coalition with the UMP and at the moment the UMP does not need the FN's support to win power. Therefore, for ideological and electoral reasons the FN remains isolated from the rest of the political class. Perhaps because of this position, the FN's support has grown over the years. At the 2002 presidential election Le Pen won nearly 17 per cent of the vote at the first ballot. To everyone's surprise, he beat Lionel Jospin into third place and qualified for the second ballot, which was a straight run-off with Chirac. At the second ballot, he gained less than 18 per cent of the vote and Chirac won the election by a landslide. Even so, Le Pen's performance was dramatic. He appeals to many of the people who feel they have no voice in the system and/or who feel threatened by the system. He wins support from people who are on short-term contracts and who feel that their economic livelihood is precarious. He wins support from people who are comfortably off and who live in areas where there is no immigration, but who are worried by what they know from television about poor and run-down inner-city neighbourhoods where the level of immigration is high. He wins the support of people who want quick and simple answers to very complex problems.

Le Pen is not a revolutionary. In that sense, his extreme beliefs do not threaten the political institutions of the Fifth Republic. However, he is proof that political beliefs in France continue to be highly polarised. In a very different way, the left provides similar proof. In contrast to the situation prior to the 1960s, the communists do not aim to overthrow the capitalist system and introduce a communist regime. Even so, the presence of a two-block multi-party system in which there are extreme political forces means that French politics remains unpredictable. The core support for political leaders is paltry. (Chirac won the support of less than 20 per cent of the voters at the first ballot of the 2002 presidential election.) To win, they need to build alliances. However, often these alliances are constructed with the support of people who hold quite radically different beliefs. Almost inevitably, therefore, leaders who come to power promising a clear set of policies will find that their allies, even those within their own party, do not share all of those policies and insist on a different set of policies in order to maintain their support. As a result, leaders in office often end up breaking their promises in order to hang on to power.

---

> **KEY POINTS**
>
> - Party politics in France is dominated by competition between left-wing parties and right-wing parties.
>
> - There are extreme parties on both the left and the right.
>
> - No single party is large enough to govern on its own for any length of time, so coalition politics is the norm.

# France's European Policy

Over the years, France has been at the forefront of European integration. (See Theme box: The Impact of the European Union.) In 1957, France was one of the founding members of the European Community. In the 1960s France was instrumental in establishing the common agricultural policy, the first policy to be determined at the European level. In the 1970s President Valéry Giscard d'Estaing helped to introduce the direct election of the European Parliament. In the 1980s, President Mitterrand was a vital force behind the Maastricht Treaty and the creation of European Monetary Union. More generally, France has been a key player at the European level. In the early 1960s France and (the then West) Germany agreed closer ties. This helped to create a Franco-German axis that spearheaded the development of the European Community for the next 30 years. French officials have often held key positions in the most important European positions—currently Jean-Claude Trichet is president of the European Central Bank—and the European bureaucracy in Brussels is organised in a similar way to the civil service in France.

While there is undoubtedly a strong ideological and political commitment to the EU in France, we should also recognise that France's support for integration is a means by which leaders have tried to pursue France's self-interest. For example, France's support for Europe is a reaction to some of the most traumatic events in the country's history. The development of an organisation in which Germany was a member and in which France and Germany had roughly equal status was a deliberate attempt to ensure that French sovereignty and territory would no longer be threatened by its neighbour. We can see the development of the EU as a way of increasing France's national standing in the face of repeated military defeats, invasions and loss of territory in the past. More recently, it is tempting to see Mitterrand's support for the European Union as a way of trying to rein in German influence in the period immediately following German unification and also as a way of trying to import Germany's post-war economic success through the adoption of the common currency and an independent European Central Bank. More mundanely, France's support for EU integration has, at times, been entirely self-interested. Here, the best example is the common agricultural policy, which, as Tony Blair is keen to point out at every available opportunity, was designed to give economic support to French farmers and which continues to do so.

Currently, France's relationship with the EU is in a period of flux. At home, most political parties

## The Impact of the European Union

The development of the Fifth Republic is inextricably linked with the development of Europe more generally. In the early years of the Republic, President de Gaulle was in favour of the general idea behind the creation of the EC, because he thought that as a block of countries working together Europe could ply an independent course between the two superpowers, the USA and the USSR. He was also in favour of the EC of the six at least, because he believed that if such a block of countries could work together, then the Franco-German alliance would be in a position to dominate the decisions taken. Thus, France would regain influence in world events. However, de Gaulle was opposed to anything akin to a United States of Europe. He believed in a confederal Europe, a Europe of sovereign states, stretching from the Atlantic to the Urals. Moreover, twice, in January 1963 and May 1967, he vetoed Britain's application to join the EC, because he felt that Britain was too close to the USA and that, if Britain joined, France's role as the main diplomatic power in the EC would come under threat. At a policy level, de Gaulle supported the creation of the common agricultural policy (CAP), because it helped French farmers, but he was still willing to paralyse the EC with his so-called 'empty chair' policy when he felt that European integration threatened French interests. This ambiguous attitude towards Europe is still present today. In the 1980s President Mitterrand was a strong supporter of European integration, and was a driving force behind the Maastricht Treaty and Economic and Monetary Union (EMU). However, this was because he thought France would benefit economically from EMU. For his part, President Chirac campaigned in favour of European integration too. Even so, it must be acknowledged that France has often delayed implementing EU reforms for as long as possible and has tried to ensure that France still benefits from the CAP as much as possible. In an enlarged Europe, France's position is more vulnerable than in the early years of the Republic. It is now much more difficult for France to be the leader at the European level. Partly as a result, there is now a fairly sceptical attitude towards European integration in France. To many, Europe is now one of the sources of France's problems, not a possible solution to them.

are either opposed to further European integration and, indeed, to membership in some cases or are at least split on the issue of further integration. The extreme left considers the EU to be a capitalist club with a liberal agenda and is opposed. The extreme right believes that EU integration threatens French national identity and is also opposed. Indeed, both extremes are sceptical of membership never mind further integration, even though neither is likely to hold sufficient political power to make the issue of leaving the EU a serious topic for discussion. For their part, the socialists and the UMP are divided on the issue of further integration. Many of the Socialist Party's leaders are in favour of European integration, but many of the party's supporters equate integration with liberalisation and see Europe as a threat to their economic livelihood and to the French model of state-centred public-service delivery. Many within the UMP favour the

EU's liberalisation programme, but also see further integration as a threat to France's standing in the international community. In the past, France was a big player in European negotiations. Now, it is one country of 25 and there is likely to be further expansion soon. All told, there is no doubt that the French are in favour of the EU, but they are sceptical of further integration. Indeed, on 29 May 2005 the French people were asked to vote in a referendum on the Draft Treaty establishing a Constitution for Europe and by a majority of nearly 55 per cent voted to reject it.

The referendum vote created a crisis for Europe and, combined with the Dutch rejection just a few days later, effectively halted the ratification process. The referendum vote also reflected a crisis in France. Many of the issues discussed in this chapter are relevant to understanding why the Draft Treaty was rejected. Key among them is the idea that the French model—the French way of doing things—was under threat. On both the left and the right, there is support for the role of the state and for public-sector service delivery. For some, the development of Europe can only threaten this way of organising economic, social and political life. For others, again on both the left and the right, European integration is a direct economic threat. In the referendum debate, reference was constantly made to the idea that workers from new member states in Central and Eastern Europe were migrating to France and taking the jobs of French workers. The economic impact of any such immigration is very difficult to determine,

but, whatever its impact, there was the perception that European integration was worsening France's already serious unemployment problem. Finally, even though the Draft Treaty has absolutely nothing to do with Turkey's possible future membership of the EU, many on the right and particularly the extreme right argued that European integration would further dilute the core values of France and the identity of the French people. For those on the right, the prospect of Turkish membership was used to create a general hostility to the EU and helped to increase the number of people opposed to the Draft Treaty.

---

**THEME BOX** ( ! )

### The Impact of Globalisation

For a long time in France, there has been a strong sense that the country has a 'universal mission'. That is to say, France has something enriching to offer the world in general. This is seen most clearly in terms of the French language and French culture. The International Organisation of French-speaking Nations (l'Organisation internationale de la Francophonie) has 50 member states and promotes the spread of the French language outside France. More generally, the French government spends millions of francs each year promoting artistic and cultural events around the world. In addition, politicians often talk of a French model. This refers to a state-supported system of public services and a well developed system of social welfare. In the era of globalisation, this sense of France's universal mission has been threatened. English has become the dominant international language. American television and culture have become ever more prevalent across the world as a whole. In terms of economics and politics, there has been a trend towards privatisation and deregulation that threatens the French model. These developments have created a sense of insecurity in France. Governments have

tried to delay liberalising the economy, but this has only put off the inevitable. The government has tried to apply cultural quotas that ensure broadcasters have to transmit a certain proportion of French-made artistic material. Some individuals have taken the law into their own hands. Most notably, José Bové has been jailed for engaging in direct action against symbolic aspects of globalisation in France. In 1997, he destroyed genetically modified (GM) crops in a protest against what he called *malbouffe*, (bad food), claiming that global food producers and distributors were damaging traditional French cuisine. In 1999, he helped to destroy a branch of McDonalds for the same reason. Globalisation is recognised as inevitable, but many people in France oppose how it is currently progressing. To this end, there is a thriving *altermondialiste* (otherglobalisation) movement, which wants to promote a different, more socially responsible form of globalisation. Politically, though, the movement is weak and more often than not French political leaders have found themselves reacting to global developments rather than shaping them.

# Conclusion

France is reflecting on its role in Europe and on the direction that European integration should take. International and European developments have created a sense that French identity is being threatened by the supposedly inexorable march of what are called 'Anglo-Saxon values', which is usually taken to mean economic liberalisation. (See Theme box: The Impact of Globalisation.) More than that, there is no doubt that France's political leaders find it increasingly difficult to make independent decisions in the face of a globalised and Europeanised decision-making process. This sense of frustration has reduced the opportunity for presidential leadership, even if the demand for such leadership remains. Moreover, this situation has also fuelled support for extreme parties on both the left and the right. All in all, this period of reflection is likely to last for some time yet.

 **QUESTIONS**

1. Why has there been so much political instability in France since 1789?
2. Why did the Fourth Republic collapse in 1958?
3. How powerful is the French President?
4. What is the role of the Prime Minister in France?
5. Why has the extreme-right National Front party done so well in the last 20 years?
6. To what extent has France been at the forefront of European integration since 1957?
7. Why did French voters reject the Draft Treaty on the European Constitution in May 2005?

 **FURTHER READING**

**BOOKS**

*History*

■ **Gildea, R. (2002),** *France since 1945***, Oxford, Oxford University Press.** A clear introduction to contemporary French history.

■ **Hanley, D. (2002),** *Party, Society, Government: Republican Democracy in France***, Oxford, Berghahn Books.** Identifies the foundations of contemporary party politics in France.

*Institutions*

■ **Elgie, R. (2003),** *Political Institutions in Contemporary France***, Oxford, Oxford University Press.** Provides an overview of political institutions and parties in contemporary France.

■ **Cole, A. (2005),** *French Politics and Society***, 2nd edn, Harlow, Pearson.** Identifies the core features of the French political system.

■ **Knapp, A. and Wright, V. (2001),** *The Government and Politics of France*, **4th edn, London, Routledge.** Provides perhaps the best introduction to the intricacies of contemporary French politics.

### Parties

■ **Evans, J. (2003), (ed.),** *The French Party System*, **Manchester, Manchester University Press.** Examines the full range of political parties in France.

■ **Bell, D. (2000),** *Parties and Democracy in France: Parties under Presidentialism*, **Aldershot, Ashgate.** Emphasises the importance of presidential elections as a factor shaping French politics.

■ **Hazareesingh, S. (1994),** *Political Traditions in Modern France*, **Oxford, Oxford University Press.** Charts the ideological differences between competing political forces in France.

### Europe

■ **McCarthy, P. (ed.), (2002),** *France and Germany in the 21st Century*, **London, Palgrave.** An overview of the relationship between the two countries with historic antagonisms but who came to be strong allies in the pursuit of European integration.

■ **Cole, A. (2001),** *Franco-German Relations*, **Harlow, Longman.** A contemporary view of Franco-German relations.

## JOURNALS

■ *French Politics*, **Palgrave.** The leading English-language political science journal focusing on French politics.

 ## IMPORTANT WEBSITES

In English:

● **www.diplomatie.gouv.fr/** Website of the Foreign Affairs Ministry with links to plenty of general information about France as well as foreign policy issues.

In French:

● **www.ifri.org/** Website of a leading research institution, the French Institute of International Relations (IFRI).

● **www.lemonde.fr/** *Le Monde* (centre-left newspaper of reference).

● **www.lefigaro.fr/** *Le Figaro* (right-wing newspaper).

● **www.liberation.fr/** *Libération* (left-wing newspaper).

● **www.elysee.fr/** Website of the President of the Republic (with a searchable speech function).

● **www.premier-ministre.gouv.fr/** Website of the Prime Minister.

 **Visit the Online Resource Centre that accompanies this book for lots of useful additional material, including an interactive map of Europe. www.oxfordtextbooks.co.uk/orc/hay_menon/**

# 3

# Italy

DAVID HINE

✔ **Reader's Guide**

This chapter places politics in Italy in the wider context of European democracy. It emphasises two paradoxes. First, Italy has often been seen as a country of endemic instability, where democracy is more fragile than in most West European states, even though until the early 1990s the same party dominated the governing coalition for four decades, and there were few changes to the basic parliamentary structure established by the 1948 Constitution. Second, despite a significant degree of recent change to both institutions and the party system, many Italians feel today that Italy is more out of line with European political values and Europe's policy-making style than in earlier post-war decades. The chapter describes the fundamentals of the ideologically polarised party system laid down after the Second World War, and the changes it experienced in the early 1990s, showing how coalition-building moved from alliances spanning the political centre, to a form of alternation between left and right. It identifies the idiosyncrasies of these two poles, showing how they are related to earlier party history, and how they generate continuing concern about the policy-making capacities of contemporary Italian government. The chapter concludes by tracing the key features of Italy's relationship with the EU, which has always been driven by a strong commitment to integration, but which in recent years has generated severe difficulties, as Italy has steadily lost economic competitiveness and has struggled to cope with the demands of deeper integration.

# Introduction

Italy was unified as a nation state relatively late in European terms. The liberal regime established in 1861—a limited form of parliamentary democracy—struggled to deal with the strongly entrenched economic imbalances of a disparate peninsula. Northern Italy was far ahead of the largely feudal south, and this gap persists to this day. Political life also reflects these differences. National governments have always struggled to reconcile different outlooks, and different social and political relationships between regions. In addition, the troubled political development of united Italy down to the Second World War left deep scars on politics. The liberal regime lasted for 60 years, but collapsed under the pressures of demands of full democratisation after the First World War. Mussolini's fascism lasted from 1922 to 1945, slowing economic development and suppressing democratic evolution. Only after 1945 did Italy have a fully fledged democracy for the first time. With it, some of the tensions of the early part of the century reappeared, with a strong communist movement on the left, and significant authoritarian and anti-democratic groups on the far right. Remarkably, parliamentary democracy has survived despite the extreme instability such polarisation has generated. No less remarkably, for several decades down to the 1980s the economy flourished, with high rates of growth, and rapid economic and social transformation. But, since the mid-1980s, this relationship between politics and economics has in part reversed itself. The party system has become less polarised, and alternation between left and right has become possible for the first time, but political corruption, an over-extended and inefficient welfare state, and the continuing burden of southern under-development, have placed severe constraints on economic performance.

# The Peculiarities of Italian Democracy

Among European states that have a continuous history of democracy from 1945, Italy has been the one with the largest number of uncertainties hanging over it. In the early decades, there was recurring speculation that democratic government would not survive. Italy's allies were constantly concerned at the risk of a communist takeover. Others feared the real threat came from the right, either from a resurgent fascist movement or an authoritarian coup. With hindsight, it is possible to see that both risks were exaggerated. The Cold War placed Italy firmly in the western camp, and both the Soviet Union and the Italian Communist Party (PCI) accepted this. In any case, it is unclear that the communists really wanted a centrally planned Soviet-style economy or a single-party totalitarian state. Many were far too pessimistic to believe such a takeover possible, and others, while not renouncing their identity as communists, from an early stage realised its fundamental flaws. Similarly, the fascist past, while alarming, was also, as in Germany, a form of historical inoculation against a revival of right-wing authoritarianism.

This polarisation and fragility nevertheless turned political competition into a struggle between so-called democratic parties and the anti-democratic extremes. However, the democratic parties themselves were quite fragmented and spanned a wide policy spectrum. Creating and sustaining governments was always difficult and their average life was less than a year. Despite this, the regime survived where the French Fourth Republic, a similarly polarised party system, collapsed after little more than a decade. There were minor changes in the composition of governments, but every one from the late 1940s to the early 1980s was headed by a Christian democrat, and Christian Democracy (DC) was the fulcrum of every coalition, and always the largest single party. Italians described themselves as living under a regime of unstable stability: the DC always in power, and the PCI always in opposition. The only political change was a form of peripheral turnover in the DC's alliance partners. Until the early 1960s, the centrist coalition excluded the third party, the Socialist Party (PSI). Thereafter it mainly included them. During the great economic crises of the mid-1970s, the Communist Party was temporarily included in the parliamentary coalition too, but the experiment was quickly abandoned.

Although coalition instability damaged the reputation of governments and the political class, it was less damaging to the legitimacy of democracy than might have been expected, and it was this, combined with the prosperity generated by three decades of rapid economic growth, which saved what by many standards was a poorly functioning political system. On the left, the fear of a resurgence of right-wing authoritarianism turned the Communist Party into one of the great defenders of liberal democratic values, and helped prepare for the day, when the Cold War ended, when the party could renounce its Soviet past entirely and transform itself into a social democratic movement. But across the political centre too, which generated the country's political rulers, the values of anti-fascism and the resistance movement were deeply embedded, while the liberal principles that the founding fathers of the Republic Constitution of 1948 had laid down were broadly respected.

As a result, Italy escaped the searing debate on its constitutional structure that France experienced in the 1950s, and the Constitution bedded down to create a form of fragile political consensus that

probably excluded only a 5 per cent fringe of monarchists and fascists on the far right. There was certainly a good deal of questioning, as time went on, about particular aspects of the political system—most notably the very pure system of proportional representation, which made it impossible for any party to win a parliamentary majority, offered a guarantee of parliamentary representation to even the smallest party, and seemed to encourage splits and schisms, especially in the 1960s and 1970s. But loyalty to the Constitution became a touchstone of legitimacy which united not only the governing parties of the centre but extended leftwards to the Communist Party as well.

This consensus began to erode from the late 1970s onwards, though in an unexpected way. The issue of constitutional reform was put more and more openly on the table, though the fact that this was possible was widely seen as a sign of democratic maturity rather than fragility. It was at last possible to question aspects of the broader system of government, because most participants in the debate were confident that this would not undermine liberal democracy itself but rather improve it. Even parties which had long defended proportional representation, either because they believed it was an inclusive system which helped legitimacy or because they were afraid of the consequences for themselves of majoritarianism, began to accept that a different electoral system might help achieve the alternation in power between competing coalitions that Italy, alone among major European democracies, had failed to achieve.

However, it was one thing to debate reform, quite another to achieve it. For over a decade through the late 1970s and 1980s, debate intensified, but the results were negligible. Meanwhile, voter satisfaction with government was diminishing as the first signs of Italy's declining competitiveness began to appear. When change came, therefore, it was not a guided or self-conscious choice either by parties or Parliament. Rather, change was forced by voter reaction to the end of the Cold War. This weakened the Communist Party, but even more the Christian democrats, because by now voters were mainly voting DC to keep the communists out, and suddenly had little reason to fear a weakened and disoriented Communist Party. In fact the end of the Cold War set off a much wider chain reaction in the political system, encouraging voters to vote for new parties, encouraging wider debate about democratic renewal, and allowing anti-corruption investigators to attack the extensive networks of political corruption on which the governing parties increasingly sustained themselves.

The political earthquake thus engendered was concentrated in the period 1992–4, out of which emerged what has often been called, erroneously, Italy's 'Second Republic'. Party politics has certainly operated differently since that time, partly because voters started to give their votes to new parties, and partly because the abolition of pure proportional representation encouraged party leaders to behave differently. But in fact there was no immediate and fundamental re-working of the Constitution as in France with the Fifth Republic. Change has been forthcoming, especially in terms of the distribution of power between central government on one hand,

and regional and local government on the other. Extensive debate has also taken place about the relative powers of executive and legislature at the centre, with everyone agreeing on the desirability of creating more stable and enduring coalitions, but so far there has been no fundamental change. (See Theme box: Democracy and Legitimacy.)

## KEY POINTS

- Italian democracy has survived where many predicted its early demise after the Second World War.

- Party fragmentation has made coalition-building a difficult and unstable process.

- Despite party fragmentation there has been a broad consensus on the liberal democratic features of the 1948 Constitution.

- Efforts to reform political institutions in recent years have had patchy success, though the early 1990s can clearly be seen as a form of watershed in the way the system works.

## THEME BOX

### Democracy and Legitimacy

Italy was for several decades after the Second World War described as a 'difficult' democracy. More recently the emphasis has been on the shortcomings of the 'quality' of its democracy. The first critique was based on the instability of coalition government, and the fear that this would lead to deadlock and conceivably even democratic breakdown. Irretrievable breakdown has never occurred, but some of the consequences of complex and short-lived coalition governments have been obvious: public disaffection from politics and the political class, a significant group of the electorate with no stable partisan identification, short-term horizons in policy-making, a weakly institutionalised executive, etc. Two cleavages—one the ideological inheritance of the Cold War and the other the territorial inheritance of southern economic backwardness—have also contributed to make policy-making more difficult. The more recent critique, focusing on the 'quality' of democracy, flows from the earlier one. Because governments have been difficult,

rational budgeting and fair and rational systems of welfare delivery have been difficult to achieve. Policies delivered via clientelism have led directly to corruption, disaffection and a degeneration of the climate of political debate. This degeneration seemed to peak in the atmosphere of the 2006 general election, conducted in the basest of terms involving paranoia and the trading of personal innuendo and insult, and concluding with a defeated prime minister, Silvio Berlusconi, momentarily hesitating to accept the verdict of the ballot box and resign. Yet despite these shortcomings, Italians seem deeply attached to parliamentary democracy, if not to their existing political class. In old-fashioned left-right terms, the system is much less polarised than in the Cold War era, and civil rights and political liberties are actively protected by the Constitution, by the Constitutional Court, by the Presidency, by extensive territorial devolution to the regions and cities, and by parliamentary vigilance.

# The Institutional Framework

Italy since the Second World War has had a classic form of parliamentary government. All European democracies have seen a long-term shift in the balance of power at central level between executive and legislature that has worked in favour of the former, but in Italy this shift came later and has moved least far. In Italy, Parliament is central to the decision-making process. It is not easily cowed or controlled by the executive, and it makes a great deal of its prerogatives. This is not to say that it exercises purposive leadership, but it is a key institutional veto player. What happens in Parliament has a vital impact on policy outcomes. Governments have had great difficulty managing public expenditure, because they have had relatively weak control of budgeting and revenue-raising. They have found it difficult to introduce purposive programmes of public-service management or reform because parliamentary lobbies alter and amend programmes as they are passing through the legislative process. They have had difficulty pursuing long-term policy because Parliament has regularly changed the composition of the government, and sought renegotiation of parts of the government's programme.

When we say 'Parliament' here, we of course mean *parties* within Parliament as much as the institution itself, but Parliament is the transformative arena in which such constant negotiation takes place, and in this sense it is more important than its counterparts in other European democracies. Members of the legislature have maintained a strong view of their own institutional privileges, so that procedural rules favourable to the government and corrosive of legislative power have been strongly resisted. The conventions that have bolstered Parliament's position and constrained the executive were laid down in the Constituent Assembly which drafted the Republican Constitution in 1946/7. Although there were critics who argued that the executive needed to be strengthened against

parliamentary excess, they were very much in the minority. The Constitution was designed to prevent a recurrence of fascism, and for Italians this meant checks and balances to limit the power of government and to curb the power of an executive-led parliamentary majority. Hence the panoply of liberal mechanisms: a written constitution with entrenched civil and social rights, entrenched regional decentralisation of power, a President with counter-powers to those of the government, a range of independent agencies to enforce the rule of law, including a constitutional court, an independent judiciary, a council of state and an independent state accounting agency, and finally an exactly co-equal bicameral Parliament. And all this was further underpinned in practice by a principle that, while not part of the Constitution itself, had far-reaching implications for the way the institutions worked, namely proportional representation (PR). Admittedly, it took some years for these institutions to work properly, following the end of the fascist period, but gradually over two decades they were put in place and by the end of the 1960s they were working largely as the founding fathers had intended.

The flaw was, of course, that the framework was not counterbalanced by anything which would help the executive to deal with such a range of checks and balances. In Germany where there had been a similar reaction to fascism, evident in the Basic Law promulgated in 1949, the political class in Germany felt more keenly another and opposite danger: that of an excessively weak executive. Thus while the Basic Law was also a power-dispersing document, it had some procedures which worked in the other direction: the constructive vote of no confidence, the bar on extremist parties, the tempering of PR through a 5 per cent threshold. Most importantly in Germany the cultural mindset of the political elite, shared by the entire parliamentary class, was that the re-establishment of Germany's democratic credentials and the bedding down of a democratic political culture required a highly consensual polity, underpinned by executive stability. Italy had none of these advantages, and the consequence was a Parliament that was seen by the parties as a legitimate arena for unbridled party competition and the frequent destruction of parliamentary majorities. Governments could not rely on their own backbenchers to support them consistently and suffered regular legislative defeats, to the point where the entire culture of the legislative process was devolved to party and committee leaders inside the legislature, and hence to extensive and complicated bargaining, amendment, withdrawal of proposals and delays. Formal rules of procedure, in particular the notorious provision for secret voting, were written to weaken government control, and it was only in the 1990s that Parliament was persuaded to give up some of the prerogatives it enjoyed over parliamentary procedure and management.

Given the brevity and fragility of governing coalitions, efforts to strengthen the executive were extremely difficult. Prime ministers were often in office for little more than a year at a time. Even the longest lasting, for example Aldo Moro in the 1960s, were forced into frequent cabinet reshuffles generated by formal crises that required their resignation and the seeking of a fresh vote of confidence. The bedding down of an effective heart to the machinery of government was very difficult in such circumstances. Two types of change were constantly advocated but until the 1990s never achieved. The first was a reduction and consolidation in the number of ministerial departments, especially in the key area of economic management and public spending. The second was an effort to inject modern management techniques into programme evaluation, public spending streams and personnel policy. Treasury management of public expenditure was just about satisfactory in the years of high growth and relatively low pressure on the welfare system, even though that control was limited largely to formal spending caps and did little for programme effectiveness. But by the 1980s

that control had been seriously eroded. Budgetary management became much more difficult when fiscal streams—the preserve of the Ministry of Finance—were out of the Treasury's control, and coalition pressures and the absence of prime ministerial authority over the Council of Ministers and the parliamentary majority forced the Treasury to resort increasingly to public borrowing and deficit spending to reconcile the disparate demands of the various parts of any given coalition. The result was a burgeoning budget deficit, which from 1980 to 1992 more than doubled, leaving the country with a fiscal overhang unparalleled among the major European economies. The problem was compounded by the fact that increasingly the Italian state was not just the instrument for governing the country, but an enormous and powerful lobby dictating policy. Public-sector employees, state-dependent beneficiaries and more generally the poorer southern regions were the electoral base of parliamentary majorities, and in these circumstances effective reform was an uphill struggle.

Italy's dispersed form of parliamentary government was therefore a limit case in European democracies, and would doubtless have succumbed to the sorts of critique which brought down the French Fourth Republic, had there not been a widespread fear, shared even by the communist left, that to attempt a serious constitutional reworking would be to destabilise a fragile democratic framework. Only when those fears receded, and when in any case the long-term consequences of policy failure were becoming inescapably evident, was it possible to start to change things. This happened during the 1990s, though even then there was no *formal* reworking of the Constitution to change the balance between executive and legislature but only ad hoc changes to the structure of central government, and to the working of the party system.

The consolidation of political authority at the centre concentrated on the financial management processes and the authority of the Treasury and the Prime Minister's office. Parliament finally agreed to changes to budgetary procedure which yielded significant control of borrowing ceilings and resource allocation, while within the executive itself over-all economic and financial authority was at last consolidated in the Treasury. It became accepted, moreover, within most coalitions and within Parliament, that the engine of policy-making had to become much more than in the past a tight and effective working relationship between the Prime Minister's office and Treasury. This was helped by the changes to the party system examined in the next section of this chapter, themselves the product of the new electoral procedure introduced in 1993. Gradually this forced coalitions to become a little more cohesive, and in turn strengthened the bargaining power of the Prime Minister *vis-à-vis* both the parties in his coalition and Parliament. However, this would not have been possible without the impact of a third factor—the changes to the external environment. As European pressures came to bear more and more heavily on Italian government autonomy, it became inescapably clear that the country faced a choice: bring important aspects of public policy into line with EU-determined rules and standards, or face relegation to an outer tier of

EU member states. This choice applied most starkly to membership of the euro area, where in the mid-1990s the overwhelming need to bring the annual budget deficit under control forced on a reluctant political class the realisation that if the core of the executive were not strengthened, then Italy could never make the changes to budgetary performance required by euro-area convergence criteria. (See Theme box: The Impact of the European Union.)

Not all changes to the institutional order worked in the direction of more concentrated powers, however. Italy was a classical unitary system of government, modelled indeed upon the Napoleonic order imposed on much of the peninsula at the start of the nineteenth century. The republican Constitution made a concession to devolution in the shape of regional government, but it took some decades to establish the system right across the country. The first regional elections took place in 1970, and in any case regions were not represented in the second chamber of Parliament, as in the German *Bundesrat*. The centre maintained financial control, in that most revenues were raised at the centre and

---

**THEME BOX** !

### The Impact of the European Union

Italy was a founding member of the original European Economic Community, and the Italian authorities have normally been among the most enthusiastic supporters of European integration. Public opinion overall remains highly supportive of integration, and successive Italian governments have been keen on treaty revisions to push forward the European constitutional framework through more majority voting in the Council, more powers to the European Parliament and wider policy remits. Yet the Italian authorities have generally been seen as less successful than some others at imposing their own specific policy choices through European institutions. Responsibility for coordinating policy across the range of Italian government departments involved has been divided, and prime ministers have rarely had a high-profile role or led from the front. Indeed, the country has often made a virtue of being tied down by European policies (for example on state aid deregulation, competition policy or budgetary policy) where, it has been

argued, the EU forces the country to do things that, left to its own devices, it would not be able to achieve because of political divisions. Recently, however, the costs of these requirements have become painful. Italy has lost competitiveness within the euro area (some estimates suggest Italian labour costs have risen by 30 per cent compared to German costs in the last decade) and, even if this is not because of its membership of the euro, the country no longer has even the short-term comfort of devaluation against its European competitors. Alongside this, Italy has found that when transatlantic divisions widen, it has difficulty reconciling its Atlanticist instincts with its European ones. Under the Berlusconi governments (2001–6) Italy shifted towards a closer relationship with the USA, but found that the divisions that US policy in the Middle East generated in Europe left Italy with less influence, in consequence, in the EU. Good relations between Europe and the USA seem important for Italy to feel comfortable in its European role.

allocated on a formula that consciously favoured the poorer regions. Most public employees were employees of the state not sub-national government. And the central authorities retained many legal as well as practical controls over the behaviour of regional authorities. In short, the scope for regional authorities to depart from nationally determined policy guidelines was very limited. The best that regional or indeed city authorities could do was to govern *better*, i.e. more efficiently, rather than according to locally distinct policy choices.

This situation began to change in the 1990s, though the nature of the changes was ambivalent. In a series of stages more power was devolved to regional government, most notably through greater devolution of control over health service provision, which was effectively regionalised, and more resources (though by no means enough) were allocated to the regional authorities to fund the system. A number of other policy areas were also decentralised. At the same time, in an effort not to replicate at local level the complex and unstable coalitions characteristic of national government, fundamentally new relationships were created between the executive and the representative assembles at these levels, with the regional president and the town or city mayor being directly elected and the lists of party candidates associated with their election automatically winning an enhanced quota of assembly seats in an effort to stabilise executive authority.

The devolution programme has been seen as a success in revitalising sub-national government. But, not surprisingly, it has had significant knock-on effects at national level, which are still working themselves out. The Italian state was certainly over-concentrated and devolution was necessary. But, in a country with wide disparities in income and wealth, and more generally in economic dynamism between regions, the decentralisation of power risks exacerbating differences rather than solving them.

If the weaker regions are left to rely on their own weaker fiscal resources or administrative capacities, they may well fall further behind. The central state cannot go far down the road of allowing local taxpayers to fund health, social welfare or education without eroding basic levels of citizen entitlements. This is the dilemma Italian governments have found themselves in, in the last two decades. It is clear that government at local level is in many respects, especially in more advanced regions, more vital and flexible than national government. But this has fed calls for even more autonomy by rich regions and, at the limit, for separatist tendencies. The poorer south, meanwhile, risks languishing in poverty and being saddled with weak local government if left to its own devices. So central government is constantly tempted to step back into the resource allocation mechanism. This, in turn, divides national governments, especially where some parties are stronger in one part of the country, and others in different parts, which, as we shall see, has been increasingly the case.

## KEY POINTS

- Italy, like the UK, has a strongly entrenched form of parliamentary democracy.

- Nevertheless, the parliamentary majority is normally weak and divided and the power of the chief executive and the key departments at the centre of the machine are relatively restricted.

- Reform has been very difficult, whether of basic institutional relationships, or of the efficiency of the machinery of government, though external pressures have done something to strengthen the authority of the centre.

- The main focus of reform has been at sub-national level, especially through the direct election of regional governors and city mayors, which has been a relative success.

# The Party System and Coalition-Building

The Italian party system is one of the best examples of what has become known as **polarised pluralism**. Its characteristics are said to be a wide ideological spectrum, with irresponsible anti-system parties at the extremes, a large number of parties (more than five), coalitions that are built at the political centre, with two main poles of competition in the electorate quite distinct from one another—one dividing moderate left from extreme left, and one dividing moderate right from extreme right. In such a system, it is claimed, centrist coalitions would be constantly embattled by attacks from right and left, coalitions would be unstable, because parties would be forced to work with one another, even when they shared little in policy terms, and voters would flee the democratic parties of the centre, dissatisfied with the compromises they had to make.

Such a model does indeed seem to capture party politics in the decades after the Second World War. The system was structured thus because almost all the main cleavages which helped create European party systems in the early decades of the twentieth century were present in Italy. Moreover, they were exacerbated by the experience of war, occupation, the resistance struggle and the Cold War, and were frozen into a complex system by the pure form of proportional representation adopted as the Republic was re-established. Thus there was a strong class-based left, but it was divided between social democrats and communists. There was a strong Christian democrat movement, which grew out of a party of religious defence present before the rise of fascism. There were secular liberals of various strands, two of which managed to re-establish themselves as minor parties, having been dominant parties in the liberal era before 1922. And on the far right there was a monarchist and fascist subculture which threw up assorted parties even more untouchable on this side of the spectrum than the Communist Party was on the left.

Although much the largest party was Christian Democracy, which got close to 50 per cent briefly in 1948, before settling down to around 40 per cent, or latterly a little less, for the next three decades, under a system of pure PR this was by no means enough to secure it a majority. The DC always had to work with minor parties—in the early years predominantly on the centre and centre-right, later on the centre-left, and this was the basic source of instability in the system.

The consequence was a very high turnover of governments. Indeed by the 1970s it became almost impossible to sustain centrist coalitions at all. And yet, against the predictions of theorists who believed that polarised pluralism would lead to extremist parties seizing power, as it had done in the inter-war years, the Italian party system did not actually collapse into stalemate and generate an anti-democratic takeover. Instead, it began a long transformation that led to a fundamentally different form of coalition-building and to a substantially different set of parties 20 years later. The reason why this happened was that polarised pluralism by the 1970s no longer captured all the features of Italian party politics. In particular, the alleged extremism of the right and left was diminishing. Indeed, it was the centre parties that had an interest in branding them as extremist, but the 'extremist' parties themselves, and most importantly the Italian Communist Party, were fast absorbing the values of liberal democracy. Although until the end of the Cold War in 1989 this did not allow the old PCI to transform itself into a fully fledged social democratic party, the PCI's brand of eurocommunism had already in the 1970s made it look like a very different sort of party from old-style communism. Hence, already during the severe economic crisis of the 1970s, the party was briefly incorporated into the ruling coalition when its parliamentary majority became untenable. And, after the end of the Cold War, both the left and right lost their anti-system connotations. Both changed their labels and identities. The Communist Party became the Democratic Left, and by 1998 one of its leaders was Prime Minister. The old neo-fascist party, the *Movimento Sociale*, had also transformed itself into a conservative party that clearly accepted democratic politics, and indeed its leader, Gianfranco Fini, went on to become Deputy Prime Minister and then Minister for Foreign Affairs.

The party transformation of the 1990s, however, was the consequence of much more than the depolarisation of the political extremes. It was also the product of an earthquake at the centre of the party spectrum. The main governing party, Christian Democracy, had become increasingly divided and unpopular. It was steeped in political corruption and heavily factionalised. It seemed unable to produce a new generation of political leaders, and—never out of power—it was increasingly seen in voters' eyes as responsible for policy stasis. It was also more and more a party of the south. In the north, voters impatient with the inefficiency and interventionism of government in Rome were turning to new movements, and especially the exotic regional separatist party, the Northern League. The 1992 general election was the catalyst for a series of events that threw the Christian democrats and their socialist allies into turmoil. Both parties lost heavily and started to split as voters, members and even elected representatives began to desert a sinking governmental ship. The judiciary, for long anxious to bring corrupt politicians to court but unable to do so because of political manipulation, seized its opportunity and brought a deluge of cases to court in a purge of the old ruling class known as **Tangentopoli**. The ruling parties imploded; there was a brief technocratic interregnum when no party was in charge; the electoral system was overhauled; and a new party framework emerged, built essentially around two broad coalitions, one on the left and one on the right. In the subsequent decade, the party system has gradually bedded down into this mould, and for the first time in the post-war era the Christian democrats, who have not fully disappeared but have split into

two small opposing camps, one in each of the two larger poles, are no longer in charge. Instead, on the left pole, is a series of parties, ex-communists, ex-Christian democrats, greens, socialists and others, while on the centre-right, former media tycoon Silvio Berlusconi has fashioned a no less heterogeneous coalition of his own, entirely new party, **Forza Italia**, conservative Christian democrats, the now modernised, far right *Alleanza Nazionale* and the Northern League. Even more than the coalition of the left, the centre-right is a complex and contradictory combination. The Northern League and *Alleanza Nazionale* represent very different regions, and are difficult bedfellows, reconciled only by the reality that without Berlusconi holding the ring they would almost certainly all lose out and leave the centre-left as the permanent governing coalition. (See Table 3.1.)

From the mid-1990s the new party system has produced a degree of real alternation that was never before possible. It seems to have offered voters a real choice. Whether it has governed any better and whether the party system has changed in a more fundamental sense is perhaps more doubtful. First, the number of parties has not diminished and the largely majoritarian electoral system introduced in 1993 has not really helped in this regard. It encourages alliances and stand-down agreements between parties in each coalition that maintains them as broad coalitions, instead of gradually reducing the number of small parties and generating more stable coalitions. But coalitions are not very much more stable than before. It is true that Silvio Berlusconi survived for a full five-year term in 2001–6, and that was a record for Italy, but the centre-left's victory in the previous legislature led to numerous governments under three different prime ministers, and was an unhappy experience. Moreover, the Berlusconi government itself has often appeared to be a stalled one, the only virtue of which has been pure survival. So while there are fundamental changes in the architecture of coalition-building, while the extremes have now largely been accommodated inside democratic politics, and while the traditional governing parties have broken up, the

**Table 3.1** Electoral Coalitions over Four Elections

| | 1994 | 1996 | 2001 | 2006 |
|---|---|---|---|---|
| | *Winner: Centre-right but significant reworking of basis of coalition in 1995* | *Winner: Centre-left but some minor reworking of basis of coalition in 1998* | *Winner: Centre-right (coalition survives largely unchanged throughout legislature)* | *Winner: Centre-left* |
| **Centre-left** | RC+PDS+VER+Si+ others | RC+PDS+VER+Ri+ PPI | Ds+VER+ SDI+Mar | *Ulivo* (Ds-Mar-Dems) +PDS+Rosa+ PDCI+VER+ UDEUR+4 other lists not winning seats |
| | **34.5%** | **44%** | **40.0%** | **49%** |
| **Centre** | PPI-Pact for Italy 15.7 Others 3,3 | LN 10.1 Others 4,7 | Others 7.0 | Others <2% |
| **Centre-right** | Northern cartel: FI+LN+CCD Southern cartel:FI-MSI-CCD | FI+CDU+CCD+AN | FI+LN+AN+Udc | *Casa delle Liberta'* (FI+LN+AN+ Udc+new PSI+8 lists not winning, seats) |
| | **46.5% (mean)** | **40.3%** | **45.4%** | **49%** |

*Notes*: The table shows the election results for the Chamber of Deputies for the main groups of parties. Many other very small and local lists competed, so that the figures shown above do not total to 100%. Several parties have changed name and, at the margin, composition. The principal switches are that of the Partito Popolare (PPI—the progressive wing of the former Christian democrats) from the centre to the left in 1996 and the temporary switch of the Northern league (LN) to non-alignment (shown here as the Centre) for the election of 1996 only. Figures in bold show the popular vote for each coalition. But note that the changes between elections reflect mainly the moving of parties and groups out of or in to coalitions, rather than shifts in voter allegiance. For the elections of 1994–2001 inclusive, the disparity in seat shares in the Chamber won by the coalitions is greater than the disparity in votes as shown in the table, due to the impact of majoritarian electoral system in operation for three-quarters of the seats in those elections. The near-tie in 2006 (under different electoral arrangements based on a reinstituted list-system of proportional representation) gave a 40-seat majority-bonus to the Centre-left, thanks to its 24,000-vote lead over the Centre-right (out of 38 million votes cast!), though its lead in the Senate, operating under different electoral arrangements, was much smaller.

*Key to main parties and lists*:
PDS Democratic Socialist Party (formerly the PCI or Italian Communist Party) which became the DS (Democratic Socialists)
RC Communist Refoundation (left breakaway from the former PDS)
PDCI Party of the Italian Communists (moderate breakaway from the RC)
PPI People's Party (ex-progressive DC); later the 'Margherita' (Mar)
VER Greens
SDI Socialists
Rosa nel pugno SDI plus Radicals

FI Forza Italia
LN Lega Nord (Northern League)
AN Alleanza Nazionale (formerly the MSI, a far-right party)
CCD (later UDC) Christian Democrat Centre (ex-conservative DC)
Nuovo PSI former Socialist Party, later on centre-right

new configurations and new parties leave much to be desired. The broad characterisation of this system which has emerged is no longer polarised pluralism, certainly, but neither is it simple bipolar competition between two cohesive teams. Instead the most appropriate label Italian commentators have found for it—**fragmented bipolarity**—sums up many of its continuing drawbacks.

Moreover, Italy remains a system of strong party government in the sense that parties occupy positions of power and absorb and control resources in a way often seen as antithetic to good governance. There is still a high degree of patronage in those parts of the state machinery that ought to be free of party influence—regulatory agencies,

public-service management teams, broadcasting, the higher reaches of the grand corps like the Council of State and even the judiciary. This is repeated at regional- and local-level agencies. And, even after the major privatisation process in the 1990s, quite significant parts of the economy, including parts of the banking system, remain under party influence; politicians clearly still vie in various ways to control the financial sector, and indeed protect it from foreign influence. The reform of the party system has not fully purged the unhealthily tight hold that parties have had on the wider political system and indeed on the economy, and this is a basic cause of the public-policy difficulties that Italy continues to experience long after liberal democracy has become fully consolidated.

# Falling Out of the European Mainstream

The Italian political system has evolved a good deal since the early 1990s. Whether or not that evolution really merits the label of a Second Republic, there has been major change. Italian democracy has certainly deepened in the sense that voters now probably have more meaningful choice in national elections than in the past, they have more vibrant systems of local democracy, there is more information available about politics and policies, there is more discussion of policy, as opposed to megaphone ideological debate, and there is at least the beginnings of a public-service revolution improving the delivery of public services and the use made of taxpayers' money. And yet paradoxically Italy seems to feel itself less at the heart of Europe than at any time during the last 50 years. It is less sure of itself, of its institutions and procedures and of its ability to compete either at a European level or a global one.

Part of the reason for this lies with the consequences of the old political order and the level of

policy stasis that was required to produce the earthquake of the early 1990s. The legacy of extremely disorderly public finances and an unmodernised administrative, legal and regulatory state has been profound. In a sense Italy has been struggling hard to catch up ever since the 1980s. The worst aspect of this is the overhang of public debt. Italy managed at least to stop the growth of the deficit by the beginning of the 1990s and to reduce the primary (net of interest) deficit to the point where, with falling international interest rates and subsequently the protection of euro membership, the deficit, if not the accumulated stock of public debt, came under control. But the measures necessary to achieve this since the mid-1990s have been painful and damaging: low levels of public investment in infrastructure, declining business and consumer confidence, and a dour and relentless struggle to contain the burgeoning costs of an over-extended welfare state that continues to have strong defenders inside and outside government. The Italian economy has, moreover, suffered more than any other European economy from fundamental structural weaknesses. Its manufacturing sector is composed disproportionately of intermediate-technology enterprises of modest size. It has few large multinational corporations and is weak in most areas of advanced technology. Its traditional manufacturing base is now challenged by low-cost producers elsewhere in the world—both in Eastern Europe and Asia—and its service-sector is weak and heavily reliant on protection. Addressing these weakness in the era of political change described above has been extremely difficult. (See Theme box: The Impact of Globalisation.)

Moreover, while political change has brought improvements they leave much to be desired. Neither the coalition of the centre-left nor that of the centre-right has been an ideal candidate to modernise the country. The latter, in particular, represented a strange paradox: led for its first decade by an entrepreneur Silvio Berlusconi, who courted political and legal controversy throughout his career, and who, through his control of virtually all private-sector broadcasting, carried with him as Prime Minister one of the most blatant unresolved conflicts of interest any democratic politician in Europe could carry. The coalition he led—an exotic blend of former fascists, populist separatists, former Christian democrats and a business party formed from scratch in three months—inspired little more confidence. Cases of political corruption have continued to erupt regularly despite the supposed purging of corruption in the early 1990s, and to outsiders the wisdom of involvement in an economy which remains heavily protected, and where business rules and practices are hard to master, and legal and administrative unreliable, looks highly questionable.

It is not surprising, therefore, if Italy suffered a severe crisis of confidence in the decade from 1995, and was left in the throws of a deep national debate about its international competitiveness. The objective data are deeply depressing: in 2006 Italy lanquished at the bottom of the European growth league. In the decade 1996–2005 its annual rate of GDP growth was only a little over 1 per cent. Nor is it surprising if this state of affairs has led to some questioning of Italy's traditional commitment to

## THEME BOX

### The Impact of Globalisation

Italy is a European power. It has a Mediterranean location which gives it what is sometimes called a Mediterranean vocation. The Mediterranean, the Mahgreb and the Balkans are its 'near abroad': areas for which it feels some special sense of responsibility (witness its relative enthusiasm for peace-keeping in the Balkans). But it had almost no colonial legacy after the Second World War, and it consciously sought to emphasise its identity as a *European* democracy, giving it an outlook very different from other north-Mediterranean countries at the time. Beyond Europe it had, like other countries in Western Europe, an Atlanticist identity, which stemmed from the need during the Cold War to shelter under the American nuclear umbrella. So Italy has never had the global vocation that the UK, France and Spain have enjoyed from their historical legacies. Nor has it had the commercial and industrial power that has given postwar Germany its international reach. Some Italian businesses became multinationals, but they were few compared to the other large European states. Italy has been a low-cost mass-producer *within* Europe, and this is its problem in the twenty-first-century world of global commercial relationships. Italy has modest foreign direct investment overseas itself, and its own economy is structured in such a way that it is very vulnerable to low-cost competitors who produce goods similar to its own. This competition comes from Central and Eastern Europe and from Asia. Nor is Italy a natural magnet in Europe for inward foreign direct investment. Its cost structures are too high, its labour market too inflexible, its system of government too bureaucratic. In this sense, Italy looks less able to cope with the pressures of globalisation than most in Europe, and it is no surprise that protectionist voices have made themselves heard in reaction to these pressures in recent years.

European integration. Historically, Italy was one of the founding member states, and most Italians believed and still believe that European integration is unequivocally in Italy's interests. Even if it has often been difficult to comply with European rules, few have until recently questioned that Italy's fate lies with faster European integration. Doubts and hesitations of the type found in more recent members states in northern Europe, or indeed in France, have never plagued either the Italian political class or the public, which has always supported institutional deepening, and rarely questioned decisions taken by the authorities to comply with European requirements—even when, as with euro membership, compliance required painful measures. Today, however, those doubts have at last begun to surface. They are not shared by the business class nor by Italy's traditional EU policy-making elite. Rather they have a more populist base, especially in the Northern League and to some degree *Forza Italia*. Berlusconi's well advertised affections for the USA and the dynamism of the US free-market have given some strength to such views, as have growing public perceptions that the introduction of the euro was not the cure-all of Italian economic ills.

In policy terms, in fact, the rise of Italian doubts about Europe are much more Italian doubts about Italy, and its capacity to cope with a world that Europe itself finds much more hostile and competitive than in earlier and gentler post-war decades. But they have focused on Europe because so many decisions affecting Italy are now taken in a European context, and the consequences of those decisions, especially in the central area of budgetary management and public expenditure, are painful and unavoidable. In this sense at least the dilemmas of Italian democracy reflect those of the wider EU: Italy has participated enthusiastically for half a century in the construction of a European quasi-polity of which it is part, but the deficiencies of that quasi-polity have a strong bearing on the quality of democracy at national level. Italy cannot do without the European Union, but it finds it increasingly difficult to reconcile its own political system with it.

# Conclusion

Italy started the post-war era as a relatively backward society, with poor prospects for democratic stability. Association with democratic and free-market Europe saved it from the fate which met many other countries of Mediterranean and of Eastern Europe. It prospered rapidly for several decades, and its democracy was gradually consolidated despite many flaws. Today, despite Italy's deep problems, both economic and political, no one questions the strength of democratic government. But there is a sense in which this modernisation has come at a high price. Italy became an advanced welfare state perhaps too early for its own good. Its commitment to welfare required a high level of state intervention, and this was executed by a political class of questionable quality in an administrative and legal environment where efficiency and predictability were never attainable. These problems have been carried over into a new and more difficult twenty-first-century era and have left legacies with which the contemporary political class struggles to cope.

**QUESTIONS**

1. Why was Italy such a latecomer as a nation state and what legacy did the history of territorial division leave on the unified state?

2. What are the features of the 1948 Republic Constitution and did its drafters intend to disperse power as widely as turned out to be the case?

3. Why have Italian governments been so short-lived?

4. Has the so-called 'Second Republic' improved coalition stability or policy effectiveness?

5. Why was Italy such fertile terrain for communism after 1945, and how did the PCI cope with the dilemma of the revolutionary party in a non-revolutionary context?

6. Is there anything repugnant to democratic principles in a business oligarch like Silvio Berlusconi forming his own party and becoming Prime Minister?

7. Why are Italians still apparently so attached to European integration when they face such difficulties living with the requirements of monetary integration?

 **FURTHER READING**

■ **Mack Smith, D. (1997), _Modern Italy: A Political History_, New Haven CT and London, Yale University Press.** Provides an extremely accessible historical overview.

■ **Bellucci, P. and Bull, M. (eds) (2003), (_Italian Politics: The Second Berlusconi Government_.** The most recent in a series of yearbooks of Italian politics.

■ **Bull, M. and Newell, J. (2005), _Italian Politics: Adjustment under Duress_, London, Polity Press.** A superb contemporary introduction to the distinctiveness of Italian political institutions.

■ **Ginsborg, P. (2005), _Silvio Berlusconi: Television, Power and Patronage_, London, Verso.** A fascinating study of the politics of patronage in Italy.

**IMPORTANT WEBSITES**

● **www.governo.it**   Website of office of the President of the Council of Ministers (the Prime Minister) (in Italian).

● **http://english.camera.it/**   English-language site of the Italian Chamber of Deputies.

● **www.iai.it/index_en.asp**   English-language website of the Italian Institute of Foreign Affairs (IAI).

● **www.astrid-online.it/**   Website of ASTRID—a major public reform research consortium (in Italian).

● **www.corriere.it/**   _Corriere della Sera_ (centrist-oriented daily newspaper) (in Italian).

● **www.repubblica.it**   _La Repubblica_ (centre-left daily newspaper) (in Italian).

 **Visit the Online Resource Centre that accompanies this book for lots of useful additional material, including an interactive map of Europe. www.oxfordtextbooks.co.uk/orc/hay_menon/**

# 4 Britain

## BEN ROSAMOND

### Chapter Contents

- Introduction
- The Historical Context: Ancient and Modern
- Political Institutions in Britain
- Political Parties in British Politics
- The European Exception?
- Conclusion

### Reader's Guide

This chapter aims to put contemporary British politics into a broad context. It notes that the modern British polity is the product of a complex historical evolution that produced a distinctive democratic state. In this context the chapter shows how politics in Britain since 1945 have been defined by three perennial and unresolved dilemmas: debates about the appropriate model of political economy though which to govern Britain, issues surrounding the appropriate global alignment of the British state and controversies over the territorial organisation of the pluri-national United Kingdom. The chapter outlines the traditional model of British politics, the 'Westminster model', and identifies the doctrine of 'parliamentary sovereignty' as the key reference point within this model. Various challenges to the integrity and workability of the 'Westminster model' are then identified. Discussion of the strategies of the main political parties is framed by an analysis of the structuring effects of electoral politics in Britain. The chapter points out that debates within political parties are often as important as conflict between parties. With this point in mind, the chapter proceeds to an overview of the interplay between British politics and the European Union. The discussion suggests that perennial party management dilemmas over 'Europe' reflect a poor fit between the European issue and the conventional cleavages structure of British politics. Moreover, it points to the explicit strategy of depoliticisation pursued by the Blair government over the question of British adoption of the euro.

# Introduction

The British political system, unlike many other European polities, does not possess an obvious moment of foundation. There has been no catastrophic military defeat leading, as in the cases of Germany and Italy after the Second World War, to the wholesale redefinition and modernisation of the political system. There has been no moment equivalent to the profound crisis of French politics in the late 1950s to force a total rewrite of the constitution and an accompanying redefinition of the purposes and roles of core political institutions. Indeed, Britain lacks even an obvious revolutionary moment in the distant past, which we can identify as the point where the modern political system emerged.

Instead Britain entered the period after 1945 as a strange hybrid political system: a parliamentary democracy and a constitutional monarchy without a codified written constitution. The evolution of British democracy is a complex story, punctuated by key moments at which democratic impulses took root, but in which ancient conventions, rituals and institutions remained intact. Its party system after the war bore a close resemblance to the structure of political competition before the war. Indeed, its core parties have displayed a common talent for adapting to changing conditions and have rarely failed to respond positively to evolving ideological frameworks. Britain's global empire, constructed over the course of two and half centuries, had covered a vast proportion of the world's surface. Its status as a world power was apparently confirmed by its central role in the international post-war settlement, yet it was confronted by a key strategic dilemma which cut to the very heart of what kind of state Britain should be within the new emerging global order. Moreover, Britain—or the United Kingdom of Great Britain and Northern Ireland to give it its technically correct title—was a pluri-national state: a composite polity consisting of four distinct national spaces: England, Wales, Scotland and Northern Ireland. Yet, unlike several other European countries (Austria, Belgium, Germany for example) Britain was a unitary rather than a federal state, governed from the centre by the Westminster parliament and the Whitehall bureaucracy.

For at least the first two decades after 1945, the British system of government and its attendant political culture were widely admired as a model of balanced democratic stability prone to neither ideological extremism nor the participatory excesses that undermined the practice of responsible government elsewhere. Yet the eventual story of post-war British politics is a story of the struggle over a series of troublesome governing dilemmas. To the issue of Britain's strategic role in the world mentioned above should be added at least two other perennial problems that have defined the scope and shape of British political debate over the past six decades. The first was the growing realisation among political elites and opinion formers that Britain's economic pre-eminence was in decline. The governing dilemma was how to manage the British economy in this context in terms of both (a) the appropriate and relative roles of the state and the market as generators of prosperity and (b) the framework (national, European or global) within which the governance of economic life should take place. The second ongoing issue concerns the internal structure of the British state. At stake has been the sustainability of Britain's unitary structure of government with the idea of the devolution of responsibilities to its constituent national parts forming a powerful alternative to the status quo.

BEN ROSAMOND

# The Historical Context: Ancient and Modern

The British political system is a peculiar mixture of the ancient and the modern, of the pre-democratic and the democratic. At first sight, it is hard to classify the British polity in terms of the main European sub-types. Where else, for example, would we find such quaintly archaic parliamentary rituals? Which other modern state subsists *without* a formal written constitution? Which other polity retains a second chamber as odd as the House of Lords? For many advocates of the British system of government, these echoes of pre-democracy are decided advantages. They show how a society can modernise without losing sight of its traditions. Many are proud of the distinctiveness of Britain's institutions and its political culture. To lose or to overturn these unique qualities in the name of modernisation—or perhaps Europeanisation—would damage fatally the essence of the body politic. For others, however, the supposedly valuable relics of ancient times actively prevent Britain from becoming a fully fledged democracy and realising its appropriate status as a modern *European* country in an interdependent and globalised world. Indeed, from this perspective, there is an intimate link between a nostalgic approach to British politics and a delusional (and harmful) presumption that Britain remains a world power.

The previous section mentioned three perennial dilemmas that frame the big picture of British politics. They may be reposed as follows:

- Which model of political economy is best suited to deliver economic growth and prosperity to Britain? Within what framework (national, European or global) should this model be realised? How, if at all, is the pursuit of economic growth compatible with the modernisation of Britain's constitutional structures?
- What is the appropriate strategic alignment of the British state? How should it position itself globally, not only within the world of international relations, but also in terms of how it inserts Britain into the international economy?
- What is the appropriate distribution of territorial power within the pluri-national British polity?

The first dilemma is in part a function of different ideological views about how Britain should be governed. Should the priorities of the state be geared towards the fulfilment of citizen welfare or should it seek to enhance economic growth? Should the state be the primary vehicle through which the goals are achieved or is the market the best device to allocate resources and achieve efficient outcomes? Should public policy be made in the name of a particular section of society: wealth creating representatives of capital whose entrepreneurial efforts will trickle down to the wider social whole, or those sections of society that suffer from the excesses of capitalist accumulation? Should society be exposed to market forces or protected from them? These alternate visions crystallise into respectively right- and left-wing narratives of British politics, which in turn find their expression within the dominant political parties, Conservative and Labour. But, as we note in the next section, these worldviews have vied with one another across the course of the past century and each has had significant periods of ascendancy and at various points parts of each have been elemental to each party's platform.

The dispute between two broad models of the good society has also, for much of the post-war period, been framed by the common perception that Britain was suffering from some form of decline. Thus, the state versus market contest came to develop into a matter of alternative solutions to supposedly profound problems. In terms of economic decline, there had been concern among elites from the late nineteenth century that, across a range of indices, Britain was being out-performed by newly industrialising rivals. While levels of absolute prosperity were on the increase, Britain's relative performance was becoming poorer. The replacement of Sterling by the dollar as the world premier reserve currency and the rise of American leadership of the capitalist world after 1945 added fuel to this debate. This was exacerbated yet further by the politics of the 1960s and 1970s which came to be organised around the conflict between polarised political economy projects—exaggerated versions of the market versus state dilemma. These in turn offered alternative takes on how Britain should be modernised, particularly in light of growing global interdependence and international economic imperatives.

The issue, for policymakers and academics alike, has not just been a question of which approach—market or state—is better or more just, but what are the sources of decline and how should these be addressed? One set of arguments is bound up with historical analyses of Britain's pathway to becoming a capitalist democracy. The lack of a seismic moment comparable to the French Revolution of 1789 or a huge shock such as military defeat meant that Britain did not undergo a full 'bourgeois'/capitalist revolution. This meant that the state was left with the curious mixture of ancient and modern elements noted above. The monarchy was not displaced but absorbed into the emerging democratic culture. The doctrine of the absolute rule of the monarch was replaced by the notion of the supremacy of Parliament, which in turn yielded (a) a highly centralised state machine and (b) a resistance to any project (such as European integration) that might threaten the autonomy and sovereignty of Parliament. Archaic institutions—such as the House of Lords—were not replaced by more rational modern variants. Civil servants were not trained in the techniques of administering a modern economy. The educational system failed to provide the technocrats and entrepreneurs needed to fuel a vibrant modern economy. This line of thinking holds that Britain had no impulse to acquire a developmental state—a predisposition to deliver forward-thinking policies geared towards the achievement of economic success. This reasoning yields strong criticisms of the

model of governance that emerged in Britain and which is discussed in the next section. Constitutional reform is seen as a central prerequisite for the reversal of decline.

It is also important to recognise the legacy of the British Empire. Not only did this give Britain significant dominion over a large portion of the Earth's surface; it also acted as a mechanism to generate huge inflows of capital into Britain. Globally oriented financial capital came to sit at the heart of British capitalism as the City of London became the world's major finance centre. The assumption here is that the British state was captured by the interests of financial capital rather than those of domestically based productive capital. The economic preferences of the British state have always been global rather than inward or even European. These long embedded factors survive the alternation of parties in office.

The second dilemma—the appropriate strategic orientation of Britain—intersects with the first. Indeed this intersection sits at the heart of many of the most contentious debates in post-war politics. Winston Churchill, Britain's wartime leader and Conservative Prime Minister between 1951 and 1955, described Britain's foreign policy as operating within the context of three overlapping circles of influence: the Empire, the Atlantic alliance with the USA and Europe. The dilemmas within the last two of these are obvious to any observer of post-war politics. Britain's awkward and ambivalent relationship with Europe discussed below may owe much to the existence of the other two circles in British foreign-policy mindsets, while the 'special relationship' with the USA perhaps explains the Blair government's decision to side with the approach of the USA rather than that of other large European states (notably France and Germany) in the war against Iraq after 2003. While the Empire circle was progressively dismantled with independence granted to virtually all of Britain's colonies after 1945, the imperial state of mind can still be seen in the prevailing assumption that Britain is and should be a world power rather than, say, a key player in the European society of states (as represented by the EU).

These rival strategic and global alignments thus provide a context within which the first set of political economy debates are played out. The evidence of the post-war period suggests that the European context has become progressively understood as the most viable way ahead for Britain, although the British reluctance to align itself fully with the European project (the continued refusal to adopt the EU's single currency, for example) suggests a continued reluctance to shed the Atlantic and global frames of reference.

At first sight, the third dilemma—the territorial organisation of the British state—would seem to stand apart from the other two. Yet the growth of the pluri-national United Kingdom is elemental to the way in which the British state was constructed. Indeed, the story of the UK is often told as one of imperial conquest by the English state over the course of seven or eight centuries, with the emergence of the British Empire as an external projection of the same process. England itself is a historical aggregation of several kingdoms and the absorption of Wales was accomplished after four centuries of struggle by Acts of Union in the 1530s and 1540s under the reign of Henry VIII. The Act of Union with Scotland created the UK in 1707 and the island of Ireland was absorbed by imperial conquest at the beginning of the nineteenth century. Six counties of Ireland achieved independence in 1921, leaving the UK composed of England, Scotland, Wales and Northern Ireland.

Two things need to be said about the territorial organisation of Britain. The first concerns its asymmetry. The UK, again because of its lack of a formal constitution, has no formal division of powers between its constituent units. That said, the Act of Union of 1707 preserved Scotland's distinctive legal system and its educational institutions operate quite differently from the rest of the UK. England and Wales is often treated as a singular legal entity, while Northern Ireland has developed its own idiosyncratic polity where the defining axis of conflict is between those who seek a united independent Ireland and those who strive to preserve the union with Britain (a conflict that has spilled over into periodic political violence). The second related comment is that, for much of the past century, the British state has sought to govern its territory from the centre—from Westminster and Whitehall.

Arguments about the constitutional reordering of territorial authority have taken the form of demands from forces within Scotland and Wales for independence, a demand which since the late 1980s has been articulated to a broader preference for an integrated Europe. But the issue of UK territoriality has also been a technical argument about the merits of devolution. It is true that devolution has been a tangible political goal for nationalists in Scotland and Wales, but the idea of delegating authority downwards to Scotland and Wales—and perhaps to England's regions and large cities—is also a technical fix to the problem of overloaded central government and is a familiar pattern across European political systems in recent decades. Indeed the highly particular type of devolution seen in Britain since 1997 (the Scottish Parliament, the Welsh Assembly and the Northern Ireland Legislative Assembly are all empowered differently) may be part of a much larger process where public authority in Europe is being reordered. National governments remain intact, but authority is delegated upwards to the EU level and simultaneously downwards to sub-national units. (See Theme box: Democracy and Legitimacy.)

### KEY POINTS

- The modern British political system is the product of a complex process of historical evolution.

- The key debates in British politics over the past century concern rival models of political economy, alternative conceptions of the appropriate global alignment of the British state and dilemmas about the territorial organisation of the United Kingdom.

- These dilemmas intersect and cut across standard party alignments.

## THEME BOX

### Democracy and Legitimacy

By most accepted measures, Britain is one of the world's higher ranking democratic states. It has also been celebrated as a model of democratic stability. In the 1950s and 1960s outside observers were prone to comment on Britain's capacity to deliver government that was representative of the popular will, yet responsible in tone. Elites were given space to govern by a respectful and deferent population, whose participation within the polity was just enough to keep the governing elites on their toes. By the 1970s this image had been shattered. Concerns were raised about the disproportionate power exercised by organised interests (notably trade unions) and the impact of party discipline that could seriously compromise parliamentary checks on a determined majority government. While the crisis atmosphere of the 1970s has largely abated, serious concerns remain about the democratic quality of British political procedures. The centralisation of power at the heart of the core executive is cause for concern, but the most obvious problem remains the electoral system which routinely delivers discrepancies between proportion of the vote won and representation in the House of Commons. Proportional representation has been a longstanding policy goal of the Liberal Democrats, but the two main parties have been reluctant to proceed with the idea, despite Labour's unfulfilled promise to offer a referendum on electoral reform for the House of Commons. A more immediate cause for concern is the dramatic downturn from 2001 in the turnout figures for general election and the evidence that younger generations are disproportionately under-represented in electoral politics.

# Political Institutions in Britain

British government is dominated by the central institutions of the British state in London. The institutional make-up of the British state and the distinctive concepts that underpin it are usually gathered together with the dominant idea of the 'Westminster model'. However, the term is rather more than a description; it is also highly charged in that invocation of the Westminster model is often about defending this traditional institutional anatomy of British politics and its way of operating against constitutional reform from within and against pressures from the outside occasioned by the likes of European integration and globalisation.

The defining features of the traditional Westminster model may be summarised as follows:

- a unitary state built around the presupposition of absolute Parliamentary sovereignty;
- the executive (the government) drawn predominantly from Parliament;
- strong Cabinet government together with majoritarian control of the executive through Parliament;
- the concept of 'the opposition', that is the aggregation of minority political forces into a single bloc within Parliament;
- an adversarial conception of debate within the polity generally but within Parliament in particular;
- a system of two-party electoral competition;
- constituency-based forms of representation based upon a 'first past the post' electoral system;
- rules and norms of procedure, but no written constitution.

Moreover, the Westminster model imagines a flow of authority through the system. This is depicted in Figure 4.1.

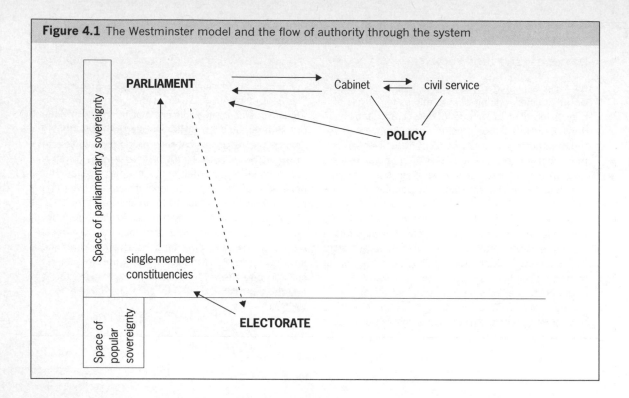

**Figure 4.1** The Westminster model and the flow of authority through the system

It is important to understand how this flow is conceived and how the transmission of popular will is both limited and potentially distorted. Popular sovereignty (the will of the people) is expressed only at those moments when Parliament is dissolved (elections). Thereafter, the majority in Parliament form a government in the form of a Cabinet that makes policy in accordance with the civil service (Whitehall). The civil service is permanent and does not change as new parties move into power. The civil service is theoretically subordinate to the executive and the executive is in turn subordinate to Parliament. Legislation cannot be made without the sanction of Parliament, hence the doctrine of parliamentary sovereignty (it has absolute authority within the system). Parliament is accountable ultimately to the electorate, but only at those moments when popular sovereignty arises in elections. Note that there is no clear separation of powers between the legislative and executive branches, as in France. The Prime Minister, Cabinet ministers and junior ministers of state almost always come from the party with the majority in the House of Commons.

The pure version of the Westminster model has been subject to several challenges that emanate from twentieth-century trends in British politics. The theory behind the model relies on the idea of Parliament as an assembly that is representative of constituency interests, but is also composed of members who operate according to their collective judgement and individual consciences. The rise of disciplined political parties ensures that party leaderships control their members to ensure conformist voting. This means that governments drawn from Parliament are able to exercise control over their Members of Parliament (MPs). Governments with sizeable majorities are, therefore, able to pass legislation without impediment. The Labour governments in office since 1997 offer a case in point with successive majorities of 177, 165 and 64. Dissent and rebellion are easily accommodated unless majorities are small as was the case with the Conservative government of John Major after 1992, when a sizeable minority of Conservative MPs habitually voted against aspects of the government's European policy. For the most part then, parliamentary scrutiny and accountability is limited.

To this must be added two further developments. The increasing power of the Prime Minister's office to exercise control over the Cabinet together with governments' shaping of the media agenda mean that power is further concentrated and centralised.

Meanwhile the model's image of the civil service is somewhat flawed. Permanent bureaucracies develop ongoing agendas and preferences. Departments of state are not 'green field sites' ready to be colonised by new policies formulated by new governments. Indeed civil service departments are notable for their ongoing historic preferences. The Treasury, probably the most powerful unit within the administrative apparatus of British government thanks to its control over expenditure allocations, is well known for its scepticism about the utility of using a European Union framework for running macroeconomic policy. This is not to say that governments have no control over the civil service. Since 1979 both Labour and Conservative governments have pursued a programme of civil service modernisation (itself part of a broader diagnosis of the failure of the British state to manage decline) involving the application of market criteria and strategic coordination into the process of policy formulation.

The other major dent in the Westminster model has been a series of developments that have further undermined the viability of the doctrine of parliamentary sovereignty. The growth of forms of authority above the nation state, be they associated with the various economic phenomena bundled together in the term 'globalisation' or the delegation of sovereignty to the European Union, seriously challenges the notion of Westminster as the final resting place of authority in British politics. Meanwhile successive governments, especially since 1979, have overseen processes of privatisation (the withdrawal of the state from the management and control of public utilities and the macroeconomy) and the application of business and market logics into much of the residual public sector. Policy-making is less a matter of hierarchical command and control relationships and more a case of governance through coordinated networks.

To these trends must be added the significant agenda of constitutional reform undertaken by the 'New Labour' governments since 1997. Within Parliament, there has been significant attention to the working practices and operation of the House of Commons and a protracted debate about how to remove the hereditary principle from the House of Lords. The Scottish Parliament and the Welsh Assembly were established in 1998, with the former having the capacity to make primary legislation in some areas and the latter quickly establishing an agenda to acquire similar powers. These acts of devolution have very obviously challenged the sovereignty of the Westminster Parliament, although it clearly retains sovereignty—in a traditional formalistic sense—over England. The 1998 Good Friday Agreement established an assembly and a power-sharing executive in Northern Ireland, although the government of the province has vacillated between this model and direct rule from Westminster ever since.

Thus, it is very hard to describe Britain as a unitary state and to discuss the totality of British politics in terms of sweeping generalisations. There are now genuine dilemmas about whether Parliament is entitled to legislate on, for example, key aspects of Scottish affairs and such issues might lead us ever closer to the conclusion that the image of a centralised, single state is no longer valid.

# Political Parties in British Politics

Post-war British electoral politics has been dominated by a competition for supremacy between two major political forces: the Conservative and Labour parties. The 17 elections since 1945 have yielded nothing but single-party governments, with the Conservatives in power for 35 years and Labour for 26 (up until the end of 2006). Periods of minority rule are rare. The Labour government of Harold Wilson continued in office between February and October 1974 without a parliamentary majority, while two of the last three years of the 1974–9 Labour government of James Callaghan were underwritten by support from the Liberal Party in Parliament.

Nevertheless, the dominance of two-party electoral politics is striking. Table 4.1 gives an overview of British general election results since 1945. It is worth noting the shares of the votes cast in each election for the two major parties. Across the 17 elections, the average share of the vote achieved by the Conservative Party is 41.19 per cent. Labour fares only a little worse, with an average share of 40.77. In other words, on average the two main parties attract over 80 per cent of the votes cast in British elections. The Conservatives have never dipped below 30 per cent. Only once (1983) has this happened to the Labour Party. In 1951, the two-parties commanded an extraordinary 96.8 of all votes cast. Compared to almost all European polities, these data are remarkable. Never has there been a need for the two-party coalitions that routinely make up German governments, let alone the delicate multi-party conglomerates that are characteristic of Italy. The French Fifth Republic has enjoyed periods of genuine single-party government, but British politics has not featured the repeated dissolution and reformation of political parties found in France.

Having said that, the data in Table 4.1 reveal some quite notable trends that might suggest a gradual unsettling of Britain's two-party system. Most obviously, there is clear evidence that the two-party share of the vote has declined since the 1970s. In the 2005 election, for example, the two main parties secured between them only 67.6 of the popular vote. Votes have clearly migrated away from the Conservative and Labour parties to other sources, notably the revived Liberal Party and its successors (see below). Also apparent is the rise, over the course of four decades, of nationalist parties such as the Scottish National Party (SNP) and Welsh Plaid Cymru (PC), reflecting the emergence of a political cleavage around the territorial distribution of power in the United Kingdom. A further trend is the decline in turnout, that is the proportion of those entitled to vote who actually go to the polls in an election. A dramatic decline was registered in 2001 when less that 60 per cent of the electorate cast a vote. The figure for 2005 represented

**Table 4.1** British Election Results, 1945–2005

| | Turnout % | Con | | Lab | | Lib/Lib Dem[1] | | SNP/PC[2] | | Others[3] | |
|---|---|---|---|---|---|---|---|---|---|---|---|
| | | % Vote | Seats | % Vote | Seats | % Vote | Seats | % Vote | Seats | % Vote | Seats |
| 1945 | 72.8 | 39.7 | 210 | 47.7 | 393 | 9.0 | 12 | 0.2 | 0 | 3.4 | 25 |
| 1950 | 83.9 | 43.3 | 297 | 46.1 | 315 | 9.1 | 9 | 0.1 | 0 | 1.4 | 4 |
| 1951 | 82.6 | 48.0 | 321 | 48.8 | 295 | 2.6 | 6 | 0.1 | 0 | 0.6 | 3 |
| 1955 | 76.8 | 49.6 | 344 | 46.4 | 277 | 2.7 | 6 | 0.2 | 0 | 1.1 | 3 |
| 1959 | 78.7 | 49.4 | 365 | 43.8 | 258 | 5.9 | 6 | 0.4 | 0 | 0.6 | 1 |
| 1964 | 77.1 | 43.3 | 303 | 44.1 | 317 | 11.2 | 9 | 0.5 | 0 | 0.9 | 1 |
| 1966 | 75.8 | 41.9 | 253 | 47.9 | 363 | 8.5 | 12 | 0.7 | 0 | 1.0 | 2 |
| 1970 | 72.0 | 46.4 | 330 | 43.0 | 287 | 7.5 | 6 | 1.7 | 1 | 1.5 | 6 |
| 1974 (Feb) | 78.8 | 37.8 | 296 | 37.2 | 301 | 19.3 | 14 | 2.6 | 9 | 3.2 | 15 |
| 1974 (Oct) | 72.8 | 35.7 | 276 | 39.3 | 319 | 18.3 | 13 | 3.4 | 14 | 3.3 | 13 |
| 1979 | 76.0 | 43.9 | 339 | 36.9 | 268 | 13.8 | 11 | 2.0 | 4 | 3.4 | 13 |
| 1983 | 72.7 | 42.4 | 397 | 27.6 | 209 | 25.4 | 23 | 1.5 | 4 | 3.1 | 17 |
| 1987 | 75.3 | 42.2 | 375 | 30.8 | 229 | 22.6 | 22 | 1.7 | 6 | 2.7 | 18 |
| 1992 | 77.7 | 41.9 | 336 | 34.4 | 271 | 17.8 | 20 | 2.3 | 7 | 3.5 | 17 |
| 1997 | 71.4 | 30.7 | 165 | 43.2 | 418 | 16.8 | 46 | 2.5 | 10 | 6.8 | 20 |
| 2001 | 59.4 | 31.7 | 166 | 40.7 | 412 | 18.3 | 52 | 2.5 | 9 | 6.7 | 20 |
| 2005 | 61.4 | 32.4 | 198 | 35.2 | 355 | 22.0 | 62 | 2.1 | 9 | 7.4 | 22 |

*Notes:*
[1] The heading 'Lib/Lib Dem' captures the electoral campaigns of the Liberal Party (1945–79), the SDP–Liberal Alliance (1983 and 1987) and the merged Liberal Democrats (1992–2005)
[2] These columns record the joint vote shares/seats won by the Scottish National Party and Plaid Cymru. These parties contest only seats in Scotland and Wales respectively
[3] These columns aggregate the results of all other contestants of British elections since 1945. All Northern Ireland results are included here

only a marginal improvement. This might suggest a growing disenchantment with the choices available to the electorate or a more general disengagement with (party) politics across the general population.

Yet the two parties continue to dominate in terms of the numbers of seats won. For example, in 2005 the two-party aggregate share of the vote (67.6 per cent) still translated into a disproportionate share of seats won in the House of Commons (83.8 per cent). This has always been the case. For instance,

Labour's 'landslide' election victory of 1945 was accomplished on the back of a share of 47.7 per cent of the votes cast, which translated into 61.4 per cent of the seats won. All post-war elections, with the exception of February 1974, delivered majority government to parties with less than half of the votes cast.

While these figures lead some to ask whether British politics delivers genuinely democratic outcomes (see Theme box: Democracy and Legitimacy), the point to make here is that the rules of the electoral game act as key shapers of two important facets of British politics: (a) the structure and functioning of the party system and (b) the electoral strategies employed by the parties.

To win a seat in the House of Commons, a party's candidate must simply secure more votes cast than any of their opponents. This is called the 'first past the post' system. Parliamentary majorities are secured on the back of constituencies won rather than votes cast. Unlike most other European states, there is no electoral mechanism to correct this distortion in favour of a proportional electoral outcome. There is no adjustment mechanism to ensure the representation of small parties, and even large national parties like the Liberal Democrats always underachieve in terms of the relationship between votes cast and seats won. The structure of the electoral system thereby provides substantial incentives for the two parties to operate as coherent, disciplined electoral machines. As we note below, both of the main parties can be described as broad coalitions with significant internal ideological discrepancies. But, within the rules of the British electoral game, there is little point in these ideological discrepancies being emphasised and cohering into separate parties as in the case of Italian polarised pluralism. Small parties do systematically badly in British electoral politics, even if—as is periodically true of both the Green Party and the UK Independence Party—public opinion is generally supportive of their party platforms. Exceptions to this rule do occur, but they are explained either by the prevalence of specific local issues affecting a constituency campaign, in which case a minority candidate may gain enough votes to take the seat, or by the growth of distinctive cleavages in Scotland and Wales, which has allowed the SNP and PC to break through in electoral terms.

Perhaps because of these structural characteristics, the main parties have—for most of the post-war period—adopted an electoral strategy that seeks to capture the centre ground. The assumption embedded in this common Labour and Conservative strategy is that the British **median voter** sits at the centre of the political spectrum and that they will punish movement by parties towards the ideological extremes of politics. Moreover, both the Conservatives and Labour have generally been able to assume that voters located respectively at the right or left margins of politics will vote for them anyway. Given the electoral system described above, there would seem to be little point in voting for a fringe party if the intention is to have some effect on the overall outcome of the election. In other words, the main parties have operated on the assumption that the key space of electoral competition (i.e. where elections are won or lost) is the ideological centre.

Two phases of post-war British politics would seem particularly to confirm this view of prevailing party strategy: the period between 1945 and the mid-1970s and the period since the early 1990s. The first period is often seen as a period of 'consensus politics', where there was little deep disagreement between the Conservative and Labour parties about the fundamentals of domestic policy. Both subscribed to a view of economic policy that accorded a role for the state intervening significantly to manage the macroeconomy. The core economic goal—in line with Keynesian economics—was the pursuit of full employment. A substantial portion of economic activity would remain within state control and there was a core commitment to the welfare state, as outlined in the Beveridge Report of 1942, and socialised medical care in the form of the National Health Service. Disagreements between the parties were not profound, but matters of degree and largely technical. The remarkably rapid adaptation of the Conservative Party to the precepts of the post-war settlement delivered by the Labour government of 1945–51 shows how deep-set this consensual and centre-seeking strategy was.

In so far as there is a consensus in the contemporary period, then it is organised around agreement that the market, rather than the state, is a better mechanism for regulating economic activity. Both parties contend that economic globalisation poses major challenges to Britain, the role of the state and the sustainability of long-standing welfare commitments, particularly in the context of an ageing population. Keynesian ideas about economic man-agement have been displaced by liberal economic thinking that regards prosperity as following from the operation of unfettered markets. The privatisa-tion of public assets, the use of market discipline in the residual public sector and budgetary discipline geared to the achievement of low inflation all stand as significant components of both major parties' electoral platforms. There is no dispute about the incoming Labour government's decision to give op-erational independence to the Bank of England in 1997, a move which arguably withdrew the capacity of British governments to make monetary policy.

The intervening period (the mid-1970s to the early 1990s) was characterised by significant ideo-logical disagreement. There was a dramatic discon-nect between the approach offered by the Conser-vative government of Margaret Thatcher elected in 1979 and that of its Labour opponents, certainly until the mid-1980s. Under Thatcher the Conser-vatives espoused an aggressive version of economic liberalism that opened the British economy to global pressures (Britain was the first European state to remove all controls on cross-border capital move-ment in 1979), denationalised public utilities, cut taxes and began the marketisation of public ser-vices. Labour, in contrast, went to the electorate in 1983 with a manifesto that sought to insulate the UK economy from global pressures by actively intervening to protect and enhance British industry in the context of an enhanced socialised economy.

None of this is to deny that there have not been profound political debates about economic management within British politics. Indeed, much of this discussion has taken place, often to an aggressive extent, within the parties themselves. The Labour Party is a case in point. The phenomenon of 'New Labour', as represented by the Labour governments of Tony Blair since 1987, stands as the culmination of decades of intra-party struggle about appropriate policy frameworks. The pro-cess of root-and-branch policy review undertaken under the successive leaderships of Neil Kinnock (1983–92), John Smith (1992–4) and Blair (after 1994) were rooted in a tradition of 'revisionism'

stretching at least as far back as the early 1960s. Labour leaders such as Hugh Gaitskell (1955–63) together with Labour intellectuals such as the MP Tony Crosland had long sought to fashion a case for the modernisation of the British so-cial democratic tradition in ways that would allow an accommodation with the institutions of cap-italism. In particular, intense battles were fought within the party over its early (1918) constitutional commitment to take 'the means of production, distribution and exchange' into public ownership. Tensions between the revisionists and the ascend-ant Labour left lay behind the foundation in 1981 of the Social Democratic Party (SDP) by a group of disaffected Labour MPs. While the idea of New La-bour looks like a straightforward accommodation to the post-Thatcher political terrain self-consciously analogous to the concept of *die Neue Mitte* in the German SPD, there are still tensions at the highest level of the party as evidenced by the differ-ent philosophies of political economy represented by Blair and his long-time Chancellor of the Ex-chequer Gordon Brown. While Brown's politics can be read as those of a modernising social democrat with redistributive instincts, those of Blair recall an earlier tradition of nineteenth-century social liberalism.

The experience of three election defeats after 1997 has left the Conservative Party grappling to fashion an electoral strategy capable of capturing the median voter once again. Historically, the Con-servative Party has been one of the most impressive election-winning machines in European politics. Unlike most other European conservative parties, the British version, whose origins lie in the landed 'Tory' faction in Parliament in the late seventeenth century, has never been rigidly or dogmatically res-istant to change. In many ways its success through the twentieth century has been down to its cap-acity to adapt itself to the immense social changes precipitated by the development of capitalism and huge political challenges posed by the advent of mass politics. The post-war Conservative Party was characterised by two clear factions: 'one nation' conservatives and economic liberals. The former were most obviously represented by Harold Macmillan, Prime Minister between 1957 and 1963. One nation Conservatism professes a belief in the virtues of social cohesion across classes and as such was easily adapted to the post-war settlement with its emphasis upon an inclusive welfare state and a mixed economy, where prosperity was delivered through a coordinated mixture of state and market.

Economic liberals became the ascendant voice within the party from the early 1970s as the British economy's performance faltered markedly. They diagnosed a prospectus which sought to remove impediments to market efficiency such as state intervention, trade union power and a top-heavy public sector. The governments of Margaret Thatcher, Prime Minister between 1979 and 1990, combined a philosophy of economic liberalism with an emphasis on nationalism (particularly with regard to European policy) and social conservatism. An overarching commitment to economic liberalism as the dominant political economy model is not in dispute within the Conservative Party, and the quest to displace New Labour as the party of government has seen the party experimenting with a mixture of social conservatism (the anti-immigration tone of the 2005 election campaign is a case in point) and socially liberal sentiments designed to appeal to the socially complex and multicultural electorate of the early twenty-first century.

The modern Liberal Democrats, Britain's third party, are direct descendants of the Liberal Party, a dominant force in nineteenth-century British politics associated with rising capitalist classes and a historic commitment to emphasise the powers of Parliament over those of the crown. The arrival of the mass franchise saw the Liberals relegated to third-party status by 1922 as the Labour Party emerged as the main alternative to the Conservatives. This is not to say that liberal ideas were without influence. Indeed the two intellectual architects of the post-1945 settlement William Beveridge and John Maynard Keynes, were both members of the Liberal Party. The Liberals began to gain electoral ground from the early 1960s at the moment when the long-run decline of the British economy was becoming apparent to the political classes. Sporadic yet spectacular by-election victories suggested that the Liberals were little more than a repository of protest votes, but the electoral alliance (1983 and 1987) and eventual merger (1988) with the SDP contributed to the party's capacity to translate proportions of the vote into concrete seats.

It is not wholly accurate to regard the Liberal Democrats as a 'centre party'. At one level, the party is able to position itself as buffer between the ideological extremes of left and right. However, the space of electoral competition between the two main parties gives the Liberal Democrats little scope to carve out a centrist territory for itself. Also, the logic of electoral politics requires the Liberal Democrats to present themselves as challengers to both of the parties. In some areas the party is best placed to beat Conservative candidates; in others it has every chance of appealing to Labour voters. In short, the appropriate and necessary electoral strategy varies according to where Liberal Democrats are standing. Under the leadership of Charles Kennedy (1999–2006) across two general elections, the party tended to adopt a mixed position where it stood to the right of Labour on economic management, but argued to its left on social issues and questions of redistribution. This reflects an ongoing and very long-standing tension in the party between economic liberals and social liberals, which boils down to a clash between the impulse to withdraw the state from the economy and the regulation of people's lives and the preference to use the state as an instrument to pursue higher levels of social and economic equality. Other European liberal parties tend to gravitate towards one of these poles. The British Liberal Democrats embody the tense relationship between both.

# The European Exception?

Britain did not join the European Communities until 1973. British governments paid scant attention to the foundation of the European Coal and Steel Community in 1951 and took no substantive part in the negotiations later that decade which led to the Treaty of Rome and the European Economic Community. However, Britain twice formally applied to join the Communities in the 1960s under respectively Conservative (1961–3) and Labour (1967) governments. Both applications were ultimately rejected by the French government and it was left to the Conservative government of Edward Heath to take Britain into the Communities.

From the late 1950s, the European issue was a bitter source of contention between, but mostly *within*, the main political parties. The question of membership did not fit comfortably into the standard left versus right, state versus market structure of political debate. Ardent supporters and opponents of British membership could be heard within both the Conservative and Labour parties, and there was no necessary correlation between positions taken on the European question and positioning within existing internal party factions. For example, economic liberals within the Conservative Party could see an obvious case for exposing Britain to the decidedly market driven ethos of the Treaty of Rome, but not all economic liberals could stomach the sacrifices to British sovereignty that would follow. The sovereignty question also raised its head within

the Labour Party. While the Wilson government (1964–70) constructed a case for centre-left economic modernisation within the large market space offered by the Communities, vocal opposition to the project usually linked membership to fears that the capacity to exercise decisive socialist interventions into the economy would be forever disallowed. Critics from both left and right organised themselves around the sanctity of parliamentary sovereignty suggesting a common affiliation across the ideological divide to certain central aspects of the British political tradition.

In other words, the arrival of the European issue into British politics in the 1960s brought with it a new political cleavage (sovereignty versus interdependence) that could not be organised into the conventional structure of inter-party competition. From the start this raised delicate issues of intraparty management. The second Wilson government renegotiated the terms of British membership and in 1975 used the extraordinary device of a public referendum to decide the question, in part because the Labour leadership was so bitterly divided over the issue. Party management questions became more acute for the Conservatives from the mid-1980s. While the Thatcher government was content enough to sign the Single European Act (1987), a major revision to the founding Treaties designed to accelerate the completion of the Communities' internal market, it bitterly opposed the suggestions of the further extension of supranationalism into Britain's social and monetary policy competence. This generated a powerful Euro-sceptic discourse in British politics, rooted in the Conservative Party, articulated by much of the tabloid press and embodied by the foundation of sovereignty-seeking political forces such as the UK Independence Party.

The Conservative government of John Major signed and ratified the Maastricht Treaty on European Union (1992), but side-stepped the issue of whether Britain should join the single currency (eventually the euro) by negotiating, along with Denmark and (when it joined the EU in 1995) Sweden, an opt-out from the Treaty's provisions on monetary integration. However, the government's low point followed its decision to enter the Exchange Rate Mechanism (ERM) in 1991. ERM membership was a crucial precondition to joining the single currency, but by fixing exchange rates it was also seen as a helpful external source of counter-inflationary discipline in the British economy. Britain was forced out of the ERM in September 1992 following a massive speculative attack on Sterling in the international currency markets. Opinion poll data suggest this moment to be the point from which the Conservatives' election chances in 1997 were fatally damaged.

Debates about whether Britain should join the single currency remain prominent in British politics. Arguments tend to take one of two forms: (a) technical arguments about the economic propriety of adopting the euro and delegating monetary policy competence to the European Central Bank, and/or (b) highly charged symbolic debates about compromises to national sovereignty and threats to national identity. Political debate in the second of these domains cannot, as we have seen, be accommodated within the traditional inter-party alignments of British politics. It divides the main parties along the sovereignty–interdependence axis regardless of preferences for models of political economy. Discussion within the first has the capacity to remain with the discourse of how best to manage the British economy under conditions of globalisation.

In 1997 the Treasury announced five economic tests, which would act as technical benchmarks against which the case for Britain adopting the euro might be measured. Such a move, undertaken by the Labour government, could be seen as a strategy of depoliticisation, designed to take contentious issues beyond the realm of public debate and thereby avoid potentially damaging controversies for the governing party. (See Theme box: The Impact of the European Union.)

As indicated above, the EU provides a clear institutional expression of one of the strategic choices available to the British state. The 'European issue'

**THEME BOX** (!)

### The Impact of the European Union

The effects of membership of the EU upon Britain are complex. At one level commitment to the Treaties and the adoption of the *acquis communautaire* stands as a profound challenge to the idea of parliamentary sovereignty. But there is no necessary incompatibility between Europeanising pressures and the general thrust of British policy. Indeed the single market programme of the European Communities Single European Act (1987) could even be read as the successful 'uploading' of British liberal economic preferences to the European level. The arrival of EU legislation into the British political system has been for the most part more straightforward than in many other EU member states. The centralised character of the British state has enabled comparatively unproblematic implementation of directives into UK law. The apparatus of the central state has been forced to adapt to the volume of legislation emanating from the EU policy process and new lines of horizontal inter-departmental communication have emerged and coordination with Britain's Permanent Representation in Brussels has become essential. Yet the evidence suggests that these changes have not threatened the bureaucratic style of Whitehall, which has adapted to European inputs in ways consistent with its own traditions. The main challenges to the British civil service have been generated by the reforming agendas of British governments rather than by any pressures brought about by EU membership.

in British politics, whether it be about the question of membership or the degree to which the British should participate in integration initiatives such as European monetary union (EMU), has been ever present since the 1950s when the inauguration of the European Communities coincided with a growing realisation among elites that Britain's status as a global power was under threat. However, it should not be assumed that European integration always stands in opposition to British preferences. For example, the dominant model of political economy within British political discourse has little quarrel with the liberal principles of the single market or, for that matter, the ideas of counter-inflationary budgetary discipline at the core of monetary union. Indeed, when a referendum in France in 2005 rejected the EU's Constitutional Treaty, one of the key sources of opposition among the French was the assumption that the EU had come to embody an Anglo-Saxon model of capitalism.

---

**KEY POINTS**

- Britain was a late entrant into the European Communities in 1973, but the European question had long been a bitter source of contention between and within the main political parties.

- European issues pose a series of dilemmas that cut across the traditional state versus market cleavage of British politics.

- New Labour has pursued a depoliticising strategy with regard to the question of British membership of the single currency.

- There is much in the economic liberal model of European integration that sits comfortably with the dominant model of political economy in British politics.

---

# Conclusion

The British obsession with decline may have receded and there may now be something of a consensus on the basic principles of economic management. But the absence of the large-scale industrial and ideological conflicts of the 1970s should not lead to the assumption that all of Britain's political dilemmas have been resolved. Indeed, the twin questions of Britain's rightful place in the world order and the structure of its internal territory steadfastly refuse to abate. The former is partly a matter of alliance strategies: Europe or the USA or some balanced permutation of the two? But it is also a question of how ultimately Britain will engage with the process of globalisation and what vision of Europe sits at the heart of Britain's globalisation strategy. (See Theme box: The Impact of Globalisation.) Should the EU be some sort of distinctive way of protecting European societies from the excesses of market power, or alternatively should the EU be a venue in which a British model of liberal capitalism is spread across the continent? The reorganisation of Britain's territorial space is well underway thanks to devolution and the extent to which this process marks the end of the United Kingdom as a singular entity remains to be seen. But the establishment of assemblies in Scotland and Wales invites the formation of distinctive agenda-driven political systems that Westminster is likely to be unable to control.

BEN ROSAMOND

**THEME BOX**

## The Impact of Globalisation

In 1918 the British Empire covered something like one-quarter of the Earth's surface. For large portions of the nineteenth and early twentieth century Britain was the world's dominant global power and its currency, the Pound Sterling was the international reserve currency. The City remains the world's largest financial centre and the British state has often been criticised for its unwavering commitment to the preferences of financial capital. In short Britain is no stranger to the global economy. However, the era of contemporary globalisation has taken place in a period when British economic supremacy has long gone. If globalisation has been about the spread of neo-liberal ideas about the relationship between state and economy, then Britain has been one of globalisation's most zealous advocates. Britain was the first European state to remove controls on capital movement in 1979 and the Thatcher governments

(1979–90) were instrumental in enacting public policies built around the orthodoxies of economic liberalism. The loss of indigenous manufacturing capacity has been offset by strenuous attempts to attract foreign direct investment and to shift the base of the economy into areas such as financial services. One striking feature of public policy since 1997 has been the extent to which policy has been premised upon claims about the determining effects of globalisation. New Labour politicians have been keen to emphasise the necessity of their policy preferences—particularly in terms of welfare reform and the general tenor of economic policy—because of the demands of globalisation. But there are no obvious assumptions from within the main political parties that globalisation either (a) should be resisted (as in France) or (b) should act as a rationale for more intensive engagement in the project of European integration.

### ? QUESTIONS

1. To what extent has the absence of a clear revolutionary juncture in British history had an impact upon the character of modern British politics?

2. How important have debates about 'decline' been to the conduct of British politics after 1945?

3. What is the relationship between debates about the management of the British economy and the question of Britain's global alignment?

4. Does the idea of 'parliamentary sovereignty' have any purchase in the analysis of contemporary British politics?

5. Does the process of devolution signal the end of the British state?

6. To what extent can 'New Labour' be described as a post-Thatcherite political project?

7. Why is Britain so reluctant to adopt the euro?

### ≋ FURTHER READING

■ **Bevir, M. and Rhodes, R. A. W. (2003), *Interpreting British Governance*, London, Routledge.** An original discussion of how to think about the transformation of British policy-making.

■ **English, R. and Kenny, M. (eds) (2000), *Rethinking British Decline*, Basingstoke, Macmillan.** A comprehensive overview of the many academic debates surrounding the issue of Britain's decline.

■ **Gamble, A. (2003),** *Between Europe and America: The Future of British Politics*, **Basingstoke, Palgrave Macmillan.** A brilliant analysis of the historical roots of 'exceptionalism' in British politics and of the strategic dilemmas that now present themselves to the British state.

■ **Geddes, A. (2004),** *The European Union and British Politics*, **Basingstoke, Palgrave Macmillan.** An impressive and comprehensive discussion of the historical, institutional and policy dimensions of British membership of the EU.

■ **Grant, W. (2002),** *Economic Policy in Britain*, **Basingstoke, Palgrave.** A crisp and lucid discussion of the debates about how the traditional economic policy priorities of the British state can be pursued.

■ **Moran, M. (2005),** *Politics and Governance in the UK*, **Basingstoke, Palgrave Macmillan.** A very clear discussion of different interpretations of the changing character of British politics.

■ **O'Neill, M. (ed.) (2004),** *Devolution and British Politics*, **Harlow, Longman.** A collection of clearly written and nicely contextualised essays on the roots and implication of the redistribution of territorial power in the UK.

 ## IMPORTANT WEBSITES

● **www.direct.gov.uk/Homepage/fs/en** The official website of the British government.

● **www.parliament.uk** The official website of the British parliament.

● **www.guardian.co.uk** *The Guardian*, Britain's leading centre-left newspaper.

● **www.telegraph.co.uk** *The Telegraph*, Britain's highest circulation right-of-centre newspaper.

● **www.palgrave-journals.com/bp** *British Politics*, a new academic journal devoted to the analysis of British politics.

 **Visit the Online Resource Centre that accompanies this book for lots of useful additional material, including an interactive map of Europe. www.oxfordtextbooks.co.uk/orc/hay_menon/**

# 5

# Scandinavia

ERIC S. EINHORN AND JOHN LOGUE

## Chapter Contents

- Introduction
- Political Institutions
- Political Actors and Policy-making
- The Scandinavian Model
- Conclusion: Current Challenges
- Notes

## Reader's Guide

The four Scandinavian countries (Denmark, Finland, Norway and Sweden) have pursued democracy beyond narrow constitutional and political terms to include social policy and, to a lesser extent, economic policy. For more than 60 years under governments dominated mainly by social democratic and labour parties they have pursued a pragmatic 'middle way' between free-market capitalism and authoritarian statism. They have developed universal welfare states resting on generous public benefits and services and financed by high taxes with resulting socio-economic equality. They have sustained these goals while reforming and recalibrating social and economic policies over the past 15 years. Their parliamentary politics are characterised by a vigorous multi-party system encouraged by **proportional representation** and steered by coalition governments of changing composition. Despite the consensual political culture, over the past 30 years there have been more frequent changes in government, new social challenges including the growing presence of non-Western European immigrants and demographic changes, and new global and regional pressures such as those emanating from the European Union.

# Introduction

The Scandinavian countries constitute, in Walter Galenson's (1949) terms of more than half a century ago, 'a social laboratory for the Western world'. More than any other group of nations, the small Scandinavian states have pioneered the policies that have ameliorated the discontents of industrial capitalism, creating societies in the last half of the twentieth century of relative equality and substantial, broadly shared prosperity. (See Table 5.1.)

This 'Scandinavian model' of a consensual and solidaristic response to the challenges of industrial capitalism was shaped by factors of historical homogeneity.[1] Denmark, Finland, Norway and Sweden are uniquely homogenous in linguistic, religious, ethnic and racial terms. The major line of division in each nation during the twentieth century was that of economics or class, and economic divisions are more subject to compromise than other patterns of community cleavage.

From the 1930s to the 1970s, the development of the Scandinavian model comprising of a strong, redistributive state managing a privately owned, capitalistic managing economy was shaped by virtually continuous social democratic government in Denmark, Norway and Sweden, creating a level of shared prosperity that became an object of envy outside the region. Finland followed the same track after the 1960s, also under social democratic dominance, and by 2000 had converged on the general Scandinavian model. That labour of reform put a safety net under all citizens, especially unskilled workers with large families; raised wage rates in the labour market through virtually universal trade union organisation; and increased the rates of labour force participation, especially among women. It brought with it an unusual policy culture that was empirical, consensual and corporatist.

Since the mid-1970s, the challenge has been how to recalibrate the welfare edifice created earlier to accommodate exceptionally high levels of female labour force participation, to train the workforce to compete in a global economy, to respond to

**Table 5.1** Size, Population and Economic Equality of Scandinavia, 2005

|  | **Denmark** | **Finland** | **Iceland** | **Norway** | **Sweden** |
|---|---|---|---|---|---|
| Population | 5,432,335 | 5,223,442 | 296,737 | 4,593,041 | 9,001,774 |
| Land area (sq km) | 42,394 | 304,473 | 100,250 | 307,860 | 410,934 |
| Population density | 128.1 | 17.2 | 3.0 | 14.9 | 21.9 |
| GDP per capita (USD)* | 32,200 | 29,000 | 31,900 | 40,000 | 28,400 |
| Ratio between income of richest 20% and poorest 20%** | 4.3 : 1 | 3.8 : 1 | NA | 3.9 : 1 | 4.0 : 1 |

*Source*: US Central Intelligence Agency, *Factbook 2005*, www.cia.gov/cia/publications/factbook/index.html. Income ratios from UN Development Programme (2005), *Human Development Report 2005*, (New York, UNDP, p. 270. GDP per capita is in purchasing power parities (PPP)
*Notes*: *2004. Compare with GDP/per capita: Canada: $ 31,500, UK: 29,600, USA: 40,100
** Compare with Canada 5.8 : 1, UK 7.2 : 1, and USA 8.4 : 1

the impact of extended life expectancy on the pension system and to the rising cost of medical care, to contain costs generally, and to reshape the tax system to produce adequate revenues to support the welfare state without as many negative side effects. This has been a work of gradual renewal, not of radical change.

## The past as prologue

Today, the Scandinavian area contains five nation states—Denmark, Finland, Iceland, Norway and Sweden—and three autonomous island provinces—the Swedish-speaking Åland Islands within Finland and the Faeroe Islands and Greenland within Denmark. All are parliamentary democracies. All are characterised by open, inclusive and consensual politics at home, and a strong internationalist, multilateralist policy abroad. Yet it was not always this way.

During the Union of Kalmar (1397 to 1523) the Scandinavian peoples were gathered under a single monarch—the Danish king or queen. The history of the last 500 years has been one of regional fragmentation. After Danish King Christian II celebrated his Swedish coronation in 1520 by executing a number of his guests for heresy, central Sweden revolted successfully under Gustav Vasa. The next centuries saw a division of Scandinavia between two states—Denmark–Norway–Iceland, ruled by Danish kings, and Sweden–Finland, ruled by Vasa and his descendants. The two were hereditary enemies; they fought each other repeatedly— by one count 12 times—between 1520 and 1814. Both were quick converts to Lutheranism between the 1520s and 1540s, and the confiscation of church lands by the crown provided resources to fuel the growth of modern states, especially in Sweden. Sweden replaced Denmark as the dominant power in Scandinavia in the seventeenth century, controlling most of the Baltic coast by the end of the century. Early in the eighteenth century, however, Sweden's adventurist Charles XII was defeated by Russia's Peter the Great in the Great Northern War

(1700–20), costing the country most of its Baltic empire.

Danish and Swedish political systems diverged. Denmark entered the modern period with a feudal system, which Frederick III converted into royal absolutism in 1665. By contrast, the Vasas created a relatively modern state administration in the new Swedish state with a balance between king and the Estates General. Following Charles XII's defeats and death in 1718, royal power was sharply restricted in the 'golden age' of Swedish parliamentarism. That lasted until 1772, when Gustav III re-established royal supremacy and, in 1789, virtual royal absolutism. He was assassinated in 1792.

The Napoleonic Wars led to geographic and political realignment. Russia won Finland from Sweden in 1808 after a short war, and it was incorporated into the Russian Empire as a Grand Duchy. In the aftermath of defeat, the Swedes ousted their failed king, Gustav IV, re-established a constitutional monarchy, and ultimately chose one of Napoleon's marshals, Jean Bernadotte, as crown prince Karl Johan. After Napoleon's defeat in Russia, Karl Johan led Sweden into the ranks of Napoleon's opponents. The Allies rewarded Sweden with Norway, which was stripped in 1814 from the hapless Danes who remained loyal to their French ally. The Norwegians sought independence and wrote a liberal constitution in 1814, but grudgingly accepted Swedish rule after Karl Johan's army arrived. Swedish kings ruled in Norway under the provisions of the new Norwegian constitution. Denmark, much reduced by military defeat, national bankruptcy (1813) and the loss of Norway, maintained royal absolutism until King Frederick VII granted a constitution in 1849 in the wake of the European revolutions of 1848.

In 1900, then, Finland was ruled by the Russian Czar under the Swedish–Finnish quasi-absolutist constitution of 1772/89; Norway and Sweden were ruled by the Swedish king under two different national constitutions; and Denmark–Iceland were ruled from Copenhagen by the Danish

King. In Denmark, Finland, Iceland and Sweden, ministers were appointed by the crown, and did not need the approval of the popularly elected lower house of parliament. Only in Norway did ministers require parliamentary approval ('parliamentary supremacy') after 1884.

This nineteenth-century political dispensation changed quickly in the twentieth century. (See Table 5.2). In 1901, after a 30-year struggle, the Danish king conceded parliamentary supremacy. Parliamentary supremacy followed in Iceland in 1903. Norway voted to dissolve its union with Sweden in Scandinavia's first referendum in 1905—the vote was 368,208 for independence and 184 against—and the Swedish government accepted the result. Finland extracted a modern parliament from the Russian Czar after a general strike in October and November 1905. The Swedish king resisted parliamentary supremacy until 1917, another revolutionary year. Finland acquired its independence as well as parliamentary supremacy following the collapse of the Russian Empire in the same year. A short, bitter civil war between Reds and Whites followed independence. The Conservatives won, and executed, imprisoned and exiled their opponents; the lines of that division marked Finnish politics for more than 50 years. Throughout the region, universal manhood suffrage was achieved between 1898 and 1918, and women's suffrage between 1906 and 1921.

The final establishment of autonomy and statehood followed. In the settlement after the First World War, Denmark granted Iceland autonomy in 1918, and recovered most of the Danish-speaking portion of Slesvig from Germany following a plebiscite in 1920. The Swedish-speaking Åland Islands, part of Finland which the Swedes had occupied in 1918, were granted autonomy in 1921 under a League of Nations settlement that awarded the islands to Finland. With the occupation of Denmark by the Germans in 1940, Iceland, the Faeroe Islands and Greenland were occupied by the Allies; full Icelandic independence occurred in 1944, and Faeroese autonomy within Denmark followed in 1948. Greenland received autonomy within Denmark in 1979.[2]

In short, modern Scandinavian political democracy was generally the achievement of a protracted, but (with the exception of Finland) peaceful, struggle that saw complex political and social alliances, confrontation and negotiation, and hard-won compromises. This laid the foundation for a modern political culture appropriately named 'the politics of compromise' (Rustow 1955).

**Table 5.2** Development of Nation States and Democracy in Scandinavia

|  | Denmark | Finland | Iceland | Norway | Sweden |
|---|---|---|---|---|---|
| Independence | always | 1917 | 1944 | 1905 | 1523 |
| Constitutional restrictions on monarch | 1849 | 1917 | 1874 | 1814 | 1809 |
| Establishment of modern parliament | 1849 | 1906 | 1874 | 1814 | 1866 |
| Parliamentary supremacy | 1901 | 1917 | 1903 | 1884 | 1917 |
| Universal manhood suffrage | 1913 | 1906 | 1913 | 1898 | 1918 |
| Women's suffrage | 1915 | 1906 | 1915 | 1913 | 1921 |
| EU membership | 1973 | 1995 | not member | not member | 1995 |

ERIC S. EINHORN AND JOHN LOGUE

# Political Institutions

The basic dynamics of Scandinavian parliamentary democracy are deceptively simple. All but Finland are pure parliamentary systems: direct election of unicameral parliaments with the largest party normally having the first chance at assembling a government. In Finland the President—now independently elected directly every six years—has historically had considerable independence in nominating the Prime Minister, but under the new constitution (2000) presidential prerogatives have been restricted. Given the multi-party political system and the generous principles of proportional representation that assure even small parties seats in parliament, Scandinavian government is inevitably either coalition or minority government and quite often both. The following discussion of the 'nuts and bolts' of democratic government will try to take the static institutions of government and give them political energy. Given the contemporary pressures for 'globalisation' and 'Europeanisation', even arcane constitutional provisions can provoke political debate and partisan manoeuvring.

## Constitutions

Scandinavian legal traditions stretch back to the Middle Ages, as do legal restrictions on government. Contemporary Scandinavia includes Europe's oldest written constitution still in use (Norway—1814) and one of its newest (Finland—

2000). Constitutions predate democracy and constitutional revision—rather than judicial reinterpretation—has been the norm. Current national constitutions in Denmark and Sweden date to 1953 and 1970, respectively.

Nordic constitutions establish the basic institutions and procedures for democratic governance. With each constitutional revision the trend has been to strengthen parliament, remove monarchical, and in the case of Finland (2000) reduce presidential, prerogatives, and add social and economic rights to the body of civil rights. While each reflects national historical and political traditions, the overall governance system among the Nordic states has become increasingly similar. Unicameralism arose out of the Norwegian experience; the ombudsman as the protector of citizens' and parliamentary rights *vis-à-vis* public administrators was borrowed from Sweden; and referenda—once largely restricted to Denmark—have a limited but notable role in legitimating constitutional changes and major decisions about the European Union.

Although all the Scandinavian countries are unitary polities, there is a strong tradition of regional and local government. In the past 40 years there have been several modifications of local government in an effort to create local governmental units capable of providing the essential services that have long been their responsibility while allowing citizens to have democratic input into these decisions. For example, counties traditionally were responsible for medical and hospital care. In recent decades medical practice has led to significant changes in the delivery of such care including larger and more technically capable regional hospitals together with the reduction of smaller hospitals. Denmark is currently abolishing its 14 county councils in favour of five 'regions' which will be primarily responsible for health care.

## Parliamentary democracy

If the basic principles of parliamentary democracy are simple, its practice in multi-party systems rarely is. Each Scandinavian constitution limits parliamentary terms to four years, but except in Norway more frequent elections are possible. A consequence of proportional representation has been the gradual disappearance of single-party majority governments. Coalition government is the practice. Denmark, Norway and Sweden are notable for their numerous minority governments including minority coalitions. By definition such governments must achieve parliamentary support from among the non-governing parties, which is the primary limitation on executive power. (See Theme box: Democracy and Legitimacy.)

Despite the ideal of parliamentary supremacy, the executive branch and the party groups dominate modern legislative procedure. The nexus between the two branches are the numerous parliamentary committees, which often correspond to main executive departments. It is here where budgetary and legislative proposals are modified to guarantee majority support. The process differs in each nation, but there are commonalities. Typical is the Swedish *remiss* system whereby government proposals are circulated to a wide range of interest and policy organisations outside of parliament. In all of the Scandinavian states major legislative proposals often begin with so-called policy commissions composed of politicians, interest organisation representatives and academic experts. These reports are expected to be based on solid

**THEME BOX**

### Democracy and Legitimacy

Although the Scandinavian countries followed different paths to democratic government, once fully established by 1920 democratic parliamentary government has not been seriously challenged. Fascist movements appeared in the 1930s, but they gained little public support other than what could be extorted during the Nazi German occupation of Norway and Denmark. Communism enjoyed two bursts of modest enthusiasm: in the wake of the 1917 Bolshevik Revolution in Russia and at the end of the Second World War. The inherently undemocratic nature of Moscow-oriented communist parties led to their rapid decline, although democratic radical socialist parties survive throughout Scandinavia and usually garner 10–15 per cent of the vote. Popular movements preceded full constitutional democracy and continue to play a significant role. Coalition government (either formal or informal) strengthens parliamentary power to question, investigate and participate in key policy decisions. Institutions like the ombudsman, which keep an eye on administrative due process, have spread from Sweden (established in 1809) to the other Scandinavian countries and beyond.

evidence and facts, not ideological abstractions. Given the pluralistic composition of commissions, unanimity is not guaranteed, but there is usually agreement on the basic facts, and the bargaining process often starts even before the parliamentary phase. The classic description by Tom Anton of Scandinavian policy-making—'consensual, open, rationalistic, and deliberative' (the 'CORD model') still holds (Anton 1969: 94).

The annual budgetary cycle, which is so technical in many democracies, has numerous bargaining phases built in. Given Scandinavia's large public sector, coalition governments must try to satisfy multiple constituencies even before a draft budget is announced. With so many public services delivered at the regional (county) and municipal levels (including social support, education, and health care), the national government undertakes extensive negotiations with the organised regional and local governments. There follows a parliamentary phase where both budgetary and programmatic committees review the financial proposals before the final budget is adopted.

The result is a complex and protracted policy-making practice where parliamentary drama is usually absent. If the government cannot obtain a voting majority, it must modify or even withdraw its proposals or, in rare cases, resign. Usually the Prime Minister and governments are 'hired and fired' indirectly by the voters; the expectation is that major initiatives in their final form will enjoy broad political support. Although Scandinavian parliamentary politics may seem deceptively placid—with neither the raucous give and take of the British House of Commons nor the occasional fistfight of the Italian Chamber of Deputies—political debates are lengthy, detailed and often emotional. The more

frequent turnover of government between the two main blocs since the 1970s has sharpened the political discourse and led to significant policy reversals.

> **KEY POINTS**
>
> - Scandinavian constitutions have evolved pragmatically to accommodate full parliamentary democracy and interventionist social and economic policies.
>
> - All the Scandinavian countries have proportional representation and multi-party systems with (multi-party) governing coalitions or minority governments dependent on ad hoc parliamentary support.
>
> - Additional oversight and input comes from parliamentary ombudsmen, royal commissions, interest organisations and an active political press.

# Political Actors and Policy-making

Since political democracy was achieved in the early twentieth century, Scandinavian citizens have participated in politics primarily through parties and interest groups. Political parties have been the focus of Scandinavian politics since they began to coalesce in the middle of the nineteenth century. Although they have changed in numbers, programmes, and methods over the decades, parties remain the core political actors. No less venerable have been Scandinavia's myriad of interest organisations which originated in the 'popular movements' of the nineteenth century. Most have represented economic interests with trade unions, farmer groups and business organisations being paramount. Many have direct links with political parties, indeed engendered them. So central have interest organisations been in Scandinavian politics that many have used the term 'democratic corporatism' to describe their role in the policy-making process.

## Parties, voters and elections

Since 1920, proportional representation in national and local assemblies throughout Scandinavia has balanced voter choice and party discipline. The countries are divided into a dozen or more regional multi-member electoral districts to assure fair geographic representation. Parties prepare lists of candidates for each district (and national supplementary seats in the case of Denmark, Norway and Sweden to ensure near perfect proportionality for qualifying parties), but in recent years voters have been encouraged to vote for their preferred candidates on the party list. Although attachment to electoral districts is much less than in the single-member districts of Canada, Britain or the USA, Scandinavian members of Parliament (MPs) have incentive to maintain local ties to their districts and the local party nominating committees.

The modern party system began to develop in the latter part of the nineteenth century in the struggle over limiting the powers of the monarch, the push for parliamentary supremacy and the expansion of the suffrage. Liberals sought to restrict the power of the crown, to increase those of parliament and to expand the electorate; they had their base in the urban middle class and independent farmers. Conservatives took the opposite position, and drew their support from the old governmental, military and economic elite in the cities and aristocracy in the countryside. The social democrats, who organised the urban working class and, eventually, agricultural labourers and tenant farmers, were the junior partner of the liberals in this process, until the expansion of the suffrage and the increasingly strong social democratic and union organisation helped them outgrow their liberal allies in the period around the First World War.

This nineteenth century three-party system grew to a five-party system by the early 1920s with splits in the liberal and social democratic parties. The five-party system—conservatives, liberals, agrarians, social democrats and radical socialists—endured for about 50 years with some minor modifications. Small fascist parties developed in the 1930s and vanished by 1945. A Christian party representing conservative social values developed in the 'free church' regions of Norway in the 1930s, giving Norway a six-party system. Moscow-loyal communist parties were either replaced by national radical socialist parties to the left of the social democrats (Denmark and Norway) or by the national communist party cutting its ties to Moscow (Sweden and Finland) in the late 1950s and 1960s.

This period corresponds to that of social democratic dominance in Denmark, Norway and Sweden. Politics revolved principally around managing the economy and the construction of the welfare state. The social democrats governed generally with the support of the liberals or the agrarians, except in Norway where the election system led to the over-representation of the largest party, giving the Norwegian Labour Party regular parliamentary majorities. Generally, governments were formed across the 'great divide' between socialist and non-socialist parties.

This changed in the 1970s and 1980s with significant party fragmentation around the issues of taxes, European Union membership, cultural conservatism and immigration. New right parties, sometimes called 'the populist right', won seats in the Danish and Norwegian parliaments in 1973 on anti-tax sentiment and continue to poll between 10 and 20 per cent of the vote there today, largely as anti-immigrant parties. Finland, also acquired a populist right party as did the Swedes in the 1990s, but both faded. The centre fragmented. Christian parties captured parliamentary representation in Denmark, Finland and Sweden. Environmentalists ('greens') won independent parliamentary representation in Sweden and Finland; in Denmark and Norway the socialist groups left of the social democrats garnered the environmentalist vote.

Currently party fragmentation has left seven or eight parties represented in the each of the national parliaments: typically these are a rightist anti-immigrant party, the traditional conservatives, liberals and agrarians, one or more new centrist parties (Christians, greens), the social democrats and a more radical socialist party filling the space on the political spectrum that the communists had once filled. Governments include coalitions across socialist–non-socialist lines (especially in Finland), but bloc governments (bourgeois parties v. socialist parties) have become more common.

During the half-century of the five-party system between 1920 and 1970, voters were exceptionally loyal to their parties, and most of the voting was along economic lines. Farmers and the rural middle class voted for the agrarian party, blue-collar workers for the social democrats or, in Finland, communists, the urban middle class for the liberals, and business owners, professionals and the old aristocracy and governmental elite for the conservatives. Party swings between elections tended to be small.

In the aftermath of the breakdown of this system in the 1970s and 1980s, voters have become much more willing to change parties within the same bloc—to move among the four or five non-socialist parties or between the radical socialists and the social democrats, or, in Sweden, the greens. Much of this voter mobility is driven by the relative attractiveness of party leaders within the blocs. Movement across bloc lines has also increased, primarily because of the exploitation of the immigration issues by the new rightist parties. Still, by comparison to most of the rest of Europe, Scandinavian voters are more likely to vote along economic lines and party (or bloc) loyalty remains a defining characteristic of voters.

## Interest groups

The other major political actors are interest groups. As befits otherwise homogenous societies, these were primarily economic in origin. Starting in Denmark in the 1880s, farmers organised purchasing, processing and sales cooperatives; farm co-ops continue to provide economies of scale for family farming today. Unions also began organising in the latter part of the nineteenth century; employers' organisations followed suit in an organisational arms race that led to massive tests of strength before and, in Finland, during the First World War. Where the test of strength resulted in a draw, as in Denmark, national systems of labour relations were established by contract; where the employers won, as in Sweden and Finland, national labour relations systems had to wait for social democratic government or, in Finland, until 1944.

Scandinavia's economic interest organisations were closely allied to their respective parties. Between them, they organised most social life prior to the 1960s. While that network of organisations broke down with the rise of television and the move to the suburbs in the post-war period, the core economic interest organisations—unions, employers, farmers, shopkeepers, professional organisations and the like—retain a density of organisation that remains the envy of their counterparts elsewhere in Europe. Unions organise 75–90 per cent of all wage and salary workers. Employers and farmers achieve comparable levels of organisation.

Moreover, Scandinavian interest organisations are increasingly active on the European and international scene. The consequence of this exceptionally high level of organisation in small societies is that interest groups have become a channel of political representation second only to parties.

In recent years, so-called grass-root groups—anti-EU organisations, anti-nuclear power groups, environmentalists focusing on saving everything from local swamps to whales, and other single issue groups—have come to the fore, supplementing the economic groups of the past. Especially notable was the revival of the women's and feminist movements after 1965.

## The Scandinavian policy-making 'model'

Under the impact of the Nazi assumption of power in nearby Germany, the Scandinavian social democrats reached a 'historic compromise' with the liberal and agrarian parties of the centre. At the core of the compromise in terms of political culture was a pattern of empirically based, consensual policy-making. Ideology took a back seat to facts. Broader majorities were preferred to narrow majorities, which meant, if necessary, further compromise. Indeed, as former Danish Social Democratic Prime Minister Anker Jørgensen put it succinctly, undertaking 'major reforms by narrow majorities is a cause for misgivings' (Einhorn and Logue 2003: 122). By contrast, in most other political systems, it is a cause for celebration.

This is obviously very different from the Westminster model of party government. Part of the Scandinavian distinctiveness stems from the rarity of single-party majorities in their multi-party systems. But much stems from a political culture in which compromise and consensus are considered virtues and in which parties and individuals who do not share those values are generally marginalised quickly. The fact that the Scandinavian political elites are small and many members are personal friends across party lines plays a role.

Moreover, because most Scandinavian parties are mass-membership organisations, their leaders can easily determine whether the party base will support a compromise—they don't have to grandstand for atomised voters as has increasingly become the case in the USA.

Furthermore, the consequence of the exceptionally high level of interest group organisation is that they have been incorporated into making and, often, implementing national policy through a routinised process of consultation before most major legislative initiatives commonly called corporatism. The government not only consults interest groups allied with it but also those that support the opposition prior to major policy initiatives or changes. Labour, employer and farm organisations are involved in researching and formulating most major reforms, and many newer, more specialized interest organisations are also involved in consultation around legislation in their areas. The nature of this process—with its exhaustive fact-finding, inclusive royal commissions' data collection, extensive consultation and input, and deliberative consensus building—built a gradualism into the reform process which has also come to be regarded as a virtue in itself.

---

**KEY POINTS**

- Scandinavian politics is party politics with a five-party system dominant from the 1920s until the 1970s. These parties included, from left to right: communists and radical socialists, social democrats, centrists (social liberal and agrarian), liberals and conservatives.

- Despite two roughly equal blocs—socialist and non-socialist—most of the major reforms creating the welfare state and the 'mixed' economy (market and state regulation) were initiated by the social democrats but required support from the centre.

- Interest organisations, especially trade unions, farmer organisations and business groups, have played a key role in policy-making in a process which has come to be called democratic corporatism. New interest groups have generally gained access to the policy process.

- During the past 30 years there has been more flux in the party system and electoral outcomes, as well as the rise of new or rejuvenated interest organisations, which has influenced but not radically changed the policy-making process.

---

# The Scandinavian Model

Denmark, Norway and Sweden were set apart in the period between the 1930s and the 1960s by a pattern of social democratic dominance of government and policy consistency that gave rise to what was probably the most coherent response to the problems of industrial capitalism among western democracies; Finland, as noted above, followed about 30 years later. Countries that were major sources of immigration in the late nineteenth century became themselves targets for major flows of immigrants in the late twentieth century. The change was most dramatic in Sweden, Norway and Finland, which, unlike Denmark, had been very slow to industrialise in the nineteenth century. Sweden, for example, which was accurately described as the 'fortified poorhouse' (*det befästa fattighuset*) in a famous political tract of 1913, would be idealised as 'the people's home' (*folkhemmet Sverige*) only a generation later, and would, for all practical purposes, have abolished poverty by 1975.

The Scandinavians did it in significant measure by adopting a new model—the combination of social welfare measures with a managed market economy—that would subsequently be generalised in the west as 'the **post-war consensus**'.

## Building the social welfare state

The Scandinavian social democrats, including Norwegian Labour, drew the appropriate lesson from the rise of Hitler to power in Germany in 1933 and from the failure of democratic governments elsewhere in Europe to respond effectively to the global Depression. They put socialisation of the means of production on the back burner and, together with the liberals and agrarians, sought to reinflate farm prices, put the unemployed back to work (preferably at union wages) and to reform the patchwork quilt of poor law and welfare measures to create a comprehensive social security net beneath the entire working population which guaranteed a decent level of income when out of the labour force temporarily (through unemployment, sickness or temporary disability) or permanently (old age, permanent disability). These basic income security programmes were supplemented by a national system of child allowances, national health insurance and housing construction that particularly benefited lower income families with large numbers of children. The push for 'social democracy' replaced that for political democracy. The welfare state—the great mechanism for social democracy and greater economic equality—became the social democrats' surrogate for socialism.

Wartime unity broadened the national consensus to include the conservatives, who proved their democratic values in the Resistance in Denmark and Norway, while totally discrediting the anti-democratic right that had been drawn to Hitler. It also established the national credentials of the social democrats in the minds of the conservatives who shared a statist approach to national development.

In the aftermath of the war, national reconstruction and development cemented these policies. It broadened the security net of transfer payments for those in the labour market to protect against temporary displacement through sickness (a general system of sick pay insurance), unemployment (higher replacement ratios and length of payments), temporary disability or pregnancy, and lower but rising rates for those permanently out of the labour market because of old age or permanent disability. These income replacement ratios were raised from 30–40 per cent in the 1950s to 70–80 per cent by the 1980s for those temporarily forced out of the labour market. It created a massive housing construction programme with various subsidies, especially for families with low incomes and a number of children; in Sweden, savings for the 1958 general supplemental pension programme financed this. It improved social services—such as medical care, education, childcare and care for the elderly—which were provided on the basis of need rather than ability to pay. In recent years, it has encouraged women's entry into the labour market through excellent (but expensive) public childcare, home assistance for the elderly and maternity and paternity leave programmes. Nowhere else in the west achieved such equality of abundance through universal, publicly financed social programmes.

The cost of transfer payments and social services soared just as the post-war economic boom fizzled. Sharp increases in income tax rates caused a political crisis in Denmark and Norway in the 1970s and ultimately led to a tax restructuring in the 1980s and 1990s across Scandinavia that reduced marginal income tax rates while broadening the tax base.

## Managing the market economy

The cost of Scandinavian social welfare provisions would have been prohibitive had it not been supported by an aggressive state management of the market economy to increase production, reduce unemployment and increase market incomes for the worst off. This has included (1) macroeconomic fiscal and monetary policies similar to those in other countries which began to be developed in the 1930s; (2) selective labour market and industrial policies which began to be developed in the 1950s that were far more extensive than those generally used elsewhere; (3) a rising level of unionisation throughout the entire post-war period coupled with a solidaristic wage policy that pushed up market incomes, especially for the least well paid; and (4) policies which supported high rates of labour force participation, particularly by women. By the mid-1970s, for example, Swedish economic policy measures included automatic stabilisers such as high pensions and unemployment compensation, basic Keynesian countercyclical fiscal policies, selective labour market measures and, more innovatively, labour 'activation' measures which forced the unemployed either into jobs or job training and resisted a culture of unemployment. Other Scandinavian countries followed suite.

Government economic policy was supplementing private measures negotiated between the union and employers' federations. Throughout most of the post-war period, five things were happening in the labour market. First, the high and rising degree of unionisation meant that practically all employees were covered by centrally negotiated labour agreements—either for the industry or for the labour market as a whole. Second, national policy encouraged high levels of labour force participation and, throughout the last half-century, Scandinavian labour force participation rates have exceeded those in the USA and the UK. Third, the combination of high degrees of organisation among employers and employees with centralised national wage negotiations created what is called 'the deterrence theory of collective bargaining': strikes were too expensive for the national economy, and the government stepped in to ensure a conclusion to the national negotiating round in keeping with national economic policy. Fourth, in the context of national collective bargaining, the unions' solidarity wage policy forced up wages for the most poorly paid—women and unskilled men—vis-à-vis skilled men until the 1990s. This policy pushed up wages in the most labour-intensive sectors, such as textiles and shoes, while restraining wages in the most capital-intensive sectors, such as machinery, aerospace and communications equipment. It forced industrial renewal

and transfer of capital and labour from less productive to more productive companies and sectors as well as increasing wage equality. Finally, in the 1970s and 1980s, a push for workplace democracy increased workers' influence through employee representatives on corporate boards of directors, co-determination of many management decisions from the shop floor to the boardroom, improved individual rights on the job and much greater worker influence on occupational health and safety.

Today pension reform—ironically often opposed by the unions and supported by the employers and non-socialist parties—is massing significant worker-controlled investment funds which also promise greater financial viability for retirement pensions than elsewhere in the Organisation for Economic Cooperation and Development (OECD). In Sweden the 'great pension reform' of the 1990s provides some measure of employee control of investment choices (see Anderson 2001). At the same time Norway created the public Petroleum Fund to insulate the national economy from the gyrations of oil prices and to build a massive source of future pension funding. By late-2006 this fund—renamed State Pension Fund—International—exceeded US $250 billion.

## Achievements of the Scandinavian social democratic model

The Scandinavian social welfare states rested upon solidarity: the 'all for one, and one for all' attitude of Dumas' *Three Musketeers*. Solidarity works best in small, closely knit groups: trade union locals, local farmers' organisations, neighbourhood associations and the like. It is perhaps an historical anomaly that, in Scandinavia, solidarity got extended from the small group—the union local—to the working class and then, thanks to the Resistance, to the national community. Ethnic and religious homogeneity until the 1970s was another contributing factor.

The result was that twentieth-century Scandinavia underwent a dramatic improvement in living standards and reduction of inequality and poverty[3] without major political or social upheaval because these changes entailed no redistribution of existing wealth and income. Rather, the growth in the national economic pie was distributed differently through national collective bargaining and through state policies than would have been the case in a pure market system. It was an optimum solution: almost no one was worse off absolutely than before, and most had their living standards improved substantially or dramatically.

The 'fortified poorhouse' was replaced by shared prosperity where, in the inspirational words of the nineteenth-century Danish theologian N. S. F. Grundtvig, 'few have too much and fewer too little'. That's not a bad definition of the good society.

## Policy in the European and global context

Just as the Scandinavian welfare state was built on and reinforced economic prosperity, so the latter rested on an early acceptance of an open trading economy. The impetus to modern political economy was provided by the recurring international crises of 1914–45. After the Second World War, the Scandinavian countries pursued international organisation and cooperation with renewed energy. The United Nations, NATO (for Denmark, Iceland and Norway) and the Nordic Council were initially the most important, and the Scandinavian countries have an unusually high profile in such international organisations. By the 1960s, however, European integration became a central issue on Scandinavian political agendas. It proved a divisive issue, and currently each Scandinavian country has its own European policy. (See Theme box: The Impact of the European Union.)

Although EU issues are generally separated from partisan politics, EU parliamentary elections and the periodic referenda (particularly in Denmark, which has had six since 1972) allow vigorous public debate. The Scandinavian countries prefer to take 'Europe à la carte' but, when they accept obligations, they have a good record of implementation of EU directives. Even Norway and Iceland, members of the **European Economic Area** (EEA) have joined the Schengen agreement on border controls and implemented much of the EU *acquis* without concessions in their politically sensitive agricultural and fisheries policies. Traditional Swedish and Finnish non-alignment has not prevented participation in the evolving European Defence and Security Policy, in which Norway occasionally joins, while Denmark exercises its 1992 opt-out.

### KEY POINTS

- In response to the global Depression of the 1930s, the Scandinavian countries expanded social programmes. This process accelerated after the Second World War to become a comprehensive welfare state by 1970.

- Accompanying social policy was active economic management (Keynesian fiscal policies), limited economic planning and pursuit of foreign trade markets. Between 1950 and 1975 these policies were successful. After 1975 new economic policies gradually responded successfully to globalisation and European integration.

- With globalisation and the expanding role of the European Union, both government agencies and interest organisations have had to develop new methods to influence policies beyond national borders. Pragmatism has prevailed.

### THEME BOX

The Impact of the European Union

The European Union divides both the Scandinavian region and opinion within each of the countries. Denmark followed Britain into the EC in 1973, but remains a moderate Euro-sceptic as indicated by four 'opt-outs' from the 1992 Maastricht Treaty and rejection of the euro currency in 2000. Sweden and

Finland joined the EU in 1995 but only Finland has accepted the full Economic and Monetary Union. Norway and Iceland remain outside the EU proper but selectively cooperate through the European Economic Area. Norwegian referenda rejected full membership in 1972 and 1994. At issue in Denmark, Finland and Sweden is the increasing intrusion of European Union laws and procedures into domestic legal and political procedures. Their governments are directly represented in the EU Council of Ministers, while 'European committees' of the national parliaments seek to keep legislators aware of EU developments have and allow parliamentary input before ministers make binding commitments. A significant number of high-ranking civil servants have gained EU experience, a pattern now being emulated by staff of leading interest organisations. Public opinion is generally favourable to economic cooperation but sceptical of 'deeper' union.

# Conclusion: Current Challenges

Scandinavia had a good twentieth century, despite some dark periods during the world wars and the international Depression (1930–40). There are four aspects to the new century's challenges that can loosely be grouped as political, economic, social and international. Each interacts and overlaps, but encompasses important trends.

## Political

As stable parliamentary democracies, the Scandinavian countries are models of effective multi-party systems. The 'politics of compromise' identified by Dan Rustow 50 years ago still functions. The failure of extremist forces to win any significant political terrain contrasts with other European states. The radical left reflects primarily a residue of socialist idealism and trenchant critique of the shortcomings of welfare capitalism. The willingness of most radical socialist parties in all of the Scandinavian countries to participate in policy reforms and compromises gives them a constructive role and discourages political infantilism. Likewise the populist right—at present only significant in the Danish People's and Norwegian Progress parties—is a determined critic of many of the social changes of the past 30 years. The transformation of relatively homogenous countries into globalised multiethnic societies has been difficult and controversial. Yet the right fully accepts the constitutional rules and, when non-socialists govern, they too are now selective participants as well as critics.

Fifty years after it was first proclaimed, the 'end of ideology' thesis may have some validity in Northern Europe, but only for *traditional*, class-based ideologies. New policy debates including environmental, gender, multicultural, European and global issues keep politics very much alive. Many of these issues have been accommodated into the pragmatic, rationalistic Scandinavian political model, but others stir deeper passions.

## Economic

Except on the leftist fringe, there is a broad consensus in Scandinavia that social capitalism—that is a negotiated market economy with strong corporatist structures and an active state—is the best way to run a post-industrial economy. Unlike some other Western European economies, the Scandinavians have developed a vigorous and competitive technological sector in areas like telecommunications, pharmaceuticals and financial services while also expanding public services in childcare, education and health and elder care. To be sure there remain lively debates about the role of privatisation and how to assure acceptable quality and efficiency from public services. The past 30 years have forced difficult economic reforms in each of the Nordic countries as old industries have declined, new competitors appeared and technological and scientific developments have changed the requirements of human, social and physical capital. Social programmes have been recalibrated to balance between competing demands for resources and changing policy priorities. Taxation remains remarkably high in Scandinavia although research indicates that similar costs must be met in other advanced industrial countries through corporatist or private expenditures.[4] Even conservatives have become cautious about promising tax cuts when well informed voters know that public revenues are necessary to pay for vital services and infrastructure.

A major challenge has been to maintain both social inclusiveness and competitiveness. In a global economy, neo-liberal ideology suggests a trade-off between egalitarianism and inclusiveness, on the one hand, and competitiveness and prosperity, on the other. So far, the Scandinavians have maintained both, perhaps because of the flexibility long required of small, open economies.

Since the mid-1990s, the Scandinavian states have avoided the economic stagnation that has gripped some of Europe's larger economies because of reforms and more flexible economic policies. Unemployment leads quickly to 'activation' policies (retraining, education and assisted relocation) which vary in effectiveness, but which seem to keep long-term unemployment at about 30–60 per cent, the 'EU-15' level. While Norway has reaped the latest petroleum boom (Denmark has also done well), investments in energy efficiency coupled with energy and carbon taxes have buffered these states from the impact of energy inflation. Wind turbines contributed nearly 20 per cent of Danish electrical supply in 2005, and alternative and renewable sources have created new industries across the region. The bottom line has been steady economic growth, lower unemployment and significant domestic and international investment that have supported rising private and public consumption. Economic pressures clearly impinge on expensive public programmes, but less drastically than in most other European countries.

## Social

The combination of two generations of solid economic growth and progressive social policy has yielded a far more democratic society than could have been imagined when the 'social question' jumped to the top of the political agenda a century ago. Although wage differentials have risen modestly over the past 15 years, most other objective measures of inequality, in education, health, housing, leisure and a host of other social indicators, reflect substantial progress towards socio-economic equality. It would be difficult to claim that the Scandinavian societies have become classless, in part because the concept of class contains many cultural, historical and other subjective factors, but the rigidities of the pre-industrial and early industrial era are largely gone.

Contemporary Scandinavia, like the rest of Europe (and the developed world) has been transformed by four decades of rising and increasingly diverse migration. Estimates suggest that between 5 and 10 per cent of the population of the Nordic countries is of non-West European origin (somewhat lower in Finland). Included are refugees and economic migrants from outside Europe whose integration into the homogeneous Nordic societies is a major challenge. Only Sweden had experience before 1980 with integration policies encouraging the learning of language, social and occupational skills that can reduce the vulnerability of immigrants to social exclusion and, among a small minority, anti-social behaviour. Even without the multicultural challenge, the elimination of poverty did not entirely eradicate a native underclass of dependent, mentally ill and anti-social people. Passive social transfers (income support) help overcome economic poverty but not social exclusion.

Another problem confronting Scandinavia is more quantitative: ageing societies and lower birthrates may auger future labour shortages. Thanks to the development of childcare facilities, women no longer must choose between children and a career. These demographic trends have given additional importance to better integration and training for immigrants, policies to increase the labour force, and reversal of ever-earlier retirement.

## International

Recurring themes throughout this book are the twin trends of globalisation and **Europeanisation**, and both are prominent in Scandinavia. This is reflected in the historic importance of foreign trade for the Scandinavian economies, the replacement of emigration before 1914 with a rising tide of immigration since 1945, and the web of interdependencies with regional (especially the European Union) and international organisations. The Scandinavian countries are strong believers in 'internationalism' but have proven quite capable of shaping their global relations to fit their national interests. Sweden and Finland remain committed to military non-alignment, but are active in international peacekeeping and peace-enforcing coalitions. Iceland and Norway remain outside the EU, but have accommodated their interests through the EEA. For 60 years the Scandinavians have been stalwart supporters of the United Nations and its affiliated organisations and have provided global leaders.

Not all Scandinavians are positive about globalising and Europeanising trends, but most political leaders have advocated pragmatic accommodation. In business, science, even culture, the willingness of Scandinavians to learn foreign languages, pursue international careers, and to apply Nordic rationalism to international public policy—not always successfully—helps to keep the Scandinavian model in the

global consciousness. (See Theme box: The Impact of Globalisation.)

Thus Scandinavians begin the new century with cautious optimism. Their five national experiences suggest that good sense and pragmatism, a broader sense of democracy and the rational search for better public policy can succeed. Despite different priorities and approaches, the common thread of the Scandinavian countries is the pursuit of democracy and equality beyond its narrow constitutional and political boundaries to include economic and social affairs in the broad sense that T. H. Marshall (1965) suggested nearly half a century ago. Political, social and economic democracy is an endless quest as R. H. Tawney noted (1920), it matters less what a society has already achieved than the direction in which its face is set.

ERIC S. EINHORN AND JOHN LOGUE

# Notes

1. Scandinavia is used here as including all five sovereign states, Denmark, Finland, Iceland, Norway and Sweden, as well as the three autonomous territories of Greenland and the Faeroe Island (with Denmark) and Åland Islands (with Finland). 'Nordic' is an alternative term for the region.

2. Space constraints dictate a focus on Denmark, Finland, Norway and Sweden to the exclusion of the smaller island societies. For coverage of Iceland, see Karlsson 2000 and, in the Scandinavian context, Einhorn and Logue 2003.

3. The World Bank (2001: 282–3) reports that Denmark, Finland, Norway and Sweden had a more equal distribution of income than any other western countries except Austria, Belgium and Japan which were in the same ballpark. The Scandinavian countries clustered around a Gini index rating of 25 (indicating that, to reach income equality, 25 per cent of the household income had to be redistributed among deciles); by contrast the UK had a score of 36 and the USA a score of almost 41. Other researchers have confirmed the relative economic egalitarianism of the Scandinavian countries, despite some modest slippage since the 1980s. (See Kenworthy 2004: 22–43.)

4. Scandinavian taxes are high and comprehensive but, when international adjustments are made, their levels of social expenditure approach the European norm. Their social programmes remain more universal than many other social insurance schemes. (See Adema 2001.)

## ? QUESTIONS

1. Scandinavia has often been thought of as a 'social laboratory' for the study of modern public policies. What is meant by this and why are the Scandinavian countries interesting cases?

2. Many Scandinavians emphasise the region's political distinctiveness from the rest of Europe in terms of party systems, public policies and political culture. Is there substance to this assertion? To what extent is there conversion on a general Western European model?

3. How democratic is the policy-making process in Scandinavia? Does the corporatist element strengthen or weaken democracy? Assess the criteria for judging a democratic system and contrast it with other European parliamentary democracies as well as forms such as the presidential democracies of the USA and France.

4. How did Scandinavian 'socialism' differ in means and ends from other Marxist and socialist movements in Europe?

5. Egalitarianism continues to play a large role in Scandinavian political and social discourse. Why and how has this affected their politics? Discuss specifically the 'new' egalitarian issues of the past 30 years.

6. How does the comprehensive Scandinavian welfare state affect political behaviour (e.g. voting, organising, administration, etc.)?

7. What are likely to be some of the political consequences as Scandinavia becomes 'multi-ethnic' or 'multicultural'?

8. How has the European Union changed domestic politics and policies in the Scandinavian countries?

 **FURTHER READING**

■ **Arter, D. (1999),** *Scandinavian Politics Today*, **Manchester, Manchester University Press.** Offers a good account of Scandinavian parties, political institutions and foreign policy; it is particularly strong on Finland.

■ **Einhorn, E. S. and Logue J. (2003),** *Modern Welfare States: Scandinavian Politics and Policy in the Global Age*, **2nd edn, Westport CT and London, Praeger.** Provides an up-to-date and comprehensive overview of all five Nordic states.

■ **Heidar, K. (ed.) (2004),** *Nordic Politics: Comparative Perspectives*, **Oslo, Universitetsforlaget.** A collection of timely essays on the current state of Nordic politics and political sociology.

■ **Ingebritsen, C. (1998),** *The Nordic States and European Unity*, **Ithaca NY, Cornell University Press.** A concise and sharply focused study of Scandinavia's complex relationship to European integration.

■ **Karlsson, G. (2000),** *The History of Iceland*, **Minneapolis MN, University of Minnesota Press.** The best history of Iceland available in English; provides good coverage of modern political history.

■ **Kautto, M.** *et al.* **(2001),** *Nordic Welfare States in the European Context*, **London, Routledge.** Surveys a wide range of social policies and makes useful comparisons between Nordic policies and other European models.

■ **Nordstrom, B. (2000),** *Scandinavia since 1500*, **Minneapolis and London, University of Minnesota Press.** Offers a concise and comprehensive regional history.

■ **Petersson, O. (1994),** *The Government and Politics of the Nordic Countries*, **Stockholm, Fritzes.** Presents a systematic and detailed review of political institutions and processes.

 **IMPORTANT WEBSITES**

● **www.scanpol.kent.edu** Has complete tables on Scandinavian elections, parliamentary parties and governments since the First World War.

● All of the Nordic countries have excellent official websites that link to various government databases and information offices. See **denmark.dk, finland.fi, iceland.is, norway.no** and **sweden.se**.

● **www.norden.org** The official website of the Nordic Council with much information about the Scandinavian countries and their regional cooperation.

● **www.psa.ac.uk/spgrp/scandinavia** The homepage of the Scandinavian politics specialist group of the (British) Political Studies Association. It has useful information and helpful links.

● **www.lib.byu.edu/estu/wess/scan** Based at Brigham Young University (USA), has links to many academic resources on Scandinavia.

 **Visit the Online Resource Centre that accompanies this book for lots of useful additional material, including an interactive map of Europe. www.oxfordtextbooks.co.uk/orc/hay_menon/**

# 6 Belgium and the Netherlands

STEVEN B. WOLINETZ

## Reader's Guide

This chapter examines politics in Belgium and the Netherlands. Although physically proximate, the two countries are quite different. Both have had pillarised or segmented social structures, and both have been considered to be consociational democracies in which the ostensibly deleterious effects of cleavage structures are said to be overcome by the self-conscious efforts of elites willing and able to compromise and share power in order to avoid system-threatening conflicts. Both have complex multi-party systems in which a large number of political parties reflecting these cleavages are represented in parliament. Consociational practices have all but disappeared from Dutch national politics. In contrast, there is continuing recourse to consociational practices in Belgium. Earlier compromises on schools and suffrage did not extend to lInguistic issues. Their increased salience led to the federalisation of Belgium politics: substantial powers were transferred to regions or Flemish and Francophone linguistic communities.

# Introduction: Belgium and the Netherlands—Similar or Different?

It is common to lump Belgium and the Netherlands together. Physically proximate, the two countries share membership in international and trans-European organisations. Both are original EU member states, until recently committed to a wider and deeper Europe. Both are parliamentary democracies with relatively fragmented multi-party systems.

This chapter compares Belgium and the Netherlands. The two are less similar than they might appear. Both are smaller European democracies which resorted to power-sharing and consociational democracy to bridge religious, class or linguistic cleavages. Substantially federalised, Belgium uses power-sharing and other consociational practices to balance its regions and linguistic communities. In contrast, consociational practices have all but disappeared from Dutch national politics.

---

**KEY POINTS**

- Both are parliamentary democracies with relatively fragmented multi-party systems.

- The Netherlands and Belgium are less similar than they might appear.

- Both have been considered to be consociational democracies. Consociational practices have all but disappeared from the Netherlands but persist in Belgium.

---

# History and Institutions

The Netherlands and Belgium share a common history, but this has divided them more than it has brought them together. United under the Holy Roman Empire, the two split when the northern provinces rebelled. At issue were religion, economy and local autonomy. Despite a sizeable Catholic minority, Calvinists were dominant in the north. In contrast, the south remained Catholic. Exploiting overseas trade, merchant capitalists in Holland and Zeeland were generating new wealth; aristocrats governed the south. The northern provinces gained independence in 1648.

The Napoleonic Wars reunited the north and south. Invading in 1795, the French imposed Napoleonic law and centralised administrative structures. Nevertheless, differences in language, mood and temperament persisted. Although French was the language of administration, Dutch was used in the north and parts of the south.

Napoleon's defeat brought further changes. Hoping to create a buffer state, the Congress of Vienna united the north and south under the Kingdom of the Netherlands. King William I's centralised rule, autocratic style and preference for Dutch-speaking Calvinists in the bureaucracy antagonised elites in the south. Liberals and Catholics rebelled in 1830 and after brief skirmishes gained independence. Belgium became a constitutional monarchy.

The two countries diverged in the nineteenth century. Belgium was a cradle of the industrial revolution. In the north, the golden age (the seventeenth century) had long since passed; substantial industrialisation did not occur until the twentieth century.

After the Second World War both countries came together in the Council of Europe, Benelux, NATO, the Organisation for Economic Cooperation in Europe, the European Coal and Steel Community and other international organisations. A forerunner of the European Economic Community, Benelux anticipated some of its policies. Border controls disappeared sooner. Later, Benelux was overtaken by the European Union.

## Institutions: an overview

Both the Netherlands and Belgium are parliamentary democracies. Each has a bicameral parliament. Lower houses are elected by proportional representation. In the Netherlands, the 75-member upper chamber or Senate is elected by provincial assemblies and serves as a chamber of revision whose assent is required for legislation to become law. In Belgium, federalisation has altered the size and composition of the parliament. The lower house was reduced to 150 members. The 71-member upper chamber now represents the regions and cultural communities. Day-to-day governing is the prerogative of cabinets which serve with the confidence of parliament. Monarchs serve as head of state. Although their duties are largely ceremonial, the Dutch and Belgian monarchs play important roles in the formation and/or maintenance of cabinets.

The principal differences are in the territorial organisation of government. Both began as unitary states whose governments performed limited functions, but have ended up administering complex welfare states. National governments guarantee citizens minimum levels of subsistence and well-being. However, the Netherlands has remained a highly centralised unitary state; provincial and local governments are subordinate to the national government. Belgium has become a federal state with important powers devolved either to regional governments in Flanders, Wallonia and Brussels or to Flemish and Francophone cultural councils.

### KEY POINTS

- Predominantly Calvinist, the Netherlands retained a substantial Catholic minority. Belgium was Catholic but divided between Francophones and Flemish-speakers.

- In 1815, Belgium and the Netherlands were brought together under the Kingdom of the Netherlands. Seceding in 1830, Belgium became a constitutional monarchy. Both are parliamentary democracies.

- Belgium industrialised earlier than the Netherlands.

- After the Second World War, both countries joined European and international organisations.

- The Netherlands is a unitary state. Belgium has become a federal system.

# Segmentation and Its Impact

Both countries were divided by religious and class cleavages, but these are no longer as salient as they once were. Language is a third, more contentious source of cleavage in Belgium: 60 per cent speak Flemish, a small percentage German, the remainder French. In both countries, religious and class cleavages were organised into cradle-to-grave networks of religious or ideologically based organisations. Class and religious cleavages ended up imprinted on party systems. The linguistic cleavage in Belgium was less salient and not channelled into the party system until the mid-twentieth century. Today, it divides parties and provides the basis for the federalisation of Belgian politics.

## Cleavage structure and pillarisation

Although language did not initially divide Belgium, religion did. Nineteenth-century Belgium was divided between liberals, opposed to Church influence, and practising Catholics, who were not. At issue was the control of schools. Industrialisation added another force—socialism. Catholics and socialists organised their followers into **parties of mass integration**. Liberals constituted a third group. Each segment or **spiritual family** constituted a separate world with its own schools and institutions (Lorwin 1966) (See Figure 6.1.).

Similar structures emerged in the Netherlands. Calvinists, Catholics and social democrats constructed segmented structures. Their joint efforts produced a segmented or pillarised social structure. (See Figure 6.2.) Each pillar constituted a separate network of religious or class-based organisations. Once state support for denominational schools was achieved, these became even more complete. Catholics and Calvinists had separate schools, universities, trade unions, agricultural organisations, newspapers, social and sport organisations. When radio was introduced, air time was divided among the four **pillars**; television broadcasting was carved up in the same way. Social democrats shared state schools

with liberals, but their social, sport and educational organisations constituted a separate pillar. General or liberal organisations constituted a fourth. Associations did not cut across religious or ideological boundaries but were delimited by them. Segmentation meant that people of different persuasions could live substantial portions of their lives without interacting (Daalder 1966; Lijphart 1975). The same was true within Belgium's spiritual families.

## Consociational democracies?

Variously called **segmentation**, **subcultural pluralism** or **pillarisation** (in Dutch, *verzuiling*), this phenomenon has intrigued social scientists. Earlier theories insisted that **cross-cutting cleavages** were needed to ensure stability and that countries which lacked them risked 'flying apart'. Different theories have been advanced to explain the relative stability of these countries. Arend Lijphart (1975, 1977) argued that stability reflected the willingness and ability of political elites to compromise and share power through devices such as grand coalition, proportional allocation, mutual veto (according each segment a veto over key issues) and subcultural

**Figure 6.1** The spiritual families in Belgium (now also divided on linguistic lines)

| Liberal | Catholic | Socialist |
|---|---|---|
| Liberal Party | Social Christian Party, Catholic church, Parish and diocesan organisations | Socialist Party |
| State schools | Catholic schools | State schools |
| State universities | Catholic university (Leuven) | State universities |
| Newspapers | Newspapers | Newspapers |
| Employers' associations | Employers' associations | |
| Trade unions and mutual societies | Trade unions and mutual societies | Trade unions and mutual societies |
| Agricultural organisations | Agricultural organisations | Agricultural organisations |
| Professional associations | Professional associations | Professional associations |
| Social and sport organisations | Social and sport organisations | Social and sport organisations |

STEVEN B. WOLINETZ

**Figure 6.2** Pillarisation in the Netherlands before 1980

| Catholic pillar | Calvinist pillar | Socialist pillar | General |
|---|---|---|---|
| Catholic Party* (KVP until 1980) | Calvinist parties* (ARP and CHU until 1980) | Social Democratic Party (PvdA) | Liberal Party (VVD) |
| Catholic church | Orthodox Reformed and Dutch Reformed churches | | |
| Parish and diocesan organisations | | | |
| Catholic schools | Calvinist schools | Public schools | Public schools |
| Catholic University (Nijmegen) and Technical schools | Free University of Amsterdam | Municipal University of Amsterdam State Universities and technical schools | State universities and technical schools |
| News papers | News papers | News papers | News papers |
| Catholic broadcasting organisation | Protestant broadcasting organisation | Broadcasting organisation | Broadcasting organisation |
| Social and sport organisations | Social and sport organisations | Social and sport organisations | Social and sport organisations |
| Trade unions** | Trade unions** | Trade unions** | |
| Employers' associations*** | Employers' associations*** | | Employers' associations*** |
| Agricultural associations | Agricultural associations | | Agricultural associations |
| Professional and occupational associations | Professional and occupational associations | | Professional and occupational associations |

*Notes:*
\* The Calvinist and Catholic parties merged in 1980 to form an inter-confessional party, the Christian Democratic Appeal (CDA)
\*\* The Socialist and Catholic trade union federations merged in 1980 to form the Netherlands Federation of Trade Unions (FNV). Originally Calvinist (Protestant Christian) the Christian National Trade Union Federation (CNV) now includes some Catholic trade unionists
\*\*\* The Calvinist and Catholic Employers' Associations merged to form the Netherlands Christian Employers' Association (NCW). The NCW subsequently merged with the liberal or secular Confederation of Dutch Entepreneurs (VNO) to form the Confederation of Netherlands Industry and Employers (Vereniging VNO/NCW)

autonomy—allowing each to regulate its own affairs. This is the theory of consociational democracy, or **consociationalism**. Others attributed stability to the strong social control or the absence of system-threatening conflicts (see Andeweg and Irwin 2005).

Lijphart's theory hinges on the willingness of self-conscious elites to rise above conflicts which had led to instability in other countries. He argues that Dutch elites worked out the pacification settlements while the First World War was fought around them. These entrenched state support for denominational schools in the Dutch constitution, granted universal manhood suffrage (women's suffrage followed quickly thereafter) and introduced proportional representation, coupled with a requirement (in effect until 1970) that voters show up at the polls. This ensured that each group would be represented in proportion to its numbers. According to Lijphart, the pacification saved the day, averting system-threatening conflict. What we cannot know is what would have happened had these agreements not been implemented.

Belgium has similar practices. There, segmentation and recourse to power-sharing did not prevent occasional conflicts, but provided ways of dealing with them (Lijphart 1981). Arguments over schools simmered in the 1950s. Liberals pressed for the expansion of 'neutral' schools. Catholics insisted on a pre-eminent role in education and additional subsidies to church-related organisations. Stalemate provided the impetus for the 1958 School Pact. This eliminated tuition fees, guaranteed the neutrality of public schools and allowed parents to send children to schools of their choice. Funding was allocated proportionally. Like the Dutch pacification of 1917, this led to the expansion of Catholic education (Witte *et al.* 2000; Lorwin 1966).

When linguistic conflicts broke out, the outcome was different; politicians reconfigured the Belgian state.

## Federalising Belgium

When Belgium split from the Netherlands, it took Flemish speakers with it. Common people spoke Flemish; elites French as did anyone who wished to advance. Limits on suffrage restricted the power of Flemish speakers; most could not vote. Flemish nationalism appeared in the late nineteenth century, but it took time and effort to advance the Flemish cause. Flemish was permitted in courts from 1873, in local and provincial administration from 1878, and in secondary schools from 1883. French remained the language of political elites.

A turning point came after 1918. Universal manhood suffrage enfranchised the Flemish majority. The University of Ghent became a Flemish-speaking university in 1930. Flemish received co-equal status with French in education and administration in 1932 and in the courts in 1935. Brussels became formally bilingual. However, the proportion speaking both languages was minuscule. Parties began operating through Flemish and Francophone wings (Witte *et al.* 2000; Keating *et al.* 2003).

Full parity came in the 1960s. Historically poorer and less developed, Flanders was modernising. Insisting on using their language, Flemish

speakers demanded greater autonomy. Francophones resisted learning Flemish. Tensions were exacerbated by economic changes. Flanders was undergoing a 'third industrial revolution'. Built on coal and steel, French-speaking Wallonia was declining. Headquarters to the EU, NATO and multinationals, Brussels was a separate world. Transferring powers to Flanders meant giving equivalent powers to Wallonia. Doing so left the question of Brussels unresolved. Predominantly Francophone, it was not only located in Flanders, but also different from Wallonia (Keating *et al.* 2003).

Solutions emerged from protracted negotiations. Because constitutional changes were required, politicians had to build coalitions capable of securing a two-thirds majority in two successive parliaments. Changes took place in fits and starts, with cabinets falling because parties could not agree.

Three packages altered the shape of the Belgian state. Negotiated in the 1960s, the first divided Belgium along its linguistic frontier. Provinces to its north became unilingual Flemish territories; those to the south, Francophone. Brussels became bilingual, with signs and services in both languages. If they were sufficiently numerous, Francophones in its suburbs—physically located in Flanders—were guaranteed 'facilities' in their own language. Francophone faculties at the University of Louvain were moved to a new town, Louvain-le-Neuf, and constituted as an independent university.

Matters did not end here: Flemish nationalists demanded the transfer of powers to a Flemish-speaking regional government. Any transfer to a Flemish government required a parallel transfer to a Wallonian government. However, Wallonia's steel industry was in decline, and a substantial portion of Belgium's Francophone population was not Wallonian, but resident in Brussels, inside Flanders, and without a sub-national identity. The solution, negotiated in the 1970s, was a dual form of federalism: regional governments accountable to regional parliaments operate in Flanders, Wallonia, Brussels and a smaller German-speaking area to the east. They deal with economic and regional questions, but not matters of culture or language. These have been transferred to Flemish-speaking and Francophone Cultural Councils. They deal with cultural and educational issues in their regions and in Brussels, where both have jurisdiction. Each can sound an 'alarm bell' delaying legislation believed detrimental to its community's interests. The Flemish Regional Government and Flemish Cultural Council coincide; the Wallonian Regional Government and the Francophone Cultural Council do not (Keating *et al.* 2003; Witte and van Velthoven 1999).

Regionalisation was not completed until a third settlement was negotiated in the 1990s. The only significant powers not transferred are raising and disbursing revenues. Although regions can tax, most revenue is raised and allocated by the national government. If it were not, the poorer Wallonian region would be starved of resources.

Linguistic conflicts have largely abated. Arguments persist about the language in which services are to be delivered. However, these are confined to the suburbs of Brussels, where attempts to extend Francophone 'facilities' antagonise Flemish nationalists. Dual federalism and recourse to consociational practices have done the trick. However, the process was neither easy nor devoid of conflict. Linguistic divisions had not been built into the previous pattern of segmentation and elite accommodation. They are now.

# Cleavage Structures Today

Cleavage structures have changed in both countries. Although still represented in party systems, class and religious cleavages are less salient than they once were. In the Netherlands, the scope and impact of pillarisation have receded. Although segmented organisations persist in schools, broadcasting and non-profit organisations involved in the delivery of services, religious or ideological content is muted. Some segmented organisations (such as trade unions and employers' associations) have merged and others, not rooted in the older pillars, have emerged. In Belgium, deeply embedded clientelism ensures the persistence of segmented structures. As in Italy, parties have 'colonised' parts of the bureaucracy, appointing followers to positions they regard as their own. Parties retain control over recruitment to the regional governments. Although ideological content has faded, deeply entrenched organisational structures persist (Deschouwer 1999).

In both countries, newer sources of division have emerged. The latter include post-materialists, demanding a better quality of life, and people opposed to immigration, multiculturalism and the EU. Neither is organised as intensively as the older class and religious cleavages once were. In the absence of dense organisational networks structuring the vote, surges of support for protest parties are common. These often subside as rapidly as they emerge.

> **KEY POINTS**
>
> - Both the Netherlands and Belgium have been characterised by pillarisation or segmentation. In Belgium, Catholic, liberal and socialist pillars (spiritual families) persist. In the Netherlands, there were Calvinist, Catholic, socialist and liberal pillars.
>
> - Lijphart's theory of consociational democracy maintains that the stability of countries like the Netherlands and Belgium depends on the willingness and ability of elites to share power and find compromises.
>
> - Linguistic conflicts in Belgium emerged later and initially were not covered by consociational bargains.
>
> - Belgium dealt with linguistic conflicts by dividing the country into regions and cultural communities and transferring powers to them.
>
> - Pillarisation has receded in the Netherlands but persists in Belgium. Clientelistic practices ensure that Belgian parties retain a strong grip over the state apparatus.

# Parties and Party Systems

Both Belgium and the Netherlands have complex multi-party systems, with as many as eight to ten parties represented in parliament. Older parties were organised around religion or social class. Newer parties typically take up post-materialist or anti-immigrant and anti-EU themes. In Belgium, parties which bridged the language divide now operate as separate entities with little to do with each other. Electoral laws are a further complication. Both countries use proportional representation with thresholds sufficiently low that smaller parties can enter parliament. This is particularly true in the Netherlands. The Second Chamber (Lower House) has 150 members. Two-thirds of 1 per cent of the national vote (0.67 per cent) is sufficient to win a seat in parliament.

Religion has been a significant but diminishing source of cleavage in both countries. In Belgium, this separates the Democratic Humanist Centre (CDH), formerly the Christian Social Party (PSC) in Wallonia, and the Christian Democratic and Flemish Party (CD&V), until recently the Christian People's Party (CVP), from secular parties.(See Background box 6.1.) The picture is different in the Netherlands. There were two Calvinist parties, the Anti-Revolutionary Party (ARP) and the Christian Historical Union (CHU) and a larger Catholic party (KVP), but all three merged to form the Christian Democratic Appeal (CDA) in 1980. (See Background box 6.2.) Christian democratic parties in both countries style themselves as centre parties bridging class divisions. There were strong links to churches and lay Catholic organisations. These barely persist in the Netherlands and are looser than they once were in Belgium.

Class and ideology separated liberals and social democrats. On the moderate left are social democratic parties, the Labour Party in the Netherlands, and the Socialist parties in Wallonia (PS) and Flanders (SP, now known as Socialist Party Differently, SPA). Historically, Dutch and Belgian social democrats favoured reform, preferring to seek power via the ballot box. Social democrats in both countries have moderated their positions, preferring to manage market economies to ensure a more equitable distribution of wealth. Social democrats now style themselves as **third way** parties, governing with liberals rather than Christian democrats in the 1990s and early 2000s.

Liberal parties are progressive on moral issues, but to the right on social and economic issues. Liberalism in the Netherlands is represented by the People's Party for Freedom and Democracy (VVD) and a newer party, Democrats 66 (D66). Established to seek a district system and an elected prime minister, D66 positions itself to the left of the VVD. Its hallmark is continuing commitment to constitutional reform. In Flanders, the Flemish Liberals and Democrats (VLD, formerly the Party of Freedom and Progress, PVV) is currently the largest party with 15.4 per cent of the national vote. Its Wallonian counterpart is the Reformist Movement (MR, formerly the Liberal Reform Party, PRL).

Both countries have left-libertarian parties, Green Left (GL) in the Netherlands, AGALEV (Living Differently) in Flanders and ECOLO in Wallonia. Reflecting religious schisms, the Netherlands has had several smaller Calvinist parties. Although opposed to elements of modern society, neither of the two currently represented in parliament is obstructionist. Belgium lacks equivalent parties. However, linguistic parties, such as the People's Union (*Volksunie*, VU) in Flanders, the Wallonion Bloc and Francophone Democratic Front (FDF) in Brussels, gained support in the 1960s and 1970, but have subsequently faded.

Other parties reflect emerging cleavages. In the Netherlands, anti-immigrant and anti-European sentiment have been articulated on the right by the Centre Party (CP) and Centre Democrats (CD) and, more recently, and more successfully, by the List Pim Fortuyn (LPF), which has since imploded and, in 2006, the party for Freedom (PvdV). On the left, the Socialist Party (SP) uses constituency work and anti-immigrant themes to mobilise remnants of the white working class. In Belgium, a new right populist party, the Flemish Bloc (VB) has gained substantial support in the port city of Antwerp.

## Voting patterns: the new volatility

The Dutch and Belgian party systems were locked into place by nineteenth- and twentieth-century mobilisation. Segmentation provided parties with stable bases of support. Relatively closed pillars ensured the transmission and reinforcement of party loyalties. Voting outside one's pillar was unthinkable for many people. In the Netherlands, church attendance or, failing that, social class were strong predictors of voting behaviour. This was apparent in the earliest voting studies. Survey data are rarer in Belgium, but religion and class have similar effects.

The scope and impact of pillarisation in both countries have receded. Fewer people attend church, class differences have eased and successive generations have been exposed to different influences than their predecessors (Andeweg 1999). Voters are less likely to be attached to any one party. Electoral volatility has risen dramatically. Recent election results in the Netherlands (see Table 6.1) show sharp drops for established parties, surprising

recoveries and the entry of anti-establishment parties such as the List Pim Fortuyn.

In Belgium, the principal changes are the long-term decline of the Christian Democrats, increased support for Liberals, and increased support for the Flemish Bloc. As Table 6.2 demonstrates, these changes are more pronounced in Flanders than in Wallonia or among Francophones. Older parties retain a stronger foothold because their support is rooted in clientelistic practices and patronage. This is a major difference between the Netherlands and Belgium. Although parties in the Netherlands reward ex-politicians with positions on the boards of para-public agencies, none has extensive patronage. In contrast, Belgian parties have colonised the state, sharing out positions among themselves (Deschouwer 1999).

## Forming cabinets

Putting cabinets together is difficult. In the Netherlands, a typical formation can take two to four months. However, the 1973 formation required 163 days; the 1977 formation, 208. After the 2003 elections, cabinet formation took 203 days. Slow to form, Dutch governments frequently survive a full four years in office. Cabinet formation in Belgium is complicated by the number of parties and the need to include equal numbers of Flemish and Francophone ministers. Differences in the strength, mood and temperament of ostensibly kindred parties complicate the process.

---

**BACKGROUND BOX 6.1**

The Belgian Party System(s)

|  | Flanders | Wallonia |
| --- | --- | --- |
| Major parties | Christian Democratic and Flemish (CD&V) | Democratic Humanist Centre (CHD) |
|  | Socialist Party Differently (SPA) | Socialist Party (PS) |
|  | Flemish Liberals and Democrats (VLD) | Reformist Movement (MR) |
| Minor parties |  |  |
| • Green | AGALEV | ECOLO |
| • New right populist | Flemish Block (VB) | National Front |

## BACKGROUND BOX 6.2

### The Dutch Party System

| | |
|---|---|
| Major parties | Christian Democratic Appeal (CDA) |
| | Labour Party (PvdA) |
| | Liberal Party (VVD) |
| Minor parties | |
| ● Left or left-libertartian | Socialist Party (SP) |
| | Green Left (GL) |
| ● Liberal/progressive | Democrats 66 (D66) |
| ● Christian (Calvinist) | Political Reformed Party (SGP) |
| | Christian Union (CU)* |
| ● New right/populist | List Pim Fortuyn (LPF) |
| | Party for Freedom |

*Note*: * Formed by merger of the Reformed Political Union (GPV) and Reformed Political Federation (RPF)

---

**Table 6.1** Recent Parliamentary Elections in the Netherlands (percentage of the vote)

| | 1986 | 1989 | 1994 | 1998 | 2002 | 2003 | 2006 |
|---|---|---|---|---|---|---|---|
| Christian Democratic Appeal (CDA) | 34.6 | 35.3 | 22.2 | 18.4 | 27.9 | 28.6 | 26.5 |
| Labour Party (PvdA) | 33.3 | 31.9 | 24.0 | 29.0 | 15.1 | 27.3 | 21.2 |
| Liberal Party (VVD) | 17.4 | 14.6 | 20.0 | 24.7 | 15.4 | 17.9 | 14.7 |
| Democrats 66 (D66) | 6.1 | 7.9 | 15.5 | 9.0 | 5.1 | 4.1 | 2.0 |
| Green Left (GL)* | 3.3* | 4.1 | 3.5 | 7.3 | 7.0 | 5.1 | 4.6 |
| Political Reformed Party (SGP) | 1.7 | 1.9 | 1.7 | 1.8 | 1.7 | 1.6 | 1.6 |
| Christian Union** | 1.9** | 2.2** | 3.1** | 3.3** | 2.5 | 2.1 | 4.0 |
| Socialist Party (SP) | 0.4 | 0.4 | 1.3 | 3.5 | 5.9 | 6.3 | 16.6 |
| Centre Democrats (CD) | 0.4 | 0.9 | 2.5 | 0.6 | | | |
| List Pim Fortuyn (LPF) | | | | | 17.0 | 5.7 | 0.2 |
| Party for Freedom (PvdV) | | | | | | | 5.9 |
| Others with seats | | | 4.5 | | 1.6 | | 1.8 |
| Others without seats | 0.8 | 0.9 | 1.4 | 1.5 | 0.7 | 1.3 | 1.0 |
| Total | 100% | 100% | 100% | 100% | 100% | 100% | 100% |

*Notes*:
*In 1986 the Communist Party Netherlands (CPN), Pacifist Socialist Party (PSP), Radical Political Party (PPR) and the Evangelical People's Party (EVP)
**Before 2002 the Reformed Political League (RPV) and the Reformed Political Federation (RPF)
*Source*: Centraal Bureau for Statistiek

**Table 6.2** Recent Parliamentary Elections in Belgium (percentage of the vote)

|  | 1985 | 1987 | 1991 | 1995 | 1999 | 2003 |
|---|---|---|---|---|---|---|
| **Flemish parties (Flanders and Brussels)** | | | | | | |
| Flemish Liberals and Democrats (VLD)[a] | 10.7 | 11.5 | 12.0 | 13.1 | 14.3 | 15.4 |
| Socialist Party Differently and Spirit (SPA + Spirit)[b] | 14.5 | 14.9 | 12.0 | 12.6 | 9.5 | 14.9 |
| Christian Democratic and Flemish Party (CD&V)[c] | 21.3 | 19.5 | 16.8 | 17.2 | 14.1 | 13.3 |
| AGALEV (green) | 3.7 | 4.5 | 4.9 | 4.4 | 7.0 | 2.5 |
| Flemish Bloc (VB) (new right populist) | 1.4 | 1.9 | 6.6 | 7.8 | 9.9 | 11.7 |
| New Flemish Alliance (NVA) (Flemish separatist) | 7.9 | 8.0 | 5.9 | 4.7 | 5.6 | 3.1 |
| **Francophone parties (Wallonia and Brussels)** | | | | | | |
| Reformist Movement (MR)[d] (liberal) | 10.2 | 9.4 | 8.1 | 10.3 | 10.1 | 11.4 |
| Socialist Party (PS) | 13.8 | 15.6 | 13.5 | 11.9 | 10.2 | 13.0 |
| Democratic Humanist Centre (CDH) (Christian dem.)[e] | 8.0 | 8.0 | 7.7 | 7.7 | 5.9 | 5.5 |
| ECOLO (green) | 2.5 | 2.6 | 5.1 | 4.0 | 7.4 | 3.1 |
| National Front (FN) (new right populist) |  | 0.1 | 1.1 | 2.3 | 1.5 | 2.0 |
| Others | 13.6 | 13.0 | 6.3 | 4.0 | 4.6 | 5.1 |
| Total | 100% | 100% | 100% | 100% | 100% | 100% |

*Notes:*
a. Formerly the Party for Freedom and Progress (PVV)
b. Formerly the (Flemish) Socialist Party (SP)
c. Formerly the Christian People's Party (CVP)
d. Formerly the Liberal Reform Party (PRL)
e. Formerly the Social Christian Party (PSC)
*Source*: www.electionworld.org/belgium.htm

In both countries, cabinet formations provide an arena in which issues can be resolved, pushed forward or put in the icebox until there is agreement. Neither a cabinet crisis, nor a long formation is cause for alarm. Caretaker governments manage day-to-day affairs.

## Coalition patterns

Cabinets take different forms. Lijphart (1975, 1977) argues that consociational democracies form over-sized grand coalitions including almost all politically significant parties. The Dutch had coalitions of four or more parties between the wars and from 1948 through 1977. Since then, no cabinet has included more than three parties. Before Belgian parties split, coalitions included two of the three major parties. The emergence of linguistic parties and the splitting of major parties injected more players into the process. Coalitions of four or more parties are the norm.

Until recently, Belgium and the Netherlands were governed either by centre-left (social democrats and Christian democrats) or centre-right (Christian democrats and liberals) coalitions. In the 1990s, both experimented with coalitions of socialists and liberals. In the Netherlands, Wim Kok's 'purple' coalition (social democrats, Democrats 66 and liberals) served from 1994 to 2002. It was replaced by a coalition of Christian democrats, liberals and List Pim Fortuyn from July to October, 2002 and a coalition of Christian democrats, liberals and Democrats 66 from 2003 to 2006. In Belgium, Guy Verhofstadt's social–liberal coalition is still in power.

---

**KEY POINTS**

- Both Belgium and the Netherlands have complex multi-party systems. The number of parties reflects proportional representation and the cleavage structure. Parties in Belgium have split along linguistic lines.

- Christian democratic parties take centrist positions. Always reformist, social democratic parties style themselves as 'third way' parties.

- Electoral volatility has increased in both countries and particularly the Netherlands.

- Cabinet formation in both countries is a time-consuming enterprise.

- Typical coalitions have included Christian democrats and liberals or social democrats or, more recently, social democrats and liberals.

- Belgian coalitions must have equal numbers of Francophone and Flemish-speaking ministers.

---

# Governing and Policy Processes

Governing in both countries requires a deft touch. Neither party system produces majorities enabling prime ministers or cabinets to secure automatic passage of their policies. In the Netherlands, premiers are not 'first among equals' like British prime ministers, but rather minister–presidents—presiding ministers. Ministers enjoy considerable autonomy within their own departments. Effective premiers can exert greater influence, but this must be earned, through stamina, as in the case of the Social Democrat Joop den Uyl, in office 1973–7, or political skill, in the case of the Christian Democrat Ruud Lubbers, leader of three cabinets between 1982 and 1994. In Belgium, premiers must contend with deeply entrenched and well organised parties as well as regional governments and cultural councils intent on ensuring equal treatment in a divided society.

The success of a cabinet depends on keeping it together and retaining the support of a parliamentary majority. Neither is easy. In the Netherlands, traditions of **dualism** separate the cabinet from the parliament. Ministers are not members of parliament; they resign their seats to serve in the cabinet. Nor are they directly accountable to parties on whose support they rely. Nevertheless, party leaders and ministers are usually in regular contact with each other. Members of parliament from parties supporting the government reserve the right to criticise it (Andeweg 1996). Cabinets can use personal connections, formal liaison and threats to resign to ensure support. Reminding dissidents that they are bound by the governing accord is another tactic. The latter is more effective in swaying members of the directly elected Second Chamber (lower house) than the indirectly elected upper house (First Chamber or Senate). Selected by provincial assemblies, senators sometimes deviate from compromises to which party leaders have acceded.

Links between parties, parliament and cabinet ministers are closer in Belgium. Anxious to retain control over patronage appointments, parties maintain a close watch on the government. So too do staff (ministerial *cabinets*) attached to each minister. Intended to be the minister's eyes and ears, they also serve as listening posts used to monitor rivals. The need to maintain consensus weighs heavily. A break can bring about the resignation of the cabinet(De Winter *et al.* 1996). Although less involved in the construction of cabinets, Belgian monarchs are involved in their maintenance. In the Netherlands, the resignation or defeat of a cabinet means that new elections will be called. In Belgium, the king often asks parties to reconsider.

---

**KEY POINTS**

- In the Netherlands, premiers are not first among equals but rather presiding ministers.

- Cabinet ministers enjoy autonomy in their own departments.

- In the Netherlands, dualism allows members of parliament supporting the cabinet to criticise it.

- Links between parties and ministers are closer in Belgium.

---

# Consensus Democracy: Sharing Space

In both countries, national governments share space with other political actors. In the Netherlands, these include **para-public agencies**, and **social partners**. In Belgium, regional governments play key roles in managing the economy and the domestic political agenda; para-public agencies and social partners are also important. Where possible, government is by consensus. If it is not, in the Netherlands legislative majorities can prevail. Constitutional requirements make this more difficult in Belgium. Dutch political scientists describe their policy process as viscous—flowing like syrup or molasses. The development of new policies proceeds slowly; changing policies is difficult. Governments since the 1980s have been trimming the Dutch welfare state. Some facets—for instance, financing health care—have been revamped. Other programmes, such as long-term disability insurance, have been under continuous review.

In both countries, trade union federations and employers' associations are involved in the formulation of social and economic policy. Both countries are examples not only of **consensus democracy** but also its Rhineland variant, **organised capitalism**. Processes are more formalised in the Netherlands. Leaders of trade union federations and employers' associations meet each other in the Foundation of Labour, a private organisation, and in the Social and Economic Council, an advisory body consisting of 11 representatives of trade union federations, 11 representatives of employers' associations, and 11 independent members appointed by the crown. Crown members include economists and professors of labour relations, balanced by party affiliation, as well the Director of the Central Planning Bureau (a macroeconomic forecasting agency) and the President of the Netherlands Bank (the central bank, affiliated with the European Central Bank).

The Foundation of Labour provides a less formal setting in which social partners can meet with each other and with government ministers to discuss the economy, wage increases and changes to the welfare state. The Social and Economic Council renders advice to the government and supervises regulatory boards governing agriculture. Both can be influential. Wage guidelines agreed to in the Foundation of

Labour have a moral force which can influence sectoral negotiations. Governments can proceed with changes to welfare measures without social partners but prefer to obtain consent if they can (Visser and Hemerijck 1997; Wolinetz 2001). The Belgian system is less formalised but offers many of the same constraints and opportunities. Social partnership is evident at the national level and in Flanders. In both countries, the fact that leaders of trade unions and employers' associations meet regularly with each other ensures that they know each other and understand opponents' positions.

## Consociational or consensus democracies?

Both the Netherlands and Belgium were considered to be paradigm cases of consociational democracy. The paradox of Dutch stability in light of the apparent absence of cross-cutting cleavages led Lijphart to develop his theory of consociational democracy. But should we consider either today as instances of consociation?

If we look at the Netherlands, there is scant evidence of power-sharing, consociation or cleavages which threaten to drive the country apart. Parties compete at election time and do not necessarily cooperate afterward. Cabinets tend to be minimum-winning coalitions, with the occasional addition of a third party to broaden its base or serve as a bridge between the principal partners. Power-sharing is more common in local politics: almost all parties participate in local governments. The contemporary Netherlands is not devoid of cleavages, but the most important divide concerns immigration and the substantial Muslim minorities who live there. The latter, however, are not part of any consociational bargain or power-sharing arrangements.

Although no longer a consociational democracy, the Netherlands is an example of a consensus democracy, a category also developed by Arend Lijphart (1999). Most policies are products of consensus emerging from the political processes we have described. That consensus is not automatic. It has to be found.

Belgium is another matter. Linguistic and other cleavages have led to conflicts. Power-sharing arrangements are common. However, they have not always worked. Bargains about schools came unstuck in the 1950s and had to be renegotiated. Nor was the language conflict accommodated until the Flemish mobilised and organised. However, the solutions negotiated fit the consociational mode (Keating *et al.* 2003). This has shifted from power-sharing based on class and religion to accommodation among regions and linguistic communities. This is based not only on balance and power-sharing—the requirement of equal representation of Flemish-speakers and Francophones in the Belgian cabinet—but also on regional autonomy. Belgium still fits the consociational mode. But it is also a consensus democracy.

## Democratic legitimacy

Consensus democracy has been a mixed blessing. Because established parties have governed with each other at one time or another, there are no clear-cut demarcations between government and opposition. In addition, parties are ineffective channels for public sentiments or anger. Although most started out with clearly defined positions, this is not true today. Positions have been adapted to changing circumstances, but not rapidly enough. Few major parties have well defined ideologies or positions which flow from them. Moreover, parties lack active members, able to take the public pulse. Clientelism gives Belgian parties greater grounding, but this does not mean that they constitute effective listening posts.

Societies have also become more complex, and governments are not necessarily well equipped to cope. The budget cuts which helped facilitate monetary union in the EU constrain the capacity of governments to deal with the problems facing them. The most severe problems facing the Netherlands and Belgium are not economic but rather social and cultural—dealing with the large number of immigrants and asylum-seekers, particularly Muslims, who live in their midst. Before 2002, the Dutch response combined political correctness and denial. Party elites paid scant attention until Pim Fortuyn, a gay and leathered former Marxist with a PhD in sociology and an ascerbic tongue, abandoned writing for politics. Leader of Livable Netherlands, a network of local protest parties, until its executive found his views on Islam too extreme—he termed it a backward religion—Fortuyn assembled his own list of candidates, the List Pim Fortuyn (LPF), and launched a concerted attack on the social–liberal coalition.

Fortuyn was assassinated by an animal rights activist nine days before the 2002 parliamentary elections. Before that, he amassed considerable support. In the aftermath, his list won 18 seats. Taken into a Christian Democratic–Liberal coalition, the LPF disintegrated. Even so, its impact continues to be felt. Despite viscous policy processes, Dutch politicians and civil servants acted rapidly, tightening up immigration and asylum procedures, and insisting that those foreigners who remain should assimilate. Although Belgium has not seen equivalent rapid growth of the Flemish Bloc, its message and that of the LPF and other new right anti-establishment parties is being heard and taken into account. (See Theme box: Democracy and Legitimacy.)

right populist parties, such as the List Pim Fortuyn (LPF) in the Netherlands and the Flemish Bloc (VB) in Flanders have gained support in recent elections. So too has a left-wing anti-immigrant party, the Socialist Party (SP) in the Netherlands. Even so, there is no challenge to liberal democracy or the legitimacy of governments in either country. Laws are obeyed, and authorities are rarely challenged in the execution of their duties. Although questions might be raised about the Flemish Bloc, none of the other parties above has challenged the tenets or processes of liberal democracy. Doubts about the efficacy of some government policies or the presence of immigrants or refugees who have failed to integrate into the larger society are another matter.

---

**THEME BOX**

!

### Democracy and Legitimacy

Citizens in both Belgium and particularly the Netherlands have become sceptical about the ability of their governments and leaders to manage problems of complex and changing societies, and new

---

**KEY POINTS**

- Both countries exhibit features of organised capitalism. Governments share space with para-public agencies and social partners. Trade union federations and employers' associations are involved in the formulation of social and economic policy.

- Dutch policy processes are viscous. Policy change proceeds slowly.

- In the Netherlands, power-sharing is more common in local than in national politics.

- Although no longer an example of consociational democracy, the Netherlands is a consensus democracy. Belgium is both a consociational and a consensus democracy.

- Consensus democracy has spurred the growth of anti-immigrant and anti-establishment political parties.

---

# External Dynamics

Both the Netherlands and Belgium were among the six founding members of the EU and, until recently, committed to its widening and deepening. Their pro-European stance reflects the First and Second World Wars. In the First, the Dutch were able to remain neutral, but Belgium was invaded. West Flanders was the site of endless trench warfare. In the Second, both were invaded and occupied.

Afterwards, both abandoned neutrality, aligned with the west, and opted for European integration.

Initially sceptical about the European Coal and Steel Community, the Dutch became committed Europeans. Like the Belgians, the Dutch depend on trade. Much of this is with other EU member states. Both have been well served by the tariff reduction, the easing of border controls and the single market. Dutch farmers benefited from the Common Agricultural Policy (CAP). Until 1990, the Netherlands was a net beneficiary of EU revenues. Since then, it has not only become a net contributor, but also the country paying the most per capita. Belgians host most European institutions and appear happy to do so. (See Theme box: The Impact of the European Union.)

The Dutch and Belgian economies are among the most open in the world. Both rely heavily on imports and exports. Historically a trading nation, the Dutch remain predisposed to international trade. Language issues in Belgium have not concerned the use of English, but learning French or Flemish. Dutch education emphasises learning English, French and German. The penetration of English-language television and films is high. Until recently, the Dutch were unconcerned about foreign influences. Immigration issues have changed that, but the issue is not globalisation, but rather dealing with immigrants who have not assimilated. The situation in Belgium is different, but not dramatically so. (See Theme box: The Impact of Globalisation.)

---

**THEME BOX**

### The Impact of the European Union

Europeanisation has not been a major issue in the Netherlands or Belgium. Both countries are original EU member states and have been staunch supporters of European integration. However, the Dutch have moved into the Euro-sceptic camp.

Both countries were victims of Nazi aggression. European integration provided the Netherlands and Belgium with greater security, a larger market and institutions through which they could make their concerns felt. Both benefited from the European Union: Belgium hosts the Commission and, with Strasbourg, the European Parliament. Dutch farmers—along with their counterparts in France—benefited from the Common Agricultural Policy (CAP).

Until recently, both countries not only supported European integration, but also took the EU for granted. That has changed in the Netherlands. The Dutch became net contributors in 1990 and now pay more per capita than any other EU member state. Annoyance with the government's apparent failure to deal effectively with problems of immigration, asylum and multiculturalism, and deterioration in the delivery of some services have spilled over into doubts about European integration. Pim Fortuyn roused many of these feelings during the 2002 election campaign. The Dutch government responded by assuming a more sceptical posture vis-à-vis the EU and calling a referendum on the draft EU constitution. Although all major parties favoured ratification, 62 per cent voted no. The 63 per cent turnout was considerably higher than elections to the European Parliament, which have attracted little interest. It remains to be seen whether this is a temporary shift or a more permanent change in public opinion.

STEVEN B. WOLINETZ

## THEME BOX

### The Impact of Globalisation

Globalisation and its effects are not major issues in either the Netherlands or Belgium. Both countries were colonial powers (the Netherlands in Indonesia, the Antilles and Surinaam; Belgium in the Congo).

The Netherlands and Belgium are two of the most open economies in the world. Although trade and investment have shifted from former colonies to Europe, increased trade makes both vulnerable to trends in the international economy. Support for international institutions is a predictable response. Some post-materialists, however, share the views of people in the anti-globalisation movement that some of these international institutions—particularly the World Trade

Organisation (WTO), the International Monetary Fund (IMF) and the World Bank—need to be redirected or made more responsive to non-government organisations (NGOs).

Reactions against the penetration of global culture—e.g. American films and television, pop music, etc.—are at best muted. Multiculturalism at home is another matter. Particularly in the Netherlands, there is concern about the presence of immigrants and refugees whose customs and moral strictures challenge contemporary attitudes towards marriage, the status of women, the rights of homosexuals and the use of soft drugs.

# Conclusion

Our comments on democratic legitimacy and anti-EU sentiment must be taken in context. Neither the Dutch nor Belgian political systems is undergoing a crisis of legitimacy or about to collapse as a result. However, Dutch citizens wonder about their government's ability to respond effectively. Issues in Belgium are different, but the failure of authorities to deal effectively with a series of child molestations (and worse), committed by a single individual, has raised questions about the effectiveness of the police and justice system.

Both governments continue to operate democratically. However, the Dutch have become sceptical about a European Union to whose politics they previously paid scant attention. When the Dutch voted against the ratification of the EU's draft constitution, they were not necessarily saying no to Europe *per se* but rather to elites who had not done a good job of explaining what they were doing and why they were doing it.

## ? QUESTIONS

1. Indicate some of the principal differences between the Netherlands and Belgium.
2. In what ways are the Netherlands and Belgium similar to each other?
3. In what ways did the Dutch system of pillarisation differ from the Belgian division into spiritual families or subcultures?
4. Is the Netherlands still a pillarised or segmented society?
5. How was the language cleavage translated into political life in Belgium? How has this changed over time?

6. Indicate why the Netherlands and Belgium should or should not be considered to be consociational democracies.

7. Are the Netherlands and Belgium consensus democracies?

8. What impact has the emergence of new right populism had on each country?

 **FURTHER READING**

## BELGIUM

■ **Deschouwer, K. (1999), 'From Consociation to Federation: How the Belgian Parties Won', in K. Luther and K. Deschouwer** *Party Elites in Divided Societies: Political Parties in Consociational Democracies***, London and New York, Routledge, pp. 74–107.** The best recent source on the Belgian party system and how it has changed.

■ **Keating, M., Loughlin, J. and Deschouwer, K. (2003),** *Culture, Institutions, and Economic Development: A Study of Eight European Regions,* **Cheltenham, and Northampton MA, Edward Elgar.** Chapter 4 provides an excellent overview of differences and similarities between linguistic communities and the federalisation of the Belgian state.

■ **Lorwin, V. R. (1966), 'Belgium: Class and Language in National Politics', in R. A. Dahl (ed.) (1966),** *Political Oppositions in Western Democracies***, New Haven CT, Yale University Press, pp. 147–87.** In conjunction with more recent sources, an excellent compact history of the Belgian system.

■ **Witte, E., Craeybeckx, J. and Meynen, A. (2000),** *Political History of Belgium from 1830 onwards,* **Antwerp and Brussels, Standaard Uitgeverij and VUB University Press, trans. R. Casert.** An up-to-date and very readable political history of Belgium.

## THE NETHERLANDS

■ **Andeweg, R. (1999), 'Parties, Pillars and the Politics of Accommodation: Weak or Weakening Linkages? The Case of Dutch Consociationalism', in K. Luther and K. Deschouwer,** *Party Elites in Divided Societies: Political Parties in Consociational Democracies,* **London and New York, Routledge, pp. 108–33.** An excellent chapter, particularly in conjunction with Lijphart (1975) and Daalder (1966).

■ **Andeweg, R. and Irwin, G. (2005),** *Governance and Politics of the Netherlands,* **2nd edn, Houndsmills and New York, Palgrave.** An advanced textbook examining Dutch institutions and arguments about how they operate.

■ **Daalder, H. (1966), 'The Netherlands: Opposition in a Segmented Society', in R. A. Dahl (ed.),** *Political Oppositions in Western Democracies***, New Haven, CT, Yale University Press, pp. 188–236.** Read with Andeweg and Irwin (2005), an excellent analysis of the Dutch system.

■ **Lijphart, A. (1975),** *The Politics of Accommodation: Pluralism and Democracy in the Netherlands* **2nd rev. edn, Berkeley, University of California Press.** The book that brought the Netherlands into the comparative literature, this should be read for its explication of consociational democracy and how it worked.

■ **Visser, J. and Hemerijck, A. (1997),** *A Dutch Miracle: Job Growth, Welfare Reform, and Corporatism in the Netherlands,* **Amsterdam, Amsterdam University Press.** The best analysis of social partnership in the Netherlands.

 **IMPORTANT WEBSITES**

● **http://area.lib.umn.edu/dupolitics.html**   Maintained by the Dutch Studies programme at the University of Minnesota, with links to Dutch and Belgian government sites (including government departments), constitutions, laws, parties and elections, this is the best site for the two countries.

## BELGIUM

● **www.politicalresources.net/belgium.htm**   Part of a larger site, Political Resources on the Net, with links to parties, organisations, governments, media and more from all around the world.

## THE NETHERLANDS

● **www.overheidslinks.nl/english/**   The official site of the government of the Kingdom of the Netherlands, with links to government departments, parliament and parties.

● **http./portal.hhs.nl/portal/page?_pageid=125,620458&_dad=portal&_schema=PORTAL**   The Hague University site contains an English-language section with information on Dutch society, economy and politics.

● **www.netherlands-embassy.org**   The website of the Netherlands Embassy in Washington, DC with an overview of institutions and numerous links.

**Visit the Online Resource Centre that accompanies this book for lots of useful additional material, including an interactive map of Europe. www.oxfordtextbooks.co.uk/orc/hay_menon/**

# 7

# Spain and Portugal

JONATHAN HOPKIN AND INGRID VAN BIEZEN

## Chapter Contents

- Introduction
- Revolution and Reform: Transitions to Democracy
- The Rules of the Game: Constitutional Basics of the Spanish and Portuguese Political Systems
- Electing Governments: Parties and Democracy in Spain and Portugal
- Beyond Consolidation: Spain and Portugal in the New Century
- Conclusions

## Reader's Guide

Spain and Portugal emerged from decades of dictatorship and international isolation in the mid-1970s, but very quickly transformed their political institutions and became members of the European Community. Although economically still among the less prosperous European democracies, the political systems consolidated by the early 1980s have been very successful in overcoming the legacy of authoritarianism. These democratic institutions do face challenges, in particular low levels of citizen participation and entrenched practices of corruption and patronage, but on the whole democracy in Spain and Portugal works as well as in most other European countries. Spain in particular has been held up as an example of how to move peacefully from dictatorship to democracy with minimal social upheaval.

# Introduction

As well as their geographical location as neighbours on the Iberian peninsula, Spain and Portugal share a number of historical similarities. Both are old nation states, Spain dating back to the late fifteenth century and Portugal proudly asserting its independence from its neighbour in 1640. Both suffered international marginalisation under authoritarian regimes in the mid-twentieth century, and initially missed out on the rapid economic development enjoyed by the rest of Western Europe in the post-Second World War period. Finally, both moved decisively from dictatorship to democracy in the 1970s, and joined the European Community on the same day in 1986. This chapter gives a brief account of political developments in the two countries in the recent period, and outlines the most significant features of their democratic systems.

# Revolution and Reform: Transitions to Democracy

Almost uniquely in Europe, Spain and Portugal were not directly touched by the hostilities of the Second World War, and therefore the authoritarian political regimes governing them both in this period remained in place while the rest of Western Europe consolidated democratic political systems. Spain's dictatorship under General Francisco Franco emerged from the bloody Civil War of 1936–9, while Portugal was ruled by a very similar regime after the military seized power in 1926. This established a dictatorship governed until 1968 by Salazar. Both regimes were remarkably resilient, yet collapsed in the space of a little over two years in the mid-1970s. The structural causes of these political changes were to some extent similar: economic modernisation and societal change created new demands for political participation and social reform, while the economic crises resulting from the oil shock of 1973 posed particular problems for dictatorial regimes lacking the moral authority to ask their populations to bear cuts in real living standards. The short-term conditions of the transitions to democracy, however, could scarcely have been more different (Morlino 1995).

In Portugal, the dictatorship was brought down in 1974 by a revolution led by junior officers in the Portuguese army, motivated by opposition to the management of the colonial war in Southern Africa. This had drained Portugal's resources throughout the late 1960s and early 1970s. This military intervention was backed by a mass mobilisation of peasants, students and workers, coordinated largely by the Portuguese Communist Party (PCP). Although the revolution's early leadership advocated relatively limited political change, a series of short-lived provisional governments presided over a leftward lurch as the most important banks and large companies were brought under state control. Land seizures by radicalised peasants in the poor agricultural regions of the south and trade union militancy further destabilised the situation. Only after the first free elections in 1975, in which the Communists performed poorly and more mainstream parties won the largest share of political representation, did the consolidation of a new democratic regime begin. The parties elected to the constituent assembly drew up a democratic constitution, and further elections were held in 1976, which again confirmed the dominance of the more mainstream democratic parties. Successive centre-oriented co-alitions governed Portugal into the 1980s, presiding over a period of political and social stabilisation. Although the military continued to play a signifi-cant role in politics until a constitutional reform in 1982, a consolidated democratic arrangement was beginning to emerge well before then.

There was no revolution in Spain. Instead, polit-ical change began with the death, by natural causes, of General Franco in late 1975. The transition was a curious mix of constitutional continuity and thor-ough democratic reform. Franco's constitutional arrangements were reformed in 1968 to provide for a monarchical succession to the dictator, in the person of Juan Carlos I, the son of the dyn-astic heir don Juan. On Franco's death, Juan Carlos replaced the dictator as head of state, but within six months initiated a democratic transition by appointing a youthful regime reformist, Adolfo Suárez, as Prime Minister (Hopkin 1999). Suárez moved quickly to negotiate with the most prom-inent anti-Francoist political groups, while trying to reassure the military and regime hardliners that there would be no radical political change. His strategy was to use existing institutional provisions to open up the political system to popular partici-pation, and then use the resulting popular backing for change to justify further reforms. Suárez's gov-ernment pushed through a Law for Political Reform which revised the constitution to allow for an elec-ted parliament, and won the strong backing of Spanish voters in a referendum in late 1976. He

then swiftly called elections and legalised political parties and trade unions. The elections of 1977 pro-duced a democratic parliament which became in effect a constituent assembly. The new democratic constitution drawn up by this parliament also won popular backing in a referendum (although with high levels of abstention in the Basque country), and a new parliament was elected which continued the reform process, re-establishing regional gov-ernments in the Basque country and Catalonia, modernising Spain's legal code and dismantling Francoist institutions. Although substantial prob-lems remained, in particular political violence in the Basque country and interventionist tendencies in the military (leading to an abortive coup in early 1981), the election of a Socialist government in 1982 effectively marked the consolidation of the democratic system (Preston 1986).

---

**KEY POINTS**

- Spain and Portugal both lived under long-standing right-wing dictatorships until the 1970s.

- The transition to democracy in Portugal began with a revolution headed by left-wing milit-ary officers, leading to a period of communist dominance.

- The Spanish transition was marked by elite nego-tiations and compromises, and the absence of any dramatic break with the previous regime.

- Despite these differences, both states had be-come consolidated, western-style democracies by the early 1980s.

---

# The Rules of the Game: Constitutional Basics of the Spanish and Portuguese Political Systems

Both Spain and Portugal adopted new constitutions in the late 1970s which established durable bases for the functioning of their democratic political systems. The Portuguese constitution subsequently underwent reforms aimed at removing provisions which enshrined the formal political role of the military and committed Portuguese governments to realising a socialist economic system. The Spanish constitution, in contrast, has remained untouched up to the time of writing. This section outlines the most important features of these two countries' constitutional arrangements. Despite their very different transition processes, the two countries' constitutions have a number of important similarities, suggesting some common influences over institutional design.

## Spain

The Spanish constitution was the result of painstaking negotiations between the major political forces which won parliamentary representation in the first post-Franco elections: socialists, communists, moderate conservatives and nationalist/regionalist parties. As such, it reflected common ground over the basic features of a liberal democracy: free elections, freedom of political organisation and expression, parliamentary government by elected representatives, and recognition of the distinctive cultural identity of Spain's 'historic nationalities'—regions, such as the Basque country and Catalonia in particular, which claimed a right to some degree of self-government. The constitution also reflected one major legacy of Franco's constitutional system: the restoration of the monarchy, initially opposed by the parliamentary left, but ultimately accepted by all parties.

Spain is therefore a parliamentary monarchy, in which the monarch acts as head of state, countersigns legislation and plays a role in the selection of the head of the government. But the real political power lies elsewhere (van Biezen and Hopkin 2005). The 1978 constitution adopted the so-called 'chancellorship' model of the Federal Republic of Germany, with the explicit objective of ensuring executive dominance over parliament, and prime ministerial dominance within the executive. The prime minister (*presidente del gobierno*) is invested personally with the confidence of the lower house of parliament, the Congress of Deputies (*Congreso*

*de los diputados*) in a vote of investiture, and only then chooses a cabinet (*Consejo de ministros*). This reinforces the prime minister's power within the cabinet itself, as only he/she can claim a direct democratic legitimacy (Heywood 1991). The prime ministerial position is further strengthened by the 'constructive motion of censure', whereby parliament can only censure the government through a majority vote for an alternative candidate for the prime minister's office. The standing orders for the Congress established in 1977 were designed to maximise the government's authority over parliament (Maurer 1999). The government has the dominant role in initiating legislation, and wide powers to issue laws by decree, as well as far superior material means for drawing up legislation. Finally, the upper house of parliament, the Senate, has only a limited revising role and no real power to challenge the majority in the Congress. Although the 1978 constitution establishes a *parliamentary* monarchy, the relationship between the Spanish parliament and the government has been skewed heavily in favour of the latter.

Part of the reason for this unbalanced relationship lies in the Spanish electoral system, which is to all effects part of the constitution, even though only its broad contours are actually written into the constitutional text. Spain's electoral law for the Congress of Deputies—passed in 1977 and barely altered since—uses the **d'Hondt system** of proportional representation in order to allocate parliamentary seats between party lists. However, several 'correctives' prevent a proportional allocation of seats (see Gunther *et al.* 1986; Montero *et al.* 1992; Hopkin 2005). Indeed the degree of disproportionality of the Spanish electoral system is similar to that of some plurality systems (Montero 1994: 76). In particular, the law makes each of Spain's 50 provinces an electoral district, electing a minimum of two deputies each, up to a maximum of 350 in total. This arrangement has two major effects. First, although more populous provinces are allocated greater representation according to their population, the two seat minimum and the upper limit on the size of the chamber means that they cannot be compensated properly, leading to a substantial over-representation of rural areas over urban areas. Second, the choice of the province as electoral district entails a large number of small districts, which has the effect of limiting proportionality. In the large number of provinces in which only three to five seats are available, the effective threshold for achieving parliamentary representation is rather high, and 'wasted' votes are not reallocated nationally.

In short, this electoral system penalises small parties with broad support across the national territory. In contrast, larger parties and parties with geographically concentrated support are over-rewarded. These arrangements reduce the number of parties in parliament, and strengthen the large mainstream parties, making single-party government the norm in post-Franco Spain. The 'limited vote' system used in the election of the Senate has a similar effect, while the Senate's constitutional role as a chamber of territorial representation entrenches the over-representation of rural Spain, with all provinces electing four senators irrespective of population. These distortions of representation allow governments to dominate over parliament, as long as prime ministers have adequate control over their own parties.

A third important feature of the Spanish constitution is its provision for regional government through the establishment of 17 Autonomous Communities (*comunidades autónomas*). The pretensions to self-government of Spain's 'historic nationalities' were a source of bitter division in the run-up to the Civil War, and the Franco dictatorship and its military support base were deeply hostile to any recognition of ethnoregional diversity. The constitution sought to compromise between this resistance to change and the strong ethnoregionalist movements in the Basque country and Catalonia by establishing a new tier of regional government through the state territory, but with a 'variable geometry' approach to the devolution of powers to the new institutions. Initially just four Autonomous Communities adopted the 'fast track' to devolution, but subsequently the remaining regions took

on responsibility for a range of policy areas including healthcare, education, transport and even some welfare and law and order responsibilities. Although until very recently Spain remained a very fiscally centralised state, in terms of policy implementation it is now among the most decentralised in Europe.

## Portugal

Portugal's democratic constitution, adopted on 2 April 1976, reflected the prevailing leftward impetus of the revolution and the prominent political role of the military at that time. The constitution sought to commit future governments to 'ensuring the transition to socialism' and institutionalised a Revolutionary Council, dominated by military representatives, which had significant decision-making and legislative prerogatives. These features of the constitution were removed once democratic consolidation was underway and the military was persuaded to return to the barracks. A constitutional revision in 1982 abolished the Revolutionary Council, placed political power entirely under civilian control and established the primacy of political parties in the new democratic system, thereby concluding the Portuguese transition to democracy some six years after it began.

In contrast, the structure of the government system established by the 1976 constitution has largely remained in place. Portugal is a semi-presidential system with a unicameral legislature. The *Assembleia da República* originally consisted of 263 seats, until this number was reduced to 226 in 1999. Like in the French Fifth Republic, the parliament is the most important source of political authority. Not only does it produce legislation and hold the government to account, it can also, as in other parliamentary systems, overturn a government through a simple absolute majority vote of no confidence, a lower standard than that required by the Spanish constitution. However, the Portuguese parliament has to share its responsibilities for government formation with the president, which amounts to a significant limitation of its power when compared with other parliamentary systems.

The president of the republic is elected directly by absolute majority in two rounds for a five-year term, with a maximum of two consecutive terms. The democratic legitimacy this affords the president has important consequences, as the parliament cannot claim to be the only institution to represent the will of the Portuguese people. Moreover, the presidential term is one year longer than that of the parliament, making the presidency less subject to the dynamics of the parliament's electoral cycle. This gives the presidency a degree of autonomy in the exercise of the powers it shares with the parliament. The 1982 constitutional revision entailed a substantial limitation of the powers of the president and turned the system more in the direction of a parliamentary system. Yet, although now more limited and more circumscribed, the president still enjoys the right to designate the prime minister, while the parliament has to confirm or reject that designation through a vote of confidence. Moreover, the president can dissolve parliament and veto legislation. In principle, an absolute majority of parliament can overrule a presidential veto, although in some cases a qualified majority is required. Although the president's ability to challenge parliament is limited in various ways by the constitution, the presidency's elective legitimacy gives it a potentially far greater role than unelected heads of state, such as hereditary monarchs, or indirectly elected presidents, such as those of Germany and Italy.

As in Spain, the dynamics of the relationship between government and parliament are heavily conditioned by the way in which parliament is elected and the extent to which parties have to cooperate in order to form parliamentary majorities. Interestingly, the electoral system adopted by the Portuguese democracy is very similar to Spain's. Deputies to the Assembly are elected for a four-year term in 22 electoral constituencies, varying in size between three and 50 seats. The seats are allocated according to a principle of proportional representation, using the d'Hondt method, which is enshrined in the constitution. There is no legal threshold to obtain parliamentary representation, although in practice the effective threshold is much higher in the smaller constituencies. Unlike in Spain, the distribution of electoral districts favours urban rather than rural areas, and therefore the distribution of seats between districts allows for a more proportional allocation. As a result, Portuguese elections tend to over-reward the larger parties with parliamentary representation, but the smaller parties are not penalised as severely and only the most marginal political forces have been effectively deprived adequate political representation.

---

**KEY POINTS**

- Although Spain is a **constitutional monarchy** and Portugal a **presidential republic**, both function essentially as parliamentary regimes.

- Both countries have an electoral system based on proportional representation using the d'Hondt method.

- Portugal is a relatively centralised unitary state, while Spain has developed a decentralised system of autonomous regions.

- The Spanish constitution has remained unchanged since its inception, while the Portuguese constitution has undergone a number of reforms.

# Electing Governments: Parties and Democracy in Spain and Portugal

Constitutions provide the basic ground rules for the working of a political system, but elections provide the raw material of modern democratic politics. This section introduces the basic contours of electoral politics in the two political systems, focusing on two aspects. We describe the major parties present in the two countries, and their ideological and organisational characteristics, and we examine the party system—the way these parties compete and interact, both in elections and in the political institutions. Perhaps surprisingly, in view of the different constitutional structures, the two party systems have mostly appeared rather similar, with two large centre-oriented parties competing for power, flanked by rather smaller and more radical formations. The Spanish case also exhibits centrifugal tendencies, with the continued growth of non-statewide parties, especially in its historically distinctive regions. In both cases, historic parties present before the dictatorship dominated the left side of the political spectrum, while new parties were developed to represent more conservative positions.

## The Spanish party system

The party system that emerged in Spain's new democracy contained both historic political parties which had been present before the Civil War and completely new political forces (Linz 1980). On the left, the two principal statewide parties both have historical roots dating back to the pre-authoritarian period. The Spanish Socialist Party (PSOE) was founded in 1879 and the Spanish Communist Party (PCE) in 1920. During the dictatorship, both parties went underground as their leaders fled into exile. The PCE proved more successful as an underground resistance movement than the PSOE and,

at the time of Franco's death, the PCE was by far the best organised political party in Spain.

The PSOE's leadership in exile lost control of the party as a new generation of activists inside Spain, led by Felipe González and Alfonso Guerra, successfully challenged them at the 1974 party congress in Suresnes (France). González guided the PSOE through a process of ideological change, leading it to abandon its Marxist ideology at the 1979 party congress, and consolidating his position as party leader through strong electoral performances (Gillespie 1989). The stunning election victory of 1982 initiated a long period of 14 years of Socialist government, which allowed González to maintain firm control over the party until his resignation in 1997. In this time the party became an organisation dominated by elected politicians, and increasingly criticised for its lack of transparency and the dubious nature of some of its funding arrangements. The election of José Luis Rodríguez Zapatero after the election defeat of 2000 has since improved the party's image, although there is little evidence of change in its rather closed organisation.

Although the PCE had hoped to turn its organisational strength into electoral advantage in the transition period, the results of the first elections were disappointing, condemning the party to a rather marginal position in the new democratic system. After internal divisions and electoral collapse in 1982, the PCE joined an electoral coalition of left-wing forces, United Left (*Izquierda Unida*, IU), formed initially to campaign for a 'No' vote in the 1986 referendum on Spain's membership of NATO. The PCE has remained the predominant component of the coalition and, under the leadership of Julio Anguita, the electoral coalition was subsequently transformed into a unified 'social and political movement' in 1992. This involved the harmonisation and centralisation of its organisational structures, although the constituent parties were not dissolved and to date continue to co-exist with IU (Ramiro 2000). The creation of IU initially brought a better electoral performance for the Spanish left, but it remains a minority force in Spanish politics.

On the right of the political spectrum there is little historical continuity, in large part because the advent of the Franco dictatorship undermined the rationale for party organisations representing right-wing and conservative interests. The main political parties of the Spanish centre and right were therefore created in the period immediately following Franco's death. The dominant party on the centre-right in this period, the Union of the Democratic Centre (*Unión de Centro Democrático*, UCD), was very much a product of the peculiar circumstances of post-Franco transition. The UCD was an ideologically heterogeneous electoral coalition created by Prime Minister Suárez to contest the 1977 elections. Although the UCD was able to dominate the new democratic parliament and its diverse components successfully worked together to complete the process of political reform, the ideological and personal differences between its major figures became increasingly bitter once the 1978 constitution had been approved. Pressurised by the difficulties of governing a serious economic crisis with untried political institutions, Suárez's government lost popularity, exacerbating the party's internal tensions. When these tensions spilled out into open conflict, the party's electoral standing collapsed, leading to key leaders defecting to other parties and contributing to a dramatic defeat in the 1982 elections in which the UCD plummeted from 34.8 to 6.8 per cent of the vote, and the party retained only 11 of its 168 seats (Gunther and Hopkin 2002). The UCD was dissolved one year later; the creation of the *Centro Democrático Social* (CDS) by Suárez proved an unsuccessful attempt to establish a party of the centre.

The main representative of hardline conservatism, Popular Alliance (*Alianza Popular*, AP), began life as an alliance of seven small parties formed by prominent servants of the Franco regime, led by Manuel Fraga, a former interior minister. AP was hostile to radical change and defensive of the record of the Franco regime, while displaying a deep suspicion of the communist left and of nationalist sentiment in the Basque country and Catalonia. Although some AP deputies refused to back the 1978 constitution, after 1979 the party moderated its rhetoric and, encouraged by the internal disputes afflicting the UCD, reached out to more moderate, centrist sectors of the electorate. It was the main beneficiary of the UCD's collapse in 1982, increasing its vote share from 6.1 to 26.4 per cent and the number of seats from ten to 107, becoming the main opposition party in parliament after the PSOE. However, Fraga's uncompromising conservatism restricted further progress, and only after several leadership changes did the party, renamed the Popular Party (PP) under José María Aznar, finally shake off its reactionary image and win electoral success. After defeating the PSOE in 1996 the PP governed for two legislatures, definitively establishing itself as the dominant force on the Spanish centre and right.

From the very first democratic elections after Franco the Spanish party system has tended to revolve around the two main parties of left and right competing for government control, partly because of the workings of the electoral system which over-rewards the larger parties, partly because of the moderation of the Spanish electorate which encourages the parties to compete against each other for centrist voters (Montero 1998). In the 1977–82 period this bipolar competition pitted the governing centre-right UCD against the PSOE who together obtained the bulk of parliamentary seats, both flanked by far smaller and more radical parties (the PCE and AP). The collapse of the UCD in 1982 unbalanced the party system, with the PSOE enjoying a long period of dominance as AP failed to provide a serious challenge. However, in 1993 the PP's electoral breakthrough ushered in a new period of more balanced electoral competition, with government changing hands in 1996 and then again in 2004. This party system has produced single-party governments, roughly half of the time with (usually small) absolute majorities, and in the remainder of cases minority administrations seeking stable parliamentary support from other forces. In a sense, therefore, party democracy in Spain manages to achieve the level of government stability associated with majoritarian democracies such as the UK, without the degree of distortion of representation caused by plurality election systems (Hopkin 2005).

One feature of the party system which has become increasingly important in recent years is the presence of significant nationalist parties, particularly in the most culturally distinctive Autonomous Communities. In particular, the Basque Nationalist Party (*Partido Nacionalista Vasco*, PNV) and the moderate Catalan nationalist party Convergence and Union (*Convergència i Unió*, CiU) have consistently won parliamentary representation, and have found themselves in pivotal positions to sustain minority governments in parliament, notably in 1993–2000, and again since 2004. Moreover, more radical parties, such as Batasuna (until it was outlawed in 2002) in the Basque country and the Catalan Republican Left (*Esquerra Republicana de Catalunya*, ERC) have also won consistent parliamentary support, the latter overtaking its rival CiU in the 2004 elections. This presence of non-statewide parties, which unlike small statewide parties are not disadvantaged by the electoral law, reflects the persisting importance of territorial issues for Spanish politics, and their role in sustaining governments is viewed with suspicion in many regions of Spain.

## The Portuguese party system

Four parties have dominated the Portuguese party system ever since the first democratic elections of 1975, providing a high degree of stability and predictability to party competition, with the exception of the short-lived success of the Democratic Reformer Party (*Partido Renovador Democrático*, PRD) of President Eanes in 1985 (Aguiar 1985). The shape of the party system emerging from the revolution was curiously similar to that of Spain, with the centre-left Socialist Party (*Partido Socialista*,

PS) and centre-right Democratic People's Party (*Partido Popular Democrático*, PPD) dominating the new parliament, and with the Communists (*Partido Comunista Português*, PCP) and conservative *Partido do Centro Democrático Social* (CDS) winning far smaller shares of votes and seats.

As in Spain, only the Portuguese Communist Party emerged from the dictatorship with a degree of organisational history and continuity. Founded in 1921, the PCP was the only effective resistance movement during the dictatorship, and was thus in a position to dominate Portuguese politics, in alliance with the armed forces, during the revolutionary phase. However, the party performed disappointingly in the 1975 elections, with only 13.5 per cent of the vote, making it the third largest party in a parliament dominated by more moderate parties. The PCP retained the classic communist principles of Marxism–Leninism until the late 1980s, when it adopted a more mainstream approach (Pereira 1988). Since 1991, the PCP has contested the elections in a coalition with the Green Party (*Partido Ecologista-Os Verdes*, PEV), although the PCP has always constituted the dominant part of this electoral alliance. In electoral terms, the hard left has steadily declined, slipping to just 7 per cent of the vote and 12 seats in the 2002 elections.

The Socialist Party was founded in April 1973 in the Federal Republic of Germany by a group of prominent socialists in exile. Initially little more than a clique of elite figures, the PS became the biggest party in both the 1975 and 1976 elections (Bruneau 1997). The party has built on this success by adopting a catch-all strategy, moving towards the centre of the political spectrum and abolishing all references to Marxism in its ideological statements. In the 1995 elections, the PS explicitly went after the middle-class vote, a strategy that proved to be successful after almost ten years of PSD rule. On this basis, the PS has been able to participate in government on several occasions. In organisational terms, the PS is a personalistic party traditionally dominated by the founding leader Mário Soares, but also highly factionalised.

The Democratic People's Party was founded shortly after the revolution by figures from the 'liberal wing' of the pre-democratic regime. The party was pushed leftwards by the prevailing revolutionary climate, leading it to claim a social democratic identity, and rename itself the Social Democratic Party (*Partido Social Demócrata*, PSD) in 1976, although it remained in effect a party of the moderate right. Like the PS, the PSD was dominated by a strong leader, Francisco Sá Carneiro, killed in an accident in 1980. The PSD is also a very factionalised party, and has not been able to move beyond its origins as a federation of elite figures, some of them entrenched in local power bases in rural areas (Corkhill 1995). Like the PS it has pitched its political appeal to the moderate centre, with a rather vague ideological profile. This pivotal position has also allowed it to form coalitions both with the Socialist Party to its left or the CDS to its right. In this way it was able to dominate government formation from 1979 until 1995.

The fourth significant party in the system is the *Partido do Centro Democrático Social* (CDS), also founded just after the revolution. A conservative organisation inspired by Christian democratic principles, the party suffered in the radical climate of the revolution. The success of the PSD closed off its main avenue for electoral growth, and the CDS has struggled to find a clear role in the party system. Its strategic confusion has provoked internal conflict among its various factions, as well as strong personality clashes. In 1992, a new leader, Manuel Monteiro, modified the party's name by adding the initials PP (*Partido Popular*, People's Party) to the original acronym and adopting a more right-wing populist and anti-European position. However, this strategy was contested by more centrist factions, who took over the party in the late 1990s.

This party system has been relatively stable over the post-revolutionary period, but this has not always provided stable government (Morlino 1995; Gunther and Montero 2001). In particular, the early phase of democratisation was characterised by extreme government instability, as governing coalitions were formed and broke down with great frequency; indeed, until 1987, no government was able to complete a four-year mandate. Part of the reason for this is that the Portuguese electoral system does not distort parliamentary representation to the same extent as in Spain, so parties are unable to easily win parliamentary majorities. As a result, various combinations of the PS, CDS and PSD (the PCP remained in opposition) formed uneasy coalitions. From 1987 onwards, the PS and PSD have been able to increase their joint share of votes and seats, and the party system has taken on a two-party dynamic, in which the two major parties alternate in power. These governments tend to be coalitions or single-party minority governments (Majone 1998).

---

**KEY POINTS**

- In both Spain and Portugal, proportional representation allows a multi-party system to operate.

- After some initial instability, the party systems have settled into consistent patterns.

- While Portugal generally has had coalition or minority governments, distortions of representation in Spain have allowed majority government to form much of the time.

- Strong communist parties in the 1970s have since declined, and in both countries electoral competition is dominated by two large centre-oriented parties.

# Beyond Consolidation: Spain and Portugal in the New Century

With three decades of uninterrupted democracy behind them, political debate in Spain and Portugal has moved well beyond problems of democratic transition and consolidation. Both countries have also completed their full integration into the 'family' of democratic nations with Spain's entry into NATO in 1981 (Portugal had joined during the Salazar dictatorship), and both countries' successful participation in the institutions of the European Union over two decades. This section outlines some of the political issues and controversies which have arisen in the two Iberian nations since democratic consolidation was completed.

## Spain: democracy in a plurinational state

The performance of Spain's political institutions since transition was completed can be considered successful, in that the kinds of tensions which many feared could re-emerge after the collapse of the Franco regime have, on the whole, not threatened the new democratic regime. The centre-oriented nature of party competition, and the abundant evidence of the essential moderation of the Spanish electorate, have put to rest fears of the kind of ideological polarisation that led to Civil War in the 1930s. Governing parties have generally adopted centrist positions, and economic and social polices have achieved a degree of consensus, with all major parties agreeing on the basics of a market economy with a substantial degree of social protection, fully integrated into the European and world economy.

For much of the 1990s, indeed, there was rather more concern about the complacent and venal behaviour of some political elites than about the intensity of ideological conflict. After a decade in office, in the early 1990s the Socialist government

had to face a range of accusations of corruption, illicit party financing and abuse of office, which the opposition Popular Party very successfully exploited to its electoral advantage. The rather closed and hierarchical nature of Spanish parties came under scrutiny, although no serious proposals for institutional reform were advanced. The 'legitimacy crisis' of the democratic system was to an extent overcome when the Socialists were finally defeated in 1996, and government turnover led to the removal from office of some of the public figures most affected by the various scandals. (See Theme box: Democracy and Legitimacy.)

This change in government pushed corruption out of the headlines, to be replaced by an increased emphasis on an issue which had never really gone away: the presence of powerful nationalist, and even separatist, movements in some of Spain's peripheral regions. There were various reasons for the renewed prominence of the territorial issue. First, for a period between 1993 and 2000 no party had sufficient parliamentary strength to govern alone, and therefore both González and Aznar were forced to rely on the support of Catalan and Basque nationalist deputies to pass legislation. This provoked widespread unease at the possibility that particular regions could win preferential treatment because of the pivotal position of their nationalist parties in parliament. Second, by the 1990s the process of transferring policy responsibilities to the regional level envisaged by the constitutional settlement of the late 1970s was largely complete, leading the most ambitious regions to begin demanding further change. Third, the Basque terrorist group ETA, which had continued its campaign of political violence throughout the democratic period, attempted to assassinate Popular Party leader José María Aznar, and stepped up its activity more generally. The Popular Party, once it had obtained a

JONATHAN HOPKIN AND INGRID VAN BIEZEN

## Democracy and Legitimacy

For a long time, Spain and Portugal were perceived, both by scholars and other observers, as fragile young democracies dogged by memories of past political failure. Difficulties in the functioning of democratic institutions were therefore interpreted as 'growing pains', which would be overcome by the passage of time. Now, more than a quarter of a century after the definitive consolidation of democracy, it makes little sense to view Spain and Portugal as 'new' democracies, and their difficulties need to be understood as typical of established democratic regimes. Indeed, many of the issues most often raised regarding the Iberian democracies are similar to those facing many other, older, western democracies: corruption, lack of accountability, citizen apathy and distrust of politicians. Although levels of political party membership and formal affiliation to civic organisations and trade unions are comparatively low in Spain and Portugal, these indicators of citizen participation are in decline, sometimes dramatically, in the majority of western democracies. It is therefore difficult to distinguish between the symptoms of democratic immaturity and those of democratic decline. Problems of corruption and partisan use of public resources do appear to be a particular problem in Spain and Portugal, just as in the other Southern European democracies, although the level of turnover in government does seem to help curb some of these practices. However, the main conclusion to be drawn in terms of democracy and legitimacy is that few in either country would seriously contemplate alternatives to the democratic institutions, and that, although democracy may function imperfectly, nostalgia for the pre-democratic period is a dying force.

parliamentary majority after the 2000 elections, adopted a hardline response to nationalist pretensions in the Basque country and elsewhere, which contributed to an increase in political tension around the issue.

In the 2004 elections the PP campaigned around a tough message on Basque terrorism, accusing the Socialist Party of planning concessions to peripheral nationalists and threatening the unity of Spain. The PP's defeat, after wrongly blaming ETA for the Madrid bombings just before the poll, brought a Socialist minority administration which governed with the support of radical Catalan nationalists. This government, under Rodríguez Zapatero, set about renegotiating the terms of Spain's territorial settlement, extending the degree of self-government enjoyed by Catalonia and several other regions too. The PP's uncompromising response to this move has ensured that the territorial issue remains an important source of political division.

## Portugal

Much of the history of post-Salazar Portugal revolves around dealing with the consequences of its revolutionary upheavals, and creating a political and economic system consistent with full membership of the European Union. The most anomalous political features of the post-revolution constitution—in particular the prominent role afforded the military—were removed fairly quickly, but economic reforms took rather longer. The 1976 constitution proclaimed the nationalisation of companies and the seizures of land which had followed the revolution to be irreversible. It also contained a series of ideological aspirations reflecting the revolutionary zeal of the 1974–5 period, committing governments to 'socialise the means of production and abolish the exploitation of man by man', and imposing restrictions on private investment and freedom of enterprise. Constitutional reforms in 1982 and 1989 removed the constitution's ideological commitments to social control of the means of production, allowing the government to privatise nationalised industries and push Portugal towards a more free market economic model. Adapting Portugal's economy to the demands of integration into an increasingly liberalised European economy has been the principal priority of governments since democracy was consolidated. The weakest economy in the EU before the 2004 enlargement, Portugal has been the beneficiary of significant investment from European structural funds, but has also undergone significant and sometimes painful reforms geared towards the liberalisation of markets and the balancing of the state finances. Portugal's economic progress has been considerable since the 1980s, but it remains one of the poorer nations in Europe, and has enjoyed less success than Spain in closing the gap with its West European neighbours. (See Theme boxes: The Impact of the European Union and The Impact of Globalisation.)

---

**THEME BOX**

### The Impact of the European Union

The EU has played a key role in the development of Iberian politics. The European Economic Community's commitment to democratic values and human rights helped convince conservative economic interests, particularly in Spain, of the need for political reform if they were to enjoy the benefits of the common market. During the transition processes, European pressure strengthened the position of democratic reformers, and helped create a sense that Western European standards of living could be achieved only if Spain and Portugal were able to develop stable democratic institutions. Full European Community membership has brought economic benefits, with a revival of economic growth in both countries from the mid-1980s on, although not without some lapses. Spain and Portugal were two of the biggest beneficiaries of the structural funds for infrastructure investment agreed as part of the package preparing Europe for monetary union, and the convergence criteria contributed to both countries achieving a level of budgetary and monetary rigour that had been absent during the tense moments of political transition. Eurozone membership has not, however, been an unqualified success. Portugal in particular has experienced low growth in the most recent period, and struggled to remain within the budgetary limits established by monetary union. Spain, in contrast, has enjoyed higher growth rates, but has also undergone a real estate boom which in the absence of any independent monetary authority has proved difficult to bring under control. Broadly speaking, however, for Spain and Portugal European membership is perceived as a great success, enhancing their political influence on the world stage and providing the conditions for improved economic performance.

---

**THEME BOX**

### The Impact of Globalisation

Both Spain and Portugal had relatively closed economic systems in the early phase of their dictatorships, with General Franco responding to political isolation by limiting trade as far as possible, and Portugal maintaining significant economic links largely with its African colonies. As western countries underwent rapid expansion in the post-Second World War period, the two Iberian nations sought to open their economies to greater trade, but political leaders remained wary of the potentially negative consequences of economic openness for social and political stability. However, isolation from external influence proved difficult to achieve. The expansion of tourism introduced the constant presence in the coastal areas of both countries of large numbers of people from richer democratic nations, whose freer lifestyles undermined the reactionary values sponsored by dictatorship. Moreover, both Spain and Portugal were exporters of labour until very recently, and returning migrants also brought outside influences with them. These commercial and human flows undoubtedly promoted democratisation. More recently, the greater openness of the Iberian nations has been largely associated with the process of European integration, although the revival of commercial links with former colonies in Latin America has been an interesting feature of the recent economic development of Spain in particular. On the whole, the political consequences of globalisation, in

JONATHAN HOPKIN AND INGRID VAN BIEZEN

terms of a decline in the decision-making autonomy of national governments, have been felt rather less in the Iberian democracies than in traditionally more powerful nation states, such as France or the UK.

A history of dictatorship and instability may have convinced many Spaniards and Portuguese that external pressures from the democratic world are not a serious threat to their well-being.

Corruption, and a sense of dissatisfaction with the performance of political parties, has also emerged in Portugal, although with nowhere near the intensity of the Spanish case. As in many other European countries, cases of illicit party finance emerged in the 1990s, and legislative changes were made in response, although as in other cases legislation has not been a conspicuous success in resolving the problem. Citizen mistrust of parties, as in Spain, is relatively high (de Sousa 2004). All in all however, Portuguese democracy since consolidation has not faced such grave problems as terrorism and threats of secession, and its political institutions have therefore been placed under less strain than those of its neighbour.

### KEY POINTS

- The period since the early 1980s has seen both Spain and Portugal successfully consolidate their democracies.

- Democratic consolidation has been accompanied by successful integration into the system of international cooperation between western nations.

- Both countries have faced problems of political corruption and popular disillusionment with the workings of the democratic system.

- Spain continues to face challenges to the constitutional settlement from strong nationalist movements in key autonomous regions.

# Conclusions

Spain and Portugal are now firmly entrenched in the European family of established democracies, with their past dictatorships and subsequent instability and threats to political freedoms an increasingly distant memory. Although the Portuguese transition created significantly more upheaval than the Spanish one, both cases have become textbook examples of how democratisation can succeed even in apparently difficult and complex circumstances. Undoubtedly the international support for democratisers received from Western, and particularly European, democracies made an important contribution to this success, as did the promise of integration into the process of European integration and its concomitant economic benefits.

The populations of both countries increasingly enjoy high material living standards, although output per head of population remains significantly lower than in the rest of Western Europe. Portugal remains the poorest of the pre-2005 EU member states by some margin, and Spain's relative position is slowly improving, though it too is still some distance behind the older Western European democracies in terms of average incomes. Both Spain and Portugal were able to join the European Monetary Union as founder members, which appears to have brought clear benefits in the form of much lower interest rates, although Portugal has struggled to meet the budgetary requirements of Eurozone membership.

Although few would doubt that the process of democratisation in the Iberian peninsula is long since complete, Spain and Portugal, like the vast majority of other democracies, do face problems of citizen disaffection with the workings of democracy. Corruption scandals and evidence of citizens' feeling of distance *vis-à-vis* the political institutions are a source of concern, and levels of political participation and voter turnout are less than impressive in both countries. However, considering the relative youth of the democratic institutions and the difficulties faced by the two countries in the recent past, the constitutional arrangements established in the 1970s have performed well. It is probably fair to conclude that political and social developments in the Iberian peninsula since the 1970s have matched even the most optimistic predictions made at the time of their political transitions.

## QUESTIONS

1. Why did Spain and Portugal democratise in such different ways?
2. To what extent is the consolidation of democracy in Spain and Portugal due to skilful constitution design?
3. Assess the benefits and costs to Spain and Portugal of joining the European Community in the mid-1980s.
4. What factors have structured party competition in Spain and Portugal since the transitions to democracy?
5. Compare and contrast the role of the Communist parties in the democratisation of Spain and Portugal.
6. Has globalisation had as much impact on Spain and Portugal as European integration?
7. What are the most significant problems facing the democratic institutions in Spain and Portugal?
8. Has the process of political decentralisation in post-Franco Spain been a success?

## FURTHER READING

■ **Magone, J. (1997),** *European Portugal: The Difficult Road to Sustainable Democracy*, **Basingstoke, Macmillan.** Comprehensive and accessible introduction to post-transition Portuguese politics.

■ **Gunther, R., Montero, J. R. and Botella, J. (2004),** *Democracy in Modern Spain*, **New Haven CT, Yale University Press.** Best and most up-to-date introduction to the post-Franco political system.

■ **Closa, C. and Heywood, P. (2004),** *Spain and the European Union*, **Basingstoke, Palgrave Macmillan.** The most authoritative treatment of Spain's role within the contemporary European Union.

■ **Van Biezen, I. (2003),** *Political Parties in New Democracies: Party Organization in Southern and East–Central Europe*, **London, Palgrave Macmillan.** Authoritative analysis of the development of political parties in post-dictatorship Spain and Portugal, placed in a comparative context.

■ **Diamandouros, N. and Gunther, R. (eds) (2001),** *Parties, Politics, and Democracy in the New Southern Europe*, **Baltimore MD, Johns Hopkins University Press.** Comparative study of political parties and electoral politics in Southern Europe, comprising some of the best available analyses of political parties in Spain and Portugal.

■ **Balfour, S. (ed.) (2004),** *The Politics of Contemporary Spain*, **London, Routledge.** Selection of essays on key themes of contemporary Spanish politics by Spanish and British specialists.

■ **Mar-Molinero, C. and Smith, A. (1996),** *Nationalism and the Nation in the Iberian Peninsular: Conflicting and Competing Identities*, **Oxford, Berg.** A comparative analysis of the phenomenon of nationalism in Spain and Portugal.

 ## IMPORTANT WEBSITES

● **www.congreso.es/**

● **www.senado.es/** Spanish Congress and Senate websites, with abundant links to various data on political and legislative issues and biographies of political representatives. Both available in Spanish and English.

● **www.lse.ac.uk/collections/canadaBlanch/** Website of the Cañada Blanch Centre for Contemporary Spanish Studies at the London School of Economics.

● **www.parlamento.pt/ingles/index.html** Portuguese parliament website, with a range of English-language links.

● **www.cphrc.org.uk/** Contemporary Portuguese Political History Research Centre website; links to a variety of sites dealing with past and present Portuguese politics.

 **Visit the Online Resource Centre that accompanies this book for lots of useful additional material, including an interactive map of Europe. www.oxfordtextbooks.co.uk/orc/hay_menon/**

JONATHAN HOPKIN AND INGRID VAN BIEZEN

# 8 Greece, Turkey and Cyprus

NATHALIE TOCCI

## Chapter Contents

- Introduction
- From the Ottoman Empire to Independence and Conflict
- Domestic Politics and Institutions in Greece, Turkey and Cyprus
- Foreign Policy in the Eastern Mediterranean
- Conclusion

## Reader's Guide

This chapter analyses domestic politics in Greece, Turkey and Cyprus and the relations between them in the wider context of European politics. It is structured thematically, examining in turn the history, domestic politics and foreign policy of these three countries. In the case of Cyprus, due to the conflict on the island, the chapter adopts a double focus, examining both Greek Cypriot and Turkish Cypriot politics. Finally, it concludes by discussing the key contemporary issues in the changing politics of the Eastern Mediterranean. It examines the domestic impact of the EU membership of Greece and Cyprus. It analyses the Greek–Turkish rapprochement as well as Turkey's process of accession to the EU.

# Introduction

The histories of Greece, Turkey and Cyprus have been and remain deeply intertwined in complex and evolving ways. Independence and nation-state building came about following wars between one another in the context of the disintegrating Ottoman Empire. In the early nineteenth century, Greece gained independence from the Ottoman Empire. In the 1920s, the Turkish Republic was established after a Greek–Turkish war in the Anatolian heartland. In 1960, Cyprus, which had also been part of the Ottoman Empire, became independent from British colonial rule. Yet, after a Greek military coup and an ensuing Turkish attack, Cyprus was partitioned into separate Greek Cypriot and Turkish Cypriot zones.

In the decades that followed, Greece, Turkey and Cyprus embarked on slow and uneven paths to **democratisation**. Despite a late start, having transited through monarchy, civil war and dictatorship, Greece was the first to establish a stable democratic system. Yet democratisation and good governance in Greece have been ongoing processes.

Turkey was the first to establish a multi-party system founded on the tenets of **Kemalism**. Yet, over the twentieth century, Turkey's domestic politics went through deep upheavals, resulting in a seriously deficient democratic system. Since the turn of the century, Turkey has been undergoing an unprecedented process of political and economic transformation.

In Cyprus, following partition, the Greek Cypriot Republic in the south succeeded in establishing a democratic system and a successful market economy. In northern Cyprus, the internationally non-recognised Turkish Cypriot *de facto* state has also established its own elected institutions. Yet the ongoing conflict has dominated domestic and foreign policy alike.

The destiny and development of Greece, Turkey and Cyprus are not only bound by history. Pending problems remain at the heart of the political development of these countries. This has been all the more true since the Greece–Turkey–Cyprus triangle has been set within the wider framework of European integration, which has both played into the changing politics of the Eastern Mediterranean and altered those very dynamics. The ongoing **Europeanisation** of Greece, Turkey and Cyprus has been a key determinant of both the domestic politics of these countries and the changing relations between them.

## KEY POINTS

- Greece, Turkey and Cyprus were born out of the Ottoman Empire. Their history and ensuing political development have been closely intertwined.

- The three countries sought to establish independent democracies. Yet their path to stable democracy has not been smooth.

- Relations between Greece, Turkey and Cyprus have affected their wider ties to Europe. Yet relations with Europe have also been a key determinant of domestic and foreign policies in the Eastern Mediterranean.

# From the Ottoman Empire to Independence and Conflict

Modern-day Greece, Turkey and Cyprus emerged from the ashes of the Ottoman Empire. Greece transited through civil war and dictatorship before establishing a stable democratic Republic. In Cyprus, a democratic bi-communal Republic was founded in 1960. But the re-eruption of conflict culminated in the partition of the island. The Republic of Turkey was established on the tenets of its founder Atatürk. Yet Turkey's path to democracy and stability has been littered with obstacles.

## From imperial control to independence and the eruption of the Cyprus conflict

Greece was the first to establish an independent monarchy in 1829, following the 1821–8 wars of independence against the Ottomans. Yet independence was the beginning rather than the end of the Greek national project. Greek nationalism was inspired by the 'Megali idea', i.e. the aspiration to unify all Ottoman territories inhabited by Christian Orthodox Greeks. This aspiration led to a Greek military campaign in western Anatolia in 1920–2.

The Greek campaign was defeated by the emerging Turkish leadership, headed by Mustafa Kemal, later known as Atatürk (father of the Turks). The Greek–Turkish war marked the final death of the Ottoman Empire and with it the birth of the Republic of Turkey. The borders of the new Republic were set in the 1923 Treaty of Lausanne.

Yet by the 1940s Greece and Turkey were again at loggerheads with each other, this time over Cyprus. Since the 1571 Ottoman conquest of Cyprus, the predominantly Greek Cypriot population had witnessed the settlement of Muslim Turks. However, given that Greek Cypriots still constituted a numerical majority on the island, Cyprus would have been

a natural candidate for the Megali idea. This was not the case in the nineteenth and early twentieth centuries, not least because Cyprus had passed from Ottoman to British control in 1878.

Nonetheless, the roots of inter-communal conflict formed in the 1920s during British colonial rule. Inspired by the decolonisation movement and Greek nationalism, the Greek Cypriots, supported by Greece, articulated their struggle for self-determination in terms of *enosis*, i.e. union between Greece and Cyprus. Fearing Greek domination and spurred by the British, Turkey and the Turkish Cypriots mounted a counter-*enosis* campaign, which crystallised in the diametrically opposed position of *taksim* (partition of the island into Greek and Turkish zones). Following years of violence between Greek and Turkish Cypriot nationalists and British colonial rulers, a compromise was found. In 1960 Cyprus became an independent bi-communal Republic, guaranteed externally by Greece, Turkey and the UK.

Greece temporarily renounced its nationalist ambitions and accepted the 1960 compromise for reasons connected to its domestic situation. Following Nazi occupation, Greece lived through a devastating civil war between government forces and communists from 1944 to 1949. In the emerging Cold War configuration, the USA played a critical role in supporting Greek government forces, giving it a key part in shaping Greek domestic politics. In those years, Greece became firmly anchored to the west, by joining NATO in 1952. Yet the USA's and the UK's strong ties with Turkey also entailed heavy pressure on Greece to abandon its expansionist aims. Hence, in 1959–60 Greece accepted Cypriot independence.

But the bi-communal Republic of Cyprus was short-lived. The Greek Cypriot leader and first president, Archbishop Makarios, remained devoted to *enosis*. By unilaterally altering the constitution in 1963, the Greek Cypriot leadership triggered the collapse of the bi-communal Republic and the ensuing re-eruption of inter-communal violence.

Back in Greece, the civil war had left the country in a state of disarray. Consequently a military coup ousted the civilian regime in 1967 and established a US-backed dictatorship led by Colonel George Papadopoulos. The dictatorship was far more overtly nationalistic than the previous regime, and accelerated subversive military activities in Cyprus in support of Greek Cypriot nationalists. In 1974 the Greek junta ousted the Makarios government, extending its dictatorship to Cyprus. The Greek coup triggered a Turkish invasion. The Greek and Greek Cypriot defeat led to the immediate collapse of the dictatorship and the return to civilian rule. In 1975 the Greek monarchy was formally abolished and the democratic Hellenic Republic was established.

In Cyprus, the Turkish invasion and the refugee flows that followed partitioned the island into two ethnically homogenous zones—a Turkish Cypriot zone in the north and a Greek Cypriot zone in the south. Despite the exclusive presence of Greek Cypriots, the authorities in the south retained the title of the Republic of Cyprus. The Turkish Cypriots in the north unilaterally declared their independence, but their *de facto* state has not been recognised by the international community. The decades that followed witnessed a series of failed negotiations, mediated by the UN and aimed at establishing a bi-zonal and bi-communal federal Republic. (See Background box 8.1.)

## BACKGROUND BOX 8.1

### Basic Chronology of Modern Greece, Turkey and Cyprus

| | |
|---|---|
| 1571 | Cyprus becomes part of the Ottoman Empire |
| 1821–8 | Greek wars of independence |
| 1829 | Greece becomes an independent monarchy |
| 1878 | Cyprus becomes part of the British Empire |
| 1920–2 | Greek–Turkish war in Anatolia |
| 1923 | The Treaty of Lausanne is signed; Atatürk establishes the Republic of Turkey |
| 1944–9 | Greek civil war |
| 1952 | Greece and Turkey join NATO |
| 1960 | The independent Republic of Cyprus is established |
| 1960 | First military coup in Turkey |
| 1963 | The bi-communal Republic collapses and inter-communal fighting re-erupts |
| 1967 | Military coup in Greece |
| 1971 | Second military coup in Turkey |
| 1974 | Greek military coup in Cyprus; Turkish invasion and partition of the island |
| 1975 | The Hellenic Republic established |
| 1977 | The first high-level agreement in Cyprus sets the principles for a bi-zonal and bi-communal federation; this is followed by the 1979 high-level agreement |
| 1980 | Third military coup in Turkey |
| 1981 | Greece enters the EC |

| | |
|---|---|
| 1983 | The Turkish Cypriots declare the Turkish Republic of Northern Cyprus; Turkey returns to civilian rule under Özal |
| 1984 | Kurdish separatist violence erupts in south-east Turkey |
| 1997 | Fourth 'silent' military coup in Turkey |
| 1999 | PKK leader Öcalan is captured; the EU recognises Turkey as a candidate to full membership; Greece and Turkey enter a period of rapprochement |
| 2004 | In separate referenda, Greek and Turkish Cypriots vote on the UN-mediated Annan Plan; the Turkish Cypriots accept and the Greek Cypriots reject the Plan; a divided Cyprus enters the EU |
| 2005 | The EU launches accession negotiations with Turkey |

## Turkey's rocky road to democracy

Turning back to Turkey, with the establishment of the Republic, Atatürk outlined the Kemalist vision, aimed at constructing a western, stable and homogenous nation state, within secure boundaries. Kemalism was essentially a blend of westernisation, secularism, nationalism, statism and populism. Atatürk's early reforms included the adoption of the Latin alphabet, the banning of traditional Muslim headwear and the adoption of western-styled legal codes and constitution. Due to the cultural heterogeneity of the country, Atatürk also attempted to create national unity by advocating the nineteenth-century French concept of civic nationalism (Poulton 1997). Hence, the constitution did not recognise any minorities, other than those mentioned in the Treaty of Lausanne (the Armenians, the Greeks and the Jews). The creation of a homogenous nation was complemented by the secularisation of the state. Turkish secularism meant both that religion was kept out of state decisions and that the state actively sought to reduce the role played by religion in private lives.

While Kemalism theoretically endorsed an enlightened vision of civic nationalism and secularism, in practice its aims were often pursued through repressive policies. For example, the Kurds, as the largest non-recognised minority, suffered greatly from state policies. Political repression coupled with economic neglect created fertile ground for the politicisation of Kurdish resentment. From the mid-1980s to the late 1990s, this took the form of Kurdish **separatism** and a resulting civil war between the Kurdish Partiya Karkeran Kurdistan (PKK) and the Turkish military in south-east Turkey. With the capture of PKK leader Öcalan in 1999 and the process of democratisation that has occurred since then, the situation in south-east Turkey began slowly and unevenly normalising.

Another source of pressure and instability has come from **political Islam**. Born in opposition to the secular Kemalist system, political Islam gained increasing electoral support in the 1970s and again in the 1990s. This led to heavy-handed state repression and a military coup in 1997 intended to weaken the Islamist movement. However, by 2002, with the rise of the moderate Islamic Justice and Development Party (AKP), radical Islamic parties aiming to reverse state secularism have been weakened. Radical political Islam has thus been defeated largely by the rise of a more appealing moderate party within the Islamic camp itself.

The threats and pressures posed by Kurdish separatism and political Islam, together with more diffuse problems of macroeconomic instability, regional inequalities, corruption and political fragmentation, have seriously destabilised Turkish domestic politics. Instability in turn triggered four military coups over the course of Turkey's republican history.

# Domestic Politics and Institutions in Greece, Turkey and Cyprus

Despite their interconnected history, the ensuing political development of Greece, Turkey and Cyprus has taken different forms. Greece was the first to establish a stable democracy in 1975. While evolving in nature and structure, Greece's political system, shaped around a right–left divide, has been the most comparable to other European states. In Turkey, domestic politics has not followed the classic right–left divide, but has been shaped by the interpretation and application of Kemalism. Post-1974 Cyprus has been dominated by the conflict between its two communities. The conflict has led to the development of separate Greek Cypriot and Turkish Cypriot polities and has been the priority issue in politics in the two communities.

## Domestic politics in post-1974 Greece

The post-1974 era in Greece has seen the establishment, evolution and consolidation of a democratic parliamentary republic. The trauma of 1974 led to an abandonment of expansionist territorial goals and a refocusing of political attention on economic development and the consolidation of democracy.

Since 1975, Greece has developed into a parliamentary democracy in which executive power lies with the prime minister and the cabinet, appointed by the president on the basis of parliamentary electoral results. The president and head of state, elected by parliament on a five-year term, does not possess decision-making power. The legislature is constituted by a unicameral parliament, elected every four years. The judiciary includes the Court of Justice, the Court of First Instance, the Court of Appeal, the Council of State and the Supreme Court.

Since 1974, the party system has been centred around and power has oscillated between the conservative New Democracy (ND) and socialist pan-Hellenic party (PASOK). Between 1974 and 1981 ND was in power under the premiership of Constantine Karamanlis. Following two terms in office, ND was replaced by Andreas Papandreou's PASOK, which remained in power until 1989. After a period of domestic instability, PASOK returned to office in 1993, and between 1996 and 2004 its governments were led by Costas Simitis. Elections in 2004 saw a return of ND under Costas Karamanlis. PASOK, in opposition, is currently led by the son of the late Andreas Papandreou, George Papandreou.

Between 1975 and 1981, Karamanlis sought to stabilise Greek democracy and to modernise the socio-economic system by anchoring

Greece within the European Community (EC). However, the ND governments also encouraged public-sector growth and an accompanying burgeoning network of corruption and clientelism. In 1981, the PASOK government exacerbated this situation. In its first decade in power, PASOK governed as a populist, catch-all party thriving on a nationalist, anti-western, anti-capitalist and anti-imperialist rhetoric. Its strong ideology and populism hindered good governance and socio-economic development.

Since the mid/late-1980s both PASOK and ND have undergone a significant process of modernisation. In turn, Greece has witnessed a remarkable transformation in its political, socio-economic and institutional structures. Until the late 1980s, the state had dominated the country's socio-economic life. This led to a pervasive clientelism, an excessive centralisation of power in Athens and an underdeveloped civil society. By the mid-1980s, the system began to transform. Successive governments loosened the state's grip over social institutions and economic activity and empowered interest groups, civil society and sub-state levels of government (Ioakimidies 2001: 77–84).

By the turn of the century, the days of military dictatorship seemed long gone. While economic and governance challenges remain, the image of the Greek state as a 'colossus with feet of clay' has been surpassed (Sotiropolous 1996). In the sphere of politics and rights, despite shortcomings (e.g. the insufficient protection of ethnic and religious minorities), Greek democracy has consolidated into a stable two-party system. Within and between both parties, discourse and differences are marked less by ideology and more by rational political arguments. In other words, despite its shortcomings, Greek democracy has matured.

## Politics and institutions in the republic of Turkey

Domestic politics in republican Turkey have been shaped by Atatürk's ideology and legacy. The head of state is the president, elected by parliament on a seven-year term. Turkey's first president was Atatürk himself. The executive is centred around the prime minister and the Council of Ministers, appointed by the president on the basis of electoral results. Legislative power rests in the Grand National Assembly, elected every five years. The judiciary includes the Constitutional Court, the High Court of Appeals, the Council of State, the Court of Accounts as well as military courts. Another key institution is the military, considered the guardian of the Kemalist republic.

With the establishment of the Republic in 1923, Atatürk set up and governed through a one-party system, the Republican People's Party (CHP). This system was retained until his successor, Ismet Inönü, legalised the opposition Democrat Party (DP) in 1946. Unlike Greece, the difference between the CHP and the DP was not based on a traditional right–left divide. Nor were party differences marked by different views over Kemalism. Both the CHP and the DP were moderate catch-all parties, which rejected class or sectarian connotations and advocated a nationalist mixed economy. Both were deeply committed to Kemalism. The principal difference between them was that while the CHP was linked to the state apparatus, the DP theoretically stood for the rural periphery and was thus more receptive to traditional values, including religion.

The evolution of the party system has not been smooth, not least because successive military coups disbanded most political parties, which reformed under different names and guises. However, the overall divide between the traditional Kemalist parties continued to oscillate around degrees and forms of nationalism and statism on the one hand, and populism and liberalism on the other. Particularly since the 1970s, there have also been different 'anti-system' parties in Turkey, including extreme nationalist right- and left-wing parties, ethnic-based (principally Kurdish) parties and Islamic parties. In the Turkish context, 'anti-system' has meant scepticism about, or outright opposition to, the Kemalist establishment (which includes the traditional parties and all public institutions).

In 1950, under the leadership of Adnan Menderes, the Democrat Party was elected and remained in power until the 1960 military coup, the outcome of which was the drafting of a new, more liberal constitution, and the disbanding of the DP (due to its increasing authoritarianism). The post-1961 party system was a fractured one, with unstable coalition governments alternating between two dominant parties: the Justice Party (as the successor of the Democrat Party) and the CHP. Rising instability led to a second military intervention in 1971, which failed to halt growing economic instability, political fragmentation and violence. As a result of the quasi-civil war in the late 1970s, the military intervened for a third time in 1980, imposing draconian measures and a new restrictive constitution. The 1980–3 regime also disbanded all political parties.

With the return to civilian rule in 1983, the party system was reshaped by the rise of Turgut Özal's Motherland Party (ANAP), which embraced conservative social values, but reversed the state's economic policy, opting for economic liberalisation over state control and import-substitution. Under the ever-rising impact of economic globalisation, the Özal government understood that sustained economic growth and stability required foreign direct investment and greater integration into the global economy.

With the death of Özal, the party system plunged again into instability, growing corruption and economic mismanagement. This remained the case until the 2002 elections, which through popular vote rather than military coup transformed Turkey's political landscape. The election brought to power the AKP, which, emulating West European Christian democrat parties, has defined itself as a conservative 'Muslim Democrat' party. The only other party to pass the electoral threshold and gain representation in parliament has been the centre-left CHP. Hence, by 2002, Turkey's party system approximated more closely the political cleavages characterising Greece and most other European party systems.

Since the turn of the century, the Turkish state has also embarked on an unprecedented process of domestic reform. Through a series of constitutional and legal packages, successive governments (but the AKP government in particular) have pursued reforms aimed at strengthening respect for human, cultural and political rights and freedoms and re-balancing civilian–military relations. Since the deep financial crisis of 2001, governments have also pursued an extensive programme of macroeconomic reform, assisted and guided by the International Monetary Fund (IMF). Turkey's political, legal and constitutional systems as well as its economy began converging on European standards.

## Politics and institutions in divided Cyprus

Due to the division of Cyprus, the sections below adopt a dual approach. Although the Republic of Cyprus has been the only recognised state on the island, the persisting conflict has seen the concomitant development of a Turkish Cypriot *de facto* state in the north. As in Turkey, both sides have seen the development of multi-party systems. As in Greece, however, party politics in Cyprus has followed a rough right–left divide. But politics on the island has been dominated by the conflict and the primary distinguishing feature between parties has been their stance on it. Based on the 1960 constitution, and unlike both kin-states, the two communities retained strong presidential systems. The presidents have also acted as communal leaders in peace negotiations.

### Politics and institutions in Greek Cyprus

In southern Cyprus, the president, directly elected every five years, is both head of state and leader of the government. The president appoints and heads the Council of Ministers, that constitutes the executive. Legislative power rests in the House of Representatives, elected every five years. Another key institution is the National Council, where all parties are represented and which determines unanimously the outlines of the community's policy in peace negotiations. The judiciary includes the

Supreme Court, the High Court of Justice and lower courts.

All political parties and public institutions in southern Cyprus share the aim of reunification, repatriation of Greek Cypriot refugees and withdrawal of Turkish troops. Yet while most actors share these basic aims, a wide array of different detailed agendas have emerged. Since 1974, nationalism within the Greek Cypriot community has taken took two forms: Greek Cypriot nationalism and Cypriot nationalism (Mavratsas 1997).

Greek Cypriot nationalists have adopted a conception of **ethnic nationalism**, emphasising the 'Greekness' in the Cypriot identity. While abandoning the aim of *enosis*, they have sought a Greek-Cypriot-controlled state organically linked to 'motherland' Greece. Their genuine commitment to a federal power-sharing and bi-zonal settlement with the Turkish Cypriots has been doubtful at best. Variants of this ideology have been espoused by the centre-right Democratic Party (DIKO), the extreme right New Horizons, the socialists (EDEK), the Greek Orthodox Church, as well as by elements in the moderate right Democratic Rally (DISY).

Cypriot nationalists have emphasised the Cypriot identity of Greek and Turkish Cypriots alike and have highlighted the civic elements of identity based on shared economic, political and social rights. They have imagined a shared history of intercommunal coexistence and have viewed Turks, and not Turkish Cypriots, as the 'enemy'. Cypriot nationalists have supported the reunification of Cyprus under a federal power-sharing agreement and have called for the end to all foreign interference (by Greece, Turkey and the UK). Variants of Cypriot nationalism have been espoused by the leftist Reformist Workers' Party (AKEL) and the liberal United Democrats (EDI).

Following the death of the first president, Archbishop Makarios, the Republic of Cyprus has had four presidents: Spyros Kyprianou (DIKO, 1979–89), George Vassiliou (EDI, 1989–93), Glafcos Clerides (DISY, 1993–2003) and Tassos Papadopolous (DIKO, 2003–). Governments have frequently been formed by coalitions between parties with different political ideologies. Currently the government is formed by the leftist AKEL together with the right-wing DIKO. In other words, while ideology has marked party stances *vis-à-vis* the conflict, domestic politics has been characterised by a high degree of pragmatism.

### Politics and institutions in Turkish Cyprus

Since 1974, the Turkish Cypriots have retained a presidential system in which the president is directly elected every five years. Unlike in the south, the prime minister is head of government. While the president acts as community leader and thus heads peace negotiations, the prime minister and the cabinet primarily manage domestic affairs. The prime minister and cabinet are appointed by the president on the basis of electoral results in the parliamentary assembly, which is elected every five years.

Beyond political differences, all Turkish Cypriots seek political equality with, and to avoid domination by, the larger Greek Cypriot community. They also call for the highest degree of self-rule and physical separation from the Greek Cypriots and for Turkey's involvement in the island's security. But, beyond these general aims, there have been wide divisions on the conflict between the nationalist camp and the centre-left and liberal camps.

The nationalist camp has emphasised the ethnic differences between Greeks and Turks and the impossibility of the peaceful coexistence between the two. It has equally stressed the organic links between the Turkish Cypriots and 'motherland' Turkey. Critics of the nationalist camp have doubted its commitment to a federal arrangement, arguing that nationalists are content to retain and consolidate partition. Rauf Denktaş has been the central figure in the nationalist camp. In addition, the two major nationalist parties are the National Unity Party (UBP) and the Democrat Party (DP). Until 2003, the UBP and DP consistently won the lion's share of the vote.

The centre-left and liberal parties have been more flexible about future solutions. They have

NATHALIE TOCCI

supported a federal settlement that guarantees maximum Turkish Cypriot self-rule and minimum interference of both Greek Cypriots and Turkey from Turkish Cypriot affairs. The two main parties on the centre left are the Communal Liberation Party (TKP) and the Republican Turkish Party (CTP). The 2003 elections witnessed the first relative victory of the centre-left camp and of the CTP in particular led by Mehmet Ali Talat. Talat replaced Denktaş as president in 2005. Normally, governments in northern Cyprus have been formed by coalitions between the nationalist parties. Most recently, however, the government has been composed of the moderate CTP and the nationalist DP. (See Theme box: Democracy and Legitimacy for further discussion.)

## KEY POINTS

- Since 1974 the conservative ND and the socialist PASOK have dominated Greek domestic politics.

- Over the decades Greek democracy has evolved, having now reached a stage of maturity.

- In Turkey the political system has been shaped by the Kemalist ideology.

- Domestic instability and frequent military interventions have resulted in a seriously deficient democracy. In recent years Turkey has embarked on an unprecedented process of political reform.

- The Cyprus conflict has led to the development of two separate polities on the island, whose domestic politics has been shaped by the ongoing conflict.

## THEME BOX

### Democracy and Legitimacy

In Greece, following the traumas of civil war and dictatorship, a democratic republic was established. Yet democratic consolidation has been an ongoing process. Ideology and populism have played decreasing roles in Greek political life, while substantive questions about economic development and good governance have come to the fore in politics. The two principal parties have been dramatically transformed, relying less on the appeal of charismatic leaders and more on the overall organisational and functional effectiveness of party structures.

In Turkey, democracy has been marred by the state's repression and violation of human rights. A particularly salient feature has been the atypical role of the Turkish military, which entrusted itself the role of guarding the Kemalist republic (Atatürk himself was a soldier before becoming a politician). After the 1980 coup, the military's role was strengthened both institutionally and through informal channels. While the military has retained key political influences, the recent wave of democratic reforms has led to a gradual

rebalancing of civil–military relations in favour of the former.

Democracy in Cyprus has suffered from the ongoing conflict. The Republic of Cyprus is recognised internationally as the only legitimate state on the island. But it does not represent nor include the Turkish Cypriot community. Its democratic legitimacy is thus incomplete. In northern Cyprus, aside from questions of international legitimacy, the democratic nature of the regime is questionable. Due to the non-recognised status of the Turkish Republic of Northern Cyprus (TRNC), the latter cannot survive without Turkey's political and economic support. As such, it has never taken any key decisions without Ankara's consent. However, this does not mean that the TRNC is a puppet regime. Having retained power longer than any Turkish politician, the Turkish Cypriot leader, Denktaş has enjoyed considerable respect and influence in Turkey, particularly among nationalist civilian and military circles.

# Foreign Policy in the Eastern Mediterranean

Relations between Greece, Turkey and Cyprus as well as wider ties to Europe have dominated foreign policy in the Eastern Mediterranean. Greece was the first to enter the EC/EU. Yet Greek attitudes towards European integration evolved gradually over time. Greek foreign policy has also shifted *vis-à-vis* Turkey. As part of the Kemalist endeavour, Turkey has sought association with the west. Yet Turkey's relations with both Europe and with its neighbours have often been problematic. Like domestic politics, foreign policy in Cyprus has been dominated by the conflict.

## Greek foreign policy

Greek foreign policy has gone through a process of radical transformation. Between 1974 and 1981, the ND government focused its foreign policy on seeking EC membership. Greece applied for membership in 1975 and entered in 1981. The government also reactivated Greece's NATO membership (Greece had exited NATO's military wing with the 1974 war in Cyprus). In contrast, the ND government took a low profile on Cyprus and Turkey, aware that Turkey's military superiority and the Cold War geopolitical setting precluded the option of a successful military confrontation.

With PASOK's election, both approaches were reversed. Greece fully re-engaged in the Greek Cypriot cause and pursued it by using its veto rights within the Council to block closer EC–Turkey ties. Yet, despite its use of the advantages of EC membership, socialist PASOK was sceptical about the liberal EC project, to the point of questioning the desirability of Greece's full membership.

PASOK's positions changed by the late-1980s. The economic benefits of membership (since the mid-1980s the Greek economy was aided significantly by EC funds) and the wider challenges posed by economic globalisation increased the appeal of European integration. In turn, openly critical Greek attitudes towards Europe were toned down; by the late 1980s, the Greek government was encouraging the Greek Cypriot Republic to apply for EC membership as well. In the late 1990s Greek foreign policy shifted further. Under Costas Simitis and George Papandreou, Greece became outspokenly pro-European and multilateralist.

Greek attitudes towards Turkey were also transformed, with Athens embarking on an unprecedented rapprochement with Ankara. To date, this has not solved the most salient disputes over Cyprus and sovereignty rights in the Aegean Sea. But, through cooperation on 'low politics' issues, the climate between the two countries has improved markedly. The rapprochement has also entailed a shift in Greek strategy towards EU–Turkey ties. Indeed, from having represented the most significant obstacle to improved Turkey–EU relations, by the turn of the century, Greece had become one of the most adamant supporters of Turkey's EU accession.

## Turkish foreign policy

Since the foundation of the Republic, Turkey has associated itself with the west in order to secure its territorial borders in a volatile environment and complement its domestic process of westernisation. Throughout the Cold War, Turkey's western orientation was based on its NATO membership in the security sphere and its association with the EC in the economic domain. Since the late 1980s, Turkey's European orientation has been a cornerstone of its foreign policy. In 1996 Turkey entered the EU customs union and in 1999 it began its **EU accession process**. However, relations between Turkey and the EU have not been smooth, not least because of the problems caused by Greece's EU membership, the wider scepticism of other European countries towards Turkey's accession and

Turkey's shortcomings in the fields of democracy and human rights. Nevertheless, Turkey launched accession negotiations with the EU in October 2005.

Turkey's ongoing commitment to the west did not preclude close attention to its neighbourhood. In renouncing any expansionist ambition, Republican Turkey sought to surround itself by a ring of friends. Yet Turkey has had difficult if not openly conflictual relations with many neighbours. The reasons for some conflicts are historical, such as the rivalry between Turkey and Russia, Greece and Armenia. In other cases, external conflicts have coincided with internal challenges. Turkish–Iranian relations have been strained over questions of political Islam, while Turkish–Syrian relations have been marred by Syria's support for the PKK. Finally, the concept of ethnic kin, in addition to strict security concerns, has also played a prominent role in Turkish foreign policy, explaining Turkey's close ties with Azerbaijan and naturally with the Turkish Cypriot community.

## Foreign policy in Cyprus

The principal and overarching foreign-policy objective of both communities in Cyprus has been the settlement of the conflict in line with their perceived interests. The conflict, representing a key existential question, has underpinned all foreign-policy decisions.

The Greek Cypriots have sought to strengthen their bargaining position *vis-à-vis* the Turkish Cypriots by seeking the internationalisation of the conflict. Internationalisation historically took place through the UN, by seeking resolutions condemning Turkey and the Turkish Cypriots. Greek Cyprus rallied international support by retaining close ties both with the USA and the Soviet Union during the Cold War. It garnered the support of the developing world through its membership of the non-aligned movement. Since the 1990s, seeking EU accession has been the principal element of this strategy. EU membership was partly sought as a means to integrate Cyprus, as a small and open economy, into a larger market in view of rising globalisation. However, the principal motivation was clearly linked to the conflict. Through the EU accession process, the Republic of Cyprus aimed to strengthen its status and to increase European pressure on Turkey in order to secure a settlement in line with its interests. The divided Cyprus joined the EU in 2004 and the Greek Cypriot side, now fully represented in the EU, has already used these advantages to further its national cause, generating new problems in EU–Turkey relations.

The Turkish Cypriots have pursued policies aimed at securing forms of recognition and the lifting of international isolation. Isolation has been felt as an increasingly pressing problem by the Turkish Cypriots, who have felt excluded from the potential benefits of globalisation. Particularly after the 2004 referendum in Cyprus in which the Turkish Cypriot community accepted and the Greek Cypriot community rejected the UN-mediated Annan Plan, the Turkish Cypriots have been pressing for the 'normalisation' of their situation especially in terms of their relations with Europe.

**KEY POINTS**

- Since 1975, Greek foreign policy has changed significantly both with respect to Europe and to its arch-rival Turkey.

- Close ties with the west and with Europe have characterised Turkish foreign policy. Yet Turkey's relations both with Europe and with several of its neighbours have often been problematic.

- The conflict has been the overarching foreign-policy priority of both Cypriot communities. In particular, Greek Cyprus sought EU entry to strengthen its hand in the conflict. But the accession of the conflict ridden-island has complicated EU–Turkey relations.

# Conclusion

This chapter has analysed the key features of the Greek, Turkish and Cypriot political systems. Greece was the first to establish a stable democratic system characterised by a dominant two-party system. Parliamentary democracy was established after the collapse of the colonels' regime, following the war in Cyprus. Since 1974, the Greek political, socio-economic and institutional systems have undergone a comprehensive process of modernisation.

Turkey was the first to establish a republic with a multi-party political system. Yet, the country's path to democracy has not been smooth. Implementation of the Kemalist vision led to frequent recourse to military rule, state repression and human rights violations. Yet, in recent years, Turkey has embarked on a momentous, albeit still incomplete, process of democratisation.

The history of Cyprus has been dominated by the conflict between its communities, supported respectively by Greece and Turkey. The conflict led to the partition of the island, and thus the separate development of two political systems. While democracy and economic growth characterised the south, the constitutional, institutional, political and economic consolidation of the country must still await a final settlement of the conflict.

One particularity of these three eastern Mediterranean countries has been the tight interrelationship between domestic and foreign policies. Greece's EC membership since 1981 has been a pivotal factor in consolidating Greek democracy and enabling the state's progressive modernisation. In turn, the maturing of the political system has allowed for the rapprochement with Turkey, spearheaded by the former PASOK government in 1999 and carried through by ND since 2004. Through the consolidation of Greek democracy, its most enlightened political leaders have understood that Greek security interests called for engagement rather than confrontation with Turkey, as well as for Turkey's progressive integration in the EU. Even starker has been the positive impact of Turkey's accession process on its ongoing domestic reforms. The causal effects have not been one way. In so far as a major stumbling block to Turkey's European integration have been the flaws in Turkish democracy and its human rights record, the unprecedented process of domestic reform has allowed closer EU–Turkey ties. In other words, following the path of Greece, democratisation in Turkey has been crucially linked to its EU accession process. While this process is far from complete, Turkey's integration into the EU, together with that of Greece and Cyprus may secure a more peaceful and stable environment in the Eastern Mediterranean in the decades to come. (See Theme box: The Impact of the European Union.)

## KEY POINTS

- Greece's Europeanisation has shaped Greek domestic and foreign policy.
- The Greek–Turkish rapprochement has been influenced by Greece's Europeanisation and has affected positively EU–Turkey relations.
- Turkey's EU accession process is both partly explained by and responsible for Turkey's ongoing democratisation.

NATHALIE TOCCI

## THEME BOX

### The Impact of the European Union

Greece's EU membership and the EU accession process of Cyprus and Turkey have profoundly affected domestic politics in these countries.

In Greece, EC/EU membership not only acted as a bulwark against a return to dictatorship, the legal and policy imperatives of membership also contributed to the modernisation of the Greek state. In seeking to meet the Maastricht criteria for monetary union, Greek governments have also engaged in a radical overhaul of Greek fiscal policy and public-sector activity. By contributing to Greece's sense of security, EU membership has also shaped Greek foreign policy, particularly *vis-à-vis* Turkey since the late 1990s.

Turkey's EU accession process has also had positive effects on democracy and foreign policy. It has provided greater strength and credibility to domestic reformers who had long sought greater democratisation and respect for human rights. The same has been true in the realm of foreign policy. Turkey's policy shift in proactively supporting a solution in Cyprus in 2004, its pursuit of rapprochement with Greece and its slowly developing dialogue with Armenia can all be linked to Turkey's EU accession process.

EU accession, to date, has not had a positive effect on the Cyprus conflict. While having contributed to greater Turkish Cypriot willingness to reach a solution, it has hardened Greek Cypriot views. The acceptance of Cyprus' membership irrespective of a settlement reduced the Greek Cypriot leadership's incentives to seal a deal. In turn, despite active UN mediation in 2002–4, the Greek Cypriot community rejected (while the Turkish Cypriot community accepted) the UN Annan Plan in the April 2004 referendum.

### ? QUESTIONS

1. What explains Greece's modernisation and democratisation?
2. What role has the north–south conflict played in the domestic politics of Cyprus?
3. Is Turkey a democratic country?
4. What factors explain Greece's changing attitudes towards Turkey?
5. What has been the impact on Cyprus of the island's EU accession process?
6. Why did Greece and Cyprus enter the EU?
7. What role has the EU played in consolidating democracy in Greece?
8. Can democratisation in Turkey be explained better by internal developments, or external relations, notably its relations with the EU?

###  FURTHER READING

#### GREECE

■ **Mitsos, A. and Mossialos, E. (2000),** *Contemporary Greece and Europe*, **Aldershot, Ashgate.** This edited volume provides a comprehensive study of the transformation of Greek domestic and foreign policies since the 1980s.

## TURKEY

■ **Kramer, H. (2000),** *A Changing Turkey: The Challenge of Europe and the US*, **Washington DC, Brookings Institution Press.** Provides a useful analysis of domestic politics and foreign policy in Turkey.

■ **Uğur, M. (1999),** *The EU and Turkey: An Anchor Credibility Dilemma*, **Aldershot, Ashgate.** Provides a convincing argument of how EU–Turkey relations have affected Turkish domestic politics.

■ **Zurcher, E. (1993),** *Turkey, A Modern History, revised edn*, **London, I. B.Tauris.** Provides an in-depth study of Turkey's republican history.

## CYPRUS

■ **Borowiec, A. (2000),** *Cyprus: A Troubled Island*, **Westport CT, Praeger Publishers.** Provides a balanced account of the Cyprus conflict.

■ **Diez, T. (ed.) (2002),** *The European Union and the Cyprus Conflict: Modern Conflict, Post Modern Union*, **Manchester, Manchester University Press.** This edited volume analyses EU–Cyprus relations from a theoretical perspective.

## GREECE, TURKEY AND CYPRUS

■ **Featherstone, K. and Kazamias, G. (eds.) (2001),** *Europeanisation and the Southern Periphery*, **London, Frank Cass.** Chapters by Ioakimidis, Pagoulatos, Featherstone, Uğur and Sofos provide an interesting account of the impact of the EU on the domestic politics of Greece, Cyprus and Turkey.

■ **Tocci, N. (2004),** *EU Accession Dynamics and Conflict Resolution: Catalyzing Peace or Consolidating Partition in Cyprus?*, **Aldershot, Ashgate.** Analyses the effect of the EU on the Cyprus conflict, in the context of politics between Cyprus, Greece, Turkey and Europe.

 **IMPORTANT WEBSITE**

● **http://website.lineone.net/~acgta**   The website of the Association for Greece, Cyprus and Turkey Affairs includes several articles on Greece, Turkey and Cyprus and the relations between them.

 **Visit the Online Resource Centre that accompanies this book for lots of useful additional material, including an interactive map of Europe. www.oxfordtextbooks.co.uk/orc/ hay_menon/**

# 9

# Central and Eastern Europe

TIM HAUGHTON

## Chapter Contents

- Introduction
- The Post-communist Challenge
- The Institutional Framework of Politics in Central and Eastern Europe
- Key Issues in the Politics of the Region
- The Role of EU Conditionality
- The Impact of EU Membership
- Conclusion: Continued Commonality or Increasing Diversity?

## Reader's Guide

This chapter explores the main features of politics in Central and Eastern Europe (CEE). It begins by defining CEE, acknowledging both the limitations of any definition and the existence of both diversity and commonality across the region. The chapter then identifies many of the challenges faced by CEE during the 1990s, especially democratisation, marketisation and state-building. After outlining the institutional framework of politics in CEE, the chapter highlights the principal issues animating politics in the region. Specific attention is paid to the role of the European Union in the politics of CEE and the role of CEE in the developing politics of the EU. It points out that during the process of accession the EU's impact varied, being much more influential at certain times and in particular policy areas than others. We examine how the transition from the status of accession states to member states is shaping the current politics of the region. The chapter concludes by highlighting diversity and commonalities in contemporary CEE and positing some possible future trends.

# Introduction

The countries of Central and Eastern Europe (CEE) have emerged from the scholarly ghetto. For so long the exclusive focus of East European studies, the rapid and radical changes in the region, not least accession to the EU, have transformed not just the politics of CEE, but European politics as a whole. Scholars and students wishing to understand contemporary European politics need to adjust their mental maps to ensure CEE is integrated into their thinking. Debates about key European issues such as changes to the EU's institutional framework, reform of the European social model and the future of EU enlargement have all been altered by the accession states of Central and Eastern Europe. Moreover, the influence of CEE on these profound challenges facing Europe is more likely to increase than decrease in coming years. Before embarking on such an analysis, however, it is important first to establish what we mean by Central and Eastern Europe.

The Cold War shaped modern perceptions of what constitutes Western, Central and Eastern Europe. The Iron Curtain created a relatively neat distinction between 'Western' and 'Eastern' Europe, with the communist states such as Poland and Hungary clearly in the latter category. Large parts of what was labelled Eastern Europe in the second half of the twentieth century, however, were historically thought of as Central Europe, not least by their inhabitants, particularly those that had been part of the Austro-Hungarian Empire.

Many of the countries sandwiched between Germany and Russia have been keen to label themselves as 'Central' Europe, conscious that the adjective 'Eastern' when applied to Europe conjures up the image of backwardness, hardship and even brutality. Czechs are keen to remind visitors that Prague lies to the west of Vienna, and both Lithuanians and Slovaks claim the geographical centre of Europe lies in their respective territories. The claim, however, is not just one of geography, but of values. Self-ascribed Central Europeans like to contrast their own adherence to liberal democratic norms with what they take to be the more autarchic character of countries to the East, especially Russia (Kundera 1984).

While cultural and linguistic boundaries can be fluid, and at times indistinct, political borders provide clearer demarcation points. Although acknowledging that the definition is imperfect, this chapter focuses on the eight states from the region which joined the EU on 1 May 2004 (the Czech Republic, Estonia, Hungary, Latvia, Lithuania, Poland, Slovakia and Slovenia) with some reference to Bulgaria and Romania which are due to join in 2007. Other countries in the region such as Albania, Ukraine, Moldova and much of the former Yugoslavia have been excluded. Many of those in the last group have faced the same challenges which confronted the eight new member states, but given the later date when they embarked on serious reform (and the comparative lack of subsequent progress made), in addition to their limited progress towards EU membership, they have been excluded.

Although there are sufficient commonalities among the eight states which form the focus of this chapter to justify treating these countries together, they cannot be considered in an undifferentiated way. Indeed, thanks to different historical experiences, and linguistic, religious and cultural differences, diversity is the 'hallmark' of Central and Eastern Europe (Batt 2003: 4). These themes of diversity and commonality in the region run not only through this chapter, but through the study of CEE as a whole.

# The Post-communist Challenge

In the 1990s comparative political scientists drew on the literature on democratic transitions in Latin America and Southern Europe to explain developments in CEE. These accounts, however, were frequently guilty of 'conceptual stretching' (Sartori 1971), prompting Valerie Bunce (1995: 112) to ask whether we were 'comparing apples with apples, apples with oranges (which are at least varieties of fruit) or apples with say, kangaroos'. Not only did the accounts suffer from the perennial temporal problem of comparing processes which occurred over different time periods, but many of the 'transitology' accounts (as they came to be known) failed to deal adequately with the legacy of the communist experience.

The communist system was officially based on Marxist ideology with its promises of equality, lack of class divisions, transcendence of alienation, communal ownership and the satisfaction of the material needs of the entire population. The reality of the communist regimes, however, proved to be very different, characterised as they were by corruption and repression. Membership of the Communist Party was usually a necessary condition for holding high-ranking positions in the political, economic and social spheres. The ideological basis of the regimes, the configuration of political and economic elites, the social structure of society, economic organisation and civil–military relations were all substantially different in communist CEE to the authoritarian regimes of Southern Europe and

Latin America. But it was not just the starting point that was different. In Southern Europe and Latin America the issue was primarily the political task of democratisation, whereas CEE faced three distinct challenges: (1) to create democracies, (2) to create market economies and, in the case of six of the eight countries, (3) to build new states. The magnitude of these tasks should not be underestimated, one alone would be difficult for any country; CEE undertook all three simultaneously.

The collapse of the communist regimes in CEE was largely the product of economic failure. The centrally planned economies failed to deliver the material abundance promised by Marxist–Leninist ideology. Although some countries such as Hungary undertook economic reforms before 1989, the collapse of the regimes changed the nature of the debate. The task shifted from one of economic reform to that of economic transformation (Batt 1991). Central to this new challenge was the building of market economies. The introduction of the market mechanism involved two key tasks: price liberalisation and privatisation. Under communism prices were fixed largely by the central planners who kept the cost to consumers of politically sensitive commodities, such as basic food stuffs, low. Moreover, the introduction of a market economy required the need for citizens to create, run and own private enterprises some of which, under market conditions, would succeed while others would fail. Factories which failed to produce products that consumers wanted to buy at a price they were willing to pay suffered losses and ultimately bankruptcy.

These changes had significant political as well as economic ramifications. The rise in the cost of bread, fuel and rent engendered discontent among the electorates of CEE. In conjunction with unemployment caused by efficiency measures and the overhaul of previously generous welfare arrangements, these economic changes fuelled political discontent. Even a decade and a half after the economic reform packages were launched politicians, such as Lithuania's Rolandas Paksas in the two-round presidential elections held in December 2002 and January 2003, have capitalised on the disappointments of those who felt they had lost out from the process of post-communist economic reform (Clark and Verseckaitė 2005). Moreover, the need for privatisation provoked further questions about how, and to whom, state-owned firms should be sold. There was a widespread feeling among the electorates of CEE that privatisation had been motivated more frequently for the benefit of politicians and their close associates than for the good of the country's finances or the well-being of ordinary citizens.

While embarking on radical economic reforms, these states also had to undertake the parallel process of democratisation. Although some of the ingredients of a democratic system such as parliaments and political parties had been in existence during communist rule, the political architecture needed to be substantially overhauled. Parliaments needed to be transformed from sham, rubber-stamp institutions into genuine assemblies and legislatures. The old communist-era constitution needed to be replaced (or at least radically amended) to remove the leading role of the Communist Party, to impose a separation of powers (between executive, legislature and judiciary) and to facilitate the functioning of a genuine multi-party democratic system. More broadly, formal and behavioural shifts from such communist shibboleths as 'the Party is always right' were required. Equally, societies which had discouraged and repressed independent political activity needed to create conditions for civil society organisations to blossom and flourish.

In addition, six of the countries (the Czech Republic, Estonia, Latvia, Lithuania, Slovakia and Slovenia) were new states, having emerged from the communist-era federations of Czechoslovakia, Yugoslavia and the USSR. The 'state' can be seen as an institution, a territory or a nation. All three needed to be built in each of the six states (although the Czech Republic inherited much of Czechoslovakia's institutional structure). Not only did ministries, agencies, regulatory bodies, law and order and internal security organs need to be created or adapted from existing federal forms, but the new territorial borders needed to be protected and staffed. These tasks consumed time and resources, but they also provoked political debate. Indeed, the process of defining these new states raised questions of nationality, citizenship and loyalty to the state. In Estonia, for example, the 'new' state was defined as the legal continuation of the inter-war republic, labelling the post-war years as the period of illegal Soviet occupation. This declaration was not just of symbolic importance; it also meant that ethnic Russians who had moved to the then Soviet Republic of Estonia were now not automatically classified as citizens, resulting in them not being accorded the same rights as ethnic Estonians. Even in the seemingly more institutionally developed cases of Poland and Hungary elements of state-building were required. During communist times the policies of both of these states were limited by what was deemed permissible by the Soviet Union, especially in the realms of foreign and defence policy.

**KEY POINTS**

- Following the collapse of the communist regimes, CEE faced the challenges of democratisation, marketisation and state-building.

- Radical economic reform entailed price liberalisation and privatisation, both of which had political ramifications.

- Democratisation required not just an overhaul of the institutional architecture of politics, but also formal and behavioural shifts to allow multi-party democracy and civil society to flourish.

- Many states in CEE were 'new' having been part of the communist-era multiethnic federations.

# The Institutional Framework of Politics in Central and Eastern Europe

Although there have been significant changes in subsequent years, such as the 1997 Polish constitution which reduced the powers of the presidency (Sanford 2002: 141), the institutional frameworks of politics in the region are largely the product of decisions made in 1989–91. These frameworks were initially forged in a melting pot of inherited structures, historical experiences, a concern for historical continuity, political actors' preferences during the transition and assorted sweeteners during the roundtable talks between the government and opposition held in many CEE countries in 1989 (Haughton 2005a: 82).

Although these different inputs produced some significant variations across the region in electoral systems and the powers of the presidency (see Table 9.1), there are several similarities in overall institutional design. The prevailing model is of a parliamentary democracy with a proportional representation (PR) electoral system (Malová and Haughton 2002: 101). This model has tended to generate multi-party systems and coalition governments. Moreover prime ministers, rather than presidents, are often the most powerful political figures in their respective countries. Initially prime ministers were regarded as often quite weak and ineffectual, but some scholars (e.g. Malová and Ilonszki 2006 forthcoming) have argued that recent years have seen the emergence of a more stable executive leadership. Nonetheless, prime ministerial power continues to be circumscribed by significant constraints, not least that associated with the need to govern in coalition with other parties. Coalition formation, maintenance and termination, therefore, are central themes of politics.

**KEY POINTS**

- Although there are many similarities across the region, there are significant variations in the institutional framework of politics in the different states of CEE.

- The diversity of institutional frameworks is due to a number of factors such as historical experiences, how the countries exited communism and the preferences of politicians during the early transition period.

- Institutional frameworks are now much more settled, but still subject to change.

**Table 9.1** The Institutional Framework of Politics

| Country | Electoral system (for lower house if bicameral) | Presidency | Bicameral/unicameral parliament |
|---|---|---|---|
| Bulgaria | PR | Directly elected, but limited powers | Unicameral |
| Czech Republic | PR | Indirectly elected with very limited powers | Bicameral (since 1996) |
| Estonia | PR | Indirectly elected with limited powers | Unicameral |
| Hungary | Mixed | Indirectly elected with very limited powers | Unicameral |
| Latvia | PR | Indirectly elected with limited powers | Unicameral |
| Lithuania | Mixed | Directly elected with significant powers | Unicameral |
| Poland | PR | Directly elected, but limited powers (since 1997 constitution) | Bicameral |
| Romania | PR | Directly elected with significant powers | Bicameral |
| Slovakia | PR | Directly elected (since 1999), but limited powers | Unicameral |
| Slovenia | PR | Indirectly elected with very limited powers | Bicameral |

# Key Issues in the Politics of the Region

Despite the diversity of the region we can identify a number of common issues which animate political debate in CEE. Among the most significant in recent years have been attitudes to the communist past; the speed, direction and extent of economic reform; EU integration; ethnic politics and minority policies; morality and values; and competence, corruption and valence. These issues rarely exist in watertight containers, but often combine, reinforcing positions and divisions in contemporary politics.

Although over a decade and a half has passed since the end of the communist regimes in CEE, the past still matters. Who held what position and who did what to whom during four decades of communist rule have not been forgotten. Even though the former communist parties in Hungary and Poland, for instance, transformed themselves into modern, European social democratic parties (Gryzmala-Busse 2002), a large slice of the Hungarian and Polish electorates resents the seemingly easy transition these politicians have made from communist apparachiks and would never vote for 'Old Communists'. Indeed, a large part of the popular appeal of the parties of the Hungarian right is their anti-communist (and anti-communist-successor party) stance (Fowler 2004). Conversely, some parties such as the Communist Party of Bohemia and Moravia in the Czech Republic have performed well in recent elections on a programme which taps into nostalgia for the certainties and security of communist-era Czechoslovakia. The desire to right the wrongs of communism also fuels calls for **lustration** (the systematic vetting of public officials for links with communist-era security services). Despite the passing of a lustration law in Poland in 1997, for example, the issue continued to be 'instrumentalised by the Polish right as part of the political power struggle' (Szczerbiak 2002: 570).

The speed, direction and extent of economic reform has been central to much political debate in CEE. In the early 1990s a number of market liberals such as Leszek Balcerowicz (Poland), Václav Klaus (Czechoslovakia/Czech Republic) and Mart Laar (Estonia) instituted radical economic reforms. Although all three were largely motivated by an ideological belief in the superiority of the market, they were also driven by a desire to distance their respective countries from the communist past. The drive for economic reform fused with others factors to produce significant consequences. Disputes between Czechs and Slovaks over economic reform, for instance, were a major factor in the break-up of Czechoslovakia. Moreover, radical economic reform in the Baltic states tended to favour the titular ethnic groups at the expense of ethnic Russians, which exacerbated ethnic tensions.

While the zeal of the market liberal pioneers in CEE won plaudits from international financial institutions, economic shock therapy was less well received at home. In consequence, reformers rarely held onto power. Although the communists performed poorly in the Polish semi-free elections in June 1989, for example, the communist-successor Democratic Left Alliance won a convincing victory four years later on a programme of more managed economic reform. An exception to this trend was former Czech premier Václav Klaus who managed to achieve re-election thanks in part to his shrewd decision to baulk at the more unpalatable marketisation measures such as the liberalisation of rents and domestic fuel prices.

Given the ethnic mix in most of the CEE countries, political parties with programmes representing and defending ethnic minorities, such as the Party of the Hungarian Coalition in Slovakia, or those seeking to represent the titular ethnic group, such as the Slovak National Party, have achieved electoral success. The case of Slovakia suggests, however, that the more successful parties in elections, such as the Movement for a Democratic Slovakia, have not based their appeal on purely ethnic grounds, but have effectively tapped into these sentiments as part of a broader strategy (Haughton 2001). Even in Hungary, which lacks a large ethnic minority, national and ethnic concerns have not been absent from politics. Not only did the Hungarian Justice and Life Party's extreme and anti-Semitic nationalism reap electoral rewards in 1998, but the main centre-right party since the mid-1990s, Fidesz, has tried to exploit discrimination against ethnic Hungarians beyond the borders of modern-day Hungary for electoral gain, albeit with limited success (Fowler 2004).

The EU has become a prominent issue in political debate, but its significance can be overplayed. Indeed, it has rarely been a dominant or decisive issue at election time. During the process of accession, whereas parties in government tended to articulate pro-European sentiments conscious of the overriding national imperative of joining the EU, during the latter stages in particular, opposition parties such as the Civic Democratic Party in the Czech Republic and Fidesz in Hungary voiced openly more critical opinions on the EU (Fowler 2004; Hanley 2004). Much of the most fervent criticism of the EU has come from the conservative right. Parties such as the League of Polish Families have attacked the secular, liberal EU imploring Europe to return to more traditional Christian values. Such criticisms are not just directed at the EU, but are part of a wider dislike on the part of Christian parties of what they see as the lack of moral values in post-communist societies. With the differences on economic policy between major parties often now rather limited, moral issues have become increasingly important, not just in terms of rallying support to a party's cause, but also in identifying a party's values. The spat in Slovakia between the then coalition partners, the Christian Democratic Movement and the liberal New Citizens Alliance, over the issue of abortion in the summer of 2003 may, therefore, be indicative of a growing trend.

Given the limits on policy choice caused by the requirements of EU accession and the demands of international financial institutions, there has been a shift in party politics towards competition based on valence issues 'associated with competence and an ability to achieve shared objectives and goals' (Szczerbiak 2003: 731). Tapping into widely held views that established politicians are corrupt and in post primarily to line their own pockets, many new parties have emerged, often led by charismatic individuals who have not spent time in government or parliament. Parties such as the New Simeon Movement II in Bulgaria, New Era in Latvia and Res Publica in Estonia scored significant victories in elections in 2001, 2002 and 2003 respectively on the basis of vague promises centred around economic competence and clean hands (Haughton 2005b). Once in government, however, new parties have frequently struggled to deliver on vague promises and have not always proved themselves immune to corruption, often suffering the consequences at subsequent elections. (See Theme box: Democracy and Legitimacy.)

With the tasks of marketisation, democratisation, state-building and EU accession largely completed, might we expect to see a more ordered pattern of party politics? As politicians and the electorate have more experience of democratic politics, there is likely to be increased voter identification with established parties, particularly those who appeal to core constituencies. Nonetheless, the continually changing political landscape will accord opportunities for politicians and parties with new and distinctive appeals.

## KEY POINTS

- The communist past still matters in contemporary CEE politics.

- Economic reform has been central to much political debate in CEE. When economic questions fuse together with political, social and ethnic questions they can be politically very salient.

- Ethnic questions are an important source of support for political parties in CEE.

- The EU is frequently mentioned in political debate, but is rarely the decisive factor at election time.

- In recent years new parties have emerged, tapping into widespread concerns about the corruption and incompetence of politicians.

## THEME BOX

### Democracy and Legitimacy

The democracies of CEE are still relatively young. Although the institutional frameworks are largely settled and citizens have had almost two decades of democratic rule, politicians and the electorate are still undergoing a process of democratic learning. Voters' expectations were raised in the early post-communist years thanks in part to wild promises which politicians found difficult to fulfil. Equally in recent years 'new' parties with vague programmes and lacking traditional ideological bases have come to the fore, promising to be more competent and less corrupt than the political elite. Such appeals tap into widespread feelings that politicians frequently put their own (material) interests and those of their associates, before the interests of their countries, especially in areas such as privatisation policy.

Nonetheless, although some of these new parties have the characteristics of anti-system parties, few citizens question the legitimacy of the democratic system. There may be much nostalgia for the economic certainties of communism among sections of the electorate, but there is not much appetite for a return to a pre-1989 political system. EU accession was generally perceived by citizens and politicians to have been a necessary step, hence the acceptance to make certain sacrifices. But with EU membership achieved questions are being raised about what decisions need to be taken at the European level and which should remain or be returned to national governments.

# The Role of EU Conditionality

Although the collapse of the communist regimes was welcomed in West European capitals, there was some reluctance to respond to the clarion call of CEE to 'Return to Europe' and immediately open the doors to what was then still the European Community (EC). At the start of the 1990s the EC was keener to press on with the deepening of the European project, especially economic and monetary union and the creation of the European Union, rather than embarking on widening. In consequence, the countries of CEE were offered financial support through the **PHARE programme** (amounting to around €5 billion in the 1990–8 period) and a series of bilateral Europe agreements offering such incentives as favourable trading arrangements, but not the prospect of membership. Like Dickens's Oliver Twist, however, the CEE states were not content with their lot and asked for more. EU leaders responded by laying down the conditions for countries wishing to join the club in June 1993. These **Copenhagen criteria** demanded that states wishing to join are democratic, functioning according to the rule of law and respecting the rights of minorities, have functioning market economies able to cope with the competitive pressures and market forces within the Union, and are able to take on the obligations of membership.

Due to their progress in meeting the criteria, at the Luxembourg European Council in 1997, five countries from the region (the Czech Republic, Estonia, Hungary, Poland and Slovenia) were invited to begin accession talks. These states were joined two years later by Bulgaria, Latvia, Lithuania, Romania and Slovakia, who were invited to start accession negotiations at the Helsinki European Council in December 1999. Following the completion of the accession negotiations at another summit in the Danish capital in 2002, the Czech Republic, Estonia, Hungary, Latvia, Lithuania, Poland, Slovakia and Slovenia were invited to join the EU. After overcoming the final hurdle of ratifying the accession treaties, these states joined the EU on 1 May 2004. (See Theme box: The Impact of the European Union.)

To what extent can we see the European Union as a key driver of change in the region? Given the complex series of hoops through which the accession states had to jump, including the laborious task of incorporating the body of EU law known as the *acquis communautaire* into domestic law, we might conclude that the EU has been highly significant in shaping policy and institutions in the region. The reality, however, has been more complex. The EU's influence has been more significant at particular stages of the process, in certain policy areas and with regard to some countries rather than others.

Vachudova (2005) distinguishes between the 'active' and 'passive' leverage of the EU. Passive leverage, in her schema, refers to the attraction or magnetism of EU membership, especially the expected economic benefits of joining the club. Active leverage, in contrast, refers to the criteria for membership laid down at the Copenhagen summit in

## THEME BOX

### The Impact of the European Union

The EU played a significant role in the politics of the region after 1989. Three distinct phases can be identified. In the first phase, from the 1989 revolutions until the conditions for entry were laid out at the Copenhagen summit of EU leaders in June 1993, Brussels did not shape significantly policy choice in CEE. Nonetheless, many of the CEE states embarked on radical economic and political reform with aspirations to join the club. During the second phase, which lasted until entry on 1 May 2004, the EU played an important role in shaping policy throughout the region, although it had greater impact in certain policy areas than others. The entry requirements for member states included a political criterion (stating that countries had to be democracies functioning according to the rule of law and respecting minorities), an economic criterion (stating that countries had to have a functioning market economy able to withstand the competitive pressures of the single market) and the demanding legal task of transposing all EU law into domestic law. The last of these tasks in particular consumed vast amounts of time and resources. Some of the reforms demanded by the EU might have been introduced regardless of the demands of Brussels, but the desire to join the EU helped determine the speed and scale of the changes. The third stage began on 1 May 2004 when the countries of CEE turned into member states. Accorded the opportunity to shape EU policy rather than just respond to EU decisions, this new two-way relationship means that although the EU remains influential in policy-making in CEE states, the new member states now have influence over the content of EU policy.

---

1993. It is difficult to discern the impact of passive leverage before the promulgation of the Copenhagen criteria, but it seems plausible to argue that the desire to replicate western liberal democratic norms and the ideological convictions of the first post-communist governments, would have ensured the broad thrust of economic and political reform even if the EC/EU had been absent.

Once the formal applications for membership from the CEE states had begun to be submitted in March 1994, however, the EU's active leverage began to take effect. Using the 'carrots and sticks of conditionality' (Malová and Rybář 2003), the EU used a number of levers to encourage the CEE states to make the requisite changes. These levers included the power to decide when negotiations would begin and whether a state would be allowed to move on to the next stage, aid and technical assistance, policy advice and twinning projects, and the use of regular monitoring reports and public criticism. In certain spheres the EU was the dominant driving force for change. Politicians in CEE knew that incorporation of the *acquis* into domestic law, for example, was a necessary condition of entry.

In order to transpose the 80,000 pages of EU law into domestic law quickly, CEE states frequently initiated fast-tracking mechanisms bypassing the normal procedures of democratic decision-making. This raised the question of whether EU demands were actually harming rather than helping democratic consolidation (Malová and Haughton 2002: 110–12). The desire to join the EU also prompted institutional change and innovation. In order to direct and manage the accession process the Czech Republic, for instance, created a raft of new institutions including a government Council for Integration and 22 separate working groups with responsibility for specific policy areas (Jacoby 2004: 44–5). Nonetheless, in certain policy areas the EU's impact was much less significant.

In seeking to explain policy change in CEE, Wade Jacoby (2004) employs the concept of emulation. Jacoby suggested that emulation can be disaggregated into four categories depending on whether the emulation is faithful or approximate on one dimension of his typology and more or less voluntary on the other: copies, patches, templates and thresholds. The EU set minimum standards for policy and institutional changes (thresholds), for example, but many standards were rough and approximate. As CEE membership drew closer the EU required soon-to-be-member states to apply patches. Many of these new laws were passed quickly with little debate, often borrowing nakedly from the EU. Moreover, he points out that in health care and consumer protection the EU *acquis* density is low, providing much more scope for choosing or ignoring 'prevailing Western models' (Jacoby 2004: 16), whereas in agriculture and regional development, not least thanks to the financial incentives for faithful emulation, there was replication of EU models.

Given the conditions laid down at Copenhagen and the politically sensitive position of ethnic minorities in many CEE states, minority policy was closely monitored. There are some clear examples of EU pressure making a difference. In Estonia, for example, a 1993 law providing for the complete transition to Estonian-language instruction in schools by 2000 was amended to allow ethnic Russians to continue being taught indefinitely in their own mother tongue (Smith 2003). Nevertheless, throughout the region there has been a reluctance to counter all aspects of discrimination on ethnic grounds, rather than just respond to specific EU demands. Moreover, there is a noticeable gap between the declared policies and implementation. Minority policy may have changed *de jure*, but not *de facto*. Ethnic Roma (gypsies), for instance, have been the subject of frequent EU reports. While much formal discrimination towards the Roma has been removed, there is still widespread prejudice and discrimination on the ground.

Slovakia arguably provides a clear example of when the EU was highly influential and when largely ineffectual in shaping the domestic policies of a CEE state with aspirations to join (Haughton 2005a: 122–31). Despite a series of *démarches* (strong diplomatic notes) and the exclusion of the country

from the first group of CEE states to begin accession negotiations for failing to meet the political criterion, the EU had very little impact on the government of the day led by Vladimír Mečiar. Compliance with the Copenhagen criteria would have placed constraints on the policies and functioning of the administration which the Slovak prime minister and his coalition allies were not prepared to accept. In stark contrast, the 1998–2002 Slovak government led by Mikuláš Dzurinda placed EU entry at the top of its agenda (Bilčík 2001). It was desperate to catch up with its neighbours and at times resembled 'an obedient dog faithfully following its master's instructions' (Malová and Haughton 2006: 326–7). Even during the first Dzurinda-led government, however, the impact of the EU can be overemphasised. Domestic politics still mattered. Some changes such the Law on the Use of Minority Languages in July 1999 and the appointment of a deputy prime minister for human rights and minority affairs, which some authors (e.g. Pridham 2002) see as a result of EU pressure, however, may have been driven more by domestic factors such as the inclusion of the ethnic Hungarian party (SMK) in the government.

---

### KEY POINTS

- From the early 1990s onwards the states of CEE expressed their desire to join the EU.

- The EU placed enormous demands on the accession states of CEE, demanding political, economic and legal changes.

- The EU's influence was more significant at particular times and in certain policy areas than in others. Moreover, the EU was influential only when the domestic elite was willing to make changes.

- The EU was often significant in changing official stated policy, especially with regard to minority policy, but was less effective in ensuring effective implementation.

# The Impact of EU Membership

The promotion of the CEE countries from accession to member states of the EU has created much more room for manoeuvre. They are no longer objects of EU decision-making, but rather have become political subjects with the ability to shape EU policy from the inside.

There are, however, clear limitations on the impact the new member states can have; and, indeed, there are limits to any member state's power in a union of 25. Although they developed institutional structures to manage the process of accession, these were often concentrated in the hands of a few officials invariably in the foreign ministry. Membership of the EU, however, requires civil servants (and their ministers) in other ministries such as agriculture and the interior not only to be fully conversant with EU laws, but also able to articulate policy positions at Council of Ministers' meetings. Hampered not least by their size and their lack of experience in dealing with European institutions many of the new member states have not (yet) become as effective at shaping policy as some of the more established member states. The exception is foreign policy, however, where arguably foreign ministry officials' intimate knowledge of the workings of Brussels has helped influence policy.

In a similar vein to the **Barcelona Process** launched soon after the accession of Spain and Portugal and Finland's **Northern Dimension Initiative**, the new member states have helped shift the focus of the EU's foreign policy towards their neighbouring states. After a decade in which Slovenia was desperate to distance itself from other former Yugoslav states, for example, with EU membership achieved it has been prominent in trying to turn more of the EU's attention towards the countries of the western Balkans. Slovene officials have highlighted their expertise in the region reminding their counterparts from other EU member states that, having been part of Yugoslavia, Slovenes are best placed of all

member states to understand the region and shape policy. Limited institutional capacity (not least due to its size), however, played a part in restricting Slovenia's impact. Holding the chair of the **Organization for Security and Cooperation in Europe** (OSCE) in 2005 meant valuable time and resources (especially staff) which could have been used to push the case for the western Balkans were consumed dealing with OSCE business in places such as Uzbekistan.

Perhaps the best example of a new member state from CEE attempting to set the agenda has been Poland's policy towards Ukraine. Although Poland had been a strong advocate of closer economic and political ties with Ukraine before joining the EU (Wolczuk and Wolczuk 2002), the **Orange Revolution** in December 2004 and Poland's new status as a member state gave Poland greater clout and ensured Ukraine was high on the agenda. It is still too soon, however, to determine whether these states have really changed the substance of policy rather than just the focus.

The new CEE member states are arguably having more impact in the economic sphere, less because of policy proposals articulated at the European level and more because of policy packages at the domestic level. Driven by an ideological belief in the free market and armed with a set of policy prescriptions inspired by the World Bank model, the Slovak government elected in 2002, for instance, implemented a series of radical reforms in healthcare, pensions and fiscal policy, including the much vaunted 19 per cent flat-rate tax. This neo-liberal agenda provoked criticism in some of the more established member states of the EU such as France and Germany who were concerned about the impact such policies may have on the future of the European social model. They feared that countries like Slovakia might act as a 'trojan horse' for the Americanisation or Anglo-Americanisation of

European economic and social policy. Slovakia's fiscal policy under the 2002–6 government, for instance, in combination with flat-tax regimes introduced elsewhere such as in Estonia, played a role in the lowering of corporate tax rates in both Germany and Austria, and in provoking debates and policy changes in Greece, the Czech Republic and Romania. Nonetheless, the Slovak government was keen to stress it was a good European. Its tax, health, welfare, labour market and pension reforms were all portrayed as solutions to the significant structural problems faced by all European countries (Malová and Haughton 2006 forthcoming). The government claimed, therefore, that the Slovak model could be seen to be a means of achieving the goal agreed at the Lisbon European Council in 2000 of making the EU the most dynamic, knowledge-based economy in the world.

The new member states still have treaty obligations to fulfil, most notably joining **Schengen** and the single currency, nevertheless membership

has transformed the relationship between the more established member states and those from CEE. For so long the largely obedient new dogs keen to impress, the young pups of CEE are now teaching the old dogs some new tricks.

---

**KEY POINTS**

- The shift from the status of accession state to member state has meant that the countries of CEE are now not just objects, but subjects of EU decision-making.

- The new member states from CEE have been active in trying to alter the EU's foreign policy towards the East.

- CEE may be having a greater impact in the sphere of economics. The neo-liberal policy packages introduced in some CEE countries have provoked changes in Western Europe.

- The countries of CEE still face the tasks of joining the euro and the Schengen zone.

---

# Conclusion: Continued Commonality or Increasing Diversity?

This chapter has argued that the states of Central and Eastern Europe have undergone significant changes since 1989. Not only did they democratise their political systems and create market economies, but many of the countries were not even states in 1989, merely constituent parts of multiethnic federations. In addition, these states undertook the arduous task of meeting the requirements laid down for entry into the European Union. Combined with four decades of communist rule this quadruple challenge had led to many commonalities in the region, but are we likely to see increasing diversity throughout the region in the coming years?

All of the states face the challenge of competing in the global marketplace. With the comparative

advantages of lower labour costs gradually being eroded within Europe and facing the emergent economic powerhouses of India and China, might we see the forces of globalisation encourage a race to the bottom? Might all CEE states have to adopt the type of neo-liberal package enacted in Slovakia? As Hay's (2006) analysis of Western Europe has shown, the argument that globalisation will automatically lead to welfare retrenchment and convergence is 'empirically suspect'. He shows that although common trajectories could be identified, changes to the social models in Western Europe tended to be implemented with varying degrees of enthusiasm and speed resulting in different outcomes. In other words, his analysis leaves space for domestic politics to matter. It seems plausible to suggest that we will see a replication in CEE. While broad patterns will be identifiable across the region, there will be significant variations from country to country. Not all the politicians in Slovakia, let alone all the politicians in CEE, are queuing up to implement the Slovak model. Global and regional pressures place limits on change, but they also create frameworks of opportunity. Different governments of different political colours in different countries will implement different policies. (See Theme box: The Impact of Globalisation.)

The EU has played a significant role in shaping the politics of the region and will continue to do so. Membership of the EU fosters aspects of convergence. Political parties from CEE, for example, are now integrated into European groupings helping to foster closer ties and policy transfer (Paterson and Sloam 2005). More significantly, in certain policy domains the EU shapes many aspects of policy. If the EU continues to develop its policies in current areas and extend into new policy areas there will, by extension, be a degree of further convergence. Both of these points, however, highlight pan-European rather than CEE trends. Indeed in many respects in the coming years CEE will reflect the diversity and commonality of Europe as a whole. Nonetheless, regional identity and the past will continue to matter. The noticeably less friendly attitude towards Russia held by the Baltic states and Poland as opposed to the stance of France and Germany, for example, is intimately linked to the communist past. Moreover, regional identities such as the Nordic Bloc have not dissolved as a result of Danish, Swedish and Finnish accession to the EU. Nevertheless, it seems likely that Central and Eastern Europe will rarely act as a bloc within the EU as the common experiences and challenges of communism and post-communism slip further into the past. The states of CEE will form alliances with other states due to national interest calculations which are based on economic, political, geographic and/or strategic grounds. In short, the countries of Central and Eastern Europe look set to act like most other member states of the European Union.

## THEME BOX

### The Impact of Globalisation

There has been a transition from one kind of globalisation, often not seen as such, to another. Prior to 1989 the states of CEE were part of a different kind of international system. The countries of Central and Eastern Europe (to greater or lesser extents) had good links with other communist regimes across the globe in Africa, Latin America and Asia, which facilitated transcontinental and interregional flows. Indeed, as a universalist ideology communism encouraged replication and uniformity, the very essence of what is often described as globalisation. The exit of CEE states from communism, therefore, ironically was a retreat from a different type of globalisation.

The policy-making capacity and autonomy of the nation state in CEE have diminished in recent years. Although the need to please international financial institutions and encourage investment has been a central concern of finance ministers, the major cause of this decline is accession to, and now membership of, the European Union. Membership, however, accords states more room to manoeuvre. Indeed, in recent years some of the new member states from CEE have been implementing radical economic packages. Much of the inspiration and justification for these policies comes from the need to compete in the global marketplace suggesting clear evidence of globalisation. But the fact that not all of the CEE states have adopted such economic packages, however, suggests such global demands merely provide broad frameworks within which politicians in CEE can make different decisions. Nonetheless, in the context of heightened competition associated generally with globalisation, CEE states have been seen as potential Trojan horses for a neo-liberalisation of Europe.

## QUESTIONS

1. What in your opinion is the difference between Western, Central and Eastern Europe? How meaningful are these differences after 1 May 2004?

2. How useful are the 'transitology' theories derived from the democratisation processes in Latin America and Southern Europe in explaining the post-communist transformations in Central and Eastern Europe?

3. Who won and who lost from the process of economic reform in CEE in the 1990s?

4. What role does the communist past play in the contemporary politics of CEE?

5. What factors have structured party competition in CEE since 1989?

6. How influential has the EU been in shaping policy in CEE in the past decade?

7. What has been the impact of the new member states from CEE on the European Union?

## FURTHER READING

■ **Jacoby W. (2004),** *The Enlargement of the European Union and NATO: Ordering from the Menu in Central Europe,* **Cambridge, Cambridge University Press.** An excellent and insightful account into the interaction between the EU and domestic politics.

■ **Lewis, P. (2000),** *Political Parties in Post-communist Eastern Europe,* **London, Routledge.** A well written survey of the first decade of party politics in CEE.

■ **Millard, F. (2004),** *Elections, Parties, and Representation in Post-communist Europe,* **Basingstoke, Palgrave Macmillan.** This detailed analysis of post-communist party politics contains lots of useful empirical material.

■ **Sadurski W.** *et al.* **(eds) (2006),** *Après Enlargement: Taking Stock of the Immediate Legal and Political Responses to the Accession of Central and Eastern European States to the EU,* **Florence, Robert Schuman Center.** A useful collection of essays which reflect on the first year of developments following 1 May 2004.

■ **Vachudova M. (2005),** *Europe Undivided: Democracy, Leverage, and Integration After Communism,* **Oxford, Oxford University Press.** An excellent analysis and overview of political developments in CEE combined with a detailed exploration of the role played by the EU.

■ **White S.** *et al* **(eds) (2003),** *Developments in Central and East European Politics 3,* **Basingtoke, Palgrave.** The best available textbook on the politics of the region. A fourth edition should be published in 2007/8.

## IMPORTANT WEBSITES

● **www.ssees.ac.uk/general.htm** Based at the School of Slavonic and East European Studies in London this site provides useful links for students studying Central and Eastern Europe.

● **www.sussex.ac.uk/sei/1-4-2.html** The European Parties Elections and Referendum Network co-convened by Aleks Szczerbiak and Paul Taggart contains links to many useful working papers and election briefs.

● **http://euobserver.com/** This site is a generally reliable and informative place for daily news from across the European continent.

● **www.euractiv.com/** A useful independent media portal with generally good coverage of European politics.

 **Visit the Online Resource Centre that accompanies this book for lots of useful additional material, including an interactive map of Europe. www.oxfordtextbooks.co.uk/orc/hay_menon/**

# PART 2

# Political Dynamics in Contemporary Europe

# 10 The European Integration Process

## DESMOND DINAN

### Chapter Contents

- Introduction
- Why European Integration?
- From ECSC to EEC
- Consolidating the Community
- Surviving the 1970s
- The Single Market and Monetary Union
- Public Unease and Political Overreach
- Conclusion

### Reader's Guide

This chapter tells the story of European integration. It begins by asking why Western European countries chose to integrate after the Second World War and goes on to show how, having decided to do so for various political and economic reasons, they established the European Coal and Steel Community (ECSC) and later the European Economic Community (EEC). The next sections demonstrate the durability of European integration in the 1960s, when faced with the challenge of French President Charles de Gaulle, and the 1970s, when faced with the consequences of the global economic downturn. The chapter goes on to examine the acceleration of European integration in the late 1980s and early 1990s, thanks to a consensus among member states on the need to pull together rather than apart in the face of intense global competition. The final section explores the roots and impact of growing public unease with the European integration process, culminating in the collapse of the proposed Constitutional Treaty in 2005.

DESMOND DINAN

# Introduction

European integration—the process by which countries act collectively through the institutions of the European Union (EU) in order to promote prosperity and strengthen security—began in the immediate aftermath of the Second World War in response to specific national and international challenges. It continues today in a radically altered international environment. Over the years, the EU—including the original European Communities—enlarged from six to 27 member states and deepened its policy remit from trade and agriculture to most other economic areas, plus cooperation on foreign policy, security, and justice and home affairs. (See Background box 10.1 and Table 10.1.)

The European integration process involves day-to-day interaction among national and EU institutions and among the EU institutions themselves. By generating a body of case law, the European Court of Justice plays an essential part in the process. Looked at more broadly and in historical context, European integration has advanced through a combination of political calculation, individual initiative and pure chance. National governments have pursued European integration because it has been in their interests to do so. Officials and politicians have played a prominent role, motivated occasionally by devotion to the ideal of European unity but usually by calculations of national and institutional advantage. Domestic circumstances have sometimes favoured further integration; at other times the political and economic situation in certain member states or throughout the EU has been uncongenial to the integration process.

Widening (of EU membership) and deepening (of EU policy scope) have come about as a result of intergovernmental conferences, the mechanism by which member states negotiate and reach agreement on accession treaties and reforms of the founding treaties establishing the EEC (1957) and the EU (1992). Apart from **enlargement**, the main intergovernmental conferences took place in 1985–6 and 1990–1. In the first case, member states sought to complete the single market programme; in the second, to achieve Economic and Monetary Union (EMU) and strengthen cooperation in the areas of foreign policy and justice and home affairs. The results were the Single European Act (1986) and the Maastricht Treaty (1992). Later intergovernmental conferences aimed not primarily to deepen the EU's policy scope but to increase its **legitimacy**, accountability and efficiency. Such efforts culminated in the Constitutional Treaty of 2004, which was put on hold following its rejection in referenda in France and the Netherlands in spring 2005. Growing public disenchantment with the EU, not least because of possible Turkish accession (however distant), is one of the most striking characteristics of the integration process today.

### KEY POINTS

- What is now the EU has expanded over the years to include 27 member states (with more wanting to join) and almost every aspect of public policy.

- The EU exists because its member states believe their national interests are best served by acting collectively through EU institutions to achieve key socio-economic objectives.

- Intergovernmental conferences are the main means through which the European integration process has advanced.

- Growing public unease is a major factor inhibiting the integration process today.

## BACKGROUND BOX 10.1

### The Ever-deeper Union

| | |
|---|---|
| 1951 | Treaty of Paris establishes the European Coal and Steel Community |
| 1957 | Treaties of Rome establish the European Economic Community and the European Atomic Energy Community |
| 1962 | Launch of the Common Agricultural Policy |
| 1968 | Completion of the customs union |
| 1970 | Launch of European Political Cooperation (foreign policy coordination) |
| 1975 | Launch of the European Council |
| 1979 | Launch of the European Monetary System |
| 1986 | The Single European Act launches the single market programme and extends Community competence in the fields of environmental policy, economic and social cohesion, research and technology policy and social policy |
| 1989 | Extension of Commission responsibility for competition policy |
| 1992 | The Maastricht Treaty on European Union sets the EU on the road to Economic and Monetary Union, transforms European Political Cooperation into the Common Foreign and Security Policy, and launches intergovernmental cooperation on justice and home affairs |
| 1997 | The Treaty of Amsterdam extends Community competence over certain aspects of justice and home affairs and sets a target date for completion of 'an area of freedom, security and justice' |
| 1999 | Launch of a common monetary policy and a single currency (the euro) |
| 2001 | The Nice Treaty reforms the EU's institutions and decision-making procedures |
| 2003 | The Convention on the Future of Europe submits a draft Constitutional Treaty |
| 2004 | National leaders agree on the Constitutional Treaty, which is put on hold following French and Dutch voters' rejection of it in 2005 |

*Source*: Dinan (2005: 3)

### Table 10.1 The Ever-wider Union

| Original member states | First enlargement (1973) | Second enlargement (1981) | Third enlargement (1986) | Fourth enlargement (1995) | Fifth enlargement (2004) | Sixth enlargement (2007) |
|---|---|---|---|---|---|---|
| Belgium | Britain | Greece | Portugal | Austria | Cyprus | Bulgaria |
| France | Denmark | | Spain | Finland | Czech Republic | Romania |
| Germany | Ireland | | | Sweden | Estonia | |
| Italy | | | | | Hungary | |
| Luxembourg | | | | | Latvia | |
| Netherlands | | | | | Lithuania | |
| | | | | | Malta | |
| | | | | | Poland | |
| | | | | | Slovakia | |
| | | | | | Slovenia | |

*Source*: Dinan (2005: 4)

# Why European Integration?

There was nothing inevitable about European integration after the Second World War. Despite strong popular and political support for closer international cooperation and new transnational arrangements in the aftermath of the war and the disastrous inter-war period, national governments were reluctant to cede any **sovereignty** to **supranational** institutions. The outcome of the Hague Congress in May 1948 proves the point. Swept up in a wave of enthusiasm for the vague notion of European union, over 600 leading European politicians met in The Hague to discuss the way forward. They ranged from ardent federalists, like the Italian Altiero Spinelli, to traditional nationalists, like former British Prime Minister Winston Churchill. Much to the disappointment of Spinelli, the majority of delegates were happy to establish not a new supranational entity, but an international organisation—the Council of Europe—based on conventional intergovernmental cooperation.

## The German problem

It was the urgent need to resolve the German problem that led within the next two years to the dramatic French proposal to establish a supranational coal and steel community and thereby institutionalise European integration. Germany was divided at the end of the war into four zones of occupation (US, British, French and Soviet). With the onset of the Cold War, the Soviets consolidated communist control in their zone and broke off contact with the Western zones. The Americans, in turn, wanted to combine the Western zones into a new West German state, whose economic revival the USA deemed essential for the prosperity and security of Western Europe as a whole. Indeed, the Marshall Plan for European recovery was predicated on full West German participation and greatly spurred Germany's economic recovery.

That terrified the French. Mindful of the two world wars and the Franco-Prussian war before that, France preferred to keep Germany down. France also wanted to exploit Germany's weakness by modernising its own steel industry, using high-grade coking coal from the occupied Ruhr. As American pressure intensified for a reversal of policy towards Germany, France abandoned its punitive approach and embraced the seemingly revolutionary idea of a common market in coal and steel under the auspices of a supranational High Authority, the forerunner of the European Commission.

To be more precise, French Foreign Minister Robert Schuman, at the urging of Jean Monnet, a senior civil servant, convinced a reluctant French government to endorse what became known as the Schuman Plan for the ECSC. A Christian Democrat from the disputed borderland of Lorraine, Schuman was strongly predisposed to make a conciliatory gesture towards Germany, especially a Germany led by Konrad Adenauer, another Christian Democrat from the border region. Monnet had no political affiliation or religious conviction, but devoutly believed that European integration was the most effective means of promoting economic security and political stability. Under other circumstances, Monnet and Schuman might not have had an opportunity to advance their ideas. Similarly, had Schuman not been part of a governing coalition that formed around other issues, he might never have succeeded in convincing a sceptical French parliament to ratify the treaty establishing the ECSC.

## The Schuman Plan

The Schuman Plan called on the countries of Western Europe to participate in the proposed ECSC. Adenauer was delighted to do so. Not only would he win French acquiescence in Germany's economic recovery, but also the ECSC would set Germany on the road to international rehabilitation and respectability. Alcide de Gasperi, Italy's prime minister, enthusiastically joined in as well in order to tie Italy into Western Europe as a means of undermining domestic support for communism. The small Benelux countries—Belgium, Netherlands and Luxembourg—had little choice economically but to throw in their lot with France and Germany. Unwilling to accept the principle of shared sovereignty, Britain remained aloof, as did the Scandinavian countries. Spain, an international pariah under the fascist rule of General Francisco Franco, was not invited to join.

The treaty called for the High Authority to regulate the coal and steel industries of the participating countries. In an early demonstration of the national governments' determination to retain as much control as possible, the ECSC's institutional architecture included also a Council of Ministers, against the wishes of Monnet, who wanted the High Authority to reign supreme. In addition, the ECSC included an Assembly of delegated national parliamentarians and a Court of Justice to adjudicate disputes among member states and among the institutions.

The ECSC was an unglamorous organisation that enjoyed only mixed economic success. Nevertheless it was an undoubted political success. By resolving the German question it amounted to a functional peace settlement for post-war Western Europe. By institutionalising supranationalism it set a precedent and provided a framework for future integrative initiatives. Nevertheless there was no spillover from the ECSC to the EEC, as early theorists of European integration posited there would be. Instead, the EEC—the precursor of the EU—emerged in response to pressure for accelerated trade liberalisation in the late 1950s. It built on the political and institutional, but not the economic, foundations of the ECSC.

---

**KEY POINTS**

- European integration was not inevitable after the Second World War.

- Public and political opinion sympathised with the idea of 'European' union but national governments were reluctant to share sovereignty.

- France eventually launched a bold supranational initiative in response to US pressure to accommodate Germany's economic and political revival.

- The ensuing ECSC amounted to a peace settlement for Europe; its significance was more political than economic.

---

# From ECSC to EEC

The launch of the ECSC in 1952 and the EEC in 1958 were punctuated by the failure of another supranational initiative, the European Defence Community (EDC), in 1954. Just as the ECSC was a desperate French response to the apparent inevitability of Germany's economic revival, the EDC was a similar French response to intense US pressure for German rearmament. Overstretched militarily after the outbreak of the Koran War, the USA wanted Germany to contribute to the defence of Western Europe. The prospect of German rearmament so soon after the end of the war understandably alarmed the French. While appreciating French concerns, Adenauer was eager to rearm, seeing it as a further step towards regaining full German sovereignty and as a means of strengthening the country's security.

The French response came in the form of the Pleven Plan for the EDC, which was analogous to the Schuman Plan for the ECSC. Monnet was the author of both initiatives. The Pleven Plan was different in one fundamental respect, however. Although it called for the pooling of military units from the participating countries under a supranational authority, it would not allow Germany to raise an army of its own. Adenauer chafed under that restriction and eventually won some changes to the original proposal. After initial scepticism, the USA supported the Pleven Plan wholeheartedly.

The six members of the ECSC signed a treaty establishing the EDC in May 1952. They also empowered a special assembly (drawn from the assembly of the ECSC) to draft a treaty establishing the European Political Community, an umbrella organisation for the other communities, with strong federal features. However, the failure of the French parliament to ratify the EDC treaty, following a bitter domestic debate, meant that the organisation never came into being and also that the proposed European Political Community failed to materialise. France was still fearful of German rearmament, which seemed less urgent in any case following the end of the Korean War and the death of Soviet leader Josef Stalin in March 1953. But the genie of German rearmament could not be put back in the bottle. France eventually went along with a British initiative to incorporate a new German army into the intergovernmental Western European Union, which in turn made it possible for Germany to join NATO in 1955.

## Beyond the EDC

The failure of the EDC left a legacy of bitterness between France and Germany and was a setback for supranationalism. Monnet, who resigned as president of the High Authority in August 1954, tried to get the ball rolling again with a proposal for a European Atomic Energy Community (Euratom) along the lines of the ECSC, but only France was interested in atomic energy cooperation. The Dutch revived the idea of a customs union that had originally been part of the proposed European Political Community, which disappeared with the collapse of the EDC in August 1954.

As a small, open economy, the Netherlands wanted to accelerate trade liberalisation through the elimination of tariffs and quotas among its principal trading partners. Key French politicians and officials wanted to pursue the Dutch proposal, but needed to overcome the opposition of vested business interests and recalcitrant colleagues. They did so by linking the success of the Euratom and EEC proposals, and by attaching to the proposed customs union provisions for a common agricultural policy and preferential arrangements for current and former colonies. German politicians and officials were also divided on the proposals, not wanting anything to do with Euratom and, in some cases, not wanting the EEC either. It took Adenauer's considerable powers of persuasion to convince the German government and parliament that Euratom and the EEC were worth pursuing primarily for the sake of Franco-German accord.

Negotiations for the two new communities were every bit as contentious as the negotiations earlier in the decade for the ECSC. There was little talk or thought of 'building Europe' in the intergovernmental conference leading to the Rome treaties in March 1957. Instead, national officials fought tenaciously for advantage, whether in the organisational design or the policy remit of the new Communities. Wrapped in the rhetoric of Franco-German reconciliation and 'ever closer union', the Rome treaties provided a regional framework for the pursuit of national economic interests in an increasingly competitive, interdependent world.

**KEY POINTS**

- Having proposed the EDC, France failed to ratify the treaty establishing the new organisation because of fear of German rearmament.

- The failure of the EDC symbolised a setback for European integration and spurred Jean Monnet to propose Euratom, another supranational organisation.

- A separate Dutch proposal for the EEC met a mixed response in France.

- French supporters of the EEC prevailed by linking the customs union—the core of the EEC—with provisions for a common agricultural

policy and concessions for current and former colonies.

- Many German politicians and officials were lukewarm about the proposed EEC and strongly opposed Euratom.

- Adenauer overcame their opposition by linking the EEC and Euratom to the overarching foreign policy goal of Franco-German rapprochement.

- Following intense intergovernmental negotiations, the same six members of the ECSC signed the Rome treaties establishing the EEC and Euratom in March 1957.

# Consolidating the Community

The EEC got off to a rocky start. Even before it came into being in January 1958, the British tried to undermine it by floating a proposal for a wider European free trade area, into which the EEC would be subsumed. At the same time, France was roiled by the political crisis surrounding the collapse of the Fourth Republic. General Charles de Gaulle, who returned to power in 1958 and launched the new Fifth Republic, had opposed the Rome treaties. Would he now renounce them and scrap the EEC?

To everyone's surprise, de Gaulle facilitated the launch of the EEC by blocking Britain's proposal for a wider free trade area, putting France on a sound financial footing, and pressing ahead with the phased introduction of the customs union. De Gaulle claimed that he was merely respecting an international agreement which the previous government had entered into. In fact, he appreciated the economic potential of the EEC for France in terms of boosting industrial competitiveness and, especially, possibly subsidising French farmers through the putative Common Agricultural Policy (CAP) rather than the overstretched French exchequer. De Gaulle doggedly pursued the construction of

the CAP, even threatening to scuttle the customs union unless the CAP came into existence in the early 1960s.

Nevertheless de Gaulle did not embrace supranationalism. In particular, he opposed the political ambition of the European Commission, whose president, Walter Hallstein, was an avowed federalist. He also objected to the introduction of qualified majority voting, an instrument of supranational decision-making, which, under the terms of the treaty, was supposed to come into effect in January 1966. De Gaulle seized upon the Commission's proposals for a permanent funding mechanism for the CAP—proposals that would have strengthened the power of the Commission and the European Parliament—to withdraw French representation from the Council of Ministers in June 1965, thereby sparking the so-called empty-chair crisis.

At issue were not only the proposals themselves but also the planned move to greater use of qualified majority voting. Thus, de Gaulle made it clear that he would not authorise France's representatives to take their seats again unless the other member states agreed to abandon qualified majority voting. The crisis ended in January with an ambiguous agreement, the so-called Luxembourg Compromise, whereby the governments decided that they would not take a vote in the Council if one of them claimed that a 'very important' national interest was at stake. Because a very important interest was impossible to determine in any objective way, the Luxembourg Compromise gave national governments—not only the French government—a pretext to block voting in the Council. As a result, Council decision-making became subject to unanimity, a notoriously arduous and inefficient devise.

De Gaulle's legacy went beyond the empty-chair crisis. He was equally notorious for blocking Britain's bid for EEC membership. The fact that Britain applied to join in 1961, having recently tried to thwart the construction of the Community, is quite extraordinary. Britain's U-turn was due to a realisation that the EEC was there to stay and that the cost of exclusion, in terms of barriers to British exports, was high. Like de Gaulle, the British were not enamoured of supranationalism and viewed the EEC exclusively in economic terms. That was not enough to endear them to the French president, however. Concerned about Britain's 'special relationship' with the USA and striving to distance Europe strategically from Washington, de Gaulle vetoed Britain's application first in 1963 and again in 1967.

De Gaulle looked to Germany, not Britain, for partnership in Europe. Surprisingly, the frosty French general struck up a warm relationship with Adenauer, the reserved German chancellor. Following the defeat, at Dutch hands, of his proposal

for a political association of EEC states based on intergovernmental cooperation and implicit French leadership (the Fouchet Plan), de Gaulle signed a bilateral treaty with Adenauer (the Elysée Treaty), which he hoped would form the foundation for a wider European organisation (excluding the British) into which the EEC could be folded. Instead, the Elysée Treaty institutionalised the Franco-German motor, which became the driving force of European integration long after both Adenauer and de Gaulle had left the political scene.

## KEY POINTS

- Political crisis in France and de Gaulle's return to power did not auger well for the success of the fledgling EEC.

- De Gaulle confounded his critics and supported the EEC for compelling economic reasons (industrial modernisation and agricultural support).

- De Gaulle triggered a major constitutional crisis in the EEC by resisting the introduction of qualified majority voting; the ensuing Luxembourg Compromise impeded effective decision-making for the next two decades.

- De Gaulle twice blocked Britain's bid for EEC membership, for both strategic and economic reasons.

- De Gaulle's most positive and enduring legacy to the EEC may be the Elysée Treaty, which institutionalised the Franco-German motor, a driving force of European integration in the decades ahead.

# Surviving the 1970s

The EEC accomplished some major objectives in the 1960s, notably implementation of the customs union, the beginning of a common trade policy and the consolidation of the CAP. The CAP still needed a permanent funding mechanism. That came about

as part of the decision by national leaders, reached at The Hague summit in December 1969 soon after de Gaulle's departure, to complete the first phase of integration. 'Completion' would complement 'deepening' and 'enlargement', the other elements of the so-called spirit of The Hague. Deepening meant cooperating more closely on foreign-policy issues and, especially, embarking on the road to EMU, for which national leaders later agreed to a target date of 1980. Enlargement meant admitting Britain, and with it Denmark, Ireland, and Norway (although a majority of Norwegians subsequently voted against membership).

## British accession and renegotiation

National governments soon agreed to fund the CAP through the Community's 'own resources' (monies that accrued to the EEC as a result of its common policies, such as customs duties). That cleared the way for the accession negotiations with the candidate countries, which ended in 1972. British Prime Minister Edward Heath, a strong supporter of membership, was happy to accept the EEC's entry terms, including a disproportionately high contribution from Britain to the Community budget. Together with the relatively low level of financial transfers that would come to Britain under the CAP (Britain had relatively few farmers), the financial aspects of Britain's membership terms were grossly inequitable.

Harold Wilson, the Labour Party leader who defeated Heath soon after Britain joined the EEC, called for a renegotiation of Britain's membership terms and a national referendum on the outcome. The ensuing renegotiation was largely cosmetic, Wilson being more interested in appeasing critics of EEC membership within the Labour Party than in reaching an equitable solution. A majority endorsed the results of the renegotiation in the 1975 referendum, the first nationwide referendum ever in British history. That should have been the end of the matter, but dissatisfaction in Britain with EEC membership grew in the years ahead.

The reason, in part, was disappointment with Britain's economic performance, which had more to do with the adverse international situation than with the fact of EEC membership. The festering budgetary question was a further source of discontent,

which Margaret Thatcher seized upon as soon as she became prime minister in 1979. Thatcher's strident demands to 'get Britain's money back' dominated EEC summits for the next five years, overshadowing other business. Resolution of the 'British budgetary question' in June 1984 removed a persistent sore in Britain's relations with the EEC and in the EEC's dealings with Britain. But it did not end Britain's wariness of Brussels, which remained entrenched and seemingly intractable.

## A mixed record

Apart from the disappointing experience (for both sides) of British membership, the EEC had a difficult time from the mid-1970s to the mid-1980s. The spirit of The Hague soon gave way to the abandonment of EMU, a goal that became increasingly illusory in the recessionary 1970s. As Europe reeled from the impact of the 1974 oil crisis and ensuing stagflation, member states diverged economically and built up regulatory and other non-tariff barriers against each other's imports. Nevertheless the picture was not entirely gloomy: the European Court of Justice managed to generate an impressive body of case law; a regional policy came into being (partly to compensate Britain for its poor return on the CAP); member states negotiated an ambitious trade and aid agreement (the Lomé Convention) with a large group of former colonies; national leaders agreed to coordinate monetary policy within the European Monetary System; and the first direct elections to the European Parliament took place in 1979.

Such progress could not disguise the fact that the EEC was floundering in the early 1980s. Intense competition from Japan and the Asian Tigers, as well as from the USA, required an urgent European response. Member states would have to abandon their beggar-thy-neighbour policies and adopt a common approach to the challenge of incipient **globalisation**. Pushed by Thatcher, who was also trying to reform the British economy through privatisation and deregulation, EU leaders agreed to go back to the future and bring about a single European market by fulfilling their obligations under the Rome Treaty. A dramatic U-turn by French President François Mitterrand, who dropped his doctrinaire socialist agenda in the face of mounting pressure on the franc, demonstrated the emerging consensus in Europe on the importance of market integration.

---

**KEY POINTS**

- Completion of the customs union and consolidation of the CAP were major achievements for the EEC in the 1960s.

- Relieved by de Gaulle's departure, national leaders agreed in December 1969 to a programme for 'deepening, completion, [and] enlargement' of the EEC.

- Enlargement took place in January 1973, but Britain never overcame its dissatisfaction with the EEC, despite the renegotiation of its membership terms and the successful outcome of the referendum.

- Only when Thatcher resolved the British budgetary question in June 1984 was the EEC able to address the pressing problem of its declining global competitiveness.

- The period from the mid-1970s to the mid-1980s nevertheless included a number of institutional and policy achievements for the EEC.

---

# The Single Market and Monetary Union

The Single European Act (SEA) of 1986 was the first major reform of the treaty establishing the EEC. It came about in response to the consensus among member states on the need to facilitate the free movement of goods, services, capital and people. Although there was consensus on the goal of market integration, member states differed over how best to bring it about. Thatcher, an ardent advocate of the single market programme, doubted the need for treaty reform. In her view, the existing decision-making machinery was adequate to bring the single market into being. Most other national leaders disagreed. Having seen the pernicious impact of the Luxembourg Compromise, they argued that a new treaty commitment to using qualified majority voting was necessary to implement the programme. Thatcher reluctantly went along with them, thereby paving the way for an Intergovernmental Conference (IGC).

A Commission white paper on the single market was one of the key documents for national governments to consider in the IGC. A report by a committee of national representatives (the Dooge Committee), which called for wide-ranging institutional reform, was another. Jacques Delors, who became Commission president in January 1985, skilfully advanced an integrationist agenda in the IGC. Delors was the right man in the right place at the right time: a former French finance minister with a grasp of detail who invigorated the Commission with his forceful personality and who assumed office just as national governments were coming round to the idea that economic integration had to be intensified.

The SEA, which came out of the IGC, called for completion of the single market by the end of 1992 and provided for the use of qualified majority voting for a majority of the approximately 300 legislative measures necessary to achieve that goal. It also committed member states to strengthening regional or **cohesion** policy through a massive increase in the amount of money allocated to the structural funds (money for infrastructural development in the Community's poor, mostly peripheral parts). The precise allocation for cohesion policy necessitated a new round of intergovernmental negotiations that culminated in agreement on the so-called Delors I budgetary package for the period 1988–92. Intense pressure from the Commission allied with a coalition of poorer countries—Ireland and the three new Mediterranean members (Greece, Portugal and Spain)—accounted for the huge increase in structural funding. Without such an agreement, the poorer member states could have blocked implementation of the single market programme.

## One market: one money

Delors saw the single market programme not as an end in itself but as a means towards the ultimate goal of EMU. No sooner had the SEA been ratified than he began to agitate for EMU, arguing that 'one market' necessitated 'one money'. Together with his open advocacy of **federalism**, that put Delors on a collision course with Thatcher. The battle between them was fought out in a number of highly publicised speeches in 1988 and 1989, with Delors promoting deeper economic and political integration and Thatcher trying to hold the line at the single market programme. French interest in EMU as a means of ending the German Central Bank's *de facto* dominance of continental monetary policy through the European Monetary System, and the pro-federalism of Germany's political leadership, strengthened Delors's position. Accordingly, Community leaders agreed in June 1988 to establish a committee of national central bank governors, chaired by Delors, to propose specific steps that would lead to EMU. Thatcher went along grudgingly with the decision. By that time, however, her influence in the European Community (EC)—as the EEC was now known—and at home in Britain was on the wane. Concerned about her strident opposition to further European integration and her increasing unpopularity, a group of senior Conservative Party members forced Thatcher to resign in November 1990.

The fall of Thatcher did not necessarily mean the continued rise of Delors. Indeed, Delors's political influence, and with it that of the European Commission, peaked at about the same time as Thatcher's demise. Having supported the single market programme, cohesion policy and the idea of EMU, many national governments began to resent Delors's, and the Commission's, influence and ambition. They sought instead to put their own stamp on the EC's rapid development in new and highly politically sensitive directions.

## German unification and European Union

Acting on the recommendations of the Delors Committee, national governments had agreed to convene an IGC to negotiate the steps necessary to bring about EMU, a decision that received an additional boost from the revolution in Central and Eastern Europe, including the fall of the Berlin Wall in November 1989. Imminent German unification gave Chancellor Helmut Kohl useful political ammunition to overcome opposition of the Central Bank to EMU. What better way for a uniting Germany to demonstrate its continuing commitment to European integration than to give up the Deutschmark in favour of the euro?

Thanks to German unification, a separate IGC on European political union took place at the same time as the previously planned IGC on monetary union. Both came to an end at the Maastricht summit in December 1991. As expected, the agreement on EMU called for a single monetary policy and a single currency, by 1999 at the latest, to encompass member states that met seemingly strict convergence criteria dealing with inflation rates, exchange rates, budget deficits and national debts. The agreement on political union included a further increase in the legislative power of the European Parliament, provisions for a largely intergovernmental Common Foreign and Security Policy, and a nascent system for cooperation in the area of justice and home affairs (covering immigration, asylum, police and judicial cooperation and the like). The supranational and intergovernmental aspects of the Maastricht agreement were incorporated into the Treaty on European Union, which foreign ministers formally signed in February 1992.

The so-called Maastricht Treaty was a remarkable achievement and represented the high point of the European integration process.

---

**KEY POINTS**

- The Single European Act (SEA) was the first major reform of the treaty establishing the EEC.

- Key provisions included a commitment to complete the single market programme by the end of 1992, greater legislative power for the European Parliament and a stronger regional (cohesion) policy.

- French and German interest in EMU, together with Commission advocacy of it, led to a decision to convene an IGC to bring about a single monetary policy and a single currency.

- Thatcher was unable to hold the line at the single market programme, eventually losing power in part because of her strident opposition to deeper integration.

- German unification added to the momentum for EMU and led to a parallel IGC on political union.

- The Maastricht Treaty, best known for its provisions on EMU, represented a major advance in the process of European integration.

---

# Public Unease and Political Overreach

It has become commonplace to say that European integration was entirely elite-driven and devoid of public input. It certainly is true that the ways in which integration moved forward—intergovernmental conferences, institutional interaction in Brussels and Strasbourg, judicial decisions in Luxembourg—involved only officials politicians and judges, and largely excluded the public. But the same can be said of national decision-making and constitution-building. Ordinary citizens in the EU could vote in national elections and thereby determine the composition of the governments representing them in the Council of Ministers. Although most national elections were fought over domestic issues, EU affairs occasionally intruded into them. Since 1979, citizens throughout the EU could also take part in elections for the European Parliament, but large numbers have chosen not to (the turnout has declined steadily over the years).

Following implementation of the SEA, the EC began to have a more perceptible impact on people's everyday lives. Despite the opportunities open to them to try to shape EC affairs in national and European Parliament elections, most people questioned the fairness, transparency and accountability of the EU decision-making process. Anticipating such popular concern, national governments had already developed the principle of **subsidiarity** or states' rights and had increased the legislative authority of the European Parliament in both the SEA and the Maastricht Treaty. The negative outcome of the Danish referendum on the Maastricht Treaty, in June 1992, and the narrow French endorsement of the Treaty in a referendum in September 1992, signalled growing public remoteness from and resentment of the emerging EU. Far from representing a triumph for European integration, implementation of the Maastricht Treaty in November 1993 was overshadowed by growing public alienation from 'Brussels'.

## Achieving EMU

Public unease about EMU, which dominated the agenda of the EU in the 1990s, exacerbated the situation. People seemed queasy about the ultimate goal as well as the steps necessary to achieve EMU. In order to meet the convergence criteria and thereby participate in the final stage of EMU (the common monetary policy and adoption of the euro), governments had to improve their public finances, often at the cost of cherished welfare programmes. Given the degree of public restlessness, it is surprising that governments stayed the course. Much of the credit belongs to Chancellor Kohl, who doggedly pushed ahead despite the misgivings of a sizeable portion of the German population. Other governments followed suit if only because the political and economic costs of failing to realise EMU seemed greater than the likely benefits.

The launch of the common currency in January 1999 was an undoubted milestone in the history of European integration. Euro notes and coins began to circulate in January 2002, bringing home to Europeans the extent of the achievement. Complaints about price rises in Germany and elsewhere reinforced public restlessness about EMU. So did the initial drop in the external value of the euro. Nevertheless the euro proved to be a stable currency, with inflation remaining at historic lows. Britain, Denmark and Sweden, which had decide not to participate in EMU, watched the launch of the euro, and subsequently the operation of the Stability and Growth Pact that supposedly underpinned the new currency, with interest but without regret for having remained on the outside.

## Enlargement

By that time the EU was well on its way to another round of enlargement that was quantitatively and qualitatively different from anything in the past. No fewer than 12 countries, ten of them from the former Soviet bloc, were negotiating membership. The road to accession was long and difficult for the Central and Eastern European countries, which were far poorer than the poorest of the existing member states and were grappling with difficult political reforms and wrenching economic modernisation. The governments and peoples of the existing member states were indifferent about enlargement, sensing that it would transform the EU in ways that were not necessarily beneficial or welcome. Farmers fretted about the future of the CAP; poor regions worried about the sustainability of cohesion policy; and the proverbial man in the street dreaded the possible influx of migrant workers from the East. The terms of the accession treaties, essentially dictated by the EU to the candidate countries, sought to reassure Western Europeans in ways that arguably discriminated against the new member states. When it finally happened in May 2004, enlargement looked less like a great accomplishment for the EU than a fateful step taken reluctantly by the existing member states and disappointedly by the new member states. The prospect of Turkish accession, which emerged after the 2004 enlargement, filled the EU with foreboding.

## Constitution-building

Partly in anticipation of Central and Eastern European enlargement, the EU had undergone two more rounds of treaty reform. This time the purpose of the IGCs was not to add substantially to the EU's policy remit but to develop the organisation's democratic credentials, improve decision-making procedures, and strengthen cooperation in the areas of foreign policy and justice and home affairs. The first of these IGCs, resulting in the Amsterdam Treaty of 1997, failed to tackle a number of pressing institutional issues, notably the allocation of votes for each national government in the Council of Ministers, the formula for qualified majority voting, the allocation of seats for each member state in the European Parliament, and the size and composition of the Commission. National governments addressed those issues again in the second IGC, resulting in the Nice Treaty of 2001. The outcome, however, was disappointing. Council votes were reallocated and the formula for qualified majority voting was changed in ways that made decision-making even more cumbersome and incomprehensible. Nor was the size or composition of the Commission, a growing problem in view of the EU's imminent enlargement into Central and Eastern Europe, adequately addressed.

Widespread dissatisfaction with the Nice Treaty and with the conduct of the IGC that preceded it led member states to call for a further round of treaty reform. This time the obligatory IGC would be preceded by a convention that would include representatives of national parliaments, the European Parliament and the Commission as well as representatives of the national governments of the existing and the candidate states. Led by former French President Valéry Giscard d'Estaing, the Convention met for more than a year before submitting a draft Constitutional Treaty to the European Council in June 2004. The adjective 'constitutional' suggested a desire to emphasise the political nature of the EU; the noun 'treaty' recognised the legal character of the EU (an organisation of sovereign states willing to share sovereignty in certain policy areas). The proposed Constitutional Treaty improved decision-making in areas such as foreign policy and justice and home affairs, gave the EU legal personality and strengthened its external representation. While far from being an ideal document, it was undoubtedly an improvement on the existing treaties, which it would replace, and was arguably the best possible outcome given the political constraints on treaty change in the EU.

Although intended to appeal to a sceptical and increasingly disaffected public as well as open up the system of treaty reform in the EU, the Convention failed to attract much interest outside Brussels. It was followed by the requisite IGC, which broke down in December 2003 over the reallocation of Council votes. Having been carefully put together by the Convention, the draft Constitutional Treaty was now being torn apart by national governments. It was not a reassuring or edifying sight. The IGC resumed in early 2004 and, thanks to unrelated political developments in Poland and Spain, ended in June of that year with agreement on a Constitutional Treaty that differed in small but significant ways from the draft submitted by the Convention.

In a stinging rebuke for the process of European integration, French and Dutch voters rejected the proposed Constitutional Treaty in spring 2005. Far from being an isolated event, this was a continuation of the expressions of popular concern about the EU first voiced by Danish voters in June 1992 and repeated in other closely contested referenda on treaty reform. The reasons for the no votes that sunk the Constitutional Treaty varied greatly and were not always directly related to the EU. Nevertheless, national leaders had little choice but to accept the limits that public unease had placed on the development of the EU in a more political direction. The EU had plenty to do on the economic front—and possessed the means if not the will to do it. European integration would continue, but in a less spectacular way than the architects of the Constitutional Treaty had envisaged.

## KEY POINTS

- The Maastricht Treaty exacerbated public unease about the EU's policy scope and institutional accountability.

- The single-minded pursuit of EMU by member states widened the gulf between governments and their constituents in the EU.

- Neither politicians nor the public in the existing member states were enthusiastic about Central and Eastern European enlargement, the other main EU agenda item in the post-Maastricht period.

- The accession of 12 poor and mostly small member states in May 2004 tested the efficiency and manageability of the EU.

- The prospect of Turkish accession filled the member states, new and old, with foreboding.

- Treaty changes intended to increase the EU's efficiency and accountability were largely unavailing in 1997 and 2001.

- Rejection of the Constitutional Treaty by French and Dutch voters in 2005 was a continuation of the expressions of popular concern about the EU first voiced in the early 1990s.

# Conclusion

European integration has changed profoundly since the early 1950s. The German question—the original impetus of the Coal and Steel Community—has long since been resolved. The EC (now the EU) has grown in size to 25 member states and in scope to cover everything from trade policy, to environmental policy, to intergovernmental cooperation on foreign and security policy. The processes of widening and deepening have complemented, not conflicted with, each other.

Nevertheless, the EU today faces a number of formidable challenges. One is expansion into Central and Eastern Europe. The accession of eight poor former communist Central and Eastern European states in May 2004 has stretched the EU logistically (by having to make the necessary institutional and operational changes) and financially (by trying to meet the demands of the new member states for agricultural subsidies and regional assistance while also meeting the demands of the existing member states without increasing appreciably the size of the budget).

The prospect of additional enlargement, especially of Turkish accession, raises these logistical and financial concerns to a new level (Turkey is a poor and populous country). It also raises serious questions about Europe's cultural and political identity. Is Turkey, a Muslim country located mostly in the Middle East, really a European state? For strategic reasons, the EU has decided that

Turkey is European. Indeed, accession negotiations began officially in October 2005. But public opinion throughout the EU is generally hostile to Turkey's accession, which is unlikely to become imminent in any case until 2015 or later. By that time both the EU and Turkey may have changed considerably. Based on their current configurations, however, it is difficult to imagine Turkey joining the EU. Rejecting Turkey, perhaps based on the outcome of referenda in a number of member states, might appease public opinion in the EU but could risk political instability in Turkey and undermine the EU's international credibility.

Even without the headache of enlargement, the EU faces the challenge of public indifference (at best) or alienation (at worst). For years public opinion acquiesced in European integration. Only as it impinged directly on them did people question the legitimacy of the project. Despite enjoying the benefits of a borderless Europe, more and more people complained more and more vociferously about the EU's institutional shortcomings and regulatory overreach. National governments have exacerbated the problem by blaming Brussels for unpopular practices and decisions instead of undertaking meaningful reform while at the same time explaining the indubitable benefits of deeper integration.

The introduction of the euro is a remarkable achievement, but one that few Europeans seems to

**DESMOND DINAN**

appreciate fully. Instead, Europeans rightly complain about the uneven economic performance of countries in the Eurozone and high unemployment in France and Germany, the traditional anchors of European integration. The governments of both countries are skittish about public opinion and fearful of the pressures of globalisation that demand greater labour market flexibility and welfare-policy reform. Public and political opinion in France, in particular, increasingly sees European integration as an agent of globalisation, and therefore something inherently hostile to the national interest. (See the discussion in Chapter 1, this volume). While trying to mould European integration into a mechanism to protect itself against what many people see as the ravages of globalisation, France is on a collision course with a country such as Britain, which has undertaken major economic reforms and generally sees globalisation as an opportunity rather

than a threat. It is hard to imagine how European integration can make much progress in the face of deep differences among key member states over fundamental issues of socio-economic policy.

The shelving of the Constitutional Treaty in 2005 in response to hostile public opinion does not mean the end of the EU or of the European integration process, however. Arguably the EU remains not only viable but also essential for Europe's economic development, overall well-being and general international standing. Managing an EU of 27 or more member states is arduous, but not impossible. The political setback of 2005 has given the EU a chance to return to first principles—economic integration—and thereby demonstrate its continuing relevance and utility in an increasingly fractious but interdependent world. It can only succeed, however, if member states reach a consensus on how best to respond to the challenges of economic globalisation.

## QUESTIONS

1. How did European integration meet French security concerns in the post-war period?
2. Is there still a German problem?
3. What was the nature of the Gaullist challenge to European integration?
4. Why did national governments decide to reaffirm their commitment to European integration in the late 1980s?
5. How significant have key individuals been in the European integration process?
6. To what extent are national interests subsumed into a broader European interest in the EU?
7. Can the EU manage with 27 or more member states?
8. Why are Europeans so dissatisfied with the EU today?
9. If the EU did not exist, would it have to be invented?

## FURTHER READING

■ Baun, M. (1996), *An Imperfect Union: The Maastricht Treaty and the New Politics of European Integration*, Boulder CO, Westview Press. An excellent account of the process of treaty reform.

■ Dinan, D. (2005), *Ever Closer Europe: An Introduction to European Integration*, 3rd edn, London, Palgrave Macmillan. A comprehensive account of the history, institutions and policies of the EU.

■ **Dinan D. (2004),** *Europe Recast: A History of European Union,* **London, Palgrave Macmillan.** Provides a good overview of the history of European integration.

■ **Gilbert, M. (2003),** *Surpassing Realism: The Politics of European Integration since 1945,* **Lanham MD: Rowman & Littlefield.** Provides a thorough synopsis of the European integration process.

■ **Gillingham, J. (2003),** *European Integration, 1950–2002: Superstate or New Market Economy?,* **Cambridge, Cambridge University Press.** A comprehensive and controversial history of the European integration process.

■ **Grant, C. (1994),** *Delors: Inside the House that Jacques Built,* **London, Nicholas Brealey Publishing.** A behind-the-scenes look at a critical period in the European integration process.

■ **Wallace, H., Wallace, W. and Pollack M. (eds) (2005),** *Policy-making in the European Union,* **5th edn, Oxford, Oxford University Press.** The gold standard of EU textbooks.

 **IMPORTANT WEBSITES**

● **http://europa.eu/** The EU's official website.

● **www.iue.it/ECArchives/EN/** The historical archives of the EU.

● **http://aei.pitt.edu** The University of Pittsburgh has a useful archive on European integration.

● **www.eu-history.leidenuniv.nl/** The University of Leiden has a website on the history of the European Union.

 **Visit the Online Resource Centre that accompanies this book for lots of useful additional material, including an interactive map of Europe. www.oxfordtextbooks.co.uk/orc/hay_menon/**

# 11

# The Institutions of the European Union

## HUSSEIN KASSIM

**Chapter Contents**

- Introduction
- EU Institutions: Origins, Structures and Organisation
- EU Institutions Today
- EU Institutions in Theoretical Perspective
- Conclusion
- Notes

**Reader's Guide**

This chapter looks at the main decision-making institutions of the European Union. It begins with a discussion of the original ambitions of the founding states. It considers how the tension between the desire of national governments to launch a joint project that would irrevocably link together their fates, on the one hand, and their concern, on the other, to ensure their control over its development led to the creation of a complex institutional system. It then examines the origins of each institution, looks at the roles, structure and organisation of each body, and considers how these have changed over time. A discussion of the main issues concerning the institutions today follows thereafter. Particular attention is paid to the question of the 'democratic deficit'. The chapter continues with a brief survey of the main theoretical debates relating to each institution. It concludes with a discussion of the wider challenges arising in relation to the European Union's institutional structure.

# Introduction

The European Union is the most successful experiment in international cooperation, but also the most complex.[1] It grew out of three original Communities—the European Coal and Steel Community, the European Economic Community and the European Atomic Community (see Chapter 10, this volume)—each of which was created with the same fundamental purpose: to bring, by their commitment to a common project, peace and prosperity to states that had fought two devastating wars against each other within a generation. The founding states wanted to establish a system that would bind them to the active and continuous pursuit of agreed goals but, at the same time, they were anxious that governments should continue to play a key role at all levels and stages of decision-making. This tension goes a long way to explaining the intricacies of the EU's institutional structure.

The solution was found in a structure that, while unlike any existing international body or national political system, combines elements of both forms of organisation.[2] Like all international organisations, the EU's competencies, decision-making bodies and procedures are set out in its founding treaties. However, whereas international organisations are generally **intergovernmental** in character—that is, their collective institutions are weak, governments dominate decision-making and signatory states are under no obligation to abide by decisions that they do not support—the European Union is **supranational**: important powers and responsibilities are entrusted to the EU institutions, which they can exercise independently, member states share decision-making power with these bodies, as well as with each other, and governments are obliged to comply with decisional outputs, even where they do not agree with particular decisions. By departing from the standard template, the founders sought to avoid the weaknesses typically associated with intergovernmental organisations, especially their tendency towards gridlock and lowest-common-denominator decision-making. By delegating key functions to EU institutions, governments aimed to ensure the **credibility of their commitments**. By entrusting independent institutions with responsibility for enforcing the treaty, governments sought to protect against **free-riding** and to minimise the **transactions costs** associated with international co-operation by handing certain functions in part or in full to EU institutions.

The EU also has features familiar from national political systems, as Simon Hix has argued (1994, 2005). It has a well established set of institutions that exercise executive, legislative and judicial power, make authoritative decisions about the allocation of economic resources and political and social values, are lobbied directly and indirectly by citizens and social groups, and are in constant interaction with public and private groups (Hix 2005: 2). Though these attributes invite comparison between the EU and national systems, the similarities go only so far. What ultimately distinguishes the EU from any national polity is the central involvement of sovereign states—actors quite different in regard to authority, resources and behaviour from those that populate domestic systems (Hurrell and Menon 1994). Governments are represented collectively in the European Council and the Council of Ministers, while national administrations and national courts have been incorporated in the wider EU system.

The central and continued involvement of governments and national actors is assured in a complex system where powers and responsibilities are shared horizontally among interdependent institutions at the EU level and vertically between the EU and the member states. Executive power in the sense of setting EU goals is shared between the European Council, the Council of Ministers and the Commission; legislative power between the Council and the European Parliament; responsibility for policy implementation between the Commission and member state administrations; and judicial power between EU-level courts—the European Court of Justice and the Court of First Instance—and national courts. According to Giandomenico Majone (2005), the principle that underlies this sharing of functions is not the **separation of powers**—the principle that informs the design of national political systems in liberal democratic states—but the representation of interests: 'Each European institution is the bearer of a particular, national or supranational interest, which it strives to protect and promote. This makes the European Community a latter-day version of mixed government. The principle of institutional balance, typical of mixed government, entails the preservation of the relative position of each interest, and of the institution which represents it.'

The EU's complexity is also a consequence of its dynamism. The EU today does not conform to a single blueprint, but represents the result of successive treaty reforms and improvised adaptations to past pressures. Its institutional system is 'fluid, ambiguous, and hybrid . . . not based on a single treaty, a unitary structure, or a single dominating centre of authority and power . . . [but] built on several treaties and a complex three-pillar structure . . . [where] the pillars are organized on different principles and supranational/intergovernmental mixes' (Olsen 1997: 165). Attempts to overhaul the Community system in order to simplify its structures have been rare. The merger of the three original Communities in 1967 was one such exception[3] but, although it simplified Community structures, its effects were not long-lasting. The EU and its institutions have increased dramatically in size and complexity since that date due mainly to successive enlargements and an accretion of competencies. New areas of responsibility have been accompanied by new decision-making procedures. The creation of the second and third pillars under the Treaty of European Union introduced cooperation in foreign and security policy and justice and home affairs, but only at the price of a departure from the traditional 'Community method' (see below), as governments insisted on retaining their control in these areas. The broadening of EU responsibilities also encouraged a tendency towards internal specialisation and differentiation within the main EU institutions (Christiansen and Kirchner 2000), adding to its institutional density and further complicating EU structures.

Partly as a consequence of these processes— though strategic action, competition between EU institutions and attempts by the member states to remedy the **democratic deficit** also played a part—the balance between institutions and between the EU and the member states has rarely been stable. The influence of the Commission has fluctuated considerably. The presidencies of Hallstein (1958–67) and Delors (1985–95) mark high points, but under other presidencies the Commission was considerably weaker. Its current decline, which has been evident since the Maastricht Intergovernmental Conference, can be attributed at least in part to the growth of Council influence and the emergence of the European Council (Kassim and Menon 2004). The European Parliament, meanwhile, has become an important legislator, though law-making was originally the exclusive preserve of the Council of Ministers.

The following section looks in turn at each of the four main institutions. It examines the origins of each. It then discusses their functions and responsibilities, before looking at their organisation and structure.

# EU Institutions: Origins, Structures and Organisation

## The European Commission

The European Commission was created to represent the general interests of the Community. Charged with key responsibilities to ensure the realisation of treaty aims and free to act independently of the member states, it was designed to act as the 'motor' of integration. Combining executive, legislative and quasi-judicial functions, the Commission is more powerful than an international secretariat, but it is not a government. It continues to play a central, if declining, role in the development and management of the Union.

### Origins

Under the Paris Treaty, the founding states had granted full executive powers to the High Authority of the European Coal and Steel Community, but they decided not to vest similar authority in the EEC Commission. Their decision was partly influenced by the different aims of the treaties. While the Paris Treaty was a set of rules aimed at creating and regulating a single market in coal and steel, the EEC Treaty was an 'outline treaty', which set out goals, defined an institutional framework and decision rules, but 'leaves many substantive policy choices deliberately open' (Majone 2005: 7). Given its broad scope, the signatory states preferred to ensure their say in decision-making. The difference also reflected experience gained since 1952. The failure of the European Defence Community (EDC) had shown that the climate was no longer hospitable to grand supranational schemes (see Chapter 10, this volume). Also, despite its formal right to act independently, the High Authority had in practice tended to seek member state endorsement.

Though not as powerful as the High Authority, with which it was merged in 1967, the EEC Commission was equipped with powers to ensure

that the Community moved constantly towards the treaty goals. In the words of Walter Hallstein, the first Commission President, it provided 'a constant reminder of a Community interest transcending the interest of each of the participants' (1965: 730), its independence enabling it 'to play the role of honest broker between the governments and [to] bring political weight to bear to ensure that formulas for agreement are found' (1965: 732).

### Functions and responsibilities

The functions entrusted to the Commission confirm the founders' conception of its leadership mission. The Commission was granted a formal monopoly over legislative initiative (Art. 211, ex 155). Action on its part was therefore essential to any progress towards meeting the treaty aims. Although the Council, and later the European Parliament, could ask it to submit a text, the Commission alone decides whether to initiate action. As well as formal agenda-setting power—the ability to choose the moment for initiating action and proposing the form it should take—the Commission is present at each stage of the legislative process. Unless compelled to amend its proposal by a unanimous vote of the Council, the Commission is the master of the text. It decides whether and what changes should be made. To maximise the chances of its proposals being adopted, the Commission has developed an elaborate machinery that allows it to consult interested parties. Before it submits a formal draft, the Commission solicits the opinion of government and non-government experts, brought together in consultative committees that it chairs.

Though these powers give the Commission considerable influence—one former official suggests that 80 per cent of its original draft survives in the final text adopted by the Council (Hull 1993)—ultimate decision-making authority is reserved to member state representatives in the Council of Ministers and, where indecision applies, the European Parliament (see below). Under the 'Community method', the term by which the traditional division of labour between the two institutions came to be known, 'the Commission proposes, the Council disposes'. As well as constant dialogue between the two institutions, this arrangement ensures that both the general interests of the Community and the particular interests of the member states are represented in the policy process. The Commission–Council relationship remains important, but other modes of decision-making (Wallace 2005: 77–89) have since developed, where the Commission's role is not as central.[4] Within the 'temple' structure introduced by the Treaty of European Union (see Figure 11.1), for example, the Commission retains its monopoly over policy initiation in the first pillar, but shares the right with member governments in the second and third pillars—common foreign and security policy and justice and home affairs respectively.

The Commission was also entrusted with executive responsibilities. In a few areas, it has direct powers. The Treaty gives the Commission responsibility for taking action to complete the customs union as the first stage in creating the common market. Mostly, the Council must first adopt an implementing measure. Thus, in competition policy, the Commission was given power to investigate and control anti-competitive agreements between firms, the abuse of dominant position, mergers and state aid. The Commission also administers various Community funds, notably concerning EU policies relating to agriculture, social affairs, development and regional development. More generally, the Treaty provides that the Council may delegate powers to the Commission to implement policies agreed by the Council. The Council has made considerable use of this provision, particularly in regard to the common agricultural policy, which is highly developed. The delegation of rule-making to the Commission is advantageous to the member states, since entrusting responsibilities to an independent body reduces transactions costs, enhances efficiency and strengthens credibility. However, because the delegating authorities cannot withdraw powers that they have conferred, unlike parliaments at the national level, governments have sought to control the way in which they are exercised. Though not foreseen in the Treaty, the Council has created a set of committees composed of national officials, referred to collectively as 'comitology', that determine to differing degrees how the Commission uses its powers.[5]

The third function entrusted to the Commission is that of guardian of the treaties (Art. 122, ex 155). The Commission can take action against the Council or member states, companies and individuals for failure to comply with their obligations, though its powers vary depending on which rules have been violated. Where a member state is suspected of having failed to apply a treaty rule, regulation or decision, or to transpose, implement or apply a directive (see Table 11.1), the Commission requests information and clarification from the government concerned. If the Commission is not satisfied with the response, it can issue a reasoned opinion, in which it specifies the infringement that has taken

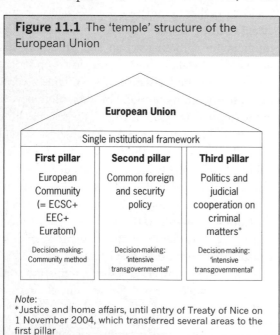

**Figure 11.1** The 'temple' structure of the European Union

**European Union**

Single institutional framework

| First pillar | Second pillar | Third pillar |
|---|---|---|
| European Community (= ECSC+ EEC+ Euratom) | Common foreign and security policy | Politics and judicial cooperation on criminal matters* |
| Decision-making: Community method | Decision-making: 'intensive transgovernmental' | Decision-making: 'intensive transgovernmental' |

Note:
*Justice and home affairs, until entry of Treaty of Nice on 1 November 2004, which transferred several areas to the first pillar

**Table 11.1** Main Types of EU Action

| Type | Powers |
|------|--------|
| Regulations | Have general application, are binding at EU and national level and are directly applicable in the member states |
| Directives | Are addressed to any number of member states and are binding with respect to defined objectives, while leaving the choice of form to national authorities, and must be transposed into law by national authorities |
| Decisions | Can be addressed to member states or private citizens, and are binding. They do not require national implementing measures |
| Recommendations and opinions | Can be addressed to any member state or citizen, and are not binding |

place and the measures to be taken for it to be remedied (Art. 226, ex 169). If the violation persists, the Commission may take the member state before the European Court of Justice. Where the Commission's position is upheld, the Court will declare that the member state has failed to respect its obligations. If, under a provision introduced by the Treaty of European Union, the member state fails to take the necessary action to comply with the Court's ruling, the Commission can return to the Court and request that a sanction be imposed. The first such ruling was made in July 2000 when the Greek government was ordered to pay a penalty payment of €20,000 per day.

In the area of competition policy, the Commission's powers are particularly far-reaching. It is effectively investigator, judge and jury. Where the Commission finds that companies are engaging in anti-competitive practices in breach of Article 81 or Article 82, it can levy fines. In the case of mergers, the Commission's approval must be sought for operations with an EU dimension. Depending on the details, the Commission can give its conditional or unconditional approval to a merger, or can prohibit it. The Commission has similar powers with respect to state aid, which is an extremely sensitive area. Governments tend to regard their financial transactions with state-owned companies as a private matter but, since the Single European Act, they have been forced increasingly

to recognise the Commission's authority to control such payments as part of its responsibilities in policing the single market.

The Commission depends to a very large degree on other bodies in the exercise of its executive responsibilities. It has no services of its own in the territories of the member states, so relies on national administrations for the implementation of Union policy and action. In the case of EU funds, the Commission is responsible for the proper disbursement of EU monies, even though around 80 per cent of EU monies are spent by national authorities over which it has little control.

The Commission's fourth function concerns external relations. While the Council, on the basis of a Commission proposal, decides the Community's position, the Commission represents the Community in negotiations with third countries and in multilateral organisations, such as the World Trade Organization, under the watchful eye of national officials on the Council's Article 133 Committee. On the diplomatic front, the Commission maintains relations with third-country missions on the European Union's behalf. The Commission's position in respect of external political relations and defence has proved difficult. Member states have attempted to maintain these as areas of essentially intergovernmental cooperation, but external policy often involves the exercise of power in areas where the Community institutions have

**Table 11.2** The Distribution of Commission Portfolios, 2005–10

| Commissioners | Nationality | Portfolio |
| --- | --- | --- |
| José Manuel Durão Barroso | Portuguese | President |
| Margot Wallström | Swedish | Institutional Relations and Communication Strategy |
| Günther Verheugen | German | Enterprise and Industry |
| Jacques Barrot | French | Transport |
| Siim Kallas | Estonian | Administrative Affairs, Audit and Anti-Fraud |
| Franco Frattini | Italian | Justice, Freedom and Security |
| Benita Ferrero-Waldner | Austrian | External Relations and Neighbours Policy |
| Louis Michel | Belgian | Development and Humanitarian Aid |
| Markos Kyprianou | Cypriot | Health and Consumers Protection |
| Vladimir Spidla | Czech | Employment, Social Affairs and Equal Opportunities |
| Mariann Fischer Boel | Danish | Agriculture and Rural Development |
| Olli Rehn | Finnish | Enlargement |
| Stavros Dimas | Greek | Environment |
| László Kovács | Hungarian | Taxation and Customs Union |
| Charlie McCreevy | Irish | Internal Market and Services |
| Andris Piebalgs | Latvian | Energy |
| Dalia Grybauskaite | Lithuanian | Financial Programming and Budget |
| Viviane Reding | Luxembourgeois | Information Society and Media |
| Joe Borg | Maltese | Fisheries and Maritime Affairs |
| Neelie Kroes | Dutch | Competition |
| Danuta Hübner | Polish | Regional Policy |
| Jan Figel | Slovakian | Education, Training, Culture and Multilinguism |
| Janez Potocnik | Slovenian | Science and Research |
| Joaquin Almunia | Spanish | Economic and Monetary Affairs |
| Peter Mandelson | British | Trade |

*Source*: http://ec.europa.eu/commission_barroso/index_en.htm

important responsibilities. Action that cuts across pillars creates logistical and often budgetary difficulties. In addition, the high representative created by the Treaty of Amsterdam is a (potential) rival of the commissioner for external relations while, at the administrative level, the Council Secretariat is increasingly involved in turf battles with Commission services.

### Structure and organisation

The Commission's central decision-making body is the College, composed of 27 commissioners. Each commissioner has a portfolio responsibility (see Table 11.2), but Commission decisions are taken by the entire College at a weekly meeting. Before 2005, the larger member states nominated two members each and the smaller countries one, but the Nice Treaty stipulated that once the EU had more than 17 members, the number should be limited to one commissioner per member state. Although the treaty provides that the College should be appointed by common accord of governments, implying that its appointment is a collective exercise, in practice each government makes its decision independently.

Unlike a national government, the College is not bound by party affiliation or coalition agreement. Its members come from diverse backgrounds and may never have met before they take up office. In order to promote greater cohesion, the Commission presidency has been gradually strengthened. The Commission president is nominated first and has a say in the composition of the College and the sharing out of responsibilities, decisions that were previously in the hands of governments. Also, under the Treaty of Nice, the president can, after obtaining the College's approval, request the resignation of an individual commissioner. Otherwise, commissioners serve a five-year term, ended by the expiry of the office, voluntary resignation, death, compulsory retirement by the European Court of Justice or a motion of censure moved successfully by the European Parliament against the whole Commission.

Members of the Commission are each assisted by a *cabinet*, a personal staff hand-picked by the commissioner. The *cabinet* has a general role to support the commissioner in respect of their portfolio responsibilities and to keep them informed about issues coming to the College in other areas. Members of the *cabinet* also liaise with the services and with the commissioner's national capital. Although collegiality and the oath taken by members of the Commission on assuming office are intended to guarantee their independence from national interests, it is accepted that commissioners will keep in regular touch with 'the country that they know best', that is, his or her home state, so that the College can be made aware of member state concerns. However, commissioners must be careful not to overstep the mark, since commissioners that become too closely identified with their home state lose influence.

While the College is responsible for political decision-making, technical work is carried out by the services, whose career officials are recruited through competitive examinations (the *concours*). The Commission's permanent administration is organised into 23 Directorates-General (DGs) and other specialist departments (see Table 11.3), which vary significantly in size. The services are the Commission's powerhouse, drafting proposals, negotiating in the Council, liaising with the European Parliament and officials in the member states, and running programmes. The Commission has a remarkably small staff—22,177 in 2004 (Spence and Stevens 2006: 153)—given the breadth of its responsibilities.

> **KEY POINTS**
>
> - The Commission was created as a supranational body to ensure that the Community moves towards the realisation of its treaty goals and that member governments and companies comply with their obligations.
>
> - The Community is formally independent, but relies on other bodies in carrying out its responsibilities.
>
> - The Commission is a small organisation with two tiers—a political College, appointed by the member states, and a permanent administration known as the 'services'.

## The Council of Ministers and the European Council

The Council of Ministers, usually referred to as 'the Council', and the European Council represent the collective interests of the member states. The European Council is the EU's leading body, the Council its main legislator, though this role is increasingly shared with the European Parliament. While the Council of Ministers finds its origins the treaties of Paris and Rome, the European Council emerged in the 1970s. Though their composition suggests they are intergovernmental bodies, in their operation and contribution to the EU system they transcend the mere interplay of national interests.

### Origins

In its first incarnation as the 'Special Council' in the ECSC, the Council was considerably weaker than the body given a central role in the EEC.

**Table 11.3** Directorates-General and Special Services of the European Commission, 2006

| Directorates-General (DGs) | Special services |
|---|---|
| Agriculture and Rural Development | Secretariat-General |
| Budget | Legal Service |
| Competition | Bureau of European Policy Advisers |
| Development | European Anti-Fraud Office |
| Economic and Financial Affairs | EuropeAid Cooperation Office |
| Education and Culture | Eurostat |
| Employment, Social Affairs and Equal Opportunities | Humanitarian Aid Office (ECHO) |
| Enlargement | Publications Office |
| Enterprise and Industry | |
| Environment | |
| External Relations | |
| Fisheries and Maritime Affairs | |
| Health and Consumer Protection | |
| Informatics | |
| Information Society and Media | |
| Internal Audit Service | |
| Internal Market and Services | |
| Interpretation | |
| Joint Research Centre | |
| Justice, Freedom and Security | |
| Personnel and Administration | |
| Regional Policy | |
| Research | |
| Taxation and Customs Union | |
| Trade | |
| Translation | |
| Transport and Energy | |

Included at the late suggestion of the Dutch delegation (Edwards 1996: 129), the Special Council had no routine role in decision-making. Once in place, however, the High Authority regularly sought the Special Council's endorsement and this practice, rather than the formal provisions of the Paris Treaty, provided the model for the EEC Treaty, which instated the Council of Ministers as its central decision-making body.

The origins of the European Council, which brings together the heads of state and governments of the member states,[6] do not lie within the treaties. The European Council developed outside the formal structures of the Communities, as political leaders sought a regular forum for informal discussion and the exchange of views. Following General de Gaulle's resignation as French president, the leaders of the member states met at The Hague in 1969 to consider the future development of the Communities. The challenges confronting Western Europe were the subject of a number of *ad hoc* summits thereafter. In 1974, at the initiative of French President Valéry Giscard d'Estaing and German Chancellor Helmut Schmidt, it was agreed that the heads of state and government would meet as the European Council three times a year. From these beginnings, the European Council became 'the most politically authoritative institution of the EC' (Bulmer and Wessels 1987: 2), contributing to all major decisions concerning the development of the Union.

### Functions and responsibilities

The Council is a decision-making forum, where member governments discuss Commission proposals, deliberate and negotiate with each other and the Commission. It also has special responsibilities in economic and monetary union, common foreign and security policy and justice and home affairs. Originally, it had the final say in all legislative decision-making, but this is no longer the case. Where co-decision applies, the final text must be agreed by both the Council and the European Parliament. The Council takes its decisions by different rules that apply in different policy areas. The main rules are: unanimity; qualified majority, where each of the member states has a vote of a given weight and a decision can be adopted only once a particular threshold has been passed (see Table 11.4); and simple majority. With each treaty reform since the Single European Act, the scope of qualified majority voting (QMV) has been extended, with the result that unanimity survives only in new areas of competence or sectors that are particularly sensitive for the member states. The progressive extension of QMV underlines the supranational character of the Union, since governments can be outvoted and have no veto power. In practice, the decision-making style of the Council is consensual. Negotiations are lengthy; strong efforts are made to accommodate the preferences of as many parties as possible; and formal votes are rare. According to Helen Wallace (2005: 61), 'votes are explicitly contested on only around 20 per cent of eligible decisions'.

The European Council assumed a leadership role from the outset. It effectively operated as an executive arm of the Council of Ministers, even though its responsibilities were only vaguely defined and, until the SEA, were not mentioned by the treaties. Though later treaties have entrusted it with specific tasks, mostly in relation to the Common Foreign and Security Policy (CFSP) and EMU, and it has taken charge of the **Lisbon Process**, the European Council's main function is to define the Union's political direction. It has carved out a role that could not be performed by any other body: it sets the Union's medium-term goals; has taken milestone decisions in relation to treaty reform, enlargement, economic and monetary union, Community financing and economic policy; and tries to clear the log-jams that occasionally arise in the Council of Ministers. The Presidency Conclusions, released after each meeting, lack legal force, but are regarded as definitive statements of policy and direction. While it has partially displaced the Commission as a source of leadership, the European Council provides the Commission president with an important interlocutor—a significant resource effectively exploited by Jacques Delors during his presidency.

### Structure and organisation

The Council's title gives an impression of structural unity but, of all EU institutions, it is the most fragmented. Looked at vertically, the Council is tripartite and pyramidal in structure. At the top, ministers from the member states meet to take final decisions. Their meetings are prepared by the Committee of Permanent Representatives (COREPER)—the middle tier—which is 'one of the most powerful organs within the European Union's institutional structure' (Westlake and Galloway 2004: 201). Though usually referred to in the singular, there are in fact two bodies. The members of COREPER II, the more senior, are permanent representatives, the heads of the national missions (Permanent Representations) comprising diplomatic staff and technical experts from the

**Table 11.4** Qualified Majority Council from the EEC Treaty to the Treaty of Nice

| | EEC Treaty 1958 | First enlargement 1973 | Second enlargement 1981 | Third enlargement 1986 | Fourth enlargement 1995 | Fifth enlargement 1 May 2004 | Nice Treaty 1 November 2004 |
|---|---|---|---|---|---|---|---|
| Belgium | 2 | 5 | 5 | 5 | 5 | 5 | 12 |
| Netherlands | 2 | 5 | 5 | 5 | 5 | 5 | 13 |
| Luxembourg | 1 | 2 | 2 | 2 | 2 | 2 | 4 |
| France | 4 | 10 | 10 | 10 | 10 | 10 | 29 |
| Germany | 4 | 10 | 10 | 10 | 10 | 10 | 29 |
| Italy | 4 | 10 | 10 | 10 | 10 | 10 | 29 |
| UK | | 10 | 10 | 10 | 10 | 10 | 29 |
| Denmark | | 3 | 3 | 3 | 3 | 3 | 7 |
| Ireland | | 3 | 3 | 3 | 3 | 3 | 7 |
| Greece | | | 5 | 5 | 5 | 5 | 12 |
| Spain | | | | 8 | 8 | 8 | 27 |
| Portugal | | | | 5 | 5 | 5 | 13 |
| Sweden | | | | | 4 | 4 | 10 |
| Finland | | | | | 3 | 3 | 7 |
| Austria | | | | | 4 | 4 | 10 |
| Poland | | | | | | 8 | 27 |
| Hungary | | | | | | 5 | 13 |
| Czech Republic | | | | | | 5 | 12 |
| Lithuania | | | | | | 3 | 7 |
| Slovakia | | | | | | 3 | 7 |
| Cyprus | | | | | | 2 | 4 |
| Estonia | | | | | | 3 | 4 |
| Latvia | | | | | | 3 | 4 |
| Slovenia | | | | | | 3 | 4 |
| Malta | | | | | | 2 | 3 |
| No. of member states | 6 | 9 | 10 | 12 | 15 | 25 | 25 |
| Total no. of weighted votes | 17 | 58 | 63 | 76 | 87 | 124 | 321 |
| Minimum no. of states for a majority | 3 | 5 | 5 | 6 | 8 or 10[1] | 13 or 17[3] | 13 or 17[2] |

*(continued overleaf)*

**Table 11.4** (*continued*)

| | EEC Treaty 1958 | First enlargement 1973 | Second enlargement 1981 | Third enlargement 1986 | Fourth enlargement 1995 | Fifth enlargement 1 May 2004 | Nice Treaty 1 November 2004 |
|---|---|---|---|---|---|---|---|
| Qualified majority (as % of total vote) | 12 (70.5) | 41 (70.6) | 45 (71.4) | 54 | 62 (71)[3] | 88 (70.9) | 232 (72.2) |
| Blocking minority (as % of total vote) | 6 (33.3) | 18 (31) | 19 (30.1) | 23 (30.2) | 26 (29.8) | 37 (29.8) | 90 (28) |

Notes:
[1] Under the Ioannina compromise, if members of the Council that account for between 23 and 26 votes oppose a decision, the Council will attempt to find an outcome that can be adopted by a minimum of 65 per cent of the votes
[2] The higher threshold applies in the case of a measure that is not proposed by the Commission
[3] The higher threshold applies in the case of a measure that is not proposed by the Commission. Any member government can ask whether the qualified majority represents 62 per cent of the EU's population of the EU. If this is not the case, the measure is not adopted

domestic ministries that each member state maintains in Brussels. The permanent representatives are of ambassadorial rank. Deputy permanent representatives, meanwhile, meet in COREPER I. Both COREPERs meet once a week and perform a dual function as 'a clearing house for the Council' and 'a bridge to national capitals' (Barber 1995).

The third and broadest tier of the Council structure—the base of the pyramid—includes 300 or more working groups, composed of experts from the member states who are based at the Permanent Representation or fly out from the national capitals. Working groups are created by COREPER and cover all areas where the Union has policy responsibilities. Council deliberations begin in the working groups. Discussions continue until issues that can be decided only at a higher level remain, at which point the dossier passes upwards. Only those matters that cannot be settled in COREPER are referred to ministers. It is estimated that up to 90 per cent of Council business has been agreed

before it reaches the ministerial level: 70 per cent is decided at working-group level and 15–20 per cent in COREPER. Since only ministers are formally empowered to take decisions, ministerial agendas are divided into A points, which have been agreed by national delegations in Council working groups or COREPER and where there is no need for further discussion, though any government can decide to reopen them, and B points, where agreement still needs to be sought.

Horizontally, the Council is segmented. At ministerial level, it convenes in nine sectoral formations (see Table 11.5) though, prior to the 2002 Seville European Council's decision to reduce the number, there were 22. Two formations are especially important. The General Affairs and External Relations (previously the General Affairs Committee) is the most senior Council, responsible for external relations and CFSP, preparing meetings of the European Council and coordinating the work of other Council formations. The Economics and

**Table 11.5** Sectoral Formations in the Council of Ministers

| Formation | Meetings | Membership |
| --- | --- | --- |
| General Affairs and External Relations (GAERC) | Monthly, with separate meetings on general affairs and external relations | Foreign ministers, high representative for CFSP (general affairs and external relations only) |
| Economic and Financial Affairs (ECOFIN) | Monthly | Economics and finance ministers |
| Agriculture and Fisheries | Monthly | Ministers for agriculture and fisheries, and the commissioners responsible for agriculture, fisheries, food safety, veterinary questions and public health matters |
| Justice and Home Affairs Council (JHA) | Six or seven times a year | Justice and interior ministers |
| Employment, Social Policy, Health and Consumer Affairs Council (EPSCO) | Every three or four months | Ministers for employment, social protection, consumer protection, health and equal opportunities |
| Competitiveness | Six or seven times a year | Ministers for industry, scientific research |
| Transport, Telecommunications and Energy | Every two months | Ministers for transport, telecommunications and energy |
| Environment | Every three months | Ministers for environment |
| Education, Youth and Culture (EYC) | Every three or four months | Ministers for education, youth, culture and communications |

Financial Affairs (ECOFIN) Council has become increasingly important, meanwhile, as a consequence of Economic and Monetary Union. At COREPER level, there is also a division of labour. COREPER II's remit includes institutional matters, the preparation of the General Affairs, ECOFIN, Development, Justice and Home Affairs (JHA) and Budget Council meetings, while COREPER I, composed of the deputy permanent representatives, manages the 'technical' Councils.[7] In addition, special high-ranking committees have been created in some areas: the Special Committee on Agriculture, the Article 36 Committee (justice and home affairs), Political and Security Committee (COPS) and Economic and Financial Committee. Council structures in some sectors, notably common foreign and security policy, justice and home affairs and agriculture, are particularly complex, with special standing working parties.

The European Council has a far lighter structure. The heads of state and government are assisted by the foreign ministers and, since 1975, the Commission president has been invited to attend. The European Council has no permanent secretariat, but the General Affairs and External Relations Council (GAERC), COREPER and the General Secretariat provide administrative support. Its flexible working methods, the seniority of its membership, and the presence of only a handful of officials are often cited as reasons for its effectiveness.

A key role in the organisation and planning of the work of both the European Council and the Council is played by the Council presidency, which rotates between the member states every six months. The tasks of the Council presidency are onerous. As well as the role of business manager, responsible for the agenda of all Council meetings at all levels, the Council president liaises with other EU institutions and has important foreign-policy responsibilities. The presidency is expected to provide a neutral chair, to negotiate compromise and issue initiatives where action is needed. Administrative support is offered by the Council Secretariat, the Council's institutional memory. In the past, the larger member states often chose to rely on their national administrations when running the presidency, but the difficulty of working with so many member states after the 2004 enlargement is likely to increase dependence on the Council Secretariat.

---

**KEY POINTS**

- The Council of Ministers is the EU's main legislative body though, with the advance of co-decision, it shares law-making powers with the European Parliament across a broad range of policy areas.

- The European Council, initially regarded as a threat to the Community, has emerged as the Union's leading institution, setting out the Union's future direction and taking key decisions.

- The European Council's select membership and simple structure give it considerably flexibility.

- The Council is a complex institution, with three tiers and nine sectoral formations at ministerial level.

---

## The European Parliament

From modest origins, the European Parliament has become a major institution. It is also the world's only elected multinational assembly. As well as important roles in law-making and the budget, the Parliament plays a significant role in the investiture of the Commission, and has various scrutiny and control powers over the Commission. As the only directly elected EU institution, the Parliament is at the centre of debates about the Union's democratic credentials.

### Origins

The European Parliament originated as the Common Assembly of the ECSC. Created to provide a check on the High Authority, which it could dismiss *en bloc*, the Assembly initially had no role in law-making. Moreover, governments argued against the direct election of its members, insisting instead that they be selected by national parliaments. Under the Rome Treaties, the Assembly became a common institution that served all three Communities. It also gained an advisory role in the EEC legislative process, while member governments agreed in principle to the direct election of its members at an unspecified date. The European Council acted on this commitment in 1975 and the first elections to the European Parliament were held in 1979. The decision to elect the European Parliament every five years was a decision that transformed the institution's status. The powers of the Parliament were further upgraded by the SEA and it has been subsequently strengthened at successive rounds of treaty reform.

### Functions and responsibilities

As noted above, the Parliament's role in law-making was initially limited. Under the original consultation procedure, the Commission and Council were required to seek the Parliament's opinion, but not necessarily to follow it. The Parliament was permitted only a single reading and had no opportunities for further input once its opinion had been transmitted to the Council. However, when, as part of the SEA, governments decided to extend QMV to enable single-market measures to be adopted expeditiously, they also agreed to upgrade the Parliament's legislative role. Decisions adopted by QMV would be sanctioned by the Parliament and thereby legitimated, even where they had not been agreed by all member governments. Also, an extension of the European Parliament's powers would compensate for the increasing inability of national parliaments to scrutinise decisions taken in Brussels. This was the context in which the cooperation procedure was introduced. Under this procedure, the Parliament acquired the right to a second reading, allowing it to respond to the Council's consideration of the Commission's proposal, now termed a 'common position', and of the amendments the Parliament has proposed at its first reading. The Parliament also acquired a legislative veto.

Six years later, the Parliament was further strengthened by the introduction of the co-decision procedure under the Treaty of European Union. Though it marked an important step towards co-equal status with the Council, co-decision was initially limited to areas within the first pillar and the Council retained the right to return to its original common position, effectively presenting the Parliament with a choice between accepting the Council's preferred text or no text at all. However, not only did the Treaty of Amsterdam extend the number of areas in which co-decision applied from 15 to 38—the Treaty of Nice added a further five, so that co-decision now covers all of the areas requiring a qualified majority in the Council except the common agricultural policy and commercial policy—but it removed the ability of the Council to return to its common position compelling the Council to negotiate with the Parliament.

Despite these advances, the Parliament's legislative influence differs markedly between and within policy domains, according to which legislative procedure applies. Influential in internal market, industry, economic policy, environment, consumer protections, telecommunications and transport policy, where 65 per cent of legislation requires cooperation or co-decision, the Parliament remains largely peripheral in competition policy, agriculture, trade and customs policy (Maurer 2003). In others areas, mostly relating to the structural funds and economic and monetary union, it has the power to give or withhold its assent.

The Parliament also shares in the 'power of the purse'. It acquired its budgetary powers in the 1970s, when the Community shifted from a system of national contributions to one of 'own resources',

where governments transferred fixed proportions of their gross national product (GNP) directly to the Community to be administered by Community institutions. The Parliament provides an EU-level check on the budget. As well as the authority to amend the budget in certain areas, it can reject it—a power it exercised in 1979 and 1984. Although the Council has the final say on 'compulsory expenditure', mostly associated with the common agricultural policy or arising from international agreements, the Council and the Parliament have the last word on non-compulsory expenditure, and the Parliament alone is empowered to approve the discharge of Community accounts each year. Its budgetary powers can be a useful tool in forcing legislative change.

Furthermore, the Parliament has important scrutiny and control powers over the Commission. Some relate to policy. As well as the many reports that the Commission is required routinely to submit to it, the Parliament can put oral and written questions to the Commission. Moreover, the Commission is required to attend all meetings of the Parliament. The Parliament has the power to set up committees of inquiry, which, as in the case of BSE, can have an important impact on policy. With respect to the appointment of the Commission, power is reserved to national governments, but the Parliament also has a role in the process. Under the Treaty of European Union, which introduced a five-year term for the Commission to commence six months after the election of the Parliament, the Parliament's approval was required to confirm member states' nominees for the president and for members of the Commission. The Treaty of Amsterdam made the appointment of the Commission president, prior to that of the other members, subject to Parliament's approval. The Parliament now holds confirmation hearings of nominee commissioners and then decides whether or not to appoint the entire College by a vote of confidence. When it became clear during the hearings for the Barroso Commission that the Parliament did not support the nomination of Rocco Buttiglione, however, the Italian government withdrew his candidature and put forward another nominee. The Parliament also has the power (under Art. 201, ex 144) to dismiss the Commission, which requires a formal motion of censure to be carried by two-thirds of its members. Conventional wisdom held that this was such a powerful weapon it would never be used, but the preparedness of the Parliament to invoke it when allegations of impropriety were levelled against the Santer Commission, ultimately leading to its resignation in March 1999, showed that this was not the case.

Finally, the Parliament has powers in relation to external policy. Under the SEA, the Parliament's approval is required before the Council can enact an international agreement. The Treaty of European Union expanded the scope of this provision from association agreements with third countries to other types of international agreement. The Treaty of Nice added the accession of new member states to the list of agreements to which the Parliament must give its assent. (See Table 11.6.)

### Structure and organisation

The European Parliament has grown from 410 members in 1979 to 785 in 2004. In terms of structure and operation, three features are important. First, the Parliament is institutionally autonomous, but organisationally dependent. Like the US Congress, it cannot be dissolved by the executive. Each Parliament sits for a full five-year term. It also defines its own rules of procedure, decides its agenda and is responsible for its internal administration. However, governments, as the 'masters of the treaty', do hold sway in two important respects: they define the scope of the Parliament's legislative powers, and decide where the Parliament should conduct its business. As the member states involved have been unwilling to forgo the privilege of hosting it, the Parliament has a 'multi-site problem'. Plenary sessions are held in Strasbourg and committees meet in Brussels, while its secretariat is based in Luxembourg.

Second, the Parliament is committee-centred. Most of its work is carried out in the Parliament's 23 committees (Table 11.7). Committees are the first stop for Commission proposals in the Parliament. A committee member is assigned the job of *rapporteur*: to evaluate the proposal and draft a response on the parliament's behalf. The key figures in each committee are the chair and three vice-chairs. Third, the political groups—the parties of the European Parliament—play a central role in the work and organisation of the European Parliament. The political groups bring together the main political families within the Union (see Table 11.8) and provide the mechanism through which financial and administrative support, as well as parliamentary privileges, are administered. They are the key players in the election of the Parliament's leadership, the appointment of committee officeholders, including *rapporteurs* according to a quota system that reflects the its overall composition, and coalition formation in the Parliament. Despite their importance, political groups are not all-powerful. They are composed of national delegations, which have their own organisation and which meet regularly. Importantly, members of the European Parliament (MEPs) are selected as candidates by their national parties, not by any EU-level grouping or federation.

---

**KEY POINTS**

- The powers of the Parliament have increased significantly and it is now a co-equal legislator in the areas where co-decision applies.

- The Parliament forms the EU budgetary authority with the Council.

- The Parliament has important scrutiny and control powers in relation to the European Commission.

---

## The European Court of Justice

Though a different kind of institution from those discussed above, the European Court of Justice forms an integral part of the EU system. Created as the ultimate interpreter of Community law and to ensure that parties comply with their obligations, the Court has made a major contribution to the development of the European Union as a

**Table 11.6** The EU's Main Legislative Procedures

| Procedure | Description (simplified) | Areas to which procedure applies |
|---|---|---|
| Consultation | Commission proposals are transmitted to the EP and the Council. The Council must consult the EP, but is not bound to follow its advice, before adopting the final text. | Agriculture, competition, discrimination, tax and legal migration |
| Cooperation | Commission proposals are submitted to the EP for a first reading, where it may propose amendments, and to the Council. The Council adopts a 'common position'. At its second reading, the EP can adopt the measure or by absolute majority propose amendments to the common position or reject it. The Council can override the EP's veto, but only by unanimity. | Certain aspects of economic and monetary union |
| Codecision, Article 251* | Commission proposals are submitted to the EP for a first reading, where it may propose amendments, and to the Council. The Council adopts a 'common position'. At its second reading, the EP can, acting by absolute majority, accept the common position, reject it, or amend it. Where it opts to amend the common position, a conciliation committee, in which the Council and EP are equally represented, is convened. The outcome must be approved at the third reading by the Council (QMV) and the EP (simply majority) for the proposal to be adopted. | Internal market, citizenship rights and free movement of labour, employment and social policy, environmental and consumer protection, development cooperation, visa and asylum policy and illegal immigration |
| Assent | The EP takes a single vote. Assent requires an absolute majority | The accession of new member states, ratification of some international agreements, imposition of sanctions on a member state in serious and persistent breach of fundamental rights |

Notes:

*For a detailed description, see www.europa.eu.int/comm/codecision/stepbystep/text/index_en.htm

**Table 11.7** Committees in the European Parliament, 2006

Agriculture and Rural Development

Budgetary Control; Budgets

Civil Liberties, Justice and Home Affairs

Constitutional Affairs

Culture and Education

Development; Economic and Monetary Affairs

Employment and Social Affairs

Environment, Public Health & Food Safety

Fisheries

Foreign Affairs

Human Rights

Industry, Research and Energy

Internal Market and Consumer Protection

International Trade

Legal Affairs; Petitions

Policy challenges & budgetary means of the enlarged Union 2007–2013

Regional Development

Security and Defence

Transport and Tourism

Women's Rights and Gender Equality

**Table 11.8** Political Groups in the European Parliament, 2004–9

| | |
|---|---|
| EPP-ED | European People's Party (Christian democrats) and European Democrats |
| PES | Party of European Socialists |
| ALDE | Alliance of Liberals and Democrats for Europe |
| G/EFA | Greens/European Free Alliance |
| EUL/NGL | European United Left/Nordic Green Left |
| UEN | Union for Europe of the Nations Group |
| IND/DEM | Group for Independence and Democracy |
| NA | Non-attached |

supranational legal order. Through constitutional-isation—the process by which the founding treaties were transformed from texts binding the member states to a source of rights that can be invoked by individuals against their governments—the Court developed 'a new legal order for the Community'.

### Origins

Like the European Parliament, the European Court of Justice traces its origins back to the ECSC and became a common institution of the Communities under the Rome Treaties. In order to ease the Court's growing workload, a Court of First Instance (CFI) was created by the SEA to hear cases in areas that involved extensive fact-finding. The Treaty of Nice provided for the creation of special judicial panels to deal with cases in particular areas, including those involving the staff of EU institutions. The European Union Civil Service tribunal, consisting of seven judges, was established by a decision of the Council of Ministers in November 2004 to adjudicate in such disputes.

### Functions and responsibilities

By entrusting the European Court of Justice with responsibility 'to ensure that, in the interpretation and application of [the] treaty, the law is observed' (Art. 220), the founders distinguished the Community from other international organisations, where treaties do not bind their signatories and there is no comparable mechanism of enforcement. The founding treaties set out six categories

of dispute which the European Court of Justice is called upon to resolve. The first, infringement actions, which can be brought by the Commission or by another member states, were discussed above in relation to the Commission's watchdog function. The second, preliminary rulings (Art. 234, ex 177), has been instrumental in the development of a Community legal system with the European Court of Justice at its apex. As the Community has no equivalent to federal courts, Community law in the member states is enforced by national courts. To ensure the uniform application of Community law, the treaty created a mechanism allowing the European Court of Justice to make an authoritative ruling on the interpretation on any aspect of Community law referred to it by a national authority. The Court's ruling in such instances is binding not only on the court that makes the referral, but in all national courts dealing with the same issue. The number of requests received by the Court has been substantial, rising from one or two a year in the 1960s to more than 100 in the late 1970s and above 200 in the late 1990s. By creating a 'set of institutionalised dialogues between supranational and national judges' (Stone Sweet 1998: 305), the system of preliminary rulings has been a major factor in the development of the Court's authority and, in particular, the penetration of national legal systems by Community law. The Court has enunciated many of its main constitutional principles cases in these rulings. (See Background box 11.1.)

---

**BACKGROUND BOX 11.1**

Key Rulings of the European Court of Justice

### Constitutional rulings

#### 'Direct effect' doctrine

*Van Gend en Loos* (case 26/62): In this ruling, which marked the initial step towards constitutionalisation, the Court held that the treaties confer rights and impose obligations on individuals which national courts are bound to recognise and enforce. It enabled

individuals to invoke the freedoms cited in the treaties as rights, thereby underlining the difference between Community law and international law, which applies only to states. Later rulings extended the doctrine to all legal acts. In *Francovich I* (case 9/90), moreover, the Court established the principle of state liability for damages where national authorities fail to fulfil their Community obligations.

### 'Supremacy' doctrine

*COSTA v. ENEL* (case 6/64): The Court ruled that the spirit of the treaties revealed the member states' intention to create a Community that limits their sovereign rights and binds them. It followed that Community law takes precedence over national law. In further judgements, it made it clear that national judges, when dealing with a conflict between national and Community law, must be capable of acting to ensure that the primacy of Community law is respected. In *Simmenthal* (case 106/77), it affirmed that national law could not hinder the application of Community law and, in *Factortame* (case 213/89), that a national judge is obliged to give interim relief.

### Other important rulings

#### Freedom of movement

*Dassonville* (case 8/74): The Court declared illegal any national provision that was 'capable of hindering, actually or potentially, directly or indirectly, intra-Community trade'.

In *Cassis de Dijon* (case 120/78), it ruled that any product legally sold in one member state can be sold anywhere else in the Union. This case gave rise to the principle of mutual recognition, which the Commission adopted in its white paper on the single market.

*Bosman* (case 415/93): The Court ruled that a footballer had the right to move to another club at the end of his contract without a transfer fee.

#### Sexual equality

*Defrenne* (43/75): The Court ruled that a Belgian air hostess had the right to equal treatment with her male colleagues.

---

The Court can review the legality of acts of a Community institution in cases brought by a member state, the Council, Commission and, in some cases, the Parliament (Art. 230), and annul them where the action is well founded (Art. 231)—a third function. Its other responsibilities are: reviewing the legality of a failure to act on the part of a Community action; determining Community liability for damage caused by the institutions or their servants in carrying out their duties; and adjudicating on the legality of international agreements.

The Court is essentially reactive like most constitutional courts: it cannot decide on the content or timing of the cases that come before it. Its deliberations are secret, decisions are taken by a majority, and dissenters do not publish their views. The rulings of the Court have had a profound impact on the development of the Communities, relations between institutions, and on the substance of policy at the EU level and in the member states.

### Structure and organisation

The European Court of Justice is composed of one judge per member state, appointed by the common accord of member governments for a renewable six-year term. Though national approaches differ, judges must be jurists whose independence is beyond doubt and who are of recognised competence. A president is elected for a three-year renewable term to direct the business and administration of the Court. The Court also includes eight advocates-general—two from the larger member states, the remainder from small countries in rotation. The advocate-general—there is no equivalent in any of the member states—works on cases with the judges and pronounces a first non-binding opinion on the issues in a particular case. Advocates-general have similar qualification to judges. Cases can be heard in chambers of three or five, or plenaries of 11 or 15 judges—since 1974, preliminary rulings have been made by chambers—though cases brought by Community institutions or member states are heard by the full Court.

The Court of First Instance (CFI), which heard its first cases in November 1989, is also composed of one member per member state by common accord of the member states to hold office for a renewable six-year term. There are no permanent advocates-general, but a similar duty is performed by one of the judges. The CFI's jurisdiction, initially limited, has been expanded to include competition cases and all actions by non-privileged actors under Articles 230, 232 and 235. Under the Treaty of Nice, it became the common court for almost all direct actions, as well as preliminary rulings in certain areas. It was also permitted to set up specialised chambers to deal with particular case categories, such as staff disputes, and allowed to appoint advocates-general. A losing party can appeal the legal findings of the Court of First Instance, but not the facts.

---

**KEY POINTS**

- The EU is unlike other international organisations in that member states are required to submit to its authority.

- The Court has responsibility for ensuring that the member states and other parties comply with their obligations under Community law.

- The European Court of Justice has played a key role in the Union's development as a supranational order and the process of constitutionalisation.

---

# EU Institutions Today

The European Union and its institutions confront several challenges. Of those that concern all four institutions, the most important is the democratic deficit. There are also several institution-specific issues that raise debate.

## The democratic deficit

The debate concerning its democratic credentials is the most urgent, but also the most intractable, issue that confronts the EU (See Theme box: Democracy and Legitimacy.). Not only are there widely varying diagnoses and, therefore, multiple prescriptions for how it should be remedied, but the very existence of a democratic deficit is itself contested. (See Table 11.9.) More broadly, the issue of the Union's legitimacy raises the question as to whether any international organisation can be democratic. The discussion here is limited to how arguments concerning the democratic deficit relate to individual institutions.

The main question relating to the European Commission concerns its alleged lack of democratic accountability, given the important functions that it performs, some of which it carries out

---

**THEME BOX**

### Democracy and Legitimacy

The democratic credentials of the EU came increasingly into question in the 1980s with the adoption of the single market project. The extension of Community competencies, combined with the greater use of qualified majority voting in the Council of Ministers, as well as the accelerated legislative output, intense activism on the part of the Commission and the mobilisation of interest groups at the EC-level, led to concerns that decision-making power was migrating from its traditional seat in national capitals to a distant authority. The difficulty is that democratic theory has historically provided a model for the nation state, based on the idea that citizens elect a government to deliver policies that serve their interests. However, it offers few prescriptions for an interdependent world, where individual governments acting alone can no longer unilaterally secure goals on behalf of their citizens. How to make democratic an international organisation, such as the European Union, which enables constrained states to achieve collectively what they can no longer attain individually, is a major challenge. While diagnoses of the EU's democratic properties vary considerably (see Table 11.9), it is unclear the extent to which a model essentially developed for sovereign states can provide a route map.

**Table 11.9** The Debate on the EU's Democratic Deficit

| Diagnosis | Argument | Comments |
|---|---|---|
| No democratic deficit (Jean Monnet, as interpreted by Featherstone 1994) | European integration is an essentially technocratic process, led by a small body of experts with the technical knowledge to develop common policies and able to engage key economic elites by persuading them of their self interest in the project of unification. | • Motivated by the functionalist belief that politicians are self-serving, but that technocrats would advance integration in the interests of Europe. |
| No democratic deficit (Majone 2002a) | The EU is a 'regulatory state', whose purpose is to implement efficient policies that benefit everyone. Efficiency is best engineered by a body of non-elected experts—a 'non-majoritarian' institution—such as the Commission. Politicisation in the form of electoral or political accountability would undermine the pursuit of efficiency and lead to policies that favour particular social groups to the detriment of the common good. | • Elections ensure that decision-makers remain responsive to citizens. There is no substitute (Hix 2005: 179).<br>• Political competition would make it more likely that citizens would form preferences in relation to policies that are currently poorly understood, such as economic reform, trade and regional development (Hix 2005: 179). |
| No democratic deficit (Moravcsik 2002) | Power is not centralised in Brussels, but under the control of national governments, who are accountable to their electorates. EU competencies are limited to areas that, at a national level, are exercised by unelected bodies ('non-majoritarian' institutions), such as independent central banks. | • The EU has broad competencies and, though decisions are taken collectively by member governments, individual governments can be outvoted. |

*(continued overleaf)*

**Table 11.9** (continued)

| Diagnosis | Argument | Comments |
|---|---|---|
| A democratic deficit exists, because EU decision-making escapes parliamentary scrutiny | 1. Strengthen the European Parliament (Bogdanor and Woolcock 1991; Williams 1991).<br><br>2. Strengthen national parliaments by:<br>• creating an EU-level chamber composed of national parliamentarians<br>• strengthening scrutiny arrangements of EU policy at the national level<br>• introducing the requirement that, where national parliaments object to a Commission proposal, that proposal is reconsidered by the Commission or withdrawn. | 1. The European Parliament has been strengthened, but remains a junior partner in many areas, the constituency link is weak, and electoral contests are 'second-order' elections.<br><br>2. As well as making the EU still more complex, a chamber of national parliamentarians would create a conflict of mandates with the Parliament and the Council.<br>• Do sufficient incentives exist for national MPs to specialise in EU policy?<br>• Would parliaments vote on the merits of the proposal before them? |
| A democratic deficit exists, because European citizens do not have the opportunity to 'throw the rascals out' (Hix 2002; Follesdal and Hix 2005) | Political contestation and an electoral link between citizens or their representatives and decision-makers are minimal conditions for democracy. The Commission president should be elected by national parliaments or nominated by the European Parliament. | • Would an electoral college of national parliaments necessarily increase citizen awareness of EU politics or encourage domestic political contestation about EU policy?<br>• Could partisanalising the Commission president *reduce* the legitimacy of the Commission, as the Commission would be identified with a faction or coalition rather than the common interest of the Union? |
| The EU suffers from a democratic deficit: it does not function like a democracy, and through its action undermines democracy in the member states (Schmitter 2000) | The EU is not a democracy. It does not have the typical attributes of a state and so must take its own path to democracy. It will need to define EU citizenship, ensure effective and widespread interest representation, and devise a constitution. | • Would a Union-wide referendum on an EU constitution be fought on its merits or would it be a domestic plebiscite on the sitting government's performance?<br>• Would simplifying EU procedures disturb the intricate balance between the three bodies representing the interests of the states of Europe, the people of Europe or Europe's general interest? |

**Table 11.9** (continued)

| Diagnosis | Argument | Comments |
|---|---|---|
| A democratic deficit exists, because there is no European demos | The existence of a demos, an ethno-cultural community or *Volk*, is a prerequisite of democracy, since only such a community, as a community of destiny, will accept the disciplines of majoritarian governance. As there is no European demos, the European Union cannot be democratic. | 'Community' can equally be defined in terms of shared values, and the ethno-cultural theory of citizenship by nationality is eminently contestable (see Weiler *et al.* 1995). A demos in this alternative sense may be the outcome of the rise of a democratic state rather than a precondition of it, as in the USA, and citizenship is linked to international bodies, not only nation states. |
| By enabling governments to achieve outcomes through joint action that is beyond their ability individually to attain, the EU serves the interests of citizens (Menon and Weatherill 2006) | According to Fritz Scharpf (2002), democracy has two elements: input legitimacy or 'government by the people'; and output legitimacy, or 'government for the people'. Historically, governments combined both, but interdependence has made it less possible for governments individually to deliver policies that benefit its citizens. Although the EU does not score highly in regard to input legitimacy, because its structures are not designed to allow for the periodic election of decision-makers, the Union does possess output legitimacy as through its common policies and action it enables member governments to realise goals that benefit their citizens, which if the EU did not exist they would not be able to bring about. | • Is Scharpf's distinction valid?<br>• Does the EU's greater output legitimacy outweigh its lack of input legitimacy?<br>• Can input legitimacy and output legitimacy be traded off? |

independently, and the fact that it is unelected. However, the areas in which the Commission has decision-making power are limited and the Commission is, in fact, 'multiply accountable' (Christiansen 1997):

- Commissioners are appointed by the member states and must be approved by the European Parliament.

- The Parliament can vote the Commission out of office by a censure motion.

- In most areas, the Commission is not a final decision-maker.

- When performing its executive functions, the Commission is controlled by the member states through 'comitology'.

- The exercise by the Commission of its financial responsibilities is scrutinised by the European Court of Auditors and by the European Parliament.

How the Commission is selected is a question that has attracted considerable interest. One radical proposal aimed at enhancing the Union's democratic credentials, as well as mobilising citizen interest, is for the Commission president to be elected by national parliaments (Hix 2002) or nominated by the European Parliament (Follesdal and Hix 2005). However, Giandomenico Majone (2002) has voiced concern about moves in this direction. He argues that strengthening its accountability in this way is likely to undermine the Commission's independence, since the Commission's ability to act in the long-term interests of the Community will be jeopardised by its concern to secure partisan support.

Three features of the Council are often raised in relation to the debate about the democratic deficit. The first concerns the impact of QMV. When a decision is taken by unanimity, it can be argued that it has the assent of all EU citizens expressed through government representatives in the Council. However, no such claim can be made to the citizens of countries whose governments are part of an outvoted minority. The high proportion of decisions that are taken within the Council before proposals reach the ministerial level is a second cause of concern. While ministers are elected representatives, the officials that attend working groups and COREPER are not. This is not a problem when officials act subject to ministerial instruction, but citizens need to be sure that this is in fact the case. The third issue concerns the extent to which national interests are effectively represented in Council negotiations and whether the positions adopted by national representatives are open to scrutiny by national parliaments. In fact, due to contrasting national arrangements, very few legislatures have the opportunity to discuss, influence or still less determine the negotiating position adopted by their government.

As the Union's only directly elected institution, the European Parliament is at the centre of debates about the democratic deficit. That decisions taken in Brussels are beyond the scrutiny of national parliaments has been an important motivation for strengthening and broadening the European Parliament's powers. However, the Parliament is not omnicompetent and EU action is unlikely to receive scrutiny from any parliament, therefore, where the European Parliament is weak. A second concern is that turnout for elections to the European Parliament remains low and in 2004 fell for the fifth time in succession. Moreover, even those EU citizens who vote tend to regard European elections as 'second-order' contests, more about domestic issues than EU-wide concerns. Furthermore, increasing support for strengthening the role of national parliaments, as in the **Convention on the Future of Europe**, suggests that expanding the European Parliament's power is not the only or even the best way of addressing the EU's legitimacy.

Arguments concerning the European Court of Justice are made from opposing perspectives. To the contention often made of national courts that the European Court of Justice as an unelected body should not overturn decisions taken by elected authorities, critics have added the allegation that the Court has unilaterally extended its own powers and established a legal order that was not anticipated in the founding treaties. However, its supporters have argued that the Court's jurisdiction should be extended in some areas, notably, justice and home affairs, to ensure that individual rights are protected, and that the range of actors who can take cases to the Court should be broadened.

## Institution-specific issues

Each institution also has issues that it would like to press or faces particular challenges. The Commission, while still a key actor, has become less influential in recent years. Since the Maastricht IGC, governments have become increasingly reluctant to entrust it with further responsibilities. 'Europe' has become a salient domestic issue and governments are under increasing public scrutiny, preferring to strengthen other institutions and to assert their own power.[8] The Commission has in addition not always helped itself. Under Jacques Delors, it enjoyed many successes but, at the same time, member governments became anxious about its expanding influence. It was also not clear that the Commission commanded sufficient resources for its new responsibilities, such as coordinating aid to former communist states in Central and Eastern Europe after 1989, or that it could easily adapt as an organisation principally concerned with producing policy ideas to one increasingly called on to manage policy. Though it sought to 'do less, better', the Santer Commission (1995–9) is likely to be remembered for its humiliating resignation in the wake of allegations about nepotism and corruption. Despite the high calibre of its members, the Prodi Commission (1999–2004) that followed was marked by ineffective leadership. The Commission of José Manuel Barroso (2005–), meanwhile, has yet to make its mark, despite the fact that, unusually, members of the College come predominantly from the same political (centre-right) background.

The Council faces managerial problems, which have become increasingly acute with the accession of ten 'new' member states on 1 May 2004.[9]

The larger member states, in particular, consider that the six-monthly rotating presidency fails to provide the necessary continuity and have argued for a more permanent arrangement. Largely at their behest, the Constitutional Treaty would have introduced a renewable two-and-a-half year term for the president of the European Council and allowed sectoral Councils to choose their own chairs, but failure to secure ratification has left that proposed new arrangement in abeyance. Though in theory the General Affairs and External Relations Council ensures coordination between the other Councils, foreign ministers are too busy with external affairs. As a consequence, 'no one is in control' (Gomez and Peterson 2001), and there is no effective mechanism to ensure that labour is divided efficiently or that the decisions taken in the various Council formations are compatible. The voting system introduced by the Treaty of Nice, which came into effect on 1 November 2004, is also problematic. As well as securing a majority of states and votes, governments can request verification that a winning coalition also carries a majority of the Union's population, establishing in effect a triple majority requirement. In addition, the weighting of votes has become an increasingly sensitive issue. Finally, the effective operation of the Council depends to a large degree on the efficiency of national systems. Though the European Council can exhort governments to ensure that EU business is coordinated effectively, it can do little more.

The Parliament has experienced a remarkable ascent since the 1980s. However, MEPs express discontent that the scope of co-decision is still limited and point to policy areas where the Parliament remains weak. Its exclusion from comitology, despite its increased role in the legislative process, is also a source of grievance. The European Court of Justice, like many constitutional courts at the national level, has attracted criticism. The pro-integrationist stance that it has historically taken made governments wary of the effects of its intervention and so they have been careful to exclude sensitive areas—notably the second and third pillars—from its jurisdiction. A different sort

194

of concern relates to the appointment of judges to the Court. As St Clair Bradley (2002: 121) points out, the Court is the only institution whose members are selected without being subject to scrutiny.

---

**KEY POINTS**

- The EU's democratic credentials are frequently questioned, but the status of the democratic deficit is contested and there are many different interpretations of it.

- Although the European Parliament has been strengthened in response to demands to make the EU more democratic, low turnout in European Parliament elections has mitigated these efforts.

- The Commission's decline and the complexity of the Council confront the EU with potentially serious managerial problems.

---

# EU Institutions in Theoretical Perspective

The relationship between the member states and the institutions, and particularly the extent to which institutions are able to act independently, has been a perennial concern of the literature on the European Union. Historically, the debate was conducted between intergovernmentalism, a theoretical viewpoint which contends that national governments control the integration process, including EU institutions, and neofunctionalism, an approach that highlights the capacities of the supranational institutions and which argues that cooperation, once initiated, would spread inexorably from sector to sector. However, though intergovernmentalism survives, neofunctionalism has increasingly given way to more sophisticated 'supranationalist' analyses, which emphasise the resources available to EU institutions and the limited ability of national governments to control them (Pierson 1996; Pollack 1996, 2003; Kassim and Menon 2004).

Though there is a general consensus about the instrumental motives that led the signatory states to create the EU institutions, only intergovernmentalism holds that the Commission and the Court remain subordinate to member state control. Scholars writing from supranational perspectives argue that these institutions develop their own preferences and mobilise the resources at their disposal to act on their agendas. For a variety of reasons, governments cannot easily reassert their control. Although created to serve the interests of the member states, therefore, both the Commission and the Council have at times demonstrated their autonomy.

These two perspectives offer competing conceptualisations of the Council. The Council is cast by intergovernmentalism as a venue for 'hard bargaining' between national governments. Each government comes to the table with a pre-formed position that it seeks to advance through negotiations, its bargaining power linked to its size and the intensity of its desire for an agreement. An alternative viewpoint, which draws on the work of early neofunctionalists and more recent sociological approaches, argues that national governments may indeed try to ensure that their interests prevail, but that the interaction between states within the Council is governed by shared norms and a collective identity that has developed within the institution as a result of repeated interaction (Wallace 1991). Rather than 'hard bargaining', the pattern is one of 'accommodation in which the participants refrain from unconditionally vetoing proposals and instead seek to attain agreement by means of compromises upgrading common interests' (E. B. Haas, cited in Edwards 1996: 128). It is less an interstate body, the internal interchanges of which take the form of classic diplomacy, and acting separately from other institutions, but rather a body at the supranational level, imbricated in a complex institutional setting and in permanent interaction with the Commission and the European Parliament.

Finally, attention in the scholarly literature has focused on why the Parliament's power has increased and on political behaviour and organisation within the Parliament. With respect to the first, some authors have pointed to the Parliament's adaptability and its ability to exploit its new powers (Bowler and Farrell 1995) or its use of discretion in interpreting rules to turn informal practice into formal procedure (Hix 2002), but others, notably Berthold Rittberger (2005), focus instead on the member states' concern to empower the Parliament in order to make the Union more democratic. In relation to the second, there is considerable interest in the political groups (Hix and Lord 1997) and their impact on the voting behaviour in the European Parliament (Kreppel 2002), as well as on the socialisation of MEPs into the Parliament's culture and norms (Scully 2005). Comparisons are frequently drawn with national parliaments, particularly the US Congress.

# Conclusion

The experiment embarked upon by the founding members of the Communities has been a remarkable success, to which successive enlargements and the prospect of further accessions, as well as initiatives at regional integration modelled on the European example in other parts of the world, bear eloquent testimony. As well as providing a path to post-war peace and prosperity, it has enabled member states to adapt to often dramatically changing circumstances. (See Theme box: The Impact of Globalisation.) The launch of the single market programme, for example, enabled governments to respond to the crisis of competitiveness that developed in the 1980s while, by coordinating assistance to the states of Central and Eastern Europe following the collapse of communist regimes, and ultimately by the extension of membership to states within the region, the Union provided an essential service in making the transformation to the post-Cold War world. Fundamentally, the Union provides a setting in which European states can develop collective responses to the problems that arise from economic interdependence, an arena for devising solutions to transnational problems, such as environmental pollution, drug trafficking and illegal immigration, and an ongoing forum that allows governments to address matters of common concern without the repeated need to create new international bodies. It has repeatedly demonstrated its usefulness and adaptability.

Despite the Union's successes and continuing achievements, however, its structure is a source of difficulties. The institutional system that member states initially created was already complex, but it has been further complicated by enlargement and the accumulation of responsibilities. The sharing of functions between EU institutions, the high level of organisational density, the mix of legislative procedures and Council decision rules and the pattern of sectorised decision-making make the system opaque to citizens and difficult for policy actors to negotiate. This complexity is rooted in a basic tension between the requirements of collective action and the desire of governments to ensure their control over the EU's direction. Though even in the late 1980s, the member states were prepared to delegate important responsibilities to the European Commission, this readiness has declined

## THEME BOX

### The Impact of Globalisation

The founding of the Communities aimed not only at enabling politically and economically interdependent states to coordinate policy and action, but to meet the challenge of post-war American economic dominance collectively. The EU has perhaps stood in a more complex relationship with regard to globalisation. Simplifying somewhat, it has, on the one hand, through the creation of the single market been able to offer member states a measure of protection from globalisation or at least has enabled them to adjust to the new pressures for competitiveness that emerged in the 1980s. On the other, the EU has acted as an agent of change externally through its support for the removal of international trade barriers and internally by compelling governments that have historically pursued policies of state interventionism to abandon protectionism in favour of neo-liberal economic and industrial policy. At the same time, the EU is an important global player economically and politically. In trade terms, it accounts for more than a fifth of global imports and exports and, with a population of more than 450 million, is an important world market. It is a key actor in the World Trade Organization, and has trade agreements with regional groupings and third countries, particularly, less developed states, across the globe. Launched in 1999, the euro is becoming a world currency. The EU is also active in many international regimes. Examples include environmental and maritime policy.

and, since the 1991 Maastricht Intergovernmental Conference, governments have generally preferred to take a leading role. The result in some areas at least has been slower and less effective decision-making.

Two other problems have come more sharply into focus. The first is coordination. The broadening of the EU's responsibilities, its growing complexity and institutional fragmentation, have made it increasingly important to avoid costly duplication and to ensure that policies are compatible. However, it is by no means clear that the need for effective improved coordination within and between EU institutions, between EU institutions and national bodies, and within national political systems has been met. At the EU level, there have been some positive developments, including a proliferation of inter-institutional agreements and greater administrative cooperation particularly among the Secretariats-General of the Commission, Council and Parliament. However, coordination between the European Council, the main source of grand policy initiatives, and the Commission, whose job it is to bring forward concrete policy proposals and manage policy programmes, remains problematic. Within all three of the law-making main institutions, moreover, coordination mechanisms

are weak and decision-making highly sectorised. In relation to EU-member state relations, there is little evidence that the European Council takes into account whether member states have the institutional infrastructure necessary for the implementation of the often grand policy objectives it pronounces (Schout and Jordan 2005). At the national level, meanwhile, there is considerable variation in the coordination ambitions and capacities of the member states (Kassim *et al.* 2000, 2001).

The second challenge concerns democracy. The debate over the EU's democratic credentials was discussed above, but there is also an important domestic dimension. A number of scholars, in particular Fritz Scharpf (2002) have argued that the European Union has been remarkably effective in building a single market and thereby in imposing constraints on the actions that governments can take in the area of economic, industrial and social policy. The design of its decision-making procedures, however, prevents it from developing the policies at the European level, notably in the area of welfare, to compensate for the loss of protection at the national level.

The member states have so far shown little interest in addressing these issues. Even at the

Convention on the Future of Europe which met 2002–2003 and the Intergovernmental Conference that followed, these topics were not the main subject of debate. However, the ability of the European Union to deliver effectively and to secure the confidence of citizens will depend upon the ability and willingness of national governments to find solutions to them.

# Notes

1. Strictly speaking, the European Union came into existence only on 1 November 1993 when the Treaty of European Union took effect. However, for stylistic purposes, the term 'European Union' is used even when reference is made to the earlier period.

2. The EU's hybrid nature has created a lively debate about the relative merits of international relations and comparative politics approaches. For a key exchange, see Hix (1994) and Hurrell and Menon (1994).

3. In practice, only the three executives had fully separate lives. According to Myles (1992: 138): 'Each of the 1957 treaties created a Court, Council and Assembly, but the new assemblies, ECSC assemblies, two new courts of justice and the ECSC court were merged into a single assembly and single court by the Convention annexed to each of the 1957 treaties, but the CEC, HA and Councils were untouched.'

4. For example, in the common foreign and security policy, justice and home affairs, and economic and monetary union, the European Council and/or the Council play key roles, the Commission is a marginal actor, and the Parliament and Court are excluded. Helen Wallace (2005: 87) terms this mode of decision-making 'intensive transgovernmentalism'. In other areas, including employment and the Lisbon Process, policy-making is even looser. National governments compare experiences and benchmark practices, but are under no compulsion to implement a common policy.

Wallace refers to this as 'policy coordination' (2005: 85–7).

5. Council Decision on comitology (1999/468 /EC) of 28 June 1999, OJ L184, 17 July 1999, distinguishes five procedures with associated committee types: advisory, where the Commission need consult only national experts; management, where it can proceed unless national officials vote by qualified majority voting (QMV) to oppose it; regulatory, under which the Commission adopts its proposed measures, only if the Council adopts it by QMV or fails to act within the specified period; safeguard, where a member state can refer the Commission's decision to the Council, which may then confirm, amend or revoke the decision by QMV; or Council itself, where the Council itself exercises direct implementing powers.

6. Only the presidents of Finland and France are actually heads of state. Other members are heads of government.

7. Certain technical aspects of agriculture are not dealt with by COREPER, but by the Special Committee on Agriculture.

8. For example, they have extended the range of issues dealt with by the European Council. At its annual spring Council, the heads of state and government deliberate on areas of economic and social policy that were previously in the Commission's domain.

9. See the Presidency Conclusions from the Seville European Council, June 2002 at http:// europa.eu.int/european_council/conclusions/ index_en.htm.

## ? QUESTIONS

1.  Why did the founding member states create such a complex institutional structure?
2.  What features distinguish the European Union from intergovernmental international organisations?
3.  Why did member governments decide to delegate functions such as policy initiation and enforcement to supranational institutions?
4.  Is the Commission too powerful or not powerful enough?
5.  Is the Council still the EU's decision-making centre?
6.  What accounts for the European Council's ability to play a leadership role within the EU?
7.  In what says is the European Parliament comparable to national parliaments?
8.  What role does the European Court of Justice play in the EU system?
9.  Does the EU have a 'democratic deficit'? If so, how might it be resolved?
10. Do member states control the destiny of the European Union?

## FURTHER READING

■ **Spence, D. and Edwards, G. (eds) (2006),** *The European Commission*, **3rd edn, London, John Harper.** Written by academics and practitioners, provides an authoritative and comprehensive examination of the European Commission.

■ **Stevens, A. and Stevens, H. (2001),** *Brussels Bureaucrats? The Administration of the European Union*, **London, Palgrave.** An interesting and accessible overview, which considers the development and operation of the Commission as an administration.

■ **Dimitrakopoulos, D. G. (ed.) (2004),** *The Changing European Commission*, **Manchester, Manchester University Press.** Looks at the European Commission in theoretical and historical perspective.

■ **Westlake, M. and Galloway, D. (2004),** *The Council of the European Union*, **3rd edn, London, John Harper.** The most authoritative text on the most powerful EU institution.

■ **Hayes-Renshaw, F. and Wallace, H. (2006),** *The Council of Ministers*, **Basingstoke, Macmillan.** The updated version of a classic study.

■ **Corbett, R., Jacobs, F. and Shackleton, M. (2005),** *The European Parliament*, **6th edn, London, John Harper.** The definitive work on the EU's only directly elected institution, written by three insiders.

■ **Rittberger, B. (2005),** *Building Europe's Parliament: Democratic Representation Beyond the Nation State*, **Oxford, Oxford University Press.** The first work to attempt a theoretical account of the rise of the institution.

■ **Dehousse, R. (1998)** *The European Court of Justice*, **Basingstoke, Palgrave.** Provides a good introduction and overview.

■ **Slaughter, A.-M., Stone Sweet, A. and Weiler, J. H. H. (eds) (1998),** *The European Court and National Courts: Doctrine and Jurisprudence*, **Oxford, Hart Publishing.** Offers theoretical and interpretive analysis from the leading writers in the field on this key relationship.

■ Rosamond, B. (2000) *Theories of European Integration*, Basingstoke, Palgrave. Provides an excellent introduction to, and overview of, the main theories applied to the European Union.

 **IMPORTANT WEBSITES**

● **http://europa.eu.int/** The official EU website is an extremely rich resource, providing a gateway to the texts of the treaties, the websites of all the institutions, and information about EU policies.

● **www.euractiv.com/** An excellent source for day-to-day commentary on EU affairs.

● **www.EuropeanVoice.com** Provides a weekly insiders' view of developments in Brussels.

 **Visit the Online Resource Centre that accompanies this book for lots of useful additional material, including an interactive map of Europe. www.oxfordtextbooks.co.uk/orc/hay_menon/**

# 12 European Parties and Party Systems

## ROBERT LADRECH

### ✔ Reader's Guide

This chapter looks at the role political parties play in contemporary European democracies. It begins with a brief discussion of the origins of modern European political parties, and then presents the main party families. The chapter then considers the internal organisation of political parties before turning to an examination of party systems. The chapter ends with a discussion of the changes and challenges facing parties in Western Europe and a brief introduction to the situation of parties in the post-communist states of Eastern Europe.

# Introduction

Political parties are critical to the working of representative politics. In Europe, party politics is central to the operation of modern government and politics. In fact, to understand the workings of European government is to essentially describe *party government*. Competitive parliamentary elections between two or more parties determine which party or coalition of parties will form a majority in parliament and therefore run government. In those few European political systems in which a president is directly elected, for example France or Finland, they are also party politicians. Unlike in the USA, most European countries have more than two significant parties that contest elections and form governments. Elections are fought between rival parties' platforms or manifestos, much more than between personalities. Many European political systems employ electoral rules that virtually ensure multi-party systems, by using a form of proportional representation (PR) based upon multi-member electoral districts. Thus, unlike the USA or Britain, where the candidate with the most votes wins the legislative seat, most European countries allot seats according to the percentage of the vote received, thereby ensuring that even medium and small parties have the chance to wins seats in a national parliament.

Political parties, and the shape of national party systems, emerged slowly over the past 200 years, in some cases simultaneously with the creation of modern states, such as Germany or Italy in the 1860s and 1870s. It has been argued that the presence of regional or sub-national parties, for example the Scottish National Party or the Catalan National Party, is due to the manner in which the British and Spanish state emerged, in which well defined identities continued to exist after the consolidation of the modern state by central elites. With the establishment of fully fledged parliamentary democracy in the twentieth century, these 'peripheral' identities were able to express themselves in parties supportive or protective of their rights. Christian democratic parties, this argument continues, owe their existence to the defence of the rights of the church from national and or secular elites during the period of state formation. Together with other major historical developments, such as the Industrial Revolution, the type of parties and the number of parties in national political systems can in many cases be traced back to these momentous events and trends.

The ideological range of parties is broad, from far left to far right, and new types of parties—such as green parties—do emerge over time, although the main parties of government are basically those of the centre-left and the centre-right. The parties of the centre-left are usually labelled variously social democratic, socialist or labour (for example, the Danish Social Democratic Party, the French Socialist Party, the British Labour Party). The parties of the centre-right are usually labelled variously Christian democratic, conservative or people's party (for example, the German Christian Democratic Union, the British Conservative Party, the Spanish People's Party). These parties belong to transnational **party families**, or groupings of ideologically similar parties. Many of these party families also have a European-level party federation to which they belong. These, in turn, are linked to **party groups** in the European Parliament. The two biggest transnational party federations are the Party of European Socialists (PES), encompassing all of the social democratic, socialist and labour parties, and the European People's Party (EPP), which began as a Christian democratic organisation but has expanded its membership to include parties such as Forza Italia of Italy or New Democracy in Greece.

Although most Western European countries have had competitive parliamentary elections since the late nineteenth or early twentieth century, it was only following the collapse of communist regimes in Eastern Europe after 1990 that this type of politics came to define Central and East European political systems (see Haughton, Chapter 9, this volume). Consequently, the challenges facing contemporary parties differ to a certain extent between parties in established Western European political systems and those in countries where parliamentary democracy is a more recent phenomenon. Much of what we know about political parties comes from the history of Western European parties and, to a certain extent, many western observers of Eastern and East-Central European politics have based their assumptions about party politics on western experiences. We will see that, if anything, party politics in former communist regimes is marked by flux in terms of ideology, organisation and electoral support.

For established political parties in Western Europe, one of the changes noted by political scientists since the 1970s has been a process known as **de-alignment**. (See Background box 12.1.) This is a process in which parties gradually lose the secure electoral support of social groups, for example, working-class support for centre-left parties. This has meant that elections are less predictable, as voting patterns are more volatile from election to election.

Another challenge confronting parties is that of turning electoral promises into government policy.

The range of public-policy choices open to parties in government has been circumscribed by the growth in the policy competence of the European Union (EU). Thus, for those EU member states that form part of the so-called Eurozone, the ability to set interest rates is no longer a national prerogative, being the responsibility of the European Central Bank (ECB). How political parties deal with this constraint on the manoeuvrability of national government is one of the challenges for parties in the twenty-first century. (See Theme box: The Impact of Globalisation.)

## KEY POINTS

- Proportional representation (PR) voting systems are common in European elections.

- There is a broad range of party ideologies, ranging from far left to far right.

- Many national parties are affiliated to European Parliament party groups.

- Western experience of party activity informs much analysis of post-communist party development.

- The development of the European Union has had an indirect effect on party legitimacy.

## BACKGROUND BOX 12.1

### De-alignment

The voter alignments analysed by Lipset and Rokkan (1967), and explained by cleavage structures, appeared to be giving way in the 1970s. Increased voting volatility suggested that patterns of electoral support for parties were perhaps eroding. Subsequent political analysis has presented several hypotheses, with electoral de-alignment one of the more prominent of them. If voting alignments had been 'frozen' for some time, then the evidence began to suggest that electorates were becoming unstructured and, furthermore, this could continue, thereby undermining or causing the decline of parties in favour of other types of political mobilisation.

The de-alignment argument has three components. First, there is a decline in party identification by voters. This decline in identification leads to a decreased urgency or feeling of obligation to vote in the first place. Survey research highlighted the decline of party identification, and the decrease in electoral turnout across most western democracies seemed to confirm the linkage between identification and motivation to vote. Second, the established parties have lost voters to new parties. Whether turning to green parties, or to anti-tax parties or extreme right-wing parties, voters were rejecting the 'old' parties. The percentage of the vote going to the older parties remains the largest in all Western European political systems, but has declined somewhat from the 1950s and 1960s. Third and last, the decline of social group cleavage linkages has meant that voting has become more individualised, and therefore election outcomes have become more unpredictable. Aggregate voter volatility, which measures levels of change from one election to the next, increased in the 1970s, declined a little in the 1980s, and increased again in the 1990s.

Without strong ties to particular parties, voters are now more susceptible to many more intervening variables as to how to vote. With less secure electorates than in the past, many parties have turned to media technology, and a more candidate-centred approach, in order to attract voters.

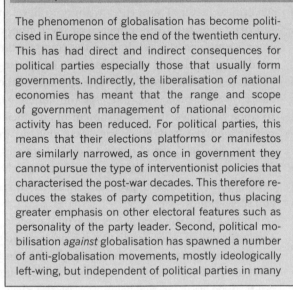

**THEME BOX**

## The Impact of Globalisation

The phenomenon of globalisation has become politicised in Europe since the end of the twentieth century. This has had direct and indirect consequences for political parties especially those that usually form governments. Indirectly, the liberalisation of national economies has meant that the range and scope of government management of national economic activity has been reduced. For political parties, this means that their elections platforms or manifestos are similarly narrowed, as once in government they cannot pursue the type of interventionist policies that characterised the post-war decades. This therefore reduces the stakes of party competition, thus placing greater emphasis on other electoral features such as personality of the party leader. Second, political mobilisation *against* globalisation has spawned a number of anti-globalisation movements, mostly ideologically left-wing, but independent of political parties in many cases. For social democratic parties in particular, this forces them to respond to an agenda not of their making. In some cases, such as at economic summits of the World Trade Organization (WTO), in which social democratic government ministers may be central players, left-wing activists may be protesting outside about the very legitimacy of their deliberations. Finally, political parties have in many cases and sometimes as a result of this popular mobilization, defined a position *vis-à-vis* globalisation. For some parties, such as New Labour in Britain, globalisation is seen as a fact of modern life that must be *adapted* to, and government policies are developed in such as response. In other parties, such as the French Socialists, globalisation is framed as a challenge, with negative as well as positive aspects, but a phenomenon that must be *controlled*.

# Origins and Cleavages

Most of the main parties of government in Western Europe trace their roots to the nineteenth century. In particular, their emergence was associated with the development of parliamentary power. The earliest parties were factions within early parliaments and, for countries such as Britain, we see that the Conservative and Liberal parties emerged from the parliament and then set up extra-parliamentary organisations in order to compete as the electoral franchise was expanded. For centre-left parties such as the British Labour Party or the German Social Democratic Party, their initial inception was *outside* parliament, establishing their extra-parliamentary organisations first in order to contest the more inclusive electoral situation towards the end of the nineteenth century (more inclusive meaning universal male suffrage). Thus, by the early twentieth century, many European countries that had parliamentary systems also had several types of parties. On the left, there were, in some countries, communist parties, some of which, such as the French, had broken away from the socialist party in order to pursue a more revolutionary path to political power. Next, we find that most European political systems had a socialist (or social democratic) party, in most cases the largest of the parties on the left. In the centre of the political spectrum, we find a number of liberal parties, parties that had sought to expand civil liberties and establish the rudiments of national welfare systems. Usually of a secular outlook, they were the main opposition to conservative and other centre-right parties in nineteenth-century political systems. On the right, we find, depending on the country, one or more of three types of party. Christian democratic parties emerged as protectors of church prerogatives, and were allied to business interests. Next we find conservative parties, in Britain but also in Scandinavia. Finally, also arising out of the nineteenth century were agrarian or farmers' parties, defending rural interests. We find these in Scandinavian and also some central European countries.

It has been argued, most significantly by Lipset and Rokkan (1967), that the political parties established in the nineteenth century—and still for the most part around today—are products of political mobilisation centred on major political and socioeconomic transformations in European history. In particular, they present a thesis that the political alignments that structure modern European politics are based upon four major historic **cleavages**. These cleavages are labelled 1) the centre–periphery cleavage; 2) the church–state cleavage; 3) the rural–urban cleavage; and 4) the class cleavage. These cleavages emerged over the past 400 years or so, and are intimately linked to state formation and the resolution of religious differences. In addition, Lipset and Rokkan argued that these cleavages vary according to the country in question and to the interactions between them.

The centre–periphery cleavage involves tensions between the 'dominant' culture and other identities—linguistic, etc.—during the formation of a modern state and its boundaries in a particular territory. 'Dominant' then translates into centre; the 'subject' identities become the periphery. The cleavage persists because the centre has not completely absorbed or eliminated the peripheral identities, and the tension emerges centuries later in support for regionalist parties such as the Scottish National Party or the Basque separatist party, Herri Batasuna.

The church–state cleavage also involves state formation, but in this case elite competition is the critical factor. Those elites wishing to develop independence from the influence of the Catholic church supported (depending on the country) the secularising tendencies unleashed by the French Revolution, or Protestant clergy. The reaction of the church was to protect its interests and adherents. In some countries, the establishment of an official state religion resolved this division, as in England; in others it persisted, as in France. In some countries, Christian democratic parties emerged during the democratisation phase to promote Christian values and social policy.

The rural–urban cleavage is one of the socioeconomic linked cleavages, in that it represents that between rising urban and commercial elites and rural interests which may have been in a dominant political position at the beginning of the cleavage formation. Interestingly, it is in Scandinavia and Eastern Europe where the tensions from this cleavage have persisted into the twentieth century.

Finally, we come to perhaps the most significant cleavage, and one that interacts with the others in structuring modern party systems. This is the class cleavage, a product primarily of the Industrial Revolution. It pits the owners of capital and their allies against the newly forming industrial working class (or proletariat). Developing urbanisation concentrated these workers in cities or mill towns, thereby prompting the self-organisation by the mid-nineteenth century of trade unions and affiliated political organisations, which, once the franchise was expanded, became the social democratic parties of today.

What is clear is that these cleavages interact with each other and are present in some but not all countries, depending upon the way each state formed and the consequences of industrialisation. In terms of interaction, the class cleavage seems to subsume others, so that anti-church (anti-clerical) forces are also pro-worker. Thus social democratic parties represent the church–state as well as the class cleavage. Christian democratic parties combine the other side of each cleavage, being supportive of the church and business interests. Where these two types of parties are unable to subsume other cleavage issues, specific parties occupy this political space, notably agrarian and regional parties. For example, in Germany the SPD subsumes the class and anti-clerical cleavages versus the CDU, which defends both business and church interests. In Britain, the resolution of the religious issue by the late seventeenth century has meant the absence of a clearly Christian democratic party.

---

**KEY POINTS**

- The earliest parties evolved from within parliaments.

- Mass parties originated outside parliaments, mobilising new working classes.

- Communist and social democratic parties occupy the left, Christian democratic and conservative parties occupy the right, with liberal parties acting as coalition 'swing' parties.

- The cleavage theory of Lipset and Rokkan proposes a historical and revolutionary origin of party systems.

---

# Party Families

Having established the origins of parties and the historic cleavages upon which they formed, we can now proceed to classify them according to party families. Party families are groupings of parties according to a set of indicators including, crucially, ideology. Party names may differ, and actual government policy may vary—especially as many European governments are made up of coalitions of two or more parties. Nevertheless, political scientists have come up with a classification of party families that has recently been reinforced by the fact that many of them belong to transnational organisations, thereby adding a self-identifying factor. We can distinguish nine party families, broadly divided into families of the left, centre and right.

## Families of the left

The largest party family on the left are the social democrats. In the wake of the Russian Revolution in 1917, communist parties were created, in some instances as splits or spin-offs from social democratic parties. The debate between those supporting a revolutionary versus reformist political path was represented in this divergence. After the Second World War, dissatisfaction with both social democratic and communist parties led to the creation of new left parties. Finally, from the 1980s, green parties were formed, initially emphasising environmental issues, but broadening their issue agendas especially once they entered parliament.

### Social democrats

The oldest of the families on the left, these parties emerged in the nineteenth century, representing directly or indirectly the interests of the industrial working classes. As political allies of trade unions—or in the case of parties such as the British Labour Party, an arm of the trade union movement—their early focus was on supporting workers' rights and contesting elections in order to enter parliament. Ideologically, these parties ranged from having a Marxist political programme, which in some cases contested the legitimacy of bourgeois (capitalist) rule, to being mildly reformist. By the middle of the twentieth century, most parties had dropped Marxist commitments to class struggle and aimed instead at developing the welfare state and representing new middle-class social groups in addition to their working-class base. In general supportive of European integration, by the end of the twentieth century these parties supported, to a greater or lesser extent, European-wide standards of social protection. Social democratic parties belong to the transnational party federation the Party of European Socialists (PES), and their national delegations to the European Parliament sit in the Socialist Group (affiliated with the PES).

### Communists

Communist parties emerged in the early twentieth century in response to the apparent success of the Russian communists (Bolsheviks) in their 1917 revolution. In some cases they were formed following splits in a social democratic party, in others, they were created independently. Early communist parties advocated a more radical approach to the capitalist economic and political order, and therefore supported the Soviet Union in its foreign policy. By the last quarter of the twentieth century, these parties were suffering electoral decline, and the fall of the Soviet Union in 1991 hastened the end of many of them. In the mid-1970s, the Italian Communist Party had polled one-third of the vote in parliamentary elections; by 2001 its successor party could poll only 6–7 per cent. Although ideologically associated with workers' rights, the remaining communist parties are still searching for political relevance.

### New left

The new left is a heterogeneous set of parties, the first of which formed in the early 1960s. It was initially comprised of communist party activists disappointed with official communist parties and hoping to 'renew' the emphasis on workers with a more radical approach to the capitalist order. By the late 1960s, the new left was enlarged by student activists from the university protest movements. These activists rejected the traditional left for being too much part of the official political system. New left parties have remained small and marginal to most electoral politics in Western Europe, the exceptions being Denmark and Norway.

### Greens

Arising out of the citizen and environmental movements of the 1970s and 1980s, green parties were founded in many Western European countries. Espousing a commitment to environmental protection, non-nuclear energy, and a more decentralised and participatory society, these parties have secured between 5 and 10 per cent of the vote in most Western European political systems. In some countries they were allied to other centre-left parties and entered into government coalitions in the 1990s, in Belgium, France and, most notably, in Germany. Their relatively fragile electoral strength at the national level is belied by their strong presence at local and regional levels of government, demonstrating their history of grass-roots activism.

## Parties of the centre and right

As parliamentary democracy became institutionalised, and with a still limited franchise, the rudiments of party competition occurred between reformers (often labelled 'liberal') and defenders of the status quo ('conservative'). Unlike parties of the left, whose nomenclature often provides clues as to party family, labels are far less clear on the right. Nevertheless, the nineteenth-century division between liberal and conservative parties does provide a common background for the subsequent development of these parties.

## Liberals

Considered as the parties representing the political 'centre', liberal parties fought in favour of extended voting rights, expanded civil liberties and against church influence in politics and, in particular, education. In the twentieth century, their primacy in Western European political systems was undermined by social democratic parties, and in most countries they are only able to enter government as a coalition partner (though in a few countries, such as Portugal or Belgium, they may actually hold the office of prime minister). In the late twentieth century, tendencies within the liberal party family demonstrated a division between left and right, with left-leaning liberal parties emphasising social justice and their right-leaning counterparts calling for less government intervention in economic affairs. Liberal parties are therefore prime candidates to form coalitions with parties to the left or right.

## Agrarian parties

According to the Lipset and Rokkan thesis, agrarian parties (many have changed their names to 'centre' party) champion the rights of rural interests, and were found mainly in Scandinavia. As rural populations have dwindled in the post-war period, these parties have sought to broaden their electoral appeal, and have fashioned an identity combining attention to rural and farming issues with an emphasis on decentralised forms of government and environmental protection. In some cases, they compete with liberal parties for voters in the centre of the political spectrum.

## Christian democrats

Christian democratic parties follow roughly the denominational divisions in Christianity. There are mainly Catholic-based Christian democratic parties, found in predominantly Catholic countries, such as Italy. Next, there are countries in which the present-day Christian Democratic party is a fusion of former Catholic and Protestant parties, such as the Christian Democratic Union (CDU) in Germany. Finally, there are Protestant parties of significant political weight in Scandinavia. Christian democratic parties, especially in the Benelux countries, Germany and Austria, have been supporters and even instigators of welfare state development. Though approaching the issue from a different ideological perspective than parties on the left, this common interest has sometimes allowed for coalitions involving both social democrats and Christian democrats (such as grand coalitions in Germany, see Chapter 1, this volume). Quite often representing the interests of business, many of these parties have, over the past 20 years, struggled to reconcile their commitment to Christian solidarity with the less fortunate with support for more neo-liberal economic practices.

## Conservatives

In countries where Christian democratic parties are weak or non-existent, Conservative parties quite often fill the void, and are the principal party opposing the left. Often promoting a strong, if not paternalistic, state—for instance in social legislation—contemporary conservative parties vary considerably over specifics. In France, the conservative party, the Union for a Popular Majority, traces its origins to Charles de Gaulle (see Chapter 2, this volume). In Britain, the Conservatives have a much longer tradition. Both parties, though, emphasise 'fiscal conservatism' and a strong national defence. They are more likely to minimise support for social welfare than Christian democratic parties when issues of economic retrenchment are considered important.

## Far right

Parties of the far right have, since the mid-1980s, risen to become part of the political landscape in many European countries. Though considered 'beyond the pale' as a coalition partner with other parties (Austria is an exception), these parties have probably exercised more influence on policy debates than their electoral strength might imply. Especially on the issue of immigration (they are against most types and levels of legal immigration), their share of the vote in some countries has led conservative parties especially to harden their stances (see Chapter 19, this volume). Sometimes referred to as right-wing populist, these parties have a varied background. Some, such as the Allianza Nazionale in Italy, trace their lineage back to Mussolini's Fascists, while others are products of a single, charismatic leader, for example the National Front in France (founded and led by Jean-Marie Le Pen) or the Freedom Party in Austria (Jörg Haider). (See Theme box: Democracy and Legitimacy.)

**KEY POINTS**

- Ideology is the most significant factor in party family identification, but government policy and election platforms also contribute.

- The green party family is the newest on the left.

- Agrarian parties, especially in Scandinavia, are finding new identities.

- Far right parties usually have anti-immigrant positions.

**THEME BOX**

### Democracy and Legitimacy

From the 1970s onwards, political scientists and others have taken notice of what could be termed a crisis or decline of party. Turnout for elections has declined, parties are losing members, and protest parties are attracting ever more votes. Added to this is the tendency on the part of some politicians to make use of anti-party rhetoric. If we add major party corruption scandals—as occurred in Italy in the early-to-mid 1990s, leading to the disappearance of the mighty Christian democratic party—public distrust of, and even hostility towards, political parties is evident. This phenomenon has been termed 'anti-party sentiment', and has the consequence of undermining the legitimacy of party government. The democratic transition process in post-communist countries often saw the 'new' politicians enrich themselves on state assets, about which they possessed inside information during the privatisation process, thereby undermining their legitimacy as well as that of competitive party politics. The conditions set down by the EU for these countries to join often had an even more constraining force on government policy choice than in older EU member states, thus motivating in part the Euro-scepticism that is widespread outside the main parties. Manipulation of electoral systems for partisan gain, as in France in 1986, and more recently in Italy in 2006, further weakens the legitimacy of party government. The trends just noted are often exploited by anti-system politicians, for example Jean-Marie Le Pen in France or Jörg Haider in Austria, who may occasionally score impressive electoral results. At such times the mainstream parties may pay attention to the specific complaints voiced by these politicians, all the while distancing themselves from them while trying to prevent them from gaining wider acceptance.

# Party Organisation

How political parties are organised internally is an important aspect of understanding European politics. Indeed, major politicians in Europe are party politicians, and it would be nearly impossible to imagine a non-party figure becoming president or prime minister. European political parties tend to be well developed organisations in which leaders have 'risen through the ranks'. Historically, as we have seen, parties were active before voting became universal (and even before universal male suffrage).

The attention to basic party organisation was limited, as most active politicians did not depend in the first half of the nineteenth century on a mass electorate. Party membership consisted primarily of notables, whether landed gentry or other members of the upper echelons of society. The formation of working-class parties in the late nineteenth century signalled a new type of party organisation, one that exploited numbers of members as well as the extended franchise. Thus, social democratic parties represented a mass party model. By the mid-twentieth century, the dynamics of competitive elections had meant that parties seeking either majoritarian status or simply to compete against social democratic parties had adopted a mass organisational structure, aiming to attract members as well as voters. Below we discuss the typical basic structure of modern parties, distinguish between parliamentary parties and the central party organisation (also known as the extra-parliamentary party), and conclude with a brief discussion of party finance.

## Basic party organisation

Apart from parties with a specific regional base, such as the Christian Social Union (CSU) of Bavaria, parties attempt to implant themselves nationally. If we were to describe a typical party organisational model, it would be one based on a local unit of organisation, usually called a branch (a constituency in Britain). In some countries, for example France, there may be regional groupings of local branches, and it is the branch that sends delegates to a party's national conference, held annually or biennially, that is involved in choosing the party leadership, generally known as the party executive. As one can imagine, there are many variations on this simple schema, but all revolve around a membership that join through a local level of organisation, are involved at a national level conference or congress in selecting a leadership, and have some input into approving the party's

political programme—sometimes a detailed statement of principles—as well as the party's campaign manifesto or platform.

The elected party executive may itself involve more than one body. At a party conference, an intermediate body, sometimes called a national council, may be elected. This body may sit three or four times a year. From this body is elected the actual party executive and, depending upon the party, the executive may appoint other figures. It is the party executive that runs the day-to-day affairs of the party. The literature on political parties sometimes refers to this dimension of political parties as the party in central office (or the extra-parliamentary party).

## Parliamentary and extra-parliamentary party relations

The other major component of parties is the body of elected party officials sitting in a national parliament, the parliamentary party. In most parties, it has a share of the vote for the party leadership at the party's conference. In some countries, such as Britain, the party leader *is* the leader of the parliamentary party. Obviously, in some countries the parliamentary party may be quite small, but in others its size can make it a pool from which party leaders are drawn. An important distinction to be made when considering politics and competition for leadership within parties is the relationship between the parliamentary and extra-parliamentary party. A very rough distinction, and one that is fading according to some analysts, is that between centre-left and centre-right parties. Essentially, since parties of the left first organised *outside* parliament, their extra-parliamentary organisation was quite well developed, and depended upon the support of a mass membership integrated in an internally democratic structure. Centre-right parties, at least those that evolved from within parliamentary groups, had certainly established by mid-century a robust extra-parliamentary organisation, but the origins of the party, its 'genetic model', still emphasised the weight of party elites in the parliamentary party over the membership.

In general, we can say that, for most parties with parliamentary representation, the two wings of the party have been roughly balanced. There are exceptions, and there have been some shifts in this relationship. Thus, the extra-parliamentary wing dominates internal party relations in France, a fact related to the weakness of the French parliament itself. In Britain, the once powerful extra-parliamentary organisation epitomized, for instance, by Labour's national executive committee (NEC), has become a mere appendage to the parliamentary party, itself dominated by the office of the party leader. Political scientists point to the role of the media in campaigns, new techniques of shaping a party's profile to voters based on focus groups and sophisticated polling, among other things, as helping to relegate the standing of the extra-parliamentary party (Farrell and Webb 2000).

## Party finance

Political parties in Europe derive their financial resources from a variety of sources. These can be divided into two general areas. The first is the party's own activities. These range from membership dues—which today represent much less than half of overall income for most parties; percentages of salary of parliamentarians and other elected officials; finally, some parties may engage in fund-raising activities, such as the sale of party merchandise. The second area of financial support is through affiliated interest groups and the state. In the first example, certain parties have very close relations, usually of longstanding, with groups that see support for the party as a means of advancing their own interests. For example, trade unions are usually financial supporters of social democratic parties (in the recent past, French and Italian communist parties were also beneficiaries), while organised business groups and organisations such as employers' associations give to conservative parties. There are normally rules governing how much money can be given and, in the interest of preventing corruption, transparency in donations is usually required.

With regard to state or public financing, this is an area that can account for the lion's share of a party's financing. Usually legislated as a means to allow parties to be independent of special interests—and to prevent corruption—state financing is usually dependent upon some measure of electoral success. For example, once the German greens first elected candidates to the German parliament, the party became eligible for state financing, which then allowed the party to enhance its organisation. Some analysts have even suggested that parties that regularly occupy government have gone so far as to 'colonise' the state, becoming far more creatures of the state rather than of civil society and, by extension, support of party members. These parties have been labelled 'cartel parties' (Katz and Mair 1995). State financing is not universal, nor is it a magic solution to corruption. In Britain in 2006, debate on party financing erupted when accusations that the Labour Party had engaged in 'selling' peerages in the House of Lords to prominent financial backers came to light. Nevertheless, suggestions for adopting state financing were tempered by a perception that taxpayers' money should not underwrite party activities.

> **KEY POINTS**
>
> - Parties normally have a local unit of organisation, from which delegates select party leaderships at regular intervals, usually every two years.
>
> - Party leaderships usually have an executive committee that runs day-to-day affairs.
>
> - Parties have two wings, one in elected office (parliament and government), and an extra- (outside elected office) parliamentary organisation, in charge of relations with the membership.
>
> - Some parties receive state (public) funding, others rely on donations and membership dues.

# Party Systems

In individual political systems there are patterns of party competition. Further investigation demonstrates that these patterns of party competition—or party systems—have long durations. Change, if it occurs, is usually very slow. Our discussion above regarding historical cleavages as explanation for the origins of modern parties also helps one to account for particular national patterns. Sartori (1976) presented a framework for analysing party systems that is widely adopted. Focusing on the number of parties in a party system and the ideological distance between them, he developed a useful classification. We therefore speak of moderate two-partyism—that is, the ideological distance between the two main parties is relatively small, as in Britain; moderate multi-partyism, where three or more parties in a system are not that distant from each other in ideological terms, for example in Germany; and polarised multi-partyism, in which there are significant differences in ideological distance between many parties, for example in Denmark or France.

A further consideration concerns which parties to include in the numerical definition of a party system. Here a notion of relevance is needed, for many more parties than are in a national parliament contest elections. In some cases, parties with a substantial number of parliamentarians may be excluded from government formation, as was the case for the large communist parties from the 1950s to the 1980s and 1990s in France and Italy, respectively. Although these parties were actively excluded from government coalitions during the Cold War, their very presence had an effect on the possible configurations of multi-party coalitions in those countries, so they could hardly be considered irrelevant.

A final consideration is possible dominance of a particular party over the others. There may be one party that, though possibly not capturing a majority of seats by itself, nevertheless dominates the party system by its sheer size and electoral success. Sweden, via its Social Democratic Party, provides an example of such a system. With only two exceptions—once in the 1970s and once in the 1990s—it has been in government since the 1930s, as the dominant member of a two-party coalition, or as a majority party or as a minority government.

Party system change, then, would imply changes in the number of parties, an increase or decrease in the number of relevant parties, a change in support for particular parties, and/or the widening or reduction of the ideological distance between parties. In the 1970s we began to witness change in Western European party systems, and many political scientists began to wonder if the cleavages that structured modern politics were beginning to fade, as new political dynamics were coming to the fore. One of the most prominent of such theses (Inglehart 1977) argued that the development of **post-materialist** attitudes and value systems in affluent western societies might account for electoral support for what Kitschelt (1988) has labelled 'left-libertarian' parties, that is parties such as the greens. Dalton (1988) expanded the scope of post-materialist political action to unconventional forms of political participation, ranging from boycotts, sit-ins, media-savvy demonstrations, and so on. By the end of the twentieth century, the parties which first arose in the nineteenth century still accounted for the majority of votes in national party systems, though certainly new parties such as the greens had emerged. The conclusion reached by most political scientists is that the 'core' of contemporary party systems in Western Europe remains intact with some 'peripheral' change (Smith 1989).

ROBERT LADRECH

# Parties and Party Systems in Post-communist States

Most of our discussion of parties and party systems relates specifically to the experience of Western European parties in the twentieth century. There were a limited number of Central European countries in the first half of the twentieth century that had parliamentary regimes long enough to see the establishment of parties and party systems (notably Czechoslovakia and, to a more limited extent, Poland). Yet these were the exceptions, as most of the regimes that emerged from the Austro-Hungarian and Ottoman empires in the nineteenth and early twentieth centuries did not establish liberal democracies. Thus the conditions that allowed for the development of parliamentary democracy in Western Europe were not replicated in Eastern Europe. Soviet domination over politics in Central and Eastern Europe until the end of the Cold War meant that the parties and party systems in post-communist Europe are still comparatively recent, and this accounts in large measure for one of their most significant characteristics: flux.

To say that parties and party systems in post-communist European countries are in flux is to say that they are still in formation. In particular, in regards to ideology, organisation and electoral support, the years since 1990 have witnessed a comparatively large amount of volatility. But this

is in itself not so surprising, given the lack of an underlying or prior party system. So, in a sense, parties in post-communist countries have the task of first constructing ties with an electorate largely bereft of party identification. Not enough time has elapsed for new cleavages to have emerged and structured social group and partisan linkages. Consequently, flux is to be expected.

## Party ideology

Western European understandings of the terms left and right were not easily translatable to the post-communist situation, especially in the first ten years or so. From a Western perspective, communist parties, were placed firmly on the left, usually to the left of social democrats. Once multi-party elections and pluralist politics became possible in the East, the former ruling communist parties had to decide whether to join a pro-reform movement or try to defend as many aspects of the former system as possible. If support for or opposition towards the development of a market economy and political pluralism became the axes upon which parties were judged to be 'reformist' ('left' in the West) or 'traditional' (usually 'right' in the West), the situation was highly variegated. For example, those communist parties opposed to reform of the economy would be considered as traditionalists, and those most supportive of as pure a market economy as possible as radical reformists, even though in the West these positions would be labelled left and right, respectively. Those communist parties that made the transition to a social democratic position were essentially supportive of developing a market economy, but also keen to ensure some level of social-welfare spending. Small nationalist parties also sprang up, often in opposition to ethnic minorities or else in fear of the intrusion of foreign capital and international organisations. Pro-reform parties dedicated to the fullest expansion of market dynamics supported business interests—though *organised* interests were as yet underdeveloped compared to the West, and so ties with parties were weak. In Poland, a peasants' party, with roots in pre-Second World War history, was revived. By the mid-1990s, all the governments in the region in which parliamentary democracy had taken hold had also applied to join the European Union, and so support or opposition to the EU became another (new) element in post-communist political party ideology. In fact, many scholars (*inter alia*, see Taggart and Szcierbiak 2007) note the beginnings of a post-communist Euro-scepticism throughout the region. By the time of elections in 2006, a pattern was beginning to emerge, at least as far as party ideology was concerned, and this typically meant a centre-left party—reformed communists or a newly created social democratic party in countries where the Communist Party refused to change—and a centre-right party, dedicated to liberal market economics.

## Party organisation

Except where parties inherited the assets of the former ruling Communist Party, all other parties had little or no organisation to speak of. Bearing in mind the experience of one-party rule, where the 'Party' was all encompassing (with few exceptions), joining a party was not in the initial post-communist

period a very popular activity. The social democratic parties that were established—either anew or from reformed communist parties—benefited from an affiliation with the transnational Party of European Socialists (PES), which lent advice and expertise on party organisation, electioneering and campaign mobilisation. Its counterpart, the European People's Party (EPP), found it harder to identify prospective members due to the fragmentation and fluidity of the centre and right of the political spectrum.

For most parties, then, organisational weakness was a common feature, and many were little more than parliamentary factions in their national parliaments, rallying around a particular individual. This would explain the relatively high rate of new party formation, divisions, splits and the disappearance of small parties in post-communist countries during the first ten years or so, especially in the centre and on the right of the political spectrum. Without strong ties to organised interests in society, all parties were largely delinked from civil society, and this was reflected in their organisation and finances. What took generations to establish in the West—mass party organisation—could not be expected to form overnight in the East, and indeed the fluidity of ideology and the absence of structuring cleavages has meant that parties are much more fragile in the East than the West.

## Parties and their electorates

Following from the above discussion, it comes as no surprise that linkages between parties and the electorate are weak in post-communist countries, and this accounts for the unpredictability of election outcomes. Unlike in the West, where a process of electoral de-alignment has been noted, the issue in the East is building these ties in the first place. The rate of electoral volatility in post-communist systems is then a result of the low level of identification with parties. The absence of long-lasting cleavages, the organisational weakness of parties and the fluidity of political ideology in post-communist systems all combine to reinforce this image of electoral volatility. According to Gallagher, Laver and Mair (2006: 301), the average electoral volatility in the post-communist countries in the 1990s was 'almost three times the equivalent figures in western Europe'. This figure of 32.7 per cent decreased in the 2000–4 period to only 30.6 per cent.

Parties and party systems in post-communist countries are characterised by weak party organisation, fluid ideological positioning and low levels of structured linkages with social groups and voters in general. If we take into consideration the swiftness of the collapse of the communist systems, it would be unrealistic to assume that full-blown 're-placement' political systems would have taken their place overnight. Indeed, what we have been witnessing since 1989 in Eastern Europe is the political disorder and chaos out of which patterns of party politics may arise. Compared to the West, where this process took generations to settle, the East might benefit from contemporary communication and organisational technology, possible state funding for

parties and much higher levels of literacy compared to nineteenth-century Western European electorates. On the other hand, just as politics in the West has changed over the past 30 years, perhaps the Western 'classic' model of party politics is not the end-point of post-communist party political development.

> **KEY POINTS**
>
> - Competitive party elections began in the early 1990s, after the fall of communist regimes, in most cases.
> - Party ideology is relatively settled on the centre-left, more unstable on the centre-right.
> - Euro-scepticism characterises many party positions on both left and right.
> - Party organisation is generally very weak.
> - The region is characterised by high levels of electoral volatility, compared to Western Europe.

# Conclusion

The political parties of the major party families in Western Europe have roots in the historic conflicts and processes in which contemporary nation states arose as well as the Industrial Revolution of the nineteenth century. Contemporary parties in post-communist East and Central European countries have a shorter history, but much of the politics in these countries reflects the state in which they found themselves after 40 or more years of single-party communist rule. Yet, despite these differences, there are some common trends or challenges with which we can conclude this chapter. The first, a phenomenon external to parties, is the impact of European integration. The second, internal to party organisations, is the relationship of parties to members.

The process of European integration was re-launched in terms of intensity and scope in the mid-to-late 1980s, with the adoption of the Single European Act (SEA) and especially the Single Market Programme (see Chapter 10, this volume). Since 2004, the European Union (EU) has enlarged to take in eight post-communist countries, ranging from former Soviet republics such as Estonia, to Poland, and the former Yugoslavian federal republic of Slovenia. All EU member states are participants in a unique form of regional governance, in which national sovereignty is pooled at the European level. What is the impact of this type of deep integration on national political parties? There are several responses that scholars have noted. First, support or opposition to further European integration has

**THEME BOX**

## The Impact of the European Union

The first direct elections to the European Parliament in 1979 instigated the formation of transnational party federations, initially representing the socialist, Christian democrat and liberal party families. These party federations acted as the extra-parliamentary party organisations to the new party groups in the European Parliament. Over the next 25 years these so-called euro-parties evolved slowly, usually in tandem with the pace of European integration. Party groups in the EP became more visible in the EU legislative process as the EP itself assumed more powers during the 1980s and 1990s (see Chapter 11, this volume). The transnational federations also experienced modest organisational development, especially in the wake of the Maastricht Treaty. European-level party politics remains distant from Europe's citizens, however, not least because elections to the EP do not determine an actual European government (in this case, the European Commission). Furthermore, many of the routine issues and policies debated at the European level do not attract national media attention, nor fit easily into the traditional left–right competitive pattern. Nevertheless, some issues have highlighted partisan differences in the EU; in 2006, the Services Directive pitted the EP's left against its right, and mobilised national member parties 'for' and 'against' the Directive, particularly in countries such as France. The further politicisation of EU politics may provide more opportunities for euro-parties in the future.

become a divisive issue in some member states. It has provided the basis for anti-EU parties, such as the UK Independence Party (UKIP) and for division within parties, such as the Swedish Social Democratic Party. Second, even if party elites are comfortable with further European integration, the results of consulting citizens in referenda, for example in France and the Netherlands on the EU Constitutional Treaty in 2005, demonstrate a disparity between mass and elite opinion. Third, especially in economic policy, the flexibility or manoeuvrability of national government is somewhat limited or constrained, and this indirectly impacts what parties can do in government as well as what they can promise voters in election campaigns. A good example of this would be the EU prohibition of 'unfair' state aid to national companies. Finally, European Parliament (EP) elections oblige national parties to engage in elections that usually result in losses for incumbent national parties, as well as to participate in the EP legislative process, thereby producing a body of party actors somewhat detached from the national parliamentary and extra-parliamentary party organisations. (See Theme box: The Impact of the European Union.)

The second trend to be noted among parties, especially in Western Europe, is the decline in party membership. One characteristic of the mass party model was that it was membership-based. There were many reasons why mass membership benefited parties in their early stages of organisational development, but with the advent of new techniques of campaigning and information technology, as well as state funding of parties in many countries, the need for a mass membership has seemed less critical. The use of focus groups, television and other factors combine to soften the impact of this decline in membership. Still, one of the classic functions of parties is to link citizens to government. This linkage function is most obvious through the participation of citizens in the activities of parties, including influencing the party manifesto. Still, a decline in numbers may not necessarily mean that parties are more remote from civil society, if instead we focus on the quality of the activities of the remaining members. It may be that the model of party organisation at the beginning of the twenty-first century has fewer, but more important, members in terms of the operation of internal party politics (Scarrow 2000). In Eastern Europe, party organisations are new by definition, and are beginning with low membership levels. But it may be that these new parties, created from parliamentary factions, or mobilised around a significant personality, can make do without a mass membership base. Indeed, Gallagher, Laver and Mair (2006: 313) even suggest that post-communist parties 'could be deliberately designed by elites as low-membership organisations'.

Political parties are crucial actors in the operation of western liberal democracies, and although they face challenges including the form of organisational development and the rise of supranational European policy-making, they continue to be central in legitimising government through competitive elections, structuring choice for voters in competing policy programmes and election manifestos, and providing the organisational format through which citizens can participate in politics.

### KEY POINTS

- Elections reveal stable patterns in Western Europe, unstable in the East.

- The EU has had a more profound and explicit impact on parties and governments in post-communist Europe than in the older member states.

- Euro-scepticism is a phenomenon across Europe.

- Parties in Western Europe have experienced a loosening of ties between themselves and voters and members; parties in Eastern Europe are trying to build these links.

### ? QUESTIONS

1. What processes lead to the emergence of modern political parties?

2. What is the difference between parliamentary and extra-parliamentary party organisations?

3. What are the main differences between parties in Western Europe and in post-communist political systems?

4. What are the arguments for and against state funding of political parties?

5. Do parties need members?

6. In what ways does the development of the European Union impact national political parties?

###  FURTHER READING

■ Dalton, R. (1988), *Citizen Politics: Public Opinion and Political Parties in Advanced Western Democracies*, Chatham, Chatham House Publishers.

■ Dalton, R. and Wattenberg, M. (eds) (2000), *Parties without Partisans: Political Change in Advanced Industrial Democracies*, Oxford, Oxford University Press. Provides chapters on most areas of party activity and trends affecting party performance, organisation and government experience.

■ Hix, S. and Lord, C. (1997), *Political Parties in the European Union*, Basingstoke, Macmillan. Covers party activity in the European Parliament as well as transnational party federations.

■ Inglehart, R. (1977), *The Silent Revolution*, Princeton NJ, Princeton University Press.

■ Lawson, K. (ed) (1994), *How Political Parties Work: Perspectives from Within*, London, Praeger. Looks at internal party organisational dynamics, including leadership, in Western as well as Eastern Europe.

■ Luther, K. R. and Müller-Rommel, F. (eds) (2002), *Political Parties in the New Europe: Political and Analytical Challenges*, Oxford, Oxford University Press. A comprehensive look at party activity in society, elections, internal organisation and at the European level.

■ Millard, F. (2004), *Elections, Parties, and Representation in Post-communist Europe*, Basingstoke, Palgrave Macmillan. A good, comprehensive introduction to the state of parties and elections in post-communist Europe.

■ Ware, A. (1996), *Political Parties and Party Systems*, Oxford, Oxford University Press. A good introduction to the study of political parties and party systems, employing a comparative approach.

 ## IMPORTANT WEBSITES

**www.pes.org**  Website of the Party of European Socialists, providing links with its member national parties in all EU member states as well as Norway and a few other European countries.

**www.epp.org**  Website of the European People's Party, providing links with its member parties in all EU member states. Does not include the British Conservative Party, which can be found at www.conservatives.com.

**www.eldr.org**  Website of the European Liberal, Democratic and Radical Parties, providing links with its member parties in EU member states.

**www.egp.org**  Website of the European Green Party, providing links with its member parties in the EU.

# 13 Social Change

## COLIN CROUCH

 **Chapter Contents**

- Introduction
- The Rise of the Services Economy
- Changes in Gender Roles
- Demographic Trends and Family Changes
- The Decline of European Religion
- Conclusion

 **Reader's Guide**

The most important social changes affecting Europe at the present time are those confronting people in Central and Eastern Europe, but in dealing with them this chapter does not see them as simply undergoing 'westernisation'. This is so if only because there is such variety among the societies of Western Europe, which are themselves undergoing considerable change. Among all industrialised economies a major factor in recent decades has been the decline in the proportion of the workforce in manufacturing industry and an increase in the proportion working in various kinds of services. Particular attention is therefore paid to this development. One aspect of it is a rise in the number of women in the workforce, which is also associated with changes in family patterns. A discussion of these leads logically to a consideration of demographic shifts, which include ageing, immigration and the position of ethnic minorities. This is in turn related to a section on the decline of religion throughout Europe. The chapter concludes with some reflections on the political implications of these changes.

# Introduction

Political systems do not exist in a vacuum, even if politicians, journalists and those around them often act as if they lived in an isolated, self-referential village. Politics operates in a constant exchange with the society around it. The actions of government clearly have an impact on that society, but society also affects how the political world behaves. Parties are based on divisions within the electorate; problems produced by society provide the agenda of political action. While this is always true, it becomes particularly obvious at times of major change when, say, the social basis of a party system is thrown into confusion.

It is often said that the present is a time of particularly great social change, from which we should therefore expect political implications. This is certainly the case, and these changes will be plotted below. However, we should not take with this the false idea that before the past few decades there had been a long period of stability. It is difficult to find any such period in the history of Europe, and certainly not during the twentieth century. The first half of that century was characterised by two world wars, revolutionary upheaval, struggles between dictatorship and democracy, and extraordinary economic change as country after country passed from being predominantly rural to mainly industrial—a process interrupted by periods of recession and crisis. A central issue was the rising power of workers in industry, who demonstrated a capacity to organise and articulate their interests rarely possessed by their rural predecessors. To varying extents, ruling elites were reluctant to accept these new actors on the political scene. The emergence of a dictatorship that claimed to be based on the power of the industrial working class in Russia, the vast country on Europe's eastern flank, added to the disquiet. The second part of the century was considerably less violent, but social changes were profound. Following the defeat of fascist and Nazi forces to which many national elites had turned in their opposition to the Soviet Union (USSR), democracy was finally accepted throughout Western Europe. In the eastern part, occupied by the USSR at the end of the Second World War, a form of dictatorial state socialism was imposed.

During the third quarter of the century the mainspring of economic development across the continent was still industrialisation. Already industrialised parts—mainly the north-west corner (Scandinavia, the UK, the Benelux group and the northern parts of France and West Germany)—moved into levels of advanced industrialism and urbanisation. In the South and much of Central and some of Eastern Europe manufacturing replaced agriculture as the dominant form of socio-economic organisation. The European peasantry, for centuries the great majority of the population, became a small and dwindling group. With these primarily economic changes came others. For example, young people started to marry earlier than they had during the difficult decades of world war and economic depression, but they took more control of their fertility and therefore had fewer children than their parents' generations. Urban society, growing mass prosperity and modern mass media brought greater variety and choice to people's leisure time.

Change continued to characterise the final quarter of the twentieth century and early years of the present one, but there were important shifts of direction. Industry started to decline as the major employer, and a number of so-called services activities began to grow instead. As we shall see below, this had major consequences for relations between men and women. It has also been a transformation with major political implications. Political conflict and party competition throughout the twentieth century was based on identities rooted in the growth of industrial society. If politics and parties sometimes seem unfocused and unrelated to people's lives today, it is partly because **post-industrial** society has not yet shaped its own politics.

But, by far the most important social changes affecting Europe at the present time, are those confronting people in Central and Eastern Europe, whose countries have, since the end of the 1980s, been experiencing a transition from a state socialist to a capitalist economy and from dictatorship to liberal politics. To some extent these changes can be seen as bringing 'westernisation', but this does not mean that these societies are necessarily coming closer to a western or Western European model of society. This is so if only because there is, in any case, considerable variety as well as major changes of direction among the latter societies. It is hard to define a stable 'western model'. In addition, the economic dislocation that has often followed the total change of economic system has in many cases led to a decline in the standard of living of Central and Eastern Europeans, increasing the gap between them and westerners.

Our review of social change across Europe will therefore be rooted in the implications of the shift from industrial to post-industrial society. Prominent among these have been changes in **gender** relations, which leads on to consideration of other changes in family life and demographic structure. Some of these latter further raise the question of the place of religion and other cultural phenomena.

---

**KEY POINTS**

- Rapid and major change has long been a characteristic of European social life and is nothing new.

- By the end of the twentieth century industrialisation had given way to the rise of services sector employment as the main motor of change.

- The experiences of Western and Eastern Europeans continue to be very different.

---

# The Rise of the Services Economy

Among all existing industrialised economies, whether European or not, whether previously state socialist or not, a very major change since the 1960s has been the decline in the proportion of the workforce in manufacturing industry. Alongside this has been an increase in the proportion working in various kinds of services (see Table 13.1). For some countries (e.g. Italy, Spain, Poland) this change was taking place before the earlier major historical shift from agriculture to industry was completed.

The decline of manufacturing employment does not mean that we are consuming fewer material goods than in the past: very much the reverse. The decline in employment has two sources. First, industrial production becomes more and more efficient over time, so that fewer people are needed

to create a given volume of output. Second is the process of **globalisation**: we increasingly buy goods made in poorer countries of the world. Western firms making capital goods benefit from this, as firms in developing countries buy most of their plant and machinery from the west. But the mass populations (as opposed to the elites) of the developing countries cannot themselves afford to buy goods back from us, producing trade imbalances. Increasingly, large firms carry out parts of their production chains in countries where labour and other costs are much lower, further reducing the number of jobs in manufacturing in the wealthy countries. To some extent the same happens in services. For example, many back-office clerical functions of large western services enterprises (for

**Table 13.1** Employment by Sector, Central and Western European Countries, c. 2004 (percentages)

|  | Primary | Secondary | Services | | | |
|---|---|---|---|---|---|---|
|  |  |  | Distributive | Business | Social, etc. | Personal |
| Austria | 5 | 27 | 22 | 13 | 21 | 11 |
| Belgium | 2 | 25 | 21 | 13 | 32 | 7 |
| Bulgaria | 11 | 32 | 22 | 6 | 20 | 9 |
| Croatia | 17 | 29 | 20 | 6 | 18 | 9 |
| Czech Republic | 5 | 39 | 20 | 7 | 20 | 8 |
| Denmark | 3 | 23 | 22 | 12 | 32 | 8 |
| Estonia | 7 | 34 | 22 | 8 | 22 | 8 |
| Finland | 5 | 25 | 19 | 13 | 28 | 9 |
| France | 4 | 24 | 20 | 13 | 28 | 11 |
| Germany | 3 | 31 | 20 | 13 | 25 | 9 |
| Greece | 17 | 22 | 23 | 8 | 18 | 12 |
| Hungary | 6 | 33 | 22 | 8 | 23 | 8 |
| Ireland | 7 | 27 | 20 | 13 | 21 | 12 |
| Italy | 5 | 31 | 21 | 11 | 22 | 10 |
| Latvia | 14 | 27 | 24 | 6 | 21 | 9 |
| Lithuania | 16 | 28 | 22 | 5 | 22 | 7 |
| Netherlands | 3 | 20 | 21 | 15 | 28 | 13 |
| Norway | 5 | 19 | 22 | 12 | 35 | 7 |
| Poland | 20 | 27 | 21 | 8 | 20 | 5 |
| Portugal | 13 | 32 | 19 | 7 | 18 | 11 |
| Romania | 33 | 30 | 15 | 4 | 14 | 4 |
| Slovakia | 6 | 38 | 19 | 7 | 22 | 8 |
| Slovenia | 10 | 35 | 19 | 9 | 18 | 9 |
| Spain | 6 | 30 | 22 | 11 | 18 | 14 |
| Sweden | 2 | 23 | 19 | 15 | 33 | 8 |
| UK | 2 | 22 | 22 | 16 | 28 | 11 |

*Source*: International Labour Office Yearbook
*Notes*:
Primary sector = agriculture, fishing, extractive industries
Secondary sector = manufacturing, construction, public utilities
Distributive services = commerce, transport, communications
Business services = financial and other services rendered to business
Social, etc. services = education, health, social services, public administration
Personal services = hotels and restaurants, cleaning, domestic and other services to households

Definitions of individual sectors may vary from country to country

example, airlines) are carried on in India and some other Asian countries where there is a large educated population working for far lower wages than in the west. But many services have to be carried on in a face-to-face manner: the provider of a service and the client need to meet for the service to be performed—the so-called front-line services. (We are unlikely to travel to China for cheaper medical services or restaurants, for example.)

On the other hand, Chinese (and many other) doctors and waiters do travel to western countries to find work. In many services, therefore, the spread of the global economy takes the form of immigration, not the transfer of production to remote sites. This has a positive rather than a negative effect on job growth in the western economies concerned. The popular idea that immigrants somehow take jobs away from local people is false. Particularly in a services-based economy, additional workers spend much of their money on locally produced services, generating more jobs: a rise in the number of people in jobs creates more jobs. This is especially the case in Europe where, as is discussed below, declining death rates and rising birth rates are creating an ageing population, with the workforce shrinking and the number of retired people growing. Immigrants are more likely to be of working age than are native populations, paying taxes that help fund the latters' pensions. In addition, the movements of people are subject to far more restrictions and controls than those of goods, reducing the extent to which globalisation affects front-line services activities. We shall examine immigration further below.

Globalisation has long been present in a minor way: the ancient Romans grew much of their corn and cotton in Egypt. But various economic, political and technological changes have made it far more prominent today. The transport of goods across vast distances has become cheaper, faster and more secure than in previous centuries; computer technology and telecommunications make possible rapid communication between distant sites, among other things making it easier to control and manage remotely. Changes in international financial regulations towards the end of the last century made it easier for investors to move large sums of capital around the world without restriction, enabling firms to pick and choose their investment locations. It is best to see globalisation as not just trade between people in different parts of the world, but as the way in which different components of the finance, product development, production, marketing and distribution chain for a single product can be spread widely around the globe.

## The diversity of services

To consider the social implications of the shift in employment from industry to services, we need to distinguish among the latter, as they include a diverse range of activities. We can identify four forms of service, more or less distinguished by their distance from manufacturing. First come the distributive services, rooted in the movement of the products of industry and therefore still close to manufacturing activities: transport and all sales activities (including shops). However, it is difficult to distinguish the transport of persons and messages from those of goods, so this sector includes passenger transport and postal services too. And, once postal services are included, it is difficult to exclude the transport of electronic messages; so the whole telecommunications sector is also included here, making this quite a heterogeneous sector. This sector, as Table 13.1 shows, is an important source of employment in most countries, though it does not vary much in size. (It does, however, change in its internal composition, as numbers employed in transport have declined and those in telecommunications have risen.)

Second, we can identify business services: activities that are not themselves part of the manufacturing process, but which are important to it: banks, insurance and other financial activities; legal services; various design and consultancy activities; cleaning, security and maintenance. Now, the growth of this sector includes some quite illusory shifts from manufacturing to services. If, say, a chemicals firm employs its own cleaning and security staff, these people count as being employed in manufacturing. But, if the firm outsources management of these activities to specialised contractors, these same people, doing the same work, pass from employment in manufacturing to employment in services. Without changing what they do or where they work, they have participated in a great historical shift. Given that there is a contemporary tendency for outsourcing, a part of the rise of the services is not really any change at all. This is a very small sector of employment, but growing rapidly (and only partly for the illusory reason mentioned). Growth is particularly rapid in Central Europe, such services not existing as separate organisations in state socialist economies.

Third, official statistics identify 'social and community services', that is services considered to contribute to some general good going beyond the individuals who receive them (such as education or health). In some cases it is not even possible to identify an individual user (maintenance of the environment, police services). Because of their communal character, many of these services have historically been provided by public authorities, though there is a current trend towards their privatisation. This is a large sector; in several countries (including, outside Europe, the USA) having become larger than manufacturing as the major source of employment. Its growth was particularly rapid during the decades of expansion of the **welfare state**, within whose auspices many of these activities are delivered.

Finally, there are services that are considered to benefit solely the individuals who consume them: cultural and sporting entertainment, domestic cleaning, repair of domestic goods, etc. This is a small, fairly static sector.

Of these sectors only business services and community and social services count as the growth that leads from a manufacturing to a services economy. The distributive sector is strongly connected to the movement and sale of industrial goods, while personal services exist in all societies from the most primitive.

The balance between manufacturing and services is one where there are particularly strong differences between Western European countries on the one hand and Central and Eastern ones on the other. This is not just because of differences in the level of overall economic development: Greece, Portugal and Spain, the least wealthy of the Western European group, have all had large distributive and personal services sectors, a characteristic common to many poorer countries. The distinctive feature of Central and Eastern Europe was that communist regimes placed a very high priority on developing manufacturing capacity and a very low one on services. A perceived need to industrialise in order to compete with the West coincided with Marxist theory that distinguished between the so-called productive labour of manual work in manufacturing and the unproductive labour of office work, sales and other services apart from transport. The fact that the socialist bloc economies were not market ones meant that far fewer people were employed in sales and marketing activities than in a capitalist economy, but, more surprisingly, communist authorities did not believe in employing larger numbers of people in public services and administration. Although those economies are stereotypically seen as being heavily bureaucratic, their bureaucracies were in fact understaffed for the huge tasks allocated to them, as all priority was placed on employing people in manufacturing. Also, since state socialist industries were mainly inefficient, they needed particularly large numbers to function.

One reason why unemployment remains high in most former state socialist economies is that the adjustment from manufacturing to services is particularly difficult. It is hard for them to develop the public services that fuelled the growth of post-industrial employment in the West, because these services normally require considerable state funding, and these countries have largely adopted economic ideologies that regard the growth of state activity negatively.

**Table 13.2** Proportion of Women among Persons in Employment by Sector,* Central and Western European Countries, c. 2004 (percentages)

| | Primary | Secondary | Services: | | | | Overall |
| --- | --- | --- | --- | --- | --- | --- | --- |
| | | | Distributive | Business | Social, etc. | Personal | |
| Austria | 45 | 22 | 45 | 51 | 64 | 60 | 45 |
| Belgium | 28 | 19 | 38 | 44 | 56 | 52 | 43 |
| Bulgaria | 34 | 43 | 43 | 55 | 63 | 57 | 47 |
| Croatia | 46 | 28 | 42 | 51 | 65 | 55 | 45 |
| Czech Republic | 27 | 30 | 44 | 50 | 67 | 53 | 43 |
| Denmark | 22 | 24 | 39 | 43 | 71 | 54 | 47 |
| Estonia | 29 | 37 | 48 | 48 | 73 | 67 | 50 |
| Finland | 28 | 23 | 41 | 48 | 74 | 63 | 48 |
| France | 31 | 23 | 41 | 46 | 65 | 60 | 47 |
| Germany | 30 | 25 | 46 | 48 | 63 | 59 | 45 |
| Greece | 43 | 19 | 34 | 48 | 51 | 52 | 38 |
| Hungary | 23 | 32 | 43 | 58 | 68 | 56 | 46 |
| Ireland | 9 | 20 | 42 | 49 | 70 | 54 | 42 |
| Italy | 30 | 24 | 35 | 42 | 54 | 52 | 38 |
| Latvia | 36 | 33 | 49 | 49 | 71 | 60 | 49 |
| Lithuania | 41 | 35 | 43 | 51 | 71 | 70 | 49 |
| Netherlands | 28 | 19 | 41 | 41 | 66 | 51 | 45 |
| Norway | 21 | 19 | 41 | 39 | 71 | 58 | 47 |
| Poland | 41 | 28 | 45 | 48 | 70 | 58 | 45 |
| Portugal | 48 | 29 | 39 | 49 | 64 | 70 | 46 |
| Romania | 45 | 39 | 45 | 47 | 57 | 55 | 46 |
| Slovakia | 23 | 31 | 46 | 55 | 70 | 59 | 45 |
| Slovenia | 44 | 33 | 44 | 53 | 70 | 52 | 46 |
| Spain | 25 | 17 | 40 | 48 | 59 | 60 | 39 |
| Sweden | 21 | 21 | 38 | 42 | 75 | 55 | 48 |
| UK | 20 | 20 | 42 | 44 | 70 | 54 | 46 |

*Source*: International Labour Office Yearbook

*Note*:

*For explanations of sectors, see notes to Table 13.1. Definitions of individual sectors may vary from country to country

# The internal social structure of economic sectors

The social structures of these different services sectors differ from each other and from manufacturing in important ways. These differences take us to the heart of some major contemporary forms of social change. First, as Table 13.2 shows, the services sectors vary considerably in their gender structure. In Western Europe (but not Central and Eastern) all employ far higher proportions of women than does manufacturing, but social and community services—the main source of recent employment growth—actually employ considerably more women than men.

There are also striking differences in the spread of educational levels among the people working in the sectors. Manufacturing, distribution and personal services have distinctly lower educational profiles than business services and social and community services—the two growing sectors. Two major components of early twenty-first century social change—rises both in the participation of women in paid employment and in the educational level of the population—are both closely related to changes in the structure of employment.

The former of these changes contains an important paradox. In general the process of change in Eastern and Central Europe since the collapse of state socialism is seen as one whereby those countries move towards social structures already embedded in western countries. However, the state socialist economies had higher proportions of women in work than did most Western European ones; to some extent 'westernisation' has involved a reduction in women's labour force participation in the East. At the same time, however, that participation has been rising in the West, suggesting a Western movement towards Eastern patterns.

Differences in the educational distribution of people working in the different sectors also contain some ambiguities, particularly when combined with the gender patterns. If we concentrate solely on the business services and social and community services sectors (ignoring the 'static' distributive and personal services ones), we can see how the trend from manufacturing to both business and social and community services corresponds to the idea of the 'learning society'. This is the popular image of the early twenty-first century as one where an increasingly **skilled** workforce works at increasingly skilled activities. As educational levels have risen, so employers have found ways of using higher levels of competence among their staffs. These changes seem to affect the services more than manufacturing for a reason already discussed: the easier replacement of staff by machines in the latter sector. Increased knowledge input into a manufacturing process—and indeed into many services activities, as the computerisation of offices has shown—frequently leads to a reduction in the overall number of staff employed. But this is less likely to happen where the service is delivered directly, as with education, health and care services. Even there it is not entirely absent, but there are also some opposite tendencies, as when scientific progress makes available new health treatments, leading to a rise in demand for medical services and therefore health service staff.

However, it would be wrong to conclude that all services employment creation has been at the knowledge-intensive end. There is also a shift in the location of low-skilled, routine work from manufacturing to services. This is partly a product of globalisation. Low-skilled workers in general have low levels of productivity, and can therefore in principle earn only low wages. Mass-production industry helped them achieve higher standards of living, because it combined their labour with high-productivity machines. It is this that enabled, for the first time in history, reasonable standards of living for relatively low-skilled people during the second half of the twentieth century. But these people depend on their wages being relatively low to find employment. If they are working in a sector where these is international trade—most manufacturing, some services—they are highly vulnerable to globalisation, to loss of competitiveness in relation to low-skilled workers in newly industrialising countries whose incomes are far lower but who can be linked to the same high-productivity machines. The same logic does not apply to low-paid workers in those services sectors that, we have noted above, are protected from globalisation—the directly provided services. Instead, these will be sectors where recent immigrants will be concentrated. In fact, some of the fastest growing occupations are in low-skilled services activities: fast-food outlets, cleaning services, security, call centres.

The growth of low-skilled work may sometimes be concealed by statistics on the educational level of different sectors. If the educational standards achieved by a population are growing (as is the case in virtually all societies today), their growth may outstrip the growth of occupations that use these levels, and many people will find themselves over-qualified for the employment they find. A sector that is growing (like many services) will be recruiting larger proportions of the young, better educated generations than one that is declining (like most manufacturing). This can give an impression of rising knowledge levels being used by the sector that is really produced by a rise in the character of the labour supply rather than its demand.

There is also evidence, that is probably related to the different skill levels used by the sectors, that incomes are higher in business services and social and community services than in the others. Now, it is well established that, on average, women's incomes are lower than men's, even though far more women work in the higher-paying sectors. Clearly, women are found predominantly in the lower-grade positions in all these (and other) sectors. Among older generations this may partly reflect the fact that male educational achievements used to be superior to female. However, virtually everywhere this has been subject to major change, and among younger generations the genders' educational performances have been reversed. Another, and continuing, reason for women continuing to occupy the lower roles in hierarchies is that their working careers are interrupted by childbirth and, in several countries, periods of

either part-time work or temporary exit from the labour force. For much of the twentieth century there was a fairly distinct division of labour in Western European (and North American and Japanese, but not Eastern and Central European) industrial societies. Men left the home to work; women stayed at home, cared for children and maintained the family home. The growth of women's employment has produced changes in that neat pattern.

**KEY POINTS**

- The rise of the services sectors is the result partly of increased productivity in manufacturing, partly of the globalisation of production and partly of growing demands for certain kinds of services.

- The services sectors can be divided among distributive, business, social and community, and personal services.

- The decline of manufacturing employment and growth of that in services (especially social and community services) is closely associated with the rise in women's employment.

- The pattern of services growth—but not of female employment—has been far weaker in Eastern and Central than in Western Europe.

- The internal structure (gender, educational level, income) of the economic sectors is diverse.

- Sectoral change is also associated with the rise of the learning society, but this is partly illusory.

# Changes in Gender Roles

Do services occupations grow because women are today available to work in them, while in earlier generations women tended to leave the labour force when they had children? Or do women go to work because there is now a growth of jobs more congenial to them than factory work? The relationship is quite complex and difficult to track down, but we

do know one thing: women's paid work is likely to create more women's paid work.

One stresses 'paid' in this context, because the change being experienced by women is a move from doing household and childcare work at home for no money to entering the paid labour market. The household and childcare work remains to be done.

This is resolved in a number of ways. First, the automation of the kitchen that took place in the West with the growth of electrical domestic appliances during the post-war decades of growing prosperity has raised the productivity of domestic labour just as factory automation did to industrial labour. Second, families today have fewer children, reducing the quantity of childcare needed. Third, particularly in Eastern Europe where there was far less kitchen automation, women acquired the 'double burden' of doing their housework when they finished their paid jobs for the day; sometimes their husbands may have shared these tasks, but not often. In some other countries (particularly the Netherlands and the UK) women work part-time in paid employment and part-time at housework and childcare. Fourth, other family members might help as a family obligation, for example grandmothers helping mothers with childcare. Finally, other people (nearly always other women) might carry out the employed woman's domestic tasks, being paid to do the work. It is this last that leads to the employment-creating spiral of women's employment.

The jobs that are created by this last process are in childcare and in other care services for the sick and the elderly that have traditionally been performed as unpaid domestic tasks by women. They can be organised in very different ways, with major implications for how the work is reported in official statistics. These are often jobs in the community and social services sector, frequently provided by the welfare state in the form of nurses, teachers and care workers, as noted above. Other jobs are for cleaning and similar services found in the personal services sector. Others again are in food preparation and restaurants, counted variously as personal services, distributive services (food outlets as shops) or even manufacturing (when people buy meals prepared in food factories). But some of these activities are traded informally among women. For example, cleaners and childminders are usually paid informally by the women who employ them; they have no contract of employment,

do not appear in any lists of persons employed, and are not registered as taxpayers. The size of this kind of female employment is therefore completely underestimated in official statistics.

As Table 13.2 shows, there is considerable diversity among countries in their patterns of female employment. Most of these differences can be explained in the following ways. Some countries, particularly the Nordic ones but to some extent also the UK and France, developed extensive direct services within the welfare state. These countries have evinced particularly strong growth of women's employment in the social and community sector, with secondary effects as the women recruited by this expansion created further demand for female labour services as carers, etc. Rather similarly, in Central and Eastern Europe places of employment provided childcare facilities for working mothers, the carers being other employed women. Elsewhere in Europe, the welfare state placed a stronger emphasis on transfer payments (pensions, disability and sickness allowances, etc.) than on direct service provision (for example Germany, Italy). This restricted primary job growth among women, and therefore the multiplier process was also weaker. In other countries again, primarily Catholic ones, acceptance of inter-generational family obligations remains strong, and women are likely to carry out as unpaid domestic work the activities that enable their daughters, nieces or sisters to enter the labour force. The work is being carried out just as much as if it was being rewarded, but as with the informal economy it does not register in the job statistics.

**KEY POINTS**

- Not just the growth of, but the particular form taken by, the services sectors is fundamentally linked to gender patterns.

- The form taken by the welfare state is similarly fundamental to the growth of certain sectors of employment.

# Demographic Trends and Family Changes

Changes in the position of women have been among a number of major changes in the structure and behaviour of families. These need to be set in the context of wider changes in population patterns. As Table 13.3 shows, Western Europeans are living longer than they did a few decades ago. The same is less the case for Central and Eastern Europeans, where economic dislocation since the early 1990s has had a perceptibly negative effect. This is particularly the case for men in Eastern Europe, who are suffering a major mortality crisis.

As death rates decline, so do birth rates (see Table 13.4). This generalisation holds across the whole continent, and distinguishes Europeans from most other world regions: only Japan shows similar patterns. Since the late nineteenth century there has been a global trend for couples to have smaller families as prosperity increases. This is valid when we look at change over time, differences between countries, and differences between rich and poor within countries. This is paradoxical, because the richer people become, the more children they can afford to support. Indeed, in the third quarter of the twentieth century the simpler association seemed to operate. Birth rates had sunk very low in the years of uncertainty around the two world wars and successive economic crises of the second quarter of that century. Young people coming to maturity in the following decades seemed to celebrate the new prosperity and economic security by marrying earlier and earlier and producing larger families than their parents did.

But any tendency for prosperity to mean higher birth rates is more than offset by contradictory factors, which started to operate from the 1970s onwards. First, there seems to be an association between growing prosperity and a belief among people that they can take control of their lives and exercise choices of a kind that seem impossible to populations sunk in poverty. An important aspect of control over life is deciding how many children one will have; improved methods of contraception towards the end of the twentieth century made this particularly easy to achieve. A further aspect of choice may also be the delay of marriage or even entry into a settled partnership until one is confident about one's choice of partner. This too began to happen; and delay in the formation of unions will tend to mean fewer children. Further still, growing prosperity has been associated with growing autonomy for women. Given that childbirth is a female experience, women's autonomy is likely to lead to more control by them over their fertility. With growing prosperity comes also growing and extended participation in education, of boys and girls alike. This tends further to delay the age at which young people embark on family building.

## Smaller households

In nearly all European countries, therefore, young people are forming couples later and having fewer children. This trend then joins with others to produce another change: households are becoming smaller. The other causes include a growing tendency for young adults and elderly people to live by themselves rather than in the same accommodation as other members of their families. This is the result of increased general prosperity, improving house-purchase loan systems and (important for elderly people) both improved health in old age and improving care facilities. There is, however, diversity within this common trend. For example, in Southern and Eastern Europe birth rates are lower than in the North-west; but young adults are more likely to live with their parents.

Decreased household size also results from a common tendency towards a decline in the number of married people. This has several causes: the rise in the age of marriage discussed above; an increase

**Table 13.3** Life Expectancy at Birth, Central and Western European Countries, 1960–2002

| | Males | | Females | |
|---|---|---|---|---|
| | **1960** | **2002** | **1960** | **2002** |
| Austria | 66.2 | 75.8 | 72.7 | 81.7 |
| Belgium | 67.7 | 75.1 | 73.5 | 81.1 |
| Bulgaria | 67.8 | 68.9 | 71.4 | 75.6 |
| Croatia | 64.3 | 70.5* | 69 | 77.8* |
| Czech Republic | 67.9 | 72.1 | 73.4 | 78.7 |
| Denmark | 70.4 | 74.8 | 74.4 | 79.5 |
| Estonia | 64.3 | 65.3 | 71.6 | 77.1 |
| Finland | 65.5 | 74.9 | 72.5 | 81.5 |
| France | 66.9 | 75.6 | 73.6 | 82.9 |
| Germany | ** | 75.6* | ** | 81.3* |
| Greece | 67.3 | 75.4 | 72.4 | 80.7 |
| Hungary | 65.9 | 68.4 | 70.1 | 76.7 |
| Ireland | 68.1 | 75.2 | 71.9 | 80.3 |
| Italy | 67.2 | 76.8 | 72.3 | 82.9 |
| Latvia | 65.2 | 64.8 | 72.4 | 76 |
| Lithuania | 64.9 | 66.3 | 71.4 | 77.5 |
| Netherlands | 71.5 | 76 | 75.3 | 80.7 |
| Norway | 71.6 | 76.4 | 76 | 81.5 |
| Poland | 64.9 | 70.4 | 70.6 | 78.3* |
| Portugal | 61.2 | 73.8 | 66.8 | 80.5 |
| Romania | 64.2 | 67.5 | 67.7 | 74.8 |
| Slovakia | 68.4 | 69.9 | 72.7 | 77.8 |
| Slovenia | 66.1 | 72.7 | 72 | 80.5 |
| Spain | 67.4 | 75.7 | 72.2 | 83.1 |
| Sweden | 71.2 | 77.7 | 74.9 | 82.1 |
| Switzerland | 68.7 | 77.8 | 74.5 | 83 |
| UK | 67.9 | 75.7* | 73.7 | 80.4* |

*Source*: Eurostat, Population Statistics 2004
*Notes*:
*Croatia 2000; Germany, Poland (female) and UK 2001
**No comparable figures available for the two Germanies of that period

in the number of couples who do not have a formal marriage; and a rise in divorce. These phenomena can be seen in all European countries and in the rest of the industrialised world. There is, however, considerable diversity. Divorce rates in particular are far higher in Northern and Eastern Europe, lower in the South. On the other hand, growing longevity in most parts of Europe means that couples who stay together can expect to have more years together before widowhood.

## The ageing of the population

Low death rates combined with low birth rates produce what is often called the ageing of the population, as the average age rises. Western Europe and Japan are experiencing this in a way unparalleled elsewhere in the world or in human history. This theme currently enters political debate in the form of a so-called pensions crisis: if the proportion of the population in work falls in relation to the proportion living on retirement pensions, there are problems for the funding of pension schemes that rely on the earnings of today's workers to fund the incomes of today's pensioners. Less noticed is the contribution that a large generation of relatively wealthy retired people makes to sustaining their adult, working children at a time of increased economic insecurity. Also, in the very long term lower birth rates eventually filter through as smaller generations of pensioners. But this is small comfort for today's managers of the welfare state and of pension funds.

## Immigration and cultural pluralism

As noted above, one aspect of globalisation has been an increase in the movement of people between nation states, the process of immigration. This too is by no means new. There has long been a tendency for people in poorer countries to move in search of work to richer ones. Some countries, in particular the USA, Canada, Australia and New Zealand, consist almost entirely of successive waves of immigrants dating back little more than two centuries. But there have also long been massive movements of people within the apparently long and stably settled countries of Europe. In the late nineteenth and early twentieth centuries there was already major immigration from poorer, rural to industrialising parts: Italians and Portuguese to France; Poles to Germany; Irish to mainland Britain. At the same time, poverty and economic depression in parts of Europe were pushing some European people to the so-called New World: Scandinavians, Germans and Poles to the USA; Irish and Scots to that country as well as to Canada and Australasia. Religious persecution brought Jews from Russia, Poland and other parts of Eastern Europe to Austria, Germany, France, the Netherlands, the UK and elsewhere, and also to the USA. Meanwhile, at the other end of the social

**Table 13.4** Total Fertility Rates, Central and Western European Countries, 1960–2002

|  | 1960 | 2002 |
| --- | --- | --- |
| Austria | 2.69 | 1.4 |
| Belgium | 2.56 | 1.62 |
| Bulgaria | 2.31 | 1.21 |
| Croatia | 2.21 | 1.23 |
| Czech Republic | 2.11 | 1.17 |
| Denmark | 2.57 | 1.72 |
| Estonia | 2.16* | 1.37 |
| Finland | 2.72 | 1.72 |
| France | 2.73 | 1.89 |
| Germany | 2.37 | 1.31 |
| Greece | 2.28 | 1.25 |
| Hungary | 2.02 | 1.3 |
| Ireland | 3.76 | 1.97 |
| Italy | 2.41 | 1.26 |
| Latvia | 1.74* | 1.24 |
| Lithuania | 2.6 | 1.24 |
| Netherlands | 3.12 | 1.73 |
| Norway | 2.91 | 1.75 |
| Poland | 2.98 | 1.24 |
| Portugal | 3.1 | 1.47 |
| Romania | 2.33 | 1.26 |
| Slovakia | 3.07 | 1.19 |
| Slovenia | 2.18 | 1.21 |
| Spain | 2.86 | 1.25 |
| Sweden | 2.2 | 1.65 |
| Switzerland | 2.44 | 1.4 |
| UK | 2.72 | 1.64 |

*Source*: Eurostat, Population Statistics 2004
*Note*:
*Estonia 1970; Latvia 1965

scale, the sons of wealthier families in France, the Netherlands, the UK, Portugal and other European countries with overseas empires went to the colonies to occupy ruling and leading business positions. In a completely different category again were enormous forced movements of people within the Soviet Union and the regions of Europe conquered by Nazi Germany after 1933. In the former case, whole populations were uprooted from their homelands and resettled elsewhere—partly to prevent them from fomenting localist movements and partly to populate remote regions. Millions died in the process. In the Nazi case, millions of Jews, gypsies and some other peoples were transported to concentration camps that became extermination camps.

There was a major increase in population movements during and after the Second World War. First, there were massive displacements of people as Jews fled Nazi-occupied Europe for the UK and the USA. Then there were movements of millions of Germans whose families had settled in various parts of Central and Eastern Europe in past centuries and who were now driven out as refugees to Germany. Next, and very differently, during the boom years of the 1950s and 1960s, when labour shortages developed in the industrial countries of North-west Europe, people were recruited to work there from certain specific backgrounds. Italians, Yugoslavs and large numbers of Turks migrated to Germany. The former imperial countries attracted people from their colonies, which were at the same time gradually achieving independence: from India, Pakistan and the Caribbean to the UK; from north Africa and Indo-China to France; from Indonesia and elsewhere in south-east Asia to the Netherlands.

In more recent decades the gap between richer and poorer countries of the world has increased, Africa in particular being left behind. Improved transport facilities have made movement around the world easier. Globalisation has spread knowledge of living conditions in the west. Civil wars and inter-ethnic or inter-religious violence in some parts of the world have led many of their inhabitants to seek a better life elsewhere. These developments have seen new waves of immigration to Western

Europe from Africa and other parts of the world. This has included parts of Europe not previously experiencing the phenomenon. The Scandinavian countries, remote and cold for most people in the Middle East, Africa and parts of Asia, but prosperous, with strong welfare states and reputations for tolerance, have attracted many. Italy and Spain, for so long countries of emigration, have found themselves attractive to people in northern Africa, geographically close. Following the collapse of the Soviet bloc, there are now also important movements of people from Eastern and Central Europe towards the West.

Unlike the immigrations of the 1960s, which took place when there were labour shortages in Western Europe, these new movements are taking place at a time when there is high unemployment in much of the latter region. Political movements hostile to immigrants have developed in several Western European countries, with anti-immigrant political parties securing representation in some parliaments. One result of this has been legislation in most countries to restrict and make more difficult immigration flows, and existing populations of immigrants frequently suffer rough treatment at the hands of police, other official agencies and elements of the general public. How do we explain continuing immigration in the face of these obstacles? First, overall unemployment exists alongside continuing labour shortages. There are continuing vacancies for particular kinds of skill, including those associated with information technology, which many Indian immigrants in particular are providing. But there is also demand for people to fill low-paid jobs that existing populations in the wealthier countries are unwilling to perform, even if they are unemployed. Second, however difficult living conditions may be for many immigrants and their descendants in early twenty-first century Western Europe, they are considerably superior to those they have left behind.

Meanwhile, half a century of immigration into some parts of Western Europe has produced second and third generations of people descended from immigrants, but born and brought up in Europe, sometimes intermarrying and forming new families with people from the host society. This produces the phenomenon known as cultural pluralism, or **multiculturalism**, whereby people from several different cultural backgrounds live alongside each other, partly maintaining their separate cultural identities, partly mixing and sharing. There usually remains a dominant existing majority culture within the plurality.

This is not an historically unprecedented experience for many Western European countries. Some (like Belgium, Spain, Switzerland, Wales) have long maintained a variety of languages. Others (including Italy, Spain and the UK) have strong regional cultures. Others again have long-standing religious diversity: different forms of Christianity, and also Jews. But, as noted above, this longer European history has also been marked by major episodes of intolerance, hatred and bloodshed. Elements of this continue to dog the creation of multicultural societies today, as dominant majorities and immigrant or post-immigrant minorities try to come to terms with each other. These difficulties sometimes create major political issues, and anti-immigrant parties, or factions within existing parties, have become among the major innovations on the party-political scene over the past decade or so.

In some cases these new cultural issues affect societies where tension still exists from older patterns of difficult relations between majorities and older settled minorities. Relations between Catholics and Protestants in Northern Ireland and between Basques and Spaniards in northern Spain have been among the most persistent in Western Europe. It is, however, in Eastern and Central Europe that this kind of tension remains strongest. During the 1990s the former state of Yugoslavia collapsed under the weight of extreme violence bordering on attempted genocide among its diverse cultural and religious (Catholic, Orthodox and Muslim) populations. These have now formed separate states more or less following these cultural contours, with continuing tensions. Elsewhere such issues as the place of Hungarians in Romania, of Turks in Bulgaria, of Russians in the Baltic states, of gypsies in many countries, continue to produce means of political mobilisation, sources of discrimination and occasional outbursts of violence.

---

**KEY POINTS**

- Both birth and death rates have reached very low levels, the latter mainly in Western Europe only. There is now population decline across the continent.

- Low birth rates, delayed couple formation, increased divorce and a greater capacity to live alone among young and old people have led to a major reduction in household size.

- Immigration into Western Europe, from South and East, has continued to be strong, despite an ever less welcoming social and economic climate for immigrants and their descendants, and problems surrounding the establishment of multiculturalism.

---

# The Decline of European Religion

While there is debate about what indicators should be used, there is little doubt that religion is an institution in major decline throughout Europe—except among some of the immigrant communities mentioned above. This trend became manifest first in a decline in attendance at religious services by people who continued to regard themselves as members of churches or other religious organisations, or at least as believers. This led some observers to say that no real decline was taking place.

They pointed to similar declines in attendance at public sporting events, theatres and cinema. In a television age, it was argued, people participated in many activities without leaving their homes. They could watch services on television just as they could watch football matches. More recently, however, there has also been a decline even in affirmations of a belief in God. Further, the European situation contrasts very considerably with that in the USA, where religious belief, church attendance and the political power of religious organisations have been growing very strongly indeed. Europe, along with Japan, stands out as a world region of religious decline at a time when the institution is rising in prominence in the USA, the Islamic world and some other areas.

There are, however, important differences in the patterns. In the UK, and more recently the Netherlands, religious observance of all kinds has sunk to very low levels. In the Nordic countries, while regular church attendance is the lowest in the world, large majorities of the population are confirmed into the church and opt to pay a voluntary religious tax to fund their churches. In some other countries, including Italy, Ireland and Poland, church attendance remained high until the past decade or so. The decline in Poland is particularly striking, as the Catholic church had been a major source of Polish national identity during the years of Soviet domination, and had played a major part in undermining the state socialist regime. It had been widely expected that there would be a major Christian renaissance, not only in Poland, but throughout Central and Eastern Europe, where churches (variously Orthodox, Catholic and Lutheran) had remained a stable symbol of popular identity during years of disorientation. At the level of political influence this has often been the case, religious leaders acquiring a dominant role in social policy in particular. However, this trend has contradicted that in popular behaviour. In fact, in Poland and elsewhere the Christian churches have declined rapidly in Central and Eastern Europe following the fall of communism, as those countries have joined a general European trend.

In general the history of religion in modern Europe has followed a clear pattern. Where the dominant church made strong demands on the loyalty of populations and exercised a strong political influence, people became divided between strong supporters of the church and outright opponents of it. This was largely the case with the Catholic church, which has always asserted an international claim above the nation state. It has also been true of Calvinist Protestant churches, which tend to flourish in embattled situations where Protestants face strong Catholic, and/or secular or other opposition (the Netherlands, Scotland, Northern Ireland, to some extent Switzerland; outside Europe in South Africa). This has been the case particularly since the 1960s, when for various reasons people have started to demand more personal freedom over their lives. The insistence by churches that people accept certain codes of, in particular, sexual and family behaviour, and their attempts to use political influence to enforce these codes, have strengthened the ranks of those hostile to them.

National churches that became content to express the common life of a nation state without making political claims other than securing their own quiet position in that life tended to attract neither the support nor the hostility to which the Catholic church was vulnerable. Declining numbers took an interest in their activities, but few challenged their claim to a place in national life. This has been the fate of the Church of England in England and the Lutheran churches in the Nordic countries. In a somewhat different way, it has also been the pattern in Eastern Europe, where the Orthodox church takes the form of a number of national churches.

Where religions of various kinds express the identity of people against, or at least separately from, an alien political power, that religion can attract powerful loyalties as in the dominant Catholic case. Here, however, this is without the antagonism attracted by a church's exercise of power over people, as this is experienced as an alternative to a more remote political authority. What such religions have to fear is the passing into insignificance of the identity they express. There are many, varied examples of this phenomenon. The Catholic church has been in this position where a Catholic population has been dominated by non-Catholics—as in Ireland (long dominated by the British) and Poland (dominated, among others, by the Russians). Those countries did not experience the strong secularist movements found in France, Italy and Spain. Long after Greek independence from Turkey, the Greek Orthodox church still plays something of a similar role for Greeks. On the other hand, the identities that were once importantly expressed by non-conformist Protestant churches such as Baptists and Methodists—usually, as in the UK, expressing some form of regional dissent against a dominant metropolitan culture—seem to have declined as those regional identities declined.

Religions often play this cultural identity role for ethnic minorities, and an earlier expression of internal local cultural diversity is replacing that of regionalism in many European societies today. Jews have long been an example of it. Following the more recent waves of immigration, Islam, Hinduism, Buddhism, the distinctive forms of Christianity found in Africa and the Caribbean, and some others, have provided valuable identities among immigrant groups and their descendants, becoming important constituents of the cultural pluralism mentioned above. Typically, therefore, ethnic minorities have far higher patterns of religious observance than native populations.

In addition to helping us understand the diversity of contemporary religious experience in Europe, these arguments about the relationship between religion, identity and political power may help us understand the striking contrast between this continent and the USA. In the latter country no one church was ever permitted to dominate national life, so there has been no historical need for a powerful secularist, anti-religious movement. Second, many people in the USA trace their roots back to various original immigrant minority populations, and assert an aspect of their identity through association with the religion borne by that minority. Third, as immigration continues and brings ever new cultural groups to the USA, these affirmations of varied identities are reinforced in importance.

### KEY POINTS

- Established religions of all kinds are in decline throughout Europe.

- The only major exceptions to this trend are among ethnic minority populations.

# Conclusion

The societies of Central and Eastern Europe have joined the general history of capitalist economic development when it is at a moment of considerable change. The late nineteenth- and twentieth-century economy built around male workers in manufacturing industry is giving way to one based around various services. This is a particularly strong challenge for the former state socialist countries, as services played a small role in employment in their economies.

Viewed as a social and not just as an economic change, this sectoral shift needs to be broken down. We can identify at least four different services sectors, each of which has a distinctive internal social structure. They differ in terms of their rates of growth, the place of women within them, and their distribution of educational levels. Only business services and community and social services conform to the stereotype of the services economy as a learning economy.

The gender changes are particularly important, at least in Western Europe. Far more women work in services than worked in manufacturing in that part of the continent. The situation is somewhat different in the East and Centre, where more women had worked in industry and where the sectoral shift is in any case lower. If anything, those parts of Europe are seeing a decline rather than a rise in female participation.

The change in the position of women is among a number of other changes that are affecting demographic and family patterns. People throughout Europe are forming couples at later ages and are having very few children; in Eastern and Southern Europe and in Germany there is actual population decline. There are also more single-parent families and a growing number of young and old people live alone. Household size is declining.

In several countries population growth depends almost entirely on immigration. In the early post-war decades immigrants came from a few identifiable countries to specific North-west European ones in response to labour shortages. Today they come from many parts of the world, including movements from Eastern to Western Europe. Even though there are no longer overall labour shortages, there are niche shortages at very diverse points of the labour market, and immigrants tend to fill these.

Immigrants and their descendants also account for a growing part of religious observance in Europe, where the Christianity of the mass of the native population is in decline. This is a phenomenon that unites all of Europe, and distinguishes it sharply from the USA.

For most of the nineteenth and twentieth centuries the politics of most European countries was shaped by two major conflictual forces. The first was struggle between religions, or between religion and secularism. The second was class struggle, first between landed aristocracy and the rising commercial and industrial bourgeoisie, and then between the latter and the rising manual working class rooted in manufacturing and mining industries. The party systems of Europe still bear the imprint of these struggles more than of any other. But they all refer to events of the past. This is not because there are no struggles over religion and class in twenty-first-century society, but they concern different issues. First, relations between ethnic and religious minorities and their host societies take the form of potential clashes between cultures rather than religious conflict in the strict sense. Second, the class conflicts around which party politics is organised still concern the role of the industrial working class.

The political agenda has responded to change. Issues of globalisation and the transition of employment forms from those designed for large-scale manufacturing to those designed around the new services sector are important everywhere. This ranges from the prosperous economies of Western Europe to those in the Centre and the East entering the scene of these new issues while they are still embroiled in the transition from state socialist to capitalist economies. Changes in the role of women, and challenges for the welfare state created by both those changes and the wider shifts in employment patterns are similarly important. Immigration is also a political issue. In this last case both racist or populist parties and parties or fractions of parties representing ethnic minorities have certainly entered the political stage. But otherwise party structures and rhetoric have remained largely static. The new issues of the transition to the services economy, and the new social groups forged by those issues, have so far found little autonomous expression. In Western Europe this may be reflected in growing popular apathy towards politics and an apparent growing gulf between political classes and the mass of the population. In Central and Eastern Europe we see a difficulty in establishing stable party structures that might express people's conflicts and aspirations, and instead a rapidly changing series of personal cliques formed around individual political leaders.

COLIN CROUCH

## QUESTIONS

1.  In what ways do people in Central and Eastern Europe face different challenges from those in the West at the present time?

2.  Why might it be misleading to generalise about *the* services sector of the economy?

3.  What links are there between globalisation and sectoral change?

4.  In what ways is the growth of the services sectors of social as well as economic relevance?

5.  On what grounds might it be argued that the position of working women is fundamental for understanding current social change?

6.  What makes the family an institution of interest to the study of social change?

7.  Why is immigration of growing social and political interest?

8.  Do you expect to see a European religious revival?

## FURTHER READING

■ **Castells, M. (2000), *The Rise of Network Society*, 2nd edn, Oxford, Blackwell.** Considers the very wide social implications of sectoral change.

■ **Crouch, C. (1999), *Social Change in Western Europe,* Oxford, Oxford University Press.** Provides a general survey of the themes reviewed here, and some others, but restricted to Western Europe and extending only to the end of the twentieth century.

## IMPORTANT WEBSITES

The following websites all provide the kind of useful statistical data crucial in mapping changes in social and demographic structures:

● **www.oecd.org**

● **epp.eurostat.ec.europa.eu**

● **www.ilo.org**

**Visit the Online Resource Centre that accompanies this book for lots of useful additional material, including an interactive map of Europe. www.oxfordtextbook.co.uk/orc/hay_menon/**

# 14 Executives

## B. GUY PETERS

→ **Chapter Contents**

- Introduction
- Types of Executive System
- Problems in Executive Governance
- Conclusion
- Notes

✓ **Reader's Guide**

Executives—prime ministers, cabinets and the public bureaucracy—have become increasingly dominant actors in contemporary European democracies. A number of changes in domestic politics and in the international environment have tended to shift power away from parliaments and towards the executive. Further, within the executive itself, there has been some shift of influence away from cabinets as collective entities and towards prime ministers and the bureaucracy. In order to understand these internal changes of power and influence within government, we need to understand the changing structures of the executive, as well as the political forces that impinge on those structures. In addition, ideas—notably the **New Public Management** (NPM)—have been important in explaining changes in public management and in fostering the increasing utilisation of private-sector managerial techniques in the public sector. Although there are a number of similarities in the changes observed in executives across European countries, there are also important differences that reflect their individual political histories and underlying conceptions of the way in which government is supposed to function. The changes occurring in the executive and in the relationships with other political institutions raise major questions about the nature of accountability in European democracy. The conventional idea of hierarchical accountability of civil servants to ministers, of ministers to parliament, and parliament to the people is no longer sufficient to capture the complex relationships in contemporary government.

# Introduction

The governments of Europe are usually described as 'parliamentary democracies', but in reality they may be better described as 'executive democracies'. Parliaments may be a principal source of legitimation for these governments, but most of the work appears to be done by cabinets, prime ministers and **public bureaucracies**. The decline of parliaments as effective governing institutions has been noted since at least the end of the Second World War, but cabinets and especially prime ministers (PMs) now dominate policy (see, for example, Bracher 1963). That formal domination of policy is supplemented by their close connections with the public bureaucracy that both supplies advice and analysis and also implements policy.

The bureaucracy also has become a more powerful actor in the policy process, in part because of the influence of reforms of the administrative system through the ideas of the New Public Management (Hood 1991; Christensen and Laegreid 2001). Both implicitly and explicitly, NPM has tended to denigrate the ability of political leaders to manage the state effectively, and has argued for a greater role for public managers. While bureaucracies may be downsized and indeed made bureaucratic in the familiar meaning of the term, they also would become the central agents in the process of governance.

The above discussion may present executives in contemporary government as monolithic actors, but in reality a number of factors divide them, and create the functional equivalent of '**divided governments**' (see Elgie 2001). Most European governments are coalitions, and increasingly these coalitions include a broad array of parties and so cannot be expected to be internally consistent. Therefore, ministers may be part of the same government but also political rivals, with few incentives to support one another. Also, some European governments are semi-presidential, with a president and prime minister dividing responsibilities for

making and executing policy; these individuals, too, may also be members of different political parties.

In addition, many political executives tend to consider the public servants in their ministries to be less than complete allies in the policy process, and some may even consider those bureaucrats to be competitors for power and control. Bureaucrats are the permanent occupants of the executive branch of government, and may consider politicians rank amateurs who are not sufficiently knowledgeable to be given responsibility for making policy. On the other side of the divide between these executives, politicians often consider their bureaucrats to be more committed to their own careers, and to particular policy ideas that have been in place within the organisation over the years, than they are willing allies who support the minister and their programme.

Finally, the bureaucracy itself is far from a unitary actor. Each of the various departments and agencies that compose government has its own interests and they often compete with each other for budgetary resources and legislative time. Although some public service systems have developed mechanisms for creating a more unified approach to governing (see below), most public bureaucracies reveal substantial internal differentiation and complexity. These differences are at the root of policy conflicts and 'bureaucratic politics' in which organisations utilise decision-making situations to maximise their own resources and power (Page and Wouters 1994). Given their control over information and their ability to influence the decisions of ministers, bureaucracies can play a major role in shaping policy choices.

This chapter discusses the nature of executive politics in European countries, focusing on the capacity of these collective actors to provide coherent governance for their societies. Further, the governance reforms that have been implemented over the past several decades have justified the role of executives, and perhaps especially bureaucracies, in governing. As implied, despite the powers that these organisations enjoy, they may find it difficult to govern in a consistent and coherent manner. In addition, I examine the mechanisms available, notably parliamentary accountability, to make executives democratic. Bureaucracy and democracy might be thought to be antithetical but, as executives become ever more central actors in governance, the need to

exercise control over these organisations is crucial for democratic governance.

# Types of Executive System

The most common form of executive system in Europe is a **parliamentary government** with a cabinet composed of members of a majority party, or members of a coalition of parties that is assembled to create a majority (see Table 14.1). The cabinet may be formed by a prime minister, who typically is leader of the largest political party in the coalition; or the individual ministers may be more or less autonomously selected by the parties who are members of the coalition. The negotiation among the parties to form the coalition may allocate ministerial portfolios among the parties, with the party then proposing the particular individual to occupy the post. In most cases a minister is responsible for a single department of government, and may be assisted by junior ministers or political assistants, but in some cases a single large and/or important department may have several ministers in cabinet. For example, in many countries the Ministry of Finance has several cabinet positions,[1] and large social and health policy organisations may also have several ministers.

The other major model of government in Europe is the **semi-presidential system**. This model combines a prime minister from the cabinet model with an independently elected president who has some executive powers. This model has been made most familiar in the French Fifth Republic (see Chapter 2,

**Table 14.1** Types of Executive System

|  | Parliamentary | |
| Semi-presidential | Majoritarian | Consensual |
| --- | --- | --- |
| France | UK | Sweden |
| Finland | Ireland (?) | Norway |
| Russia | Germany (?) | Denmark |
|  | Spain (?) | Netherlands |
|  |  | Belgium |
|  |  | Switzerland |
|  |  | Luxembourg |
|  |  | Italy |
|  |  | Austria |

this volume), although Finland had been using it for several years before the constitution of the Fifth Republic in France was written (Nousiainen 1996). In semi-presidential systems, president and prime minister divide executive powers between themselves, usually on a constitutional basis, and each will have ministers or other political executives responsible for those policy areas. There are, however, no purely presidential models such as that of the USA or the Latin American democracies found in Europe.

As well as the descriptive categories of cabinet government, semi-presidentialism and presidentialism, we can also think about executive systems (and governments) in more analytic terms. Arend Lijphart has argued (1984) that there are fundamental differences between majoritarian, winner-take-all democratic systems and more **consensual political systems**. The UK is usually used as the example of a majoritarian system. The electoral system is designed to magnify differences among the votes for parties and to produce one-party majorities in parliament and therefore relatively strong governments. With a cabinet formed from a single party, such a government should be able to impose its own perspectives on public policy more readily than one in a coalition. Although they tend to have coalition governments, Ireland and Germany have relatively small coalitions with a dominant partner, so they may act somewhat like majoritarian systems.

In contrast to the dominance of a single party and variations in policy when there are changes in parties, consensus political systems are characterised by coalitions composed of numerous parties, often parties with extremely different political views. These countries also tend to be corporatist or corporate pluralist systems in which a full range of social actors are included directly in public decision-making (see, for instance, Chapters 5 and 6, this volume). The continuing involvement of a range of political parties, as well as of social actors, means that policies are less likely to change rapidly than in majoritarian systems. Further, executives in consensus systems may have as strong a role in policy-making as they do in majoritarian systems, and there may be an even greater tendency for bureaucracies to dominate over the political executives.

The consensus nature of politics in many European countries is being emphasised by the tendency towards broad-based coalitions and over-sized coalitions. In other words, governments now tend to involve more parties than they might need simply to form a government, and the parties involved may not appear to be natural allies. For example, in 2006, governments in the 25 European Union countries were governed by coalitions that included an average of 57 per cent of the members of parliament. In countries such as Finland and Belgium, the parties involved in cabinets tended to span the political spectrum from right to left, in apparent attempts to reduce conflict in parliament and enable more effective governing.

## Cabinet government

The fundamental notion of cabinet government is that parliament selects from among its number a group of individuals, the cabinet, who will become ministers and serve as the executive of government. Further, one of those members of the cabinet will be selected as the prime minister. Although it is usually known in advance who the likely candidates for prime minister are, no citizen ever votes for a candidate for prime minister, but only for a member or members of parliament. The cabinet has that executive authority so long as it maintains the confidence of the parliament, but, under varying rules, the parliament may remove the cabinet—often also referred to as the government—either singly or collectively. Therefore, the executive is dependent upon maintaining control of a majority of the legislature if it wishes to maintain power, and the fundamental source of power in the system is the parliament elected by the people.

In contemporary European political systems, the control of parliament is more apparent than real. Power has shifted to the executive for several reasons. First, as political parties have become more institutionalised, tending to control the electoral fortunes of individual members, parliamentarians of government parties may be loath to be seen opposing the government, even when that government has performed poorly. In addition to the concerns about the electoral futures of ordinary members of parliament, governments have proven to be less willing themselves to resign in the face of criticism or the failure of a government bill. Should a bill fail, the government will often call a vote of confidence and mobilise party members to maintain it in office.

Governments sometimes survive because the political traditions of their country do not favour elections other than at predetermined intervals, and therefore the government formed after an election may survive as a minority until the next election, even if it loses substantial amounts of support from member parties. This pattern is especially prevalent in the Nordic countries, and has been adopted in some of the new democracies in Eastern and Central Europe as a means of attempting to create greater stability. In the extreme, a Norwegian government from 1972–3 was supported by only 25 per cent of parliament (Strom 1990). More formal rules may sustain a government even when unpopular. For example, in Germany, Belgium and now in a number of other countries a 'constructive vote of no confidence' is required to dismiss a government (see Metcalf 2000, and Chapter I, this volume). It is not sufficient simply to vote against a sitting government—a replacement must be elected first.

The powers of cabinet go beyond simple survival. Perhaps the most important of these is the capacity to control the agenda of parliament, and therefore to determine what bills will even be considered, much less passed. Although some countries (Norway, the Netherlands) permit private members more power, the clear pattern is that government bills comprise the large majority of the bills considered (De Winter 2004) and are much more likely to be adopted than private members' bills. The government also has the public bureaucracy at its disposal when drafting legislation; while individual members of parliament may have access to experts in their political party, or experts in a union or other interest group, they still cannot match the expertise at the disposal of the government.

Finally, the increasing power of the media has tended to move power upward from parliaments to the executive. Ministers are much more likely to appear on television and to be able to shape public perceptions of policy. Those ministers who are effective at using the media are able to enhance their own careers, and to enhance the position of the government as a whole. Ordinary members of parliament are less likely to have these opportunities,

and may not be able to get their ideas into the public domain nearly as readily. As the public shifts its attention from print media to the thirty-second soundbite, the tendency is to focus as much on the personality of the minister (the image) as on the details of complex public policies.

## Cabinets

We tend to say that cabinets are central actors in government, but not all ministries and all ministers are the same. Cabinets are composed of a number of different types of ministers and ministries. Although nominally all equal members of the collective structure, in reality they have very different functions and different levels of power and prestige. The types of ministries found in contemporary cabinets include:

- *Central agencies.* Some ministries, for example ministries of finance, budgeting and public administration, are responsible for the internal management of government and provide few if any services to the public. These ministries tend to be among the most powerful in government, and control the resources available to the other ministers. In several cases, the minister of finance, when in agreement with the prime minister, can veto actions of their cabinet colleagues.

- *Defining functions.* These are the old functions of government that are essential for any government. These include justice, foreign affairs, defence, tax collection and so on. These are often powerful and prestigious ministerial posts in a cabinet, and may overlap with the category of central agencies. In particular, as globalisation proceeds and increases the international importance of almost all policy areas, foreign affairs ministries become central agencies that must approve a wider array of actions by other ministries.

- *Economic functions.* Most European governments have had, or continue to have, extensive involvement in the economy. All have at least one ministry dealing with trade and industry, one for labour, one for agriculture and some continue to have ministries for particular industries, such as the merchant marine in Greece. Neo-liberal reforms and associated privatisation have reduced the level of economic involvement but some persist.

- *Social functions.* European governments are all welfare states of one type or another and therefore also have an extensive array of ministries for health, social services and education. In some cases these organisations are combined with employment ministries, given the close connection of these activities. These ministries are often among the largest employers of personnel in government, given the large number of teachers, social workers and health care personnel needed to provide social services.

- *New ministries.* In addition to the rather familiar ministries described above, newer functions have been added to the public sector. The most common have been ministries for environmental protection. Also, a number of ministries have been created for client groups—families, women and even the middle class. Other ministries have attempted to deal with cross-cutting issues that affect a range of clients or portfolios, e.g. ministries for women and for families.

Cabinets are composed of ministers responsible for the above types of organisation, and all governments will have some ministries of each of these types, with the possible exception of the new ministries. These categories are not, however, watertight, and to some extent everything in government is related to everything else, so that the actual configurations of ministers may cut across these categories. For example, a labour ministry might conventionally be categorised as an economic ministry, but might have strong social missions as well. As the EU's Lisbon growth and employment goals have become more central, the linkage of social and labour policies has become more common in Europe (see Mosher and Trubek 2003).

Cabinets among the European countries have been tending to become smaller. (See Table 14.2.)

**Table 14.2** Average Cabinet Size (number of ministers)

| 1990 | 1995 | 2000 | 2005 |
|------|------|------|------|
| 18.3 | 16.8 | 15.3 | 16.2 |

Whereas in 1990 there was an average of over 18 members in cabinets, in 2000 there were only just over 15. That number has increased slightly because of the larger cabinets in Eastern European countries. This reduction in the size of cabinet has been a result of several factors. First, governments have been shedding a number of economic functions, especially nationalised industries, so need fewer ministers to manage those activities. Further, although policies have always had a number of interconnections, those connections have become more apparent and there has been a tendency to create 'mega-departments' integrating and coordinating a range of policies. For example, in Sweden a range of industrial policy departments was assembled into one large department designed to integrate the policies administered by these departments.

## Prime ministers

I have already argued that power has been shifting from parliament to the cabinet as a whole, but within cabinet the shift of power towards prime ministers is perhaps even more pronounced. The governance processes within these governments are increasingly dominated by the prime minister and their agenda. Some of the same dynamics that have produced increased powers for cabinets in general have also tended to enhance the powers of prime ministers. Perhaps the most important of these has been the role of the media and the focus of so much public attention on national leaders. While it is difficult to argue that these officials are not important, it is important to remember that their original styling was as *primus inter pares* (first among equals) rather than as a dominant figure in government.

In addition to the external changes that have tended to improve the position of prime ministers, they have themselves been working to enhance their powers. For example, the staffing of prime ministerial offices has been increasing significantly so that PMs have greater capacity to monitor and control other parts of government. For example, the Cabinet Office and the staff in No. 10 Downing Street have increased markedly in each recent government, and the creation of a Strategy Unit and other new structures, as well as the enhancement of the media office, now give the prime minister in Britain substantially greater control over the remainder of government (Hennessy 2005).

Some other prime ministers, such as the chancellor in Germany, have had such support for some time, but some such as the Danish prime minister continue to struggle along with little or no staff support (Peters, Rhodes and Wright 2000). To some extent these differences in staffing represent something about politics and governance in these governments. Danish politics remains very egalitarian, despite the shifts in visibility of prime ministers, and parliament remains more important than in many other parliamentary democracies (Damgaard 1992). German politics, on the other hand, has tended to focus on the central role of the chancellor as a means of providing leadership to integrate society and economy.

The shift of power in the direction of the prime minister is often described as being 'presidential', but in formal terms this is not at all the case (Peters 1997; Hefferman 2005). The fundamental point of presidential government is that the executive, while apparently extremely powerful, is in fact often highly constrained. Rather than necessarily having the consent to hold office and to govern from the legislature, a president is independent from that legislature and may be opposed by it. That opposition may be partisan, based on differences in the political parties controlling the two institutions, or it may be strictly institutional. That is, legislatures may defend their prerogatives in the face of the potentially growing powers of executives.

## Semi-presidential government

As already mentioned, semi-presidential government in France, Finland, and many of the newer democracies in Europe have both a directly elected president and a prime minister who is responsible to parliament. In addition to their own sources of political legitimacy, these two executives also have different policy responsibilities, and perhaps also different capacities to influence the overall direction of governing. For example, in most semi-presidential systems the president has control over issues such as defence and foreign affairs, while the prime minister has responsibility for most domestic policy issues. Further, presidents tend to have some responsibility for the constitutional order in the system, while prime ministers have more limited responsibilities for governance.

Semi-presidential governments are relatively easy to manage if the two executives come from the same political party, but more problematic when the two are drawn from different parties. In France, the first period of *cohabitation* between a conservative president and a socialist prime minister was successful, with the two executives in question playing their constitutional roles very precisely (Duverger 1980). In later periods, the relationship between presidents and prime ministers were not so successful and real conflict over power and responsibility emerged (Massot 1997; see also Chapter 2, this volume). In Finland, as a more consensual political system, *cohabitation* has not been as much of a political problem and indeed is to be expected given the number of parties involved in governing. Still, the semi-presidential system almost inherently involves the potential for conflict, and political systems must develop mechanisms for coping with that potential.

A number of the new democracies in Central and Eastern Europe have adopted the semi-presidential form of government, believing that this system combines some of the permanence of the presidential system with the responsiveness and apparent democracy of parliamentary governments. As such, semi-presidentialism was conceptualised as a means of creating a central figure for the new state, while at the same time offering the opportunity for greater responsiveness to changes in public opinion, and greater accountability for the new governments. While the level of success of these new governments has of course varied, the evidence to date is that the level of cooperation across the two executive institutions has been much as was intended by the institutional designers, and that these are viable mechanisms for these governments.[2]

## The public bureaucracy

Cabinets and prime ministers are executives who come to office by political means, but the vast bulk of the executives in European countries are appointed through processes that depend more upon merit principles than election. The public bureaucracies in European countries are recruited and managed through a range of different means (Peters 2006) but they share the characteristic of having formal organisational structures and hierarchical controls within the organisations. The public bureaucracy consists of more than paper pushers in the national capital—most public employees are employed to supply public services. Most of the scholarly attention (Aberbach *et al.* 1981; Wright and Page 1999)

has been directed at the top of the bureaucracy—the so-called policy-making positions—but for most citizens the relevant actors are at the bottom of the hierarchies whom they actually encounter on the street.[3]

There are at least four major traditions—Anglo-American, Napoleonic, Germanic and Scandinavian—among the European bureaucracies that produce very different patterns of governance, and relationships between the bureaucracy and political officials, and with civil society. (See Table 14.3.). Although all of these have to some extent been affected by the ideas of New Public Management (NPM), many of their fundamental principles persist. Further, the receptiveness of the bureaucracies to the reforms of NPM has been affected by their underlying organisational and legal patterns. The most important dimensions for understanding the differences among the patterns of bureaucracy are the role of law in administration, the linkages with civil society, the linkage of political and administrative careers and the degree of uniformity of administration.

The first factor differentiating among types of public bureaucracies is the emphasis on law as training and as a source of guidance in making decisions. Napoleonic and Germanic administrative systems are based more upon law than upon management. Almost all German public servants are

**Table 14.3** Administrative Traditions

| Anglo-American | Napoleonic | Germanic | Scandinavian | Hybrid |
|---|---|---|---|---|
| UK | France | Germany | Sweden | Netherlands |
| Ireland | Italy | Austria | Norway | Belgium |
| Luxembourg | Spain | Switzerland | Denmark | Finland |
| | Greece | Most of | Iceland | Baltic republics |
| | Portugal | Central Europe | | |

trained as lawyers, and they tend to conceptualise their role almost as a judge would, applying the law in an impartial manner. French senior civil servants are not trained as lawyers *per se* but they are expected to consider the legal aspects of public decisions as the primary issue. Further, the instruments for controlling bureaucracy in France, Italy, Spain and other countries influenced by the Napoleonic model tend to be formal and legalistic (see below).[4]

The legalism of Germanic and Napoleonic administration can be contrasted with the more managerial approach of the Anglo-American and Scandinavian systems. Especially in the Anglo-American systems, the emphasis in administration is on managing programmes to produce results, rather than on strict legalism. This is not to say that these administrative systems condone illegality. Rather, this is meant to imply that the first thing that enters the mind of an administrator is not legal constraints but the need to make programmes work. The Scandinavian countries (perhaps especially Sweden) have some of the Rechtstaat tradition of Germany, but they increasingly are concerned with management (see Christensen and Laegreid 2001). Given these fundamental characteristics, it is not surprising that the Napoleonic and Germanic systems have adopted relatively few of the reforms associated with the New Public Management (but, on local government in Germany, see Reichard 1994).

A second factor differentiating among the various approaches to public administration is the role of administration in politics, and conversely the role of politics in administration. The Anglo-American system has the sharpest distinction between politics and administration. The doctrine in these systems has been that public administration should be apolitical and be capable of serving any political party. Therefore, a political career is incompatible with an administrative career, and the alleged **politicisation of administration** (see Sausman and Locke 2004) is therefore more of a concern in these societies than it is in others. The Scandinavian administrative systems also have a strong sense of this separation, although the long-term dominance of social democratic parties in most of these cases

has tended to blend politics and administration somewhat more.

In contrast to the norm of separation found in the Anglo-American and to a large extent in the Scandinavian approaches to administration, the Germanic and Napoleonic approaches see little incompatibility, and indeed in some cases almost mandate a political role for the bureaucrat. For example, the top civil servants in Germany almost all have some linkages with political parties, and change when parties change. So, when Angela Merkl became chancellor in 2005, a large number of top civil servants with Social Democratic Party memberships left office and took a form of early or temporary retirement. They were then replaced by civil servants with CDU/CSU affiliations. The assumption behind these arrangements is that a minister requires a committed official to run the ministry, and to assist in making policy that conforms to party programmes, rather than someone who may be merely an expert.[5]

The Napoleonic model for the civil service is less overtly politicised than the German, but still lacks the norm of separation. In the case of France, and to some degree also in the other cases, the civil service elite is an all-purpose elite for the society. Students trained in the National School of Administration (ENA) may begin their careers in public administration but many of them move into politics and the private sector. This produces much greater integration between the public and the private sectors than found in most countries, as well as integration between the administrative and the political aspects of governing.

The third point of differentiation among these administrative systems is their linkages with civil society. Again, the Anglo-American approach tends to have less integration of civil-society actors than do the others, although the demands of contemporary democracy do involve some openness to the public. There are mechanisms for citizen involvement in the UK and Ireland, but these tend to be more *ad hoc* and involve some capacity for government to pick and choose among interest groups which may want to participate in the process. The Napoleonic systems also tend to permit relatively minor influence for social groups, given the *etatiste* philosophy that has dominated them.

The Scandinavian systems have the strongest level of integration between state and society, with **corporate pluralist** structures permitting interest groups of all sorts to have some direct involvement with making and implementing public policy. Each ministry has advisory committees that involve a range of social actors, and the ministries and agencies are also expected to circulate petitions requesting the views of those interests about policies. The assumption in Scandinavian administration is that any decisions must reflect not only the views of the political parties in control of government, but also the views of the full range of interests (see Chapter 5, this volume).[6] The Germanic model of administration also permits a range of actors to be involved in policy decisions, but has not developed the elaborate structures for inclusion that are found in Scandinavia.

The final factor differentiating administrative systems is whether there is a strong emphasis on uniformity in administration or not. At one end of that continuum, Napoleonic administration historically has emphasised almost absolute uniformity and equality in administration. The assumption is that republican values of citizenship demand such equality.[7] This demand for equality is associated with institutions such as *préfets* in France, designed to ensure that standards are enforced throughout the country. The Scandinavian countries also have strong norms of equality but, despite being unitary regimes, do allow some decentralisation and some differences across local governments.

At the other end of a continuum of uniformity, the Anglo-American systems, and to some extent Germanic systems, do permit a good deal of differentiation across different parts of the country. For example, in the UK the four constituent countries have rather different legal systems, with Scottish law being derived to some extent from French civil law, as well as common law. The federalism central to Germanic systems also creates a good deal of difference across different parts of countries such as

Germany, Austria and in the extreme Switzerland, although the legalism of governing in these systems helps to dampen the range of options that may be considered. The German administrative style relies on sub-national governments to implement a great deal of central government law, with the consequence that central bureaucracies are relatively small, while the state and local bureaucracies are relatively large.[8]

These characteristics are abstractions from the complex realities of individual administrative systems. The French administrative system is an almost perfect representation of the Napoleonic model, while that of Italy or Spain may have many of the characteristics, but also have some national characteristics. Although there are these differences within and across administrative traditions, all these organisations face common problems of administering public programmes in as effective and efficient a manner as possible. They also face the common problem of finding some means of relating effectively to civil society, given the *etatiste* nature of governance characteristic of these systems.

I have mentioned the role of the New Public Management in reforming administration in many countries. There have been marked improvements in many cases, but the consequences have not all been positive. For example, although the individual programmes may be managed better, the emphasis on managerial freedom and organisational autonomy has increased problems of coordination within government (see below). In addition, the emphasis on managerial autonomy makes conventional mechanisms for accountability less viable, given that if organisations pursue their own goals they are no longer merely administering programmes in what they consider to be the most efficient and effective manner, as expected.

## Politicians and bureaucrats

The public bureaucracy represents a set of expert organisations, increasingly skilled in management and in policy-formulation. On the other hand, politicians have substantial democratic legitimacy but they often lack the skills necessary to be effective in modern government. Although government does attract individuals with extraordinary commitment to certain policy goals and in many cases to the general improvement of the society, these individuals often do not have any particular knowledge about the programmes they must administer.[9] Further, relatively few politicians have much experience in managing large organisations, and some ministries are among the largest, not to mention most complex, organisations in their societies. Further, given that managing in the public sector is more difficult than managing in the private sector, the demands on these ministers are extraordinary. Finally, ministers have equally extraordinary demands on their time, as practising politicians, (often) members of parliament, members of cabinet and then managers of a department.

Given that politicians do encounter all these barriers to being effective in controlling their departments and placing a personal stamp on public policy, we should examine the instruments that can be used to assist ministers in achieving their goals. I should emphasise at this point that the main competitor for ministers for governance capacity is not parliament but rather the public bureaucracy. The minister in their ministry is attempting to make the organisational machinery perform in certain ways, and to use the expertise within the bureaucracy to create new policies. The question is whether that bureaucracy will be as receptive to the ideas of the minister as it might be expected to be.

One way to assist ministers is to give them more time to be ministers. In Westminster political systems the tradition is that ministers must be members of parliament, but in some cases those two roles are incompatible. The constitution of Fifth Republic France, for example, forbids a minister from remaining in parliament once selected as a minister, therefore freeing the minister to be a full-time executive. In practice, Norwegian and Dutch ministers also are removed from their parliaments, and can spend their time as executives (Andeweg and Nijzink 1995). In other cases, governments can bring in ministers who have not been elected, bringing expertise into government and also eliminating the need of those ministers to spend as much time in parliament. For example, Austria tends to recruit its minister of finance from among economic experts, rather than depending upon the talent available in parliament, giving that minister freedom from parliamentary duties.

Another means of making ministers more effective is to give them greater advice, and especially advice that does not come up from the bureaucracy within the department. The Austrian example above involves recruiting ministers who have the requisite expertise themselves, but that technocratic solution may not be acceptable in every political system. While the use of cabinets and special advisers to ministers is often conceptualised as being politicisation, ministers may see these practices simply as attempts at restoring some balance between the influence of the bureaucracy and the capacity of politically selected officials to make policy.

Finally, ministers may be assisted by reducing the workloads on ministries and ministers. Part of the logic of NPM and other reforms in governing is to give greater discretion to public managers and thereby to limit the necessity for civil servants. Creating agencies (see below), privatising and simply emphasising the policy roles of ministers as opposed to their implementation functions all have helped to give them more time to perform their ministerial tasks, but at the same time they may have weakened the control that ministers can exercise over policy, and especially over implementation.

In summary, although there are some common problems that political executives encounter when they attempt to govern, the design of executive institutions can help to ameliorate, if not eliminate, some of those weaknesses. Cabinet governments differ along several dimensions that can affect the capacity of the political executives to govern effectively, in relation both to their parliaments and to the bureaucracy (see Siaroff 2003). The national differences in executive governance capacity are important for understanding how these countries are able to manage the numerous policy demands that they regularly must confront, as well as how they manage the problems of balancing efficiency with democracy.

## Other executive structures

The above discussion of ministries is less inclusive than it once would have been. Part of the reforms of the public sector during the past several decades has been to create more autonomous and quasi-autonomous organisations. This trend is usually associated with the creation of 'executive agencies' in the UK (James 2003), but any number of other governments have adopted this model of organising the executive branch (Pollitt *et al*. 2004). The Scandinavian countries (Pierre 2003) had used this mode of governing for decades, if not centuries, but the model of governing did not become widespread until the British adoption of the concept, and the ideas of NPM emphasised the separation of implementation into the devolved structures. This organisational form is now widespread in European governments, and has also been adopted by the European Union (Keleman 2002).

The basic idea of agencies is to create organisations that have greater autonomy from political control than the typical ministry, or any component of a ministry. Delegating responsibility for programme administration to an agency is intended to permit public managers to make the programme more effective and efficient, and also to enable it to make potentially unpopular decisions that might be difficult for a politician. The idea of using agencies has been adopted by any number of countries, often in more extreme forms than that adopted in Britain. For example, in the Netherlands, ZBOs (*zelfstandige bestuursorganen*) were used to deliver a range of public services, managed largely by boards composed of stakeholders (van Thiel 2001). This model of governing did not, however, persist because of the extreme difficulties in accountability and control that were encountered.

Although agencies are a relatively new format for many countries, there have been and continue to be a large number of organisations that are to some extent autonomous from direct control by ministries and parliaments. Although many have now been privatised, there are still a number of public enterprises in European countries. Further, in a number of countries major components of the welfare state are managed at arm's length from government and are, in principle at least, private organisations (Bach *et al*. 2005). In addition, the quasi-governmental or parastatal sector of government has been increasing as governments attempt to hide some of their costs and employee statistics from a sceptical public, and also attempt to avoid responsibility for programmes that may go badly wrong.

### KEY POINTS

- Each of the styles of executive organisation has strengths and weaknesses.
- There have been large-scale reforms of the public bureaucracy.
- Executive structures have become more diverse and more decentralised.

# Problems in Executive Governance

## Coordination

One of the central problems of executives in government is the coordination of the numerous organisations and functions within the executive branch. The specialisation of organisations and their linkage to powerful social interests make it difficult for politicians, or bureaucrats in central agencies, to create coherent approaches to public problems. While interest groups and bureaucrats in departments and agencies may want to maintain their own policy regimens, actors in the core executive of government (Hayward and Wright 2002; Marsh *et al.* 2001) generally want to create greater coherence among programmes and a more co-ordinated pattern of governing.

Although coordination has always been a major problem for governing, the need for it has been increasing. This need is in part a result of the processes of administrative reform that have increased the number of organisations in the public sector and the autonomy of the managers in public organisations. In addition, the idea of 'joined-up government' (Bogdanor 2004) and the need to enable presidents and prime ministers to impose their own perspectives on government policies have pressed governments to engage in greater efforts at coordination. Finally, changes in the clientele groups central to government—the increasing role for women, children, the elderly and immigrants among others—require programmes that provide the range of services needed by these groups.

European governments have adopted a variety of mechanisms in order to attempt to create higher levels of coordination. Many countries rely on their central agencies, especially ministries of finance, as central coordination agencies (Jensen 2004). The budget is a central instrument for pulling together the full range of policies and imposing central priorities. Further, some cabinet systems have created ministerial positions, as junior ministers or as ministers without portfolio, that are charged with coordinating their colleagues. In addition, one common reaction to the need to coordinate has been to create large departments (see above) that bring together a number of related functions, with the hope that the one minister can make them create more coherent policy. Finally, some governments such as Finland have institutionalised procedures that establish central priorities in policy and link line ministries to those programmes.

## Holding executives accountable

If our analysis is correct, and parliamentary governments are increasingly becoming dominated by their executives, whether it be the cabinet, the prime minister or even the public bureaucracy, then conventional models of democracy face major challenges. (See Theme box: Democracy and Legitimacy.) Although cabinets and prime ministers do have an electoral connection with the public, their control over organisations and over political parties means that political constraints are not as capable of exercising control as implied in models of parliamentary democracy. If political executives are indeed so powerful then perhaps the only real democratic constraint is the threat of electoral defeat. Such a situation undermines one of the basic ideas of parliamentary government, that the executive can be dismissed at any time for poor performance, malfeasance or whatever reason.

We have already mentioned that the European Union has been an important locus for enhancing the visibility of political executives, and especially prime ministers, but working through this venue also can be used as a means of avoiding some traditional forms of accountability. The nature of EU policy-making is such that any number of important decisions are made in the Council, containing ministers from the member countries, or made through bilateral negotiations among the members. These mechanisms provide few, if any, checks for national parliaments over the executive.[10] Some countries such as Denmark do attempt to impose some close parliamentary controls over the actions of their executives in European bargaining, but for most cases there are few effective controls.

This lack of political control in the European context became apparent in late 2005 when Tony Blair was attempting to reach an agreement on the European budget towards the end of the UK presidency. The British prime minister was making the rounds of national capitals attempting to reach an agreement with the newer members of the Union that would trade some portion of the

## THEME BOX

( ! )

### Democracy and Legitimacy

Accountability has always been a central concern for executives, and the changes documented in this chapter may have increased those concerns. The traditional means of enforcing executive accountability in European democracies has been to hold ministers accountable for the actions of their ministries in parliament. This mode of accountability was effective so long as ministries were integrated service delivery organisations, and as long as ministers were willing to resign in the face of criticism in parliament. Both of those conditions appear to have been weakened significantly.

First, the ideas of New Public Management have tended to devolve a good deal of administration to autonomous organisations such as executive agencies. As well as these structural changes NPM has tended to empower senior managers to make more of their own decisions, thereby reducing the capacity of politicians to exert control. Budgets and law remain useful means of control over organisations but these are to some extent countered by links with clients, markets and networks of social actors interested in the programmes. Further, the use of contracts for service delivery with non-government actors has also reduced capacities for control.

As well as changes in the bureaucracy itself, expectations about the behaviour of politicians have also changed. In part because of the separation of implementation from policy-making, ministers may be reluctant to resign for failures within their department or the agencies attached to their departments. While this reluctance may represent a more realistic conception of their responsibility for programme failures, it also makes use of conventional mechanisms for accountability more difficult.

Accountability in modern governments has become more diffused and more complex. In part the role of the public itself has been enhanced, both through greater transparency and through the use of consultation and citizen engagement in programmes. That very democratic element of accountability is being augmented by the use of performance management and a number of techniques of measurement to hold programmes accountable for what they have produced for citizens. This change in accountability makes the process less political, and may also direct attention to the daily performance of organisations rather than the egregious errors that often were the focus of traditional parliamentary accountability.

British rebate.[11] These negotiations affect both the budget in the UK—historically a central locus of parliamentary control over the executive—and the budgets of the ten new member countries. Despite the importance of these financial negotiations, they were conducted largely out of the control of parliaments and the public, and once concluded there was little or no possibility for reconsideration. (See Theme box: The Impact of the European Union.)

Many of the changes introduced into the public sector as components of the NPM and other reforms in governing have tended to create problems for enforcing the accountability of executives. The creation of the executive agencies mentioned above has meant that there are now a number of relatively autonomous[12] organisations that may presume that they are entitled to act with less direct supervision from ministers. Likewise, the use of

instruments such as contracts and partnerships limits scrutiny of the actions of the executives, given that these arrangements with the private sector may be made with little opportunity for parliaments or other accountability structures to review them (Mulgan 2000). In some cases these instruments may have been created by legislation, but in many cases they represent merely the exercise of executive authority.

Even if the scenarios above are too apocalyptic, and there are more democratic constraints, contemporary democracy may require some consideration of the mechanisms for holding those officials to account. To a substantial extent accountability is an internal process, with the various executive actors exercising some levels of control over each other. This is most noticeable for the bureaucracy, as ministers and even prime ministers invest substantial

## The Impact of European Union

Although the individual countries of Europe retain their national identities and control over many aspects of policy, they are now embedded in a process of Europeanisation that affects how they must conduct their government business. This is of course true for the members of the European Union, but to some extent it is also true for the relatively few countries outside. For executives, Europeanisation poses two particular challenges, as well as some opportunities. One of the most important challenges coming from Europeanisation is to coordinate activities effectively with the other countries of Europe and create more or less consistent responses to policy questions. The need for coordination requires members of the bureaucracy, and in some cases (European Council) ministers to participate in numerous meetings negotiating the exact nature of European regulations. These requirements for involvement in Europe are not just for foreign ministries but also for all the functional departments. National governments, and their bureaucracies, are also responsible for implementing European regulations. While these regulations have been harmonised with national laws, their implementation still requires consultation and some interpretation, and hence poses additional challenges for the national administrations if effective coordination is to be achieved. The challenges of European administration are perhaps the greatest for the Anglo-Saxon and Scandinavian systems of government that govern rather differently from the continental model that dominates the EU.

The European Union presents some opportunities for executives, especially the political executives. Europe is another political arena in which executives have the opportunity to engage in policy-making, and to attempt to advance the interests of their national constituents. It is particularly useful as a locus for obtaining grants and contracts to benefit their constituents, and to demonstrate their effectiveness in 'bringing home the bacon'. The European arena can also provide a great deal of visibility for politicians, especially presidents and prime ministers, when they attend European summits with numerous photo opportunities. Even for politicians who are not pro-Europe appearances on that stage are an important political opportunity and tend to direct attention to the executive.

energy in getting the bureaucracy to perform as desired by their political masters. That investment may increase as service delivery and policy performance become more central to the evaluation of governments. A concern with controlling bureaucracy also helps to emphasise the point that the civil servants in the central agencies may be the crucial actors in controlling other parts of the bureaucracy (Jensen 2003).

The various forms of government discussed above present different opportunities for controlling the political executive and the bureaucracy. The relatively majoritarian political systems in Europe present perhaps the greatest difficulties for control. As noted, the executive in these systems tends to be drawn from a single political party, or perhaps from a dominant party with some support from a smaller party, and therefore there is a common interest in retaining power and not exposing any failures of any of the ministers. They may have a strong incentive to attempt to control the bureaucracy, but will tend to do so rather quietly so that any failures in the delivery of services will be attributed to failures of ministers.

In contrast, consensual political systems and the coalition governments that tend to characterise them may provide somewhat greater opportunities for control. Given that the members of the coalition will come from different parties they may be more willing to expose the failures of other ministers. While members of a coalition may be expected to have at least some loyalty to one another and to the preservation of their collective government, political ambition cannot be suppressed entirely. A party that believes it can improve its own position by a new election, or simply by a reshuffle of the government, may be very interested in 'blowing the whistle' on failures from other ministers. For example, parties or individual ministers always have the option of resigning from a coalition, and they may use failures by their 'colleagues' in the cabinet as a pretext for a resignation.

Napoleonic administrative systems present an additional form of control over the executive, both the political executive and the bureaucracy. These systems have a number of control organisations built into their constitutional and legal frame that are intended to prevent the executive from exercising as much autonomy as appears available at first glance. Unlike the political controls over executives that have been discussed to this point in the chapter, many of the control structures in Napoleonic systems depend more on law and hierarchical oversight of the bureaucracy. For example, the *Conseil d'État* and its analogues in the other countries of this type review legislation and regulations coming from the executive and must approve such acts prior to their being implemented. In addition, a number of inspectorates supervise the finances of government organisations, as well as many of the engineering and social-service functions of government.

Although these administrative systems have been using a number of means for enforcing accountability for decades, if not centuries, they are also institutionalising performance methods for enforcing accountability (Bouckaert 2001). Most conventional methods of accountability are based upon political mechanisms, notably using parliaments as the means of exposing and punishing malfeasance by ministers and their civil servants. Performance management, on the other hand, emphasises more objective indicators of the activities and outputs of public organisations. While these indicators are far from perfect, they do provide a means of understanding how well organisations are performing on a day-to-day, month-to-month basis, rather than focusing on egregious cases of failure as is often the case for political forms of accountability. Further, performance-based ideas of accountability emphasise improvement and learning, rather than punishment as is often the case for the traditional instruments.

---

**KEY POINTS**

- The problems of coordination and accountability persist after reforms, and may have been made worse by reforms.

---

# Conclusion

Most of the work of governing is performed by executives, whether they are politically elected or are career public servants who attain office through merit recruitment. This major role for the executive has always been the case, but the power of executives has been increasing. The power of the political executive has been increasing relative to parliaments, so that the notion of governing through parliament, while important as a legitimating device, does not appear a realistic description of contemporary governing. Likewise, even within the executive, a great deal of power has shifted from the cabinet as a collectivity to the prime minister. Increasingly governing is lodged in the person of the prime minister. (See Theme box: The Impact of Globalisation.)

The major competitor to the cabinet and the prime minister is the other component of the executive, the public bureaucracy. Although ministers may have nominal control over their departments, and have the democratic legitimacy coming from their connection to the electoral process, they have a number of deficiencies in the actual process of

## The Impact of Globalisation

Globalisation may not have had as much impact on the internal structure of governments and their processes as it has on the content of policy, but there certainly are impacts of the increased openness of European governments to the international environment. One of the most important impacts of globalisation has been that all issues now have an international dimension, and therefore foreign ministries become more central players in government. The foreign minister has always been one of the most important of cabinet posts, but that importance had been a function of the importance of diplomatic relations *per se* for any country. In an era of globalisation almost all policy issues have an international dimension. Given that increased centrality for international issues the foreign minister must play a role in a wider range of policy debates and may have to assist in international negotiations in those policy areas. Likewise, presumably domestic ministers and ministries must be cognisant of the international implications of their activities.

A second impact of globalisation is that it tends to empower prime ministers and presidents. One aspect of the politics of globalisation has been, just as with Europeanisation, the increasing visibility of chief executives on the international stage. Meetings such as the G-8 focus attention on the role of these leaders in representing their countries and makes them appear perhaps even more central in the policy process than they are. The role of these chief executives is also more than just a construct of the media. Their role in negotiating international agreements, perhaps especially on the economy, has been increased.

Finally, just like Europeanisation, globalisation has increased the demands for coordination among policy areas. This change can be seen most clearly in economic policy. Rather than using only economic instruments, the need to enhance international competitiveness requires the involvement of education, labour market, social policy and a range of other ministries and programmes in order to enhance the capacity of a country to compete effectively in the international market.

governing. On the other hand, the bureaucracy has a pronounced capacity for making and implementing policy, it may not be considered a legitimate institution to determine policies that have major impacts on citizens. Therefore, one of the principal challenges to governance in the executive branch of government, as well as more generally, is to find the means of balancing the virtues of political legitimacy with the virtues of efficiency and expertise.

# Notes

1. For example, the Ministry of Finance in Finland has two ministers, the first coming from the Social Democratic Party and the second coming from the Swedish People's Party (which represents Finland's Swedish-speaking minority).

2. The 'carrot' of membership in the European Union has been helpful in maintaining democratic practice which had been threatened by some presidents with apparent ambitions for maintaining their positions as president, even if by means that stretched the usual norms of democratic practice.

3. These 'street-level bureaucrats' such as social workers, tax inspectors and even postal clerks determine the outcomes of individual decisions for citizens, and also affect the perceptions that

citizens have of their government. See Meyers and Vorganger (2003).

4. The Netherlands is an interesting case having some characteristics of this model, as well as the Germanic model, but increasingly is adopting the more managerialist perspectives of the Anglo-American systems (but see Kickert 1997).

5. Austria as an example of Germanic administration tends to divide posts in government between the two large parties rather than having more of a winner-take-all approach. This *Proporzdemokratie* has maintained social consensus by dividing posts in government and in semi-public organisations between the two large parties.

6. As Stein Rokkan commented (1967) famously, 'Votes count but resources decide'.

7. This norm of equality may have some pathological consequences. The inability to differentiate among different types of citizens, e.g. those of Arab descent living in the suburbs of the large cities.

8. For example, of the roughly four and a half million public employees in Germany only less than half a million are employed by central government, almost all in the state railways and post. The UK has a relatively centralised bureaucracy, but most other systems derivative from this model use a more federalist principle for administration.

9. For a detailed and perceptive analysis of the problems faced by politicians attempting to govern, see Rose (1974).

10. In fairness, the European Parliament has gained an increasing level of control over policy choices at the EU level, although national parliaments generally do not have such influence except in a few cases.

11. Because the UK receives relatively little benefit from the Common Agriculture Policy that accounts for over 40 per cent of EU spending, Margaret Thatcher was able to negotiate an annual rebate of some 3 billion pounds. These funds have been a source of contention in the EU budget, especially when the ten new members were admitted in 2004.

12. On the concept of autonomy in organisations, see Verhoest *et al.* (2004).

## ? QUESTIONS

1. What are the relative advantages of parliamentary and semi-presidential systems for effective governance?

2. How do consensus forms of parliamentary government provide means of mitigating social and political conflict?

3. What forms of administrative structure are most effective in providing public services and in linking citizens to government?

4. Does bureaucratic recruitment on the basis of expertise or general ability provide for the most effective forms of governing?

5. What elements are most important for defining administrative traditions?

6. What are the most effective ways of holding bureaucracies accountable?

255

**EXECUTIVES**

 **FURTHER READING**

■ **Bekke, H. G. M. and Meer, F. van der (eds) (2000),** *Civil Service Systems in Western Europe*, **Cheltenham, Edward Elgar.** A collection of highly comparable discussions of public administration in most Western European countries.

■ **Blondel, J. and Müller-Rommel, F. (2001),** *Cabinets in Eastern Europe*, **Basingstoke, Palgrave.** A companion to an earlier book by the same editors on Western Europe, containing detailed information on the structure and dynamics of cabinets in Central and Eastern Europe.

■ **Müller, W. C. and Strom, K. (2000),** *Coalition Governments in Western Europe*, **Oxford, Oxford University Press.** A thorough examination of the characteristics of cabinet governments in European countries.

■ **Peters, B. G., Vass, L. and Verheijen, T. (2005),** *Coalitions of the Unwilling?: Politicians and Bureaucrats in Coalition Governments*, **Bratislava, NISPAcee.** Examines the relationships between civil servants and politicians in both Eastern and Western Europe.

■ **Poguntke, T. and Webb, P. (2005),** *The Presidentialization of Politics*, **Oxford, Oxford University Press.** Discusses the now common argument that parliamentary systems are becoming more presidential, in the context of a number of European countries.

■ **Verheijen, T. (1999),** *Civil Service Systems in Central and Eastern Europe*, **Cheltenham, Edward Elgar.** The only systematic treatment of the development of post-communist civil service systems.

 **IMPORTANT WEBSITES**

● **www.sosig.ac.uk/roads/subject-listing/Europe-cat/heads.html** The Social Science Information Gateway linking to most prime ministerial offices in Europe.

● **www.lib.umich.edu/govdocs/foreur.html** Extensive links to European government websites from the University of Michigan.

● **www.oecd.org/topic** A good source on changes in public administration and governance in Europe and in other industrialised democracies from the OECD.

● **www.nispa.sk** Excellent information source on Central and Eastern European governments from the Network of Institutes and Schools of Public Administration in Central and Eastern Europe.

 **Visit the Online Resource Centre that accompanies this book for lots of useful additional material, including an interactive map of Europe. www.oxfordtextbooks.co.uk/orc/hay_menon/**

# 15

# Courts

LISA CONANT

**Chapter Contents**

- Introduction: The Development of European Courts
- Separation of Powers Doctrine and Transformations in Judicial Power
- Judicial Politics and Liberal Democracy
- European Integration and the End of Sovereignty?
- Conclusion: Politics as Usual?

**Reader's Guide**

This chapter examines the role of courts in European politics. It begins by charting the post-war emergence of courts as political actors. It then explains why the judiciary was historically subordinate to other branches of government and discusses how its influence increased after 1945. It continues by analysing how two European courts transformed politics by adding a new layer of rights and obligations. It then examines competing accounts of judicial authority in the European Union (EU). The chapter concludes with a discussion of the extent to which judicial politics is distinctive from other kinds of politics.

# Introduction: The Development of European Courts

Before the Second World War, few observers attached much political significance to courts outside the USA. **Constitutional review** powers predated 1945 in Denmark, Ireland, the Weimar Republic and countries that broke away from the Austro-Hungarian and Ottoman empires including Austria, Czechoslovakia, Greece and Romania. However, courts rarely invoked their review powers and, with the exception of Ireland, soon lost all authority in the wake of domination by the Nazis or authoritarian regimes. The post-war proliferation of constitutional review powers, however, fundamentally altered European politics, enhancing the authority of the courts. Constitutional courts began to review laws for compatibility with the constitution, sometimes overturning the decisions of elected leaders. Austria's specialised constitutional court, established first in 1920 and reestablished in 1945, became the model that new post-war European democracies emulated. Democratisation in post-fascist Italy initially provided for constitutional review by the regular judiciary in 1947, but this was abandoned in favour of a specialised constitutional court in 1956. The Federal Republic of Germany also adopted this approach in 1949. The French Constitutional Council operates largely according to this model, which Greece, Portugal and Spain adopted when they democratised in the 1970s. Another wave of specialised constitutional courts emerged as communism collapsed in Eastern Europe: Poland established its constitutional tribunal in 1986, even before its transition to democracy, and most other post-communist democracies followed suit.

The judiciaries of a number of established European democracies lack extensive constitutional review powers, but many experienced empowerment in recent decades nonetheless. The UK lacks a constitution in the form of a single document, and its judges lack the authority to overturn legislation on the ground that it is unconstitutional. Despite these limits, UK judges have increasingly exercised

**judicial review** of (1) government action for conformity with laws passed by Parliament, (2) national law for conformity with EU law, and (3) national law for conformity with the Convention for the Protection of Human Rights and Fundamental Freedoms (CPHR). The Netherlands also forbids its courts to consider the constitutionality of legislation but, as in the UK, Dutch judges have reviewed government actions for their legality and can overturn national laws that are incompatible with EU and CPHR provisions. In Belgium, the 1989 constitution introducing federalism permits judicial review concerning the distribution of power in government, and Belgian courts also review law for compatibility with European provisions. The judiciaries of Nordic countries tend to avoid political controversies, but judicial review is possible in Denmark, Finland, Norway and Sweden, and all face constraints from EU or European Economic Area (EEA) rules as well. Switzerland allows its Federal Tribunal to strike down legislation adopted by the cantons, but not the federal parliament, and voters have the right to determine the constitutionality of law through referenda. International commitments to the rights of asylum seekers compelled the Swiss parliament to limit citizen initiatives in 1996, however, and Switzerland is subject to the CPHR.

The post-war expansion in judicial power within states has been accompanied by the empowerment of two supranational courts: the European Court of Justice (ECJ) in Luxembourg City and the European Court of Human Rights (ECHR) in Strasbourg. The ECJ and ECHR are the most influential 'international' courts in the world: their caseloads far exceed those of other international jurisdictions, and they command the respect granted to domestic institutions. The ECJ interprets EU law, resolving disputes between individuals, firms, member states and EU institutions. While some cases reach the ECJ directly, national courts also send references with questions about EU law that the ECJ answers in **preliminary rulings** that the national court then applies. By ruling that EU law was supreme to national law and could be directly enforced by national courts in many instances, the ECJ invited national courts to exercise judicial review of national law, overturning legislation that was incompatible with EU legal obligations (for more on the ECJ, see Chapter 11, this volume). As a result, the ECJ empowered most national courts and created a decentralised means of enforcing its own interpretations of EU law. The ECHR enforces the CPHR, protecting the rights of individuals who have exhausted domestic remedies. National courts often assist in protecting European human rights as well because many signatory states have incorporated the CPHR into domestic law.

### KEY POINTS

- Courts exercised little political power in Europe before 1945.

- Judicial power expanded most dramatically in the post-war era in European states that democratised after an experience of fascism, authoritarianism or communism.

- Judicial power in established democracies expanded in recent decades, particularly in response to opportunities that emerged through European institutions.

- European courts that resolve disputes about EU law and human rights are the world's most influential international courts.

# Separation of Powers Doctrine and Transformations in Judicial Power

Doctrines that each branch of government should exercise separate powers were historically prevalent in Europe. The exercise of distinct powers by the executive, legislative and judicial branches reflects the confidence that Europeans originally placed in elective democracy. In this approach, representatives who are directly accountable to citizens through regular elections are most likely to make laws that benefit society. The demise of democracy and human rights abuses during the Second World War challenged commitments to elective democracy and contributed to an emphasis on liberal democracy, where the protection of particular rights and freedoms takes priority over the preferences of a majority of citizens or their elected representatives. This shift transformed the powers of courts, who became the core institutions to safeguard the liberties of liberal democracy.

## The French Revolution and the civil-law tradition

French ideas about the appropriate role of different branches of government once dominated most emerging European democracies. The political philosopher Montesquieu advocated a strict **separation of powers**, where the legislature makes all laws and the judiciary merely applies the correct law in individual disputes. Similarly, Rousseau considered the legislature to be the institution that would best reflect the general will of society. These ideas appealed to those on the winning side of the French Revolution of 1789, partly because many associated the courts with the interests of the monarchy rather than the people. As a result, early reformers concentrated law-making powers in the legislature and expressly forbade the regular judiciary from reviewing legislation. French leaders also rejected the idea that judges could bind themselves to decisions from previous cases since such a binding **precedent** would become a source of law, which only legislatures could rightfully make. In an attempt to rationalise law and limit judicial discretion, Napoleon pioneered the first modern **legal codes** after the Revolution. The French codes established rules to provide a foundation for the entire legal system, where judges make legal decisions by applying the appropriate article from the code. Together, the separation of powers doctrine, rejection of binding precedents and the system of code law prevent the development of a 'government of judges'.

Napoleon's conquest of Europe led to the widespread adoption of legal codes and suspicion of a powerful judiciary. The impact of the French codes is evident in Belgium, Italy, Luxembourg, the Netherlands, Portugal and Spain. Germany adopted a distinct code in 1900 that influenced legal systems in Denmark, Finland, Iceland, Norway and Sweden. Transforming judges into legal technicians who applied pre-existing code laws appealed to democratic reformers across Europe. These countries, along with most others in the world, belong to the **civil-law tradition** whose characteristics typically include a legal system founded on legal codes and a judiciary comprised of officials with the character of civil servants who are subordinate to the representative branches of government.

## Judicial law-making, the common-law tradition and legislative supremacy

The other major European legal system, the **common-law tradition** of the UK and Ireland, accepted judicial law-making through precedents, but still limited the power of the judiciary and subordinated it to the legislature. The common law refers to laws that originate in the precedents set by court rulings over time. Under the principle of *stare decisis*, which means 'let the decision stand', judges in common-law systems normally consider themselves to be bound by the judgments given in previous similar cases. The precedent set in a case becomes the law by which judges settle other related cases. In this way, common-law judges create and change law over time as they establish precedents and also overturn them as judicial opinion evolves. The judicial law-making role, therefore, is dynamic and independent of other branches of government. Yet common law developed through precedents evolves slowly, in small steps that mirror conventional practices. The complexity that characterises the common law is the main reason that it appears only in the UK (excluding Scotland) and many of its former colonies, where it could be imported wholesale, with English lawyers and judges knowledgeable about its precedents. Moreover, under the UK tradition of **parliamentary sovereignty**, statutes adopted by the legislature are supreme to common-law precedents. While judge-made common law was prevalent for centuries, parliamentary statutes began to dominate by the twentieth century.

Despite the differences in the civil-law and common-law systems, all European countries historically subordinated the judiciary to other branches of government. The executive branch, typically headed by a monarch, traditionally used the judiciary to enforce its conception of justice. As countries moved towards democratic rule, the legislature became the dominant source of law and citizens looked to competitive elections as the best means to assure a responsive government. Judges were not entirely powerless since common-law judges indeed made law and even civil-law judges found it necessary to interpret ambiguous codes and construct rules where gaps existed. Efforts to weaken the French judiciary also led to the creation of alternative 'councils', which are courts in all but name, to take on tasks denied the 'regular' courts. The Council of State has reviewed the legality of administrative action since 1799 and advises governments about the constitutionality of proposed legislation. Although the Council of State is formally part of the administration, it has gained respect by protecting citizens from arbitrary acts of the bureaucracy. Yet, while courts or court-like bodies always possessed some authority, they nonetheless tended to be overshadowed by the power of the more explicitly 'political' and eventually democratically representative branches of government before 1945.

## Disciplining democracy through courts, constitutions and conventions

Faith in an unfettered democratic process faltered in the aftermath of the Second World War as the full extent of the atrocities of the Holocaust became apparent. Adolf Hitler's Nazi party won a plurality of the vote in the 1933 elections in Weimar Germany, and wrote laws to justify its actions as it overthrew the republic and instituted a totalitarian regime directly responsible for the murder of over 10 million civilians. Benito Mussolini's fascist dictatorship in Italy and contempt for individual rights also underscored the need for stronger institutions to uphold democratic processes and basic civil liberties. France's swift fall to the Nazis in 1940 and Marshal Pétain's collaborationist Vichy regime cast doubts that even a long democratic heritage guaranteed protection of individual rights. The states that pioneered the strongest constitutional courts and most extensive constitutional review powers in the post-war era were Italy, the Federal Republic of Germany and Austria, which, although forcibly united with Nazi Germany, had also been a base of Nazi support. Italians, Germans and Austrians committed to liberal democracy, and US occupation forces in Germany and Italy, supported the adoption of constitutions that bound governments to limit their power. Constitutional courts would ultimately enforce those individual rights and freedoms that deserve protection regardless of the whims of mass sentiments.

The origins of the ECHR and CPHR also stem from the post-war desire to entrench rights and freedoms. Andrew Moravcsik demonstrates that leaders of new post-war democracies readily ceded sovereignty to an international human rights regime in order to prevent any authoritarian regression. By

agreeing to binding human rights norms, enforceable in an international court, leaders signalled their commitment to maintain liberal democratic institutions and created the mechanisms that would constrain future governments (Moravcsik 2000). The subsequent ratification of the CPHR and acceptance of ECHR jurisdiction in other signatory states marked the beginning of an increase in supranational judicial control over political outcomes.

In 1958 France adopted a new constitutional review process, although its initial motivation was to increase, rather than limit, state power. Charles de Gaulle supported the creation of a Constitutional Council as a mechanism to strengthen the executive relative to the legislature. In his view, a powerful legislature was the major cause of weak and short-lived French governments. Because only the president of the republic or the presidents of either house of the legislature could originally bring suspect legislation to the Constitutional Council, political leaders controlled all challenges. Since De Gaulle's party presided over governing majorities while he was president, few measures faced challenges. The constitutional amendment in 1974 that enabled either 60 senators or 60 deputies to challenge legislation then transformed constitutional review into a meaningful constraint. Minorities have taken advantage of this opportunity since the early 1980s to dilute majority reforms.

In states where established democratic regimes endured, even if interrupted by Nazi occupation, courts experienced less dramatic increases in power. With the exception of Ireland, where judges capitalised on pre-existing post-colonial constitutional review powers, the primary source of judicial empowerment in long-standing democracies was European. EU membership and acceptance of ECHR jurisdiction following ratification of the CPHR brought disputes under the authority of the two supranational courts even in countries with no tradition of constitutional review. Moreover, the EU legal system empowered national judges to overturn national law on the grounds that it is incompatible with EU legal obligations. While British and Dutch judges gained completely new 'constitutional' review powers, therefore, the regular judiciary of other EU member states began to exercise this power that had previously been reserved exclusively for constitutional courts. The eventual incorporation of the CPHR into domestic law in many signatory states also confers powers on national courts to enforce human rights.

With the exception of federal reform in Belgium, all the other countries that embraced new constitutional review powers adopted reforms as authoritarian or communist regimes gave way to democracies. A newly democratic Spain buried the legacy of Francisco Franco's dictatorship with a Constitutional Court with extensive powers of review, and Central and East European states followed the pattern of their Western counterparts in entrenching their new democracies with constitutional courts.

The proliferation of constitutional review powers in Europe has contributed to a broader globalisation of judging. (See Theme box: The Impact of Globalisation.)

---

## KEY POINTS

- French ideas about the separation of powers dominated Europe before 1945. Under separation of powers doctrine, the legislature is the exclusive lawmaker, and judges may not exercise judicial review.

- Civil-law ideals expect judges to apply legal codes mechanistically, but judges must be creative because codes and statutes can be vague and incomplete.

- Judges create laws through precedents in the common-law system of the UK, but parliamentary sovereignty subordinates precedents to legislated statutes.

- Colonial, fascist, authoritarian or communist experience inspired the creation of constitutional courts and review powers in newly established democracies.

- French President Charles de Gaulle created the Constitutional Council to strengthen executive powers relative to the legislature, but a 1974 expansion in access transformed constitutional review into a constraint on government.

- EU law and the CPHR function as a higher law that national courts can use to exercise judicial review of national law.

---

## THEME BOX

### The Impact of Globalisation

Europe has been a key site of what observers call a global expansion of judicial power. Yet the post-war proliferation of constitutional review by courts has not been limited to Europe, but has been a prevalent feature of democratisation processes in the second half of the twentieth century in Africa, Asia and Latin America. Judicial review and constitutional rights protection have also expanded in established democracies such as Canada, Israel and New Zealand since the 1980s.

As the number of politically influential courts has grown, judges from around the world have also begun to interact as they search for solutions to common problems. Anne-Marie Slaughter writes of a 'new world order' that operates through networks of government officials who exchange information and coordinate activity to address contemporary challenges on a global scale. Judges increasingly participate in these networks by attending international judicial summits, meeting and observing their counterparts abroad, reading each other's judgments, and communicating via modern information technologies from the comfort of their desks. An increasing number of courts have their judgments translated into English to facilitate the global judicial dialogue, and electronic databases of case law such as Lexis and Westlaw are adding foreign and international holdings. Although judges do not consider the decisions of foreign or international jurisdictions as binding precedents within their own legal systems, many are open to what Slaughter calls the 'persuasive authority' of well reasoned judgments from around the world (2004).

LISA CONANT

# Judicial Politics and Liberal Democracy

The empowerment of courts has transformed politics in Europe. Parliaments are no longer free to rule in the absence of constraints imposed by courts, whether those courts are intervening on the basis of national constitutions or European sources of law. Liberal democracy, with its emphasis on protection of fundamental rights and freedoms, appears to have triumphed over elective democracy, with its emphasis on popular accountability. Yet the extent to which courts determine political outcomes remains disputed.

## Towards juristocracy?

Accounts of bold judicial intervention in contemporary controversies suggest that juristocracy, or rule by judges, now characterises the politics of many democratic states (Hirschl 2004). Constitutional courts contribute to political debates by ruling on the legality of anti-democratic parties and anti-terrorism measures, ratification of EU treaties, boundaries between church and state, contraception, abortion, divorce and sexual identity (Stone Sweet 2000). In France, Alec Stone (now Stone Sweet) considers the Constitutional Council to be a third legislative chamber, issuing the final word on all important law (Stone 1992). Government ministers in the UK and Netherlands endeavour to avoid judicial review of their actions, and the once sovereign legislators in each country defer to European legal obligations. The new constitutional courts of post-communist democracies have also enjoyed successes in patrolling the division of power and gaining respect for their rulings. Even where regimes attacked their constitutional courts, which occurred in Bulgaria, Russia, and Slovakia, the courts fought back and contributed to democratisation (Schwartz 2000). The Ukrainian Supreme Court's invalidation of the 2004 presidential election amid allegations of electoral abuses represents one of the more dramatic demonstrations of judicial independence and the rule of law in a new democracy plagued by corruption and Russian interference. By requiring a new run-off, the Court defied the incumbent government and changed the outcome of the election. Even concerted efforts to circumvent judicial interference backfired: the Irish Supreme Court used a 1983 'pro-life' amendment to the constitution, intended to preclude legalisation of abortion, to confer a right to an abortion if a woman's life was threatened by continuation of her pregnancy.

Citizens are the most active participants in this new judicial politics in countries where they are given direct access to pursue constitutional challenges. For example, individuals initiate the majority of constitutional claims in Germany, Ireland, Italy and Spain even though elected representatives have the power to request review of legislation prior to its coming into effect. By contrast, only sets of elected elites may refer bills to the French Constitutional Council and Portuguese Constitutional Court. Although parties in the opposition frequently challenge government proposals, the restrictive rules of access in France and Portugal exclude citizens from contributing to the constitutional agenda. While most analysts of juristocracy applaud the rise of courts, others are more critical of its implications: Ran Hirschl argues that constitutional reform can entrench elite preferences as they come under challenge from the democratic representation of new groups (2004). Ambivalence about the legitimate role of courts in democracies remains evident. (See Theme box: Democracy and Legitimacy.)

## Limits of judicial power and the lack of a 'final word'

The rise of courts invites the question Martin Shapiro asked in his 1988 book, *Who Guards the*

*Guardians?* The record of judicial protection during national security panics, when citizens are most likely to face threats, is rarely inspiring. The German Federal Constitutional Court's (GFCC) approval of indiscriminate police investigations when the terrorist Red Army Faction was active and the US Supreme Court's acceptance of the internment of US citizens of Japanese descent during the Second World War are typical and do not bode well for the judicial protection of civil liberties in countries battling terrorism today. Even in more mundane disputes, J. A. G. Griffith argues that courts in the UK consistently support more conventional and established interests (1997). Shapiro suggests that the ideal of independent rights protection is a myth given that courts, particularly at the highest appellate levels, are fundamentally institutions of the regime, enforcing its norms and interests (1981).

Another important question is whether courts can actually control the state. Scholars of US judicial politics, who have long studied a powerful system of courts, articulate a nuanced view of judicial power, drawing attention to its limits as well as its promise. Many agree that, while courts may delay or modify particular reforms, they rely on the support of other branches of government to exert much influence. For example, the 1998 Human Rights Act in the UK, which incorporated the CPHR into national law as of 2000, allows individuals to bring claims based on the CPHR before national courts but does not actually permit judicial overruling of national law. Judges may issue declarations of incompatibility, but government and Parliament possess the power to bring legislation into conformity with human rights norms. The variable impact of the constitutional protection of fetal

---

**THEME BOX**

### Democracy and Legitimacy

The relationship of courts to democracy has undergone a major transformation in Europe. Until the post-war era, few Europeans associated courts with the protection of democracy. The more common view was that powerful courts potentially threatened democracy: most notably, the practice of judicial review allows unelected judges to reject the decisions of the majority in elected legislatures. This is problematic in terms of democratic accountability because citizens rarely play any direct role in selecting judges and the typically long terms of judicial appointments mean that judges often stay in office after the elected officials who appointed them have left office. In countries where judicial appointment proceeds largely through bureaucratic channels, the judiciary possesses no democratic credentials whatsoever. As a result of this political insulation, judicial review was long considered to be an illegitimate interference with the will of the people. Contemporary critics of the post-war expansion of judicial power in Europe complain that judicial interventions in politics remain biased in favour of more established interests. By contrast, supporters of recent judicial empowerment argue that an independent institution is necessary

to tame the potential excesses of majority rule. Unfair treatment or even persecution of an unpopular minority may achieve majority support, and, during periods of crisis, the executive may exploit fears to concentrate power and even dismantle democratic institutions. In this view, courts are essential institutions to enforce fundamental individual rights of citizens, safeguarding a liberal democracy where guarantees of certain freedoms limit the range of democratic choice. Empirically, it is not clear that the expansion of judicial power has generated any real crisis of democratic legitimacy. Surveys from opinion polls such as the *Eurobarometer* show that citizens in many European democracies rank their constitutional courts as among the most trusted of political institutions. Many observers of courts also note that it is rare for courts to remain seriously out of sync with public opinion for long periods of time. Finally, a number of scholars find that courts need allies in order to exert much influence in the political process: unless other governing institutions and societal groups support judicial opinions, implementation of court orders can be very limited.

life in Germany is also illustrative of the limits of judicial power: abortion has been more readily available in *Länder* controlled by parties that support legalised abortion than in *Länder* controlled by parties that support most prohibitions of abortion (Prützel-Thomas 1993: 472–3). Even the GFCC softened its stance in the wake of sustained pressure for liberalisation, arguing that abortions, while not legal, could nonetheless remain unpunished in circumstances commonly used to justify legal abortions in many countries: fetal defects, pregnancies resulting from rape, and health risks or social hardship for the woman. The constitutional doctrine that abortion is a criminal procedure, therefore, is hardly a meaningful final word.

While courts face implementation problems in trying to impose unpopular decisions, they can also face threats to their institutional integrity when they intervene in important political controversies. Charles de Gaulle considered abolishing the Council of State after it declared that the establishment of special military tribunals to try suspected terrorists during the Algerian war was illegal (Provine 1997: 189). Schwartz observes that judicial efforts to check

political power resulted in the abolition of the constitutional court in Kazakhstan, the suspension of the constitution and its court for a year and a half in Russia, and judicial failures to uphold democracy in Albania, Armenia, Belarus and Romania (2000). As a result, constitutional protections cannot be only what courts make of them, but what the political regime and its citizens ultimately make of them as well.

> **KEY POINTS**
>
> - Courts regularly intervene in contemporary political disputes in European countries.
>
> - Individuals actively participate in setting the constitutional agenda of courts whenever they are given direct access to courts to wage constitutional challenges.
>
> - Courts do not necessarily protect individual rights against abuses of power, particularly when national security is at stake.
>
> - Courts remain dependent on the exercise of power by other branches of government.

# European Integration and the End of Sovereignty?

The expansion of judicial power in the context of European integration was surprising because conventional understandings of international relations expect that states act as they wish, without regard to the constraints of international law and courts. In this view, national interests and the power to pursue them explain behaviour. The use of EU law as a higher law that trumps national law directly challenges state sovereignty, subjecting national independence to the will of an international court. Conventional accounts would predict that ECJ judgments would remain largely unenforced, as EU member states refused to comply with unwelcome rulings. Yet, while delays

in compliance occur, states more typically obey EU law (Conant 2002; Zürn and Joerges 2005). To explain this puzzling phenomenon, scholars of international organisation, regional integration and comparative politics developed competing accounts.

## Member state dominance

Geoffrey Garrett and his collaborators explain EU judicial politics in terms that are largely consistent with traditional expectations of international relations. In this approach, national governments adopt common EU rules to promote beneficial interactions, and they rely on the ECJ to identify who is violating rules and resolve disputes about interpretation. Garrett argues that the ECJ panders to the preferences of member states because national governments retaliate against unfavourable rulings by simply disobeying them or by overturning them through revisions of EU law and treaties. The costs of compliance and the relative difficulty of overturning unwelcome rulings determine the likelihood of such retaliation. Although the ECJ enjoys some autonomy in this approach, it is largely consistent with conventional understandings about international politics, where states are dominant actors (Garrett 1992; Garrett *et al.* 1998).

## Court dominance

Another group of scholars reject this approach, contending that legal integration eroded the dominance of states. Anne-Marie Burley (now Slaughter) and Walter Mattli argue that interactions among private litigants, lawyers, national judges and ECJ justices created a binding system of European law that constrains national governments. Blending legal and political logic, they explain that the ECJ encouraged national judges to refer cases for preliminary rulings by developing convincing legal reasoning and offering the opportunity to exercise judicial review. As a result, cooperation between national and ECJ judges became mutually empowering. Meanwhile, lawyers and litigants gained an additional avenue to pursue their interests. National governments gradually lost control as case law incrementally developed EU rules, with careful justifications to 'mask' political implications and 'shield' judges from attack (Burley and Mattli 1993; Mattli and Slaughter 1998). Danny Nicol verified the extent to which legal masks can obscure by demonstrating that the British Parliament did not realise it was abandoning parliamentary sovereignty by joining the EU even after the ECJ had made its decisions on supremacy and direct effect (2001). Meanwhile, others demonstrated that rising EU trade corresponded with rising EU litigation rates in a manner

that contributed to the increasing scope and effectiveness of EU law (Stone Sweet and Brunell 1998).

## The EU: comparative or international politics?

This debate, and the effectiveness of the EU legal system, inspired scholars to look to comparative politics, where study focuses on politics within states. Karen Alter compared French and German courts to explain why national courts began to cooperate with the ECJ. Observing resistance in some courts, Alter argued that the EU legal system empowered lower and intermediate-level courts but actually demoted supreme courts from their position at the top of national legal hierarchies. Already possessing review powers, constitutional courts faced the greatest relative loss of influence in a world where EU law takes precedence over all national law. As a result, Alter finds that activism from lower courts was largely responsible for generating the cases that the ECJ needed to construct the EU legal system. Many national supreme courts eventually participated as a means to influence a stream of cases that otherwise escaped their control, but they also refused to accept all of the ECJ's legal justifications in order to maintain opportunities to give precedence to national constitutional norms in some instances (Alter 2001). Judges are central actors patrolling the boundaries of legal integration, therefore, but the ECJ is not necessarily *the* dominant court in a clear judicial hierarchy.

Also drawing on domestic judicial politics, Lisa Conant argued that court rulings usually have a narrow impact, affecting parties to the litigation and not necessarily the universe of individuals in parallel situations. When individuals have a very strong interest in a particular ruling and actually possess the financial means to litigate, governments may face a trickle of lawsuits as those in similar situations demand equal treatment. In many instances, however, citizens lack the knowledge and resources to sue. More commonly, governments face serious pressures to adapt to legal developments only when organised interest groups, enforcement agencies such as the European Commission or coalitions of business interests support change. These actors have the resources to litigate frequently and lobby for change at the national and European levels. As a result, reactions of other institutions and actors in society mediate the influence of the ECJ, which cannot easily impose major change in the absence of broader support (Conant 2002). (For an example of this policy dynamic, see Theme box: The Impact of the European Union.)

In contrast to the approaches claiming member state or court dominance, these comparative politics approaches tend not to assign predominance to either national governments or the ECJ, but see legal integration as a process that is shaped by the contributions of actors across levels of government within the EU.

## KEY POINTS

- The emergence of a binding EU legal system challenges ideas about the independence of states in international politics.

- Some international relations scholars explain this puzzle by arguing that the EU legal system serves the interests of national governments, who still control integration.

- Other scholars counter by arguing that judges, lawyers and litigants operate in a legal context largely independent of the logic of state power.

- Comparative politics scholars argue that legal integration proceeds through interactions between governing institutions at the EU *and* national level in a process characterised by compromise.

## THEME BOX

### The Impact of the European Union

Citizens of EU member states enjoy the legal right to work all over the EU thanks to Article 39 of the EC Treaty on the free movement of workers, but countries can still restrict employment in the 'public service' to their own citizens. Because governments defined public service differently and excluded migrant workers from all public-sector jobs in some countries, individuals seeking employment began to contest official personnel policies before national courts. In response to a reference from a German court, the ECJ ruled in 1974 that national definitions of public officials could not determine the public-service category. After the European Commission brought infringement proceedings against Belgium in 1980 for the closure of virtually all public-sector employment to migrant workers, the ECJ defined public service narrowly, arguing that nationality could be a requirement only where national loyalty and allegiance to the state were necessary to perform a particular job. Despite this ruling, which was reaffirmed in a subsequent infringement proceeding against Belgium in 1982, individuals continued to challenge discriminatory practices before national courts throughout the 1980s. Cases concerning the same professions emerged in different member states, making it clear that governments were not responding to the ECJ case law by opening their public-sector employment to migrating EU workers. As a result, in 1988 the European Commission issued a formal communication that called on national governments to eliminate nationality requirements in all fields of employment that did not correspond to the ECJ's narrow definition of public service. When national discrimination continued anyway, the European Commission then initiated enforcement proceedings against all member states who continued to ignore the policy implications of ECJ case law. In response to these systematic infringement proceedings, which involved ten of all 12 member states, national governments began to adapt national legislation to the requirements of EU law as the ECJ interpreted it. Yet, even as they eliminated provisions that constituted clear violations of EU law, national governments left in place other discriminatory practices that continued to pose obstacles to labour mobility in the public sector. For example, some individuals found that their past experience or pension contributions were not considered relevant in a new national context. This case illustrates that ECJ interpretation does not automatically result in policy changes, and that vigilant enforcement of EU rules can be crucial to encourage reform. (Adapted from Conant 2002.)

# Conclusion: Politics as Usual?

Courts have become prominent institutions in European democracies. Although courts have exercised more limited powers in many long-established democracies, they appear to play a central role in transitions to liberal democracy after experiences of authoritarianism, colonialism, fascism and communism. Democratisation that represents a sudden and significant break with past regimes generates strong demands for protection of the democratic process and citizens' rights. With recent memories of government abuses and fears that supporters of past regimes may try to regain power, backers of new democracies have an incentive to articulate constitutional rules and establish courts to enforce these rules. Intended to preserve democracy, constitutions also limit democracy by removing certain decisions from the hands of elected leaders and citizens. This conservative element of constitutions may help to strengthen new democracies, but it may also constrain efforts to respond to new social needs. If consensus persists that existing constitutional arrangements are beneficial, relying on courts that are insulated from popular demands may play a stabilising role that is consistent with democratic ideals. To the extent that consensus breaks down, however, such entrenched rules and their enforcement mechanisms may undermine the democratic responsiveness of European governments.

In addition to the explicit creation of constitutional constraints, judicial power also expanded unintentionally. Recall that Charles de Gaulle intended to control the legislature with the creation of the French Constitutional Council, but a decision to broaden access in 1974 ultimately generated a process of constitutional review that constrains the executive as well. In the EU, member states did not design EU law to serve as a higher law that could be used to overturn national law, but ECJ decisions on the supremacy and direct effect of EU law, along with national judicial cooperation, eventually produced this result. Many observe that these unintended consequences of institutional change are not easily reversed because change would involve constitutional or treaty amendment, both of which require high degrees of consensus. As long as any significant minority appreciates the expansion of judicial power, it will be difficult to reverse.

In summary, judicial politics has many features in common with ordinary politics. Even though courts are created to exist 'above politics' in order that they can protect the most fundamental rules of democratic politics, their very creation is the product of self-interested actors attempting to entrench a particular set of values as permanently as possible. Because societal demands change over time, judicial efforts to preserve particular norms, especially when impervious to legislated change, generate political conflict. Although judicial interpretation can unsettle existing relations to the benefit of less privileged individuals and groups, more established and resourceful elites remain advantaged in judicial venues that require knowledge and money for access and that look overwhelmingly to entrenched rules for guidance. As logical and technical as legal reasoning may appear, the law itself originates in the political imposition of particular values in constitutions and legislation. Courts may display considerable independence in interpreting and applying the law, but the laws still typically advantage and disadvantage different individuals in society.

## KEY POINTS

- Courts and constitutions have been central features of transitions to democracy.

- Courts protect democratic procedures but also limit democratic choices.

- Judicial politics often concerns entrenched rules that are difficult to reverse.

- Judicial interference in democratic politics can benefit either elites or less advantaged groups.

## QUESTIONS

1.  Why was judicial power originally so limited in Europe?
2.  How important are the differences between civil-law and common-law systems?
3.  What explains the rise of courts as political institutions in Europe?
4.  Can courts be trusted to control the state?
5.  What limits courts' control of the state?
6.  How did the ECJ create opportunities for judicial review by national courts?
7.  Which explanation of legal integration is the most convincing?
8.  To what extent is judicial politics distinct from ordinary politics?

## FURTHER READING

■ **Börzel, T. and Cichowski, R. (eds) (2003),** *The State of the European Union*, **vol. 6, Oxford, Oxford University Press.** Provides an interdisciplinary analysis of the interaction between law, politics and society in the EU.

■ **Epp, C. (1998),** *The Rights Revolution*, **Chicago IL, University of Chicago Press.** Examines how the democratisation of access to courts promotes the protection of rights in four countries, including the UK.

■ **Jacob, H.** *et al.* **(1996),** *Courts, Law and Politics in Comparative Perspective*, **New Haven CT, Yale University Press.** Brings together specialists to examine the role of courts in five advanced industrial democracies.

■ **Kommers, D. (1997),** *The Constitutional Jurisprudence of the Federal Republic of Germany*, **2nd edn, Durham NC, Duke University Press.** Examines the importance of the Federal Constitutional Court of Germany in policy-making.

■ **Sterett, S. (1997),** *Creating Constitutionalism*, **Ann Arbor IL, University of Michigan Press.** Examines how judicial review constrains governments and officials in the UK even in the absence of a written constitution.

## IMPORTANT WEBSITES

● **www.law.nyu.edu/library/foreign_intl/country.html** This website compiled by the New York University School of Law provides links to national collections of legal materials and databases.

● **http://curia.eu.int/en/index.htm** The website of the ECJ provides information about the Court and a link to search case law.

● **www.echr.coe.int/** The website of the ECHR provides information about the Court and a link to search case law.

**Visit the Online Resource Centre that accompanies this book for lots of useful additional material, including an interactive map of Europe. www.oxfordtextbooks.co.uk/orc/hay_menon/**

# PART 3

# Public Policies of Europe

# Economic Management in the Eurozone

GRAHAME F. THOMPSON

✓ **Reader's Guide**

This chapter investigates how the arrival of the euro in 1999 has affected economic policy-making in the European Union (EU) area. It concentrates on institutional changes like the formation and operation of the European Central Bank (ECB) and how monetary policy was formulated and conducted by the ECB. The role of fiscal policy is also discussed, which is crucially linked to the emergence and fate of the Stability and Growth Pact as well as to monetary policy. Issues associated with the liberalisation of services across the EU and the attempts at creating financial integration are also discussed. Finally, the newly emerging international role of the euro is raised and the prospects for the new entry countries and further enlargement beyond assessed.

# Introduction

This chapter focuses on key developments in the EU economy since the advent of the euro in 1999. It concentrates on the challenges this has posed for economic policy-making and the governance of the EU's expanding economy. A central feature of the post-Maastricht governance environment has been the attempt to create a 'single market in services' for Europe. If the 1990s was the decade of the **single market programme** (SMP) which concentrated on the integration of product markets, then the early decades of the twenty-first century promise to be those of an equivalent attempt to create a single market for professional, financial and other services. The famous **four freedoms** embodied in the EC's (later EU's) founding Treaty of Rome (1957) involved trade, labour, capital and services. Up until the late 1990s the EU had concentrated upon trade, labour and real investment matters, rather to the neglect of services and the financial system. But, while this chapter focuses on services and particularly financial services and capital flows, this has to be set in the context of the evolving macroeconomic management environment created by the introduction of the euro.

In many ways the introduction of the euro both begged the question of an integrated financial system for Europe (or the **Eurozone** in the first instance) and was stimulated by the relatively smooth passage of the euro's introduction. Thus a central issue to deal with in the chapter is the institutional changes that **economic and monetary union** (EMU) has occasioned and benefited from. The key institutional development here is the creation of the **European Central Bank** (ECB) and how it has gone about conducting monetary policy. But monetary policy cannot be properly dealt with without at the same time considering fiscal policy.

Just as the SMP was so important in forging a convergence and integration of the EU's real product economy in the 1990s, so the concentration on the services sector in the current decade could be equally as important for the EU's future economic development. The emphasis on the services sector arose in the context of the **Lisbon Agenda** initiated in March 2000. What this Agenda amounts to, and the political conflict it has engendered among EU leaders is discussed below.

Of course, the euro is not only a common currency for the Eurozone but it is also a major international currency. The characteristics of the euro's role as an international currency are considered in this chapter. And connected to this are issues thrown up for the monetary and financial future of Europe by the expansion of the EU from 15 members to 25 in May 2003, and the further **enlargement** to come.

But, before all of this, it is useful to remind ourselves of the importance of the EU in the international economic context relative to other main potential competitor economies and zones. This is the object of the next brief section.

# Comparative Importance of the European Union

Just to put things into perspective it is useful to provide an outline picture of the size of the EU compared to the USA and Japan. While a lot is made of the rise of China and India as potential competitors to these and other economies, as yet they remain rapidly expanding economic giants

**Table 16.1** Comparative Economic Data, 2003

| | Population (millions) | GDP at market prices (US$ 000bn) | GDP at PPP adjusted price (US$ 000bn) | GDP per capita at market prices (US$) | GDP per capita at PPP adjusted prices (US$) |
|---|---|---|---|---|---|
| China | 1,288 | 1,410 | 6,435 | 1,100 | 4,990 |
| India | 1,064 | 600 | 3,096 | 530 | 2,880 |
| EU12 | 306 | 8,175 | 8,115 | 22,850 | 26,260 |
| USA | 291 | 10,882 | 10,870 | 37,610 | 37,500 |
| Japan | 127 | 4,326 | 3,583 | 34,510 | 28,620 |

*Source*: World Bank, Online data services, accessed April 2005

whose main impact will probably arise in the decade following this one. Comparative data on these two economies and the EU12, USA and Japan is given in Table 16.1 (note that these data are measured in terms of US dollars). Several measures of economic size are provided in Table 16.1: GDP and GDP per head both measured at market prices and at purchasing power parity (PPP) unit prices. This latter PPP measure adjusts GDP to reflect what income can actually comparatively purchase in an economy.

The differences between market prices and PPP prices are striking (and they are somewhat controversial), but they show that although China (and to a lesser extent India) are significant economies in absolute terms, when compared to the three advanced economies their GDP *per head* remained small in 2003. Table 16.2 provides data that signal some of the key characteristics of these economies presented in terms designed to bring out the importance of differences *within* the EU as well as between the EU and the USA and Japan (note that these data are measured in terms of the euro).

The main points to be noted from Table 16.2 are:

- The population of the EU15 was already larger than that of the USA before the ten new members joined in 2004.
- If the three next most likely new large members (Turkey, Romania and Bulgaria) were to join,

another 100 million people would be added to the EU total. (In fact Romania and Bulgaria will join in January 2007).

- The existing EU and USA are almost the same size in terms of GDP, but both the USA and Japan have higher GDP per head than the EU.
- The average US citizen was estimated to have a 42 per cent greater PPP adjusted income than the average EU15 citizen in 2005.
- In terms of growth rates, the EU's performance was poor compared to the USA. Japan demonstrates the weakest performance.
- The Romanian and Bulgarian economies shrank over the transitional period 1990–2002.

The fact that the majority of the ten countries who joined the EU in 2000 were considerably less prosperous than the EU15 was part of the reason for them wanting to join. However, the economic challenge posed by this is obvious. The EU15 had achieved a considerable degree of convergence and integration by 2000; the members had developed common rules and policies that suited their stage of development. As will be discussed later in this chapter, the advent of a large number of new, less prosperous and somewhat differently organised economies may upset the delicate balances forged between the EU15 and require a radical rethink of how the expanded EU economy can be managed and governed. (See Theme box: The Impact of the European Union.)

**Table 16.2** Comparative Economic Data for the EU, USA, Japan and the Main EU Candidate Countries (estimates for 2005)

| | Population (millions) | GDP at market prices (€ 000bn) | GDP at PPP (€ 000bn) | GDP per capita (EU15 = 100) | GDP per capita at PPP rates (EU15 = 100) | Growth rates: annual % change, 2001–4* |
|---|---|---|---|---|---|---|
| **EU15** | 385 | 10.0 | 10.0 | 100 | 100 | 1.5 |
| **EU25** | 460 | 10.5 | 11.0 | 87.8 | 91.9 | 1.6 |
| **USA** | 300 | 10.3 | 11.0 | 133.0 | 142.0 | 2.6 |
| **Japan** | 128 | 4.2 | 3.5 | 124.0 | 104.6 | 1.0 |
| **Turkey** | 73 | 0.262 | 0.442 | 13.8 | 23.2 | 3.1 |
| **Romania** | 21 | 0.055 | 0.165 | 9.9 | 29.4 | −0.1 |
| **Bulgaria** | 8 | 0.021 | 0.067 | 10.7 | 30.5 | −0.7 |

*Source*: Derived from 'The EU Economy: 2003 Review', *European Economy*, 6, 2003, EU Brussels, 2004, and 'Economic Forecasts: Spring 2005', *European Economy*, 2, 2005, EU Brussels, 2005
*Note*: For Turkey, Romania and Bulgaria, growth rates are averaged over the period 1990–2002. The source for these data is the World Bank, Online data services

## KEY POINTS

- The EU15/25 represents a continental-sized economy, able to compete with the USA (and China and India somewhere down the line).

- The new EU members who joined in 2004, and those lining up to join later, are at a different level of development to the existing EU15.

- This will pose considerable challenges for those managing and governing the newly expanding EU economy.

## THEME BOX

### The Impact of the European Union

In as much as the European Union has successfully integrated in respect to a range of economic dimensions associated with the four freedoms first embodied in the Treaty of Rome, its impact has been profound at both the domestic level for member states and for the international system to which it is connected. However, the EU is neither homogeneous as an entity in itself not the sum total of 'Europe'. There are several important European countries that remain outside the EU, and within the EU there are various divisions, notably that between those in the Eurozone and the rest. These divisions, inclusions and exclusions mean that the 'European economic space' is both bigger than just the EU and more differentiated than often recognised. However, increasingly the EU itself is having a major impact on its 'near neighbours' within Europe and various configurations on its periphery and beyond. Few could dispute the EU as a major continental-sized economy, providing it with the potential to compete with other economic giants like the USA, China, India and Japan.

# The Euro and Macroeconomic Policy

The development of an integrated and inter-dependent EU economy, with a single currency—one gradually including other European countries—raises important new issues for macroeconomic management. Central from the point of view of economics is whether the EU is an **optimum currency area** (OCA) or moving towards it. An OCA would have a sufficient degree of underlying structural convergence between the economies involved to make the establishment of a common currency a viable proposition. Whether the EU as a whole—or just the Eurozone in particular—can be considered an OCA is a difficult issue, but there are several features to be considered.

- The first concerns the relative inflation rates between countries. If there were widely variable inflation rates, accommodating a single currency would require major and potentially disruptive domestic economic adjustment in the countries (significant interest rate changes, for instance). In large part this accounts for the central concern of the EU authorities—and the ECB in particular—with maintaining price stability in the EU/Eurozone.

- A closely related issue involves monetary policies and interest rates. Monetary policy can be restrictive, neutral or expansionary depending upon whether governments are trying to dampen down economic activity, maintain it at about the existing level, or trying to stimulate more economic activity. If these policies were being perused differently in different countries, because their business cycles were out of synchronisation for instance, then a single monetary policy could be jeopardised. In particular, the imposition of a common currency implies a single interest rate so, if rates differed significantly, a common monetary policy would be difficult to establish.

- The establishment of an economic union requires the fixing of exchange rates (indeed, their elimination) among the countries involved, so if there were continued variability and volatility in these rates this is another signal that monetary union is unlikely to be successful.

- A further point concerns the expectation of a high degree of bilateral trade intensities between the prospective participants. This would indicate that they have already effectively integrated in product and service markets, so that structural interdependency was secured, making a monetary and financial union more likely to be successful.

- We should note the extent of comparative labour market conditions (e.g. unemployment rates, participation rates) and how far labour mobility had been achieved between the prospective participants. Only if unemployment is low and labour mobility high will there be enough flexibility to enable a union to work effectively.

- Finally, there needs to be at least some institutional convergence in the way that the economies operate and are managed so that the mechanisms of economic policy-making and adjustment can work reasonably effectively, without this leading to institutional conflict between incompatible regulatory regimes.

Of course, not all of these features are likely to be fully in place in the EU context but, as we will see in later sections, they have provided the organisational context in which economic policy-making by the EU institutions has been formulated. And they are not uncontroversial. The idea of an OCA is often challenged by those who wish to promote the EU as a normative political project, rather than a purely economic one.

And, even from within the conventional wisdom, there are problems associated with exactly *how* the EU authorities are to encourage or ensure the movement towards an OCA or full economic convergence. For instance, the ECB has been charged with controlling inflation, but first it has to decide operationally exactly what inflation means and then which instruments to use to effectively tackle this objective.

A second major problem is the relationship between monetary policy as stressed by the OCA approach and fiscal policy. Formally, fiscal policy in the EU is left to individual governments to decide, while—in Eurozone countries—monetary policy is the responsibility of the ECB, a supranational institution. Such a split in responsibilities is fraught with difficulties.

> **KEY POINTS**
>
> - EMU poses the question as to whether the EU/Eurozone is or is nearing an OCA.
>
> - An emphasis on monetary and financial policy for an OCA also raises issues about fiscal policy and institutional convergence.

# The Arrival of the Euro and the European Central Bank

The ECB is a formally independent body charged with defining and implementing monetary policy for the EU. It holds the reserves of the national banks of those participating in the Eurozone, and also has responsibility for the euro exchange rate (see below). Independence is ensured by the fact that the ECB does not have to 'take instructions' from any EU government or institution and it does not act as the 'banker' to the EU or its governments by granting them credit or managing their debt (a task undertaken by national treasuries or finance ministries). But its overriding goal is delivered to it by the Maastricht Treaty: to achieve price stability—though exactly how this is defined and how to achieve it is left up to the ECB to decide.

The central problem encountered by the ECB in its management of monetary policy almost since its inception has been to balance its main concern with inflation—which implies a 'conservative' or restrictive stance *vis-à-vis* interest rates (i.e. keeping them high) with the fact that the EU economy has been performing relatively badly in real comparative terms which has implied the need to keep interest rates low to stimulate business and commercial activity. It has generally opted for caution in its interest rate and money supply policy.

In the initial phase after the euro was established there was some uncertainty over the way the ECB should operate and the reaction of the financial system to its policies. But the ECB may have added to this uncertainty by adopting a dual approach to monetary policy: neither a pure inflation-targeting approach nor a monetary aggregate approach, but a combination of both of these. It established its definition of price stability as a 2 per cent or below increase in consumer prices per year. To achieve this it would monitor a money growth aggregate in the economy (known as 'M3') and take this 'money supply growth' as indicator of possible inflationary pressures. But it would also look at other relevant aggregates (various asset prices and macroeconomic measures) in making final decisions about interest rate changes. So there is a range of possibly conflicting measures and aggregates that the ECB was to concentrate on in making its decisions about monetary policy, which was thought to add to the confusion over what was actually being measured and monitored. In addition, Eurozone actual inflation has been above 2 per cent over most of the operational period of ECB activity so far, though it has not acted to explicitly suppress this. All this has gone towards raising concerns over the adequacy of its capacity to meet the goal commitment to defeat inflation.

A further issue for the ECB has been the way it is governed internally. Central to this task is the Governing Council made up of a six-member Executive Board and the governors of the national central banks of those member states that participate in the Eurozone. This Council makes the decisions—thus monetary policy decision-making is centralised—but monetary policy operations are left to the participating national central banks to implement on the instructions from the Board; they are decentralised. It is this functional centralised and decentralised structure that imparts another level of uncertainty and potential conflict into the overall running of monetary policy. In addition, if all the current EU members were to eventually participate in the Eurozone the decision-making Council would expand to a possible 32 members, making it almost impossible to reach sensible decisions. To address this issue the ECB Council has been restricted to a maximum of 24 members with a rotating membership, but this is still a very large number for effective decision-making.

The final issue circulating around the ECB concerns the transparency of its decision-making and its political accountability. The ECB is formally independent as outlined above. But there has been the inevitable political wrangling over the appointment of its president. Furthermore, to whom does the ECB report on its conduct of monetary policy? Unlike several other central banks (including the Bank of England) the ECB does not publish the minutes of its meetings that decide monetary policy. This is thought to undermine its transparency. And it is only through a rather ill-defined process of 'dialogue' with the European Parliament that the ECB can be formally called to account for its actions. Thus, political accountability and transparency are thin and lack comprehensiveness.

> **KEY POINTS**
>
> - The ECB is a formally independent body charged with securing price stability in the Eurozone.
>
> - It has adopted a dual approach to monetary policy: direct inflation-targeting and aggregate monetary supply targeting. This may sow confusion within the financial system.
>
> - The ECB's internal governance and decision-making mechanism looks cumbersome.
>
> - The political accountability of the ECB lacks transparency and comprehensiveness.

# The Fate of the Stability and Growth Pact

## Nature of the SGP

With the advent of EMU and the euro the question of the **Stability and Growth Pact** (SGP) embodied in the Amsterdam Treaty of 1997 was raised once again. This Pact is designed to ensure that EU member states' *fiscal policies* (involving government taxation and expenditure decisions) do not clash with their *monetary policies* (or, in the case of the Eurozone countries, with the monetary policy pursued by the ECB).

Formally at least, under the SGP all EU governments are free to conduct their own fiscal policy, but national budgets are to be controlled by limiting government borrowing to a maximum of 3 per cent of GDP per annum, and keeping overall public debt to a maximum of 60 per cent of GDP. In fact, this latter criterion has never been seriously enforced (Greece and Italy have public debts of over 100 per cent of GDP), though the former one has been the subject of fierce dispute. But the question this raises is how far an independent fiscal policy is compatible with a common currency, and a single monetary policy? Does *convergence* organised around the euro sit comfortably with *divergence* in respect to fiscal policies?

## Struggles over the SGP

The real political struggles over the SGP emerged at the end of 2003 when France and Germany were called to account by the Commission for overtly breaking the 3 per cent deficit rule. The background to this dispute can be seen in the data presented in Table 16.3. France and Germany went into a larger than minus 3 per cent deficit from 2002 onwards.

It might be noted that the Netherlands and Portugal also recorded deficits of greater than 3 per cent of GDP in the early 2000s, as did Greece (−6.1 per cent in 2005). But it was the fact that the two largest countries 'at the heart of Europe' moved into this position that really challenged the SGP. The Council of Ministers met in November 2003 ostensibly to condemn France and Germany on

the recommendation of the Commission, but this was rejected. This unprecedented decision in effect killed the SGP. The rule now lacks credibility; there is little chance it could be realistically applied to any other country given its suspension in these cases. And what was happening to Italy in 2005 seemed to confirm this prognosis since its deficit was forecast to rise from −3.5 per cent in 2005 to −4.6 per cent in 2006, and even the UK was predicted to possibly break the rule in the not-too-distant future. The political lesson to be learned from this episode is that whatever sovereignty countries may cede to the Commission, the large ones at least will claim this back if they feel it in their interests to do so (Alesina and Perotti 2004).

But the problem remains. Can a single currency and single inflationary objective coexist with such potential variability in fiscal positions? In addition, how is 'fiscal discipline' to be organised and guaranteed if there is no effective SGP? These points are important from the point of view of the financial integration objective considered in a moment. Financial convergence across the Eurozone is in large part predicated upon the 'confidence' that inflationary pressures can be coped with. But, if 'fiscal discipline' fades, and the different EU countries were to expand their economies by indulging in competitive reflations via significantly increasing government expenditures financed by borrowing, this would increase local risk factors at the expense of the carefully crafted common position forged across the Union as a whole. Inflationary pressures could emerge, interest rates rise and confidence in the euro be undermined. As a result, a 'one-size-fits-all' monetary policy would no longer be viable (if, indeed, it ever has been). Indeed, Gros *et al.* (2005) suggest that Italy is becoming the weakest link in the EMU chain largely because of its deteriorating fiscal position, which might result in it either being forced out of the Eurozone or withdrawing from it.

Within the SGP rules only differences in tax rates or contributions would allow for differences in government expenditure levels, so the way that fiscal policy was constrained is clear. What this

**Table 16.3** General Government Deficits or Surpluses (as percentage of GDP at market prices); 2001–5

|      | EU15 | Germany | France | Italy | UK   |
|------|------|---------|--------|-------|------|
| 2001 | −0.9 | −2.8    | −1.5   | −2.6  | +0.7 |
| 2002 | −1.9 | −3.5    | −3.1   | −2.3  | −1.5 |
| 2003 | −2.7 | −4.2    | −4.2   | −2.6  | −2.8 |
| 2004 | −2.6 | −3.9    | −3.8   | −2.8  | −2.7 |
| 2005 | −2.4 | −3.4    | −3.6   | −3.5  | −2.4 |

*Source*: 'The EU Economy: 2003 Review', adapted from table 75, p. 626

imparts in the system as a whole is a deflationary bias in economic activity almost regardless of the explicit monetary policy stance adopted by the ECB. But, given that the ECB's monetary policy has also been restrictive—always operating in the shadow of the need to fight inflation—a double deflationary bias operates. Autonomous large-scale increases in government expenditure for redistributive or stabilisation objectives are ruled out.

But, for those not committed to the EU's current overall policy stance (supported by the Commission and the Council of Ministers alike it would seem)—one that can be termed **neo-liberal** and pro-market (i.e. generally in favour of liberalisation and deregulation)—this change could open up some intriguing opportunities. A **Keynesian**-inspired fiscal policy as the key stabilisation and management tool could come to the fore once again as monetary policy and an obsession with inflation-targeting retreated; fiscal discretion and flexibility could replace fiscal rules (Sapir *et al.* 2003). From the point of view of the Commission's orthodox position, however, fiscal discretion and flexibility mean fiscal indiscipline and inflation.

In fact, a much looser compromise on policy was forged in March 2005. The SGP was renegotiated to allow countries to operate 'close to the reference value' of 3 per cent deficits rather than to adhere strictly to it. And several new 'particular circumstances' were introduced—among them expenditure on 'international aid', on 'European policy goals' (like R&D and e-Europe expenditures) and on 'European unity' objectives (e.g. convergence and solidarity expenditure)—that were to be given 'due consideration' in judging the underlying fiscal position of countries. In effect, this opened the Pact for further political fudging and creative accounting. It was condemned by the ECB and a number of smaller EU countries.

---

**KEY POINTS**

- An issue raised by the SGP is the compatibility of a common single monetary policy target designed to defeat inflation with different fiscal policies ostensibly at the discretion of the individual governments.

- When France and Germany contravened the SGP fiscal rule, effectively the SGP was suspended and it broke down. This was a case of the Council of Ministers asserting control over the European Commission.

- It is possible that inflationary pressures will grow without the fiscal discipline afforded by the SGP.

- Alternatively, undermining the SGP could lead to more active and discretionary fiscal policies that would be expansionary and correct the deflationary bias built into the existing EU policy regime.

---

# Services and Financial Integration

## The Lisbon Agenda and liberalisation of services

After the successful introduction of the euro between 1999 and 2002 (euro cash was launched on 1 January 2002), the attention of the EU authorities turned to a related matter, namely services and financial integration. A key event in this was the Lisbon European Council Meeting held in March 2000.[1] This Council announced the now famous Lisbon Agenda: within ten years to make the EU 'the most dynamic and competitive knowledge-based economy in the world, capable of sustainable economic growth with more and better jobs and greater economic cohesion'.[2]

This strategy involved a whole raft of policy measures in areas from research and education to the environment and employment. It was particularly concerned with putting Europe into the forefront of the 'knowledge economy'. Its macroeconomic objective was to generate economic growth of 3 per cent per year for the EU as a whole and to create 20 million new jobs by 2010. But as well as these general targets the initiative contained a vast range of more localised, specific and precise targets.

Laudable though most of these objectives were, they indicate a tendency to try to 'micro-manage' many key aspects of economic and social life on the part of the Commission (Alesina and Perotti 2004). And the fact that there were so many areas and targets led to a lack of focused attention on achievable outcomes. By 2004 the strategy was adrift, with too many detailed goals and too little coordinated attempt at the national level to implement the policies associated with each of the targets. After a 'high level review' in 2004, in March 2005 the new president of the EU Commission, José Manuel Barrosoa, initiated a revised Lisbon Agenda in an attempt to revitalise the process.[3]

The Lisbon Agenda was particularly concerned with the services sector. As a direct result, in 2004 the Commission set about preparing a Services Directive, the aim of which was to allow services to operate more easily across borders which would affect a vast range of businesses such as hotels and restaurants, car hire, construction and estate agencies. It also covers advice provided by professionals such as architects and lawyers. It even mentions certain public services such as health care and environmental services. The European Commission argued that this could create 600,000 new jobs and could contribute an additional €33bn to output in the EU economy. The service sector already amounts to as much as 70 per cent of EU GDP and accounts for 63 per cent of jobs.

But this Directive set off a furious row, one in which French President Jacques Chirac described the Directive as an 'example of Anglo-Saxon neo-liberal economics' the extreme version of which was 'the new communism of our age'. Along with Germany's President Gerhard Schroeder, he campaigned against the Directive at the March 2005 Council of Ministers meeting and defeated it. The row centred on the 'country of origin principle'. This means that a company could operate according to the rules and regulations of its home country, rather than the country it was operating in. So, for example, a building firm based in Poland could offer its services in the UK and France, but would operate under Polish rules.

This upset some countries because they argued it could undermine standards. A company from a country with laxer labour regulations could set up business in a country which would normally require higher standards and price its competitors out of the market, critics argued. They also feared there could be a 'race to the bottom', with firms relocating to countries with less regulation and lower standards. This was all summed up under a concern for 'social dumping'. So, for the moment at least, the Services Directive is on hold.

## The Financial Services Action Plan (FSAP) and financial market integration

However, in the area of financial services the story has been somewhat different. The Lisbon summit also set a date for the full implementation of the **Financial Services Action Plan** (FSAP): to be completed by 2005. Integration of financial markets lies at the heart of the FSAP. It is designed to remove the regulatory and market barriers that exist in cross-border financial services and the free flow of financial capital within Europe. In this it mirrors the Single Market Programme set up by the Maastricht Treaty, which concentrated on the 'real product economy'. It is largely agreed that by the late-1990s an effective single market in goods (and, nominally in labour) had mostly been established within the EU (as indicated by the convergence of prices for products across the Union), so it was thought appropriate that attention be directed to the 'financial economy' in terms of integration (and of course, the ill-fated Services Directive).

The problem with financial integration across the EU is that traditionally the range and nature of financial institutions in the EU countries have differed, and the various financial markets have also operated differently and are regulated differently. It is often suggested, for instance, that the 'organised economies'—of which Germany is the exemplar in Europe—have a much more bank-orientated financial system, whereas 'Anglo-American' economies, such as the UK and Ireland, rely much more on stock exchanges, and this fundamental difference inhibits successful financial integration (Moran 2001). In addition, the French financial system has involved heavy state intervention and ownership, while Italy and Spain have influential family-based financial holdings and networks.

In fact, these differences were probably never quite as stark in Europe as had been originally claimed (Allen *et al.* 2004). However, this is not to suggest that there remain insignificant differences, or that the attempt to engineer a single operational financial system for the EU area as a whole has not involved considerable effort and common institution-building.

But what of the successes more generally in terms of financial integration in various European financial markets? Here the results have differed considerably by market segment. In some cases a substantial degree of integration has been achieved though elsewhere it is still quite limited, testifying to the continued difficulties and obstacles to full integration. The **money markets** show the greatest degree of integration, as might be expected given the introduction of the euro (Baele *et al.* 2004). There has also been a high degree of integration in the government **bond market** (involving loans to governments). However, even here convergence was not yet complete in 2004 (Pagano and Von Thadden 2004) and this could be exacerbated by the emergence of serious Stability Pact problems as discussed earlier.

But there is still substantial fragmentation in European stock exchanges and securities settlement systems, so **equity markets** are less integrated than are money and government bond markets, and the corporate bond market still shows a low level of integration. Integration in these markets remains fragmented because of the continuation of separate stock exchanges operating across Europe. As far as **retail financial services markets** are concerned, these demonstrated the least integration in 2004. The greatest cross-border interest rate differentials existed in the market for consumer loans. There was little foreign branching by banks, and bank mergers had in general occurred within countries rather than across borders. (An exception was the takeover of Abbey National Bank in the UK by Santander Central Hispano Bank of Spain in 2004.)

## The future for financial integration

What is the EU doing to overcome these problems from the point of view of fostering greater financial integration? Here several possible initiatives and trends could develop. The first would be for the Commission to initiate a new round of legislative programmes in a concerted effort to harmonise across Europe and eliminate barriers to integration and reform domestic regulatory arrangements. In the longer term it might even involve the setting up of some kind of Federal Supervisory Authority to oversee a common EU-wide financial regulatory regime. However, the idea of jumping straight to a centralised European authority is unlikely (particularly given the experience with the wider Services Directive discussed above).

More likely is a 'policy' that leaves it very much up to the market mechanism to decide; the encouragement of market agents to work within the new rules laid out with the arrival of the euro, the ECB and the FSAP, so as to create barrier-free infrastructures as mergers and acquisitions in the financial system take place across frontiers, accompanied by private initiatives to consolidate consumer awareness and promote their choice of financial vehicles for borrowing and lending. In the face of this, the EU itself is likely to press on with its 'home-country passport principle'—those practices and regulations recognised in one home country territory should be accepted in other territories within the EU, given continued home country control (much like the 'country of origin principle' mentioned above in the context of the discussion of the Services Directive).

In part this latter trajectory is already underway. The EU has not been slow to advance one of its most favoured 'modes of governance' in this area, namely the establishment of committees (the practice know as **comitology** in EU parlance). Two such 'policy networked' committees have been very active in this field: the **Giovannini Group** and the **Lamfalussy Committee**. It is important to note, however, that the Lamfalussy Committee was established after the decision to go ahead with the FSAP had been taken by the Council of Ministers at Lisbon; so there may be more political will behind this proposed programme than behind the Services Directive. In addition, there seems more political commitment to seeing financial services liberalised across Europe because the job implications are fewer (or less obvious).

## Implications for political governance

All this is important and emblematic of a change in the trajectory of EU policy-making since the EMU process in the 1990s. The EMU process and the Delors Committee and Presidency probably represented the high point of supranationalism in recent economic (and other) policy-making in the EU. The Commission, and the policy networked committees close to it, drove economic policy-making, while the Council of Ministers in particular, and the EU Parliament, followed closely behind, but essentially endorsed the Commission's initiatives. (See Theme box: Democracy and Legitimacy.)

Since then, however, the Council of Ministers has assumed the driving seat again. Between 2000 and 2005 a series of meetings of ministers reset the economic policy agenda and, crucially, re-established control over the dynamic of the EU's development in an essentially inter-governmentalist fashion. It is primarily the Council, and then the Parliament, that will act on the recommendations of the Lamfalussy Committee, for instance, though in consort with the Commission. Although the Commission has the sole right to propose legislation, it is assuming a more back-seat role in this case. This demonstrates the attempt by the Council of Ministers to win back

**THEME BOX**

### Democracy and Legitimacy

The EU is often accused of facing a democratic deficit and of lacking legitimacy. These terms are applied to the EU to describe the lack of democratic control over the decision-making processes of the EU as a political system. Deficits have been identified along various dimensions, including the relatively weak powers of the European Parliament; the fact that European Parliament elections tend to be 'second order' to national elections; the lack of national parliamentary scrutiny and control over national executives conducting intergovernmental negotiations; and the weak sense of European citizenship in EU countries. These issues arise very acutely for this chapter in respect to the European Central Bank. Unlike several other central banks (including the Bank of England) the ECB does not publish the minutes of its meetings that decide monetary policy. This is thought to undermine its transparency and legitimacy. And it is only through a rather ill-defined process of 'dialogue' with the European Parliament that the ECB can be formally called to account for its actions. Thus political accountability and transparency are thin and lack comprehensiveness.

control over the policy-making process from the Commission—thereby reasserting the authority of national governments in an intergovernmentalist fashion. It parallels the discussion above about the fate of the SGP, where once again the Council (but particularly France and Germany) were seen to be reasserting their powers *vis-à-vis* the Commission. Perhaps governments have so far been only partially successful in this, though there are good arguments to suggest this is not a unique or simply passing phase (Kassim and Menon 2004).

---

**KEY POINTS**

- The attempt to initiate full liberalisation in services has had to be put on hold after considerable political opposition.

- Initiatives to complete a 'single market in financial services' have so far had patchy results. It is most advanced in the money market and sovereign bond market, but less advanced in the equity and corporate bond markets, and least effective of all in the retail financial markets.

- A key component in the EU's decision-making structure in this area has been the role of expert committees and 'comitology'.

- The attempt to introduce financial integration demonstrates the way supranationalism has given way relatively to inter-governmentalism as the current *modus operandi* of EU decision-making.

---

# The Euro, the Wider World and Enlargement

## A 'two currency' world?

The introduction of the euro threatens to have a significant impact on the international monetary economy as well as on the economies of the EU countries themselves. As yet, this impact is not altogether clear since the euro has been operating only for a few years. But certain trends are emerging and the possibilities are opening up. It is the main features of these trends that we concentrate upon in this section.

A preliminary point is that the euro exchange rate is not a policy variable or a policy target in the EU context (European Commission 2005: 79). The exchange rate is set by 'market forces'. The ECB has not intervened in the currency markets to try to influence the value of the exchange rate. All it does is 'monitor' exchange rate developments as part of its task of assessing prospects for the Eurozone and setting interest rates.

Given the analysis of bond market integration in the previous section, it is useful to look at this in a more international context. The international bond market is huge and growing; towards the end of 2000 outstanding accumulated bond issues were well over US$30,000 billions, with government bonds comprising three-fifths of this total. Table 16.4 sets out the trends in the total global issue of bonds (both government and corporate).

The general trends shown in Table 16.4 are:

- It is the two main currencies of the international system—the US dollar and the EU euro—that are consolidating their hold over the international bond market.

- After the euro launch in 1999 there was a big jump in the issue of euro-equivalent denominated bonds.

- The US dollar and the Eurozone currencies/EU euro accounted for 54.3 per cent of the

**Table 16.4** Global Net Issuance of Bonds (Debt Securities), 1994–2002 (US$bn)

| | 1994 | % | 1995 | % | 1996 | % | 1997 | % | 1998 | % |
|---|---|---|---|---|---|---|---|---|---|---|
| US dollar | 664.3 | 33.1 | 796.9 | 37.2 | 1125.4 | 44.9 | 1255.5 | 57.5 | 1726.4 | 62.0 |
| Euro | | | | | | | | | | |
| Eurozone currencies | 425.3 | 21.2 | 366.3 | 17.1 | 528.7 | 21.1 | 326.9 | 15.0 | 435.3 | 15.6 |
| Yen | 336.7 | 16.8 | 434.6 | 20.3 | 458.7 | 18.3 | 237.9 | 10.9 | 185.8 | 6.7 |
| Other currencies | 578.3 | 28.8 | 544.1 | 25.4 | 392.6 | 15.7 | 362.4 | 16.6 | 438.9 | 15.6 |
| Total | 2004.6 | 100 | 2141.9 | 100 | 2505.4 | 100 | 2182.7 | 100 | 2786.4 | 100 |

| | 1999 | % | 2000 | % | 2001 | % | 2002 | % |
|---|---|---|---|---|---|---|---|---|
| US dollar | 1511.9 | 45.1 | 1053.5 | 42.0 | 1302.1 | 45.1 | 1443.6 | 49.3 |
| Euro | 876.4 | 26.1 | 626.3 | 25.0 | 562.9 | 19.5 | 714.0 | 24.3 |
| Eurozone currencies | | | | | | | | |
| Yen | 496.1 | 14.8 | 450.6 | 18.0 | 570.6 | 19.8 | 280.6 | 9.6 |
| Other currencies | 470.7 | 14.0 | 375.9 | 15.0 | 450.6 | 15.6 | 494.3 | 16.8 |
| Total | 3355.1 | 100 | 2506.3 | 100 | 2886.2 | 100 | 2932.5 | 100 |

*Source*: Calculated from Pagano and Thadden (2004), table 2, p. 533

total in 1994 compared to 73.6 per cent in 2002.

- This growth was at the expense of the yen and other currency denominations, such as the UK pound.
- These trends confirm the idea of a growing two-currency world.

## Consequences of introducing the euro into the international system

The jump in the euro as currency of choice for bond denomination in 1999 in part reflects the advent of the euro as a common currency across the Eurozone. But is has also encouraged those countries in the EU who are not in the Eurozone, or those not in the EU at all, to borrow in euros as well. The point about the consolidation and integration of the euro bond market discussed in the previous section is that this adds depth and liquidity to the market. These features increase the attractiveness of euro-denominated bonds, and in principle allow borrowers to borrow at lower interest rates and at reduced risk. (See Theme box: The Impact of Globalisation.)

In as much as the euro becomes a stronger currency, and the euro-economy itself performs better in terms of growth, eventually there will be competitive pressures upon the traditional dominance of the US dollar in the international system. Given, also, that there are pressures to diversify away from dollar-denominated bonds (because of its balance-of-payments difficulties) the USA may find itself facing difficulties in continuing to fund its external position. Whenever an 'adjustment' happens this could prove to be quick and painful for the USA (and the global economic system at large).

And this point is reinforced by the way exchange rate adjustment mechanisms are evolving in this

**THEME BOX**

## The Impact of Globalisation

'Globalisation' is typically taken to refer to the economic processes whereby national economies are becoming increasingly porous and interdependent—as measured by the intensity of trade and investment flows across borders, migration and technological connectedness. Globalisation is thought to imply diminished national economic sovereignty, with states less able to pursue policies that are contrary to market trends. It is associated with the ascendancy of a (neoliberal) market order over a (Keynesian) regulatory order. These trends can be seen in operation across the EU countries as a consequence of integration and convergence, but some individual governments still seem able to impose their positions if they feel their interests are strongly threatened. In addition, the EU is a major player in the international system, and the euro an emerging global currency. This will give the EU enormous authority and power in the international system, which may imply and foster the move towards a supranational regional configuration rather than a strictly global one.

emerging two-international-currency world. With a bipolar currency world, where there are two possible 'safe havens' when economic difficulties arise, the system could become more unstable. Thus the development of the euro as a potential rival international currency could lead to greater instability in the international financial system rather than less. Under these circumstances exchanges rates between the US dollar and the euro could tend to oscillate more widely and move more rapidly, hence destabilising the relationships between the two currencies and the international economy more generally. What becomes crucial under these conditions is the careful management of these relationships. But exchange rate management (involving coordination and intervention) goes against the grain and sentiment of economic policy-making in this field. It is widely believed that complete flexibility in exchange rates, built upon market sentiment, must not be tampered with.

## Enlargement

There is another problem hovering in the background in respect to the euro's international role, namely that of the enlargement of the EU. Both monetary policy and fiscal policy issues are involved, raising questions about the costs of enlargement for the new members and those set to join somewhere down the line. We concentrate on the monetary issue of joining the Eurozone first and then go on to look at fiscal issues.

### Monetary issues

For all the new members there will be a process of 'catching up' with the older members before the former can join the Eurozone. In 2002, GDP per capita was 60 per cent of the EU average for Slovenia and the Czech Republic (in PPP terms); it dropped to 50 per cent for Hungary, 40 per cent for Poland, Estonia and Latvia, and just 35 per cent for Lithuania. So, if these states want to join the Eurozone, there must first be some further GDP convergence, which itself will entail a sizeable influx of capital for investment. In addition, there will need to be some appreciation in their real **exchange rates** before entry can be justified. The problem is that none of this may be compatible with the exchange rate 'stability' required for Eurozone entry. To join the Eurozone candidate countries must pass through a phase termed **Exchange Rate Mechanism 2** (ERM 2) similar to ERM 1 that characterised the run-up to the introduction of the euro for the older members prior to 1999. This is a form of the 'pegged' (to the euro) or semi-fixed rate systems, which historically have been vulnerable to speculative attacks. To achieve the required stability, therefore, will either take a long time or will cost a lot of resources to ensure

**Figure 16.1** Monetary and fiscal rules with enlargement

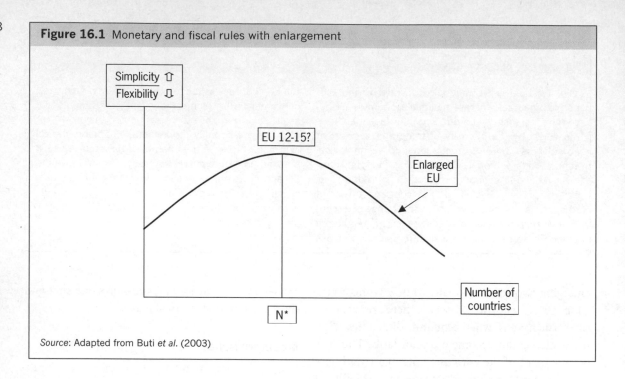

Source: Adapted from Buti *et al.* (2003)

adequate 'catch-up' first and ability to withstand speculative pressures later.

### Fiscal retrenchment?

If we turn to fiscal issues, at the time of entry to the EU in 2004 six of the ten entry countries had government deficits in excess of the SGP 3 per cent of GDP rule; the Czech Republic (−5.9 per cent), Cyprus (−4.6 per cent), Hungary (−4.9 per cent), Malta (−5.9 per cent), Poland (−6.0 per cent) and Slovakia (−4.1 per cent). Thus these countries could be required to cut back on their public expenditures or increase taxes so as to move into a more or less balanced budget position as required by the SGP. But, as we have seen, the SGP is in some disarray. So who or what is going to impose 'fiscal responsibility' on the recalcitrant countries? And they could be asked to retrench fiscally just at a time when it might be appropriate for them to increase public expenditures, on welfare say, so as to ease the adjustment of their populations to all the competitive and regulatory pressures associated with a transition into the EU.

Thus with both monetary and fiscal polices there are a newly emergent set of problems for the EU to grapple with as it expands. And this could add to the pressures for change just as the traditional mechanisms of rule-based policy come under a wider scrutiny. Figure 16.1 shows how we might judge the relationship between simple rule-based monetary and fiscal policies as the enlargement process proceeds (Hallet 2004). It shows a humped-shape relationship.

The political preferences for simple rules increases with the number of participants but only up to a point like N* in Figure 16.1. Beyond that number, however, the need to take account of a much wider set of country-specific economic circumstances (recall the above discussion and data in Table 16.2) makes very simple across-the-board rules sub-optimal. Country diversity requires more flexible rules, even if these are set by a single central authority, and preferences change, hence the downward slope in Figure 16.1. Quite where the curve inflects is, of course, highly judgemental, but in the EU circumstances it is probably somewhere close to the 12–15 country mark given the existing and likely future accession members. And this relationship looks even more likely since we have seen that there are already trends towards more flexibility in relationship to the SGP and financial services.

---

**KEY POINTS**

- There is now emerging a bipolar currency world, made up of the US dollar and the EU euro.

- Exchange rate fluctuations between the US dollar and the EU euro could increase as a result of the introduction of the euro.

- A key feature for the stability of the international financial system in the future will be to effectively 'govern' the relationship between the US dollar and the EU euro.

- The process by which the accession countries can enter the Eurozone will be long and will possibly lack stability.

- According to the rules of the SGP fiscal retrenchment is called for in some countries because of government-sector imbalances.

- The issues thrown up in connection with the accession countries and those waiting to enter further down the line could serve to put pressure for change on the traditional mechanisms of fiscal and monetary management and governance.

---

# Conclusion

Several concluding points are worth highlighting. First, it is clear that the general thrust of EU policy-making, whether this be pushed by the Commission or the Council of Ministers, is one that embodies a market-based liberalisation and deregulatory agenda (something forcefully expressed by President Chirac of France quoted above) though, as with any programme of this kind, there are anomalies and reversals to this overall trajectory.

Second, the EU remains an arena of political contestation at a number of levels. At the ministerial level there is still a lively debate about supranationalism and inter-governmentalism in respect of the development of the EU. In addition, there remain significant differences *between* the EU members over economic policy and institutional reform, even among those fully committed to the widening and deepening of the Union. For instance,

there are the differences of interest between those *in* the Eurozone and those *outside* it, whether they would like to keep out of it (like the UK and Sweden) or those who would like to get into it (like many of the accession countries). And this is all independent of the differences within 'Old Europe' between large countries like France and Germany and the smaller ones like the Netherlands and Austria (who strongly supported the Services Directive, for instance).

Finally, we have the possible consequences of the development of a bipolar currency world. Under these circumstances, it becomes increasingly difficult to see the advantages of remaining aloof from the development of these supranational regional configuration, and of presenting oneself as an essentially free-floating world-trading economy, unencumbered by the collective responsibilities of managing such a system (as is the case with the most

Euro-sceptic wing of UK public opinion). The larger issue that this throws up is how exactly to govern this emergent system so as not to encourage the re-emergence of autarkic economic policy-making and a complete retreat from liberal internationalism and multilateralism in the international economy.

## Notes

1. (See *An Agenda of Economic and Social Renewal of Europe*, COM DOC/00/7 March 2000, Brussels, http://europa.eu.int/growthandjobs/pdf/lisbon_en.pdf.).

2. See ibid., http://europa.eu.int/growthandjobs/key/index_en.htm.

3. See *Working Together for Growth and Jobs: A New Start for the Lisbon Strategy*, DOC COM/2005/25, Brussels, http://europa.eu.int/growthandjobs/key/index_en.htm.

##  QUESTIONS

1. What is economic and monetary union?

2. What is meant by an 'optimum currency area'?

3. Are a Eurozone monetary policy and fiscal policy compatible under existing policy and institutional arrangements in the EU?

4. How will enlargement of the EU affect policy-making and economic management?

5. Has the attempt at EU financial integration been successful?

6. What will be the impact of the euro on international economic relationships?

7. Why did the Services Directive collapse in 2005?

## FURTHER READING

■ **Thompson, G. (ed.) (2001), *Governing the European Economy*, Sage, London.** Provides a series of essays that introduce the trajectory of the European economy and EU policy-making over the post-war period until 2000.

■ **European Commission (2005), 'EMU after Five Years', *European Economy Special Report No. 1, February.*** The Commission's own thorough assessment of the impact of EMU.

■ **Gros, D., Mayer, T. and Ubide, A. (2005), *EMU at Risk*, Centre for European Policy Studies, Brussels.** A critical independent commentary on the EMU process which points to some of the problems and dangers ahead.

## IMPORTANT WEBSITES

- **http://europa.eu.int/pol/emu/index_en.htm** The EU website for the latest developments and analysis of EMU.

- **http://europa.eu.int/growthandjobs/key/index_en.html** The website for the Lisbon Agenda and service sector liberalisation.

- **www.ecb.int/home/html/index.en.html** The website for the European Central Bank.

- **www.HM-treasury.gov.uk/about/information/recent_pubs.cfm** The UK Treasury (HM Treasury) provides information and analysis of the UK's position in respect of the EU and the euro.

 **Visit the Online Resource Centre that accompanies this book for lots of useful additional material, including an interactive map of Europe. www.oxfordtextbooks.co.uk/orc/hay_menon/**

# 17 Welfare Policy

LINDA HANTRAIS

✔ **Reader's Guide**

This chapter is primarily concerned with social welfare, but it also looks at the boundaries with economic welfare, and at theories that probe the relationship between economic, labour market and social policies. The chapter begins with a review of the concepts and definitions of welfare used at national and European level. It considers the main theoretical approaches adopted in analysing welfare and examines different welfare models. The development of European social welfare competence and legitimacy is then tracked since the founding of the European Economic Community. Attention is paid to the interactive relationship between European Union (EU) and national-level governance of welfare, as both have sought to establish and maintain democratic legitimacy. The conclusion explores the prospects for greater social integration within an expanding Union, and asks whether the pressures of European integration and globalisation are resulting in convergence of welfare policies.

# Introduction

Apart from the inherent interest of debates over welfare trajectories for developing an understanding of contemporary European societies, three main reasons can be adduced to explain the enduring importance of welfare policies for social scientists and, more especially, for students of European politics.

First, from the time when the European Economic Community (EEC) was established in 1957, welfare has remained a contested area at the centre of controversy over national sovereignty. Social welfare, therefore, provides an appropriate lens through which to examine the politics of the European integration process (see Chapter 10, this volume). Opinions differ over the extent to which control over social policy has shifted from nation states to supranational institutions. Some observers comment on the strong resistance of governments to the erosion of national sovereignty over social welfare. Others contend that, under the pretext of pursuing market integration, European law, supported by decisions of the European Court of Justice (ECJ) (see Chapter 15, this volume), has operated to undermine the authority of national governments. There may be no winners. While the Union's competence and legitimacy to act in social policy areas have been constrained by institutional barriers, national autonomy has gradually been eroded.

The second reason why political scientists are interested in welfare is that the history of social-welfare policies within the European context in the second half of the twentieth century is tightly bound up with economic integration and cannot be understood without considering the relationship between social and economic policies. Within the European context, social policy has variously been portrayed in a subordinate role as the handmaiden of economic policy, the action necessary to counter or correct the possible adverse spill-over effects of the completion of the internal market for the social area, a means of avoiding a two-speed Europe and as a trade-off between equity and efficiency (Kleinman 2002; Hantrais 2007).

Third, the development of welfare policies within the Europe Union has to be understood as part of a complex and dynamic relationship between national welfare systems and social policies, which vary significantly in scope, range and character, and the wider processes of European integration and globalisation.

This chapter attempts to unravel these multifaceted relationships and processes by looking at how national welfare states have evolved in an ever-widening and deepening Union in the face of internal and external constraints and forces for change. The chapter examines whether these processes are contributing to the production of an identifiable **European social model**, and whether they are driving national welfare systems to become more similar or to merge.

**KEY POINTS**

- Social welfare is relevant to the study of European politics because it draws attention to issues surrounding national sovereignty.
- Another source of interest is the ambivalent relationship between welfare and economic policy.
- Analysis of social welfare is informative about the development of the political process within the context of European integration and globalisation.

# Conceptualising, Theorising and Measuring Welfare

In the western world, the creation of the welfare state was heralded as a major achievement of the post-war years. The concept is, however, contested and controversial, and has given rise to prolonged theoretical wrangling. This section examines how welfare has been conceptualised and theorised before going on to consider some of the indicators available for measuring the development of welfare provision within the EU.

## Concepts of welfare

Welfare is already difficult to conceptualise within national contexts. It is more difficult still to define and delimit in the international arena. In addition, a terminological distinction is often made between social and economic welfare, although the two are highly interdependent and intertwined.

Administrative definitions of welfare generally refer to state or collective provision of financial support and services in areas such as health, housing or education, designed to maintain income and improve the quality of life of members of society where markets are failing to do so. In democracies, welfare provision is expected to offer 'social security' against certain risks or contingencies, which are held to pose a threat to individual and collective well-being. According to the European System of Integrated Social Protection Statistics (**ESSPROS**), applied by **Eurostat**, the European Commission's statistics office in Luxembourg, the financing and provision of 'social protection' (the term used for social welfare in European documentation) 'encompasses all interventions from public or private bodies intended to relieve households and individuals of a defined set of risks or needs, provided that there is neither a reciprocal simultaneous nor an individual arrangement involved' (Eurostat 1996: 12).

The state intervenes in the provision of welfare primarily through its capacity to determine policy and control expenditure. Although vertical redistribution of resources to reduce inequalities may be implicit in administrative definitions of social welfare, it is not necessarily their stated objective. The redistributive function is, however, a necessary component in the definition of economic welfare, and is generally expressed in terms of the redistribution of national or public income through state regulation, the aim being to enhance the well-being of citizens (Pennings *et al.* 1999: 304).

Economic policy can influence social welfare in a number of ways: for example, by generating the resources needed to fund social-welfare policies, by determining the level of unemployment and the degree of income inequality and poverty, or by stimulating the housing market. In turn, social policy may affect economic policy and performance by directing government spending towards the main welfare services. Schemes to combat unemployment involve trade-offs between social-welfare payments made to unemployed people and the economic cost of unemployment due to the loss of state revenue from unpaid social insurance contributions and taxes (see Chapter 16, this volume). In another policy area, public provision of education and training contributes to the skills base and, thereby, enhances the productive capacity of the labour force (Gough 2003: 137). Human capital formation, in turn, feeds the imperatives of competitiveness in an era of globalisation, to the extent that social policy may be recast to contribute more effectively to competitiveness (Cerny 1997).

The term 'welfare' is ambivalent in other ways. In Anglo-Saxon and Nordic countries, 'welfare' is widely used to refer to the 'welfare state' and 'welfare systems', more especially in debate about the rationale for developing a 'European welfare state'.

Latin countries generally prefer terms such as 'social security', 'social protection' or 'public policies' to collocations involving 'welfare'. With enlargement of the EU to the East in 2004, reference was made to the 'social security gap' to signal differences in the level of welfare provision between the old and new member states. Expressions such as 'being on welfare', 'welfare dependency' or 'welfare to work' have taken on negative connotations, resulting in the last case in a change of name in the European context to **activation policies**. By the turn of the century, the 'activation of welfare policy' had become the mantra for proponents of the modernisation of the European social model, symbolising an approach designed to develop more efficient welfare systems (Wincott 2003).

---

**KEY POINTS**

- Social welfare refers to the collective provision of financial support and services to protect members of society against defined risks or needs and to improve standards of living.

- The state is involved in welfare provision through its role in determining policy and controlling expenditure.

- Social welfare is closely bound up with the workings of the economic system. The two policy areas may be mutually supportive, but more often they are in competition, with economic policy as the dominant partner.

- The term 'welfare' may take on negative connotations. In the European context, reference is more often to 'social protection'.

---

# Perspectives on welfare trajectories

Many different perspectives have been developed in the analysis of welfare in modern societies and have been influential in determining the paths taken by welfare states at critical junctures in their histories. Social policy students, therefore, need to be aware of their main tenets. These approaches also help us to understand why welfare trajectories and

welfare reform have been such contentious and divisive topics in the European context (Alcock *et al.* 2003).

## Socialism and welfare

The interdependency of economic and social welfare is most clearly illustrated by the Marxist view that welfare played an ideological role in legitimating capitalist social relations and in reducing the reproduction costs of labour, thereby serving as a means of social control. According to the core principles of socialism, collective social-welfare measures and institutions are required, first, to meet welfare needs and eliminate social inequality; second, to enable a radical democratisation of the state and civil society, and to allow the development of social solidarity and popular power; third, to replace exploitation, unemployment and private profit by community ownership and industrial democracy.

Within socialism, views diverged about the extent to which capitalism would have to be transformed to achieve socialism. Whereas Marxism, as practised in Eastern Europe, called for the abolition of the capitalist state as a precondition for socialism (see Chapter 9, this volume), social democrats in Western Europe believed that capitalism could be transformed by gradually extending the welfare state and democratic institutions. Social democracy, as applied in Sweden, was based on the notion that needs are universal, as too is societal responsibility for responding to them through legislation and by underwriting the costs using redistributive taxation (see Chapter 5, this volume). In Britain, post-war social democrats saw the state as essentially neutral and considered that expert administrators were capable of ensuring the delivery of social citizenship rights through the creation of a universal welfare state (see Chapter 4, this volume). Until the economic crises of the 1970s, the aim of British social democrats was to ensure horizontal rather than vertical redistribution of resources, thereby responding to social needs and acting as a shock absorber without setting out to deliver social justice.

### Neo-liberalism and welfare

By contrast to socialism, the neo-liberal perspective on welfare supports a competitive market economy, portrayed as underpinning democracy by preventing the concentration of power in the hands of a minority, and by ensuring that the rule of law is based on specific regulations rather than individual discretion. Within neo-liberalism, a distinction is usually made between two traditions. On the one hand, are economists or behaviourists, who see people as 'rational utility maximisers' with a limited ability to make choices, and who favour a welfare system that pays out low benefits and avoids moral judgements. The Thatcher years in Britain are often taken to represent this tradition (see Chapter 4, this volume). On the other, are those who see people as moral agents constantly faced with difficult choices between right and wrong, and in need of at least minimal support to enable them to become self-reliant. Within this perspective, concepts such as 'civil society', 'mediating structures' and 'social capital' have come to the fore, bringing this strand of neo-liberalism closer to the social democratic perspective on welfare.

### The third way and welfare

These concepts are also part of the vocabulary of proponents of the 'third way', sometimes referred to as the 'new social democracy'. The third way influenced thinking about welfare policy within the European context by promoting economic efficiency and social justice as two sides of the same coin, and by emphasising redistribution of opportunities, rather than considering welfare as a safety net (Giddens 1998). Proponents of the third way argue in favour of a mixed economy of welfare, involving public–private partnerships and other more cost-effective alternatives to state welfare. The influence of third-way thinking is apparent in the development of new modes of welfare governance at EU level, where traces can be found in the activation policies, target-setting and benchmarking contained in the **open method of coordination** (OMC), as implemented from the late 1990s in the **European employment strategy**, with its emphasis on employability, flexisecurity and making work pay.

### Feminism and welfare

Feminism cuts across these various perspectives. Whereas socialist feminists focused on the relationship between state welfare and capital and its impact on the position of women in society, radical feminists were more concerned with power relationships between men and women. Liberal feminists emphasised issues concerning equality of opportunity and treatment, which have progressively been incorporated into European law. Within the socialist tradition, feminist critics argued that, despite their universalistic pretensions, post-war welfare policies were premised on the subordination of married women, thereby perpetuating the economic and social dependence of society on women as carers. They criticised the welfare state for being patriarchal in its assumption that male breadwinners would earn a family wage capable of supporting a female partner, who would act as an unpaid domestic service provider, at the same time as carrying out the reproductive functions for workers and caring for children and older dependants. In post-war welfare systems, married women were denied access to benefits in their own right, but could, nonetheless, be called upon as a reserve army of labour when needed, shouldering the double burden of paid and unpaid work (Lewis 2003).

In the early years of the twenty-first century, feminists are keen to remind politicians that women are at one and the same time clients, paid and informal providers, as well as agents of welfare. The extent to which they are supported in these different functions varies markedly from one EU member state to another, with the Nordic states having moved furthest away from the male breadwinner to the dual-earner model and the concept of individualised citizenship rights as a basis for welfare provision. Other countries, where full-time female employment is less widespread, have had more difficulty in deciding whether women should be treated as citizen-mothers, citizen-workers or both, a dilemma that is reflected in policy developments at EU level (Hantrais 2000).

## Measuring welfare spending

Many of the indicators used to measure the performance of welfare policies reflect the interdependence between social and economic welfare and, more especially, the bias in favour of economic parameters, which are the main concern of governments. Given the considerable cost of delivering welfare, when in government, politicians are constantly preoccupied with how to pay for welfare benefits and services. Government departments are always working within tight budgetary limits and looking for ways of making savings and raising additional income, without compromising their policy objectives.

### Availability and comparability of data sources

A number of indicators are used to measure welfare spending and receipts on both an individual and collective basis at national and EU level (see the examples in Table 17.1). The main source of indicators for EU member states is ESSPROS, which collates data supplied by member states. No comparable trend data are available across the EU for the period prior to the 1990s. As the ESSPROS methodology was changed in 1996, data collection is also inconsistent for the 1990s. Many of the social-welfare indicators used in international comparisons are unreliable because national welfare arrangements vary considerably from country to country, national accounting systems are not fully standardised, and policy is constantly in a state of flux. The available data do not cover the whole range of human services or the variety of funding sources and providers. In addition, for pragmatic reasons, ESSPROS figures for expenditure are gross of taxes and social charges. Since countries differ markedly in the extent to which benefits are subject to taxes and social contributions, ESSPROS cautions that the value of benefits and the real cost to governments may be over- or understated. Variations in the ways in which benefits and services are funded and delivered compound the difficulty of measuring and comparing their relative generosity across countries and over time, and complicate assessment of their effectiveness in reducing risks.

### Patterns of welfare spending

Despite the many classificatory and measurement problems, some broad patterns can be discerned in welfare spending for EU15 member states from national and EU data. National statistical sources suggest that social protection expenditure on welfare benefits expressed as a percentage of gross domestic product (GDP) grew rapidly when co-ordinated nationwide welfare systems were being established in the post-war years and during the subsequent period of high economic growth. Real spending continued to increase despite the slowdown in economic growth in the 1980s and 1990s. From 1996, however, welfare expenditure was stabilising or falling in relation to GDP in almost all EU member states. ESSPROS data for 2001 show that social protection expenditure accounted for

**Table 17.1** Social Protection Indicators for EU Member States

| | Social protection expenditure as % of GDP | | Expenditure per head of population in PPS | Social protection receipts as % of total receipts | | | |
|---|---|---|---|---|---|---|---|
| | | | | Government | Employers | Protected persons | Other |
| | 1996 | 2001 | 2001 | 2001 | 2001 | 2001 | 2001 |
| Austria | 29.8 | 28.6 | 7289 | 33.0 | 38.5 | 26.8 | 1.8 |
| Belgium | 28.6 | 27.7 | 6641 | 25.3 | 50.4 | 22.1 | 2.2 |
| Cyprus | — | 15.2 | 2777 | — | — | — | — |
| Czech Republic | — | 19.5 | 2637 | 23.3 | 50.8 | 24.6 | 1.3 |
| Denmark | 31.4 | 29.2 | 7610 | 62.6 | 9.3 | 21.1 | 7.0 |
| Estonia | — | 13.6 | 1247 | 27.0 | 72.8 | 0.0 | 0.2 |
| Finland | 31.6 | 25.5 | 6001 | 42.7 | 38.8 | 11.5 | 6.9 |
| France | 31.0 | 29.5 | 7006 | 30.4 | 45.9 | 20.8 | 2.8 |
| Germany | 29.9 | 29.3 | 6731 | 32.4 | 37.9 | 27.7 | 2.1 |
| Greece | 22.9 | 27.0 | 4084 | 27.8 | 38.5 | 23.5 | 10.2 |
| Hungary | — | 19.8 | 2287 | 33.2 | 45.6 | 13.1 | 8.2 |
| Ireland | 17.8 | 15.0 | 4025 | 60.3 | 24.4 | 13.9 | 1.4 |
| Italy | 24.8 | 25.6 | 5825 | 41.0 | 42.8 | 14.7 | 1.5 |
| Latvia | — | 14.3 | 1093 | 25.2 | 74.8 | 0.0 | 0.0 |
| Lithuania | — | 14.7 | 1234 | 38.6 | 53.7 | 6.2 | 1.5 |
| Luxembourg | 24.1 | 21.3 | 9303 | 42.4 | 27.4 | 25.3 | 4.9 |
| Malta | — | 17.7 | 2669 | 27.4 | 48.5 | 21.8 | 2.3 |
| Netherlands | 30.1 | 26.5 | 7018 | 16.3 | 31.5 | 35.4 | 16.8 |
| Poland | — | 21.5 | 2014 | 46.4 | 29.7 | 23.4 | 0.4 |
| Portugal | 21.2 | 22.8 | 3789 | 37.8 | 36.4 | 18.0 | 7.8 |
| Slovakia | 19.8 | 19.1 | 1924 | 32.5 | 46.6 | 18.5 | 2.5 |
| Slovenia | 24.7 | 25.3 | 3896 | 32.6 | 26.5 | 39.3 | 1.5 |
| Spain | 21.9 | 19.4 | 3767 | 26.6 | 53.0 | 16.3 | 4.1 |
| Sweden | 33.9 | 31.5 | 7501 | 45.3 | 43.1 | 9.3 | 2.3 |
| United Kingdom | 28.0 | 27.5 | 6441 | 48.5 | 30.2 | 19.5 | 1.8 |
| EU15 | 28.4 | 27.6 | 6426 | 36.0 | 38.9 | 21.7 | 3.4 |
| EU25 | — | 27.1 | 5576 | 36.1 | 38.9 | 21.7 | 3.3 |

*Source*: Eurostat, System of Integrated Social Protection Statistics (ESSPROS)
*Note*: The PPS figure for Luxembourg is artificially inflated due to the fact that a significant proportion of benefits, particularly family benefits and pensions, are paid to persons living abroad. Even after correction of this anomaly, the figure remains the highest across EU25

close to 28 per cent of GDP in EU15. For EU25, it was nearer to 27 per cent. The internal variation between member states was considerable, with percentages ranging from below 15 per cent in Estonia, Latvia and Lithuania to over 30 per cent in Sweden (Table 17.1).

ESSPROS measures expenditure per head of population, using **purchasing power standards** (PPS) to take account of differences in price levels and exchange rates between member states. Data for 2001 put Luxembourg at the top of the rank order. One of the Central and East European member states that joined the EU in 2004, Latvia, recorded the lowest level of expenditure: it spent almost nine times less than Luxembourg on this budget head. (See Table 17.1.)

Information about receipts is also indicative of the implications of the different principles underlying funding mechanisms in welfare systems: schemes may be based on social insurance contributions from employers and/or protected persons; they may be non-contributory, providing cover on a universal (residence or citizenship) and/or means-tested basis according to individual or household income. Whereas central government contributions account for a relatively large proportion of receipts in Denmark and Ireland, employers contribute more than 70 per cent in Estonia and Latvia, but less than 10 per cent in Denmark. Protected persons contribute more than a third of the total in the Netherlands and Slovenia but 0 per cent of it in Estonia and Latvia (Table 17.1).

Aggregate data say relatively little about how the living standards of individuals are affected by welfare provision, although they do give an indication of who the main welfare clients are likely to be,

how resources are redistributed and the possible impact of welfare benefits and services. Analysis by the European Commission (2004a: 70–1) of the effectiveness of social policy in improving living standards, protecting individuals from risk and reducing social inequalities suggests, for example, that the reduction in the percentage of the population at risk of poverty due to benefit payments is greatest in Denmark, the Czech Republic, Hungary and Poland and smallest in the Southern European member states.

---

**KEY POINTS**

- European indicators for welfare spending are based on national data that are not always reliable or comparable over time and across countries.

- The available data on welfare expenditure indicate that social protection accounts for more than a quarter of GDP for EU15 member states, but with wide variations between countries.

- The source of funding for welfare varies markedly between countries reflecting different funding mechanisms.

- The impact of welfare benefits and services on poverty rates also differs between member states.

---

# Differentiating National Welfare Systems

The concepts, theories and measurements of welfare outlined in the previous section provide some indication of the forces shaping welfare systems. Social-policy analysts and political economists have long been interested in identifying dominant welfare models that they might apply to help them gain a better understanding of national systems. This section begins by reviewing some of the models proposed before summarising the main characteristics of welfare systems in EU member states by wave of membership.

## Models of welfare

National welfare states were founded on different principles, and have followed diverse developmental paths. Funding mechanisms, provision and coverage continue to vary from one country to another. During the early post-war period, attempts were made to characterise social-welfare states by identifying 'models of welfare'. Already in the 1950s, models emanating from the USA distinguished between residual welfare, where needs were met primarily by markets or families, with the state providing a low-level safety net when other support systems broke down, and an institutional model offering universal, rights-based, non-stigmatising redistributive welfare (Wilensky and Lebeaux 1958). For Titmuss (1974), the residual model was exemplified by the USA and the institutional model by the Scandinavian countries. He added a third 'industrial achievement' model, typified by West Germany, where needs were met on the basis of work performance and status.

For so long as economies remained buoyant and economic and population growth continued, state welfare provision was seen as part and parcel of democratic societies. In the 1980s, in a context of low economic growth and industrial restructuring, attempts by political economists to make sense of changing welfare systems stimulated the search for new ways of classifying welfare states (May 2003).

Esping-Andersen's (1990) taxonomy of welfare state regimes has been most widely cited and influential. He analysed indicators of the scale, scope and entitlements of public provision in capitalist countries, with reference to policy-making styles and processes, underlying patterns of class formation and political structures. State welfare was seen as sustaining social citizenship insofar as it frees individuals from market forces and enables them to maintain a socially acceptable standard of living independently from the labour market, described as 'decommodification'. The second dimension in the taxonomy, 'stratification', indicated the extent to which state welfare differentiates between social groups or promotes equality and **social inclusion**. Esping-Andersen developed a series of indices to measure the accessibility, coverage and performance of social security systems in 18 OECD countries in the 1980s, among which he identified three ideal-type welfare regimes: social democratic, as typified by the Scandinavian countries, and demonstrably the most decommodified welfare type; conservative/corporatist, exemplified by Germany, France and Austria, and partially decommodified for certain sectors of the population; and liberal, as manifested by Anglo-Saxon

countries, where welfare was most commodified, and state welfare operated mainly on residual lines to provide little more than a safety net for the poor.

Esping-Andersen's classificatory system has been criticised for its many omissions and for not producing a dynamic model (reviewed by Arts and Gelissen 2002). He did not, for example, refer to the gender, family and race dimensions of welfare provision. When the data were collected, the Netherlands, the UK and Southern European countries did not fit neatly into his three categories. In subsequent work, Esping-Andersen (1999: 74) admitted that his typology was static. It reflected prevailing socio-economic conditions at a time when the economy was still dominated by industrial mass production, when the class structure was characterised by the male manual worker, and when households were stable with one earner.

Revisiting the three worlds of welfare capitalism two decades later, he acknowledged that no regime could be considered 'pure', and even less so an individual country. He, therefore, identified examples of 'regime-shifting': the UK had, for example, moved from being social democratic in the post-war period to become liberal by the 1980s. If the focus was on income maintenance, the Netherlands could be classified with the social democratic states, whereas emphasis on the role played by families in services delivery placed it in the conservative category. He maintained that the strong familialist traditions in Southern European countries justified setting them apart as a sub-regime within the conservative category rather than creating another world of welfare. Esping-Andersen did not include the Central and East European member states in his original or revised typology. It seems likely that they would today be classified as hybrids: their adoption of employment-based funding principles places them among conservative welfare states, whereas their heavy reliance on marketised services locates them with liberal welfare states.

The attributes chosen and the way they are measured clearly influence how welfare systems are classified, which is an important factor to remember when examining the relationship between different waves of EU membership and the development of a European social model.

# EU member state welfare systems

A major obstacle to European social integration and convergence has been the great diversity of national welfare systems. Although the six founding member states had a similar conception of welfare principles, each subsequent wave of enlargement brought different conceptions of welfare, making harmonisation or even coordination more difficult to achieve and the prospect of a single European model of social welfare more distant. (See Theme box: The Impact of the European Union.)

### *Corporatist, insurance-based welfare*

The original EEC member states—Belgium, France, Germany, Italy, Luxembourg and the Netherlands—shared an approach to welfare founded on the corporatist, work-based social insurance principle. The EU membership of Austria in 1995 further reinforced this dominant continental model of welfare, whereby employers and employees paid

---

**KEY POINTS**

- Early post-war models of welfare identified residual, institutional and industrial achievement welfare.

- Esping-Andersen's 1990 typology focused on welfare regimes using indices for decommodification and stratification.

- His three welfare regimes were labelled as social democratic, conservative/corporatist and liberal.

- Not all countries fit neatly into a particular welfare typology, and countries may shift between regimes.

- The Southern European member states can be considered as a subcategory of the continental model, whereas the Central and East European member states are hybrids.

---

**THEME BOX**

### The Impact of the European Union

From the origins of the European Economic Community, the relationship between European and national welfare policies has been interactive. The founding treaty provided a framework for European-level action to promote the welfare of workers, but national governments retained responsibility for determining how their social protection systems were structured, financed and organised, and how policy measures were implemented and delivered. Member states participate in the formulation of European law, which they are then required to transport into national legislation, as a condition of membership. Proceedings can be brought against national governments for infringement of European regulations and directives. The European Court of Justice plays an important role in interpreting legal provisions and in enforcing a strong legally binding regulatory framework, resulting in governments being required to amend national legislation. Governments react to European intervention in a variety of ways. They may refer to European law to justify introducing contentious national legislation. They may press for reform at European level in an attempt to offset the competitive advantage of other member states with, for example, less restrictive labour or social security law. The softer social sanction of naming and shaming applied in the open method of coordination may act as an incentive for member states to comply with rules and standards laid down at European level. As countries with different welfare principles and systems have joined the EU, the need has developed for a specifically European way of combining economic growth and social cohesion. The compromise embodied in what is described as the European social model allows member states to operate in accordance with their own institutional procedures and practices, while working to achieve a common set of values, principles or objectives, encompassing democracy, social dialogue and social solidarity.

contributions calculated according to wages, in return for which workers received benefits as of right when faced with certain contingencies, including ill-health and retirement. The assumption was that employment qualified individuals for welfare benefits as well as wages, and that benefits should be funded primarily, if not exclusively, from contributions paid by employers and employees as part of the cost of labour.

This approach was intrinsically non-egalitarian in that access to employment and pay are known to vary with age, gender, ethnic origins and qualifications, among other factors. In addition, over the post-war period, schemes were perpetuated that offered different arrangements to different categories of workers, ensuring distribution of income over the lifetime of individuals. The system was less concerned with redistribution from one sector to another across society. Although they share several broad characteristics, the social protection systems in the founder EU member states are today far from being uniform, either structurally or in terms of their funding arrangements, as demonstrated by the way that different proportions of receipts are distributed between sources (Table 17.1).

### Social democratic welfare systems

The three states that joined the Community in 1973—Denmark, Ireland and the UK—shared a general conception of social protection closer to what can be described as the citizenship approach. They had built their welfare systems on the principle of universal coverage of needs, funded from general taxation. According to the social welfare schemes in Britain and the more consistently social democratic model in Denmark, the right to a pension, health care and family benefits was granted on the basis of social citizenship. The assumption was that employment provided a living wage, whereas welfare benefits were distributed through taxation to all citizens on equal terms, whatever their employment status. The social security systems in these three countries continue to be distinguished from the 'continental' model by their preference for fiscal resources, especially Denmark and Ireland, rather

than insurance contributions, and by the principle of universal provision rather than income-related benefits. When Finland and Sweden joined the EU in 1995, they reinforced the tax-based, social democratic approach.

In Ireland and the UK, however, the aim was to ensure subsistence by providing low flat-rate payments or means-tested benefits. Following EEC membership, in the 1970s, the New Right under Thatcherism responded to the dilemma of how to reconcile a successful market economy with the extension of state welfare provision by resorting to privatisation and marketisation, thus bringing the UK closer to the (neo-)liberal welfare perspective (see Chapter 4, this volume). By the turn of the twenty-first century, the British welfare state was characterised by pluralism and, under New Labour, by the search for a third way between state and market. The shift from the welfare state to the welfare mix was based on the notion of partnerships between the state and other providers. The state had become the subsidiser and regulator, with the aim of ensuring that social-welfare policy intervention could shape investment and production (Alcock 2003).

### Southern European welfare states

Compared to previous waves of membership, Greece, Portugal and Spain, which joined the Community in the 1980s, were characterised by less advanced and less coherent social-welfare systems, further increasing internal European diversity. Apart from the core labour market, these countries continue to rely heavily on traditional forms of support through family and kinship networks and the church, with emphasis on discretionary provision at local level (Hantrais 2004). The social welfare systems they have developed are broadly based on corporatism, as in the continental model, with employers carrying the major burden of the cost of providing benefits in Spain. As in many other member states, the system is mixed. In both Portugal and Spain, a national health service is largely funded from taxation. In the early years of the twenty-first century, Greece still did not have a general scheme guaranteeing a minimum income. Welfare in Greece, therefore, continues to rely heavily on private support, most often from family members.

### Post-Soviet welfare states

When they became EU members in 2004, the Central and East European countries were in the process of reshaping their welfare systems following many years of Soviet rule, during which welfare had been state controlled but delivered through the enterprise in a context of full employment for both men and women (see Chapter 9, this volume). Given their low levels of per capita GDP, and the economic problems still facing them when they joined, the fifth wave of EU membership was expected to follow the more residual pattern of welfare provision of the Southern European states.

Despite their shared tradition of state socialism, in the 1990s the Central and East European countries did not constitute a homogeneous grouping, corresponding to one of the three welfare regime types outlined above. The preference in most countries was to move away from state financing towards provision based on social insurance contributions and oriented towards the needs of workers, as in continental welfare systems, to which several of them had subscribed in the pre-socialist era. Most governments introduced earnings-related rather than flat-rate benefits, albeit at a relatively low level of support due to fiscal restraints. Private and semi-private solutions were adopted, particularly in the area of pensions, with a minimal safety net subject to local discretion. Means-testing largely replaced universalism, as in the Anglo-Saxon welfare model, creating another permutation of the social-welfare mix.

> **KEY POINTS**
>
> - The welfare systems in the EEC founder member states followed the corporatist, work-based, social-insurance principle, which was not concerned with vertical redistribution of resources.
>
> - The countries that joined the Union in the 1970s were based on social democratic principles, providing universal coverage of needs, funded from general taxation. Finland and Sweden strengthened this mode when they became EU members in the 1990s, by which time the UK had moved towards a neo-liberal system.
>
> - The Southern European welfare states were less advanced and less coherent when they joined the Union in the 1980s. While developing in line with the continental model, they continue to rely heavily on self-provisioning by family members.
>
> - The Central and East European countries that joined the Union in 2004 have moved away from the state welfare of the Soviet era and adopted a hybrid system combining social insurance, work-based arrangements and private-sector provision.

# European Social Welfare Competence and Legitimacy

The many different ways of conceptualising and theorising welfare and the path dependencies of national welfare systems may help to explain why welfare has not, hitherto, played a more central role in the process of European integration. This section looks at the development of European competence in the area of welfare and the extent to which European institutions have gained legitimacy as social welfare actors. (See Theme box: Democracy and Legitimacy.)

**THEME BOX**

**Democracy and Legitimacy**

Democracy and legitimacy operate as symbiotic partners in the area of European social welfare. In what is sometimes described as the post-war welfare settlement, state welfare provision was seen as a legitimate activity for governments in democratic societies. In democracies, electorates have come to expect the state to make provision to protect them against any contingencies likely to affect individual and collective well-being. The legitimacy of European institutions as welfare actors is less widely accepted. Over the years, directives, recommendations and communications emanating from the Commission have gradually moved social policy up the European agenda. Cases brought before the European Court of Justice have reinforced a regulatory framework that severely restricts the autonomy of member states and limits their sovereign rights. Opposition to the extension of the powers of the Union in the area of social protection has, however, prevented the development of a European welfare state under the control of European institutions. National governments may use European legislation as a pretext for introducing unpalatable measures, but they continue to be accountable to their own electorates for the effectiveness of their responsiveness to welfare needs. In successive treaties, the right of member states to define the fundamental principles of their social security systems and to ensure their financial equilibrium has, theoretically, been left intact. At the same time, national governments are constantly being brought into competition with European institutions for authority and control over welfare policies.

## Building European welfare competence

When the Treaty of Rome was signed in 1957, the founding member states had already created their own welfare states and were developing their own styles of welfare provision. Since the EEC was established as a 'common market', 'social policy', as it was described in Title III of the founding treaty, was relevant only insofar as it contributed to the achievement of economic goals by improving the working conditions and standards of living of the working population. Harmonisation of social systems was expected to ensue automatically from the functioning of the common market, the procedures provided for in the Treaty and the **approximation** of provisions, regulations and administrative actions (Art. 117). It was anticipated that sustained economic growth would result in social development, with social harmonisation as an end product. The task of the European Commission was to promote closer cooperation between member states in the social field in matters relating to employment, labour law and working conditions, education and training, social security, health and safety at work, collective bargaining (Art. 118) and equal pay for equal work between men and women (Art. 119). The only area in which common measures were envisaged at European level was in dealing with migrant workers moving between member states (Art. 121). The European Social Fund was set up to facilitate the employment of workers and increase geographical and occupational mobility within the Community (Art. 123). Under the same section of the Treaty, the Council was empowered to lay down general principles for implementing a common vocational training policy, with the aim of contributing to the harmonious development of national economies and the common market (Art. 128) (Hantrais 2007).

Most of the early policy statements about social welfare in the European context were based on a conception of social policy as a spill-over from economic policy. By the 1990s, the social dimension had moved up the agenda and was gaining legitimacy due largely to the efforts of the European Commission under the leadership of Jacques Delors. In the Maastricht (1992) and Amsterdam (1997) treaties, social policy was again cast in a supporting role, with the social chapter relegated to a protocol and agreement annexed to the Maastricht Treaty as a result of the UK's opt-out. The search for a common approach to social policy became a topical issue during the 1990s, when the Union was facing major social problems due to slow economic growth and persisting long-term unemployment, population ageing, the increasing cost of providing social protection, pressures to meet the targets for Economic and Monetary Union (EMU) and the prospect of further enlargement (see Chapter 21, this volume).

Progressively, attention has shifted away from harmonising welfare systems towards promoting **convergence of social protection objectives**. Softer alternatives to binding legislation were introduced during the 1990s in the form of framework directives, recommendations and communications. The decision to write employment into the Treaty of Amsterdam, in response to public concern about high levels of unemployment, marked another turning point for social policy. The Union affirmed its commitment to achieving a high level of employment by adopting a more proactive and concerted approach, as expressed in the employment guidelines produced at the Luxembourg summit in 1997. This approach culminated at the end of the decade in the OMC, which was formerly launched by the Lisbon European Council in 2000, and subsequently extended to other areas including education, poverty and social exclusion, pensions and immigration.

---

**KEY POINTS**

- When the EEC was founded, social-policy provisions were intended to support the development of the common market.

- By the 1990s, social policy was gaining greater legitimacy but still with the aim of supporting economic integration during the process of EMU.

- The social policy chapter was not written into the Maastricht Treaty due to the British government's veto.

- As employment became a central concern for the Union, governments adopted a more proactive and softer approach to welfare policy, epitomised in the open method of coordination, introduced in the European employment strategy and, subsequently, extended to other social areas.

---

# EU and national legitimacy in the field of welfare

Political analysts often claim that national social-policy competences have been progressively eroded, that national sovereignty is under threat, and that the legitimacy of national governments has been undermined, as the Union's regulatory powers have been extended into most areas of social policy (see Theme box: Democracy and Legitimacy). They also recognise that the Union still has relatively limited formal competences or legitimacy in the field of social welfare (Leibfried 2005). On the one hand, member states still retain responsibility for formulating, implementing and delivering policy. On the other, as new member states join the Union, they are obliged to sign up to the substantial body of social legislation gradually put in place over half a century. Even governments that have strongly opposed the notion of a European social welfare state are not exempt from being taking before the ECJ for infringing European law. These observations make it difficult to argue that national sovereignty has not been undermined.

Given the ever greater diversity in national welfare systems, the OMC offers a softer alternative to the legislative route, since it involves setting common objectives for social protection at EU level, and measuring the progress of member states in relation to targets and benchmarks. The interest for national governments of pursuing the OMC option is that it leaves them to choose the most suitable mechanisms for implementing policies, even though, in a context of cost containment and stricter controls on public spending, choice remains heavily constrained by economic factors, and the onus is on member states to demonstrate the effectiveness of their welfare system by their performance. OMC lessens the caseload of the ECJ, because no legal sanctions are applied for failure to meet targets. It reduces the regulatory burden on the Commission but increases the monitoring and co-ordinating function.

The limits to the Union's social welfare competence and legitimacy were further affirmed in the

**Charter of Fundamental Rights of the European Union**, signed and proclaimed at the European Council meeting held in Nice in 2000. While subscribing to a set of common values encompassing human dignity, freedom, equality and solidarity, the signatories to the Charter expressed their continued commitment to respect the national identities of member states and the organisation of their public authorities. References in the Charter to social solidarity and social welfare, notably Articles 27, 28 and 30 on workers' rights, Article 34 on social security and social assistance, and Article 35 on health care, are all qualified by the phrase: 'in accordance with the procedures laid down by Community law and national laws and practices'. Under the general provisions, Article 51 reiterates that the Charter addresses the institutions and bodies of the Union, but 'with due regard for the principle of **subsidiarity**'. Furthermore, Article 51 stipulates that 'the Charter does not establish any new power or task for the Community or the Union, or modify powers and tasks defined by the Treaties'. The Charter thus reasserts the boundaries of the Union's competence and legitimacy as a welfare actor and the responsibility of member states for determining how welfare policy is organised and delivered.

> **KEY POINTS**
>
> - The regulatory powers of the Union have been extended, but without creating a self-contained European welfare state.
>
> - In recognition of the importance of diversity in national welfare systems, national governments retain their power to decide how social policy is formulated and implemented.
>
> - OMC offers a compromise solution in support of the interests of the Union and member states.
>
> - The Charter of Fundamental Rights of the European Union reaffirms the principles of national sovereignty in the area of social-welfare policy.

# Conclusion: European Integration, Globalisation and Welfare Convergence

The history of welfare within the EU in the second half of the twentieth century must be seen as part of a complex relationship between national welfare systems and social policies and the wider processes of European integration and globalisation. The extent to which these various influences have contributed individually or collectively to welfare convergence and the development of a European social model is periodically debated and contested. This concluding section briefly reviews the conflicting arguments and evidence in the convergence debate and examines the prospects for greater European social integration.

The EU is not intended to deliver a European welfare state. Nor does the Union have the fiscal resources or legitimacy to become one. Indeed, the progressive enlargement of the Union would seem to have made the prospect of such an institution becoming a reality ever more distant. Confirmation is regularly found of the underlying divergence and ambivalence of national interests, and the need to preserve diversity in the scope, form and content of national welfare states. In the absence of a fully developed European social competence, to the extent that social integration has occurred, it would seem to be due to the delegation of responsibility to the Commission and the ECJ and to the space that the Union's institutions have thus been able to carve out for themselves. Through its rulings, the ECJ has, for example, helped to open up traditionally closed

**THEME BOX**

## The Impact of Globalisation

Views are divided about the impact of globalisation on the autonomy of governments in the field of welfare. Early claims that globalisation is an unavoidable force for change were speculative rather than being based on rigorous empirical studies. As more evidence has become available about the various forces driving reform, such theories have been largely discredited or modified to take account of the many other factors influencing the reform process, not least the power of individual welfare states to resist external pressures. Change may be indirectly related to globalisation, but national policies and institutions mediate reform. Economic globalisation creates pressures on welfare states in terms of their ability both to fund and deliver welfare. The options available to governments have, thus, become more constrained when they are deciding whether to support, restructure or retrench their welfare systems. In the continental welfare states, globalisation would seem to have created an agenda for change rather than being the direct cause of adaptations or fundamental restructuring. Any changes introduced in the Nordic countries in response to globalisation of the economy have not affected their commitment to the underlying ideology of social justice and equality on which their welfare systems are based. In the Southern European countries and Ireland, globalisation can be seen as a positive force promoting social cohesion as governments seek to demonstrate that they have a stable working population and commercial environment ready to confront economic competition. In some cases, the role of international organisations may be far more important than globalisation in promoting the reform process. Nowhere is this more apparent than in Central and Eastern Europe, where the World Bank and International Monetary Fund were influential in prescribing how welfare reform should be shaped against a backcloth of regime change and preparation for EU membership.

systems by upholding the rights of mobile workers and their families to social protection across the Union, forcing national governments to comply with European legislation.

Arguments such as these help to explain why member states may have lost more autonomy and control over national welfare-state policies than the EU has gained in transferred authority (Leibfried 2005: 244). The implication is not that welfare systems have become more similar. If they can be said to be converging at all, it may be towards a mixed system of welfare, but where the nature of the mix continues to be determined largely by each country's welfare history and the balance sought between state, private and voluntary sectors, and families. Nor does convergence of policy objectives and coordination of methods mean that national welfare systems are being dismantled or that national diversity is being eliminated.

While the EU has been building its own path dependency and constructing its own modes of governance (Wincott 2003), theories of critical junctures suggest that European economic and political integration may have provided the necessary catalyst to breach national path dependencies and allow social integration to develop. The processes of incrementalism and institutional harmonisation have thus been able to increase the chances of developing and legitimising European social policy, making necessary the renegotiation of the boundaries between European and national-level responsibilities for social welfare. Low economic growth, high unemployment, labour market restructuring, socio-demographic change and the high costs of welfare reform, particularly in the Central and East European countries, have also made social integration even more necessary to deal with the negative consequences of economic integration and avoid any levelling-down of social welfare provision in what might otherwise become a 'race to the bottom', pending the closing of the social security gap.

The impact of external forces, most notably globalisation, is a further component in the controversy about the extent to which national control over social welfare policies is being eroded. (See Theme box: The Impact of Globalisation.) The literature exploring the relationship between globalisation and welfare states proposes three main perspectives on the impact of globalisation: for some, it has a strong effect due to the increasing dominance of the market economy, leading inexorably to welfare retrenchment; for others, it has a less powerful effect on welfare states than do other social and economic processes; according to the third perspective, the effects of globalisation are mediated by national politics and policies, and change depends largely on pre-existing national welfare ideologies and institutional frameworks (Prior and Sykes 2001; Sykes 2003).

The Union is portrayed at one and the same time as a body promoting and resisting the pressures of globalisation, and as a constraining and enabling force. A similar comment could be made about individual member states with regard to the pressures of economic integration. In responding to self-imposed EMU, national governments have been forced to adapt their systems for financing social welfare. In responding to economic integration, they are adopting new forms of governance aimed at

achieving common policy objectives and targets in areas including employment and social protection. National welfare states are not, however, in the process of being dismantled, and governments seem set to continue to act in ways that reflect their individual conceptions of social welfare, thereby producing different outcomes despite their common interest in upholding a European social model.

**KEY POINTS**

- Any convergence of welfare systems towards a welfare mix that has occurred as a result of economic integration has not reduced the path-dependent diversity between welfare states.

- A combination of external and internal forces may be making social integration more necessary to prevent levelling-down of social provision.

- Globalisation may be creating the need for change, but national policies and institutions mediate reform and produce different outcomes.

- National welfare systems are not being dismantled and national diversity has not been eliminated.

**? QUESTIONS**

1. Why are political scientists interested in studying social welfare?

2. What are the different meanings of welfare?

3. How are social and economic policies linked together?

4. What are the characteristics of different theoretical perspectives on welfare?

5. Analyse the main features of national welfare arrangements in EU member states using the social protection indicators presented in Table 17.1.

6. What do you understand by 'welfare models'?

7. How has the development of national social-welfare systems been influenced by membership of the EU?

8. What are the main factors preventing harmonisation and coordination of national welfare arrangements?

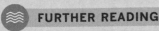
 **FURTHER READING**

■ **Alcock, P., Erskine, A. and May, M. (eds) (2003),** *The Student's Companion to Social Policy*, **2nd edn, Oxford: Blackwell.** Provides a comprehensive and accessible guide to social policy, with the main focus on the UK.

■ **Esping-Andersen, G. (1990),** *The Three Worlds of Welfare Capitalism,* **Cambridge, Polity Press and idem (1999),** *Social Foundations of Postindustrial Economies,* **Oxford, Oxford University Press.** Present and critique the author's influential work on welfare-regime theory.

■ **Hantrais, L. (2007),** *Social Policy in the European Union*, **3rd edn, Basingstoke/New York, Palgrave/St Martin's Press.** Provides an analysis of the development of national and EU-level social-policy competence.

■ **Kleinman, M. (2002),** *A European Welfare State? European Union Social Policy in Context,* **Basingstoke/New York, Palgrave.** Explores the development of a European welfare state and looks at the impact of European economic integration and globalisation on welfare states.

■ **Sykes, R. Palier, B. and Prior, P.M. (eds) (2001),** *Globalization and European Welfare States,* **Basingstoke/New York, Palgrave/St Martin's Press.** Assembles a useful collection of contributions to theoretical and conceptual debates about the impact of globalisation on European welfare states.

 **IMPORTANT WEBSITES**

● **http://europa.eu./documents/eur-lex/index_en.htm** and **http://europa.eu.int/scadplus/ scad_en.htm** European Commission websites that can be searched for information about treatles and European social legislation.

● **http://europa.eu.int/comm/dgs/employment_social/index_en.htm** The website of the Directorate General for Employment and Social Affairs, providing regularly updated information about policy matters that fall within the Directorate's remit.

**Visit the Online Resource Centre that accompanies this book for lots of useful additional material, including an interactive map of Europe. www.oxfordtextbooks.co.uk/orc/hay_menon/**

# 18 Environmental Policy

## WYN GRANT AND JANE FEEHAN

✔ **Reader's Guide**

This chapter looks at the extent to which environmental policy has been one of the success stories of European integration, and also at whether its place in the European agenda is being challenged by a growing emphasis on growth and competitiveness. The **precautionary principle** is of central importance in understanding environmental policy and provides a basis for resisting an excessive emphasis on economic growth. The old division between 'leader' and 'laggard' states in terms of how environmental policy is driven forward is no longer very meaningful, but new challenges are presented by the accession states with their inheritance of environmental problems. Non-governmental organisations have played a key role in stimulating and shaping environmental policy. Environmental policy has become increasingly fragmented in a way that can undermine an overall ecological perspective, but this makes it important to examine what happens in particular policy areas such as air pollution.

# Introduction: Environmental Policy as a Success Story?

Is environmental policy one of the big success stories of European integration as is often claimed? There are a number of imperatives that create a demand for an effective environmental policy at the EU level. Pollution is no respecter of national boundaries. Rivers like the Rhine and the Danube flow through several member states, while air pollution is a transboundary issue and climate change a global problem that requires a European effort to maintain pressure for international agreement. Environmental policy is also an area where the EU can connect with the aspirations of its citizens for a better quality of life, including a better standard of environmental health. Since 1987, when the Single European Act confirmed that environmental management was one of the formal policy goals of European integration, EU environmental policy has moved steadily up the agenda. (See Background box 18.1 and Theme box: The Impact of the European Union.)

However, within Europe the challenges in this area are changing. During the 1980s the challenge was to regulate point sources of pollution, reining in industry from its damaging excesses. In the twenty-first century we have moved on from this confrontational approach, and the EU finds itself in a very different environmental-policy landscape. The priorities are now climate change and sustainable development; the pollution problems—greenhouse gases, low-dose chemicals in the environment—arise from diffuse sources that are more difficult to regulate, and the tools that we use, increasingly, are economic instruments and sectoral integration. As environmental policies become

---

## BACKGROUND BOX 18.1

### What Is Sustainable Development?

At its heart, sustainable development means a better quality of life for everyone, now and for generations to come. It is a vision of progress that gives equal attention to environment, economy and society. The need to link these three pillars—protection of the environment, economic development and social justice—is recognised by democratic governments and political movements around the world, and sustainable development is now at the core of modern environmental policies.

The concept of sustainable development emerged onto the global political stage with the 1987 United Nations Brundtland Commission report, *Our Common Future*. The 1992 'Earth Summit', the UN Conference on Environment and Development in Rio de Janeiro, made ground-breaking progress with the Rio Declaration on environment and development, as well as the Agenda 21 Action Programme.

According to the Organisation for Economic Cooperation and Development, sectoral integration is the most important tool for achieving sustainable development. Sectoral integration means the instigation and pursuit of environmental considerations from *within* sectors, such as energy, transport and agriculture, rather than their imposition from outside. Since 1997, environmental integration has been a requirement under the EC Treaty: Article 6 states that 'environmental protection requirements must be integrated into the definition and implementation of the Community policies...in particular with a view to promoting sustainable development'. The importance of integration was reaffirmed in the Sixth Environment Action Programme, which stipulates that 'integration of environmental concerns into other policies must be deepened' in order to move towards sustainable development.

subsumed into the policies of industry, agriculture, transport and other sectors, can we conclude that the work of Europe's environmental policies has been done? Is the ebb of the environmental agenda's distinctive, separate identity due to the fact that the zeal to 'save the world', having peaked in the 1980s, has given way to a more mature, cooperative and integrated approach to solving environmental problems? Or is it because the environment is steadily losing ground to the ever-strengthening drive towards competitiveness, economic development and the nurturing of the European Union's 'knowledge economy'?

## Clean, clever and competitive

It is certainly the case that at the heart of the European Union's sustainable economic development is quality of life for citizens, and safeguarding of essential natural resources: the quality and safety of water, soil and air. Environmental legislation is sometimes cited as a barrier to industry, but in fact environmental legislation can promote innovation, and the wider benefits speak for themselves—although the value of clean air doesn't fit neatly into a balance sheet.

The Dutch presidency of the European Union in the second half of 2004 heralded the launch of a new partnership for a 'clean, clever and competitive' Europe to move eco-efficiency and eco-innovation higher up the EU's political agenda. Dutch State Secretary Pieter Van Geel proposed a partnership between the Dutch environment ministry and the World Business Council for Sustainable Development (WBCSD), a coalition of 170 multinational companies dedicated to sustainable development. Van Geel explained that 'economy and **ecology** go hand in hand and that eco-efficiency can contribute to European competitiveness'. 'Strengthening competitiveness by improving the market perspective for eco-innovation is in the interest of EU member states as well as companies operating in Europe', he said (VROM 2004:7). In a further demonstration of the important role that the Dutch play in shaping the EU's environmental agenda, former Dutch prime minister Wim Kok produced a report on the progress of the Lisbon Strategy, which aims to make the EU 'the most competitive and dynamic knowledge-based economy in the world by 2010' (Kok 2004:7). The report includes recommendations on how to best use the synergies between environment and economy to make Europe more competitive.

**KEY POINTS**

- Environmental policy has been claimed to be one of the success stories of European integration.

- The level of environmental protection is higher than would have been achieved by independent member states.

- New challenges are being faced and environmental policy may be losing ground to economic policy objectives.

- A new effort is being made to achieve a 'clean, clever and competitive' Europe.

# The Development of EU Environmental Policy

When the EU was first established as a common market it did not have an environmental policy, reflecting the fact that its original purpose was economic integration. There was no reference to environmental policy in the Treaty of Rome. Stimulated by the first United Nations conference on the environment held in Stockholm in 1972, the 1972 summit of EU leaders called on the Commission to draw up an environmental policy and give a group of Commission officials specific responsibility for environmental protection. In 1972 the Commission set up an Environment and Consumer Protection Service but as part of the directorate concerned with industrial policy. It was not until 1981 that a distinct directorate-general was set up with responsibility for the environment. This was an important development because in an organisation like the Commission it is important to have a distinct group of officials with the 'mission' of looking after the environment who can argue the case for enhanced protection from within 'the house'. Within the college of commissioners, however, there was no commissioner with sole responsibility for environmental policy until 1989.

Environmental policy still lacked a treaty basis, a deficiency that was not remedied until the Single European Act (SEA) of 1987. This gave explicit recognition to the improvement of environmental quality as a legitimate Community objective in its own right. The SEA stated that in harmonising national regulations the Community would take as its base a high level of environmental protection. The commitment to an environmental policy was strengthened in the Maastricht Treaty which introduced sustainable development, i.e. development that will meet the needs of the present without undermining the prospects of future generations, as a guiding principle. The Treaty specified that the EU's environmental policy must aim at a high level of protection and that environmental protection

requirements must be integrated into the definition and implementation of other EU policies. The draft Constitutional Treaty produced by the European Convention maintains this commitment to an environmental policy that aims at a high level of environmental protection.

When environmental policy first emerged as a distinct policy area at the beginning of the 1970s, there was an emphasis on the ecosystem as a whole. It was recognised that changes in one area of human activity could have unforeseen and harmful consequences elsewhere. Pollution or the deterioration of natural resources had to be viewed within the context of the carrying capacity of the planet, and its ability to sustain a human population of a given size. As environmental policy has developed, it has tended to become a series of discrete sub-areas that often have little connection with each other. In part, this reflects the distribution of technical expertise so that someone who is an expert on noise will usually know little about water pollution. The EU has sought to improve its competence in this area and has made extensive use of temporary appointments, consultants and research projects to improve its understanding and expertise. However, the fragmentation of policy between different forms of expertise can undermine its coherence and its potential contribution to sustainable development.

## Environment action programmes

The EU has been aware of this problem and has sought to frame policy within the context of a series of environment action programmes (EAPs). The first programme covered the period from 1973 to 1977 and the sixth programme was announced in 2002. The first two programmes established some basic principles that have been carried forward into later programmes:

- Prevention is better than cure.
- The polluter pays.
- Environmental impacts should be taken into account.
- Environmental action should be taken at the most appropriate level (what came to be known as the subsidiarity principle).

The third and fourth programmes that ran from 1983 sought to provide an overall strategy for protecting the environmental and natural resources. The emphasis shifted from pollution control to pollution prevention, and the concept of environmental protection was broadened to increase land-use policy and the integration of environmental concerns into other EU policies. However, land-use planning policies remain largely under the control of the member states. The integration of environmental concerns into other EU policies was not really tackled until the introduction of the so-called 'Cardiff process' (named after the EU summit at Cardiff) in 1998, and although some progress has been made in that area there is still a long way to go. A recent review of environmental policy integration (EPI) in Europe indicated that inadequate capacity and resources are believed to be dedicated to EPI, particularly positive financial incentives, and that the Cardiff process is impeded by the lack of an institutional anchor (EEA 2005: 45). Although EAPs provide a framework for legislative action—setting out objectives, targets and time—their aspirations cannot always be easily achieved. The fifth programme emphasised sustainable development and the need to encourage optimum reuse and recycling of raw materials. However, in a detailed analysis of the programme, the Commission admitted that while the scheme was full of good intentions, many of its recommendations were never put into practice. The sixth programme adopted in 2002 took a new approach, setting out objectives, actions and key horizontal aims in four priority areas: climate change, biodiversity, health and quality of life and sustainable use of resources. The contents of this programme caused some controversy within the

Commission with the enterprise commissioner, Erkki Liikanen, arguing that early versions gave too much ground to green campaigners and should be more industry-friendly. The environment directorate argued that the proposals concentrated on 'greening the market' with an emphasis on the use of policy instruments such as financial incentives for polluters to clean up their act rather than greater use of rules-based regulation. Returning to the theme of the need to adopt a holistic approach to environmental policy, the sixth programme identified seven key environmental issues, the so-called Thematic Strategies. (See Background box 18.2.) The draft Strategies were under threat due to concerns over their potential to impede Europe's economic competitiveness but, after extensive examination and debate, the Commission collectively agreed in July 2005 to allow them through. They will complement the existing work on climate change and biodiversity, completing the strategic underpinnings of European environment policy for the medium term. These Thematic Strategies represent a new approach to making policy by taking an integrated, holistic approach to environmental issues. They focus on themes, rather than specific economic activities or pollutants, and they identify all the actors that need to be involved in resolving the issues at stake. They take a long perspective—up to 20 years—to ensure

---

**BACKGROUND BOX 18.2**

Thematic Strategies in the Sixth Environmental Action Programme

- Clean air for Europe (CAFE)
- Soil protection
- Sustainable use of pesticides
- Protection and conservation of the marine environment
- Waste prevention and recycling
- Sustainable use of natural resources
- Urban environment.

a predictable, stable policy and regulatory framework. They are based on an in-depth scientific review of existing environment policy, and have been through extensive, wide-ranging consultations and rigorous impact assessment. The European environmental community awaits these Strategies with great interest, two having been published by October 2005.

---

> ### KEY POINTS
>
> - The EU did not originally have an environmental policy.
> - It was given a basis in the treaties only in 1987.
> - Environment action programmes have played a key role in framing policies.
> - The Cardiff process is supposed to ensure the integration of environmental policy into all aspects of EU policy.
> - Seven Thematic Strategies make up a new framework for Europe's environmental policies, aiming to take a long-term, integrated, holistic approach.
> - Land-use planning remains a member state responsibility.

---

# Precautionary Principle

The precautionary principle lies at the centre of EU environmental policy, but is also the subject of some controversy. The Rio Declaration on Environment and Development adopted in 2002 calls for the precautionary principle to be widely applied and recognised. 'This principle means that the absence of scientific proof for a risk of environmental harm is not a sufficient reason for failing to take preventative action' (McEldowney and McEldowney 2001: 10). Thus, according to the Commission, 'Recourse to the precautionary principle presupposes that potentially dangerous effects deriving from a phenomenon, product or process have been identified, and that scientific evaluation does not allow the risk to be determined with sufficient certainty' (European Commission 2000: 4). As the Court of First Instance emphasised in a judgment in 2002, a risk assessment is vital and must comprise both a scientific and a political component.

In its 2000 communication on the precautionary principle, the Commission emphasises that it must be used in a way that is proportional to the chosen level of protection: 'A total ban may not be a proportional response to a potential risk in all cases. However, in certain cases, it is the sole possible response to a given risk' (European Commission 2000: 4). Decisions should also be based on an examination of the potential benefits and costs of action or lack of action. This should go beyond an economic cost–benefit analysis to include 'non-economic considerations such as the efficacy of possible options and their acceptability to the public' (European Commission 2000: 5).

## Difficulties in implementation

It is this mixture of political and scientific discourses that has caused considerable difficulty in the implementation of the principle. Green organisations have sometimes in effect argued that a negative must be proved, i.e. that there is no risk from a given product or process. This is very difficult to do and in international trade disputes the USA has argued that the principle has been used to halt the application of controversial new technological developments such as genetically modified crops. Majone (2002b: 89) argues that 'the approach purports to provide a legitimate basis for taking protective regulatory measures even when reliable scientific evidence of the causes and/or the scale of potential damage is lacking'. He maintains (2002: 90) that 'the precautionary approach is deeply ambiguous, and . . . this ambiguity is abetted by a lack of clear definitions and sound logical foundations'. However, European environmental policy has to operate against a background in which a series of incidents, primarily in the food safety area rather than in relation to the environment as such, have made European citizens highly risk averse. Whether the precautionary principle has actually guided EU environmental policy in a way that meets these concerns is open to question. Eckley and Selin (2004: 98) note:

'Precaution has been a part of Community discourse for fifteen years and treaties for ten years, yet despite substantive changes in debate and international pronouncements . . . the precautionary principle has had little effect on actual policy-making . . . making it a case of all talk and little action.'

---

**KEY POINTS**

- The precautionary principle is at the heart of EU environmental policy.

- Policy responses must be proportional to a given risk.

- The principle involves a mix of scientific and political considerations.

- Its effect on policy may have been more limited than is sometimes claimed.

---

# Policy-making Process

## 'Leader' and 'laggard' member states

The strength of environmental sentiment in member states of the EU varies considerably from one country to another. (See Theme box: Democracy and Legitimacy.) These differences feed through to the stance that member states take in the Council of Environment Ministers and the European Parliament. Of the 34 greens elected to the European Parliament in the 2004 elections, over a third (13) came from Germany. In contrast, no greens were elected from any of the new member states. When the EU was made up of 12 member states, Germany was seen as having a leading role in driving forward environmental policies, reflecting the importance of green sentiment in its domestic politics. Denmark and the Netherlands were seen as the principal allies of Germany in pushing for stricter

environmental policies. The enlargement of the EU in 1995 that brought in Austria, Finland and Sweden was seen as strengthening the grouping of states with a strong commitment to the development of environmental policy. Britain, on the one hand, was often portrayed as the 'dirty man of Europe' during the period of Conservative government, while the Southern member states were seen as having a weak commitment to environmental policy and inadequate mechanisms for its implementation and enforcement.

The salience of the distinction made between 'leaders' and 'laggards' in the formation of EU environmental policy was always capable of being overstated. Even within the group of states identified as a 'green core', 'Alliances between the "green" member states . . . are by no means given. They have to be formed on an issue-by-issue basis and remain liable to defection' (Liefferink and Andersen

## THEME BOX

### Democracy and Legitimacy

EU environmental policy aims to lift standards across the whole of Europe for the benefit of its citizens. However, tensions may arise between EU-level initiatives and policy preferences at the level of the member state. These often arise at the stage of implementation. For example, when the Bathing Waters Directive was passed, Britain, worried about the cost of new sewage treatment plants, managed to designate only 27 'bathing waters' compared with 37 in Luxembourg. Popular resorts such as Brighton, Eastbourne and Blackpool were excluded. The Commission brought legal proceedings against Britain, focusing on the beaches at Blackpool and Southport, and eventually compliance improved. One interpretation would be that this was an interference with the ability of the UK to control its own budgetary costs. An alternative interpretation was that the Commission was seeking to protect the right to swim in waters free of untreated sewage which can be a source of disease. In other words, it was seeking to enhance its legitimacy with citizens even though the process through which the Directive was passed in 1975 involved only indirect democratic participation through the governments of the member states.

With the increased role of the European Parliament, direct democratic input into environmental policy has increased, although it often seems a rather remote institution to EU citizens.

been claimed, nevertheless Britain did adopt more of a leadership role in EU environmental policy. The Labour government made environment one of its three priorities during its presidency of the EU in 1998.

As the content of environmental policy has changed, the old division between leaders and laggards among member states has become less helpful in explaining the direction that policy takes. It was found to be of little help in explaining national differences towards environmental policy integration (Lenschow 2002: 16). According to Sbragia, new cleavages have emerged that 'have much more to do with how environmental protection is achieved'. Sbragia goes on to argue that Germany's emphasis on traditional command-and-control regulation based on the best available technology has been challenged by the development of new policy instruments. 'The combination of this new policy agenda and the unexpectedly high costs of unification have eroded Germany's leadership role' (Sbragia 2000: 295). It could be argued that environmental policy has become more like other areas of EU policy in that it has become embedded in political and administrative routines and less reliant on a political push from a particular group of member states.

## The new EU member states

New member states have been given long accession periods before they have to comply with EU environmental rules. For example, Poland does not have to comply with the EU directive on municipal waste treatment until 2015. The cost of implementing EU environmental policies in the new member states is considerable. In the case of Poland, the Commission has estimated that the overall cost of applying EU environmental policies will be something between €22.1 and €42.8 billion. Despite the long transition periods, the new member states may find it difficult to meet all the targets they have been set. These problems will be exacerbated by the accession of Bulgaria and Romania which have serious problems with ageing industrial plants in industries such as chemicals. New member states may therefore seek

1998: 262). Germany could be a vigorous defender of its own particular national interests and, domestically, the environment ministry had a lower status than longer established ministries. 'In some cases, such as climate policy, Germany appeared as the most reluctant "green" member state' (Liefferink and Andersen 1998: 268). In Britain, the change to a New Labour government in 1997 led to a changed approach taken to environmental policy which was given a higher priority, reflecting a 'manifesto commitment to strengthen co-operation within the EU on environmental issues' (Young 2000: 63). Although it could be argued that this new policy commitment was more superficial than might have

to bargain for further extensions and may also be reluctant to commit to further developments of environmental policy.

## The Directorate-General and the Commissioner

Environment policy did not have its own Directorate-General (DG) until 1981 and its own Commissioner until 1989. For a long time DGXI, as it used to be known, was seen as one of the weaker component parts of the Commission. Cini (1997: 81) argues: 'DGXI [now Environment DG] is generally considered to be a weak DG within the Commission. Its inability to win arguments or to have its priorities translated into EU priorities provides ample evidence of its marginal character.' Nevertheless, the administrative resources available to the directorate-general have been built up over time. From just 50–60 professional staff in 1987, their number had grown to 450 by 1997. 'This growth was accompanied by a move to new and improved offices and owed much to the administrative and diplomatic skills of the director-general throughout the period, Laurens-Jan Brinkhorst' (Weale 1996: 598).

Much can also be achieved by the profile given to the Directorate-General's work by the Commissioner. Margot Wallström of Sweden who was the Commissioner from 1999 to 2004 was very effective at communicating the objectives and policies of the Environment DG, even if she was only given a 'mixed' rating by the Green G8. Her reward was to be promoted to take charge of the Commission's general communication efforts. She was replaced as Commissioner by Stavros Dimas from the Greek conservative party New Democracy who was believed to have a less strong commitment to the environment than Wallström. Some interpreted the change as an indication that the Commission was giving a lower priority to the environment.

One problem for the Environment DG is that it has always been viewed with suspicion by other parts of the Commission as having too green a tinge to its outlook. As Weale (1996: 608) notes: 'A number of the officials clearly have a commitment to environmental protection that is personal as well as professional. It may be this tendency which creates the impression among some other officials that DG XI has a limited perspective.' Proposals made by the Environment DG often face opposition from other DGs with close links to business interests. In the Prodi Commission, Energy and Transport Commissioner Loyola de Palacio was criticised as being the most anti-environment commissioner by green groups. The Barroso Commission has prioritised growth and jobs, creating a perception that a back seat has been given to environmental issues.

## The European Parliament

Advocates of environmental policy have often looked to the European Parliament as the institution best disposed towards the advancement of environmental policy. Most of its work on policy has been done in committees and it first set up an environment committee in 1973. This committee has had a number of titles becoming the Environment, Public Health and Food Safety Committee in the Parliament elected in 2004. The committee has built 'prestige and legislative importance . . . over the years' (Judge and Earnshaw 2003: 187–8). For a long time the problem for environmental-policy advocates was that, although the Parliament was the greenest of the EU institutions, it was also one of the least influential. The introduction of co-decision has changed that, although the Parliament's influence still has to be exercised ultimately through the process of bargaining known as 'trialogue' involving the Commission, Council of Ministers and Parliament.

## European Environment Agency (EEA)

During the 1990s, the Commission began to take a broader and more strategic approach to environmental issues, developing instruments for environmental protection that were more flexible and responsive to regional situations. Fewer new

**Figure 18.1** The EEA's DPSIR framework: a basis for analysing the interrelated factors that impact on the environment

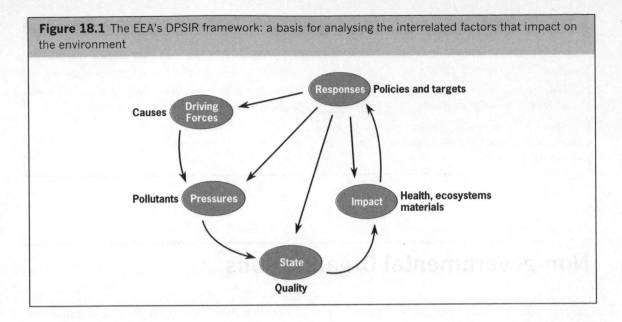

laws were being proposed, and attention was focusing on improving the implementation of existing laws. Better data were needed to more accurately assess the extent of environmental problems, and the progress—or lack thereof—of member states in addressing those problems. An essential precondition for this is the availability of reliable, standardised and comparable information on the environment. In response to these needs, the European Environment Agency (EEA) was established in 1994.

The EEA is the leading public body in Europe dedicated to providing sound, independent information on the environment to policymakers and the public. Based in the Danish capital Copenhagen, the EEA is the hub of the European environment information and observation network (Eionet), a network of around 300 bodies around Europe through which it both collects and disseminates environment-related data and information. Although an EU body, the Agency is open to all nations that share its objectives. It currently has 32 member countries: the 25 EU member states, three EU candidate countries—Bulgaria, Romania and Turkey—and Iceland, Liechtenstein, Norway and Switzerland. The west Balkan states—Albania,

Bosnia and Herzegovina, Croatia, the former Yugoslav Republic of Macedonia, and Serbia and Montenegro—have applied for membership of the Agency.

The EEA's aim is to help the EU and member countries make informed decisions about improving the environment, integrating environmental considerations into economic policies and moving towards sustainable development. To do this, it provides a range of information and assessments, covering the *state* of the environment and its *trends*, together with *pressures* on the environment and the economic and social *driving forces* behind them (see Figure 18.1).

The regulation creating the EEA (1210/90) included an article providing for a review to assess the possibility of giving the EEA more powers in monitoring compliance. This review took place in 1995, concluding that the EEA should focus on provision of environmental information and analysis, not compliance (McCormick 2001:146). Nevertheless, its work has improved the accuracy and reliability of environmental data in Europe, revealing a clearer picture of the extent of environmental problems and the effects that EU laws are having.

# Non-governmental Organisations

Interest representation in Brussels in terms of resources and the exercise of influence has long been dominated by business interest groups. For example, 'an alliance of automobile and oil interests is widely perceived as having been successful in weakening the "Auto-Oil" programme of DGXI relating to vehicle emission standards' (Long 1998: 117). However, the environmental groups organised in the Green G8 (see Background box 18.3) have made an increasing impact on the policy-making process. In part this is because even more than other non-governmental organisations (NGOs), they are effective at the evidence-based policy-making which a technocratic organisation like the Commission prefers. The 80 staff they have between them is still a small number compared with the combined resources of business groups, but through the deployment of their expertise they have been able to gain the ears of Commission decision-makers, as illustrated by the example of Climate Action Network–Europe. (See Background box 18.4.) Environmental organisations do receive some financial assistance from the Commission which, according to one informant in one of the organisations, might account for 20 per cent of their Brussels office costs. However, Greenpeace has always refused to accept such funding.

'For almost fifteen years, the European Environmental Bureau (EEB) with its European network of member groups was the only significant environmental organisation in Brussels' (Long 1998: 105). Indeed, as other environmental groups have made their presence felt in Brussels, the EEB has faced adjustment issues. They tended to think that they were first among equals, the first interlocutor with the Commission and the European Parliament. With the passage of the Single European Act, a number of environmental groups established offices in Brussels in the late 1980s, including Friends of the

## BACKGROUND BOX 18.3

### Members of the Green G8

BirdLife International

Climate Action Network–Europe (CNE)

European Environmental Bureau (EEB)

European Federation for Transport and Environment (T&E)

Friends of the Earth Europe (FoEE)

Greenpeace Europe

International Friends of Nature (IFN)

World Wide Fund for Nature European Policy Office (WWF)

## BACKGROUND BOX 18.4

### Climate Action Network–Europe (CNE)

CNE was set up at the height of international concern about increasing concentrations of greenhouse gases in the atmosphere. It forms part of a global network of organisations concerned with these issues. It is a coalition of 90 NGOs. It acts as an information service and has come to be regarded as the definitive voice on climate-related matters at the EU level. CNE has sought to build alliances with a number of clean-energy companies and trade associations such as those dealing with energy conservation and wind energy. It has nurtured a range of contacts with EU institutions and is often invited to attend relevant meetings. Its influence strategy is essentially a subtle, long-term one, educating decision-makers to improve their understanding of climate change issues and change their perceptions. However, much of the time of its staff has to be spent putting together grants to enable the organisation to survive. In the recent past it has received funding from the European Commission and the Belgian and Dutch governments.

*Source*: **Newell and Grant (2000)**

Earth (FoE), Greenpeace and the World Wide Fund for Nature (WWF). Greenpeace pulled its national member organisations out of EEB in 1991, but a number of groups continued to find its federal structure a useful umbrella.

## The Green G8

The four leading groups in Brussels—FoE, Greenpeace, WWF and EEB—developed into a 'Gang of Four'. This grouping 'developed close working relations with the head of the NGO liaison unit in the Environment Directorate-General of the Commission, which resulted in regular reporting back sessions to the environmental groups following the normally secretive meetings of the Council of Ministers' (Long 1998: 114). Subsequently, it evolved into the Green G8, the last organisation to join being the International Friends of Nature,

an Austrian-based organisation with a special interest in tourism issues. Sometimes reference is made to the G7/G8 as Greenpeace's involvement can be more distanced given that it retains an interest in protests that stretch understandings of legality.

Some of the organisations within the Green G8 have broader interests than others, although even the more broadly based organisations have an informal division of labour with recognised specialities, e.g. Greenpeace is an authority on genetic modification, FoE on nuclear power and WWF is known for its expertise on biodiversity. The alliance is able to function because of its flexibility so that members are able to choose to act collectively on some issues and independently on others. There are also policy clusters that exist below the G8 level that involve some, but not all, of the organisations. Green organisations may also build much broader coalitions with other non-governmental organisations that do not have explicit environmental objectives. 'When two of the Green 8 (EEB and the European Federation for Transport and Environment) joined consumer, citizen and public health organisations in the European Coalition for Clean Air (ECCA), they entered into a temporary coalition to pursue two related issues, vehicle emissions standards and European legislation on air quality' (Webster 2002: 4).

Long argues that the environmental movement failed to consolidate its position in Brussels when interest in the environment was at its peak in the late 1980s and early 1990s. He detects 'a number of worrying signs concerning the decline in the status of the environmental lobby in Brussels *vis-à-vis* the Commission' (Long 1998: 116). He concludes that 'the environmental movement is "punching below its weight" in Brussels despite the important advances which it has made in its institutional presence in the city over the past few years' (Long 1998: 118). The position does not seem to have been improved too much in the period since 1998 to judge from the extent to which business interests have been successful in diluting and delaying the REACH (Registration, Evaluation

WYN GRANT AND JANE FEEHAN

and Authorisation of CHemicals) reforms on testing of chemicals. On the other hand, there are some signs of environmental groups forging constructive relationships with business organisations where there is a commonality of interest. For example, one environmental group has held meetings on a non-attributable basis with food companies to discuss common perspectives on the reform of the CAP. It may be that more influence will be exerted in the future through a constructive dialogue between previously opposed interests designed to find solutions to environmental problems.

# Policy Areas

## The fragmentation of policy-making

As noted in the introduction to this chapter, early initiatives on environmental policy-making in the 1970s tried to adopt an ecosystem approach to policy development. Pictures of the Earth taken from voyages to the Moon created a sense of the fragility and wonder of the planet and the need for it to be cherished. Organisations like WWF have tried to maintain this emphasis on the planet as an entity that has to be protected and nurtured for future generations. (See Background box 18.5.) However, over time environmental policy has become fragmented into a number of distinct policy areas with their own agendas and policy instruments. Thus, for example, **ground-level air pollution**, discussed as an example here, is treated as a discrete policy area. This is then subdivided into air pollution from mobile (cars and trucks) and stationary (power plants and factories) sources and again into particular pollutants (carbon monoxide, nitrogen dioxide, etc.) This fragmentation reflects the fact that different interests are focused on particular issues (the oil and auto industries in the case of air pollution) and also that expertise is fragmented into a number of distinct 'epistemic communities'

of experts. Someone who is an expert on air pollution may know little about water pollution and someone who is an expert on carbon monoxide may know much less about nitrogen dioxide.

## Climate change

This fragmentation of knowledge poses particular problems when one comes to the most serious long-run environmental problem, **climate change** or global warming. Modelling long-run climate changes is particularly difficult, even with sophisticated mathematical models and powerful computers, because there are so many variables and their interactions with each to consider. For example, will climate change eventually lead to a colder climate in Britain more commensurate with its latitude because of the diversion of the Gulf Steam that currently gives the British Isles a relatively temperate climate? A small minority of qualified scientists contest the view that human activities have played a significant role in increasing recent temperatures, insisting that the causes are natural. These sceptics underpin the reluctance of the US government to commit to measures to tackle climate change, undermining the efforts of the EU to move policy

## BACKGROUND BOX 18.5  Ground-level air pollution

### The Living Planet Index

WWF sees its Living Planet Index as a measurement tool comparable to the Dow Jones Index for the economy. The fifth Living Planet report produced in 2004 measures humanity's 'ecological footprint' in terms of the resources we consume. This increased 2.5 times over the last 40 years. On average each person on Earth consumes 2.2 hectares of land when only 1.8 hectares are available. Americans have an ecological footprint of 23.5 hectares because they consume such large quantities of natural resources. Energy consumption is the fastest-growing component of the index, increasing by nearly 700 per cent between 1961 and 2001. A separate index tracks populations of more than a thousand animal species. Populations fell by 40 per cent between 1970 and 2000, an average of one species disappearing every 13 minutes. With humans consuming 20 per cent more natural resources than the Earth can produce, the Earth's capacity to regenerate is placed in danger, ultimately putting humanity itself under threat from ecological disasters. Critics argue that humans can intervene to increase the carrying capacity of the environment, e.g. through renewable energy schemes.

*Source*: www.worldwildlife.org/about/viewpoint/living_planet.cfm

Initial efforts to tackle ground-level air pollution were motivated by concerns that different standards being adopted in different member states were undermining the common market. In the 1980s, concerns about the impact of acid rain on forests became a focus of concern and led to the Directive on Large Combustion Plants that came into force in 1988. In the 1990s, the focus of attention switched to health issues associated with air pollution for which the principal source was increasingly motor traffic. It was recognised that the approach of tackling one pollutant at a time had not worked very well. The Commission therefore proposed a new strategy based on new EU-wide air-quality objectives, as well as setting minimum standards for monitoring air quality and passing on the results to the public embodied in the Air Quality Framework Directive of 1996. This was then put into effect through a series of 'daughter' directives dealing with particular pollutants.

As part of its efforts to move away from 'command and control' regulation to new environmental policy instruments, the Commission also set up the AutoOil I programme in 1993. This has been described as 'one of the most important policy initiatives launched by the Commission in the environmental field during the 1990s' (Freidrich *et al.* 2000: 593). It was an attempt to find practical solutions to vehicle emission problems by working in a tripartite dialogue with the oil and motor vehicle industries. Indeed, NGOs and the European Parliament were initially excluded from the policy-making process. The Council and the Parliament eventually adopted more stringent standards than those originally proposed by the Commission, although some observers saw the concessions as marginal (Peterson and Bomberg 1999: 179). The measures introduced as a result included mandatory limit values for emissions and a two-stage programme for tightening fuel quality requirements.

forward in this area. Uncertainties do exist regarding how much climate change should be expected in the future, and a hotly contested political and public debate exists over what actions, if any, should be taken. However, even if all the proposed policy measures were put into place, it is likely that global warming would be slowed down rather than reversed. Therefore, the EU argues that we should put in place measures to adapt to some degree of climate change, combined with steps to mitigate more severe long-term changes, thus tackling the rising emissions of greenhouse gases being produced by human activities around the world.

**WYN GRANT AND JANE FEEHAN**

# Biodiversity

**Biodiversity** is a big, inclusive concept: it is defined as the variety of all life. This variety does not just mean types of animals and plants (species), but also the variation at genetic level, and the range and variety of habitats, ecosystems and landscapes. Many people think of biodiversity as being untouched wilderness—rainforests, exotic coral reefs, the otherworldly creatures living in deep-sea hydrothermal vents—but in fact in Europe we have many semi-natural, managed landscapes and regions which are highly valued for their beauty, cultural importance and amenity value, and which are also places with a rich variety of flora and fauna.

Europe is the most urbanised and, together with Asia, the most densely populated continent in the world. This means that Europe has a relatively impoverished natural heritage. Nonetheless, it does have a vast range of natural habitats stretching from the Arctic Circle in the north to the warm Mediterranean waters in the south. Intensive land use makes it all the more important to take care of what remains, and places an even higher premium on the beauty and cultural value of our landscapes, and on the essential ecosystem services that they provide: nutrient cycling, water purification, natural flooding defence.

The story of biodiversity policies in Europe is a story of shrinking scope: from the exotic and global (policies to protect elephants and seal pups), to the local (making the link between biodiversity and quality of life). Until recently in the hands of member states, biodiversity policy was never a core community competence. Unlike water quality, air, waste and acidification for example, there has been no obvious relationship between protecting nature and building the single market. This is changing with a greater realisation that the protection of natural resources—air, water and soil—on which everyone depends, is important at a European level, and this is inextricably linked with the careful management of European landscapes and biodiversity. It is also because our collective understanding of what biodiversity is has changed: it is something that enriches our home place, enhances our local area and benefits quality of life. These things are, it seems, worth legislating for.

## The Wild Birds and Habitats Directives

The EU's biodiversity policy centres on two key pieces of legislation: the 1979 Wild Birds Directive (79/409/EEC) which aims to protect wild birds and their habitats, and the 1992 Habitats Directive designed to protect natural habitats and wildlife. Several other laws developed during the 1980s illustrated the global character of many EU activities in this area, and had significant public support, for example a ban on the import of seal pup skins (Directive 83/129) and products from whales (Regulation 348/81), and a ban on African elephant ivory imports (Regulation 2496/89). This was also a time when the European Community became party to international laws including the Convention on International Trade in Endangered Species of Fauna and Flora (CITES), which was opened for signature in Washington DC in 1973, and which the Community implemented in 1982.

By the 1990s, protected areas existed in a confusing array of categories developed under various international conventions, the Wild Birds Directive (see Background box 18.6) and national laws. The need for a more strategic approach to wildlife and habitat management, integrated with policies on fisheries, forestry, transport, tourism and above all agriculture, was becoming clear. Momentum gathered in 2001. When EU heads of state and government launched the EU Sustainable Development Strategy in Gothenburg, they declared that the decline in biodiversity must be halted by 2010. A 2010 target also exists at the international level: during the 2002 World Summit on Sustainable Development in Johannesburg, world leaders committed themselves to significantly reducing global biodiversity loss by 2010. The aim of EU policy is to reach these targets and to include nature protection into other policy areas, such as farming, fishing and industry.

## BACKGROUND BOX 18.6

### Twenty-five Years of the Wild Birds Directive

Directive 79/409/EEC, the Wild Birds Directive, is a key piece of European conservation legislation. Birds have always been the stars of the biodiversity world: they are a high-profile and popular group, such that legislating for their protection enjoys plenty of public support. Their protection benefits many other, less 'famous' creatures and plants—the general public of the biodiversity world—that share their habitats.

The Directive's twenty-fifth anniversary was celebrated during November 2004 at a conference in the Netherlands. Taking stock of the Directive's effects during this time, BirdLife International's new study, *Birds in Europe*, reveals that 226 species of birds—no less than 43 per cent of all those occurring regularly in Europe—are facing an uncertain future. Some species are now so threatened that they may disappear from parts of Europe altogether in the very near future. Some familiar urban birds such as the house sparrow and the common starling have declined to such an extent that they are no longer seen on our garden birdtables or city rooftops. Many waders, including the northern lapwing, have declined as a result of drainage of lowland river valleys and upland habitat. Migratory birds wintering in sub-Saharan Africa and farmland birds such as the corn bunting are also rarer. On the other hand, BirdLife notes that the Directive's measures appear to have contributed to the increased numbers of 14 bird species. Better protection has benefited Audouin's gull, once one of continental Europe's most threatened seabirds, together with the Eurasian griffon and the white-tailed eagle, two of Europe's largest birds of prey.

The principal policy tool in achieving this aim is the 1992 Habitats Directive (92/43), which aimed to protect Europe's wildlife species and their habitats. (See Background box 18.7.) It also aimed to develop a single network of protected areas across Europe. Despite delays, each member state's list of its Special Areas of Conservation (SACs) was finalised in 2006 but the full implementation of Natura 2000 will be a very expensive affair. However, the new regulations for the Structural and Rural Development funds may offer opportunities in this regard.

## BACKGROUND BOX 18.7

### Implementing the Habitats Directive

The EC Habitats Directive aims to conserve natural habitats and wild fauna and flora within the European Union. Member states must propose sites for protection of the habitats and species listed in the Annexes to the Directive. In such a region of intensive land use and population density as the European Union, the establishment of such a network is a very ambitious goal.

Designation of sites has proved to be a slow process, beset by conflicts between site designation and infrastructural developments, difficulties in agreeing appropriate management solutions, and local objections due to fears that landowners' activities will be curtailed. Despite serious delays, more than 15 per cent of the EU's territory was in 2006 proposed for or included in Natura 2000 (European Commission 2006).

The planned network of sites has been completed by more than 80 per cent. By September 2004, Belgium and the Netherlands had fully completed their site proposals for protecting all the species and habitats of the Directive occurring in their countries. (Marine species and habitats are not considered.) Progress in the remaining member states is good, and now seven additional member states (Denmark, Greece, Italy, Luxembourg, Spain, the UK and Sweden) have more than 90 per cent sufficiency in proposing sites. Three member states (Finland, Ireland and Germany) have decreased in sufficiency since November 2003, having deleted sites from their previous proposals.

The EU's Wild Birds Directive, despite having been around for 25 years, continues to be a relevant and important tool for these more recent and integrated developments in the management of Europe's biodiversity. (See Background box 18.6.) It requires member states to complete and appropriately manage a network of Special Protection Areas (SPAs) for birds. The broader importance of this is that many of these SPAs are areas of high nature value, harbouring a range of habitats and species that can benefit, hitch-hikerlike, from the attention attracted by the birds that frequent the region. However, this highlights the danger of managing an area for the benefit of one species alone: management of the habitat needs to be managed with its varied complement of plants and animals in mind, not birds alone.

## KEY POINTS

- Environmental policy-making has become increasingly fragmented into discrete policy areas.

- Despite emerging scientific consensus, the debate over what actions to take on climate change is hotly contested.

- An effective policy framework has developed to tackle ground-level air pollution.

- Biodiversity policy offers major challenges for the EU with the Wild Birds and Habitats Directives making an important contribution.

# Conclusion

As we have noted, perhaps more than other policy areas, environmental policy exemplifies the benefits of European integration. Pollution is no respecter of national boundaries. It is possible to devise more effective policies to tackle, for example, the problems of the North Sea or the great European rivers such as the Danube and the Rhine if they are dealt with by one authority rather than by several different countries. Although member states may differ in the priority that they attach to environmental policy, there has been a shared adherence to the goal of creating a more sustainable environment in Europe. This may be diluted by the accession of less prosperous member states but, as they become better off, there will be an increasing demand from their own citizens for a better quality environment. (See Theme box: The Impact of Globalisation.)

This is an area in which Europe has a united voice on the international stage and often a very distinctive one, as has been evident in relation to climate change policy. Of course, a problem here has been the antipathy of the Bush administration in the USA to an environmental agenda, in large part based on concern about the effects on American growth and lifestyles. This, however, gives the EU an opportunity to articulate and pursue an alternative model to that of the USA and to offer a model of effective environmental policies in the rest of the world. Within Europe, environmental policy is an area in which the EU can demonstrate that it is bringing real benefits to European citizens that would not be available if the EU did not exist. It therefore offers a means of tackling the legitimacy deficit of the EU and the view held by many Europeans that it does not make any practical difference to their lives.

Nevertheless, we have also noted a number of challenges to environmental policy in the EU. Other objectives such as growth, employment and competitiveness are often given greater priority, fuelled by the persistence of high unemployment in many parts of Europe, although the pursuit of these objectives is by no means incompatible with a sustainable environmental policy. Non-governmental organisations have been very effective in the area of environmental policy because of the way in which they have been able to use evidence to back their

## The Impact of Globalisation

The EU has taken a leading role in securing and enforcing multilateral environmental agreements designed to tackle problems that extend beyond the borders of the continent: climate change, biodiversity loss, damage to the ozone layer, trade in toxic wastes and so on. The EU seeks to play a leading role in the pursuit of global sustainable development. It is the world's largest donor of development aid, the world's biggest trading partner, and a major source of direct private investment. But how do these globalised patterns of trade and consumption impact on the rest of the world?

The 'ecological footprint' concept is a useful indicator of Europe's demand on nature. It is calculated by estimating the total area of biologically productive land and sea required to provide the resources consumed by a population—food, clothing, housing, transport—and to assimilate the waste generated, using current technology.

Europe now uses ecological capacity from the rest of the world at almost twice the rate as it does within its own borders. In contrast to the global average demand of 2.2 global hectares per person, the European average in 2002 was 4.7 global hectares per person. Europeans rely on the biocapacity of the rest of the world to make up this growing deficit.

The EU buys inexpensive goods, often raw materials, and sells more processed, higher-value goods. The 'ecological rucksacks' made up of physical imports may be about twice as 'heavy' as all the materials used within Europe. This is reflected in Europe's ecological footprint: over the past 40 years, Europe has used about 75 per cent of its domestic biocapacity. But its use of ecological services from the rest of the world is three times this and increasing. In other words, Europe has a deficit in 'traded' biocapacity: we're displacing the impacts of our consumption beyond our borders.

---

arguments, but their influence may be on the wane. There is no longer a clearly identifiable group of 'green' leader states and many of the accession states face considerable difficulties in applying EU environmental standards. The reputation of the environment DG has, however, been enhanced by effective leadership and the increased influence of the Parliament in the policy-making process may offer new opportunities for greening EU policy.

Over time environmental policy has become less holistic in character and more organised around discrete policy areas based on distinct communities of expertise. Progress can be made in these compartmentalised policy areas as the examples of

biodiversity and ground-level air pollution show. Climate change is a more contested area in terms of knowledge, particularly outside the EU, and progress relies on securing international agreements that can be difficult to achieve. The precautionary principle was meant to provide an objective test for policy, but has to some extent become contested and politicised. Overall progress increasingly depends on how far environmental principles can be integrated into other areas of EU policy-making and also on the extent to which the developing jurisprudence of international trade law constrains environmental policy.

**? QUESTIONS**

1. Why should the EU be able to develop a more effective environmental policy than individual states working on their own?

2. Why is there a risk that environmental policy may slip down the policy agenda?

WYN GRANT AND JANE FEEHAN

3.  Why did the EU not have a treaty-based environmental policy until 1987?

4.  Who are the key actors in EU environmental policy-making?

5.  Why are non-governmental organisations particularly important in environmental policy-making?

6.  Why has environmental policy become more fragmented?

7.  How would EU citizens benefit from a policy to tackle ground-level air pollution?

8.  Why does the EU need a policy on biodiversity?

 **FURTHER READING**

■ **McCormick, J. (2001),** *Environmental Policy in the European Union*, **Basingstoke, Palgrave.** Provides a comprehensive overview of EU environmental policy.

■ **Grant, W., Matthews, D. and Newell, P. (2000),** *The Effectiveness of European Union Environmental Policy*, **Basingstoke, Palgrave.** Examines the effectiveness of EU environmental policy.

■ **Barnes, P. M. and Barnes, I. G. (1999),** *Environmental Policy in the European Union*, **Cheltenham, Edward Elgar.** A very thorough and systematic treatment of EU environmental policy.

■ **Weale, A. (1992),** *The New Politics of Pollution*. **Manchester, Manchester University Press.** A powerful and thought-provoking extended essay that tackles some of the key questions in environmental policy.

■ **Lowe, P. and Ward, S. (eds) (1998),** *British Environmental Policy and Europe*, **London, Routledge.** A collection of essays written by leading experts in various aspects of environmental policy.

■ **Zito, A. R. (2000),** *Creating Environmental Policy in the European Union*, **Basingstoke, Macmillan.** An analysis of the development of environmental policy in the EU.

■ **Golub, J. (ed) (1998),** *New Instruments for Environmental Policy in the EU*, **London, Routledge.** An examination of the move towards new policy instruments in environmental policy.

 **IMPORTANT WEBSITES**

● **www.europa.eu.int/comm/environment**  Access to comprehensive materials relating to EU policy on the environment.

● **www.un.org/documents/ga/conf151/aconf15126-1annex1.htm**  Text of the Rio Declaration.

● **http://europa.eu.int/comm/environment/eussd/**  Sustainable development strategy of the European Union.

● **www.eea.europa.eu**  The European Environment Agency's homepage.

**Visit the Online Resource Centre that accompanies this book for lots of useful additional material, including an interactive map of Europe. www.oxfordtextbooks.co.uk/orc/hay_menon/**

# 19 Migration Policy

RANDALL HANSEN

✓ **Reader's Guide**

Until 1945, European countries had little experience of non-white migration. Since then, all have become countries of immigration. This chapter examines immigration, immigration policy and the politics of immigration in Europe. It explains the key components of immigration; discusses the main post-war migration flows to Europe and how they affected European politics (including far-right politics); traces the recent new openness of some European countries to immigration; asks whether migration threatens social solidarity and the welfare state; and considers the European Union's emergent immigration policy framework. It argues that we are witnessing a subtle shift in Europe's policy towards migrants: whereas from 1973 until the 1990s, Europe treated its earlier waves of migrants with relative generosity while shutting out new migrations, since then Europe has become relatively open towards new migrants while hardening its attitude and policy towards old ones.

# Introduction

The 1990s and early years of the millennium have been a defining period in the political history of immigration policy and politics, as a number of events have converged to place immigration at the centre of the domestic and EU political agendas: major European states renounced their previous restrictionist paradigm and sought to expand avenues for labour migration; asylum applications increased, and in some cases (such as the UK) exploded; far-right political parties made further gains and for the first time joined national coalitions; and, finally, the EU made substantial strides in harmonising and communitarising aspects of immigration and asylum policy.

At the same time, this modest loosening of migration controls in the area of labour migration has been matched by a renewed concern in some EU member states about integration and by an intense suspicion of multiculturalism. Countries that had gone furthest in encouraging ethnic minorities to retain and publicly promote their own culture, language and religions—particularly the Netherlands—have reversed these policies. Both the Netherlands and Denmark have embraced a robust, and some would argue illiberal and intolerant, integration policy placing the onus squarely on migrants and their descendants to prove their 'fit' with—and loyalty to—their society. Since the mid-1990s, Europe has become something of the

mirror image of what it was. Whereas from 1973 until the 1990s, Europe treated old migrants with relative generosity while shutting out new migrants, since the 1990s Europe has become relatively open towards new migrants while hardening its attitude and policy towards old ones.

This chapter proceeds in six steps. First, it describes the components of immigration policy. Second, it places migration to Europe in its historical context, explaining how and why traditional European emigration countries became countries of immigration. Third, it reviews changes in immigration policy since the millennium. Fourth, it considers how immigration has shaped electoral and party politics in Europe. Fifth, it discusses the relationship between immigration and welfare policy. Finally, it examines the role of the European Union (EU) in the immigration and asylum fields.

## KEY POINTS

- Immigration is at the centre of national and European politics.

- European states have reversed a decades-long opposition to new immigration.

- States that had embraced multiculturalism have questioned this commitment.

# The Components of Migration Policy

Migration policies include a complex of informal and formal measures designed to govern the entry, stay and return of migrants. They include

- Visa policies. Visas cover transit and entry. Transit visas allow individuals to pass through

a third country, while tourist visas allow individuals to present themselves at the border of a country for temporary entry (which is usually granted). Within Europe, the Schengen visa allows individuals to enter and to travel freely within the 13 member states of the Schengen zone (the pre-2004 enlargement EU minus Ireland and the UK). Entry visas allow individuals to live and/or work in a third country for a limited or unlimited period of time. Other legal categories—Leave to Remain in the UK, the *carte de séjour* in France or the *Aufenthaltserlaubnis* in Germany—perform the same function as a visa by governing the length and/or conditions of residence. Visa policy thus cuts across the second and third components of migration policy.

- Policies governing temporary migration. There are three categories of temporary migrants: students, who are admitted for the duration of their course of study; temporary skilled or unskilled workers who enter for a fixed period of between a few months and several years (including seasonal workers); and migrants fleeing repression, war or natural catastrophe who are granted temporary protection.

- Policies governing permanent migration. Permanent migration streams are made up of skilled and unskilled workers, family members and categories of individuals granted privileged access to a particular country (Jewish migrants under Israel's law of return, ethnic migrants to Germany, or pre-1962 Commonwealth migrants to Britain).

- Policies governing refugees. Individuals given refugee status under the 1951 United Nations convention relating to the status of refugees are allowed to remain permanently, as are individuals denied this status but granted permanent residency on other humanitarian or compassionate grounds.

---

**KEY POINTS**

- Visa policies govern the transit and entry of migrants.

- Temporary migrants include students, skilled and unskilled workers.

- Permanent migration includes family migrants and labour migrants.

- Refugees are granted permanent residence and social/economic rights on the basis of a 1951 United Nations convention.

---

# Migration and Migration Policy in Context

Europe has for centuries been defined by a complex interplay of inward and outward migration. During the nineteenth century, tens of thousands of Germans, Britons, Italians and others left Europe for the USA and Australasia. By 1870, there were as many Irish abroad as there were in Ireland, and the island's survival depended on an explicit policy of emigration. After 1871, migrant workers, particularly Poles, were attracted to Germany by the country's industrial boom. At the same time, anti-Jewish agitation in Russia and Eastern Europe led to a refugee-like movement through Hamburg, to London, and

on to the USA. Many stayed in Hamburg and above all in the British capital, giving birth to London's East End Jewish communities and to a nativist backlash, one that has repeated itself with every new wave of migrants. During the inter-war period, the economic Depression, combined with a wave of immigration restrictions in major receiving countries, led to a sharp decline in international migration.

The most numerically significant migration to Europe, and the one that continues to define Europe's politics to this day, occurred after 1945. It was a market-driven phenomenon: migrants travelled to and within Europe in response to the needs of the buoyant post-war economy, particularly in the Franco-German core. Migrants arrived in response to this demand through two distinct channels. The first were the **guestworker schemes** operated by Belgium, France, Germany, Austria, Switzerland, Sweden, Denmark and Norway. All these countries sought to fill labour shortages with migrants regarded as least troublesome and most likely to return: Southern Europeans. Large numbers of Italians, Greeks, Spanish and Portuguese migrated north for work. Once this initial pool of workers had been exhausted, these labour-importing countries had to look outside Western Europe. Austria, Switzerland and Germany had no colonies. As a result, they expanded their guest-worker programmes to include Yugoslavia and Turkey.

It was at this time that the second migration channel emerged. Unable to compete with Swiss and German wages, Britain, France and the Netherlands found themselves increasingly reliant on **colonial migration**. The process was a passive one insofar as none of these countries was keen to encourage large-scale, non-white colonial migration. Nonetheless, they all maintained citizenship and/or migration schemes that provided privileged access for colonial migrants. The combination of labour market demand and open or relatively open immigration channels could only have one consequence: West Indians and South Asians migrated to Britain, North Africans to France, and Surinamese to the Netherlands. Most of these migrants were young men, and they later brought their wives and had families. The same process occurred in the guestworker countries. Although many guestworkers did return home, enough stayed—3 million (out of 14 million) in the case of Germany—to ensure that, following **family reunification**, these countries would have substantial ethnic minority populations. Some half-hearted efforts were made to ensure the guestworkers' return, but these were blocked by domestic courts. A defining case was heard in Germany. It involved an Indian national who had entered Germany on a

temporary work visa, which he regularly renewed. As the deadline for his departure approached in 1972, he applied for German citizenship. While his application was pending, the authorities withdrew his work permit in 1973 on the grounds that he intended to stay in Germany permanently, and ordered his departure. The matter went before the constitutional court, however, which argued in a landmark 1978 decision that the repeated renewal of the work permit had built up a 'reliance interest' on his part. His deportation would thus violate the 'protection of legitimate interests' principle of Article 19 of the German constitution.

Up until the 1970s, post-war migration in Europe was a story of migration *within* and *to* Europe. Guestworkers were expected to return, but activist courts, imbued by a post-war, post-Holocaust concern for individual rights against a heavy-handed state, drew on national constitutions and jurisprudence to ensure their stay. For their part, colonial migrants entered in the main as citizens, and there was little question of compelling their return. All countries introduced incentives for voluntary return, but these programmes were limited, symbolic in intention (designed to placate the restrictionist right) and rarely used except by those migrants who had intended to return anyway. The result, by the mid-1970s, was a large and stable migrant population—numbering in the millions in the larger, Northern European states. When the European economy entered recession in the early 1970s, all the northern receiving countries ended **primary migration** (migrants who have no familial ties to the destination country) and limited new migration to family reunification. As a result, migration patterns stabilised, and migration was limited to a predictable core of yearly migration. This changed in the 1980s.

In 1951, a United Nations Convention was signed relating to the status of refugees. It was drawn up in response to the experience of the 1930s, when boat loads of Jewish refugees sailed the world vainly seeking a port that would allow them to land. The Convention defined a refugee as one who 'has a well-founded fear of persecution' on one or more grounds: race, religion, nationality, membership of a particular social group, or political opinion. An **asylum-seeker** is one who applies for asylum under the 1951 Convention; a **refugee** is one who is granted asylum under that convention (there are also individuals who are not given this status but who are allowed to remain: non-convention refugees). Those who signed the document are not obliged to grant asylum, but they are obligated not to return a refugee/asylum-seeker to a country where they face persecution (the **non-refoulement**) requirement. The document was originally temporally and geographically limited to events occurring before 1951 in Europe. A 1967 protocol to the Convention removed both restrictions.

From 1980, the new protocol interacted with a series of other factors to create what was known as the asylum crisis of the 1990s. Refugee-producing events (in Vietnam in the 1970s, Central America and Afghanistan in the 1980s, Yugoslavia in the 1990s) escalated; the price of intercontinental travel plummeted as its availability increased; other options for entering Europe legally disappeared; the end of the Cold War provided a new and large access point to Europe; and criminal organisations illegally transported migrants to Europe, often in appalling conditions, in exchange for a fee, indentured labour or both. These factors converged to create an explosion in asylum applications: whereas there were 175,000 applications for asylum lodged in Europe in 1985, the figure for 1992 was 695,000. Throughout these years, Germany's liberal and constitutionally entrenched right to asylum made it the preferred destination for asylum-seekers: 74,000 (42 per cent) of all 1985 asylum applications were lodged in Germany, as were 438,000 (63 per cent) of all 1992 applications. Germany amended its constitution in 1993, and asylum applications dropped to 128,000 in that year, but the Federal Republic and Europe as a whole continued to receive large numbers of asylum applications throughout the rest of the decade. In the UK, which processed as few as 5,800 applications in 1988, asylum applications rose sharply in the late 1990s, reaching 100,000 in 2000. The result, as during previous waves of migration, was a tabloid politicisation of the issue, a public backlash and a raft of anti-asylum policy measures.[1]

European states responded to increased numbers with a series of national and European responses:

- *Visa regimes* have been expanded. Any country that constitutes a substantial source of migration and asylum-seeking (Morocco, Nigeria, Rwanda, India, Pakistan, Russia and many others) will find its citizens subject to a visa requirement when visiting Europe.

- *Carrier sanctions* have been levelled on sea, air and land carriers that bring foreign nationals without proper documentation or visas to state territory. Austria, Belgium, Denmark, France, Germany, Italy and the UK all use such sanctions.

- *Pre-inspection regimes* in foreign countries preventing unwanted arrivals are another, more innovative, example of 'migration policy by remote control'. By the end of the 1990s, European states including the UK, Sweden and France had employed an advance guard of immigration staff, commonly referred to as airport liaison officers, in select foreign airports to detect potential illegal entrants. The Netherlands and Norway, among others, have sent immigration officials abroad to train airline staff at foreign airports to recognise fraudulent or incomplete documentation.

The primary goal of visa regimes, carrier sanctions and pre-inspection is to prevent the arrival of unwanted and illegal entrants.

While pre-inspection regimes *extend* migration boundaries, some states have also contracted their boundaries to evade asylum claims. Switzerland, France, Germany and Spain have all declared parts of their airports international zones. Such zones are established to function as areas in which officials are not obliged to provide asylum-seekers or foreign individuals with some or all of the protections available to those officially on state territory (for example the right to legal representation, or access to a review process) in order to enable speedy removal from the country. American use of Guantánamo Bay, at which the USA detained first Cuban refugees and then terrorist suspects, follows the same logic.

In summary, post-war migration to Europe occurred in three broad phases: colonial and guest-worker migrants from 1950 to 1973; family migrants from the 1960s to date; and asylum-seekers from the 1990s to date. The vast majority of migrants in Europe are connected directly (they have travelled themselves to Europe as family members or refugees) or indirectly (they are the descendants of colonial migrants or guestworkers) to these movements.

**KEY POINTS**

- Guestworker schemes were pursued by all major European receiving countries after the war, and account for the majority of post-war migrants to Germany, Austria and Switzerland from the 1950s to the 1970s.

- Britain, France and the Netherlands drew on their colonies to satisfy their post-war labour shortages in the 1950s, 1960s and 1970s.

- From the 1970s, family reunification dominated migration to Europe.

- Asylum-seekers migrated to Europe in larger numbers in the 1980s, and arrivals skyrocketed in the 1990s.

# Migration Policy in the New Millennium

In the 1990s, those writing on immigration policy in Europe emphasised, incessantly, its increasingly restrictive quality. As late as 2005, a Google search of 'immigration' and 'Fortress Europe' produced 76,000 hits. The phrase was repeated so often that it became a cliché, and those repeating it overlooked a subtle change in policy. Europe quietly shifted towards a moderately pro-immigration stance in the 1990s. The most dramatic cases of policy reversal occurred in Germany and the UK. Citing labour shortages in high-tech industries, Germany's SPD/Green coalition announced, in May 2000, a 'Green Card' visa programme granting well paid workers temporary visas. A year later, the interior minister proposed allowing a set number of skilled applicants to migrate to Germany each year, according to a quota and Canadian-style points system,[2] but avoided specifying any number. The skilled migrants would be offered permanent residence. After one failed attempt and lengthy negotiations with the opposition CDU/CSU (which held an upper house majority and which sought restrictions on asylum and a tougher return policy), Germany

introduced Europe's most comprehensive immigration bill: it provides for an unspecified number of skilled migrants to be admitted every year, channels them directly into permanent residence and provides funds for language training. (See Theme box: The Impact of Globalisation.)

**THEME BOX**

### The Impact of Globalisation

Immigration has for centuries been bound up with globalisation. During the age of empire (sometimes called 'Globalisation I') Europeans travelled to their colonies, and colonial workers travelled between colonies (such as the Indian workers who moved throughout the British Empire). Today, increasingly integrated capital and services markets ('Globalisation II') have led to two movements: an elite class of educated migrants who choose between the benefits packages offered by countries, and a mass of unskilled, badly paid migrants who fulfil the mundane jobs necessary to keep the service economy running (see Chapter 13, this volume).

Although receiving less attention, a similar shift occurred in Britain. Once described as Europe's only successful 'country of zero immigration' (Layton-Henry 1994), the British government had been encouraged to reconsider more open policies in the light of Germany's new openness to immigration. Responding to labour shortages, notably in the information technology (IT) sector, the Department of Education and Employment (DfEE, now the Department of Education and Skills) announced in May 2000 that British businesses would be given the power to bypass normal immigration rules and rapidly to employ non-European workers in areas of severe labour shortage, notably IT and health (especially nursing). In September of that year, the government announced new immigration rules easing the requirements for workers entering the country and allowing them to stay longer. The DfEE drew up a list of professions requiring labour, notably IT personnel, but also service staff such as Indian restaurant chefs. In January 2002, the Home Office introduced a programme allowing skilled foreign nationals to enter Britain. Modelled on the Canadian points system, it rewards education, work experience and earning. A month later, the new thrust of migration policy was confirmed by a 7 February 2002 white paper concluding that attracting skilled migration was important to secure the UK's prosperity. In 2002 and 2003, the number of work permits (the main scheme through which non-EU migrants enter the UK) granted reached a post-war high of approximately 135,000 (including dependents). The majority of migrants came to the UK under the work permit scheme. In 2006, the government introduced a points system, closely following the Canadian example, which consolidates all existing tiers of visa applications. Finally, the UK and Ireland were the only two EU countries that granted citizens of the ten new members of the EU an immediate right to work following accession in May 2004.

This shift was not restricted to Northern Europe; indeed, developments in Southern Europe have, in some instances, been still more striking. Altering a decades-old pattern in which large-scale illegal migration was followed by periodic legalisation programmes, Italy adopted its first avowedly pro-migration policy on 6 March 1998. The legislation allowed employers to hire foreign workers directly (including those in Italy illegally, if they left the country and re-entered with the requisite paperwork), and allowed public entities to sponsor migrants to come to Italy and look for work. The Berlusconi government abolished the second provision in 2002, but continued to allow employers to issue contracts—subject to national quotas—to foreign workers. Likewise, Spain adopted in 1993 a quota system for channelling labour migrants into specific regions and economic sectors; since 1994, some 30,000 worker permits are granted annually to immigrants already living in the country. In early 2005, Spain adopted a legalisation programme (following early programmes in 1986, 1991, 1996 and 2000–1) for hundreds of thousands of clandestine migrants resident in the country. Some 700,000 people applied by the deadline. The move prompted criticism from Spain's European partners, who feared the proposal would serve as a magnet for new migrants. At the same time, the government created a catalogue of high-demand jobs—truck-driving, catering, domestic labour and restaurant staff—for which employment visas were easily obtainable. The programme is notable in that it explicitly and publicly targeted unskilled workers. Previous immigration reforms in Europe (such as Germany's) have targeted skilled workers. By contrast, unskilled migration has been either quietly tolerated or regulated through low-profile bilateral accords.

These policy developments have been motivated by two concerns: immediate and prospective. In terms of the former, immigration policy was reformed in response to sectoral shortages in the high- (Germany, UK) or low-skilled (Spain, Italy) sectors of the economy. In the latter, policymakers have woken up to the dangers inhering in demographic trends. Britain, France, Italy, Spain and Germany all have birth rates below the replacement rate and, all things being equal, face an ageing population and (Britain and France excepted) probable population decline over the next 50 years. Whereas

336

in the 1950s there were two people under 20 for every one over 60 in Germany, demographers argue that, in the absence of immigration, the ratio would be reversed by 2050. Given low German birth rates, the population of a Germany without immigration would fall from 82 million to 52 million by that year. In the context of the country's generous pension and health system, Germany would face a crippling financial crisis due to a lack of tax revenue. Birth rates in Italy and Spain are lower still.

There has, of course, never been a Germany, or indeed a Europe, without immigration. Immigration can, however, at best temper demographic decline; it cannot prevent it. Its greatest effect is on population levels. Without immigration, Germany's population would have been in decline since the mid-1990s, while the vast majority of Britain's predicted increase in population over the next decades will come from immigration. Retaining the ratio between workers and retirees is an entirely different matter: maintaining current labour market participation levels requires a level of immigration that would be politically and sociologically impractical. In even the most optimistic scenarios, it can provide only a partial solution. In 2000, the United Nation's Population Division released a report, *Replacement Migration: Is It a Solution to Declining and Aging Populations?* Based on different scenarios, it provided estimates of how much migration

would be required to maintain the overall population and its working-age component. To retain its current population of 82 million by the middle of the century, Germany would need to accept 17.8 million net migrants, or 324,000 per year. To maintain the current size of its working-age population, it would need many more: 6,000 migrants per 1 million inhabitants per year, or approximately 480,000. No one believes that Germany, or any other country in Europe, could absorb so many migrants without radically altering its welfare policy. What's more, as migrant birth rates tend to converge over the medium term with those of the broader population, migration really only delays population ageing. Nonetheless, there is general recognition that while immigration cannot solve demographic problems, it can make coping with them easier.

**KEY POINTS**

- Northern and Southern European countries have expanded opportunities for migration.
- This new openness was motivated by immediate and long-term concerns.
- Labour shortages, particularly in the high-tech sector, were the immediate concern.
- The long-term concerns were demographic: ageing and in some cases declining populations.

# The Far-right Parties and Politics

Immigration is an issue around which the far right has mobilised. It is not the only one: far-right parties—the British National Party in the UK, the Freedom Party in Austria, the Republikaner/German People's Union/New Democratic Party in the Federal Republic of Germany, the National Front in France, the National Alliance party in Italy—are also motivated by national and

local concerns. In Germany, the far right opposes the country's assumption of responsibility for its crimes during the Second World War; in Austria, it rejects consensus politics and what it takes to be corruption endemic to grand coalitions; in France, it is hostile to any form of devolution or special status for Corsica. Nonetheless, hostility to immigration and foreigners is the one position that

## Democracy and Legitimacy

Migration raises several issues for democratic theory. Democracy is expressed through the nation state, and implies the capacity of nationals to control the borders of that nation state. At the same time, liberal democracy is based on a number of principles—procedural equality and basic human rights—that dictate the manner in which those controls are implemented and, in particular, how migrants are treated once on national soil. The legitimacy of an immigration control regime depends on public confidence in it. In the area of welfare policy, some have argued that large volumes of immigration undermine interpersonal trust and thus the legitimacy of wealth redistribution.

unites far-right parties across Europe. Hostility to European integration is a close second. (See Theme box: Democracy and Legitimacy.)

Although much has been written about the far right's inexorable rise, its basis of support has been largely stable in Europe. In France, the *Front national* achieved 15 per cent of the vote in the first round of the 1988 presidential elections, and its support has plateaued at that level. The dramatic events of the 2002 presidential election, in which Jacques Chirac and the *Front national*'s Jean-Marie Le Pen went through to the second ballot, were caused by an interaction of contingent factors and particularly by France's electoral system. This allows only the top two candidates to go ahead to the second ballot. This requirement usually leads to a large number of candidates from all parts of the political spectrum entering the first ballot, followed by a clear left/right division in the second. In 2002, however, the French left splintered between numerous parties, allowing Le Pen to squeak through just ahead of the Socialist candidate Lionel Jospin. The final ballot was written up in the press as a battle for the very soul of France, but the result was a foregone conclusion: Jacques Chirac swept the election with 80 per cent of the vote.

The far right's support has been similarly stable in other European countries. In Germany, neither the Republikaner, the German People's Union (DVU), nor the New Democratic Party (NPD) ever breaks the 5 per cent threshold nationally. The far right saw a drop in support during the 2002 general election, which occurred in the middle of a recession. Periodically one of the parties enjoys breakthroughs of 5–15 per cent locally (such as 1998, when the DVU garnered 12.9 per cent of the vote in Saxony-Anhalt state elections), but these are generally reversed at the next election. In Britain, where the far right faces the discouraging effects of Britain's electoral system (the plurality system punishes small parties with a vote evenly distributed across the country), neither the National Front nor the British National Party has secured more than a few percentage points at each general election since 1979.

If the far right's support has been largely stable since 2000, it has not been entirely so. Two developments marked a break with post-war far-right politics in Europe. The first was the decision by Austria's Christian Democratic Chancellor Wolfgang Schlüssel to form a coalition with Jorg Haider's Freedom Party, rather than renewing its coalition agreement with the social democrats. The Freedom Party had done particularly well, securing 27 per cent in the 1999 parliamentary election, on the back of anti-immigration sentiment, opposition to EU enlargement (Austria lay on the EU's eastern border), and frustration with decades of grand coalition rule. Schlüssel's decision provoked mass protests across Europe and in Austria itself, and led to a short-lived decision on the part of the rest of the European Union to cease cooperation with Austria. Europe's leaders made a point of ostentatiously ignoring Schlussel at EU summits, but they eventually found this practice, and the non-cooperation regime more generally, unworkable. Both ended by the summer of 2000, though the coalition remained unchanged. In the end, the Freedom Party was kept away from the interior and foreign affairs ministries, and had little effect on policy. Schlüssel's Faustian pact appeared to pay off: the Freedom Party was reduced to 10.7 per cent of the vote in the 2002 parliamentary elections, and did worse still in regional elections. Schlüssel's party increased its support correspondingly, and the Chancellor has subsequently been able to largely ignore the Freedom Party. In 2005, the Freedom Party split, and Schlüssel immediately transformed his coalition with the Freedom Party into cooperation with the splinter party, the Alliance for the Future of Austria.

The second development was the meteoric rise of the Danish far right. In 2001, the Danish People's Party, which had been formed only six years previously, stunned everyone by winning 22 seats and becoming the third largest party in the Danish Parliament. The party threw its support behind the conservative–liberal coalition in exchange for a series of hard-line immigration policies. Shortly thereafter, Denmark adopted some of the most restrictive immigration polices in Europe. New legislation abolished the right to asylum on humanitarian grounds (Denmark had until then among the highest recognition rates for refugees in Europe), restricted the grounds under which asylum-seekers could claim refugee status under the 1951 convention, and cut social rights for asylum-seekers by some 30 per cent. The legislation also tightened the rules on family reunification, effectively creating a three-year waiting period and introducing an 'attachment requirement' (the need to provide evidence of attachment to Denmark). Finally, the law tightened the rules on naturalisation, requiring applicants to pass a stringent language test.

---

**KEY POINTS**

- Far-right parties are united across Europe in their opposition to immigration.

- Far-right support has stabilised in France and Germany.

- Far-right parties came to power in Denmark and Austria.

- Proportional representation and the need to govern by coalition makes far-right political gains easier on the continent of Europe than in the UK.

---

# Islam, Immigration and the Turn from Multiculturalism

Since 11 September 2001, migration policy has been affected by a renewed concern with terrorism and Islamic extremism. This concern affects all of Europe, but does so particularly forcefully in countries directly affected by either. EU member states have responded to this concern in two ways: through expanded police powers and through a renewed policy interest in minority integration. The effect on immigration policy itself was less than originally predicted: the trend has been modestly expansive. Following the events in New York and Washington, and particularly following terrorist attacks in Madrid and London, EU member states have expanded powers of detention and deportation. In Germany and the UK, high-profile radical Islamists have been arrested and deported. In the UK, the home secretary, shortly after 9/11, passed legislation giving the UK the right to detain indefinitely terror suspects whom it could not deport. In 2004, the House of Lords ruled that indefinite detention violated the European Convention on Human Rights. In 2005, the government proposed to replace the provision with legislation allowing terrorists to be detained for 90 days without charge, but the proposal was defeated in the House of Commons.

Following riots in the UK and France in late 2005, 'integration', once almost a dirty word, has again been on the lips of politicians and journalists. It is, however, the Netherlands that presents the starkest example of this development. Since 2001, two public figures grounded their opposition to further immigration in the threat of Islamic extremism, and both paid for it with their lives. The first was Pym Fortuyn. Fortuyn was the most intriguing anti-immigrant candidate in European politics because he did not hail from the usual morally conservative, anti-European, xenophobic right. He was, rather, an openly gay politician who embedded his opposition to Muslim immigration in a defence of Dutch progressive values. Because of Muslims' failure to reconcile themselves to secular, liberal Europe, he argued, they represented a threat to the rights achieved by, among others, Dutch gays and women. It was the sort of anti-immigration sentiment that confused the left. Before the electoral and political appeal of such a position could be tested, Fortuyn was gunned down by a radical vegan Volkert Van der Graaf who claimed to be acting on behalf of Muslims. Fortuyn's party secured a high sympathy vote at the elections, which took place shortly after his murder, but has foundered since.

If Fortuyn's assassination shocked the Netherlands, a subsequent murder shook the country to its core. On 2 November 2004, the controversial filmmaker Van Gogh was taking his usual bicycle path to work. A 26-year-old Dutch-Moroccan national Mohammed Bouyeri was waiting at the side of the road. He stepped out and shot Van Gogh eight times. The film-maker crawled to the side of the road, turned to face his attacker, and begged for mercy. Bouyeri unsheathed two swords, and slashed van Gogh's throat. He implanted the knives in van Gogh's body, pinning a note threatening Jews, western governments and Hirsi Ali—author of the controversial short film *Submission*, which showed partially clothed and bleeding women with misogynist Qur'anic verses. Van Gogh had directed the film which, along with his habit of referring to Muslims

as 'goat f\*\*kers', made him a controversial figure, and the object of intense radical Islamist hatred.

The murder had particularly significant ramifications in the Netherlands—the European country that hitherto had taken multiculturalism most seriously. It was among the first in Europe officially to embrace the concept in the early 1980s, and—drawing on structures employed during the pillarisation area—encouraged migrant groups to organise along ethnic lines. The Dutch government subsidised a wide spectrum of migrant organisations on an ethnic and religious basis; co-opted their leaders in ethnicity-based representative councils; aired children's programmes in four languages; fully funded education in migrants' 'own language and culture'; and allowed Muslims and Hindus to establish dozens of separate denominational schools (Koopmans 2005). At the same time, the country did not (in this respect in common with much of Europe) pursue avowedly integrationist policies. Following the murders, Dutch policymakers initiated a volte-face: new *and* settled immigrants are forced to pass an integration test; newcomers who fail to do so within five years will be fined. Rules on family reunification were also tightened: the minimum age for spousal immigration was raised to 21, and the sponsoring party must earn 120 per cent of the minimum wage. The policy shifts were embedded in a broader paradigm shift: policymakers officially declared multiculturalism a failure, and explicitly embraced 'integration' as a policy aim.

A milder version of this shift is also discernible in the UK. Following riots between Asian and white gangs in northern England, the government made naturalisation dependent upon a language test, a citizenship exam and an oath of allegiance. In July 2005, four men—all of whom were Muslim and three of whom were British—blew themselves up on London's transport system. Four months later, riots broke out between members of Birmingham's black and Asian communities. The riots were triggered by a rumour that a young Black girl had been raped by between three and 25 Asians. The violence left one man, a 23-year-old bystander, dead, and 35 seriously injured. These events and evidence of endemic socio-economic deprivation among some (but certainly not all) ethnic minority communities have led many to question the UK's post-1997 embrace of multiculturalism. For many, as the head of the UK's Commission for Racial Equality (the body overseeing the implementation of race relations legislation), Trevor Phillips, put it in April 2004, multiculturalism is 'dead'.

Is it? On one level, it is absolutely not. The rights of ethnic minorities to practise their religion, speak their language, join ethnicity-based associations and lobby for group-based causes are fundamental to liberal democracy, in Europe and elsewhere. At the same time, it is widely viewed as illegitimate (in a way that it was not before the Second World War) to force a dominant culture upon minority groups. It is not at all clear what that culture would be anyway: a far-left Berlin devotee of the capital's leather scene will share few cultural references with a deeply religious CSU-voting Bavarian farmer. All anyone else can agree is that both have the right to live their lives as long as they do not prevent the other from doing the same. To this degree, multiculturalism flows from liberalism: it manifests itself in group-based claims and activities, but they derive their logic and justification from individual rights, grounded in national constitutions and defended by the courts.

On another level, there have been two important paradigmatic and policy shifts. The first is a new concern with language. In a service-based economy, mastery of the national language is a perquisite to educational and economic success and thus to integration. As a result, across Europe governments have introduced language tests for naturalisation, increased funding for language training and scaled back policies that allowed or encouraged separate language schools. Second, commentators, governments and citizens have reacted against multicultural (or putatively multicultural) policies that privilege group claims over individual claims. Critics react to forced closings of plays in Birmingham (in response to Sikh protests), to the extension of the British Public Order Act to cover religions as well as racial hatred, and even to the murder of van Gogh because in all of these instances there is a danger of placing the good of multiculturalism before the right of liberalism.

Given the current almost trendy hostility towards multiculturalism, it is importance not to exaggerate the 'ism's' importance. In the same way that Canadian commentators tend to overstate the role of Canada's official multiculturalism in Canada's relative success in immigrant integration,[3] some European critics lay the blame for all the ills that plague ethnic minority integration at the door of multiculturalism. The Netherlands' early embrace of multiculturalism failed to ensure lower unemployment, better educational achievement or less spatial segregation than other European countries. In an important paper, Ruud Koopmans (2003) argues that against all these measures the Netherlands does worse than Germany, which has long been criticised for failure to accommodate its Turkish population. Yet nor is the rejection of multiculturalism a guarantee of minority integration. Policymakers in France have traditionally been highly sceptical of multiculturalism and group-based claims, and the country has a more robustly integrationist ideology than Germany or Britain. Neither has been a notable success: ethnic minorities in France have lower educational attainments, suffer high levels of unemployment, and are spatially segregated in the suburbs that were the scenes in 2005 of France's worst rioting since 1968. Neither pillarised Dutch multiculturalism nor republican French integrationism has worked particularly well.

---

**KEY POINTS**

- After 2001, the immigration debate in Europe has been affected by concerns over terrorism and religious extremism.

- Two high-profile murders have led the Netherlands to abandon its commitment to multiculturalism in favour of a more integrationist approach.

- The July 2005 terrorist attacks in London, in which British citizens were involved, has solidified a rhetorical turn away from multiculturalism in the UK.

# Immigration and Welfare

In 2004, the editor of *Prospect*, David Goodhart, made national headlines by arguing that excessive levels of immigration would undermine social solidarity, the willingness of one citizen/resident to pay for another, and thus the welfare state. Goodhart cites American research showing that hostility to economic redistribution in the USA is a function of racial heterogeneity (the poor are disproportionately Blacks and other minorities, and voters view distribution to them as unappealing) (Alesina *et al.* 2001). The article was reproduced in *The Guardian*, and provoked strong views in favour and against. The argument is not a new one: people have long worried about the impact of immigration on a community's character and cohesion, and in 1998 Milton Friedman declared: 'It's just obvious that you can't have free immigration and a welfare state.'

The Goodhart–Friedman claim is debatable. Above all, Goodhart's use of the evidence is selective. By his own admission, Denmark and Sweden (whose homogeneity he exaggerates) suggest conflicting hypotheses: both have generous welfare states, but Sweden has sought to incorporate migrants/minorities into welfare while Denmark sought to exclude them. The results of the US research are also not as clear-cut as Goodhart suggests. The authors argue that racial heterogeneity, *and* majoritarian institutions *and* a peculiarly American belief (not shared in Europe) that the poor are lazy rather than unfortunate *collectively* explain the USA's limited welfare state. One could also add that one of the most popular social programmes in the USA—social security—is universal rather than means-tested. Finally, racial heterogeneity in the USA does not result, as in Europe, solely from immigration, but from a long history of slavery and segregation. This experience may have generated political dynamics and sentiments that make it poorly comparable with Europe.

Does this suggest that Goodhart is wrong? Not entirely. As so often, the academic jury is out. On the one hand, there is as yet no clear evidence that immigration undermines support for the welfare state. In France, Germany, the Netherlands and Scandinavia, strong support for the welfare state combines with high levels of immigration and ethnic diversity. The clearest case of the welfare retrenchment in Europe—the UK—had little to do with immigration (though the great retrencher, Margaret Thatcher, thought little of the poor and less of immigrants). On the other hand, academic research does seem to show that high levels of diversity do correlate with lower levels of interpersonal trust ('social capital', in the currently fashionable phrase) (Costa and Kahn 2002). It is possible, but by no means certain, that these lower levels of interpersonal trust will undermine support for redistributive welfare policies. There is as yet no case for restricting immigration on the basis of such speculative arguments.

> **KEY POINTS**
>
> - Some commentators are concerned that increased immigration will undermine social cohesion and the welfare state.
>
> - Continental European countries combine strong support for welfare with high levels of immigration.
>
> - Academic research shows that ethnic diversity is related to lower levels of interpersonal trust.

# Migration at the EU Level

Parallel to these national developments, the European Union has furthered its role in immigration policy. (See Theme box: The Impact of the European Union.) The EU plays a key role in regulating the free movement of EU citizens within the EU as well as in asylum and immigration policy. In the latter cases, the most significant developments occurred in the post-1995 period. The Schengen agreement which took effect in that year, abolished border checks among the 13 participating states. The agreement also created a common Schengen visa, and expanded police cooperation (including the right to pursue suspected criminals into another country's territory). The 1990 Dublin Convention, which took effect seven years later, attempted to prevent 'asylum shopping' (asylum-seekers applying for refugee status in multiple member states) by requiring them to apply in the first EU country they reach and in establishing a (largely ineffective) mechanism for returning asylum-seekers to this first country.

The 1997 Amsterdam Treaty committed EU member states to maintaining and developing the Union as an area of freedom, security and justice. Rights to movement and residence across the EU are basic to this commitment. The Treaty took the furthest step towards 'supranationalising' migration policy: it partially communitarised the policy area, bringing the Schengen agreement and key elements of the Dublin Convention out of the intergovernmental third pillar and into the European Community. Following a five-year transitional period that ended in 2004, decisions in these areas are governed by qualified majority voting (a 71 per cent weighted vote in the Council of Ministers). At Tampere in 1999, the European Council committed itself to implementing a 'comprehensive approach' to managing migration flows based on fair treatment of third-country nationals, partnerships with countries of origin and a common policy for asylum. In the last, the Council issued a call for a common European asylum system by 2004. The common system was meant to equalise burdens across the EU and to avoid 'asylum shopping' by offering one access point to the same basket of legal, social and economic entitlements. Since then, there has been fitful, but by no means insignificant, progress in the development of an EU migration policy. By 2004, the EU had agreed to a 'reception directive' harmonising policy towards asylum-seekers; a 'qualification directive' and 'asylum proceedings directive' (creating common standards on recognising refugees and for granting them social rights).

The EU has also made progress on the other two policy areas. In 2004, a Council Directive calling for the harmonisation of the rights of third-country nationals with those of citizens took effect, with an implementation deadline of January 2006. Like all directives, however, it contains many qualifications and leaves the member states substantial discretion. The EU and individual member states have also expanded avenues for international cooperation between sending, transit

---

**THEME BOX** ⚠

## The Impact of the European Union

The EU plays a key role in regulating the movement of EU citizens across the Union, in asylum and in immigration policy. The Schengen agreement, which took effect that year, abolished border checks within the EU and established a common visa. The 1990 Dublin Convention tackled 'asylum shopping' by limiting asylum-seekers to one application at their first point of entry in the EU. More recently, the 1997 Amsterdam Treaty partially communitarised migration policy, and the EU committed itself to a common asylum system and a 'comprehensive approach' to managing migration flows.

and receiving states. The EU joined the 'Budapest process', which encouraged Central and Eastern European countries (particularly accession countries) to reform their visa policies, border policies and policies on international crime and the trafficking of migrants. France, Spain, Italy, Portugal and Malta also joined the '5 + 5 dialogue', through which they discuss common approaches to north–south migration with Algeria, Libya, Mauritania, Morocco and Tunisia. These arrangements reflect the general recognition in Europe that managing migration requires the participation of all countries—sending, receiving and transit—involved. Their effect on policy is, however, variable, and they clearly work best when European countries have a carrot to offer sending countries in exchange for reformed emigration and immigration controls. The most attractive carrot has been EU membership itself, which cannot be offered indefinitely (see Chapter 21, this volume).

**KEY POINTS**

- The EU plays a substantial role in immigration and asylum policy.
- Thirteen EU member states have abolished border controls and adopted a common visa policy.
- The Dublin Convention and its successors limit asylum-seekers to one application at the first point of entry in the EU.
- The EU and its member states have expanded cooperation in immigration control with sending and transit countries.

# Conclusion

Immigration is now at the centre of European politics, and presents the EU and its member states with three distinct challenges. The first is the need to cope with the failure of integration—characterised by high levels of unemployment, chronic poverty and pockets of intense alienation (manifested in riots in the UK in 2001 and France in 2005)—of second- and third-generation migrants. Their parents found themselves ill-equipped to cope with post-1973 changes in the European economy and a complex of factors has limited their capacity to enjoy economic success and to participate fully in political life. Second, they must confront Islamic extremism, which—in its vilification of Jews, its denial of full rights to women and its hatred of homosexuals—is anathema to Europe's basic values. Yet they need to do so in a manner that does not compromise their values: Europe's large Muslim communities, the vast majority of which view violence with the same abhorrence as everyone else, are part of Europe, and efforts to ensure that their members are able to live free of abuse, intimidation and violence must be redoubled. In this context, high-profile deportations of foreign radical Muslims may be necessary, and may play a role in reassuring public opinion, but they themselves risk giving the impression to the moderate Muslim majority that the state's approach is invariably based on heavy-handed police tactics, repression and securitisation. Similarly, British proposals for detention without charge not only violate basic common law principles; they risk further alienation of elements of the Muslim community. Finally, European governments have to prepare themselves for the next wave of immigration: the looming demographic shortfall, and attendant skills shortages and pension requirements, means that Europe needs immigrants; it can only accommodate them, however, if its economic and social policies are reformed.

# Notes

1. The next two paragraphs draw heavily on Gibney and Hansen (2005).
2. The Canadian system assigns intending migrants a series of points for factors such as education, language skills and age (the target population being young, educated migrants), and defines a minimum number of points. Applicants' points are then tallied up, and if they are above this bar they are granted entry to Canada.
3. On this, see Joppke and Morawska (2003).

## QUESTIONS

1. Why and how did European countries become countries of immigration?
2. What role does the far right play in national politics?
3. Why did asylum applications sharply increase in the 1980s and 1990s?
4. What role does the EU play in immigration and asylum policy?
5. How can the shift from 'intergovernmental' to 'supranational' EU responses to migration be explained?
6. Have EU countries turned from embracing multiculturalism to demanding integration? If so, why?

## FURTHER READING

### BOOKS
#### History

■ **Green, S. (2004), *The Politics of Exclusion: Institutions and Immigration Policy in Contemporary Germany*, Manchester, Manchester University Press.** Provides comprehensive overview of immigration and citizenship policy in Germany.

■ **Hansen, R. (2000), *Citizenship and Immigration in Postwar Britain*, Oxford, Oxford University Press.** Based heavily on archival sources, this book traces the UK's transformation into a multicultural society.

■ **Weil, P. (1995), *La France et ses étrangers*, Paris, Gallimard.** Provides a comprehensive overview of immigration to France, and furnishes evidence that French President Giscard d'Éstaing sought to encourage the return of colonial migrants.

#### Immigration policy and asylum

■ **Cornelius, C. *et al.* (eds) (2004), *Controlling Immigration: A Global Perspective*, Palo Alto CA, Stanford University Press.** Examines immigration policy in the traditional countries of immigration, in Europe, and in Japan and South Korea.

■ **Gibney, M. (2004),** *The Ethics and Politics of Asylum*, **Cambridge, Cambridge University Press.** Combines an account of asylum policy in the main receiving countries with an original normative account of asylum.

■ **Gibney, M. and Hansen, R. (eds) (2005),** *Immigration and Asylum from 1900 to the Present*, **Santa Barbara CA, ABC- CLIO.**

■ **Helton, A. C. (2005),** *The Price of Indifference*, **Oxford, Oxford University Press.**

### Far-right politics

■ **Eatwell, R. (2004),** *Western Democracies and the New Extreme Right Challenge*, **London, Routledge.**

■ **Messina, A. (2005), 'Far-right Parties', in M. Gibney and R. Hansen (eds),** *Immigration and Asylum from 1900 to the Present*, **Santa Barbara CA, ABC-CLIO.** A detailed encyclopedia entry providing a succinct introduction to far-right parties and their fortunes in Europe.

■ **Ignazi, P. (2003),** *Extreme Right Parties in Western Europe*, **Oxford, Oxford University Press.**

### European Union

■ **Geddes, A. (2003),** *The Politics of Migration and Immigration in Europe*, **London, Sage.** The key source on the EU's evolving immigration policy.

■ **Guild, E. (2004),** *The Legal Elements of European Identity: EU Citizenship and Migration Law*, **New York, Kluwer Law International.** Provides a detailed legal overview of EU citizenship and the Europeanisation of migration policy.

■ **Joppke, C. (1998),** *Challenge to the Nation-state*, **Oxford, Oxford University Press.** Presents and evaluates the main theoretical positions on immigration and integration policy.

## JOURNALS

*Ethnic and Racial Studies*

*International Migration Review*

*Journal of Ethnic and Migration Studies*

 **IMPORTANT WEBSITES**

● **http://migration.ucdavis.ca**  Migration News provides updates of the most important immigration and integration developments in the preceding quarter.

● **www.unhcr.ch**  The website of the United Nations refugee agency provides up-to-date information on refugee and refugee-like situations around the world, and contains a wealth of research reports and statistics.

● **www.georgetown.edu/sfs/programs/isim/index.html**  The Institute for the Study of International Migration's website provides links to free publications, as well as information on migration-related conferences and other events.

 **Visit the Online Resource Centre that accompanies this book for lots of useful additional material, including an interactive map of Europe.**
**www.oxfordtextbooks.co.uk/orc/hay_menon/**

# 20 Competition and Industrial Policy

## LEE MCGOWAN

### Chapter Contents

- Introduction
- Competition Policy: Emergence and Ascendancy
- Industrial Policy
- Conclusion: Pursuing Competitiveness
- Notes

### Reader's Guide

Fewer areas of contemporary European public policy may appear so initially unappealing than the study of both competition and industrial policy. Both, however, are fascinating in their own right and go to the very heart of economic governance. They matter and when considered together reveal the different strategies that have been pursued by Western European governments since 1945 to bolster economic growth and competitiveness. Accounting for the misfit between significance and actual interest may find explanation in a variety of factors: partly, the substantial volume of material on both; partly, the more dominant presence of other academic disciplines, notably economics and law, in these two areas; and partly, the salience of more seemingly attractive policy areas. Competition and industrial policies matter. They have been *en vogue* at different time periods and deployed to varying degrees across states. Which approach is better served to promote employment and secure prosperity has until recently been a major bone of contention in the respective views of capitalism and government/industry relations in the states of Western Europe (consider the contrasting position in France and the UK). Competition policy has gradually exerted itself as the dominant force. In contrast, support for industrial-policy considerations have diminished. This chapter explores both policies and accounts for the rationale behind them at the European level and sets their changing fortunes within the context of an increasingly globalised environment.

# Introduction

The ultimate purposes of both competition and industrial policies are similar insofar as they seek to stimulate economic growth and foster competitiveness, but the means to this end have been approached in different ways and means. In retrospect, both competition and industrial policies have found favour at different times and to varying degrees in recent European economic history. They have been deployed as alternative solutions to aid industry. A degree of tension (and this is essentially the leitmotif of this chapter) has often existed between the older concept of industrial policy (that was largely synonymous with a steered economy, interventionism and even outright protectionism) and competition policy (about rationalisation and increased efficiency). The latter has emerged as the driving ethos and mantra since the mid-1980s in promoting competitiveness and even compelled a rethink of industrial-policy considerations. But what are competition and industrial policies?

From the 2007 perspective, industrial policy can broadly be defined as a wide range of government action and intervention that seeks to promote competitiveness and efficient industrial structures. It is **dirigiste** in style and confers preferential treatment on targeted industrial sectors which assumes various guises, for example, in the form of monies allocated to research and development (R&D), government procurement programmes, education and infrastructure initiatives, tax incentives, export assistance schemes or, more controversially, efforts to provide special assistance to particular industries or firms through the means of direct or indirect subsidies. Competition policy, on the other hand, strives to secure the maintenance of genuinely competitive markets and is predicated on the conviction that a state of genuine competition between firms unleashes dynamic effects that result in greater efficiencies, innovation and, ultimately, lower prices for the consumer. The notion of fair and free competition has a long pedigree that can be traced back to early economists in the late 1700s and early 1800s, such as Adam Smith and David Ricardo. Both thinkers regarded competition and free trade as basic rights and decried all examples of protectionism as a scam and an example of overt nationalism that thwarted economic growth and progress. Such views on the functions of the economy find resonance today and underpin the turn to competition policy in the 1980s; competition policy is very much regarded as a precondition for a successful market economy.

The existence and operation of EU competition policy has come to epitomise the European integration process. Its rise has been enshrined not only in the development of individual domestic competition regimes, but also in an ever-growing and puissant series of European rules, that have ultimately impacted upon and transformed the domestic legislation itself. In marked contrast, industrial policy, which might have been expected to emerge as a leading EU policy competence, has remained very much more an uncoordinated and underdeveloped area of EU activity that is primarily the preserve of individual states. This reality owes much to the divergence in views and approaches within member states on the role of the state, but also the growing impact of globalisation and notions of **competitiveness**. There has been a noticeable shift away from industrial policy to competition policy as the predominant mode of economic governance in this area. It occurred essentially in the 1980s when the traditional notions of industrial policy became increasingly perceived as a synonym for protectionism that was deemed to be outmoded and no longer either defensible or sustainable in the context of globalisation.

It may seem strange in the early twenty-first century that the influence and salience of competition policy was not readily appreciated in the

1950s and 1960s. It took time, however, to develop and for most of its early history competition policy very infrequently hit the main policy radar screen. A sudden metamorphosis in the mid-1980s brought competition to the fore and this transformation finds explanation in a number of factors. First, timing was certainly crucial and changing economic philosophies (boosted by a **neo-liberal** agenda) pushed competition as a means to encourage innovation and efforts to restore European competitiveness, especially in the UK and West Germany. Second, the European Commission had matured sufficiently enough by this stage to assert its own analyses and powers and, third, was assisted by the rulings of the Court of Justice in Luxembourg and the accumulation of a considerable amount of competition case law. Personalities, as a fourth explanatory factor, also played a substantial part at the European level as a series of dynamic and forceful competition commissioners (including Peter Sutherland, Leon Brittan, Karel van Miert, Mario Monti and Neelie Kroes) all propelled competition forward as the only credible solution to European economic dynamism as vociferously as they challenged state intervention in the economy.

Finally, although competition policy was not specifically identified as a specific non-tariff barrier to be eradicated under the 1992 **single market programme** its pursuit was very much an integral aspect of the project. In short, national government mindsets and strategies on competitiveness had changed significantly enough during the 1980s and the coming of competition not only exerted

an irrevocable impact on the domestic competition arena, but also heralded a transformation in national approaches, albeit to varying degrees, to the acceptance and acceptability of industrial-policy tools. Clashes between both policies became inevitable and the tension, which also reverberated among the EU member states, centred on the forms of government support at aiding, protecting and preserving potentially uncompetitive, profit-losing or inefficient industries (such as aircraft manufacture, information technology and shipbuilding).

---

**KEY POINTS**

- Both competition and industrial policies represent contrasting visions of how governments have sought to establish and maintain successful and competitive enterprises.

- The study of competition policy has been a rather neglected area from a political-science perspective and has remained principally the preserve of law (developing case law and interpretation) and economics (theories of competition).

- This omission is curious as both the domestic and EU competition regimes are well established by a system of rules and regulations that embody a distinct system of competition governance.

- Industrial policy has long represented a feature of government activity though its use has varied considerably from state to state and there has been considerably much less industrial policy development at the EU level.

---

# Competition Policy: Emergence and Ascendancy

The pursuit of perfect competition has long been a cherished concept of classical economics where the market has been regarded as the most effective instrument to allocate resources and determine prices. Of course, much depends on the level of

competition within the market. Economic theory illustrates the argument through two ideal types. The first type refers to a world of perfect competition where the existence of numerous suppliers prevents any likelihood or possibility of collusive agreements to control price. This ideal model remains largely utopian in nature especially as the model assumes that the products are always homogeneous. The realities of many actual markets are typified more by models of imperfect competition (type 2), i.e. where considerably fewer players exist and can therefore determine price and do deliberately set out to thwart competition through the pursuit of anti-competitive agreements.

Consequently, a state of actual competition cannot simply be taken for granted even if there are ethical and social objections to the absence of competition. Markets can be manipulated by firms to deliberately distort the benefits and efficiencies of competition. In the lack of strict competition application and enforcement such incentives are easily lost and, without it, as the command-led economies of the former communist states in Eastern Europe readily illustrated, prosperity and growth suffer. Some firms resist such calls for competition and seek to undermine such objectives by engaging in a number of anti-competitive practices that include dividing up markets and fixing prices. Thus, the market has to be 'policed' and this in turn requires the establishment of an institutional regime and a clear system of rules and regulations that require strict enforcement. In practice, competition policy needs to strike a balance between the imposition, by legislation, of necessary restrictions upon unbridled economic competition, and the elimination of harmful restrictive practices that prevent a coherent integration of markets. (See Background box 20.1.)

## Competition policy in the European Union

From a European perspective the development of a competition-policy framework has been a gradual process and largely a post-war phenomenon. The foremost substantive steps towards the first coherent regimes developed in the UK (from 1948) and West Germany (from 1957).[1] From the outset the adoption of these policies reflected new thoughts on industrial structures and competitiveness and were influenced indirectly and directly by the well established US competition model (initiated under the Sherman and Clayton Acts in 1890 and 1914 respectively). This US **antitrust** legislation had sought to ensure that economic power (in the shape of banks, oil and railroad companies) was not concentrated in the hands of a few powerful trusts. Competition law essentially seeks to balance the perceived benefits of economic collaboration against the potential economic and political problems that could ensue. The UK, West German and the later national competition regimes in Europe would all differ slightly in terms of structure, institutional design and decision-making processes. For example, the main characteristic of the UK system (see Wilks 1999) is its institutional and statutory complexity. Considerable room was built into the process for substantial ministerial discretion. In contrast, the German system which was centred on the Federal Cartel Office was largely a bureaucratic and judicial model with some more limited possibility for ministerial control.

Despite such different approaches they all share the same objective of promoting competitive market structures and breaking up anti-competitive behaviour such as market-rigging, price-fixing cartels and abusive monopolies that were an endemic feature of the European business environment for the first half of the twentieth century. They remain very much a threat in the early twenty-first century. Consequently the national regimes often find themselves ill equipped to tackle and investigate international activities and this has led to both greater inter-regime cooperation and new modes of international competition governance. The notion of competition policy, for example, assumed central importance in the European integration process and found reflection in both the objectives of the European Coal and Steel Community of 1951 and the European Economic Community Treaty of 1957 (Cini and McGowan 1998). Article 3(g) of the EEC Treaty explicitly declared that competition should not be distorted in the common market while the substantive law was spelt out in Articles 81–90.[2]

## BACKGROUND BOX 20.1

### The Regulation of Competition Policy

| Requirements and issues | Actors |
| --- | --- |
| To promote economic efficiency | Requires regulators to provide an economic assessment. |
| To ensure the appropriate design of a competition policy regime (institutions and laws) | The setting up of independent national and EU regulatory agencies, such as the Office of Fair Trading in the UK and DG Competition. Their powers, procedures and responsibilities are established in relevant laws and statutes. |
| In order to deal with competition cases that transcend national borders it becomes necessary to seek international cooperation and establish international regimes | The EU developed a supranational competition regime, and common goals have led to a considerable degree of policy convergence of national competition laws to fit with the EU model. The pressure for common approaches has also led to, and so far unsuccessful, greater cooperation between competition agencies outside the EU, for example between the EU and US authorities in the long-running Microsoft case. It has also led to, and so far unsuccessful, calls for an international regime based on the WTO. |

Set within the context and ambitions of a customs' union it would have been counter-productive to dismantle trade barriers between the member states if private industry had been allowed to remain free to engage in cartel-like restrictions on competition and undermine the advantages of opening up the markets in the first place. In short, the realisation of a truly integrated market and flourishing intra-EU trade could be ensured only if the marketplace were actually policed. EU competition policy constitutes one of the largest, if often unheralded, success stories of European integration and has two main objectives: first, to create and sustain a single market that fosters intra-EU trade and competitiveness; second, to promote economic and political integration. It has achieved both. The most distinguishing feature of EU competition policy is its clear example of European governance, but what issues does it deal with, who are the principal actors behind competition policy and to what extent has the policy become Europeanised?

It was clear that only some form of institutionalised control at the **supranational** level was sufficient to secure and maintain competition discipline within the common market. Consequently, the six original member-state governments established the European Commission's legal competence (and simultaneously sidelined the Council and the European Parliament) to operate as an autonomous and quasi-judicial competition policy-making institution. To aid its policing of the European market DG Comp (formerly DGIV) was equipped (under Regulation 17) with exclusive powers of investigation (including the infamous 'dawn raids') into suspected violations of the EU competition rules and enabled it to codify, exempt and impose fines on offending firms.[3] In effect, the Commission operates as the investigator, judge, jury and executioner and only the European courts have the power to overturn Commission decisions. The Commission is highly active and investigates several hundred cases of alleged infringements each year. This nascent European regime laid the basis for the development of a competition policy that was constructed on increasingly shared norms and gradually helped to disseminate a competition culture throughout the Community and beyond.

## The focus of the EU competition rules

The EU rules extend over five substantial areas: these target the endemic existence of cartels and restrictive practices (such as price-fixing and market-sharing agreements) under Article 81. Cartel policy has emerged as the core activity in terms of staff, time and resources and is the most developed aspect of policy. The malignant threat posed by cartelisation to both the business environment and the consumer was recognised under Article 81 which prohibits all agreements 'which may affect trade between member states and which have as their object, the prevention, restriction or distortion of competition within the common market'. Framed in very general terms it was designed to catch and prohibit (para. 2) all agreements that restrict the free spirit of competition. Some types of anti-competitive agreement were entitled to exemptions if they improved the production or distribution of goods, promoted technical and economic progress or ensured that consumers reaped considerable benefits.

The second and most glamorous activity centres on merger control and the Commission's power to prohibit mergers. Merger policy (originally omitted in the Treaty of Rome) was added as a belated weapon to the Commission's arsenal in 1990 after the member states bowed to the wishes of the Commission and demands from the business community for a level playing-field and a one-stop shop for assessing EU mergers. In effect this regulation bestowed a Community dimension on the Commission's responsibility for all mergers that exceeded specified thresholds.[4] The handling of mergers has drawn almost universal praise from industry for its speediness (with almost 95 per cent of cases being formally cleared within one month).

The third and fourth key aspects of EU competition policy focus on monopolies that are abusing their dominant position in the marketplace (under Art. 82) and efforts to inject greater competition into the public-utility sectors such as telecommunications and energy (under Art. 86) respectively.

All four areas bring the Commission into direct dealings with the business world, but uniquely the fifth area which centres on the granting of state subsidies (under Art. 88–90) involves direct contact with member-state governments and has proven the most contentious aspect of the EU competition brief. State aids have featured as an aspect of government-industry relations to varying degrees across Western Europe since 1945. These have often been justified as an essential aspect of government-driven industrial policy and are designed as ways to secure employment particularly in peripheral and economically depressed regions, as issues of national prestige (e.g. Air France and Olympic Airways), or attempts to create European champions (e.g. Bull, to compete directly with US and other international companies).

## Member-state resistance

Industrial restructuring can be both economically and politically sensitive for governments and the Commission's pursuit of state aids had traditionally proven particularly difficult, because of the tendency of governments to shield their own money-losing and inefficient companies from competition through a variety of techniques and mechanisms, which may or may not amount to state aid. These include government subsidies to firms that can take the form of direct payments, debt write-offs, tax breaks and preferential borrowing. Subsidies are effectively industrial-policy tools that governments have used to deal with the pressures of increasing integration in both European and global markets and are often interpreted as responses to the insecurity and inequalities that are associated with economic openness. They were most often directed towards specific sectors that were facing decline.

The Commission's 'meddling' is often resented and this particular aspect of competition policy remained largely underdeveloped until the late 1980s. The Commission's initial reluctance to act, however, was replaced by a determination, and one buoyed by changing neo-liberal values and ideals, to address the issue as recognition grew over concerns about the effects of such aids on competition, the degree to which they were in the longer term a waste of valuable resources as well as doubts about how they impacted on EU economic and social cohesion policy. Although combating state aids rapidly emerged as a target of Commission interest and activity they continue to persist as a particular source of concern and led the Commission to publish a regular scoreboard to illustrate how much progress individual member-state governments are making towards the targets of the Lisbon Agenda. The total amount of state aid granted by EU member-state governments in 2003 amounted to approximately €53 billion. Wide variations naturally exist across the EU in the extent and scope of such aids and the Commission has been trying to tighten the rules: member-state governments are now requested to inform the Commission when they plan to grant aid. In absolute terms most aid was granted by Germany (€10 billion), followed closely by France (€9 billion) and Italy (€7 billion). In contrast both Sweden and the UK continue to offer least in the way of state aids. Significantly, since the 1990s there has been a shift away from aid to individual companies and towards horizontal objectives such as the environment. In 2003, 79 per cent of all granted aid was directed at the former category with only some 21 per cent being granted at specific sectors and restructuring initiatives. By means of further illustration some €14 billion was earmarked for agriculture and fisheries with just over €5 billion for coal.

In any analysis of state-aids policy it is necessary to distinguish between legitimate aid (for regional development, for small and medium-sized enterprises) and aids that distorted competition. State aids that do the latter and confer economic advantages to firms that they would otherwise not have realised are normally deemed illegal under Article 87 of the EEC Treaty. Nevertheless, the provisions do allow for a range of exemptions and these include, for example, aid having a social character, aid to facilitate the development of certain economic blackspots, aid to promote culture and heritage and, most notably of all, other categories determined by the Council. Categories of state aid that have been exempted from the general rules include grants to areas afflicted by a natural disaster and aid to economically depressed regions to assist the development of new forms of economic activity. The Commission has also issued guidelines governing state aid to industries severely affected by recession, but has insisted that such aid must have a specific purpose and fixed duration, and be regarded as totally exceptional. In the past, shipbuilding, steel, synthetic fibres and textiles have benefited from these guidelines. Member states wishing to provide aid to companies are expected to inform the Commission of their intentions. If the Commission rejects the plan, and if the latter goes ahead, it has the authority to demand the repayment of unauthorised subsidies, and even to impose fines on recalcitrant member states. Where disputes arise between the Commission and the member states they may be resolved in the last resort by the courts.

The recent history of the European airline industry provides an excellent example of the issues and sensitivities at play. Indeed, airlines and state aids have often gone hand in hand. Many airlines were effectively national 'flag carriers' and were regarded as sources of pride. Many, such as Sabena of Belgium, were, however, largely inefficient and were kept in business by direct government aid packages. Even prior to the events of 11 September in New York and Washington the sector had been in difficulty and there was general recognition, and particularly given the rising complaints from both low-cost airlines such as Easyjet and private companies such as British Airways over the level of state aids being handed out to their competitors, that some degree of restructuring and consolidation was long overdue. The Commission ordered the ailing Greek-owned Olympic Airlines in September 2005 to repay some €540 million (£364m) of illegal state aid to the Greek government. It is expected that the shape of this sector will change radically over the next few decades with more mergers taking place, as has already occurred in the case of Air France and the Dutch KLM, or with decisions to cease operation completely (like Sabena).

Competition policy represents the EU's first genuinely supranational policy, i.e. where decision-making power lies with the Commission and the European courts, and is one that over time has grown significantly in stature in terms of dealing with cross-border trade. The EU regime has exerted pressures that have culminated in a substantial convergence in both policy and design across Europe as the EU15 modified their existing domestic competition legislation and practices to conform to the EU rules with reference to both cartels and monopolies and has led to the emergence of a genuine system of European competition governance that comes very close to replicating a 'federal' regime (Gerber 1998). In the UK, for example, this trend found illustration in the both the 1998 Competition Act and the 2002 Enterprise Act (Whish 2003). It went further and as part of the accession negotiations the Europeanisation dynamic exerted even more pressure and compelled the newest member states from Central and Eastern Europe to adopt national competition laws that reflected the principles of the *acquis communautaire* (body of EU laws and regulations). The reach and extent of EU influence have been further advanced through the radical overhaul of the competition administrative machinery in the EU that came into force in May 2004. The latest changes (Council Regulations 1/2003, dealing with restrictive practices, and 139/2004, dealing with mergers) both decentralised and modernised the system of competition governance in Europe.

On the one hand these radical changes provide for closer cooperation between the Commission and the national authorities and thereby enable the Commission to prioritise its own caseload and to determine which cases should be left to the national authorities who are now entitled to apply and interpret EU competition law directly. The Commission hopes that these reforms will enable it to concentrate its limited resources on the more problematic cases and to aid its quest it has been awarded tougher powers of enquiry. These reforms have consolidated what effectively constitutes a federal regime in all but name (McGowan 2005) where the Commission very much remains the ringmaster.

> **KEY POINTS**
>
> - Substantive domestic competition-policy regimes only truly emerged for the first time in Western Europe after 1945.
>
> - The salience of competition policy found reflection in the European integration process and emerged as one of the few policy areas given its specific chapter in the EEC Treaty.
>
> - The activities and responsibilities of both domestic and European competition policies developed from the original focus on cartels and monopolies to cover mergers in the 1970s and 1980s and the public utilities in the 1990s.
>
> - Both the national and EU regimes underwent a Europeanisation process as policies converged through policy learning and demands from industry for similar rules and a level playing-field.

# Industrial Policy

Although rather less easy to define than competition policy, industrial policy has traditionally centred on direct intervention by government into the market in order to create and maintain the conditions in which industry can flourish. The rationale for government intervention or arguably interference with market mechanisms finds explanation for a variety of reasons and can take various forms, such as financial support for new industries (e.g. information technology); incentives for small and medium suppliers who provide the backbone of European employment; monies for research and development objectives; a desire to enable national/European industries to compete alongside foreign companies and to protect employment. To this end industrial policy can be deemed as both a *laissez-faire* approach (i.e. about government investment, R&D initiatives, encouraging open trade, and promoting competition). Alternatively, it can assume a much more aggressive form that centres on government planning, as in France where government sought to work alongside industry. This latter *dirigiste* approach was typified by successive government attempts at targeting and protecting specific economic sectors through subsidies, corporation taxes and public procurement policies. This raises a raft of questions. Is government intervention necessary or desirable? Should inefficient or unviable firms be supported through public funds? Should European champions be fostered through state subsidies and other favourable (e.g. fiscal) incentives? (See Background box 20.2.)

Understanding why some national governments are more inclined to provide aid necessitates consideration of a selection of economic, political and cultural variables. State intentions differ and the contrasting approaches of European governments towards notions of competitiveness were most clearly reflected in both France and the UK. All the French governments of the Fifth French Republic from President Charles de Gaulle to Jacques Chirac have favoured aiding industry and many have been ready to advocate almost a centrally planned industrial policy that is heavily *dirigiste* in tone. Indeed, it could even be argued that in the French case thinking on industrial policy forms almost a facet of cultural policy. This position contrasts starkly with the very much more non-interventionist approach of UK governments, particularly after the arrival of Margaret Thatcher as prime minister in 1979. They rejected industrial policy motivations on the grounds that any immediate short-term benefits (e.g. in terms of employment) were ultimately overridden by continuing and encouraging inefficiencies in the longer term.

## A historical overview of European industrial policy

Any examination of the history of post-1945 European industrial policy uncovers four relatively distinct time periods. In the first period from the late 1950s until the 1970s industrial policy did not feature in any comprehensive or integrated form at the EU level. Instead, individual member states were left to determine how they wished to deal with industry and coordinate industry–government relations at the national level. So, for example, the French and West German governments, acutely aware of US competition, opted to both foster European champions and protect existing national industries through the pursuit of an industrial policy that advocated the use of subsidies and other mechanisms (Geroski 1989). Interestingly the seeds of some highly ambitious European industrial projects such as Concorde and Airbus were sown. A second phase from 1973 until roughly the mid-1980s involved a much more interventionist policy that saw domestic capitals trying to bolster national industrial giants through a range of government subsidies to car manufacturers, shipbuilding plants, steel plants, as well as more positive efforts to invest in new 'sunrise' industries such as telecommunications and electronics and a growing recognition for greater cooperation in the field of R&D (Curzon Price 2001). This clearer example of *dirigisme* was intensified further when individual member states sought to respond to the after-effects of the oil price rises of the 1970s that led to an energy crisis, added fuel costs for industry and rapidly rising unemployment and inflation.

The response of the member states seemed to reinforce the limits or inadequacies of the European economic integration project. The difficulties of forging any EU reaction reflected differing member-state attitudes towards industrial policy. Nevertheless, as fears grew about the future competitiveness of European companies in world markets and the dangers of potential economic dependency on Japan and the USA, two substantive initiatives were launched on both the supranational and

## Aiding Industry—The Airbus Consortium

Airbus is one of the success stories of European industrial cooperation. Founded in 1967 as a consortium of European aircraft manufacturers, the aim of Airbus was to design and build large passenger aircraft that could compete with the large US corporation Boeing. Since 1992, Airbus's share of the large civil aircraft market has grown steadily from over 30 per cent to more than half by 2004 and its future successes seemed assured with the launch of the new double-decker-style aircraft (Airbus A380) in 2005. This new plane has been specifically designed to carry 500 passengers and has been marketed to fly to a series of hub international airports and is set to revolutionise the nature of air travel in much the way that the jumbo jet has done since the 1960s. However, Boeing has met the challenge by building a smaller plane which will be able to land in smaller airports. Consumers and their preferred choice of hub plus further plane connection to smaller airport or direct flight to their destination will play a significant role in determining the success of both ventures.

Airbus comprises four partners: British Aerospace, Construcciones Aeronáuticas SA (CASA) of Spain, Daimler-Benz Aerospace of Germany and Aérospatiale of France. Each of the four partners specialises in producing different parts of the aircraft. The lucrative aircraft-manufacturing industry provides a rare example of the tensions between competition and industrial policies. Boeing, for example, has continually complained about the massive government subsidies being channelled into Airbus in order to make it viable, and has labelled such activity as constituting nothing less than unfair competition. Tension was particularly acute in the 1980s, until a bilateral agreement on civil aircraft, which capped government support for new aircraft, was reached in June 1992. Nevertheless, relations between the world's two largest aircraft manufacturers were still tense, as was evident in the EU's total opposition to the planned merger between Boeing and McDonnell Douglas in 1997. This merger aimed to create the world's largest aerospace and defence company. As Airbus was the only other major competitor, the European Commission raised its concerns about the potential dominance in the world market of this new company, and threatened to oppose the merger and to impound Boeing aircraft if they landed on EU soil. The USA saw EU competition policy being used as another means to protect Airbus. Rumours of a trade war between the EU and the USA grew and the sensitivity of the issue led to intervention by US President Bill Clinton. The issue was resolved only when the Commission sanctioned a merger providing that many of the clauses that would have tied Boeing customers to the new company for 20 years were removed.

Tensions between Airbus and Boeing over the degree of subsidies supporting the activities of both companies have become almost a permanent feature of the EU–US trade discussions. In October 2004 both companies launched the largest trade dispute in the World Trade Organization's short history. However, aware of the economic repercussions of any damaging ruling against them, both parties agreed in January 2005 to return to the negotiating table in an effort to consider how to cut subsidies. The ongoing bilateral negotiations certainly proved intense and a renewed bitter row erupted between both companies in May 2005. The difficulties centre on the failure of both Airbus and Boeing to agree on the level of subsidies and led to both sides reviving their charges before the WTO. EU Trade Commissioner Peter Mandelson placed responsibility for this latest problem with Boeing. The Europeans resent the illegal subsidies that centre on the way in which Boeing is facilitated through a number of military contracts and tax breaks, while the Americans resent the aid being given in the construction of the new A380. It seems highly unlikely that subsidies will ever disappear altogether and both sides are certain to complain about unfair competitive advantages for some time to come.

Indeed, the US government raised its objections in February 2006 to a £5.2m grant from the Welsh Assembly to train new workers at the Airbus factory in Broughton. This factory is the largest manufacturing plant in Wales and employs some 6,000 people. It makes wings for the A380 and the new A350. The US authorities claimed that this subsidy breaches WTO rules of fair competition. Both parties are also certain to clash over assistance in the construction of new middle-sized aircraft (the 787 or 'dreamliner' and the A350). Airbus confirmed the development of the A350 in October 2005 and stated that it had deliberately turned down contentious state support for one year in an attempt to calm the ongoing row with Boeing. Airbus and Boeing will remain fierce competitors for some time to come.

intergovernmental levels. In the first, the European Commission, with full member-state approval, presented its plans in 1985 for the creation of a genuine European single market by 1992.[5] This project heralded a third phase of, and major shift in, European industrial-policy considerations. Policy content now moved significantly away from being about aids for declining industrial sectors to creating the right environment in which business could operate successfully. The single market programme was the launching pad for this new approach. The single market encompassed objectives to eradicate the damaging non-tariff barriers (customs posts, varying technical specifications, protected public procurement policies and widely diverging excise taxes and VAT rates) that thwarted intra-EU trade and economies of scale.

But it went much further and as part of the drive to bolster European competitiveness the European Commission sought to develop a series of horizontal and regional subsidies that included the promotion of a research and technological development (RTD) policy as a means to encourage collaborative Europe-wide research networks, foster synergies (e.g. in information technology) and to avoid costly duplication. Put simply, the Commission sought to provide aid for small and medium-sized companies and to encourage cooperation and was prepared to countenance a degree of antitrust dispensation. It is important to stress that this decision did not in any way herald the return to old-style industrial policy and was not an attempt by the Commission to 'pick winners'. On the contrary, the emphasis was firmly placed on pre-competitive research projects and agreements where technological development would be the end product.

There were several examples of this attempt to Europeanise research and innovation. They included the evolution of EU programmes such as ESPRIT (European Strategic Programme for Research and Development in Information Technology), BRITE-EURAM (Basic Research in Industrial Technology for Europe/European Research on Advanced Materials), JET (Joint European Torus), RACE (Research and Development in Advanced

Communications Technology in Europe) and the development of Europe-wide research projects through the multi-annual frameworks programmes (MFP). It these were examples of supranational initiatives the EUREKA (European Research Co-ordinating Agency) project typified a second and intergovernmental approach towards industrial considerations that reflected concerns over the lack of any coordinated industrial policy at the EU level.

EUREKA was launched by then French President François Mitterrand in 1985 as a direct response to his concerns over the advances in American technology and specifically the Strategic Defence Initiative programme. With this and the endorsement of ten other European states and an initial budget of approximately $26 billion EUREKA aimed to encourage and provide support for Europe-wide and later international research and development programmes. Progress was monitored by a secretariat in Paris, but its role was merely supervisory and at no time has it sought to devise any form of coherent policy. It has brought mixed fortunes. For example, one of the most notable and infamous failures included the very well funded but ill fated High Density Television (HDTV) programme. Still, there have also been successes such as the JESSI (Joint European Submicron Silicon Initiative) and overall the EUREKA programme.

A fourth phase in industrial policy development in the 1990s firmly signalled the shift away from state aids towards a pro-competition ethos. Martin Bangerman, the European Commissioner for Industry from 1989 to 1999, underscored the acceptance of market forces and competition (Bangermann 1992). Although elements of the old-style industrial policy continued at national level, times had changed and member-state governments were coming under intense pressure to abandon such aid packages. The contentious nature of aiding industry and its effects on competition were clearly illustrated in the very first EU merger prohibition order on the proposed deal between the European aircraft manufactures Aerospatiale of France and Alenia of Italy with the Canadian giant De Haviland in 1992. The DG for competition was convinced that the merged company would be far too dominant in the marketplace and accordingly advocated prohibition. As ensuing disagreements raged within the Commission with DGIV (Competition) and DGIII (Industry) on opposing sides of the argument and with lobbying of both the French and Italian governments, the outcome was hard to call. Ultimately, the argument against the merger won and the proposed merger was prohibited, albeit by an extremely narrow pro-competition majority (nine votes to seven) in the **College of Commissioners**.

## The rise of competitiveness

Approaches to industrial policy have undergone a sizeable change. The 1992 Treaty on European Union may have provided industrial policy for the first time with its own specific article (Art. 157) and empowered the member states to secure the conditions necessary for the competitiveness of EU industry and to take special measures to boost industry, but only so long as these measures did not interfere with or distort competition. The focus on competition and competitiveness was reflected in the Commission's language and documentation, such as its proposals for a coherent industrial policy in its 1993 white paper, *Growth, Competitiveness and Employment* and its green paper on innovation (COM(95)688 final) in 1995. Both underscored the centrality of competitiveness in the EU agenda and represented nothing less than a complete transformation in Commission thinking and a means to confront a number of problems that threatened European growth. These were: the impact of globalisation; the rising costs of capital and labour; the need to create a competitive market (pro-competition); and greater social cohesion and environmental protection. How should industrial policy tackle and overcome these difficulties?

The Commission provided some answers in its 1995 action programme (EC(95)437 final) on the 'Implementation of Council Resolutions and Conclusions on Industrial Policy' which outlined four major priority areas to strengthen industrial competitiveness. These were: solidifying the internal market; encouraging research and technological development; promoting the information society; and encouraging industrial cooperation. Collectively, however, EC enterprise policy, research and development policy, regional policy, social policy, competition policy, workers' rights, energy policy, transport policy and environmental policy can be said to constitute an industrial policy. The basic concern has been to increase the efficiency and competitiveness of any industry within a free-market ethos. These changes to policy design were mirrored by changes in institutional design within the European Commission and saw the former Directorate-General (DG) III (Industry) being rebranded first as DG Enterprise and then DG Enterprise and Industry.

Competitiveness, innovation and entrepreneurship have emerged as the central tenets of EU enterprise policy and it is intertwined closely with other policies, in particular those on the single market, research and innovation and the information society. These latest developments illustrate how far industrial policy has come since the very *dirigiste*-driven regimes and crisis cartels of the 1970s. There has been a real shift away from directly supporting inefficient companies and sunset industries towards encouraging greater collaboration and pre-competitive R&D strategies. Of course, degrees of tension between the intergovernmental and supranational levels persist as some states have shown a greater reluctance to move away from old-style intervention strategies that have been driven by political considerations, but the levels of such aid have diminished. Responsibility for this reduction owes much to the Commission's ongoing pursuit of illegal state aids. The European Commission is the focal point for ensuring that innovation policy is coherent and cohesive across the EU, for benchmarking performance, for disseminating best practice, for assisting small and medium-sized enterprises (SMEs) and for highlighting lessons to be learned from any failure of the market economy that might justify state intervention. Through its Entrepreneurship Action

Plan, the Commission is promoting a more entrepreneurial mindset, encouraging more people to set up businesses, helping those businesses grow and become more competitive, improving the flow of finance and creating a more SME friendly regulatory and administrative environment.

---

### KEY POINTS

- Industrial policy is about incentives and aid from government to enable enterprises to flourish.

- Attitudes towards industrial-policy considerations have varied widely across Europe since 1945.

- Industrial policy has been more pronounced in countries such as France and Italy, where it has often represented an integral aspect of governmental planning.

- The clear demarcations between member-state positions and preferences have ensured that a

*dirigiste*-motivated industrial policy did not materialise in any serious fashion at EU level.

- Common concerns about the state of competitiveness in Europe have resulted in both intergovernmental (e.g. EUREKA) and supranational (e.g. RACE) initiatives to bolster European companies.

- Industrial policy has undergone four rather distinct phases and has increasingly become subservient to competition-policy considerations.

---

# Conclusion: Pursuing Competitiveness

Competition and industrial polices are principally about visions of how best to ensure and encourage economic prosperity and sustain a high level of competitiveness. They need not necessarily clash as alternative policy approaches but can and have when *dirigiste* industrial-policy considerations are deployed to support what amounts to inefficient and profit-losing industries or when efforts are made to protect employment. There may be sound arguments in certain cases but, overall, few benefit from such overt aid and any widespread return to them threatens further spiralling subsidies that in the long run damage efficiency. For the moment this older form of industrial policy at the European level has more or less disappeared in favour of efforts at creating the right environment in which firms can operate effectively and fairly or where enterprises can be assisted to develop into main players.

It would be naive to assume that industrial-policy considerations have vanished altogether from national agendas as two recent cases in France highlight: the French government agreed in January 2005 to assist the struggling French wine industry with a package of €70 million and in 2004 to rescue Alstrom, the producer of high-speed trains and employer of some 100,000 people. Such examples are increasingly the exceptions rather than a rule as competition rationale has begun to bite ever harder and is pushing the EU member states to open up their energy markets. Indeed in October 2005 it was announced that Airbus had opted to forgo government aid in developing its new A350 plane in a bid to calm a subsidies row between Europe and the USA. Both the newer version of industrial policy and competition policy are clearly set to play an integral part of the commitment by both the Commission and the 25 EU member states (set at the 2000 Lisbon Summit and modified with more achievable targets in 2005) to make Europe the world's most competitive and dynamic entity by 2010. It is clearly an ambitious target.

## BACKGROUND BOX 20.3

### Resistance to More Competition

The Bolkestein Directive or, to give it its proper name, the Directive on Services in the Internal Market, sparked huge debate and controversy in various EU countries and especially Belgium, France, Germany and Italy in the first half of 2005. The Directive had been put together by Frits Bolkestein, the former Commissioner for the Internal Market, and aimed to establish a single market for services within the EU. Services are a rapidly growing sector and account for around 70 per cent of EU economic activity. The Directive contained two key principles. The first centred on the 'freedom of establishment' and sought to ensure that any company or individual who provided a service in one EU member state should be allowed to provide it in all EU member states. The second, the 'country of origin principle', sought to establish that if goods were produced in one EU member state then it was legitimate and acceptable to sell such goods in other EU member states. Critics maintained that the Directive would unleash unwelcome competition between workers in different parts of the EU and result in a decline in income levels. Trade unionsists argued vociferously that such changes would culminate in 'social dumping' practices. The dangers of companies opting to relocate to low-cost economies led to a series of mass protests that culminated in a 100,000 strong march through Brussels in opposition to this Directive in March 2005. The pressure of public opinion led the European Council (and especially France) effectively to postpone the Directive and call for alterations before it could be considered. The issue will return as the EU is determined to open up this sector. There can be little doubt that this example of liberalisation fed into the discussions on the Constitutional Treaty for Europe in France.

The study of competition and industrial policies raises important questions about how best to achieve and nurture economic success, but it also raises issues about governance and how it operates and should function at the national, supranational and global levels. What has been occurring in the competition policy arena amounts effectively to a process of harmonisation or convergence (Drahos 2001) by stealth where the national competition laws in the EU25 have converged with EU rules in relation to practices on cartels and mergers to create a truly European regime. It should be recognised that in some member states, such as France, competition has not been welcomed in plans to open up the services industry (see Background box 20.3) as it is still regarded as a threat to jobs.

Competition and industrial policies are to be judged by their outcomes, achievements or failures at fostering greater competitiveness in Europe and beyond. Yet both policies seem and are far removed from EU citizens. There is little doubt that they impact upon the citizens but the technical and economic rationale behind actual policy content scarcely can be expected to enthuse public interest. In fact decisions about competition and industrial policies remain primarily the preserve of economic and political elites. The competition *cognoscenti* meet, debate and discuss the salient issues on a regular basis at national and European conferences and other international fora. For example, each six-month presidency of the European Council now hosts a Competition day to review practices and procedures. The policy is effectively regulated by a series of independent institutions. Majoritarian institutions (parliaments) are simply not involved in day-to-day decision-making. This reality raises a number of pertinent questions on power, accountability and legitimacy that are echoed at both the national and EU levels but also on the wider international front. But how significant are they here? Do efficient outcomes overcome such democratic deficiencies?

The answer has to be in the affirmative. The WTO is the latest example of an international organisation that is trying to tackle competition cases that transcend European borders. It is considerably more unaccountable than the EU regime. Since 2000 the European Commission has devoted considerable effort to creating an International Competition Network (ICN). This network was established in October 2001 as, essentially, an informal forum in which competition authorities from around the world exchange and discuss the issue and function of competition policy and its enforcement. It is almost a purely virtual network, but it is emerging as a credible forum that seeks to encourage and spread best practices. It is and will remain an elite network that seeks to secure high degrees of competitiveness among European firms and is one that is being facilitated at times through the tools of the new-look industrial policy. Both deserve much closer attention.

# Notes

1. The frameworks for these evolving competition regimes were laid down in the 1948 Monopolies Act and the 1956 Restrictive Trade Practices Act in the UK and the *Gesetz gegen Wettbewerbsbeschränkungen* (Law against restraints on competition) in West Germany. For an overview of the historical evolution, see Wilks (1996) and Sturm (1996).

2. In the EEC Treaty this general objective was to be found under Article 3(f) and the articles pertaining to competition ran from 85 to 94. The numbering of the latter was amended under the 1997 Treaty of Amsterdam.

3. Fines have been steadily increasing. For example, in 2001 the European Commission imposed fines of €462m on Hoffmann-La Roche (vitamins cartel); €296m on BASF (vitamins cartel); and €184m on Arjo Wiggins (paper cartel). In 2002, €250m was levied on Lafarge (plasterboard cartel) and €149m on Nintendo (for price-fixing); while in 2003 Hoechst was fined €99m (food preservative cartel). The 'hitlist' will continue to grow, but so too does the determination and resolve of many companies to conceal their anti-competitive activities, by all means possible.

4. The Commission automatically became the one-stop shop for processing merger applications where the firms involved had an aggregate worldwide turnover of more than €5m; where at least two of the firms involved had an aggregate EU-wide turnover of more than €250m; or where at least two of the companies involved held more than two-thirds of its aggregate EU-wide turnover within one and the same member state.

5. The initiatives taken to complete the internal market, which were announced in the Commission's white paper *Completing the Internal Market* (COM(85)310), gave the Community's industrial policy a major boost. An integrated market will give European industry the advantages already enjoyed by its US and Japanese competitors in their large internal markets. These advantages include opportunities for mass production, specialisation, economies of scale, transnational cooperation among enterprises, technical harmonisation, research, innovation, investment and Community-wide tendering.

## QUESTIONS

1. To what extent should competition and industrial policies be of interest to students of government and political science?

2. How far are competition policy and industrial policy compatible?

3. To what extent has competition policy emerged as one of the prime success stories of European integration?

4. Is this example of supranational governance to be welcomed?

5. Should European champions be fostered through state aids?

6. Should the EU and its member states try to pick and support 'winners' such as the Airbus consortium?

7. How do you foresee industrial policy developing in the future?

8. To what extent have both competition and industrial policies been influenced by the processes of Europeanisation and globalisation?

9. Which policy and approach best secures greater competitiveness in Europe?

## FURTHER READING

■ Commission, *Annual Reports on Competition Policy*, Luxembourg, Office for Official Publications of the European Communities. These are (and remain since 1973) the best guide to the evolution of EU competition policy and provide a comprehensive review of Commission and court activities as well as highlighting the priorities of the Commission.

■ Commission (2005), *Competition Policy in Europe and the Citizen*, Luxembourg, Office for Official Publications of the European Communities, at http://ec.europa.eu/comm/competition/publications. A very useful introduction to the objectives, institutions and activities of EU competition policy.

■ *European Competition Law Review*. An indispensable tool for all those who wish to seriously study and analyse competition policy.

■ Goyder, D.G. (2003), *EC Competition Law*, Oxford, Clarendon Press. Presents one of the most authoritative works on competition law. Although written for lawyers, any student of political science who wishes to engage in postgraduate study is strongly encouraged to read the opening and closing chapters.

## IMPORTANT WEBSITES

● ec.europa.eu/comm/competition/index_en.html  The best starting point for an examination of EU competition policy is the European Commission's site where DG Competition provides excellent and exhaustive coverage of all five key aspects, provides information on individual cases and lists links to other competition agencies.

● ec.europa.eu/enterprise/index_en.htm  The changing nature of industrial policy and the focus on competitiveness in the European Union is clearly displayed in DG Enterprise's extensive website.

● **www.mmc.gov.uk/our_role/index.htm    www.oft.gov.uk/default.htm**    For information on the substance of UK competition policy, see the Competition Commission's website and the site of the Office of Fair Trading.

● **www.bundeskartellamt.de/**    For further information on all aspects of the German competition regime in operation.

 **Visit the Online Resource Centre that accompanies this book for lots of useful additional material, including an interactive map of Europe. www.oxfordtextbooks.co.uk/orc/ hay_menon/**

# PART 4

# Europe in the Wider World

# 21

# European Union Enlargement

ANIA KROK-PASZKOWSKA AND JAN ZIELONKA

## Chapter Contents

- Introduction
- Successive Enlargements
- European Power Politics
- Diversity and Integration
- Nature of the Enlarged EU
- Conclusion

## Reader's Guide

This chapter argues that enlargement has been a dominant factor in the process of European integration. It begins by examining how successive enlargements have shaped the process of European integration and how they have affected the nature of the European Union. It then goes on to show that the most recent (fifth) enlargement was different from those that preceded it in that it subjected applicants to tougher membership conditions and was aimed at influencing their domestic and foreign policies. This policy of conditional accession represents a unique European manner of handling an unstable environment. The last wave of enlargement was thus guided by strategic rather than merely economic or institutional considerations. The chapter describes how this enlargement has resulted in greater political, economic and cultural diversity and it shows how much the enlarged Union deviates from the dominant statist paradigm.

# Introduction

Since its creation in 1957 the European Union has grown from a European Economic Community of six member states to a Union of 25 members with a population of over 450 million citizens. The EU is now the world's largest trading bloc, generating about a quarter of world GDP and more than a fifth of global trade. It is the world's largest single market. It has a common currency shared by 12 of the member states and a fledgling common foreign and defence policy.

There have been five **enlargements**. All states joining the EU have had to accept the **acquis communautaire**, comprising the rights and obligations derived from the EU treaties, laws and court rulings existing at the time of entry. Over the years the EU has expanded to new policy areas, making the process of adjustment and adaptation more arduous for each successive wave of applicants. In exchange, the Union gave acceding states access to its decision-making, markets, financial aid and transfers.

With each new round of enlargement, institutional and procedural changes have been made to the EU system. European integration has been an ongoing process involving a mixture of widening (enlargement) and deepening (closer integration). Every time the Union has enlarged in terms of members it has also enlarged its policy remit. Enlargement thus fits well into one of the main themes of European integration, that of constant evolution and change. (See Background box 21.1.)

The most recent enlargement to include ten new member states was the largest and the most challenging to date. It created pressure for far-reaching reforms of the Union's institutional structure. Indeed, the depth and scope of the latest enlargement is likely to change the very nature of European integration. Most notably, this particular enlargement resulted in an enormous and unprecedented increase in structural diversity in terms of wealth, law, administration, local habits and culture. In practice this may mean that not all members will be able or willing to implement EU policies in a uniform way. The Union will be forced to adopt complex institutional solutions including what is known as **variable geometry**, whereby different member states participate in different EU activities. Moreover, more and more policies and programmes are likely to reach beyond the Union's borders.

Within the Union itself there has been growing scepticism about the ability of its institutions to cope with the challenges of such a large and increasingly diversified body of members. EU institutions are seen as increasingly remote from ordinary citizens. National referenda on EU issues such as treaty ratification, the single currency and EU membership have been close-run affairs and there have been several examples of national publics rejecting them. A partial exception has been the high

---

**BACKGROUND BOX 21.1**

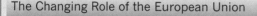

### The Changing Role of the European Union

'For its first half century, Europe was essentially introspective and obviously so, as it created the new institutions and the economic integration to give effect to the vision of a Europe at peace. But now it is confronting a much greater and broader challenge that has to turn it outward: the challenge of globalisation. Everywhere, every nation, every region, is finding its economy, security, even culture turned upside down by globalisation.... In the era of globalisation, nations like ours need to come together as allies and fashion the new Europe for our and others' national interest. To make it outward, not inward; to make it economically effective, not economically feeble; to use Europe to make our voice heard louder and stronger in the world.'

" Tony Blair's message to Poland on joining the European Union, Warsaw, 30 May 2003 "

level of support and relatively high turnouts in the most recent EU accession referenda held in nine of the ten new member states. However, the average turnout of 45.7 per cent in the most recent (June 2004) elections for the European Parliament (EP) was the lowest since direct elections to the EP were introduced in 1979. And the rejection of the Constitutional Treaty by Dutch and French voters was largely due to anxieties caused by the most recent enlargement and reluctance to extend EU membership to Turkey.

Indeed, the issue of enlargement is likely to preoccupy the EU for some time to come. The Union will continue to be faced with the widening v. deepening dilemma. Two more countries—Bulgaria and Romania—are set to join by 2007. Croatia and Turkey have already started **accession negotiations**. Several more countries in the Western Balkans have been promised membership, while others such as Ukraine and Moldova are clamouring to be considered. All the official and unofficial candidates are economically less developed than most current EU members. Many have had recent experience of war and ethnic cleansing; some are still engaged in ongoing territorial disputes. Many are still struggling with a communist legacy. A crucial question confronting the Union relates to whether it will really, as in the past, be able to claim that further enlargement would ensure stability and security in Europe and promote economic growth and general well-being.

> **KEY POINTS**
>
> - The process of European integration has involved a mixture of widening (enlargement) and deepening (closer integration).
>
> - The fifth enlargement has been the most ambitious and challenging to date.
>
> - The EU will probably have to accept the principle of variable geometry to accommodate the latest enlargement.

# Successive Enlargements

Enlargement has been a leitmotif of European integration and successive enlargements were of crucial importance in shaping the process. Each round of enlargement has been accompanied by consolidation of the European project. (See Background box 20.2.)

## The first enlargement

The first enlargement took in the UK, Ireland and Denmark. The UK had refused to join the six founding members in a project that would lead to 'an ever deeper union', but later changed its mind. However, British politicians faced the ignominy of seeing two applications vetoed by France under

> **BACKGROUND BOX 21.2**
>
> ### Enlargement as a Motor of Integration
>
> '...enlargement is shaped by and itself shapes internal policy in profound ways. Bringing in new countries requires the EU to reform various internal policies, practices and institutions to accommodate newcomers. Enlargement in its own right is therefore a motor of integration.'
>
> " Lykke Friis, 'EU Enlargement ... And Then There Were 28?', in Elizabeth Bomberg and Alexander Stubb (eds), *The European Union: How Does it Work?*, Oxford, Oxford University Press, 2003, p. 179. "

President Charles de Gaulle who viewed Britain as a potential American 'Trojan horse' in the EEC. A new opportunity presented itself when de Gaulle left office. Accession negotiations with the UK, Ireland and Denmark started in 1971 and the three states joined the EEC on 1 January 1973. Despite the rather negative atmosphere surrounding Britain's entry, enlargement from six to nine members was followed by a number of significant institutional and policy developments such as the creation of a regional policy and a common fisheries policy as well as the launching of the European Monetary System (EMS). The European Council, i.e. regular meetings of the heads of state or government of the member states, first met in 1975. The first direct elections to the EP were held in 1979. Careful steps were also taken to extend the aims, powers and procedures of the European Political Cooperation (the precursor of the CFSP) through the 1973 Copenhagen Report, the 1981 London Report and the 1983 Solemn Declaration on European Union.

## 'Southern' enlargement

The second (Greece in 1981) and third (Spain and Portugal in 1986) enlargements are usually taken together and referred to as the 'Southern' or 'Mediterranean' enlargement. All three countries were new democracies that had recently thrown off authoritarian rule and their membership of the EC was seen as the best guarantee that their fragile democracies would be strengthened and consolidated. They were also relatively poor countries. Among the nine existing members there were fears of large numbers of economic migrants from Greece, Spain and Portugal, as well as worries that their economic and administrative capacities would not allow them to function effectively within the EC. For their part, the three new members were interested in regional aid and access to European markets as a way of stimulating economic growth. The EC proved an important catalyst for their economic development and political modernisation. These countries became strong supporters of regional aid and the common agricultural policy (CAP).

These two enlargements were followed by the adoption of the Single European Act (SEA), signed in 1986, which laid the groundwork for the projected completion of the single market in 1992. It also brought environmental policy into the treaty, as well as committing the EC to greater funding of regional development (cohesion policy). Cohesion policy increased in importance and became a key policy area largely due to pressure from the three new Mediterranean members. The SEA also put in place procedures for foreign-policy cooperation. Institutional changes—greater use of qualified majority voting and an enhancement of the European Parliament's legislative role—were introduced with the aim of ensuring greater efficiency and democratic legitimacy in a larger community.

## Institutional restructuring

A mini-enlargement took place in 1990 when the five East German *Länder* were absorbed by the Federal Republic of Germany and hence the EC. Europe was undergoing a profound geopolitical transformation that could not but affect the process of European integration. At the time, the 12 were primarily concerned with consolidating—notably by completing the internal market—and deepening. However, this effort highlighted the fault-lines between different members' views of the European project. The Treaty on European Union was signed in Maastricht in 1992. The Treaty produced some changes in the structure and competences of the EU. It set forth a series of objectives, including the establishment of a single currency, EU citizenship, a more assertive role for the Union in foreign policy, and closer cooperation in justice and home affairs (JHA). However, ratification of the Maastricht Treaty proved to be a very complex and difficult process. Britain negotiated a number of **opt-outs** from provisions on the common currency, the Social Charter and later refused to participate in the **Schengen regime** on the elimination of internal borders. Denmark obtained opt-outs in defence and JHA areas. Maastricht thus represented the first officially sanctioned moves towards a multi-speed Union. In an ever wider and more diversified Union one-size-fits-all solutions were proving to be increasingly inadequate.

## 'Nordic' enlargement

The end of the Cold War opened the way to a far larger potential membership of the EU than ever before. The fourth enlargement in 1995 took in the three neutral countries of Austria, Finland and Sweden. Prior to 1990 their geographical location in the 'shadow' of the Soviet Union and their non-aligned status had been held to preclude membership of the EU. However, the disintegration of the Soviet empire and the end of the Cold War era deprived their neutral status of much of its meaning. All three countries had belonged to the European Free Trade Association (EFTA). In the early 1990s, with the creation of the internal market, the EFTA countries joined the European Economic Area (EEA) which, by linking the EU and EFTA, allowed unrestricted access for most of their industrial products to the wider European market without internal frontiers. In exchange, members of the EEA had to accept most EU legislation related to the internal market. This, however, left them in the uncomfortable position of conforming to the EU's rules and regulations, while having no influence over policy-making in the Union. As a consequence, membership became a logical choice.

However, in 1994, the EP had threatened to block the EFTA enlargement unless the member states agreed to hold a new Intergovernmental Conference (IGC) on institutional reforms. This was all the more necessary given that by the mid-1990s ten Central and Eastern European (CEE) countries (as well as Cyprus and Malta) had formally applied for membership and it was clear that enlargement on this scale would require a radical rethinking both of core EU policies and of the Union's institutional design.

Although the Nordic enlargement proved relatively unproblematic as the accession states were relatively small and prosperous, with well developed economic and welfare systems and significant experience of intergovernmental cooperation within EFTA and the EEA, the decision-making process in the EU was becoming increasingly complex.

## 'Eastward' enlargement

Despite growing concerns with the internal functioning of an ever-wider Union the next, fifth enlargement, was set in motion in response to dramatic developments in Central and Eastern Europe following the fall of the Berlin Wall in 1989. When communism abruptly collapsed, it was far from certain whether the newly liberated CEE countries would manage to secure peace, prosperity and democracy within their borders. If they did not, problems would be bound to spill over into the Western part of Europe. The EU's initial response was to offer these countries financial assistance through the PHARE programme (Poland/Hungary Assistance for Reconstruction of Economies—later applied to all CEE candidate states) and to sign **Association Agreements** (also known as **Europe Agreements**) with them. Although these agreements provided for a large degree of political cooperation and liberalisation of trade in non-agricultural goods, they fell far short of full membership as a result of fears that a large-scale enlargement could threaten the progress the Union had already made. There was also uncertainty about the cost of enlargement. However, in June 1993 at the European Council in Copenhagen the EU officially recognised that 'the associated countries in Central and Eastern Europe that so desire shall become members of the European Union. Accession will take place as soon as a country is able to assume the obligations of membership by satisfying the economic, democratic and social conditions'. This was the first time the EU had laid out membership conditions and linked them to the capacity of the

**BACKGROUND BOX 21.3**

### The Copenhagen Criteria

Candidate states must have:

1. Stability of institutions guaranteeing democracy, the rule of law, human rights, and respect for and protection of minorities.

2. The existence of a functioning market economy, as well as the capacity to cope with competitive pressure and market forces within the Union.

3. The ability to take on the obligations of membership, including adherence to the aims of political, economic and monetary union.

The EU must have:

4. The capacity to absorb new members without endangering the momentum of European integration.

Union to absorb new members. (See Background box 21.3.)

The next decade witnessed intense political squabbles, hectic diplomatic negotiations, wide-ranging economic and legal adjustments, and sporadic public recriminations. The basic conditions for enlargement that were spelled out in the Copenhagen criteria in 1993 were subsequently specified in a large document entitled **Agenda 2000**. The document provided the first detailed explanation of what the conditions of enlargement actually were. It covered four main areas. The first dealt with the Commission's opinions on the extent to which candidates met the Copenhagen criteria. The second outlined a framework enlargement strategy—basically explaining how the negotiations were to be structured. The third area was an examination of the effect enlargement would have on the Union's internal policies and how they might be reformed to cope with an enlarged Union. Finally, the budgetary impact of enlargement was examined and proposals made on a financial framework for 2000–6. Indeed, the seriousness with which the Union approached this particular wave of enlargement was truly unprecedented. As Marise Cremona (2003: 1) put it: 'For the first time, specific political, economic, and legal conditions have been applied, regular **progress reports** have been produced, a **pre-accession strategy** has been developed, founded on bilateral treaty commitments but also incorporating "Accession Partnerships", technical assistance and participation by the candidate states in Community programmes'. It was 'an experience of change and adaptation by the European Union as well as by the candidate states'. Nevertheless, despite the complexities of the process, Estonia, the Czech Republic, Hungary, Latvia, Lithuania, Poland, Slovakia and Slovenia joined the Union on 1 May 2004 together with Cyprus and Malta.

**KEY POINTS**

- Enlargement affects the whole range of EU policies.

- Each round of enlargement has engendered significant internal institutional restructuring.

- New countries joined the EU for a variety of economic, political and cultural reasons.

# European Power Politics

The fifth enlargement was also special because of the strategic context in which it occurred and the diversity it created among the membership. When the decision was taken to accept applications for membership, these were tied to strict conditions. This gave the EU the possibility to control democratisation and the development of a market economy through the adoption of EU laws, through opening markets to EU goods, and through the export of values, norms and institutions.

The entire process evolved gradually and the formal accession negotiations were completed in a period similar to the previous cases of enlargement. For instance, the overall process for Hungary and Poland from application to accession took about ten years compared to almost nine years in the case of Spain and Portugal. (See Background box 21.4.)

However, none of the previous cases of enlargement involved such a striking projection of the EU's political and economic power upon the applicant states. And the geopolitical considerations behind enlargement had never been so salient. What was at stake was the establishment of peace, democracy and prosperity in the region. The EU tried to export its institutions, norms and practices in the hope that this would help these countries to maintain economic growth, stabilise their political order and secure their borders. Integration had helped Western Europe to achieve all this in the post-1945 period and the same recipe was used for Eastern Europe in the post-1989 period. This enlargement was less about institutional and financial bargaining and more about power politics.

One can look at the objectives of actors involved in this power political game either in functional or in power terms. From the functional point of view, one would try to establish what kind of European Union the member and applicant states were striving for through the accession process in terms of security, economics and culture. If one were looking at the objectives of actors in terms of power, one would try to establish how they attempted to gain or maintain power through the process of accession. (See Background box 21.5.)

**BACKGROUND BOX 21.4**

### Chronology of Enlargement

1991—first Europe agreements signed (in Preambles, accession was recognised as a wish of the associated country, but not as the express objective of the EU

1993—Copenhagen criteria, i.e. conditionality as feature of accession process

1994—First two CEE applications for membership. Essen summit agrees on a pre-accession strategy mapping out technical preparation

1995—Commission publishes white paper outlining sequence in which associated countries should set about bringing their legislation into line with the *acquis*

July 1997—Commission publishes detailed report on enlargement including 10 Opinions on the CEE applicants and Agenda 2000 with recommendations for EU's financial framework 2000–6

December 1997—Luxembourg summit approves opening of accession negotiations with six states

December 1999—Helsinki council approves negotiations with remaining candidates (six except Turkey)

December 2002—Copenhagen council officially concludes accession negotiations with ten countries and also declares that the objective is to welcome Bulgaria and Romania as members of the EU in 2007

April 2003—The Treaty of Accession between the EU and Cyprus, the Czech Republic, Estonia, Hungary, Latvia, Lithuania, Malta, Poland, Slovakia and Slovenia is signed in Athens

May 2004—the ten countries officially become EU members

December 2004—Croatia and Turkey are invited to start accession negotiations in 2005 subject to certain conditions

May–June 2005—French and Dutch referenda on EU Constitution are held. Anxieties over the EU's enlargement to the east and over the Turkish candidacy are cited as reasons for a 'no' vote

**BACKGROUND BOX 21.5**

The Purpose of Enlargement

'Throughout my life, I have been a convinced European. From my youth I remember the last world war, and I know the value of the peace, stability and prosperity which we have today. I understand how much we have gained from the process of European integration in the past half-century. The wars and atrocities in former Yugoslavia have demonstrated what Europeans can do to each other when forces of disintegration are allowed to overtake the wish for unity. The enlargement of the European Union to me, therefore, is the fulfilment of a vision—a vision that is too easily forgotten in times when security and prosperity within Europe are taken for granted. But if we pause to reflect, we see that this vision is what the EU and its enlargement are really about: the reunification of Europe's peoples in a constitutional framework that encourages them to work in peace and stability.'

Wim Kok, former Prime Minister of the Netherlands, *Enlarging the European Union: Achievements and Challenges*, Florence, European University Institute, 2003, p. 2.

## Functional objectives

Functional objectives in terms of security, economics and culture were spelled out on many occasions by various negotiating actors. Most candidates from Eastern Europe wanted to join a club of secure, prosperous, democratic and relatively well governed countries. They saw themselves as naturally belonging to Europe, but deprived of the opportunity to benefit from democracy and the free market by Soviet hegemony and Western European acquiescence with it. With the fall of communism this historical injustice had to be remedied, and accession to the European Union was to make their return to Europe complete. Eastern Europeans looked at enlargement as a means to move from Europe's periphery to its centre. They also viewed the EU's membership conditions as largely in line with their strategy of modernisation and democratisation. In other words, a significant proportion of the political and economic reforms required by the EU would have to be carried out whether these countries joined the EU or not (see Chapter 9, this volume).

Within the EU, the emphasis was less on historical justice and more on tangible common interests. Western European leaders argued that the EU had to open up to the countries further north, south and east in order to safeguard security, prosperity and democracy in Europe. As Tony Blair put it in November 2002: 'Enlargement will extend Europe's area of peace, democracy and prosperity. We will also be safer and more secure through better cooperation on border controls, asylum and immigration, joint efforts to tackle cross-border crime, and shared environmental standards.' There would also be greater stability, greater access to markets and investment opportunities.

## Power: access and control

Enlargement emerged as the Union's prime instrument of gradually acquiring control over the former communist space. The promise of accession persuaded states in Eastern Europe to adopt EU laws and regulations, to open markets for EU goods and services, and to settle internal and external disputes in a peaceful manner. The Union was acquiring control over the post-communist space by promising access to its decision-making and resources. If this was an exercise in empire building, as some have claimed, then it is important to state that the process was voluntary rather than coercive, and based on incentives rather than punishments.

However, for the old members, there was a price to pay for enlargement. Enlargement means that more states have access to decision-making. And these states have new and perhaps conflicting priorities. There is more pressure on limited resources and there is far greater structural diversity within the EU in terms of income and wealth, law and administration, local habits and culture and language. Hence the attitudes of the general publics in several existing member states were often cautious and somewhat ambivalent with respect to enlargement.

For the acceding states, membership represented not only access to EU funds, but to decision-making. For new states emerging from state socialism (communism) it meant greater economic credibility and political legitimacy.

## Scope of conditionality

The scope of the conditionality for membership was enormous, especially if compared with previous enlargements. The agenda for Eastern European adjustment required by the EU ranged from free elections and property rights to export quotas and unified standards for the production of the most trivial items. Moreover, a similar blueprint was applied to all the applicants.

As with all previous entrants, CEE countries were asked to adopt the *acquis communautaire*. This *acquis* had steadily grown since previous enlargements and was now made up of some 20,000 laws, decisions and regulations, spanning nearly 80,000 pages. The undertaking was thus unprecedented especially if one considers that most of the new entrants were relatively weak states in economic and institutional terms.

Another key feature of the EU conditionality policy was its intrusiveness. The EU not only told Eastern European applicants what they should do—for instance in terms of new legislation or administrative reform—but it also sent representatives to specific ministries there to make sure that

the changes were being made as prescribed through its 'twinning' programme. The whole process of readjustment was carefully monitored. At every stage, the champions and laggards were identified at regular review sessions through the publication of the European Commission's regular reports on the candidate countries.

The normative power of the EU should also be taken into consideration. EU fundamental norms of democracy, market economy, human rights and social justice were seen as an example to follow by all applicant states. Moreover, the EU was in a position to provide authoritative interpretations of these norms, to accord or deny international recognition of certain policies, and to confer international legitimacy upon the applicant states' behaviour.

The EU's structural dominance over Eastern European applicants was thus enormous, allowing it to put in place a very broad, detailed and intrusive package of conditionality. However, at the end of the accession process, the candidate countries were getting seats at the EU table. Structural inequality was thus not to be indefinite. Moreover, the EU conditionality package was vague and ambiguous. This created a degree of flexibility in complying with the EU conditions for accession. For instance, there was no single model of democracy, administration or social policy that the EU expected the candidate states to adopt. Nor has the Union ever articulated the vision of Europe for which it is striving. Indeed, its policies have often been guided by an accidental combination of internal and external pressures rather than broader strategic considerations.

The enlargement taking in eight CEE countries together with Cyprus and Malta was thus a complex and quite sophisticated response to the huge number of challenges and problems facing Europe since the end of the Cold War. It has shown that the Union is able to apply its power and leverage abroad in a purposeful and effective manner. It has also shown that export of institutions and regulatory frames can be an efficient means of foreign

ANIA KROK-PASZKOWSKA AND JAN ZIELONKA

## BACKGROUND BOX 21.6

### Dilemma of Inclusion and Exclusion

'The European priority now is to construct a stable and workable institutional order for a broad region without definable boundaries, within which it will nevertheless be necessary to draw demarcation lines. The most difficult task will be to construct a mutually satisfactory framework for relations with the dependent states on Europe's periphery, to associate them with Europe's prosperous and secure Western states: to find a formula that allows them access, through borders which are at once permeable and secure.'

> William Wallace, 'Where Does Europe End?', in Jan Zielonka (ed.), *Europe Unbound: Enlarging and Reshaping the Boundaries of the European Union*, London, Routledge, 2002, p. 93.

Turkey, Serbia, Ukraine, Belarus or Russia would obviously represent an even greater challenge, but then the interests at stake are also arguably greater. The EU can hardly afford major political or economic instability in these rather volatile states. (See Background box 21.6.)

### KEY POINTS

- The last wave of enlargement was the EU's response to the events of 1989.

- The fifth enlargement involved a striking projection of the EU's political and economic power upon the applicant states.

- From the EU perspective enlargement was chiefly about securing peace and prosperity in the future Europe through the skilful use of EU membership conditionality.

- For the CEE states, EU membership conditions were in line with their strategy of modernisation and democratisation.

- EU membership for the CEE states meant a move from Europe's periphery to its centre.

policy. The success of this enlargement is likely to encourage the Union to act towards its new neighbours in a similar fashion. Countries such as

# Diversity and Integration

Not all visions of European integration are compatible with enlargement. The problem is not only that widening makes deepening more difficult. The danger is that poorly designed and implemented enlargement may paralyse European institutions, erode western democratic standards, produce economic chaos and even undermine Europe's security.

One of the main sources of anxiety has been the perceived level of diversity in the enlarged EU. The fear is that, despite the intensive process of mutual adaptation, the post-communist new member states are not yet truly compatible with Western

European states. The new members are functioning democracies which share the core values of the EU. However, upon joining the Union they had been democracies only for just over a decade. In some cases even their statehood was newly established. Faced with taking in fragile democracies, the EU devised the Copenhagen political criteria but with no guarantees that liberal reforms would continue after accession. Moreover, although these countries' transformation to competitive market economies has been virtually completed, they are much poorer than West European states. Their institutional infrastructure constitutes the basis for good governance, but their economic, legal and administrative structures are less developed. They also have their own distinct histories, societies and cultures. They have different foreign and security preoccupations. The European Union will thus be a much more diversified entity following this particular wave of enlargement. (See Background box 21.7.)

The existing literature on enlargement usually views diversity in the fields of economics, democracy and foreign policy as being somewhat problematic.

## Welfare gap

The welfare gap between the old and new EU members is significant. At the time of accession, the new members had an average GDP per capita of only 40 per cent of that of existing members (at purchasing power parity). This compares with Spain's and Portugal's average per capita GDP of 70 per cent of the existing EC when they joined

in 1986. Such economic disparities are said to create pressure for large financial transfers from rich to poor member states, prevent the new members from fully implementing the existing *acquis*, and disrupt smooth functioning of the EMU and the single market. However, it should also be remembered that the total GDP at market prices and current exchange rates of new members is less than 5 per cent of the GDP of the former EU15. The small economic size of new members also facilitates economic transfers. Even a tiny sacrifice by the old richer members means a lot for the new poorer members. Besides, under Agenda 2000 the Union was able to keep financial transfers under control.

Growth rates are generally higher in the states which have recently acceded to the EU than in the old member states, and are expected to rise still more. Experience with previous enlargements shows that EU membership is a powerful factor fostering growth rates in new members, and this in turn helps to achieve convergence in income. Moreover, welfare gaps existed within the EU15 and they caused few economic problems. For instance, Austria's gross national income (GNI) per capita is more than double that of Portugal. The gap between Sweden and Greece is even greater. And Luxembourg's GNI per capita is nearly twice as high as that of Sweden or Austria.

The accession of Eastern European states will make differences in welfare more visible, more striking and probably more challenging, but the Union is quite accustomed to living with such kinds of differences.

## Democracy and political culture

In the field of democracy and political culture, there is no clear East–West divide, at least from the formal point of view. All new members are either parliamentary or semi-presidential republics. They all have constitutions providing checks and balances between different branches of power. Citizens' basic

---

**BACKGROUND BOX 21.7**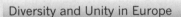

### Diversity and Unity in Europe

"Europe is one political entity whose security is indivisible. The idea that there could forever be two Europes—a democratic, stable and prosperous Europe engaged in integration and a less democratic, less stable and less prosperous Europe—is, in my opinion, totally mistaken. It resembles a belief that one half of a room could be heated and the other half kept unheated at the same time. There is only one Europe, despite its diversity, and any weightier occurrence anywhere in this area will have consequences and repercussions throughout the rest of the continent.'

" Address by Vaclav Havel, President of the Czech Republic, before the members of the European Parliament, Strasbourg, 16 February 2000, cited in www.hrad.cz/president/havel/speeches/2000/1602_uk.html "

rights and freedoms are also guaranteed by law. NGO membership density per million of population, although it varies from country to country, does not show particular differences between the eastern and western parts of the Union. In sum, a comparison of formal laws and institutions does not reveal any particular pattern of divergence between old and new EU members. Nor is there a striking East–West divide when we look at independent evaluations of democracy, rights and freedoms.

Nevertheless, in the former communist states the effort required to achieve a liberal democracy and a participatory political culture has been greater than initially expected. Successive governments have pursued neo-liberal economic policies and largely ignored their social impact. This has led to a wide gulf between political elites and their electorates. Political parties are weak and often alienated from society. There is a danger of charismatic leaders emerging with promises of easy solutions to economic and social hardship by preaching intolerance, exclusiveness and a rejection of compromise. So far such populist appeals have enjoyed limited electoral success. Moreover, several Western European states such as Austria or Belgium have also seen the rise of populist politics based on symbols, myths and nationalism.

There are still problems of transparency, inefficiency and corruption in the state apparatus of new member states, despite far-reaching reforms. Again this has been largely due to legacies of a command economy and the party state and the need rapidly to set up entirely new public institutions and increase administrative capacity to manage privatisation and the EU accession process.

## Foreign policy and attitudes towards the USA

In terms of foreign policy, and more specifically attitudes towards the USA, the Central and Eastern Europeans have tended to see alliance with the USA as a means of escaping from centuries of domination by Germany and Russia. Indeed, for historical reasons, and due to their geographical proximity to Russia, CEEs are probably more sensitive to possible security threats than states in the western part of Europe. The pro-American stance of a new member state such as Poland led to it being described by some—as had Britain by de Gaulle some 30 years earlier—as an 'American Trojan horse' within the Union. However, there is little evidence of a clear and consistent cleavage between old and new EU members when it comes to the USA. Individual member states have a complex set of diplomatic relationships within and across EU borders and they pursue their security in a different manner depending on the case and circumstances of the day.

## Managing diversity

For those who advocate a unified, homogeneous federal EU, differences in structure and behaviour are seen as something to be overcome or even as something fundamentally undesirable. However, homogenising tendencies in the process of European integration have been countered by the development of concepts of subsidiarity and flexibility. Moreover, until recently, member states have been able to obtain temporary or permanent opt-outs in certain policy fields. In the case of eastward enlargement, however, the applicants were denied the opportunity for the various opt-outs that had already been negotiated by some current member states in the areas of foreign, monetary, social or border-related policy (e.g. the Schengen *acquis*). The negotiating process was aimed at streamlining and unifying where possible, with transitional periods kept to a minimum.

The EU policy of enlargement was thus very much about reducing diversity through political crafting and institutional engineering. The applicant states were required to implement a set of conditions that were aimed at making them

EU compatible. Their progress in meeting these conditions was subject to regular screening. Accession was meant to take place only once the applicants had met the envisaged targets. However, accession conditions were often imprecise, impractical and contradictory. They represented general principles rather than well established and uniformly applied norms. Moreover, they were not applied consistently. The screening process was superficial and subject to discretionary interpretation. And the successive decisions taken within the process of enlargement resulted from hard and largely unpredictable political bargaining rather than from a carefully crafted blueprint.

---

**KEY POINTS**

- The accession of Eastern European states highlighted differences in levels of economic development and welfare but, while this was undoubtedly a challenge, there have always been significant welfare gaps within the Union and they have been managed successfully so far.

- There were no clear structural differences between the eastern and western parts of the Union in the fields of democracy and political culture, but new ways would have to be found to accommodate a more diversified set of cultural orientations in the enlarged EU.

- Greater legal, economic and cultural diversity requires a different kind of governance than practised in the original EU. In the enlarged EU we are likely to see a further shift from a hierarchical type of governance to a polycentric one based on incentives rather than sanctions.

---

# Nature of the Enlarged EU

What is the nature of the enlarged European Union and how can it address the challenges posed by enlargement? Since its inception the EU has continuously evolved and adapted. Its scope in terms of policy remit and its size in terms of membership have grown, although this has not always been matched by its capacity to manage its own affairs. During the early stages of European integration, it was unclear whether power would rest with the member states or would be transferred to the emerging European polity. Opinion has been, and remains, divided between adherents of different models of European integration. Those who favour an intergovernmental model would prefer a Union in which member states would bargain among themselves to reach compromises on policy outcomes that would serve their economic interests. This would leave them free to choose how the EU should function. Federalists envision a Union taking on more attributes of a nation state, such as clear-cut borders, a common army and police force, a central budget funded by direct taxation as well as a common currency and a common foreign and security policy. However, these models are not mutually exclusive and indeed the EU has always been a hybrid. The nature of this hybrid is still in flux, however. No doubt, one of the factors behind the current change is cascading globalisation, but enlargement has also stimulated change and often in the same direction. Both enlargement and globalisation make simple hierarchical governmental structures unworkable if not redundant altogether. They both put pressures on Europe's borders, making them soft rather than hard. And both enlargement and globalisation

**BACKGROUND BOX 21.8**

### The Widening and Deepening Dilemma

'If we are to be able to meet this historic challenge and integrate the new member States without substantially denting the EU's capacity for action, we must put into place the last brick in the building of European integration, namely political integration.'

From 'Confederacy to Federation: Thoughts on the Finality of European Integration,' speech by Joschka Fischer at the Humboldt University in Berlin, 12 May 2000

stimulate cultural exchanges and subsequent cultural differentiation of the European public space. The following sections will deal with these three major changes prompted by enlargement (and globalisation). (See Background box 21.8.)

## Multi-layered polity

Since the late 1990s there was mounting evidence that European leaders were afraid that enlargement was going to paralyse the EU institutional structure. This is why the Union embarked on major institutional reform prior to the eastern enlargement. However, accomplishing these reforms proved extremely difficult. The 1996 Intergovernmental Conference on institutional reforms resulted in the 1997 Amsterdam Treaty which provided for the progressive establishment of an area of freedom, security and justice, extended the scope of communitarian policy-making in justice and home affairs, and produced a new set of tools in the field of foreign and security policy. It also introduced the concept of 'flexibility' which allowed for further integration by less than the full complement of member states. However, many of the institutional reforms necessitated by enlargement towards the CEE countries, the so-called Amsterdam leftovers, were postponed until the next IGC in 2000 which took place against the background of negotiations with the CEE candidate states.

The 2000 Nice Treaty was limited to dealing with the three Amsterdam leftovers (size and composition of the Commission, weighting of votes in the Council and extension of qualified majority voting). The negotiations were very protracted and the final compromise complicated rather than simplified the Union's decision-making process. After the disappointing results of the EU treaty revision at Nice, European leaders opted for a spectacular institutional 'big bang': a new European constitution. However, with the apparent failure of the Treaty any major institutional reform of the Union is unlikely for several years. This means that the Union will be a very complex and multi-layered polity. We are likely to see inter-penetration of various types of political units operating in a system without a clear power centre and hierarchy. For instance, European, national and regional levels of government will compete for resources and competence. (One should add that in Central and Eastern Europe independent regions have usually been created only through the process of European integration, with the European Commission insisting that regional institutions be set up in order to manage the structural funds.) European agencies responsible for different domains of European administration will also have different formal powers and geographic reach. For instance, the European Central Bank is not in Brussels but in Frankfurt and its formal powers apply only to countries belonging to the Eurozone. (In 2006, none of the new EU members belonged to the Eurozone). It is difficult to resist the impression that such a multi-layered, multi-centred and heterogeneous European polity will resemble a neo-medieval empire rather than a classical federal state. (See Background box 21.9.)

## Fuzzy borders

The enlarged EU will also lack another important attribute of a state, namely relatively hard, centrally governed and geographically fixed borders. Although new communitarian solutions for organising the EU's borders are being introduced they are

## BACKGROUND BOX 21.9

### The (Failed) Constitutional Treaty

'The new treaty makes it clear that the EU is not a state. The Union lacks most of the administrative and coercive powers that characterize sovereign countries.... Under the constitutional treaty the EU will be far more diverse and flexible than it is now. Different groups of member-states will be able to pursue integration—in defence, or criminal law or even the harmonization of tax bases—while others can choose to watch from the fringes.... [The draft treaty] opens up the possibility that member-states will take a "pick'n'mix" approach to future integration, in line with their very different capabilities and ambitions.'

❝ The CER guide to the EU's constitutional treaty', Centre for European Reform, *Policy Brief*, London, July 2004, available at www.cer.org.uk ❞

Nor would it be easy to fix the EU's borders. Although further enlargements of the EU to countries such as Turkey, let alone Ukraine or Serbia are being resisted in most of the member states, it would be extremely difficult to halt the enlargement process. This is because the Union needs to address mounting threats just outside its borders and the policy of conditional admittance to the Union has proved to be a powerful tool for stabilising the external environment. It is increasingly obvious that alternative solutions in the form of strategic partnerships or neighbourhood policy are inadequate to shape political and economic developments in the western Balkans, Maghreb and in some former Soviet republics. (See Background box 21.10.)

As a consequence, the Union is likely to end up with soft border zones in flux rather than with hard and fixed external borderlines as envisaged by Schengen. In due time, the EU's borders will probably be less territorial, less physical and less visible.

## Cultural plurality

Democracy and legitimacy are not only about institutions, they are also about culture understood in broader political, legal and economic terms. Nations are bound by a common history, language, culture and ethnicity and it is often argued that it is

constantly being questioned by a variety of political groups and countries. On the one hand, the system of Schengen is criticised by those who believe that nation states can control borders better, especially in the age of terrorism. On the other hand, others point to a growing body of evidence suggesting that the system is unduly harsh, impractical and at odds with the Union's major foreign-policy objectives. In an era of increasing interdependence it is difficult to seal any borders, especially those that are in constant flux due to successive waves of enlargement. A hard border regime does not necessarily help mitigate concerns about terrorism, cross-border crime and migration. At the same time, hard borders hamper profitable trade, alienate the EU's current and future neighbours and jeopardise the existing western system of civic rights and freedoms. Some of the new member states from Eastern Europe are particularly unhappy about the Schengen *acquis* because it frustrates cross-border human links of their respective nationals, curbs flourishing economic relations resulting from these links and even causes some legal problems.

## BACKGROUND BOX 21.10

### Will the Union Enlarge Further?

'If Europe is seen as closing its door to Turkey, the Balkans and the Ukraine, it should know it is opening the door for other forces and risks creating instability on its very doorstep in the decades ahead. Different satellite arrangements, whatever glorious labels they are given, will do next to nothing to compensate as long as that door is closed.'

❝ Carl Bildt, former Prime Minister of Sweden 'Europe Must Keep Its "Soft Power"', *Financial Times*, 1 June 2005, p. 17 ❞

only on this basis that polities can be built. As stated earlier, enlargement has further diversified the cultural map of Europe and has broadened the democratic public space. As a consequence, democratic decision-making within the EU will have to accommodate a more diversified set of interests and cultural orientations. It is also difficult to imagine the emergence of a single or easily identifiable pan-European identity, let alone a European *demos*.

Of course, *demos*, ethos and identity are not primordial and stable categories. They evolve over time through experiences and discourses in a certain public space. The role of various political agents in engineering them cannot be underestimated. In fact, the European Union promotes various European symbols, such as for instance the European flag, which are aimed at strengthening European identity. European citizenship is also part of this effort, as are various cultural and educational exchange programmes. Likewise, structural funds or the euro play a role in enhancing European identity. The question is, however, whether this is enough to create a cultural basis for a well functioning democracy at the European level. The question also is whether efforts to engineer a European identity are plausible on either political or cultural grounds. Czech President Václav Klaus expressed the anxiety of millions of fellow Eastern Europeans by asking: Shall we let our identity 'dissolve in Europe like a lump of sugar in a cup of coffee?' (Klaus 1994: 136). This view has been confirmed by opinion polls. According to the 2004 Eurobarometer, the majority of those polled in the new member states consider themselves as 'their nationality only' rather than calling themselves 'European to some extent'. (In the old member states the result is reversed.)

The situation seems rather hopeless. However, rather than trying to build a European nation-writ-large we can think about enhancing a sense of constitutional patriotism across the continent reflecting common rights and duties of all European citizens. There is a lot of wisdom in the European Commission's slogan 'United in diversity'. After all, identity that does not recognise pluralism, individualism and multiculturalism can hardly be conducive to a democratic system.

---

**KEY POINTS**

- The enlarged EU will lack some basic state characteristics such as a central government in charge of a fixed territory.

- In the absence of strong cultural links the enlarged EU will have to rely on some kind of cultural patriotism based on common civic norms and values.

- The borders of the Union are likely to remain soft and fuzzy partly due to the pressures of globalisation and partly due to further enlargement on geo-strategic grounds.

---

# Conclusion

The official EU policy is that the widening of the Union goes hand in hand with its deepening. The Union is trying hard on behalf of its member states to regain a degree of control over the forces of globalisation and to assert its sovereignty within its borders. It is gradually introducing some forms of central European government not only in the fields of foreign, monetary and social policy, but even in the fields of defence and JHA. The Union is also trying to improve its democratic credentials and enhance a common European cultural identity, for instance through the European citizenship project.

The enlargement process has been accompanied by efforts to deepen EU integration through the expansion of the *acquis communautaire*, the creation of a single market and the imposition of a strict external border regime. New countries can join the European Union, but only after meeting an ever-growing list of conditions that would make them compatible with the current members and fit them into the existing system.

However, it can be somewhat misleading to apply statist terms and analogies to the Union. The EU is not a typical state, but a complex international institution in search of purpose and legitimacy. It is an actor of multifaceted character, full of paradoxes and contradictions. The EU is aspiring to become a powerful international actor without turning itself into a super-state. It has ambitions to stabilise its external environment, but its policies are being guided by internal rather than external pressures. The EU has no effective monopoly over the legitimate means of coercion. It has no clearly defined centre of authority. Its territory is not fixed. Its geographical, administrative, economic and cultural borders diverge. The Union also lacks a strong and coherent sense of cultural identity, let alone of a European *demos* or *patria*. Globalisation with its massive labour and capital flows makes it difficult for the Union (or in fact for any other actor) to maintain a minimum degree of sovereignty, hierarchy and order.

Decision-making will become more complex with 25 members. However, European actors (the Commission and the member states) have been very resourceful in finding ways out of and around deadlock situations. Various scholars have argued that in heterogeneous polities (which the EU undoubtedly is) the diversity of interests creates opportunities for trade-offs among actors thus increasing the likelihood of agreement. Such polities are characterised by accommodation, bargaining and compromise-seeking. There is a growing body of literature arguing that variable geometry and competing jurisdictions should be applied to such a complex and highly diversified environment as the enlarged EU. Flexible governance arrangements and overlapping, polycentric jurisdictions are said to serve well both efficiency and redistribution. They allow decision-makers to adjust the scale of governance to reflect heterogeneity. They provide more complete information on constituents' preferences, and are more adaptive in response to changing preferences. They are also more open to experimentation and innovation, and facilitate more credible commitments. Indeed, diversity may prove not only an important prerequisite of democracy, but also of efficiency, in that it may be argued that it is only highly diversified and pluralistic societies acting in a complex web of institutional arrangements that are able to succeed in conditions of modern competition.

The fifth enlargement is part of an unprecedented historical process generated by the fall of communism and the East–West division of Europe. It represents an enormous import of diversity that can hardly be addressed by the new members' formal adoption of the *acquis communautaire*. It has also opened the door to further EU accessions on strategic rather than strict economic, legal or cultural grounds. In other words, this particular wave of enlargement has dramatically and irreversibly transformed the nature of the Union.

---

**? QUESTIONS**

1. What impact have previous enlargements had on the process of European integration?

2. Which objectives have guided the EU's enlargement into post-communist Europe?

3. What did EU conditionality towards the candidate countries involve and how successful was conditionality in ensuring candidates were ready to take up the obligations of membership?

4. How will enlargement to 25 member states affect the way the institutions of the Union work?

5. Will the enlarged EU be able play a greater role in world affairs?

6. What can the EU offer to those who are not candidates for membership, but who want to share in the area of peace, prosperity and security on their doorstep?

7. How will the Union be able to cope with the economic, social and cultural diversity after enlargement?

8. Are there territorial limits to further EU enlargements?

 **FURTHER READING**

■ **Cameron, F. (ed) (2004),** *The Future of Europe: Integration and Enlargement*, London, Routledge. Gives a detailed account of the state of the EU on the eve of eastward enlargement and considers its future prospects in several key areas.

■ **Cremona, M. (ed) (2003),** *The Enlargement of the European Union*, Oxford, Oxford University Press. Examines the process of the fifth enlargement and its impact on both the candidate states and the institutions and policies of the EU.

■ **Jacoby, W. (2004),** *The Enlargement of the European Union and NATO: Ordering from the Menu in Central Europe*, Cambridge, Cambridge University Press. Compares the two processes of enlargement and sets them in a broader geopolitical context.

■ **Mair, P. and Zielonka, J. (eds) (2002),** *The Enlarged European Union: Diversity and Adaptation*, London, Frank Cass. Assesses the political and economic diversity in the enlarged EU and investigates what the implications of this diversity are likely to be.

■ **Rupnik, J. and Zielonka, J. (eds) (2003),** *The Road to the European Union. Vol. 1: The Case of the Czech Republic and Slovakia*, Manchester, Manchester University Press and Pettai, V. and Zielonka, J. (eds) (2003), *The Road to the European Union. Vol. 2: The Case of Estonia, Latvia and Lithuania*, Manchester, Manchester University Press. These two volumes reveal the Eastern European part of the enlargement story and show how enlargement has been played out in the domestic politics of the candidate countries.

■ **Schimmelfennig, F. and Sedelmeier, U. (eds) (2005),** *The Politics of European Union Enlargement: Theoretical Approaches*, London, Routledge. Focuses on a theoretical approach to the EU's eastward enlargement and combines this with comparative analyses.

■ **Tsoukalis, L. (1981),** *The European Community and its Mediterranean Enlargement*, London, Allen & Unwin. Analyses one of the previous waves of enlargement in the 1980s to Greece, Spain and Portugal.

■ **Vachudova, M. A. (2005),** *Europe Undivided: Democracy, Leverage, and Integration After Communism*, Oxford, Oxford University Press. Reveals how variations in domestic competition put democratising states on different political trajectories after 1989, and how the EU's leverage eventually influenced domestic politics in liberal and particularly illiberal democracies.

■ **Zielonka, J. (2006),** *Europe as Empire: The Nature of the Enlarged EU*, Oxford, Oxford University Press. Analyses the evolving nature of the European Union following the last wave of enlargement. It sets forth a novel way of thinking about the European governance in the field of economics, democracy and foreign policy.

■ Zielonka, J. (ed) (2002), *Europe Unbound: Enlarging and Reshaping the Boundaries of the European Union*, London, Routledge. Shows how moving the EU's borders further south and east changes the nature of European integration.

## IMPORTANT WEBSITES

● **www.europa.eu.int/comm/enlargement/index_en.htm**  This is the website of the European Commission DG Enlargement, and provides background information and state of play with respect to acceding countries, candidate countries and potential candidate countries.

● **www.europarl.eu.int/enlargement/default_en.htm**  The website of the European Parliament with information on enlargement, state of negotiations, Eurobarometer and the role of the European Parliament in the enlargement process.

● **www.cer.org.uk/enlargement/index.html**  The Centre for European Reform is a think-tank and forum for discussion about the challenges facing the EU. The website includes analyses, archives, list of upcoming seminars and publications by the Centre.

● **www.ceps.be/Default.php**  The Centre for European Policy Studies is a policy research institute. The website provides a list of publications and activities of the Centre.

● **www.euractiv.com**  Provides news about EU policies and activities divided into policy sections, including one on enlargement with news, interviews, analyses and web links.

**Visit the Online Resource Center that accompanies this book for lots of useful additional material, including an interactive map of Europe. www.oxfordtextbooks.co.uk/orc/hay_menon/**

# 22 External Economic Relations

## ALASDAIR R. YOUNG

→ **Chapter Contents**

- Introduction
- Europe and the Global Economy
- External Economic Policies
- Trade Policy-making in the EU
- Europe and Global Economic Governance
- External Economic Policies as Foreign-Policy Tools
- Conclusion

✔ **Reader's Guide**

European politics and external economic relations intersect in four particularly salient ways. First, common external economic policies have been central to the project of European integration since its inception. Second, nonetheless, there has been persistent tension among the member states and between the member states and the European institutions about the appropriate location of authority in external economic relations. Third, external economic relations are the interface between the state and processes of globalisation, influencing how globalisation affects Europe and how Europe seeks to 'harness' globalisation. Fourth, the implications of globalisation have led to significant changes in the politics of Europe's external economic relations. This chapter develops and explores these four crucial intersections. It begins by providing the necessary background about Europe's importance to the global economy and how the global economy affects Europe and by describing Europe's principal external economic policies. It then examines the location of authority for various external economic policies and the implications for the politics of policy-making. The chapter then considers the European Union as both a model for economic relations among states and as an actor seeking to shape the governance of the global economy. The final section of the chapter examines how the EU uses its economic relations to pursue foreign-policy objectives.

# Introduction

External economic policies—how high tariffs (taxes) on imports of goods are, how extensive are restrictions on the provision of services across borders or on investment in production or service provision (foreign direct investment (FDI)) or in stocks and bonds (portfolio investment) and whether a currency is freely traded—are crucial to determining the impact of globalisation upon a state. European integration has sought progressively to eliminate these impediments to economic exchange among its member states, but it has also sought to establish common policies in these areas towards the rest of the world. As a consequence, Europe has emerged both as an important player in shaping **global economic governance** and as an example of how deeper economic integration might be pursued.

This chapter, therefore, examines both how the global economy impacts on Europe and how Europe affects the global economy. It concentrates on four particularly salient interactions between external economic relations and European politics. The first is the central role that pursuing common external relations has played in the development of the European Union, both at its inception and more recently as it has sought to establish itself as an international actor. The second is the enduring tension over the appropriate location for external economic relations: the EU or the member states. The third interaction concerns the impact of globalisation on Europe and Europe's influence on globalisation, particularly as an example of deep economic integration and prominent advocate of a rule-based system of economic governance. The chapter also considers how the changing nature of trade politics in response to the changing nature of international economic exchange and the development of global economic governance have affected Europe.

This chapter examines these four salient intersections with reference to the four most important economic policies: trade, foreign direct investment, development and monetary policy. It pays particular attention to trade policy both for its importance in its own right and because of the extent to which the EU uses trade policy to pursue other policy objectives, including promoting development and encouraging human rights and democratisation.

This chapter begins by establishing Europe's importance in the international economy and establishing how important the rest of the world is economically for the EU's member states. It then introduces Europe's external economic policies affecting trade, foreign direct investment, development and monetary policy. It also examines the increasingly important external effects of some of the EU's principal internal policies: the common agricultural policy and the single European market. Having established Europe's importance in the global economy and the principal ways in which it interacts with the rest of the world, it analyses how the EU's member states decide how to pursue these policies, especially the extent to which they are pursued collectively. The chapter then considers the EU's efforts to influence global economic governance, before turning to how it seeks to use external economic policies to pursue foreign-policy objectives.

# Europe and the Global Economy

External economic relations in Europe have two distinct, but related dimensions. One is among the member states of the European Union. Eliminating obstacles to economic exchange among the member states has been a defining characteristic of European integration from the outset. Although such barriers have not been entirely eliminated, and probably never will be, the remaining obstacles pale into insignificance when compared to those found among most states of the world. This chapter, therefore, focuses on the second dimension of Europe's external economic relations: its relations with the rest of the world.

Taken together, the member states of the EU have the world's second largest economy, only slightly smaller than the US economy in purchasing power parity terms, and slightly larger at official exchange rates. (See Table 22.1.) The EU is the world's largest merchandise exporter, accounting for nearly one-fifth of world trade, and largest services exporter, accounting for over one-quarter of world trade. It

is the world's largest importer of commercial services and second only to the USA as an importer of goods.

Significantly, however, most European trade occurs among the member states of the EU. (See Figure 22.1.) If trade among the EU member states is included, Germany emerges as the world's leading exporter of merchandise goods, ahead of the USA and China, and is second only to the USA as a merchandise importer. Belgium, France, Italy, the Netherlands and the UK are also all among the world's top ten merchandise importers and exporters. (See Table 22.2.) Thus trade within the EU is more economically, and potentially politically, significant than the EU's trade with the rest of the world. (See Theme box: The Impact of Globalisation.)

Europe is also a major home to and host of foreign direct investment. (See Table 22.1.) As with trade, the majority of Europe's FDI flows occur among the member states of the EU. During 2001–3, for example, just over a third of EU FDI outflows were

**Table 22.1** The EU's Importance in the Global Economy

| | Share of world GDP (PPP) 2005 | Share of world trade 2004 (excludes intra-EU) | | | | Share of global FDI 2004 (includes intra-EU) | | | |
|---|---|---|---|---|---|---|---|---|---|
| | | Goods exports | Goods imports | Services exports | Services imports | Inflows | Outflows | Inward stock | Outward stock |
| EU25 | 20.5 | 18.1 | 18.3 | 27.8 | 25.1 | 33.4 | 38.3 | 45.2 | 53.3 |
| USA | 20.8 | 12.3 | 21.8 | 20.7 | 17.1 | 14.8 | 31.4 | 16.6 | 20.7 |
| China | 13.7 | 8.9 | 8.0 | 4.0 | 4.7 | 9.4 | 0.2 | 2.8 | 0.4 |
| Japan | 6.5 | 8.5 | 6.5 | 6.2 | 8.8 | 1.2 | 4.2 | 1.1 | 3.8 |
| Canada | 1.8 | 4.8 | 4.0 | 3.0 | 3.7 | 1.0 | 6.5 | 3.4 | 3.8 |

*Sources*: GDP: CIA, *The World Factbook,* estimated. Trade: WTO, *International Trade Statistics 2005*. FDI: UNCTAD, *World Investment Report 2005*

**Figure 22.1** European trading partners, (2005)

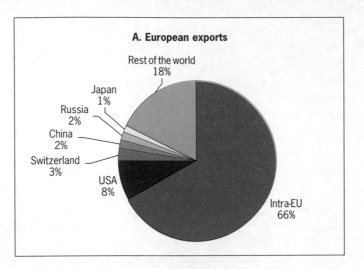

A. European exports

Rest of the world
18%

Japan
1%

Russia
2%

China
2%

Switzerland
3%

USA
8%

Intra-EU
66%

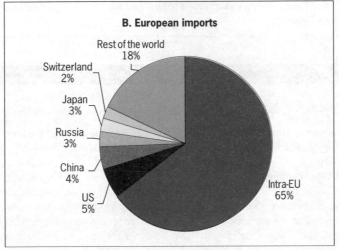

B. European imports

Rest of the world
18%

Switzerland
2%

Japan
3%

Russia
3%

China
4%

US
5%

Intra-EU
65%

*Source*: Author's calculations based on DG Trade, 'Top Trading Partners' and 'EU Trade in the World' available at http://ec.europa.eu/comm/trade/issues/bilateral/data.htm (Acessed 20 August 2006)

to non-EU25 countries and just over a quarter of FDI inflows came from outside the EU25 (author's calculations based on Eurostat 2004). Also, as with trade, individual EU member states rank among the top ten homes to and hosts of FDI. (See Table 22.3.)

Europe also influences the world economy through its currencies. (See Chapter 16, this volume.) The euro is second only to the dollar as a reserve currency, and accounts for over 20 per cent of foreign-exchange reserves, compared to over 60 per cent for the US dollar. Moreover, the euro was used in 37 per cent of extra-Eurozone international transactions in 2004, compared to 89 per cent for the US dollar. The British pound was used in 17 per cent.

Europe's importance to the global economy is significant for three reasons. First, it gives the EU a major stake in the governance of the global

ALASDAIR R. YOUNG

**Table 22.2** Top Ten World Traders, including Intra-EU Trade, 2004

| | Imports | | | Exports | |
|---|---|---|---|---|---|
| **Rank** | **Country** | **% world** | **Rank** | **Country** | **% world** |
| 1 | USA | 16.3 | 1 | Germany | 10.3 |
| 2 | Germany | 7.9 | 2 | USA | 9.1 |
| 3 | China | 5.6 | 3 | China | 6.9 |
| 4 | France | 5.1 | 4 | Japan | 6.0 |
| 5 | UK | 5.0 | 5 | France | 5.1 |
| 6 | Japan | 4.9 | 6 | Netherlands | 4.1 |
| 7 | Italy | 3.8 | 7 | Italy | 4.0 |
| 8 | Netherlands | 3.4 | 8 | UK | 3.9 |
| 9 | Canada | 3.3 | 9 | Canada | 3.6 |
| 10 | Belgium | 3.2 | 10 | Belgium | 3.5 |

*Source*: DG Trade, 'Top Trading Partners', available at http://ec.europa.eu/comm/trade/issues/bilateral/data.htm, accessed 25 February 2006

**THEME BOX**

## The Impact of Globalisation

External economic relations policies are the interface between Europe and globalisation. They both moderate how exposed Europe is to the pressures of globalisation and provide the means through which to try to 'harness' globalisation.

Several factors have led to Europe's economy being relatively open to international economic exchange. As a consequence of trade liberalisation through the multilateral trade rounds the EU has relatively low tariffs on most manufactured goods. The single European market programme made it easier for third-country products to circulate in the EU, liberalised services and abolished exchange-rate controls. At the same time the member states have, despite the odd hiccup, liberalised their foreign investment regimes, for both FDI and portfolio investment.

Despite this relative openness to the world, Europe's states are far more open to each other. As a consequence more than 60 per cent of Europe's trade and foreign direct investment occurs among the member states of the EU. This suggests that the greatest pressures from international competition come from within the EU. Moreover, as the USA, Japan and Switzerland are among the top five exporters to the EU, more than 75 per cent of EU imports, including intra-EU, come from developed countries.

Nonetheless, globalisation provokes considerable concern in Europe, particularly in the context of the capacity to maintain the European welfare state. In part as a consequence, the EU has been at the forefront of efforts to, in the Commission's word, 'harness' globalisation. It has sought to do so through promoting, albeit only modestly, common core labour standards and rules on environmental protection. Although it has been unsuccessful within the WTO due to opposition from some developing countries, it has used preferential access to its market to encourage other developing countries to embrace existing international rules in these areas.

The intensity of economic competition within Europe and the EU's use of its market power to seek to 'harness' globalisation underpin two competing views of the relationship between the EU and globalisation: one sees the EU as intensifying the pressures of globalisation; the other depicts the EU as a buffer against it.

**Table 22.3** Top Ten World Hosts of and Homes to FDI, (2004)

| | Imports | | | Exports | |
|---|---|---|---|---|---|
| Rank | Country | % world | Rank | Country | % world |
| 1 | USA | 16.6 | 1 | USA | 20.7 |
| 2 | UK | 8.7 | 2 | UK | 14.2 |
| 3 | France | 6.0 | 3 | Germany | 8.6 |
| 4 | Hong Kong | 5.1 | 4 | France | 7.9 |
| 5 | Netherlands | 4.8 | 5 | Netherlands | 5.6 |
| 6 | Germany | 3.9 | 6 | Hong Kong | 4.2 |
| 7 | Spain | 3.9 | 7 | Switzerland | 4.0 |
| 8 | Canada | 3.4 | 8 | Japan | 3.8 |
| 9 | Belgium | 2.9 | 9 | Canada | 3.8 |
| 10 | Australia | 2.9 | 10 | Spain | 3.4 |

*Source*: author's calculations based on UNCTAD, *World Investment Report 2005*

economy. Second, the size of its economy and its share of global imports means that its policies can have important implications for other countries. Third, because its economy is important to other actors it is able to exercise influence by making access to its valuable market conditional on domestic-policy changes or trade concessions.

**KEY POINTS**

- Europe is very important to the international economy in terms of its market size, participation in trade and foreign direct investment and, to a lesser extent, because of the euro.

- This gives it a stake in and influence over the development of global economic governance.

- The vast majority of Europe's international economic exchange, however, occurs among the members of the EU, and European integration, therefore, is a more significant pressure than is globalisation.

# External Economic Policies

Having established Europe's importance in the international economy in terms of activity, it is now necessary to consider how it interacts with the rest of the world, i.e., to consider the policies the EU and its member states pursue.

This discussion includes both those policies that are intended to affect economic exchange with the rest of the world—trade, foreign direct investment, development and monetary policy—and internal EU policies that have significant external impacts—the common agricultural policy and the single European market programme.

## Trade

The principal tools of trade policy are tariffs (taxes) or restrictions on the quantity of a particular good that can be imported. Both have the effect of raising the price of foreign goods and thus protect domestic producers from competition at the expense of consumers (individuals and firms) who must pay higher prices. The EU is at its core a **customs union**, which means both that all tariffs and quantitative restrictions on trade are eliminated among the member states and that the member states pursue a common trade policy towards the rest of the world.

Since the end of the Second World War international efforts to liberalise trade have centred upon the General Agreement on Tariffs and Trade (GATT), which was transformed into the World Trade Organization (WTO) in 1995. As a consequence of multiple rounds of multilateral negotiations, the EU's average most-favoured-nation tariff is quite low by international standards, only 4.2 per cent (WTO 2002). In addition, products falling into 20 per cent of the EU's tariff lines enter duty free. Further, the vast majority of the EU's trading partners, including many developing countries (about which more below) enjoy some kind of preferential access to the EU market, which means they face even lower tariffs. These arrangements are negotiated bilaterally between the EU and the other country(ies).

The EU's 'nominal' liberalism, however, is tempered by a number of very important exceptions (Winters 2001: 25). The most extensively protected sector is agriculture. The common agricultural policy (CAP), which was initially aimed at boosting European food production, operates through a system of price supports: governments, if necessary, will buy food in order to maintain high prices. This has two important implications for EU trade policy. The most direct is that high domestic prices can be maintained only if foreign products are excluded.

Thus, the EU's tariffs on agricultural products average over 16 per cent and are much, much higher on particularly sensitive products, such as wheat, sugar and dairy (Winters 2001). The second trade-policy implication is that elevated prices produce surplus production that must be disposed of outside the EU's market. This occurs through subsidising exports, which can make it very difficult for foreign farmers to compete.

The EU also has a few particularly high tariffs (tariff peaks) on some manufactured goods, particularly footwear, leather, textiles and clothing. In addition, duties can be imposed on specific foreign producers following complaints by domestic producers of 'unfair' competition. The EU is an extensive user of such measures and has been making increasing use of them. As a consequence, fertilisers, VCRs, integrated circuits, photocopiers and clothing are heavily protected (Winters 2001).

As tariffs have (generally) fallen and quantitative restrictions have been eliminated, the negative impact of different national regulations on trade has become more economically and politically important. As a product sold in a country must comply with that country's rules, any rule affecting the character of a product may impede imports from another country where a different rule applies. Regulatory differences are particularly important with respect to the provision of services, some of which, for a variety of reasons, tend to be heavily regulated. The EU's single European market programme was aimed, in part, at eliminating such regulatory barriers among the member states. Although the objective was internal liberalisation, the single market programme has also generally benefited non-EU firms. This is because rather than having to comply with different rules in each member state a firm needs to comply with only one rule in order to be able to sell its product throughout the EU. In some cases, however, the single market programme has resulted in very strict common rules being adopted, thereby increasing regulatory barriers to imports. These 'regulatory peaks' cluster where the regulatory differences among the member states are most pronounced (Young 2004).

Thus, while the multilateral trading system has encouraged the lowering of explicit trade barriers, the trade effects of internal EU policies have become more important in absolute and relative terms.

## Foreign direct investment

Regulatory barriers are also the principal impediment to foreign direct investment. In contrast to trade, however, the EU does not have a common policy on foreign direct investment by non-EU firms. As a consequence, the member governments pursue quite different policies. Although there has been significant convergence around a more liberal approach to foreign direct investment, significant national differences in restrictions on FDI persist (Langhammer 2005; Young 2002). In addition, the EU's member states individually conclude agreements with other countries concerning the treatment of foreign investment.

A number of European policies, however, affect FDI in the member states. The European Commission can prohibit a merger involving foreign companies if it feels that the merger would hurt competition within the EU. The application of EU competition rules can even extend to mergers between non-EU companies—such as Boeing–McDonaldDouglas and GE–Honeywell—or to the practices of non-EU firms, such as Microsoft. The EU's rules on state aids restrict the incentives that national and local governments can use to attract foreign firms. In addition, in a few sectors, such as air transport, the privileges of the single market are restricted to firms controlled by EU citizens. For the most part, however, the regulation of foreign direct investment is a national responsibility.

## Development policies

European development policy combines both national and common policies. This is not surprising as development policy is made up of a combination of preferential market access for imports (trade policy and thus an exclusive EU policy)

and development aid, which is primarily a national prerogative. Europe's development policy has traditionally focused on its former colonies, the 79 African, Caribbean and Pacific (ACP) countries (Holland 2004). The centrepiece of the EU's relationship with the ACP countries is the 2000 Cotonou Partnership Agreement, which sought to remedy the shortcomings of earlier policies (the Yaoundé (1964–76) and Lomé (1976–2000) Conventions). The Cotonou Agreement provides preferential access to the EU's market, but also requires that the ACP countries liberalise their trade with each other and the EU, and provides development assistance. The Agreement makes these benefits conditional on respect for human rights, democratic principles, the rule of law and good governance.

The development assistance under the Cotonou Agreement comes from the EU's common European Development Fund, but the member states also provide development assistance directly. The individual and common aid provision combined make Europe by far the world's largest aid donor. (See Table 22.4.) There are, however, big variations in the level of generosity of the European governments, despite having agreed common minimum targets as part of the 2002 Monterrey International Conference on Financing Development. In 2004 Denmark, Luxembourg, Sweden and the Netherlands all exceeded the United Nation's target of aid equalling 0.7 per cent of gross national income, while Italy gave only 0.15 per cent. In addition, while Portugal massively increased its level of development assistance in 2004, Belgium and Italy cut theirs substantially. The Central and Eastern European states give very little in development aid and are not members of the OECD's Development Assistance Committee (DAC), which brings together the world's largest aid donors (Carbone 2004).

Although development assistance is primarily a national prerogative, the EU is involved in trying to improve the coordination and complementarity of the member states' and the EU's own aid policies. In December 2005 the Council of

**Table 22.4** Development Assistance Committee (DAC) European Members' Net Official Development Assistance, 2004

| | $ million | ODA/GNI % | % change 2003 to 2004 in real terms |
|---|---|---|---|
| Denmark | 2,037 | 0.85 | 4.1 |
| Luxembourg | 236 | 0.83 | 8.2 |
| Sweden | 2,722 | 0.78 | 2.1 |
| Netherlands | 4,204 | 0.73 | −4.5 |
| Portugal | 1,031 | 0.63 | 188.3 |
| Belgium | 1,463 | 0.41 | −29.8 |
| France | 8,473 | 0.41 | 4.3 |
| Ireland | 607 | 0.39 | 6 |
| UK | 7,883 | 0.36 | 9.5 |
| Finland | 655 | 0.35 | 5.9 |
| Germany | 7,534 | 0.28 | 0.1 |
| Spain | 2,437 | 0.24 | 9.6 |
| Austria | 678 | 0.23 | 19.6 |
| Greece | 465 | 0.23 | 13.3 |
| Italy | 2,462 | 0.15 | −10.5 |
| EU DAC members combined | 42,886 | 0.35 | 2.9 |
| EC | 8,704 | | 8.3 |
| USA | 19,705 | 0.17 | 18.3 |
| Total DAC | 79,512 | 0.26 | 5.9 |

*Source*: OECD, 'Statistical Annex of the 2005 Development Cooperation Report', table 1, www.oecd.org/dac/stats/dac/derannex

Ministers, the European Parliament, the Commission and representatives of the member states adopted a 'European Consensus on Development', which sets out a European vision of development shared by the member states and the Commission and lays down guidelines for implementing this common vision at the EU level.

In a break from the past practice of focusing primarily on the former colonies of the member states, in 2001 the EU adopted the 'Everything But Arms' initiative, which permits the 49 least developed countries to export to the EU duty-free all products except arms. The full liberalisation of certain sensitive products was delayed—bananas (January 2006), sugar (July 2009) and rice (September 2009). The EU has been actively pushing for other developed countries to adopt similar initiatives and had some success at the December 2005 WTO ministerial meeting in Hong Kong.

## Monetary policy

The fourth dimension of Europe's external economic relations concerns monetary policy. Fluctuations in exchange rates can disrupt economic exchange and an overvalued currency can make one's own products more expensive on world markets while making imports cheaper. Consequently, governments, or often more accurately central banks, may change their interest rates or buy/sell their own or other currencies in an attempt to adjust the foreign exchange rate.

As noted earlier, there are two European currencies of global importance: the euro and the British pound. The euro is more important because it is the currency for a much larger economy, encompassing 12 of the EU's member states, including Germany, France, Italy and Spain. (See Chapter 16, this volume.) There are two dimensions to European external monetary relations; one between the Eurozone and the non-Eurozone members of the EU, the other between Europe, particularly the Eurozone, and the rest of the world.

There are two different monetary arrangements between the Eurozone and the other members of the EU. (See Table 22.5.) As of 2006, eight of the

---

**Table 22.5** Monetary Relations within Europe, March 2006

| ERM 2 | Floating |
|---|---|
| Cyprus | Czech Republic |
| Denmark | Hungary |
| Estonia | Poland |
| Latvia | Sweden |
| Lithuania | UK |
| Malta | |
| Slovakia | |
| Slovenia* | |

Note:
*Slovenia is due to join the euro on 1 January 2007.

---

non-Eurozone EU member states participate in the Exchange Rate Mechanism 2, which is a system of managed exchange rates. (See Chapter 16, this volume.) Slovenia will join the euro on 1 January 2007. The other members of the EU allow their currencies to 'float' against the euro, that is their exchange rates are determined by market forces and there is no obligation to intervene to damp down fluctuations.

Some other countries have chosen to 'peg' their currencies to the euro, which means that the exchange rate between the two currencies is fixed. The 14 West African members of the *communauté financière africaine* (CFA), for example, have pegged the CFA franc to the euro. Against most other currencies, however, the euro's exchange rate is determined by market forces. Although the Maastricht Treaty establishes that the Council of Ministers (Economics and Finance) can conclude formal agreements with other countries regarding the euro's exchange rate or formulate general orientations for the euro's exchange rate policy it has not done so. In part this is due to a lack of clarity regarding the locus of authority among the European Central Bank, the Commission and the Council of Economic and Finance Ministers (McNamara and Meunier 2002).

In addition, the European Central Bank's overriding concern has been with maintaining price stability within the Eurozone rather than with the euro's exchange rate, for which it has received some criticism. Consequently, there has been no external monetary policy to speak of, the euro has fluctuated with the market in response to external events and to ECB decisions taken for internal reasons. Thus, with the exception of the countries in the ERM 2, European exchange rate policy is conducted more by accident than by design.

# Trade Policy-making in the EU

As the preceding discussion made clear, the extent to which European governments can pursue external economic relations individually varies significantly between policy areas. The authority of the EU is particularly great with respect to trade policy, which is also an important component of Europe's development policy and increasingly of its efforts to play a more active international role (see below). I, therefore, concentrate on how trade policy is made in the EU. There are three aspects to this issue that deserve particular attention: (1) the transfer of authority for trade policy from the member states to the EU; (2) how collective policy is made; (3) how the changing nature of trade politics is affecting the EU.

## The transfer of authority to the EU

Although trade policy is one of the policy areas in which EU competence (authority) is greatest, this was not a foregone conclusion and has been a persistent source of tension among the member states and between the member states and the European institutions. Over time, however, the extent of EU competence has increased.

As noted earlier, the EU is at its heart a customs union, which requires the pooling of decision-making with regard to trade policy. The establishment of a customs union was not the only possibility, however, and several other options were considered in the run-up to the 1957 Treaty of Rome, which created the European Economic Community. One was to continue to pursue liberalisation through existing multilateral and pluri-lateral fora (the GATT and the Organisation of European Economic Cooperation—now the Organisation for Economic Cooperation and Development). Another was to create a free trade area, in which trade barriers would be removed among the members, but there would be no common external policy, such as the subsequent European Free Trade Association (EFTA), to which Iceland, Liechtenstein, Norway and Switzerland belong. Strong support for a customs union from the French government and slow progress on liberalisation within existing fora contributed to the decision to pursue a customs union (Lindberg 1963; Parsons 2002). As a consequence, the conduct of trade policy became an exclusive 'Community competence'.

Significantly, however, this agreement reflected only the trade concerns of the time, most notably tariffs and quantitative restrictions. Over time, however, the EU became involved in external negotiations on a much wider range of economic issues, not least as other forms of economic exchange, such as trade in services and foreign direct investment, became more important. In many cases, the member states have been reluctant to cede authority in areas seen as important to economic development and other public-policy objectives. Thus tension over the allocation of authority has been a persistent feature of the EU's foreign economic policy. For the most part, this tension has not presented a problem in the EU's ability to participate in international economic negotiations, as the member states have been willing to cooperate in areas beyond what is strictly required by the treaty (Young 2002).

Tensions have arisen, however, over the formal arrangements for concluding agreements. This has led to a series of judgments by the European Court of Justice (ECJ) regarding whether authority for a particular negotiation lies with the EU or with the member states. During the 1970s and 1980s the ECJ tended to find in favour of the European institutions, leading to the gradual accumulation of greater EU authority over foreign economic policy. In a major decision regarding ratification of the outcome of the particularly wide-ranging **Uruguay Round** of GATT negotiations (1986–94), however, the ECJ established the limits of expanded EU competence on the basis of interpretation of the existing treaty (Young 2002). The 2001 Treaty of Nice sought to resolve this issue by explicitly transferring authority over a wider range of policy issues to the EU. Some issues that are of particular concern to certain member states, however, remain subject to joint EU and member-state authority (such as trade in audio-visual, health and education services), while others (such as FDI in manufacturing) remain largely within the competence of the member states. Thus any international agreement that addresses these issues must be ratified by both the EU and by each member state.

## Trade policy-making

The location of authority for trade policy is only the starting point for understanding how European trade policy is made. Also crucial are the institutional arrangements through which any collective decisions will be taken. The institutional arrangements are important because they influence the power relations among the member states of the EU and thus have implications for the substance of EU foreign economic policy.

Having agreed to establish a customs union, the founding states had to decide how they would agree common trade policies towards the rest of the world. The smaller states—Belgium, Luxembourg and the Netherlands—supported delegating decision-making entirely to the European Commission, while the French government wanted to retain some control (Lindberg 1963). The outcome was that under the common commercial policy the actual conduct of negotiations is delegated to the Commission, but the member states maintain close oversight through a special committee of national officials (the 133 Committee) and the Council of Ministers ratifies all agreements.

The more liberal governments—those of Belgium, Germany, Luxembourg and the Netherlands—wanted ratification to be by qualified majority vote, which would prevent the most protectionist member state from blocking liberalisation. The more protectionist governments of France and Italy favoured unanimity. In the end the more liberal governments won the institutional argument. This established the basic structure that is in place today: where the EU has competence, the Commission negotiates trade agreements, assisted and overseen by a committee of national trade officials, and the Council ratifies agreements by qualified majority vote.

Although only a qualified majority is formally required to conclude agreements under the common commercial policy, in practice the member governments tend to proceed on the basis of consensus, albeit one that is reached in the 'shadow of the vote' (Johnson 1998; Woolcock 2005b). This emphasis on consensus contributes to the tendency of the EU's member governments to accumulate each government's protection of particular sectors into a common policy (Winters 2001). As noted earlier, however, many international economic agreements include issues that also fall within the authority of the member states. In such circumstances, the decision rule effectively becomes unanimity, which strengthens the hand of the most protectionist member state.

The EU's institutions for aggregating the member governments' trade policy preferences are extremely important because of the pronounced differences among those preferences. Although there is some danger in characterising the member states as protectionist or liberal, as these positions can change with the electoral and business cycles and on specific issues, most of the member governments have tended to pursue fairly consistent approaches to trade policy, at least until recently (Johnson 1998; Woolcock 2005b). The British, Danish, Dutch, Finnish and Swedish governments tend to adopt fairly liberal positions. The German government has tended to be liberal on goods, but less so on agriculture and services. The Irish government tends to be liberal on trade in goods and services and on foreign investment, but is more protectionist on agriculture (Woolcock 2005b). The Italian, Spanish and Portuguese governments tend to be protectionist. In many respects France is the most protectionist member state, especially on agriculture, although it is liberal with respect to most services, with the exceptions of audio-visual, education and health services (Lehmann 2005). The French government is also keen for the EU to stand up to its trading partners, particularly the USA (Woolcock 2005b).

Indications are that the 2004 enlargement will not significantly alter the balance of trade policy preferences within the EU, because it introduced both liberal and protectionist states (Johnson with Rollo 2001; Woolcock 2005b). The Estonian government is now perhaps the most liberal member government, and the Czech, Hungarian and Slovenian governments have also reinforced the liberal wing, although the Hungarian government is now a strong defender of the CAP. The Polish and Slovak governments, by contrast, have bolstered the protectionist wing, particularly with respect to agriculture.

Although the most recent enlargement does not seem to have altered the liberal–protectionist balance among the member governments, it is possible that it has affected the balance between the member states and the Commission, shifting more influence to the latter (Woolcock 2005b). In part this is an outgrowth of the enhanced power of an agenda-setter when there are more participants because finding an alternative point for agreement is harder. At the same time, however, the need to reconcile more interests may restrict the range of options that will command sufficient support for ratification.

In addition to affecting the substance of the negotiating positions, the EU's institutions influence how effective it is in pursuing them. In particular, where unanimity applies it is harder for the EU to make concessions—all of the member states, including the most protectionist, must agree. This means that in order to overcome such opposition the EU's negotiating partner(s) must make significant concessions of their own in order to build sufficient support for the agreement within the most protectionist member state that it is willing to accept the agreement. Thus the EU's institutional structure enhances its negotiating leverage when it is on the defensive (Meunier 2005). Conversely, in areas where unanimity is required, it can be harder for the EU to agree a common position; however, once it has done so the need for unanimity does not appear to reduce the EU's negotiating capacity (Young 2002). (See Theme box: The Impact of the European Union.)

**THEME BOX** (!)

## The Impact of the European Union

The extent to which the EU intrudes into national external economic relations varies across policies. Trade policy can be conducted only through the EU. Members of the Eurozone have a common external monetary policy. There are both common and national development policies. Foreign direct investment is subject largely to national rules.

Where the EU has authority it can have a significant impact on the substance of policy. Decision-making under qualified majority voting, for example, undermines the influence of the most protectionist member state. In other areas, the impact of the EU has been even more profound. During the process of creating the single market the need for a qualified majority in favour of common rules enabled more liberal states

to block the creation of protectionist common policies to replace most national quantitative restrictions, although not with regard to bananas or cars, or market access rules in services. Given the free movement of goods and services within the single market, this meant that the most liberal member state's policy was effectively the EU's policy.

In general the intrusion into national sovereignty and the degree of liberalisation that accompanies the single market is far greater than anything that might be agreed in a multilateral forum. As a consequence, the development of multilateral rules, at least along EU lines, holds no fears for the EU member governments because it will not impose stricter disciplines than they already face.

## The EU and the new trade politics

The preceding discussion focused on the relationship between the Commission and the member states, which has traditionally been the key to understanding EU trade policy (Woolcock 2005a). In large part this is because, with the prominent exception of agriculture, the EU's trade policy institutions are quite insulated from societal pressures, which play a much more important role in shaping trade policy in other polities, most notably the USA.

One reason for this relative isolation is that aggregation of trade-policy interests still occurs primarily through the member states. Although European interest associations do engage on trade-policy issues, they often have trouble reconciling the different preferences of their members. Moreover, the Commission is not elected, nor does the European Parliament have much say in trade politics, which further dilutes the impact of societal interests at the EU level. The most notable exception is agriculture, where a combination of electoral leverage and close ties to ministries in a number of member states accounts for farmers' considerable influence in EU trade policy (Keeler 1996).

Other producer interests have considerable leverage when seeking to influence the EU's unilateral trade policies, such as anti-dumping or market access.

Because of the relative weakness of societal actors in EU trade policy-making, the academic literature has effectively treated the EU's engagement with the rest of the world as a **two-level game**, with the member states acting at domestic level and the Commission being the negotiator at the international level (Woolcock 2005a). This simplifying approach has been facilitated by the member states' trade-policy preferences being fairly stable. Changes in the politics of trade, however, suggest that this may no longer reliably be the case.

Since the mid 1980s, and particularly since the mid 1990s the nature of trade has changed with the growth in importance of trade in services and foreign affiliate sales. At the same time the focus of the international-trade agenda has changed. With and since the Uruguay Round of multilateral trade negotiations the international-trade agenda has become much broader both in terms of the sectors covered, now encompassing agriculture and services, and the types of measures that are addressed, going 'beyond the border' to address the trade effects of domestic rules and regulations, such as food safety, environmental protection and the protection of intellectual property rights. In addition, the way in which trade barriers are addressed has changed, with a much greater emphasis on adopting common disciplines on national practices (Dymond and Hart 2000) and the increasing legalisation of the multilateral trading system (Keohane *et al.* 2000). In response to these changes in the 'what' and 'how'

of trade diplomacy new bureaucratic and non-governmental actors have become actively engaged in trade politics, politicising what had been a private and technocratic realm (Hocking 2004: 264). (See Theme box: Democracy and Legitimacy.)

Although there has been an increase in the number and variety of interest groups lobbying the Commission and in the involvement of the European Parliament, the main impact of the new trade politics on EU trade policy has been

---

**THEME BOX**

## Democracy and Legitimacy

Democracy and legitimacy have a complex relationship with external economic relations. Even within national contexts both trade policy and monetary policy have been intentionally insulated from democratic politics in the name of enhanced legitimacy. In trade policy the argument has been that because the benefits from protection are concentrated and obvious, while the costs are diffuse and opaque, those that want protection will be better mobilised than their opponents. Thus, if politicians are responsible for trade policy they are likely to respond to this asymmetric mobilisation and provide protection to special interests, which will be detrimental to the economy as a whole. In monetary policy, the idea has been that if politicians control the levers of policy they will be tempted to try to boost the economy in the run-up to elections, leading to a boom-and-bust cycle that is hostile to sustainable economic growth.

The EU's institutions very much reflect this thinking. Trade negotiations are delegated to the unelected Commission; the European Parliament is kept out of trade policy. The member states expressly set up a non-majoritarian body (the ECB) to be responsible for monetary policy in the Eurozone. While the orthodoxy of central bank independence remains largely unchallenged, the lack of democracy in trade policy has become a matter of public concern.

This concern is in response to the multilateral trading system addressing the trade effects of domestic rules and regulations and becoming more legalistic. This shift in the focus has transformed the domestic politics of trade by altering the distribution of costs and benefits from trade liberalisation (Evans 2003).

Traditionally, trade liberalisation hurt the few (the protected producers) and benefited the many (consumers and user industries). When national rules are the focus of liberalisation, however, the distribution of costs is quite different, with the benefits of cheaper products competing with benefits from measures adopted to achieve desired public policy objectives.

At the same time increased legalisation raises the prospect that national rules could be found to be incompatible with multilateral obligations and have to be changed. These concerns seemed to be confirmed by a number of high-profile WTO rulings against national measures protecting the environment (the USA's ban on shrimp caught without the use of nets friendly to sea turtles and the EU's moratorium on approvals of genetically modified organisms) and food safety (the EU's ban on hormone-treated beef). Although arguably these rulings showed considerable deference to governments on broad principles while challenging specific aspects of the rules, they have served to fuel popular concerns about the lack of transparency and democracy in trade politics.

In response to such concerns the European Commission's Directorate-General for Trade set up a consultative 'Civil Society Dialogue' to provide a forum for discussions with societal interests, including producers. Although this forum provides an opportunity for the actors of the new trade politics to consult with the Commission, it does not appear to have had any discernible impact on policy. Rather the impact of societal interests on trade policy has come through the governments of the member states, which are responding to electoral pressures.

through the member governments. A number of the new trade policy issues—particularly the environment and labour standards—resonate particularly strongly with European publics (Evans 2003). A number of social democratic member governments have picked up and championed these concerns. The British government has particularly pushed the development agenda (Holmes 2005). The German government also supported development, as well as international environmental and labour standards (Falke 2005). The Scandinavian governments have championed international environmental rules and labour rights (Young *et al*. 2000). These positions influenced the EU's negotiating position in the **Doha Round** of multilateral trade negotiations (see below). Thus national politics seem to be mattering more than they did in explaining EU trade policy.

---

**KEY POINTS**

- The location of authority over foreign economic policy has shifted towards the EU, but continues to be contested.

- The EU's institutional framework affects both the substance of the EU's negotiating positions and its negotiating leverage.

- EU trade policy has been largely insulated from societal interests, with the exception of agriculture, but national politics are becoming more important.

---

# Europe and Global Economic Governance

One reason why EU trade policy-making matters is that the EU is a crucial player in the development of global economic governance. As a consequence of its economic importance, the EU's support is necessary for the development of the multilateral trading system. In this capacity, the EU is distinctive because it is both an example of deep economic integration and a particularly vigorous proponent of the development of multilateral rules.

## The EU as model for global economic governance

The multilateral trading system has only recently begun to wrestle seriously with the negative trade effects of differences among national regulations. Dealing with such obstacles to trade in goods and services was one of the central objectives of the EU's single market programme. The EU itself therefore provides an example of how these issues might be addressed at the multilateral level.

The EU has developed some innovative ways of tackling regulatory barriers to trade. One of the most innovative is the mutual recognition principle, which holds that when another government's regulation is equivalent in effect, if not detail, products complying with it should be accepted in the domestic market. In practice, however, the EU has encountered many instances where such equivalence cannot be assumed. In these instances the EU has sought either to replace all national rules with a common rule ('approximation') or agree common minimum standards (Young 2005). Such rules have often been difficult to agree even within the EU where the member states have relatively similar preferences and where decisions are taken by qualified majority vote.

## The EU as advocate for global economic governance

Although the conditions for developing common rules is much less favourable at the multilateral level, the EU has been one of the main proponents of the development of a rule-based multilateral trading system, albeit one that is not as developed and intrusive as that found within the EU. During the Uruguay Round the EU became one of the main advocates of greater legalisation and the establishment of binding, third-party dispute resolution (Woolcock 2005a).

Even more strikingly, the EU was the principal advocate of adopting new common disciplines as part of the Doha Round. In particular, it was the principal proponent of the so-called 'Singapore issues'. These included agreeing minimum standards for national competition-policy regimes, a common framework for investment, common rules on transparency in government procurement and new disciplines with regard to trade facilitation. The EU also advocated, albeit less vigorously, provisions on environmental protection and core labour standards. In the face of vigorous opposition from the governments of developing countries, all of these issues, except for trade facilitation and the relationship between the WTO and multilateral environmental agreements, came off the Doha agenda long before the talks were suspended in July 2006. Here the EU has not been able to translate its negotiating leverage into concrete developments.

## Global economic governance beyond trade

Although the EU is most visibly involved in shaping global economic governance through the multilateral trading system, European states are key participants in the other main institutions of global economic governance. France, Germany and the UK are members of the G8 group of leading industrial countries, which meet regularly to discuss major economic and political issues, including occasionally the coordination of monetary policies. The EU has participated in meetings of the G8 (then G7) since 1977, represented by the president of the Commission and the leader of the country holding the EU's rotating presidency, but

it does not bring a formal mandate to summit meetings.

The EU's member states, but not the EU, are also members of the International Monetary Fund (IMF), which lends money to countries having balance-of-payment crises, and the World Bank, which provides money (loans and grants) for development projects. By arrangement, a European is always the managing director of the IMF and the member states combined command a blocking minority within the IMF's Board of Governors, controlling nearly one-third of the votes. The nomination of the managing director is, however, the only issue on which the EU's member states formally coordinate their positions. There is likewise, no formal coordination with regard to European participation in the World Bank, where again European states wield considerable influence. For example, France, Germany and the UK, along with Japan and the USA, each nominate one of the 24 executive directors, who are responsible for the Bank's general operations. Thus, although European states have important roles in the main international institutions of global economic governance in areas other than trade, they do not wield collective influence and therefore have less say (McNamara and Meunier 2002).

### KEY POINTS

- The EU is itself an example of international economic governance, but there are limits both to the success of the EU's own economic integration project and to how well it might translate to the global stage.

- The EU is one of the major architects of the multilateral trading system and the most outspoken advocate of its further development.

- Europe does not play a leadership role in global financial governance because only the individual states are members of the main international monetary and financial institutions.

# External Economic Policies as Foreign-Policy Tools

As the discussion of conditionality in European development policy above noted, the EU seeks to use access to its market as a carrot to encourage domestic-policy changes. This is a feature not just of its development policy, but is applied much more widely, not least in the accession process (Meunier and Nicolaïdis 2006). The EU tends to use positive conditionality—promising benefits, preferential market access or more development assistance, in exchange for desired policy changes—rather than negative conditionality—the withdrawal of benefits (Smith 2005). An example of positive conditionality is the awarding of enhanced preferential access to the EU's market under the General System of Preferences scheme for developing countries that accept the main international conventions relating to social rights, environmental protection and governance, including the fight against drugs (known as GSP+). There is also an element of negative conditionality, however, as the extra preferential market access can be withdrawn if a country is found to be systematically failing to meet those obligations.

Negative conditionality plays a part in many of the EU's bi- and pluri-lateral agreements. Conditionality clauses concerning the protection of human rights, the development of democracy and respect for the rule of law were part of the Europe Agreements that structured the EU's relations with the countries of Central and Eastern Europe before their accession. Since 1995 the EU has included a standard 'Human Rights and Democracy Clause' in all of its agreements with third countries (Youngs 2001). Such clauses can be found in the Cotonou Partnership Agreement and the European Neighbourhood Policy.

The EU, however, has not always been effective in exercising this conditionality (Smith 2005). With the exceptions of association agreements and accession decisions, the EU has been slow to exercise the conditionality clauses embedded in its framework agreements. In large part this is due to the member governments having trouble agreeing to take a tough stand (Smith 2005). To an extent, differences among the member governments reflect their commercial and strategic interests in the country in question, but they are also influenced by doubts about the merits of applying sanctions (Smith 2005). Thus, when the EU has exercised conditionality clauses, it has tended to do so where the human rights abuses have led to serious instability or where the government in question pursues a foreign policy contrary to EU interests (Youngs 2004).

## KEY POINTS

- The EU seeks to use its trade power to pursue foreign-policy objectives by attaching conditions to access to its market.

- It is more likely to use positive conditionality than negative conditionality, because it finds the latter harder to agree.

- Differences among the member states stemming from their relations with the country in question and their views on the use of sanctions mean that negative conditionality is applied only rarely and then in extreme circumstances.

ALASDAIR R. YOUNG

# Conclusion

European external economic relations occur among the member states of the EU and between them, individually and collectively, and the rest of the world. Governing the external relations of the member states has been a central focus of European integration from the outset. As a consequence, international economic governance within the EU has progressed further than anywhere else in the world. This means that intra-EU economic relations are more important than the EU's relations with the rest of the world, though the latter are very important in their own right. This also means that the EU provides an example of how deeper economic integration might be pursued in other contexts, including multilaterally.

Because of the size of its economy and the success of its integration project, Europe is a crucial player in the global economy and a key interlocutor on issues of global economic governance. The coherence and effectiveness of its engagement, however, vary across the range of external economic relations. Where European integration has progressed the furthest, trade policy, the EU plays a pivotal role. Its participation is necessary, if not sufficient, for further development of the multilateral trading system. In development policy, where the member states and the EU share authority, it is also a crucial actor, as collectively Europe is the world's largest aid donor. Due to a combination of fragmented external representation and the internal institutional confusion, the euro has not enabled Europe to play a leading role in international monetary policy. Foreign direct investment from and to third countries is largely governed by the individual member states.

This variation in EU authority reflects the importance that the member states have attached to external economic relations, not least because of the implications of international competition for their national economies. While some European states have embraced economic openness as a way to prosper, others regard increased international competition with trepidation, fearing that it will undermine treasured objectives. As a consequence, some member states have been reluctant to cede authority to the EU, wanting to be able to control the terms of economic openness. Therefore issues of authority in external economic relations remain highly contested within Europe.

The member states' reluctance to cede authority contributes to European external economic relations having been relatively insulated from politics. It accounts for both the two-tier system of interest aggregation—first within member states and then between them—and the European Parliament's limited role. The general increasing politicisation of external economic relations means this insulation is eroding. European external economic relations will become more complex and more volatile as European politics intrude.

## ? QUESTIONS

1. To what extent should Europeans be concerned about globalisation as opposed to regional integration?
2. Should the EU be seeking to export its model of market integration to the global level?
3. Is the increased politicisation of European external relations a good thing?

4. Why do member states guard their policy authority more jealously in some areas of external economic relations than in others?

5. How do the EU's institutions affect the substance of its preferences regarding external economic relations?

6. How effective has the EU been in pursuing its objectives through external economic relations?

7. How does the location of policy authority affect Europe's capacity to pursue external economic relations?

8. Should greater authority for external economic relations be transferred to the EU?

 **FURTHER READING**

■ **Johnson, M. (1998),** *European Community Trade Policy and the Article 113 Committee,* **London, Royal Institute of International Affairs.** Provides a very detailed, if somewhat dry, insider's account of trade-policy decision-making within the EU.

■ **Meunier, S. (2005),** *Trading Voices: The European Union in International Commercial Nego-tiations,* **Princeton NJ, Princeton University Press.** Illustrates how the EU's institutional structure affects its negotiating leverage, focusing on transatlantic trade relations.

■ **Peterson, J. and Young, A. R. (eds) (2006),** *The European Union and the New Trade Politics,* **special issue of the** *Journal of European Public Policy,* **13,6.** The contributions in this volume engage with many of the issues discussed in this chapter, including how the new trade politics are affecting the EU, Europe as a model of and advocate for global economic governance and how the EU seeks to use its external economic relations to influence policy developments in other countries.

■ **Young, A. R. (2002),** *Extending European Cooperation: The European Union and the 'New' International Trade Agenda,* **Manchester, Manchester University Press.** Explores the application of the two-level game to the EU and charts the development of EU competence in foreign economic policy, trade and FDI.

 **IMPORTANT WEBSITES**

● **http://europa.eu.int/comm/trade/index_en.htm** The European Commission's Directorate-General for Trade website provides extensive statistical information on the EU's relations with different countries. There is also a wealth of EU policy documents and position papers, including proposals and offers in the Doha Round of WTO negotiations.

● **www.europa.eu.int/comm/development/index_en.htm** The European Commission's Direct-orate-General for Development website contains information about the EU's relations with developing countries, including texts of agreements, policy papers and statistics.

● **http://ue.eu.int/showPage.asp?id=388&lang=en&mode=g** The website of the General Affairs and External Relations Council of Ministers, which is responsible for trade and development policies, among others. The website contains overviews of policies and links to conclusions of Council meetings.

 **Visit the Online Resource Centre that accompanies this book for lots of useful additional material, including an interactive map of Europe. www.oxfordtextbooks.co.uk/orc/hay_menon/**

# 23

# Transatlantic Relations

JOLYON HOWORTH

✔ **Reader's Guide**

This chapter assesses the impact on transatlantic relations of three major events: the end of the Cold War; the emergence of the EU as an international actor; and the 11 September 2001 terrorist attacks on New York and Washington. These events radically changed a relationship between Europe and the USA which had spanned the Cold War: one of hegemony on the one side and dependency on the other. The end of the Cold War dissipated the existential threat to 'the west' posed by Soviet communism (thereby weakening the security dimension of the transatlantic relationship) and heralded, in the medium term, the withdrawal of US forces from Europe. This, in turn, forced Europeans to think seriously about their own military requirements for the twenty-first century. The al Qaeda attacks of 11 September 2001 shifted USA foreign and defence policy from cautious realism to crusading idealism and forced all European countries to redefine the nature of their relationship with the USA. But, while the EU–US relationship has been dominated by security issues, other policy sectors have also grown in significance. The emergence of the EU as a unified and enlarged market gradually closed the gap with the USA in terms of market size, GDP, trade in services and foreign investment. Moreover, 'values-based' issues such as human rights and environmental policy increasingly provoked transatlantic tensions.

JOLYON HOWORTH

# Introduction: Europe and the Problem of 'America Policy'

The member states of the EU struggled for several decades to coordinate their global impact and speak to the rest of the world with a single voice. However, since the 1990s, the adoption of the Common Foreign and Security Policy (CFSP) has gradually seen the emergence of a more coherent European diplomatic mindset (Ginsberg 2001; Hill and Smith 2005). As the EU became a unified market with a currency shared by most member states and a single frontierless space, and as it asserted growing political ambitions, the national interests of its member states slowly converged and European declaratory policy towards most of the main regions of the world became gradually less cacophonous. The one major exception to this rule has been 'America policy'. When faced with the challenge of defining their relationship to the world's sole superpower, especially in terms of that superpower's global grand strategy, European nations have often found themselves at sixes and sevens. Nowhere was this more dramatically illustrated than during the Iraq crisis which broke out in 2002–3. The American capacity for attraction, coercion and patronage is such that a united European response is often difficult to achieve. The fact that two leading EU states, the UK and France, have, since at least the Suez crisis in 1956, adopted diametrically opposite policies towards the USA (the one seeking never to break ranks with, the other never to be dependent on, the USA) does not make this any easier.

At the same time, broader trends deriving from all three of the historical events referred to above have marked a further growing tension between the EU and the USA. On the one hand, the EU as an international actor has sought to transcend the **Westphalian system** based on sovereign nation states, and to construct a new grammar of international relations based on multilateralism, international institutions, international law, human rights and 'values' (Whitman 1998; Leonard 2005a). On the other, the USA, dominant in a 'unipolar' world, has refused to yield sovereignty in any domain (including the environment, the international criminal court and international law), and has asserted its right to intervene unilaterally wherever it felt its national interests require it to do so (Mann 2004; Walt 2005). Asymmetry has always characterised the transatlantic relationship. Since the mid-1980s, the nature of that asymmetry has changed markedly.

There are three distinct levels to the transatlantic relationship. The first is the systemic interplay of great-power politics; the second derives from the specific circumstances of the post-Cold War era; and the third is the more recent 'Bush factor'. At the first level, there is nothing *automatic* about transatlantic harmony. The EU and the USA share various values, cultural norms, historical experiences and strategic interests. However, the fact is that each side constitutes a massive great-power bloc. According to the once dominant (but increasingly challenged) theory of international relations, **structural realism**, 'great powers always compete with each other for power' (Mearsheimer 2001: 2). From 1776 to 1989, the USA was regularly involved in wars—hot or cold—with most major European powers. The good news at this level is that, while disputes remain unavoidable, serious confrontation is now unthinkable. Wars between democracies and particularly between nuclear democracies do not happen (Russett and Oneal 2001). Moreover, the main reasons for past conflicts have disappeared. The USA traditionally found itself at odds with European nations either over European imperialism and/or a US demand for 'open door' trading policies, or over the advent, in continental Europe, of a regional hegemon such as Germany or the USSR. Those sources of conflict have now been transcended.

The second dimension of the relationship stems from the end of the Cold War. It is only normal for Europeans and Americans to have squabbled in recent years given that the type of asymmetric relationship they shared during the Cold War was a historical aberration. Since 1989, we have witnessed a new chapter in a centuries-old process of adjustment. This jostling for position was rendered all the more dramatic because the emergence from the Cold War, which would have engendered jostling under any circumstances, coincided with the rise of Europe to quasi-superpower status. Under these conditions, a reordering of the transatlantic relationship was practically inevitable A painful part of that reordering will be for the USA to accept a more balanced partnership (Rifkin 2004; Reid 2004; Leonard 2005a). This will be all the more delicate in that Europe is no longer in the centre of the US international radar screen. Paradoxically, as the EU becomes less important to the US in terms of security, it is becoming more important in other policy areas. Asymmetry remains but shifts its scope.

A third level has entered the transatlantic equation, rendering what would have been a difficult adjustment in any event all the more difficult because of both the style and the substance of US policy under the administration of President George W. Bush. In 2003, favourable impressions of the USA fell to all-time lows in most European countries. The leading determinant of this collapse was the Bush administration's foreign policy, particularly with respect to Iraq. When French and German populations were asked if they thought the problem was 'mostly Bush', 74 per cent of Germans and French agreed—along with 59 per cent of British respondents (Pew 2004). In another poll, up to 58 per cent of Europeans found strong US leadership 'undesirable' (German Marshall Fund 2004). A growing number of Europeans in all countries (77 per cent in Poland; 71 per cent in France, Italy and Portugal; 61 per cent in the Netherlands and Spain; and even 59 per cent in the UK and Turkey) hope the EU will become a military power 'in order to become more independent of the U.S.'. Moreover, while almost 80 per cent of Americans polled said they wanted the EU and the USA to become closer partners, the figure across Europe was only 46 per cent—with more than 50 per cent saying they actually wanted the two blocs to move further apart (German Marshall Fund 2004). In a BBC poll conducted in 21 countries after November 2004, huge majorities in European countries felt that the Bush re-election was a negative factor for peace and security in the world (BBC 2004). This is an unprecedented phenomenon in the history of the transatlantic relationship. While the second Bush administration (2005–9) initiated damage-control measures, and while transatlantic relations improved markedly, the challenge ahead remains considerable. The EU–USA relationship between 2001 and 2003 passed through an area of extreme turbulence. Turbulence is an appropriate metaphor because, while it reflects a surface phenomenon generating both fear and nausea in those experiencing it, it tells us nothing about the deeper currents flowing below.[1] It is to those deeper currents of EU–USA relations that I now turn.

---

**KEY POINTS**

- It is on the response to US global strategy that Europeans disagree most seriously.

- Since 1989, the EU and the USA appear to be diverging rather than converging on their fundamental approach to the international system.

- While military conflict between the EU and the USA is unthinkable, tensions are almost inevitable.

- The situation was initially made worse by the advent of the George W. Bush administration in 2000.

# Contending Visions of the Transatlantic Relationship

## Architects of a 'transatlantic community'

Since the end of the Second World War, many political actors and theorists have sought to forge a unified 'transatlantic community' (Sloan 2005b). In June 1947, the **Marshall Plan** revealed not only extraordinary generosity, but also extraordinary vision. The Plan was not just about reviving the shattered economies of Europe, nor just about building Europe up as a buffer against a looming Soviet threat. It was also about laying the bases for a healthy and competitive *rivalry* which would forge a true *partnership* between the USA and Europe. The influential editor of *Foreign Affairs*, Hamilton Fish Armstrong, argued: 'The European economy . . . must be helped to reconstruct the plant that, in turn, will enable it to be independent of us and to compete with us. . . . Europe will resist becoming the satellite of American capital and industry, and it is not to our advantage that she should so become' (Armstrong 1947). Europe, he concluded, in order to be a true partner of the USA, must be encouraged to become autonomous. The notion that a strong, united Europe was in the USA's national interest became an article of faith with every US administration. (See Background box 23.1.)

Political scientists also began theorising the contours of a values-based, culturally homogeneous Atlantic community (Deutsch 1953). At the height of the Clinton administration, in December 1995, the EU and the USA signed the New Transatlantic Agenda (NTA), asserting: 'We, the United States of America and the European Union, affirm our conviction that the ties which bind our people are as strong today as they have been for the past half century.' They gave themselves four basic objectives:

**BACKGROUND BOX 23.1**

'Declaration of Interdependence' with Europe (1962)

'We do not regard a strong and united Europe as a rival but as a partner. We believe that a united Europe will be capable of playing a greater role in the common defense, of responding more generously to the needs of poorer nations, of joining with the United States in lowering trade barriers, resolving problems of commerce, commodities, and currency, and developing coordinated policies in all economic, political, and diplomatic areas.

I will say here and now, on this Day of Independence, that the United States will be ready for a Declaration of *Inter* dependence, that we will be prepared to discuss with a united Europe the ways and means of forming a concrete Atlantic partnership, a mutually beneficial partnership between the new union now emerging in Europe and the old American Union founded here 175 years ago.'

" President John F. Kennedy, speech on 4 July 1962 "

- promotion of peace, stability, democracy and development around the world;
- responding to global challenges;
- contributing to the expansion of world trade and closer economic relations;
- building bridges across the Atlantic (NTA 1995);

Significantly, one reason why the signatories of the NTA felt the need to reassert transatlantic bonds was precisely the fact that, by the mid-1990s, many analysts and politicians were beginning to predict the demise of the transatlantic community model.

## American Euro-scepticism rears it head

Only five years after the NTA, the allies found themselves in the throes of what Henry Kissinger called 'the most serious crisis in transatlantic relations since 1945' (CFR 2003). Earlier declarations of transatlantic solidarity can be contrasted with the disingenuous question posed by President George W. Bush at a White House meeting of European experts called to brief him prior to his first visit to Europe in June 2001: 'Do we really want the EU to succeed?' (Garton Ash 2004: 102). Contrast them also with the suggestion made by Secretary Rumsfeld that Europe could be subjected to a policy of divide and rule, with the good guys of 'New Europe' distinguished from the bad guys of 'Old Europe' (See Background box 23.2.) This was accompanied by the replacement of fixed alliances by cherry-picked 'coalitions of the willing'. When, on 12 September 2001, NATO, for the first time in its history, invoked its key article 5 which regarded an attack on any one member state as an attack on all of them, the response from Washington was: 'Don't call us, we'll call you!' (Pond 2004). Or consider the opening words of Robert Kagan's polemical essay *Of Paradise and Power*: 'It is time to stop pretending that Europeans and Americans share a common view of the world, or even that they occupy the same world'. Kagan's conclusion was: 'the United States and Europe *have parted ways*' (Kagan 2003: my emphasis). Period! No room for conditional tenses in this analysis. Contrast those earlier declarations of transatlantic community with an article in the December 2004 issue of the journal *Foreign Affairs*. The author, subjecting the new EU Constitution to a withering critique, declared: 'The political integration of the EU presents the greatest challenge to continuing US influence in Europe since World War II'. He concluded that Washington should now *end* its 'uncritical support for European integration' (Cimbalo 2004). Six months later, the EU's Constitutional Treaty was in crisis. Should Americans rejoice? The sound of hands rubbing in glee was almost audible across

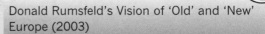

the Atlantic. Isolationists, conservatives and radical economic liberals in the USA have been arguing ever since the end of the Cold War that the political 'west' is not a natural construct but a highly artificial one. They insist that it was only the presence of a hostile 'east' that brought it into existence and maintained its unity. Its demise spells the end of Atlanticism (Carpenter 2000). In 2004–5, a pleiad of US structural realists, finally realising that something was stirring in Europe, began to take a closer look at a continent which had been of little interest to them for over 20 years. What they believed they had discovered was that the EU was **balancing** against its

**BACKGROUND BOX 23.3**

Is the EU 'balancing' against the USA? (2005)

- The leading theorist of structural realism, John Mearsheimer, defines balancing as taking place when 'threatened states seriously commit themselves to containing their dangerous opponent...they are willing to shoulder the burden of deterring, or fighting if need be, the aggressor' (2001: 139).

- Barry Posen argues: 'The EU is balancing against US power, regardless of the relatively low European perception of an actual direct threat emanating from the US...US strategists and citizens should thus follow carefully the EU's efforts to get into the defense and security business. The Europeans are useful to the US, but if present trends continue, they will have the wherewithal to decamp, and they could even conceivably cause some mischief'. (2004: 2–7).

former hegemon. (See Background box 23.3.) The USA, they all concluded, had better start looking after its own national interests (Art 2004; Posen 2004; Walt 2005). Transatlantic relations, all of a sudden, seemed to be in free fall.

## Iraq 2003: catalyst or consequence?

The transatlantic crisis referred to by Henry Kissinger was produced by the events surrounding the vote, in the UN Security Council (UNSC) on 8 November 2003, of Resolution 1441 which called on Iraq to cooperate with the UN weapons inspectors (UNMOVIC) or face 'serious consequences'. It is ironic yet revealing that a UNSC resolution which produced a unanimous favourable vote should give rise to such subsequent discordance (Gordon and Shapiro 2004). Was the crisis over Iraq a consequence of prior strategic divergence between the two sides, or rather a catalyst which led to a structural stand-off? Both interpretations are equally plausible. Whenever analysts or commentators speak of 'the Europeans' in the context

of transatlantic relations, they are invariably engaging in unwarranted generalisations. As noted earlier, a majority of European governments actually supported US policy over Iraq, some of them enthusiastically, others after a little arm-twisting (Anderson *et al.* 2003). However, opinion polls consistently demonstrated that, even in 'pro-US' countries such as Britain, Poland, Italy and Spain, large majorities of the public rejected both the US policy and their government's support for it. In a Pew survey conducted in June 2003, the world leader who received the highest ratings for 'trust to do the right thing' was French President Jacques Chirac. It was undoubtedly Chirac's very public defiance of the US administration from within the UNSC (rather than his murky tenure as mayor of Paris) which accounted for this rating. Chirac, for many around the world during the Iraq crisis, came to represent 'Europe'.[2] However, the reality is that there are, where European-American relations are concerned, two very different 'Europes'.

It has become fashionable to speak of a divide within Europe between 'Euro-Atlanticists' (led by the UK), who seek systematically to support US diplomacy, and 'Euro-Gaullists' (led by France), who seek to oppose it (Garton Ash 2004). The reality, however, is even more complex. France has never systematically opposed US policy. Whenever push really came to shove (the Berlin crisis 1958; the Cuban missile crisis 1962; the Euromissiles crisis 1980–3; the Bosnian crisis 1995), France proved to be a rock-solid US ally (Cogan 1994). De Gaulle remained until his dying day a believer in the necessity of the Atlantic Alliance. But the key concept for de Gaulle was *non-dependence*—which, as an outcome, is not the same thing as *independence*, itself more of an objective (Colard and Daille 1992: 63). More generally, for de Gaulle, once an allied country lapsed into what he called 'vassalisation', that country became, *ipso facto*, a weaker ally. It ceased to think strategically and thereby to contribute to the vitality and dynamism of alliance options. No less a witness than Henry Kissinger concurred with this judgement: 'the most consistent, the most creative, the most systematic thinking on strategy in

Europe today takes place in France' (Kissinger 1994: 337). Jacques Chirac, at the time of the Iraq crisis in 2003, repeated the same basic point: 'In life', said Chirac, 'one must not confuse friends with sycophants. It's better to have only a few friends than a lot of sycophants.' French officials constantly made the distinction between being 'allied' and being 'non-aligned' (de Villepin 2003: 328–49). One 'European' view of the Iraq crisis, as articulated by France, was relatively clear-cut.

President Chirac, in a *New York Times* interview on 8 September 2002, formulated most of the arguments which all French spokespersons were systematically to deploy thereafter. Two key elements of French policy emerged clearly. War should be an option of last resort. Saddam could and should be contained. France was in broad agreement with the USA on four key points. Iraq under Saddam Hussein presented a danger, both to its neighbours and to the Iraqi people. Saddam personally was a problem and it would be desirable if he were to leave power. Any existing weapons of mass destruction (WMD) must be declared and the weapons destroyed (in conformity with existing UNSC resolutions). If absolutely necessary, military force should be used to bring about this result. Above all, for Paris, the struggle against global terrorism required the forging and maintenance of a broad international political coalition such as that which Washington had generated to support the war in Afghanistan. However, there was real disagreement on five issues. First, France insisted that the west did not know whether Iraq possessed WMD. In order to find out, the inspectors should return. Second, while the USA advocated a single resolution authorising both the return of the inspectors and military action in the event of any further 'material breach', France insisted that recourse to military action should be the subject of a second UNSC resolution. Third, France was not opposed to pre-emptive war on principle, but rejected unilateral US pre-emption unsanctioned by the UN. Fourth, to French minds, regime change as a policy objective was unacceptable since it would open a Pandora's box in international law. Fifth,

France insisted there had been no significant contact between the Iraqi regime and al Qaeda. With nuances (sometimes significant, such as Germany's refusal to be part of any military operation, even if sanctioned by the UN), this analysis of the situation was broadly shared by a clear majority of European citizens. (See Background box 23.4.)

However, these approaches ran directly counter to many of the policy preferences of the Bush administration in the post-9/11 world. As became clear in 2004–5, not only had decisions been taken by Bush's inner circle as early as the spring of 2002 to invade Iraq in March 2003, but the (exceedingly flimsy) evidence of the existence of WMD was manipulated in order more effectively to sell the invasion to the US public. The link between the al Qaeda attacks of 9/11 and the Saddam Hussein regime was made repeatedly—despite the total absence of any evidence of such a link.[3] And a far-reaching ideological crusade to 'export democracy' to the broader Middle East underpinned the entire exercise. Most of these policy preferences were

---

**BACKGROUND BOX 23.4**

**Key Features of the European Analysis of the Iraq Crisis (2003)**

- Recognition that Saddam Hussein poses a challenge to the world

- Need to sustain an international coalition to manage the crisis

- Central role of United Nations and of international law

- Preference for containment over use of military force

- Worry about US talk of pre-emption, regime change and unilateralism

- Agnosticism over existence of Iraqi WMD—need for inspections

- Refusal to conflate al Qaeda and Iraq

- Concern not to exacerbate tensions in the broader Middle East

attributable directly to the Bush administration rather than to a bi-partisan consensus reflecting an earlier general shift in US policy. To that extent, the Iraq crisis was indeed a catalyst which led to a deeper EU–USA rift. Nevertheless, the USA's role as a lone superpower (particularly one which felt a new and unprecedented sense of vulnerability) with the capacity to act unilaterally if it so desired, was a structural reality which argues for the crisis also being a consequence of shifts in the world's tectonic plates since 1989.

Two major consequences arose from the 2003 crisis over Iraq. The first was the gradual realisation, across the USA, that, while the US armed forces are indeed capable of successfully taking on any military challenger anywhere in the world, the broader political, social and cultural challenge of democratisation, nation-building and post-conflict reconstruction is a far more complex problem for which the USA has very few answers (Walt 2005). By December 2005, a consensus seemed to be emerging within the USA that the US military should withdraw before it sustained irreparable damage to its own morale and recruitment potential. This was probably an overly pessimistic view of reality, but it reflected a growing awareness that the strategy of the Bush administration in 2003 was almost certainly a mistake. The second consequence was that the 'Europeans' gradually realised that, as long as they continued to be divided into 'Atlanticists' and 'Gaullists', their influence in Washington DC would be negligible. From the summer of 2003, one can date a new willingness on the part of Europe's leaders to consult with one another and to try to find common ground in their 'America policy' in order to exercise some real influence over the shape and direction of US foreign policy (Menon 2004). This new course has reaped rewards in a number

of areas: policy towards Iran, Israel–Palestine, the broader Middle East partnership and China. The prospect of partnership between the two sides of the Atlantic has emerged as the desired objective of both. When President Bush visited Europe in February 2005—after his re-election - he stressed repeatedly the words he had first used in his 2005 inaugural address: 'All that we seek to achieve in the world requires that America and Europe remain close partners'. The prospects for transcending the 2003 rift, while challenging, are far from insuperable (Dassù and Menotti 2005; Grant 2003; Lindstrom 2003; Zaborowski 2006). In the remainder of this chapter, I argue that the original architects of the transatlantic partnership were correct and that recent American sceptics are misguided. The USA needs the EU and vice versa. The relationship is not a zero-sum game. In today's world, cooperative and complementary contingency planning should be the name of the game. (See Background box 23.5.)

---

**KEY POINTS**

- The default position in US administrations from 1945 to 2000 was that European integration served the interests of the USA.

- This was called into question by the incoming Bush administration which attempted to play strategically on European divisions over 'America policy'.

- The Iraq war exacerbated those divisions and produced the 'most serious crisis in transatlantic relations since the end of World War Two' (Kissinger).

- Under George W. Bush's second term, transatlantic relations have improved, in part owing to the diplomacy of Secretary of State Condoleeza Rice.

# Seven Policy Areas in Search of Complementarity

## Security and defence policy

Throughout the Cold War, the USA urged its European allies to put more resources into collective defence (Kennedy 1979; Sloan 1999). But the Europeans believed their security was guaranteed by the US nuclear umbrella. Whether or not **extended deterrence** would have worked in practice, the end of the Cold War removed the centrality of the nuclear option. The most important consequence of the fall of the Berlin Wall (the 'European 9/11'—9 November 1989) was that US conventional force disengagement from Europe became an inevitability. This left the Europeans with two options. Either they could dispense altogether with military accoutrements and just wallow in the soft Kantian paradise that Robert Kagan (2003) caricatures.[4] Or they could develop their own military capacity. The choice was never a serious one. It was *made for* Europe in the Balkans, in the Middle East, the Mediterranean and in a host of civil wars in Africa. Europe's 'backyard' is not exactly a lagoon of tranquillity. The development of an EU military capacity was the logical corollary to gradual US disengagement (Howorth and Keeler 2003).

From December 1998 onwards, the European Council has been working on a common defence policy for which the EU must develop, in the words of the Franco-British Saint-Malo Declaration of December 1998, 'the capacity for autonomous action, backed up by credible military forces, the means to decide to use them, and a readiness to do so in order to react to international crises'. (See Background box 23.6.) The EU has comparatively rapidly put together a military capacity designed to carry out the three so-called Petersberg Tasks: humanitarian assistance, peacekeeping and peacemaking. It is working hard to transform its outdated Cold War military capacity—designed to halt the Red Army in its tracks at the Fulda Gap—into a usable, projectable force capable of tackling crisis management missions more or less anywhere in the world.

Initially, in the face of these developments, the USA demonstrated signs of schizophrenia if not actual paranoia. Americans have had difficulty adjusting to this new reality for three main reasons. First, the European Union is not a nation state and, according to all the rules of international relations since at least 1648, only states can 'do' security effectively. Second, while the USA has long

**BACKGROUND BOX 23.6**

The Franco-British 'Saint Malo Declaration', December 1998

**"The Heads of State and Government of France and the UK are agreed that:**

**1.** The European Union needs to be in a position to play its full role on the international stage. ... This includes the responsibility of the European Council to decide on the progressive framing of a common defence policy in the framework of CFSP. ...

**2.** To this end, the Union must have the capacity for autonomous action, backed up by credible military forces, the means to decide to use them, and a readiness to do so, in order to respond to international crises. ... In strengthening the solidarity between the member states of the European Union, in order that Europe can make its voice heard in world affairs, while acting in conformity with our respective obligations in NATO, we are contributing to the vitality of a modernised Atlantic Alliance which is the foundation of the collective defence of its members."

been nagging the Europeans to get their military act together, it requires some cognitive adjustment when they actually begin to do so—especially when the buzzword is autonomy. Fears that the Europeans were seeking to decouple the Alliance surfaced immediately in Washington. Third, generations of US theorists have been weaned on structural realism and tend to see all power relations around the world in terms of balancing. (See Background box 23.3.) The confused debate within the USA over what the European Security and Defence Policy (ESDP) actually is has thrown up four different schools of thought. The 'yes please' group embraces a variety of analysts who believe, for one reason or another, that ESDP will strengthen the transatlantic partnership. The 'yes but' camp includes official spokespersons from both the Bill Clinton and George W. Bush administrations who are officially supportive of ESDP, but only under certain conditions. The 'oh yeah?' cohort features sceptics who refuse to believe that

Europe is capable of emerging as a military actor. The 'no way!' brigade sees ESDP as a threat to US national interests. The proliferation of these different schools reflects a number of basic misunderstandings about the nature of the ESDP project (Hamilton 2002).

In fact, what Europe is developing, is a completely different type of military. The European Security Strategy of December 2003 suggests that the key concept is that of 'comprehensive security'. Security is seen as indivisible; it addresses basic human rights and fundamental freedoms, economic and environmental cooperation as well as peace and stability. It is based on 'consultation rather than confrontation, reassurance rather than deterrence, transparency rather than secrecy, prevention rather than correction and interdependence rather than unilateralism'. It is closely linked to the concept of global public goods associated with debates inside the UN. It is deeply rooted in current concepts of human security (Biscop 2005; Dannreuther and Peterson 2006). As such, it is the perfect complement to the US military. It is a truism (with the notable exception of the UK and France) that the USA fights the wars and Europe does the dishes. The EU has done this systematically in Bosnia, in Kosovo, in Afghanistan and, to some extent, even in the Persian Gulf. But the deeper point about the complementarity between the USA and the EU in this area is twofold. First, the EU's development of a military capacity relieves US forces from duties in Europe which were hardly essential, and it allows for their redeployment to more urgent theatres. Second, the EU genuinely does have expertise in post-conflict reconstruction, in nation-building, in peace-keeping—expertise which is sorely lacking in the US armed forces. As Condoleeza Rice said during the election campaign in 2000, 'The 101st Airborne is not trained to escort students to kindergarten' (Rice 2000). However, EU armed forces are so trained. It is precisely this type of expertise in which the EU intends to specialise. If the objective is to win hearts and minds, post-conflict reconstruction is a crucial part of the equation. However, complementarity will not just happen. It will have to be planned, discussed, organised and gradually introduced. If the Iraq war taught one single overwhelming lesson, it was that the initial military entry campaign and the subsequent post-conflict follow-up campaigns must be tightly coordinated from the outset. Both sides have been thinking hard about this (Lindley-French 2002; Dobbins 2005).

## Trade and economics

Here, also, a natural symbiotic partnership—the type envisaged by Hamilton Fish Armstrong—has begun to develop. The USA and the EU are overwhelmingly one another's largest trading partner, largest investor and fiercest competitor. (See Background 23.7.) Europe and the USA are more inextricably interdependent in trade and economics than any two entities have ever been in the history of the world (Quinlan 2003). However, there is another side to this story. The EU overtook the USA in the late 1990s as the world's biggest market. It overtook the USA in 2005 as the world's largest GDP ($11.8 trillion as opposed to the US's $11.2 trillion). More significantly perhaps, the EU in 2000 also overtook the USA for world trade in services ($640bn v. $600bn). The EU exports much more than it imports, running a $200 plus billion surplus while the US trade deficit is over $500bn. Europeans have long been aware of the presence among them of US commercial giants: Coca Cola, McDonalds, Starbucks. Americans are largely unaware that such quintessentially 'American' household names as Donna Karan, Hellman's, Plymouth, Dodge, Chrysler and Jeep, Random House, the *Chicago Sun Times*, Verizon, Amoco, 7-Up, Stop and Shop, Dunkin Donuts, Ben & Jerry's, Dr Pepper, Holiday Inn, Lucky Strikes, Miller Lite and hundreds of other 'all-American names' are owned by European companies (Reid 2004: 116). Fourteen of the 20 largest commercial banks in the world are European, as are eight of the top ten insurance companies. Europe's rise

---

**BACKGROUND BOX 23.7**

Transatlantic Trade and Investment Complementarity 2003

- The total output of US foreign affiliates in Europe ($333 billion in 2000) and of European affiliates in the USA ($301 billion) is each greater than the total gross domestic output of all but a dozen nation states.

- Europe's investment stake in the USA grew to almost $1 trillion in 2000, which is nearly one-quarter larger than the USA's stake in Europe. European firms have never been as exposed to the US economy as in the first decade of the twenty-first century.

- There is more European investment in Texas alone than all US investment in Japan.

- US assets in Germany alone—$300 billion in 2000—were greater than total US assets in all of South America.

- US firms in the 1990s ploughed nearly twice as much capital into the tiny Netherlands ($65.7 billion) as they sank into Mexico ($34.1 billion).

**Joseph P. Quinlan (2003)**

---

is partly due to the disinterested launch of global competition implicit in the Marshall Plan. Significantly, while the EU (with the major exception of agriculture) has increasingly embraced institutional mechanisms, rules-based procedures and pooling of sovereignty, in these matters, the USA, for long the universal high priest of free trade, has increasingly frequently resorted to protectionism (Baldwin *et al.* 2003). Although the media tend to highlight high-profile trade battles such as those between Boeing and Airbus, in reality fewer than 2 per cent of all EU–US commercial ventures give rise to disputes. However, there is no doubt that the era of absolute US hegemony in this sector is ending. New players—China, India, Brazil—are making their voices heard in international trade, particularly within the World Trade Organization (WTO). Globalisation has become an extremely powerful force which neither the USA nor the EU can any longer properly control (Friedman 2005). Faced with the challenges of the new international economic order, the two sides have everything to gain from acting in partnership. They have much to lose from confronting the future along diverging paths.

## Human rights and democracy

Human rights and democracy are central to the US founding documents and to its universal ambitions. Many Americans migrated to the USA to escape European human rights abuses. It was the USA that insisted on the Nuremberg trials after the Second World War. The USA helped design the UN Human Rights Commission and draft the Universal Declaration on Human Rights. In 2004, the Bush administration embarked on what it had little hesitation in calling a crusade to introduce democracy into the Middle East and to persuade countries such as China to respect basic human rights norms (Halevy and Shafeeq 2003). Yet the USA remains strangely reluctant to ratify human rights treaties. The US Senate was one of the last to ratify the Genocide Convention. The USA is the only nation not to have ratified the 1990 Convention on the Rights of the Child. It still has not ratified the Convention on the Elimination of all Forms of Discrimination against Women (Mowle 2004: 85). The USA is one of only seven states (together with China, Iraq, Libya, Qatar, Yemen and Israel) to vote against the International Criminal Court. US policy on the death penalty clashes with Council of Europe strictures. In late 2005, the USA found itself convulsed with controversy over the role of torture in military or CIA detainee centres, unleashing major enquiries by both the Council of Europe and the European Parliament into the policy of *rendition* (transferring detainees to countries where they can 'legally' be tortured). In short, US credibility in a crucial area of contemporary international relations is increasingly undermined by its own domestic preferences (Ignatieff 2005).

Europe, on the other hand, has become the greatest force for democracy the world has ever seen. In 1939, most of Europe's great nations had been sucked into the totalitarian vortex: Spain, Portugal, Italy, Germany, Austria and Russia. Only the UK, France—and Poland—held out among the larger nation states. And even Poland and France were not to hold out much longer. Since the late 1950s, however, the EU integration process has seen the definitive reconciliation of France and Germany, the democratisation and integration of Greece, Spain and Portugal, and, most recently, the democratisation, prior to their incorporation, of 11 former communist states. The prospect of EU membership has had a dramatic effect on democracy and human rights in Romania, Bulgaria, Croatia and Turkey and is set similarly to transform the countries of the western Balkans (Vachudova 2005). Europe has, similarly, taken over the role of spearheading the cause of human rights worldwide, particularly with respect to the International Criminal Court (Sands 2003). In this capacity, as the row over rendition has demonstrated, it has inevitably been cast in the role of a critic of the perceived inadequacies of the US record in this increasingly crucial field of international relations.

How do we explain this strange *chassé croisé* in the respective trajectories of the two partners in this one policy area so central to the values of each? The US attitude, once again, reflects the dominance of realism. The USA's unique status as a superpower explains the strong resistance to any restrictions on US 'sovereignty'. Moreover, the distinctiveness of the US judicial process is such that few Americans can countenance the notion of subjecting US citizens to the imponderables of an international court. The EU, as we have seen, has no fear of 'pooling sovereignty' or of subjecting its activities to the scrutiny and (if necessary) to the arbitration of international institutions. It does this all the time. The EU attitude reflects the Union's growing embrace of multilateralism and multinationalism as a way of life appropriate to the post-Cold War world. The USA and the EU would both like to bring democracy to the Middle East and to promote the cause of human rights around the globe (Halevy and Shafeeq 2003). But democracy does not follow in the wake of precision-guided missiles. And EU membership for Middle Eastern countries is not on offer. Alone, neither the EU nor the USA is likely to achieve these grandiose objectives. Together, they might just stand a chance. Complementarity is indispensable. But this will require the USA to make some distance towards the EU's essentially post-modern and highly moralistic, values-based stance. Recent studies, demonstrating that, even by calculations of 'national interest', the USA could stand to gain from the introduction of international human rights regimes, suggest that such a development is not entirely out of the question (Gilligan 2006). However, there is growing concern across the Atlantic that those much cherished *values* which allegedly underpinned the Alliance for 40 years can no longer be considered as compatible. On issues such as the death penalty, gun control, abortion and the role of religion in public life, the two sides are manifestly moving in opposite directions (Drinan 2001; Hood 2003; Sloan 2005a).

## Environmental policy and sustainable development

In the area of environmental policy—arguably the most crucial policy area for the future of the planet—the two sides also appear to have traded places. The USA led the world on environmental issues in the 1970s and 1980s (lead-free gas, CFCs, ozone layer). But the EU took over that lead from the mid-1990s (growth hormones, biodiversity, global warming). Since the advent of the Bush administration, the USA has withdrawn its signature from (and effectively abandoned) the Kyoto Protocol (Victor 2000), the fate of which is now increasingly in European hands. A harsh critic of the USA position would focus on the increasing role of big business in driving US international policy, together with the abandonment of many values the USA has traditionally held dear (Bodansky 2003). A rather

more indulgent explanation would suggest that this probably reflects less a shift in values between the two sides and more an accident of circumstance. Since the 1980s, Europe has been the theatre of numerous environmental crises (Chernobyl, BSE, HIV-contaminated blood) and its citizens have demanded action at international level because they simply do not trust their own national regulatory agencies. This has translated into a vibrant green politics which is unnecessary in the USA since citizens trust governmental agencies to protect their environmental interests (Vogel 2003). In fact, the EU and the USA have similar percentages of voters who vote green. But a green vote in the EU delivers 40 green MEPs and green ministers sitting in governments in numbers of EU countries. A vote for Ralph Nader in the USA helped elect George W. Bush (twice).

This does not mean that the USA has abandoned global environmental objectives, but it does mean that, for the moment, the EU is in the driver's seat. Perhaps in the future some new environmental disaster in the USA will put the boot back again on the other foot. The succession of hurricanes in 2005 certainly set many thinking again about the relationship between human agency and weather patterns. The bottom line, once again, is that together the USA and the EU have made practically all the running, worldwide, on environmental issues. The challenge is phenomenal. Under the Clinton administration, despite many obstacles, the two blocs made significant joint progress towards accomplishment of the three objectives set at the Earth Summit in Rio de Janeiro in January 1992: the Convention on Biological Diversity, the Framework Convention on Climate Change and the Kyoto Protocol. All three of these were blocked either in the US Senate or by executive action under President George W. Bush. There are no signs that the Bush administration is contemplating shifting in this area. Yet, here again, faced with the environmental consequences of the rise of new industrial giants, the two blocs can only hope to make progress in tandem. Complementarity is unavoidable.

# Nuclear proliferation

While the USA—an 'Asian power'—was instrumental in trying to resolve the problem of nuclear proliferation in North Korea, Europe did most of the early heavy lifting in Iran which emerged as a potential nuclear weapons power at the turn of the century. In 2002, France, Germany and the UK engaged with Tehran and teased out the bases of a negotiated process (Everts 2004). The EU's commercial attraction, both as supplier and as market, gave it a measure of bargaining power with the Iranian regime. However, although the USA has effectively taken a back seat, no overall deal could be concluded without Washington's approval, since Tehran sought both a security guarantee and commercial concessions from the USA. The first round of negotiations (2002–5) was probably flawed. In retrospect, it seems highly unlikely that Iran was ever going to accept, as the basis for negotiation, constraints on its domestic nuclear programme which it was not required to accept under the terms of the **Non-Proliferation Treaty** (NPT). Although the early negotiations were conducted entirely by the EU3, the hard-line stance which sought to deny Iran any domestic control of the nuclear fuel cycle, was adopted with a wary eye on American realism. Yet US policy towards Iran since the revolution of 1979 has been a complete failure. The USA, in early 2005, associated itself formally with the EU negotiations, but its involvement remained ambivalent. While the official US position was supportive of the EU3 negotiation process, most US officials remained convinced of the eventual failure of the negotiations (Perkovich 2005). The view from Tehran was that the EU3 were no longer entirely autonomous or credible interlocutors.

In August 2005, the EU–Iran negotiations collapsed and Tehran recommenced its nuclear conversion and processing activities, challenging the International Atomic Energy Agency (IAEA) and the UN to deny it the right to do so. Yet such was Tehran's desire to emerge from its international isolation, and such was the power of attraction of the EU, that in October 2005 Iran invited the EU3, in association with Russia, to engage in a new round of negotiations. Iran has sought to have the international community accept its right to the full fuel cycle in exchange for cast iron guarantees that it will not develop a nuclear weapon. On that issue, the USA and the EU needed urgently to coordinate their responses. Although the USA at first took a hard-line position and threatened immediately to take Iran before the UN Security Council, a number of factors coalesced to allow the EU to re-engage the negotiations: the cooperative role of Russia in proposing assistance to Iran's peaceful nuclear ambitions, the political and military impasse in which the USA found itself in Iraq, and the internal political struggles taking place in Iran between the volatile new President Mahmoud Ahmadi-Nejad and the more cautious conservatives within the Guardian Council. Iran is a large, complex and unpredictable player in one of the most unstable areas of the planet. The EU clearly emerged as the 'indispensable partner' of the USA in defusing one of the thorniest issues of international relations (Leonard 2005b). After protracted negotiations, in which the EU and the US carefully coordinated their positions, the IAEA, in February 2006, voted to refer the Iranian nuclear programme to the United Nations Security Council. In March 2006, the UNSC issued a 'Presidential Statement' calling on Tehran to halt uranium enrichment. In all these negotiations, the partnership of the EU and the USA in bringing Russia and China 'on board' was crucial. US sabre-rattling (threats of both sanctions and military action) was seen in Europe as counterproductive. The Iranian problem was, in mid-2006, the most serious problem of international relations. Without tight EU–US coordination through the relevant international institutions, it ran the risk of running out of control.

## Regional peace: the Israel–Palestine question

The EU–US partnership has been all too invisible, however, in another key problem area of international relations: the Middle East peace process (MEPP). While both partners have an equal commitment to the two-state solution, they have very different historical experiences with the Middle East and very different approaches to the task. (See Background box 23.8.) The EU has constantly drawn up point-by-point blueprints for a final settlement. The USA, by contrast, has eschewed blueprints and tried to act as 'honest broker' (Gordon 1999). In fact, the USA has given staunch backing to Israel, while the EU has bankrolled the Palestinian Authority. The USA has underwritten the military side of the equation, while the EU has emerged as by far the biggest commercial partner both of Israel and of the Palestinians. But none of this has been coordinated. As early as 1980, the EU called for recognition of the Palestine Liberation Organisation (PLO) as a legitimate partner and for an eventual Palestinian homeland. Both notions were at the time rejected by Washington and by Israel ('Munich-like capitulation to totalitarian blackmail'). Rarely, since the Suez crisis of 1956, had the two sides been so far apart on a major issue of international relations. After the Gulf War of 1991, the USA emerged as the only serious player in the MEPP. Divisions between the different EU member states,[5] the collapse of the Soviet Union and the disarray of the Arab world guaranteed US predominance in the peace process. But the US initiative was gradually succeeded by the Oslo process, the forefather of the present peace process, itself essentially the detailed reformulation of the main points of the EU's Venice blueprint (Behrendt and Hanelt 2000). In the late 1990s, President Clinton worked in cooperation both with the EU's special envoy, Miguel Angel Moratinos, and with the EU's High Representative for the CFSP, Javier Solana. Both sides had important inputs into the current 'road map', which is underwritten also by the UN and Russia.

> **BACKGROUND BOX 23.8**
>
> ### The Middle East 'Road Map' (2002)
>
> **Phase I: Ending Terror And Violence, Normalizing Palestinian Life, and Building Palestinian Institutions—Present to May 2003**
> In Phase I, the Palestinians immediately undertake an unconditional cessation of violence according to the steps outlined below; such action should be accompanied by supportive measures undertaken by Israel....
>
> **Phase II: Transition—June 2003–December 2003**
> In the second phase, efforts are focused on the option of creating an independent Palestinian state with provisional borders and attributes of sovereignty, based on the new constitution, as a way station to a permanent status settlement.
>
> **Phase III: Permanent Status Agreement and End of the Israeli–Palestinian Conflict—2004–5**
> Phase III objectives are consolidation of reform and stabilization of Palestinian institutions, sustained, effective Palestinian security performance, and Israeli–Palestinian negotiations aimed at a permanent status agreement in 2005.
>
> **www.jewishvirtuallibrary.org/jsource/Peace/road.html**

During the first Bush term (2001–5), the EU and the USA once again found themselves at cross-purposes. The US administration disengaged from the MEPP, effectively stalling the road map process and allowing Prime Minister Ariel Sharon a relatively free hand to crack down on Palestinian 'terrorists'. The EU for its part pressed hard for US re-engagement. It was not until early 2005, with the death of Yasser Arafat and the arrival at the State Department of Condoleeza Rice, that the partnership cranked back into gear. No definitive solution is possible without US political involvement. But none is imaginable without the EU's regional and economic commitment. If Turkey were to join the EU, the Union would have borders with Syria, Iran and Iraq. Israel and Palestine would become immediate neighbours. For the Palestinians, the USA lacks the credibility to be an honest broker.[6] The EU, for its part, has never been seen by Israel as objective. That is why the USA and the EU are, once again, indispensable partners in the implementation of any eventual peace plan. Neither, on its own, can really secure political change in this part of the world. Together, they just might. Together, they can coordinate the necessary pressures on both Israelis and Palestinians which will be necessary to break the impasse. Together, they could construct a far-reaching economic plan for the region which would allow it to escape its dependency on oil. There is still a long way to go (particularly since the twin elections of Hamas and Kadima in 2006), but nobody can doubt the centrality to the entire process of EU–US cooperation (O'Gorman 2004; Gordon 2005).

## The 'Global War on Terror'

The final 'big issue' on the planetary agenda today is yet another policy area in which EU–US cooperation is vital. A rapid comparison of the US National Strategy for Combating Terrorism (February 2003) and of the EU Declaration on Combating Terrorism (March 2004) suggests that the two blocs are very much on the same wavelength. Indeed, there is nothing in one side's approach that is not replicated in some form or another in that of the other side. (See Background box 23.9.) In June 2004, EU and US leaders issued the EU–US Declaration on Combating Terrorism, which reads like a perfect synthesis of the two national documents. There is no doubt that EU–US cooperation on counter-terrorism has been substantial and growing ever since 9/11. Intelligence-sharing has been more intense and more effective than ever before. France has passed on highly sensitive intelligence, which President Bush has gratefully acknowledged to have been crucial. Cooperation between law-enforcement agencies and prosecutors has been massively stepped up. In June 2003, the two sides concluded an Extradition and Mutual Legal Assistance Agreement facilitating extradition for many

more offences than previously. Agreement was reached in May 2004 on communication of passenger name records (PNRs) in connection with international travel. In September 2004, wide-ranging agreements were reached on the safety of container transport (the Container Security Initiative), including extensive customs cooperation and the facility for US officials to check container cargoes in European ports. Joint US–EU investigative teams are being planned. A wide-reaching Policy Dialogue on Border and Transport Security is attempting to narrow the gap on issues such as sky-marshals and biometric data. Substantial legal and banking cooperation has been agreed on countering terrorist financing. New measures have been agreed for cooperation in response to the consequences of terrorist attack. This amounts to a substantial package of agreements, many of which would have been virtually unthinkable before 2001. Yet, the two sides continue to spar over the priority to be attached to the immediate hunt for active terrorists as against the long-term problem of addressing root causes. Obviously, both are essential and, once again, for both to happen, tight cooperation between the EU and the USA is indispensable (CSIS 2004; Keohane 2005).

### KEY POINTS

- On every major foreign-policy and security-policy issue, the USA and the EU can only gain from coordinating their efforts.

- However, on most of those key issues, there are major strains in the relationship deriving from domestic political preferences, distinct political cultures and shifting asymmetries.

- On some (human rights, environment), the EU has taken over the lead from the USA, on others (Middle East, nuclear proliferation), the USA remains the 'indispensable actor'.

- On a third set of issues (security, trade, terrorism) a workable partnership seems to be emerging.

## BACKGROUND BOX 23.9

### Major EU and US Statements on Terrorism

■ *The 9/11 Commission Report. Final Report of the National Commission on Terrorist Attacks upon the United States*, New York, Norton, 2004, available at www.9-11commission.gov/report/index.htm

■ European Union *Fight Against Terrorism*, available at http://ue.eu.int/showPage.asp?lang=en&id=406&mode=g&name=

■ *European Union Factsheet: The EU and the Fight Against Terrorism*, June 2004 available at http://ue.eu.int/uedocs/cmsUpload/europa.pdf

■ European Union *Declaration on Combating Terrorism*, 2004, available at http://ue.eu.int/uedocs/cmsUpload/79635.pdf

■ United States, *National Strategy for Combating Terrorism*, available at www.whitehouse.gov/news/releases/2003/02/20030214-7.html

■ *EU–US Declaration on Combating Terrorism*, available at http://ue.eu.int/uedocs/cmsUpload/10760EU_US26.06.04.pdf

# Overall Conclusions

The United States is the world's only global superpower, with unprecedented and unparalleled influence in almost every area of public policy (Bacevich 2002; Ferguson 2004; Ikenberry 2002; Lieber 2002). The European Union is emerging as an international actor, with considerable resources in the area of 'soft power' (Nye 2004; Hill and Smith 2005) and a growing reputation as a stabilising force around its perimeter and even beyond. While the EU has matched US power in terms of trade, economics and investment, it still lags behind in terms of growth, employment and dynamism. While the EU has recently taken the lead in issues such as human rights and environmental policy, its global impact in these areas would be more effective through partnership with the United States. In the area of 'hard power', the EU is developing a military capacity geared to crisis management and post-conflict reconstruction, but this is not—nor is it intended to be—comparable with US military might. Under President George W. Bush, US military power has been projected to Central Asia and the Middle East in an unprecedented show of unilateral resolve which has generated vociferous

protest across Europe. The USA has ridden roughshod over international treaties and appeared to backtrack on a fifty-year record of commitment to multilateralism, international institutions and international law. The EU remains firmly committed to internationalism in all its guises and to the further development of international law. These mismatches and contrasts have highlighted a growing divide between the two sides of the Atlantic which has seen many question the compatibility of European and American values.

A further complexity arises from public opinion. Americans, by and large, remain convinced that, whatever its international shortcomings, their country remains basically a force for good in the world. Seventy per cent of Americans are 'very proud' of their nationality and 79 per cent believe it to be a good thing that 'American ideas and customs are spreading around the world' while almost 80 per cent believe that the US does either 'the right amount' or 'too much' to solve global problems (Walt 2005: 63). By contrast, a minority of Europeans—with only slight national variations—are 'proud' of their nationality. More tellingly, large percentages of Europeans have a negative image of the USA and view its influence in the world as 'mainly negative'. This negative image of the USA rose to unprecedented heights in the spring of 2003 as the USA invaded Iraq. A key question in transatlantic relations as the George W. Bush administration entered the mid-point of its second term in 2006 was whether the impact of 9/11 and of **neo-conservatism** had so radically changed the parameters of European–American relations as to rule out a return to the partnership patterns of the past. This question has been hotly debated in a variety of collected editions (Lindberg 2005; Levy, Pensky & Torpey 2005; Zaborowski 2006). The precise answers will depend to a large extent on the fortuitousness of 'events' over the coming years. But, as this chapter has tried to argue, despite the serious and growing transatlantic problems of the early twenty-first century, the US and the EU still retain more in common—in terms of history, project, culture and values—than that which divides them. They also share more with one another than either does with any other region of the world. As one of the most high-profile and fiercest European

critics of the war in Iraq put it, 'For so much of my lifetime, America has been an education to the world—to every nation, every continent and every civilization. It has been a living lesson, a paradigm to which others could aspire, an example for others to follow. I hope that Europe can help America to be that again' (Patten 2006: 293). However, while Europe can certainly 'help' America move back towards the more consensual internationalism of the post-1945 years, such assistance, on its own, will not suffice. As long as Americans remain convinced that the USA and its system represent a 'city on a hill', a unique example to all mankind, a model exportable to and adaptable by every nation and every culture, one which epitomises good and sees it as its duty to extirpate 'evil' wherever it is to be found, there will be a fundamental problem for transatlantic relations. Europeans are moving, if they have not already moved, beyond the narrow confines of the Westphalian state system (Cooper 2002). The USA remains the most complete embodiment of that system. Under these circumstances, there are distinct limits to the potential for harmonious cooperation.

## Notes

1. I am grateful to Alyson Bailes, Director of the Stockholm International Peace Research Institute, for devising this metaphor.
2. For the interventions by Chirac's then Foreign Minister Dominique de Villepin, see Villepin (2003: 37–145). For Chirac's own views, see his speeches in *La Politique Etrangère de la France* and his two major interviews with the *New York Times* (Chirac 2002; Chirac 2003).
3. Richard Clarke, who was National Coordinator for Security and Counter-terrorism under both President Clinton and President Bush, recounts in his memoirs (Clarke 2004: 32) that Bush

instructed him on 12 September 2001 (the day after the attacks on the World Trade Center): 'go back over everything, everything. See if Saddam did this. See if he's linked in any way . . .'.
4. 'It is absurd to depict Europe as a carefree oasis of security when it depends on the outside world for 40 per cent of its trade and 50 per cent of its energy. Germany is 60 per cent dependent on outside suppliers for energy, Italy 82 per cent. Europe's periphery is within range of missiles belonging to several potentially hostile states, some nuclear capable. It has lived for hundreds of years with violent terrorism

and contains some 15 million Muslims with full citizens' rights' (Bailes 2004).

5. France tended to be the most 'pro-Arab', while Germany was objectively 'pro-Israel'. The UK attempted to steer a middle course by remaining close both to the USA and to France.

6. In spring 2006, John Mearsheimer and Stephen Walt caused a firestorm in the USA with their article on 'The Israel Lobby' (Mearsheimer and Walt 2006). The fact that such an analysis, highly critical of US policy towards Israel, could not be published in the USA and had to be published in the UK, and the fact that the ensuing row suggested the impossibility of engaging a serious debate about the issue, speak volumes in this regard.

 **KEY WORDS**

**Balancing:** in structural realist international relations theory, nation-states, when faced with a rising or current hegemon, will seek to "balance" that hegemon's power through alliances, coordinated action at a variety of levels, or even war.

**Extended deterrence:** the policy whereby the nuclear deterrent of a given nation state is declared to "protect" from the aggressive attentions of a potentially hostile third party the territory and political existence of an ally or friendly state. Sometimes referred to as the "nuclear umbrella".

**Marshall Plan:** The European Recovery Programme enunciated by US Secretary of State George C Marshall in June 1947, whereby a total of US$ 12.6 billion (equivalent to over $100 billion in 2005 dollars) was granted to European nations to assist their recovery from the destruction of World War II.

**Neo-conservatism:** a political movement in the US at the turn of the 21st century in which an ideological mix of left-leaning democratic idealism and right-wing military unilateralism resulted in a doctrine of pre-emptive warfare and the crusading "export" of democracy around the world.

**Non-Proliferation Treaty:** An international Treaty, signed in 1970 (currently by 187 states) whereby the five officially nuclear states (US, Russia, China, France, UK) agree to reduce their nuclear arsenals and the non-nuclear states agree not to develop nuclear weapons, while having the right to develop, with the assistance of any state, nuclear energy for peaceful purposes.

**Structural Realism:** Sometimes referred to as neo-realism. The international relations branch of theory which sees war and conflict as the inevitable outcome of systemic anarchy (the absence, in the international system, of any overarching authority capable of influencing the policies of nation-states).

**Westphalian system:** The system of nation-states, enjoying external and internal sovereignty, which was initiated by the Treaty of Westphalia in 1648. According to this system, which underpins the United Nations Charter, nation states may not normally intervene in the internal affairs of other nation states.

**? QUESTIONS**

1. What are the principal asymmetries between the nature of US and of EU power?

2. Why is it that the EU, in formulating a common policy towards the outside world, has the greatest difficulty agreeing on policy towards the USA?

3. To what extent do you believe that the US and the EU have espoused and still espouse similar values?

4. Why do structural realists believe that the EU must necessarily find itself "balancing" against the United States?

5. In what ways have the events of 11 September 2001 and their consequences had a complicating effect on European–American relations?

6. To what extent has the administration of President George W. Bush exacerbated relations between Europe and the USA?

7. Why have the USA and the EU switched roles in terms of taking the leadership on issues such as human rights and the environment?

8. What are the prospects of the EU and the USA jointly helping to solve the Iranian nuclear proliferation problem?

9. Do the EU and the USA really see eye-to-eye on the solution to the Middle East problem?

10. Is the dominant trend in transatlantic relations currently one of convergence or one of divergence?

 **FURTHER READING**

■ **Baylis, J. & Roper, J. (eds),** *United States and Europe: the Future Divide***? London, Routledge.** A comprehensive set of essays on the main tensions between the two sides.

■ **Garton Ash, T. (2004),** *Free World: America, Europe and the Surprising Future of the West,* **New York, Random House.** A lively survey of transatlantic relations, advocating tight 'Anglo-Saxon' style US links for the EU as a whole.

■ **Gordon, P. and Shapiro, J. (2004),** *Allies at War: America, Europe and the Crisis Over Iraq,* **Washington DC, Brookings.** A superbly balanced analysis.

■ **Kagan, R. (2003),** *Of Paradise and Power: America and Europe in the New World Order,* **New York, Knopf.** Much cited but essentially polemical essay about Mars and Venus.

■ **Levy, D., Pensky, M. & Torpey, J. (eds.) (2005),** *Old Europe, New Europe, Core Europe: Transatlantic Relations after the Iraq War,* **London, Verso.** Leading intellectuals from both sides ponder the crisis.

■ **Patten, C (2006),** *Cousins and Strangers: America, Britain and Europe in the New Century,* **New York, Holt.** A *cri de coeur* from one of Europe's leading statesmen for a revitalised partnership.

■ **Pollack, M.A. and Shaffer, G.C. (eds) (2001)** *Transatlantic Governance of the Global Economy,* **Lanham, Rowman and Littlefield.** Offers key insights on trade and economic policy.

 **Visit the Online Resource Centre that accompanies this book for lots of useful additional material, including an interactive map of Europe. www.oxfordtextbooks.co.uk/orc/hay_menon/**

# 24

# Conclusion

COLIN HAY AND ANAND MENON

**Chapter Contents**

The preceding chapters have covered much ground, dealing with political processes and dynamics specific to individual European country cases and those which characterise the politics of Europe more generally. Yet, despite this breadth and diversity, a range of common processes, practices and concerns animate and inform each chapter. To some extent, of course, this is precisely because, as the editors of this text, we sought to make such themes the focus of attention. Yet we did so because it was clear to us from the outset that the impact of both globalisation and European integration and the question of the democratic legitimacy of the processes, practices and institutions with which this volume has been most concerned were likely to emerge as common themes. Having explicitly identified such themes in advance and having focused the attention of the chapter authors on them, we are now in a position to draw these various threads together in a brief conclusion.

Before turning to each in turn, however, it is important to state that, though clearly separable as sets of issues, the impact of the processes of globalisation and European integration and the question of democratic legitimacy are by no means unconnected. Arguably, the popular legitimacy of democratic institutions at the domestic level throughout Europe is challenged as never before precisely by virtue of the extent to which transnational processes (those of European integration and globalisation) wrest or are seen to wrest sovereignty and autonomy from the domestic level. Similarly, the extent to which the process of European integration counters, mediates, tempers or accelerates that of globalisation is the subject of considerable controversy. As this suggests, it is important that we do not see these three sets of issues as discrete and self-contained.

# The Impact of Globalisation

We began the introduction to this volume by noting that, for many, the condition of globalisation serves to challenge and compromise the ease with which we might identify national or even regional political processes and dynamics. In many respects the preceding chapters present a powerful refutation of that thesis. Domestic and regional political trajectories are remarkably resilient and the story of European politics in recent years is most definitely not one of the declining significance of political processes and institutions at the domestic and regional level. Yet this is most certainly not to suggest that globalisation has had no impact.

But quite what that impact has been is not easy to specify precisely and is the subject of considerable controversy—not least in the analysis of European politics (compare for instance Garrett 1997, Hay 2000 and Kurzer 1993 on the future of European social democracy). That controversy has, in essence, two sources—one semantic, one empirical. The semantic problem is easy to grasp. Different authors mean different things by globalisation. Whether globalisation is happening and whether the effects so often attributed to it can legitimately be attributed to it depend, unremarkably, on what globalisation is taken to mean—and there is no great consensus on the subject. The more inclusive one's definition, the more credible the claim that globalisation's impact is considerable; the more exacting the definitional standard, the more difficult it is to show that globalisation is even occurring, let alone decisively reshaping political processes at the domestic and regional levels. This brings us to the empirical debate. For there are those who argue that the term globalisation captures increasingly poorly the complex interdependencies which characterise contemporary Europe. Take economic interdependence. The conventional

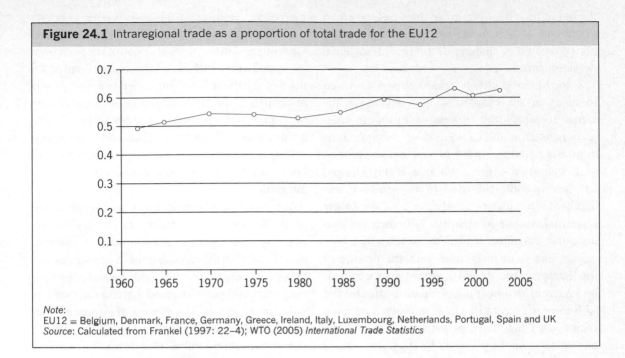

**Figure 24.1** Intraregional trade as a proportion of total trade for the EU12

*Note*:
EU12 = Belgium, Denmark, France, Germany, Greece, Ireland, Italy, Luxembourg, Netherlands, Portugal, Spain and UK
*Source*: Calculated from Frankel (1997: 22–4); WTO (2005) *International Trade Statistics*

wisdom—in Brussels, among political elites across the continent, and among academics alike—is that the European economy is globalising. Accordingly, European economies must increasingly prove their competitiveness in genuinely global terms if they are to survive. Yet, the sceptics argue, this is simply not the case. In fact, they argue, pointing to data like that in Figure 24.1, that an ever greater share of Europe's trade is internal to the European economy (a point also noted by Lee McGowan in Chapter 20 and Alasdair Young in Chapter 22).

In the early 1960s, less that 40 per cent of the EU12's trade was intraregional in character. That figure has risen slowly but surely ever since and is now in excess of 60 per cent. This is not, they suggest, a globalising economy but a Europeanising economy.

This may seem like a purely empirical dispute. Yet a moment's further reflection reveals this, too, to be a largely semantic controversy. The point is that, for many authors, data such as those shown in Figure 24.1 are perfectly compatible with an (albeit somewhat less exacting) definition of globalisation. For such authors, whether globalisation is occurring or not depends not on the geographical composition of trade (the degree to which European trade is intraregional in character) but the overall volume of trade. While that volume continues to rise, they will continue to refer to the European economy as a globalising economy. Once again, whether globalisation is happening or not depends on what globalisation is taken to imply.

Yet debates about globalisation in contemporary European politics are by no means purely semantic in nature. A common theme in the preceding chapters is the extent to which the European Union might increasingly be seen as a global actor. This clearly varies considerably between issue domains. In Chapter 18, Wyn Grant and Jane Feehan show how the European Union has indeed become a global agenda-setter in the field of environmental policy. Yet the same could most certainly not be said in the field of foreign policy, where internal divisions between member states, especially over the war in Iraq, have prevented the development of a common, or even an effective foreign and security policy capable of shaping decisively international developments.

A further, and closely related theme discussed in many of the chapters of this volume is the extent to which the process of European integration itself might be seen as a reaction to, or even as a potential means of shaping, the process of globalisation. Again, this is a highly charged and heavily contested set of issues—in both academic and popular political discourse. As Robert Elgie makes clear in Chapter 2, French political discourse has often tended to associate the process of European integration with the defence of the 'European social model' against encroachment by agents of neo-liberal globalisation. If attitudes to European integration in France are now more critical than they have perhaps ever been in the past then, it might plausibly be suggested, this is as much as anything else bound up with the fear that the process of European integration and the institutions to which it has given rise are no longer capable of defending French and European traditions from the ravages of an increasingly global free market. If this is so, it is in turn associated with the rising influence of more liberal and neo-liberal ideas on the European stage. These have often been associated with, but are by no means limited to, the British. Indeed, as Tim Haughton makes clear in Chapter 9, the process of enlargement itself may be changing the political character of the Union, giving renewed impetus to liberal and neo-liberal voices, and weakening the historic influence of France on the trajectory of the process of European integration.

Yet, however influential this view has become, it would be wrong to see the contemporary process of European integration as a simple capitulation to neo-liberal globalisation. European economies and European societies remain highly regulated by contemporary comparative standards and their welfare states are generous. The process of European integration has, certainly thus far, tended to reinforce rather than to undermine that distinctiveness. It is this which makes credible the claim that Europe offers an alternative conception to the neo-liberal orthodoxy of a dynamic, open and competitive economy—an alternative vision of globalisation to that offered by the USA.

# The Impact of European Integration

If the impact of globalisation on contemporary European politics is a contested subject, then scarcely less controversial, both academically and in popular political debate, are the impact and character of the process of European integration. Much of this we have already touched on in the section on globalisation—again, the two topics are almost inextricably interwoven. But, in addition to the points already made, a number of general and specific themes emerge from the chapters which together comprise this volume.

The first of these is the question of convergence, which was touched upon briefly in the introduction and has been a consistent theme of the chapters which follow. Though globalisation has often been associated in the academic literature with convergence, there is in fact scant evidence for the kind of convergence the globalisation thesis predicts within Europe. European economies, as already noted, remain extremely open economies by comparative standards, yet their politics in recent years has not been characterised by significant welfare retrenchment, deregulation and a dismantling of a long tradition of state intervention. Indeed, while all European social models have undoubtedly liberalised to some extent, it is those that were already the most liberal in character (notably the British and the Irish) which have embraced neo-liberalism most enthusiastically. The result is not the much anticipated convergence of European social models, but instead their continued distinctiveness, indeed arguably even their divergence (for such an argument, see Hay 2004).

Moreover, insofar as there are pressures for convergence within Europe, these are far more credibly associated with the process of European integration than they are with that of globalisation. First, as already noted, the European economic space is very closely integrated internally. As a consequence, many of the challenges it faces are common, many of the determinants of its economic success or failure rather closer to home than is often assumed. Arguably, for instance, the poor performance of the Northern European economies in the early years of the 1990s was far less a consequence of any innate lack of competitiveness in global markets than it was of trade dependence on a large German economy undergoing the deflationary shock of reunification. This was merely compounded by the deflationary effects of the Maastrict Convergence Criteria on the whole European economy. Tempting, then, though it is to look for general explanatory factors like globalisation, the devil of European politics invariably lies in the details. Second, as the process of European Monetary Union demonstrates very well, the European Union has been very effective at the institutional imposition of convergent policy choices. The harmonisation of currencies, and with it the harmonisation of exchange rates and interest rates, imposes convergence in a previously almost unprecedented manner. As this suggests, to explain convergence in macroeconomic policy choices in Europe, and much else besides, we simply do not need to invoke globalisation.

A further set of issues which is explored in almost all chapters, particularly those of Parts 2, 3 and 4, is the character and indeed the changing character of the process of European integration itself. A traditional concern here, already touched upon in the previous section, is whether the process of European integration has served to promote the interests, institutional templates and agendas of particular national models over others. Historically, the Union's architects in France and Germany have been identified as those in whose image European institutions have been forged. Yet the contemporary debate is rather different, as a number of chapters suggest. France's influence over the developmental trajectory of the Union has been significantly weakened in recent years—and has been *seen* to have been weakened, with a variety of both domestic and European-level consequences. Germany's place at the heart of Europe seems destined to continue, but the character of the agendas and policies it is promoting has changed significantly since reunification. And, as the process of reunification reminds us, the most significant and still ongoing process of reform in recent years has been that of enlargement. That has already served decisively to recast the nature and character of EU politics—increasing the complexity of the Union, altering the relative balance of liberal and more statist voices within the Union, tabling an entirely new set of issues and policy challenges, and leading to a more intergovernmental, diplomatic and less Commission-driven style of integration (Menon 2007; Kassim and Menon 2004). The consequences of such changes, many of them still ongoing, are difficult to predict at this point and will need to be closely followed in the years ahead.

A final set of concerns relates to the growing salience in European domestic politics and at a pan-European level of Euro-scepticism. There is, of course, nothing especially novel about Euro-scepticism. But the levels to which this has risen in recent years, the near exponential rise in the prevalence of such attitudes, and the fact that such a rise is common to virtually every European case are unprecedented. This undoubtedly speaks to broader issues of democratic legitimacy and accountability to which we will turn in the final section. It is manifest in the rise of political parties, of right and left, which are explicitly anti-EU, anti-European or both in the policy stances they adopt, in the increasingly defensive tone adopted by ostensibly pro-European politicians and policymakers towards the process of European integration, and in the seemingly increasing difficulties found achieving a popular consensus for progress on institutional, constitutional or foreign-policy matters.

# Democratic Legitimacy

As the above paragraphs perhaps serve to indicate, there is virtually no facet of contemporary European politics which is not bound up with concerns about democratic legitimacy and accountability. Trust in politicians at all levels is unprecedently low; levels of formal political participation scarcely less depressing. Of course, Europe is by no means alone in experiencing such high levels of political disaffection and disengagement; nor, indeed are they uniform—the Nordic states continue to enjoy among the highest rates of political trust and participation in the world today. Yet even here there is a palpable sense of democratic malaise at both the domestic and European levels.

In a way, the European political space today encapsulates the more global problem of democratic legitimacy, accountability and participation. We live in worlds characterised by complex interdependence, yet by and large we are governed by institutions which were either designed to deal with issues which were narrowly domestic in character or were modelled on precisely such designs. Moreover, we have yet to devise effective means of holding power to account to citizens at levels above that of the nation state. As a consequence, in a complex and multi-level polity in which policies are shaped, developed and often even implemented at levels above the national, citizens of democratic polities are likely to feel increasingly alienated and remote from the decision-making process—scarcely able to identify, let alone hold to account, those making decisions on their behalf. That describes well the contemporary European predicament, as arguably it does the attitudes of citizens throughout the world to such institutions of global governance as we have thus far devised. It also describes well the contemporary challenge which faces European politics. Europe, as a region, is characterised politically by a greater density of national and regional-level institutions than any other and its politics has had to deal with the complex relationship between the domestic and the transnational for longer than anywhere else. It is, then, one might think, the context out of which solutions to the problem of democratic legitimacy, accountability and participation in a multi-level polity are most likely to emerge. Yet if there is a single lesson of this volume, it is surely that such solutions have yet to emerge. Our hope, as editors, is that the chapters we have commissioned and assembled in this volume will contribute in some small way to the development of an understanding of the European polity on the part of a new generation of students capable of fashioning some answers to this most pressing of challenges in the years ahead. If this is indeed the case, then Europe will emerge as an alternative model of globalisation from which we can all benefit.

# Glossary

**Accession negotiations** Aimed at examining the applicant's capacity to fulfil the requirements of EU membership and apply the *acquis* at the time of accession.

***Acquis communautaire*** The body of laws, rights and obligations that bind member states together in the EU. Applicant countries have to transpose the *acquis* into their national legislation and implement it upon accession.

**Activation policies** The activation approach to welfare moved onto the European agenda with the European Employment Strategy in 1997. The term is used mainly to describe the relationship between social policy and employment. It involves a shift from redistributive social policies to regulation and implies an emphasis on cost effectiveness.

**Ageing** When used in demographic discussion in relation to entire populations, as opposed to individuals, this refers to the rise in the mean age of a population that occurs if birth rates fall while life expectancy rises.

**Agenda 2000** Strategy paper which set out the reform of EU polices in the light of enlargement towards Central and Eastern Europe and the financial framework for the period 2000–6.

**Allies** The nations that opposed the Axis Powers during the Second World War: the USA, UK, France and the USSR.

**Antitrust** Essentially an American term and synonym for competition policy. See the title, for example, of the prestigious academic journal *The Antitrust Bulletin*. Antitrust is designed to combat trusts (concentrations of wealth in the hands of the few) and cartels, i.e. by preventing them from using monopolistic business practices to make unfair profits.

**Approximation** The means used to overcome the disruptive impact on the common market of differing national provisions laid down by law, regulation and administrative action. Article 100a of the EC Treaty provides for the approximation of provisions that have

as their object the establishment and functioning of the single market.

**Association (Europe) Agreement** A treaty between the EU and a non-EU country that creates a framework for cooperation between them.

**Asylum-seeker** A migrant outside their country of origin who applies for refugee status under the 1951 Convention relating to the status of refugees.

**Balancing** In structural realist international relations theory, nation states, when faced with a rising or current hegemon, will seek to 'balance' that hegemon's power through alliances, coordinated action at a variety of levels, or even war.

**Barcelona Process** Agreed by the member states of the EU and ten states from the Mediterranean in 1995, the Process established the Euro-Mediterranean Partnership (EMP) with the overall objective of turning the Euro-Mediterranean basin into an area of dialogue, exchange and cooperation guaranteeing peace, stability and prosperity.

**Biodiversity** The abundance of life on the planet measured by the variety of species and their genetic variability and the ecosystems and landscapes in which they occur.

**Bond market** A financial market centred on the issuing of, and trading in, fixed interest securities issued by firms (corporate bonds) and governments (treasury bonds). Stock exchanges transact this activity.

***Bundesrat*** lit. 'Federal Council', the upper house of the German Parliament.

***Bundestag*** lit. 'Federal Diet', the lower house of the German Parliament.

**Candidate countries** Countries with which accession negotiations have started.

**Charter of Fundamental Human Rights** Signed and proclaimed by the European Parliament, the Council and the Commission at the European Council meeting held in Nice in 2000, it entered into force in the same year. The Amsterdam Treaty affirmed the Union's commitment to human rights and freedoms by referring to the European Convention on Human Rights. The Charter sets out in a single text the range of civil, political, economic and social rights of European citizens and all persons resident in the EU with regard to dignity, freedoms, equality, solidarity and justice.

**Civic nationalism** A form of nationalism which rallies around the concept of citizenship and the political, economic and social rights that this entails.

**Civil-law tradition** This legal system is prevalent in continental Europe and much of the rest of the world. Its central feature is a set of legal codes designed to establish the general framework for national law and limit judicial discretion. The civil-law ideal expects judges to apply codes to disputes with a minimum of creative interpretation.

**Cleavage** A political division whose characteristics involve (1) social division; (2) the social group must be conscious of its collective identity; and (3) there must be an organisational dimension.

**Clientelism** A form of political exchange, also known as patron–client relationships, in which political parties (or others with access to or control of the resources of the state) channel minor benefits or patronage to individuals in exchange for political support. One or more patrons act as intermediaries. Clientelism is more likely in less developed societies in which clients at the base are dependent on the state for their well-being.

**Climate change** Changes in the Earth's climate, at global and regional levels, over any time scale from millions of years to decades. Recent usage of the term refers to ongoing changes in modern climate, including the average rise in surface temperature known as global warming. These changes arise from several sources including internal processes and external forces, and most recently human activities.

**Co-determination** The participation of employees on the board of directors of private firms. Usually represented through unions, such representatives would share information and strategic decisions with management. Particularly in Sweden in the 1970s such policies were established by legislation modelled loosely on West German laws.

**Cohabitation** Where there is a president from one party and a prime minister from an opposing party.

**Cohesion** An EU policy that aims to close the socio-economic gaps between richer and poorer regions through financial transfers from the central budget for development projects.

**College of Commissioners** Comprises 25 individuals (currently, one is nominated from each EU member state). Once the College has been approved by the European Parliament the Commissioners assume responsibility for their own policy areas (as selected for them by the Commission president. Neelie Kroes holds the competition portfolio. Formal decisions on competition cases are not made by the competition commissioner but by the College and by means of a simple majority vote.

**Colonial migration** Migration from former European colonies (India, Indonesia) to the colonising country (e.g. the UK, Netherlands).

**Comitology** The Commission is able to instigate regulations as 'implementation measures'. The Commission establishes an 'implementation committee' which expresses a view on proposed measures or approves these. The procedures of this committee are called comitology. The membership is made up of policy experts who arrive at decisions through consensus after comparison and benchmarking across different states. Comitology may also refer to 'open methods of coordination'.

**Common-law tradition** This legal system is prevalent in the UK and its former colonies. Its central feature is that judges create the common law through the consistency of their decisions, where one decision serves as a binding precedent to guide future judicial rulings in similar cases.

**Competitiveness** A highly popular concept and slogan since the mid-1980s but it is actually very difficult to define. The best definition of national competitiveness is a country's ability to produce products that can penetrate international markets and pass the test of international competition both abroad and at home. At its core the term implies a comparative angle as countries must continually gauge their own performance against that of others.

**Conditionality** EU membership and pre-accession assistance are dependent on the extent to which a country applying for membership complies with the conditions laid down by the EU.

**Consensus democracy** A form of liberal democracy whose political organisation and patterns of political competition are characterised more by consensus than adversarial relations. From Lijphart (1999).

**Consociational democracy** A form of consensus democracy characterised by extensive power-sharing. According to Arend Lijphart (1975, 1977), political elites in subculturally plural or segmented societies agree to share power to avoid the potentially deleterious effects of system-threatening conflict. They do so via grand coalition, mutual veto (according key segments a veto), proportional allocation and subcultural autonomy (allowing key subcultures to regulate their own affairs).

**Consociationalism** See 'consociational democracy'.

**Constitutional monarchy** A democratic regime in which the head of state is a hereditary whose powers are clearly defined by a democratic constitution. This allows the hereditary principle of monarchy to coexist with the democratic principle.

**Constitutional review** Judges exercise this process when they consider whether laws and actions are compatible with constitutional rules. If judges find laws and actions to be unconstitutional, they overturn, or invalidate, the legislation and order governments to refrain from the actions.

**Convention on the Future of Europe** The gathering of representatives of the Heads of State and Government from the 15 EU member states (15) and the candidate countries (13), national parliaments of the EU15 (32) and the candidate countries (26), the European Commission (2) and the European Parliament (16), called by Heads of State and Government at the Laeken European Council in December 2001 to draft proposals on an EU Constitution for submission to an Intergovernmental Conference. The Convention opened in February 2002, closed in June 2003, and submitted its Draft Constitutional Treaty to an Intergovernmental Conference in October 2003. An amended version of the text was adopted by the Heads of State and Government in June 2004. Following negative votes in referenda in France and the Netherlands in May and June 2005 respectively, the ratification process was suspended.

**Convergence of social protection objectives** Council recommendation of 27 July 1992 on the convergence of social protection objectives and policies (92/442/EEC) designed to encourage member states to work towards common objectives and policies in the area of social protection. The recommendation proposed non-binding incentives as a way of preventing differences in social security arrangements from acting as a brake on free movement of workers and exacerbating regional imbalances.

**Copenhagen criteria** Agreed at the Copenhagen European Council in 1993, these criteria specified that any country wishing to become an EU member state must have achieved the stability of institutions guaranteeing democracy, the rule of law, human rights and respect for minorities, have a market economy able to withstand the competitive pressures of the single market, and the ability to take on the obligations of membership.

**Corporate pluralism** A system of interest representation that provides groups rights to participate similar to those found in corporatist arrangements, but which provides those rights of participation to a much wider array of organisations.

**Corporatism** Democratic corporatism legitimates representation and participation in policy-making by interest organisations such as trade unions, business and professional groups.

**Countercyclical fiscal policies** Based on the economic theories of John Maynard Keynes and other inter-war economists (especially in Sweden) these policies see the government stimulating a sluggish economy with spending increases and/or tax cuts and the reverse when inflation or excessive demand become a problem. The goal is to balance the business cycle and avoid deep recessions, soaring inflation and economic stagnation.

**Credibility of commitments** The extent to which arrangements put in place to ensure the parties to a contract will comply with its terms are likely to succeed.

**Cross-cutting cleavages** A pattern of cleavage in which economic and social cleavages cut across each other rather than coincide, e.g. when key religious groups are divided by social class, ethnicity or language.

**Customs union** An economic association of states that seeks to maximise the benefits of free trade by building a common external tariff around its members and devising a common commercial (trade) policy.

**De-alignment** A decline in voter identification with political parties and a turn towards supporting other types of organisation, such as social movement.

**Democratic deficit** A term applied to nominally liberal democratic states that are deemed to fall short of democratic standards in significant respects.

**Democratisation** The process of domestic political change including both the establishment of democratic political systems and their consolidation in terms of human rights, political participation, the rule of law and good governance.

**Demographic structure** The overall size, age and gender structure of a given population, including its characteristic rates of birth, family formation, life expectancy and death.

**Depoliticisation** A governing strategy designed to take potentially contentious issues out of public debate.

**Devolution** The delegation of designated powers to sub-national units of government. In Britain this has involved the creation of assemblies and executives.

**d'Hondt system** A variant of proportional representation in which seats are allocated by dividing each electoral list's vote share successively by 1, 2, 3, 4 etc., and distributing seats to the highest quotients. This method tends to over-reward high vote shares and penalise smaller ones.

**Dirigisme** A model of economic and social development that emphasises the role of the state in addressing a country's economic and social problems. It is mostly associated with France. It is applied in this context to a capitalist economy where the government seeks and is able to exert strong influence. Most modern economies are dirigiste to some degree—for instance, governmental action may be exercised through subsidising research and development of new technologies, or through government procurement, especially in relation to the purchase of military equipment.

**Divided government** A government in which the executive and at least one house of the legislature are controlled by different political parties. In a parliamentary system this usually means that the upper and lower houses are controlled by different parties.

**Doha Round** The first comprehensive multilateral trade negotiations since the WTO was established in 1995. The negotiations were officially launched in 2001 in Doha, Qatar. The negotiations are officially intended to benefit developing countries, hence the name the Doha Development Agenda. The negotiations were suspended in July 2006.

**Dualism** The separation between parliament and cabinet in Dutch parliamentary politics.

**Ecology** The study of the relationships that organisms have with their natural environment.

**Economic and Monetary Union (EMU)** The process of the economic and monetary union of EU member states launched by the Maastricht Treaty. Various convergence criteria were established to move in stages to full monetary union.

**Electoral volatility** A measure estimating the proportion of the electorate which has changed parties between elections. High rates of electoral volatility indicate decreasing attachment to political parties.

**Enlargement** The expansion and 'widening' (as opposed to 'deepening') of the EU as new member states join the existing Union. A number of issues are raised by the process (for example, the need to reform decision-making procedures, the demands placed on the EU budget, and so on).

**Equity market** A type of financial market involving the financing of firms through the issue of new shares (primary market) and the buying and selling of existing shares (the secondary market). Equity markets have traditionally been a prominent aspect of Anglo-American economies rather than organised forms of capitalism.

**ESSPROS** The System of integrated Social Protection Statistics (ESSPROS) was developed in the 1970s by Eurostat, jointly with representatives of member states. ESSPROS introduced a new methodology in 1996, allowing more detailed classification of social benefits and introducing greater flexibility into the system. A core system provides standard information on social protection receipts and expenditure, based on data regularly provided by member states. Supplementary modules cover subjects determined by the needs of the Commission and member states, applying less strictly the definitions adopted in the core.

**Ethnic nationalism** A form of nationalism that emphasises the ethnic bonds uniting people. Rallying around primordial elements such as culture, language and religion has been a common form of such nationalism.

**EU accession process** The process of preparation for membership undertaken by EU candidate countries and EU institutions, which normally concludes with entry into the EU.

**European Central Bank (ECB)** Established in 1998 and based in Frankfurt. It is the supranational central bank that sets a single interest rate for the euro economies (which, at the time of writing, do not include the UK, Denmark and Sweden). The ECB is technically independent from operational political control and committed to price stability (low inflation).

**European Economic Area (EEA)** Norway, Iceland and Liechtenstein are affiliated with the European Union without full membership. These countries enjoy full access to the EU market (including for labour) but do not participate in agricultural, developmental or fisheries policies. They must accept the EU 'acquis' (rules and regulations) fully in the relevant areas but do not participate directly in EU policy-making.

**European employment strategy** Launched at the Luxembourg Council in 1997. Its legal basis is the Treaty of Amsterdam. Guidelines and quantitative indicators are agreed at EU level, and member states are required to draw up national action plans describing the measures taken to meet the EU objectives. The Council and Commission then produce a joint employment report, comparing and benchmarking the performance of each member state. The strategy involves targets for increasing employment rates, making labour markets more inclusive and creating more equitable social conditions across the Union.

**European integration** The voluntary pooling of sovereignty by European states at the supranational level of governance in a set of decision-making institutions: the European Commission, European Council, Council of Ministers, European Parliament and European Court of Justice.

**European social model** The term has been used since the 1990s to refer to a politically feasible alternative to unregulated capitalism. No single European social model can be said to exist in the sense that there is not a social equivalent for a common European currency. The European Commission uses the term to suggest that EU member states subscribe to a common set of values, principles or objectives, encompassing democracy, social dialogue and social solidarity.

**Europeanisation** This complex term is generally taken to mean both the impact of European institutions on domestic politics in European countries, as well as the convergence between political systems across Europe. The trend for several decades has been for the EU to gain policy power in a growing number of areas, especially involving the economy.

**Eurostat** The Statistical Office of the European Union in Luxembourg produces and publishes regular statistical analyses and forecasts. Eurostat supplies EU institutions with harmonised data provided by national statistical offices as a basis for decisions and actions.

**Eurozone** Comprises those 12 countries of the EU that adopted the euro as their currency in 1999. These were Austria, Belgium, Finland, France, Germany, Greece, Ireland, Italy, Luxembourg, Netherlands, Portugal and Spain. Of the then existing 15 members of the EU, Denmark, the UK and Sweden did not join.

**Exchange Rate Mechanism 2 (ERM 2)** The new exchange rate mechanism that replaced the European Monetary System in 1999. It was designed to govern the exchange rate movements (the value of domestic currencies relative to the euro) of countries who wish to join the euro. Accession countries (the ten who joined in 2004) are obliged to participate in ERM 2 for at least two years in order to establish the exchange rate stability criterion set out in the Maastricht Treaty.

**Exchange rates** The value of traded currencies relative to each other. A vital convergence criterion before the adoption of the single currency (the membership of which rules out any change in currency value). The *real* exchange rate is the money exchange rate minus domestic inflation rate.

**Extended deterrence** The policy whereby the nuclear deterrent of a given nation state is declared to 'protect' from the aggressive attentions of a potentially hostile third party the territory and political existence of an ally or friendly state. Sometimes referred to as the 'nuclear umbrella'.

**Family patterns/life** Families in the European context typically comprise groups of persons who recognise special links to each other through blood ties or through marriage or sexual cohabitation. When these links lead to people sharing the same household or recognising particular obligations to each other, we may talk of family patterns or family life. These may range from the living together that is characteristic of parents and their growing children to the recognition of a need to help each other in times of difficulty among family-linked adults.

**Family reunification** A migration stream through which family members of a migrant join them in the country to which they have migrated. In many countries, family reunification makes up the majority of migration.

**Federalism** A form of political organisation between states that allocates responsibility for decision-making on various issues among at least two levels of governance, with responsibility for national security and international trade residing at the central (federal) level.

**Financial Services Action Plan (FSAP)** An EU initiative aimed at constructing a single market in financial services through harmonising regulations across the member states. It was put forward by the Commission as a Framework for Action in 1998. It forms a key part of the Lisbon Agenda where agreement was reached by the member states to implement the FSAP by 2005.

*Forza Italia* The archetypical business party, formed overnight by tycoon Silvio Berlusconi, which quickly became Italy's largest party, essentially on the basis of a business structure and a massive injection of personal resources.

**Four freedoms** The freedoms of trade, investment, services and labour contained in the Treaty of Rome. The customs union and single market are based on an economic doctrine in which the factors of production are mobile and allocated to maximise efficiency and welfare.

**Fragmented bipolarity** A party system in which two broad teams of parties compete, but in which no party on either side is sufficiently powerful to dominate and control the coalition.

**Free-riding** Where one or more parties to an agreement disregards their obligations, while at the same time benefiting from the compliance of other parties.

*Führer* lit. 'leader'; when used to refer to Hitler as der Führer, better translated as 'dictator'.

**Gaullists** Supporters of General Charles de Gaulle.

**Gender** The distinction between male and female persons viewed from a sociological perspective rather than from a biological or genetic perspective. The concept of gender serves to draw attention to the social implications of the distinction rather than its simple biological meaning.

**Giovannini Group** A group of financial-market participants formed in 1996, under the chairmanship of Alberto Giovannini, which advises the European Commission on financial market issues. It is widely acknowledged as having been a major force in forging a common approach to the redenomination of public debt into euro and in establishing common bond market conventions for the Eurozone.

**Global economic governance** Efforts at the global level to regulate economic activity among the states of the world. These activities are centred upon the main international economic organisations the G8, the International Monetary Fund, the World Bank and the World Trade Organization.

**Globalisation** The process whereby the financing, manufacture, organisation and sales of economic activities are increasingly distributed across different countries of the world, so that nation-state boundaries have a declining relevance to both markets and the internal organisation of large firms. This is often detrimental to low-skilled jobs and expensive social-welfare programmes in developed countries.

**Grand coalition** A coalition of either all parties or the largest parties. Grand coalition was used in Austria from 1946 to 1966 and the Federal Republic of Germany from 1966 to 1969.

**Ground-level air pollution** The presence of contaminants in the air below the stratosphere in concentrations which when breathed in pose a threat to human health.

*Grundgesetz* lit. 'Basic Law', constitution substitute adopted in West Germany in 1949; revised in 1989, it is now the constitution for all of Germany.

Immigration The movement of persons from one nation state to another, with the aim of more or less permanent settlement. The term should be distinguished from the wider term 'migration', which describes all major movements of this kind whether or not they cross national boundaries (as in movement from the countryside to towns).

**Guestworker schemes** Programmes operated by Germany, Switzerland and Austria (among others) after the Second World War. They were designed to bring workers to Europe for temporary contracts, but many remained, giving rising to these countries' ethnic minority populations.

**Industrialisation** The process whereby the economic activity of a society becomes dominated by the machine-powered manufacture of goods, typically in factories. Normally, this replaces economies based almost entirely on agriculture with some handicraft and services activities.

**Intergovernmental** A traditional form of cooperation among states based on the right of each state to veto or not abide by a decision that it considers to be against its national interest.

**Intergovernmental Conference** The formal meeting of representatives of EU member states to negotiate treaty amendments.

**Judicial review** This can be a synonym for constitutional review, but is often used in the European context to discuss the review of government actions for compatibility with legislation, or the exercise of constitutional review by the regular judiciary.

**Kemalism** The tenets of nationalism, westernisation, secularism, republicanism, statism and populism underpinning the Turkish Republic founded by Mustafa Kemal Atatürk.

**Keynesian economics** The economic theory associated with the economist John Maynard Keynes, in which macroeconomic policy is geared to managing aggregate demand (the key determinate of overall economic activity). An interventionist approach in which government fiscal policy can control the level of demand to ensure low unemployment and mitigate market volatility. See 'countercyclical fiscal policies'.

**Lamfalussy Committee** Part of the broad process of implementing the Financial Services Action Plan. Established after the Lisbon summit of July 2000, it is a committee of 'wise men' charged with enquiring into the regulation of European securities markets, chaired by Baron Alexandre Lamfalussy.

**Legal code** A comprehensive set of rules that serves as the foundation of a civil-law system. Legislated statutes will supplement the code, and judges will ultimately have to interpret the code as they apply it to disputes.

**Legitimacy** Public acceptance of the legal authority of a political entity, based on key principles such as participation, representation, accountability and transparency.

**Lisbon Agenda** The arrangements put in place by the Heads of State and Government at the Lisbon European Council in 2000 to deliver the goal of making the European Union 'the most dynamic and competitive knowledge-based economy in the world capable of sustainable economic growth with more and better jobs and greater social cohesion, and respect for the environment by 2010'. Rather than the traditional Community method, centred on the Commission and using legislation to achieve common action, the Lisbon Process relies on the non-coercive practice of diffusing best practice among the member states. Progress towards the Lisbon goals is monitored by the European Council at an annual meeting in spring.

**Lustration** The systematic vetting of public officials for links with communist-era security services.

**Marshall Plan** The European Recovery Programme enunciated by US Secretary of State George C. Marshall in June 1947, whereby a total of US$12.6 billion (equivalent to over $100 billion in 2005 dollars) was granted to European nations to assist their recovery from the destruction of the Second World War.

**Median voter** A theory suggesting that there is an average voter placed at an identifiable point along a left–right political spectrum. This voter's allegiance must be won if a party is to win an election.

**Minority government** A government of one or more parties lacking a formal parliamentary majority. It requires the passive or *ad hoc* support of additional parliamentary parties to govern.

**Money market** A type of financial market for securities. Essentially, inter-bank lending: day-to-day transactions and short-term debt. In addition the money market includes a range of specific securities or financial instruments that are traded by financial institutions.

**Multiculturalism** Situations in which groups of persons from different cultural backgrounds (usually derived from historically rooted ethnic, geographical and/or religious differences) live alongside each other, interacting in daily life while maintaining their differences with mutual toleration, respect and interest.

**Nazi** German pronunciation of the first two syllables of the Nationalsozialistische Deutsche Arbeiterpartei, the National Socialist German Workers' Party.

**Neo-conservatism** A political movement in the USA at the turn of the twenty-first century in which an ideological mix of left-leaning democratic idealism and right-wing military unilateralism resulted in a doctrine of pre-emptive warfare and the crusading 'export' of democracy around the world.

**Neo-liberal ideology** Revival of the belief in the superiority of 'free markets' with minimal governmental regulation. Seeks as well to introduce market mechanisms into many public policy sectors including education, health care and social insurance.

**Neo-liberal policies** The set of policies, replacing Keynesian demand management, introduced in the 1980s (especially in the UK but less vigorously in continental Europe) to tackle high inflation and unemployment. Control of the money supply (through monetary policy—interest rates) was seen as vital to containing inflation, while labour market reforms (weakening the bargaining power of trade unions) were designed to reduce unemployment by allowing the price mechanism to work.

**New Public Management** A set of ideas for reforming the public sector involving greater use of private-sector management techniques and empowering public managers to make more of their own decisions.

**Non-Proliferation Treaty** An international treaty, signed in 1970 (currently by 187 states) whereby the five officially nuclear states (the USA, Russia, China, France and the UK) agree to reduce their nuclear arsenals and the non-nuclear states agree not to develop nuclear weapons, while having the right to develop, with the assistance of any state, nuclear energy for peaceful purposes.

**Non-refoulement** The duty states have under international law not to return a person to a country where their life would be threatened or where they would face persecution.

**Northern Dimension Initiative** The Northern Dimension was launched to promote security and stability in Northern Europe, as well as helping build a safe, clean and accessible environment for all people in the region.

**Open method of coordination (OMC)** Formally introduced as a method of intervention at the Lisbon Summit in 2000, to be used on a case-by-case basis. It is a way of encouraging cooperation, the exchange of best practice and agreeing common target and guidelines for members states, usually backed up by national action plans, as in the case of employment and social exclusion. It relies on regular monitoring of progress to meet the targets set, allowing member states to compare their efforts and learn from the experience of others.

**Optimum currency area (OCA)** An economic space in which there has been sufficient structural convergence and integration to justify the introduction of a common currency, generating net benefits across the participating economies.

**Opt-out** Exemption granted to a member state that does not wish to join the others in a particular area of EU cooperation.

**Orange Revolution** In response to allegations of massive corruption, voter intimidation and direct electoral fraud in the Ukrainian presidential elections of November 2004, a series of protests and political events took place throughout the country provoking a rerun of the second round and the election of opposition leader, Viktor Yushchenko.

**Organization for Security and Cooperation in Europe (OSCE)** Established in 1973 as the Conference for Security and Cooperation in Europe, it is concerned with early warning, conflict prevention, crisis management and post-conflict rehabilitation in its 55 member states from North America, Central Asia and Europe.

**Organised capitalism** A form of capitalism characterised by cooperation rather than competition between capital and labour. The opposite of liberal capitalism, this may involve corporatism or social partnership. Sometimes known as an organised market economy.

**Para-public agencies** Private or quasi-public bodies which fulfil public functions. Examples include advisory boards in which key interest groups and non-elective authorities have defined responsibilities for certain tasks, such as provision of parks or water management.

**Parliamentary government** A government in which the executive power depends upon being elected by, and maintaining the confidence of, the lower house of parliament.

**Parliamentary sovereignty** Parliament is formally able to exercise the last word in decisions about the validity of law. As a result, judicial review cannot be directed against acts passed by parliament, but only against actions taken by government that exceed the bounds of parliamentary statute.

**Party family** A classification of parties in different countries according to common ideological positions. Some party families are further defined by membership in transnational party organisations, e.g. the Party of European Socialists.

**Party groups** The parliamentary parties in the European Parliament, composed of national delegations belonging to the same party family, except most notably in the case of the European People's Party–European Democrats, which is composed of a combination of Christian democrats, conservatives and some liberal parties.

**Party of mass integration** An earlier form of party organisation used by class- or religious-based parties in Europe. Socialist or Christian democratic parties attempted to organise a large proportion of their followers as members and involve them in extended networks of religious or ideologically based organisations. These provided services and, for many, a spiritual home.

**PHARE programme** Originally designed to assist economic reconstruction and political change in Central and Eastern Europe, PHARE has become an important instrument to prepare countries before they begin the process of accession to the EU.

**Pillar** A Dutch term for spiritual family, segment or subculture. See 'pillarisation'.

**Pillarisation** The phenomenon of subcultural or vertical pluralism, the division of a country's population into distinct and mutually isolated networks of religious or ideologically based organisations or subcultures.

**Pillarised social structure** See 'pillarisation'.

**Polarised pluralism** A party system characterised by wide ideological distance, a substantial number of parties, centrifugal electoral tendencies and large irresponsible parties at the extremes.

**Political Islam** The use and manipulation of the Muslim faith by political parties intended both to raise their popular appeal and to undermine secularism.

**Politicisation of administration** Civil service systems have tended to stress their apolitical nature, but political leaders often attempt to inject political criteria into the selection, rewards, assignment and termination of civil servants.

**Post-industrial** Post-industrial societies are those in which the proportions of the workforce employed in manufacturing are declining and those in services are rising, without any necessary decline in the overall purchase and consumption of the products of manufacturing.

**Post-materialist** A label to describe a value and attitudinal orientation associated with voters belonging to the post-war baby-boom generation. It manifests itself in support of issues emphasising aesthetic concerns, self-actualisation, individual autonomy and collective well-being, for instance environmental issues, participatory democracy, feminism, gay rights, etc.

**Post-war consensus** Following the Second World War there was broad political support for policies that increased and maintained sustainable economic growth, low unemployment and expanding social-welfare programmes. While differing in emphasis and details, this consensus avoided the political stalemates of the pre-war period.

**Pre-accession strategy** 'Structured dialogue' between the associated countries (seeking membership) and EU institutions.

**Precautionary principle** When there are threats of serious or irreversible harm to the environment or human health, precautionary measures should be taken even if there is scientific uncertainty about cause and effect relationships.

**Precedent** A judicial decision that establishes a rule to decide future similar cases. Judges in common-law systems normally consider themselves bound by precedents. However, they overturn precedents when they are no longer useful and they distinguish the facts of cases which may seem to be governed by prior precedents, but which are different in some crucial way.

**Preliminary ruling** An interpretation of European Union law provided by the European Court of Justice in response to a reference from a national judge who asks a question about the meaning of EU treaties or legislation. The national court actually applies the EU law to the case that generated the dispute, guided by the ECJ's ruling.

**Presidential republic** A form of regime in which the head of state is a president directly and democratically elected. There are various types of presidential republic, some of which give the president unfettered authority over the executive, others of which involve the executive needing parliamentary backing to be constituted, thus restraining presidential power.

**Primary immigration** The immigration of people with no familial ties in the country to which they are migrating.

**Progress reports** The Commission submits reports on the progress achieved by each country preparing for accession to the Council. This serves as a basis for the Council to take decisions on the conduct of the negotiations.

**Proportional representation** Parliamentary representation primarily based on a party's overall share of the vote. Usually includes some regional multi-member constituencies with supplementary seats distributed to parties underrepresented in the constituencies once they have reached a minimal threshold: e.g. 4 per cent in Sweden and 2 per cent in Denmark.

**Prussia** Former duchy of the Hohenzollern kings, this small country in north-eastern Germany near the Baltic Sea was passed to the electors of Brandenburg in 1618, and was proclaimed a kingdom in 1701, its capital in Berlin. Under Frederick the Great, it became a major power during the eighteenth century, and would dominate other German states by the 1860s. Prussian supremacy ended in 1918 at the end of the First World War.

**Public bureaucracies** Formal organisations responsible for the implementation of public programmes and often for providing advice to ministers. The employees of these organisations are usually career civil servants.

**Purchasing power standard (PPS)** A common reference unit that can buy the same amount of consumer goods and services across member states in a given year.

**Refugee** An asylum-seeker granted refugee status under the 1951 Convention relating to the status of refugees.

**Reich** lit. 'empire' or realm, commonly used to refer either to the Second Reich (Imperial Germany, 1871–1918) or to the Third Reich (Nazi rule, 1933–45). The Holy Roman Empire was regarded as the First Reich.

**Religion** A system of belief about the character of the spiritual world outside human experience and about the obligations that this world places on human conduct. For sociologists the main points of interest of religions are the character of these obligations and the forms of social organisation that religions develop, and their implications for life styles.

**Retail financial services market** Commercial banks, building societies, insurance companies, etc. that provide a range of financial products to consumers (savers/borrowers).

**Schengen** An agreement between EU states which ended border checkpoints and controls between those countries. Some states such as Britain, however, remained outside.

**Screening** Evaluating the compatibility of each applicant country's legislation with EU rules.

**Segmentation** See 'pillarisation'.

**Semi-presidentialism** Where the people directly elect the president, but where there is also a prime minister who is elected and dismissed by parliament. The president tends to be responsible for foreign and defence policy while the prime minister tends to be responsible for domestic policy.

**Separation of powers** The doctrine prevalent in Europe before 1945 that each branch of government exercises distinct powers. The executive enforces and administers the law, the legislature makes the law, and the judiciary interprets and applies the law in discrete disputes. Judicial or constitutional review of law is typically not allowed, as this would involve the judiciary encroaching on the law-making powers of the legislature.

**Separatism** The attempt to secede and establish a separate state normally undertaken by ethnic, linguistic or religious minorities within a state.

**Services** When used to describe sectors of economic activity, the term denotes forms of work where the product is not a physical product (as in agriculture or manufacturing), but a set of activities from which the recipient derives some benefit (as in the provision of sales, medical, educational or clerical services).

**Services (Bolkestein) Directive** The directive prepared by the Commission (under the Dutch commissioner Bolkestein) in 2004 aimed at creating an internal market in services. This was part of the Lisbon Agenda.

**Single market programme** The '1992 programme' proposed by the Commission to build a single internal market in 1985. These legislative proposals and the timetable were aimed at addressing the many non-tariff barriers that prevented the realisation of factor mobility (see 'the four freedoms') and the economic and social benefits of an integrated single market space.

**Skill** When used in relation to paid work activities, this denotes learned or otherwise acquired attributes of a worker or job category that are recognised in the allocation of job titles, pay and seniority levels.

**Social capitalism** A liberal market economic system characterised by private enterprise moderated by comprehensive publicly funded social welfare programmes and governmental regulations to deal with poverty and other economic problems. In addition corporatist policies ensure broader participation in making economic policy decisions. It is similar to the German concept of the 'social market economy'.

**Social inclusion** A process which ensures that those at risk of poverty and social exclusion gain access to the opportunities and resources necessary to enable them to participate fully in economic, social and cultural life, and to enjoy a standard of living and well-being that is considered normal in the society in which they live. The process implies that individuals are involved in decisions affecting their lives and gain access to fundamental rights as defined in the Charter of the Fundamental Rights of the European Union.

**Social partners** Key producer groups, such as trade union federations and employers' associations, which work together in organised capitalism.

**Solidaristic wage policy** A policy of the Swedish labour movement from the late 1950s until the 1980s to gain wage increases for low-paid workers that were equal to or greater than those gained by higher-paid workers in the most profitable firms. With the help of government training and mobility measures, the effect was to move labour from stagnating or declining industries to expanding and profitable sectors.

*Sonderweg* Term, particularly during the Wilhelmine and Weimar eras, for trying to steer a unique German path between undesirable political and economic alternatives (liberalism v. conservatism; culture v. civilisation; socialism v. capitalism).

**Sovereignty** Authority, usually vested at the national level, for binding decisions on public policy issues.

**Spillover** A concept developed by early theorists of European integration, notably Ernst Haas and Leon Lindberg, to describe the way in which the policy scope of the EC would progressively broaden due to the vested interests of key economic actors and the linkages between different policy areas.

**Spiritual family** A Belgian term for pillar or segment. A distinct subculture with a religious or ideological basis.

**Stability and Growth Pact (SGP)** A supplement to EMU (Maastricht) contained within the Treaty of Amsterdam. This was intended to prevent deficit spending by national governments from undermining the credibility of monetary policy set by the European Central Bank and the stability of the euro. Government borrowing is limited to 3 per cent of GDP and overall national debt is capped at 60 per cent of GDP.

**Structural realism** Sometimes referred to as neo-realism. The international relations branch of theory which sees war and conflict as the inevitable outcome of systemic anarchy (the absence, in the international system, of any overarching authority capable of influencing the policies of nation states).

**Subcultural pluralism** See 'pillarisation'.

**Subsidiarity** A federal principle whereby on policy issues other than those formally accorded to the central (federal) level, decisions are taken at the lowest level possible (closest to the people). The Treaty on European Union, signed in Maastricht in 1992, introduced the principle of subsidiarity into the EC Treaty (Art. 3b). This means that the Community may take action in areas that do not fall within its exclusive competence 'only if and in so far as the objectives of the proposed action cannot be sufficiently achieved by the Member States and can therefore, by reason of the scale or effects of the proposed action, be better achieved by the Community'.

**Supranational** Describes international organisations where individual governments do not have the final say in decision-making and where they may be obliged to comply with decisions that they do not support (for example, where they have been outvoted by other states), and/or where organisations created to implement the terms of the founding treaty or to monitor compliance (for example, an executive body or a court) have the authority to compel member governments to comply with the terms of the treaty or policy decisions and rules agreed subsequently.

**Tangentopoli** The extensive series of corruption scandals which broke out in the early 1990s forcing a large part of the political class out of office and destroying the two main governing parties, the Christian Democrats and the Socialists.

**Third way** An alternative to socialism and liberalism as proposed by Tony Blair's New Labour in the UK.

**Transactions costs** The costs incurred by an actor in making the effort to achieve a particular objective.

**Two-level game** A metaphor, developed by Robert Putnam, to capture the interaction between domestic and international politics, particularly in the context of negotiations. At the domestic level there is a 'win set' of possible outcomes for which ratification can be secured. All international agreements must fall within the win sets of all participating states. Each state's chief of government (COG) operates in both the domestic and international games. The COG may be able to increase the likelihood of agreement by manipulating their own or their negotiating partners' win sets through inducements (e.g. subsidies or other side payments) or threats (e.g. the imposition of sanctions).

**Tutelage** Guardianship, instruction.

**Unicameral** Parliamentary assemblies with only a single chamber, typical of the Scandinavian countries.

**Uruguay Round (1986–94)** The last round of multilateral trade negotiations conducted under the auspices of the 1947 General Agreement on Tariffs and Trade (GATT). Saw the expansion of the multilateral trade agenda to include agriculture, services, intellectual property rights and (arguably) investment. Created the World Trade Organization.

**Variable geometry** Proposal for a method of differentiated integration that would allow separate levels of integration, i.e. separation between a group of member states and a number of less developed integration units.

**Vichy regime** French government (1940–4) led by Marshal Philippe Pétain following the invasion of France by German forces and sited at Vichy in central France. A dictatorial regime with the slogan 'Work, Family, Fatherland'.

**Welfare state** A state that, in addition to the historically important activities of maintaining internal law and order and preparedness for external war and securing the privileges of the most powerful social groups, also devotes resources and services activities to advancing the welfare of the mass of the population.

**Wessis** Mildly derogatory East German term for those who have moved from West Germany to work (and sometimes live in rather than commute) in the East; the comparable term for East Germans is Ossis.

**Westphalian system** The system of nation states, enjoying external and internal sovereignty, which was initiated by the Treaty of Westphalia in 1648. According to this system, which underpins the United Nations Charter, nation states may not normally intervene in the internal affairs of other nation states.

# References

Aberbach, J. D, Putnam, R. D. and Rockman, B. A. (1981), *Politicians and Bureaucrats in Western Democracies*, Cambridge MA, Harvard University Press.

Adema, W. (2001), 'Net Social Expenditure', 2nd edn, *Labour Market and Social Policy Occasional Papers*, 52, Paris, OECD.

Aguiar, J. (1985), 'The Hidden Fluidity in an Ultra-stable Party System', in E. Ferreira and W. C. Opello (eds), *Conflict and Change in Portugal, 1974–1984*, Lisbon, Teorema, pp. 101–27.

Alcock, P. (2003), 'The Subject of Social Policy', in P. Alcock, A. Erskine and M. May (eds), *The Student's Companion to Social Policy*, 2nd edn, Oxford, Blackwell, pp. 3–10.

——, Erskine, A. and May, M. (eds) (2003), *The Student's Companion to Social Policy*, 2nd edn, Oxford, Blackwell.

Alesina, A., Glaeser, E. and Sacerdote, B. (2001), 'Why Doesn't the US Have a European-Style Welfare State?', Harvard Institute of Economic Research Discussion Paper 1933.

Alesina, A. and Perotti, R. (2004), 'The European Union: A Politically Incorrect View', *Journal of Economic Perspectives*, 18, 4, 27–48.

Allen, F., Chui, M. K. F. and Maddaloni, A. (2004), 'Financial Systems in Europe, the USA, and Asia', *Oxford Review of Economic Policy*, 20, 4, 490–508.

Alter, K. (2001), *Establishing the Supremacy of European Law*, Oxford, Oxford University Press.

Anderson, K. (2001), 'The Politics of Retrenchment in Social Democratic Welfare State', *Comparative Political Studies*, 34, 9, 1063–91.

Anderson, S., Bennis, P. and Cavanagh, J. (and E. Leaver) (2003), *Coalition of the Willing or Coalition of the Coerced? How the Bush Administration Influences Allies in its War on Iraq*, Washington DC, Institute for Policy Studies, available at www.ips-dc.org/iraq/COERCED2.pdf

Andeweg, R. (1996), 'The Netherlands', in J. Blondel and M. Cotta (eds), *Party and Government: An Inquiry into the Relationship between Governments and Supporting Parties in Liberal Democracies*, Houndsmills, Macmillan; New York, St Martin's Press), pp. 128–52.

—— (1999), 'Parties, Pillars and the Politics of Accommodation: Weak or Weakening Linkages? The Case of Dutch Consociationalism', in K. Luther and K. Deschouwer, *Party Elites in Divided Societies: Political Parties in Consociational Democracies*, London and New York, Routledge, pp. 108–33.

—— (2001) 'Lijphart versus Lijphart: The Cons of Consensus Democracy in Homogeneous Societies', *Acta Politica*, 36, 117–28.

—— and Irwin, G. (2005), *Governance and Politics of the Netherlands*, 2nd edn, Houndsmills and New York, Palgrave.

—— and Nijzink, L. (1995), 'Beyond the Two Body Image: Relations between Ministers and MPs', in H. Döring (ed.), *Parliaments and Majority Rule in Western Europe*, New York, St Martins.

Anton, T. J. (1969), 'Policy-making and Political Culture in Sweden', *Scandinavian Political Studies*, 4, 90–102.

Armstrong, H. F. (1947), 'Europe Revisited', *Foreign Affairs*, 25, 4.

Art, R. (2004), 'Europe Hedges its Security Bets', in T. V. Paul, James J. Wirtz and M. Fortmann (eds), *Balance of Power Revisited: Theory and Practice in the 21st Century*, Stanford CA, Stanford University Press.

Arts, W. and Gelissen, J. (2002), 'Three Worlds of Welfare Capitalism or More? A State-of-the-Art Report', *Journal of European Social Policy*, 12, 2, 137–58.

Bacevich, A. (2002), *American Empire: The Realities and Consequences of US Diplomacy*, Cambridge MA, Harvard University Press.

Bach, T., Fleischer, J. and Hustedt, T. (2005), 'A Survey of the German Non-ministerial Federal Administration', unpublished paper, Lehrstuhl fur Verwaltung und Staatswissenschaft, University of Potsdam.

Baele, L., Ferrando, A., Hördahl, P., Krylova, E. and Monnet, C. (2004), 'Measuring European Financial Integration', *Oxford Review of Economic Policy*, 20, 4, 509–30.

Bailes, A. J. K. (2004), 'US and EU Strategic Concept: A Mirror for Partnership and Difference?', *International Spectator*, 39, 1, January–March.

Baldwin, M. *et al.* (2003), 'Trade and Economic Relations', in J. Peterson and M. Pollack (eds), *Europe, America, Bush: Transatlantic Relations in the Twenty-first Century*, London, Routledge.

Bangermann, M. (1992), *Meeting the Global Challenge: Establishing a Successful European Industrial Policy*, London, Kogan Page.

Barber, L. (1995), 'The Men Who Run Europe', *Financial Times*, 11–12 March.

Batt, J. (1991), *East Central Europe from Reform to Transformation*, London, Pinter.

—— (2003), 'Introduction: Defining Central and Eastern Europe', in S. White, J. Batt and P. Lewis (eds), *Developments in Central and East European Politics 3*, Basingtoke, Palgrave, pp. 3–22.

BBC (2004), www.globescan.com/news_archives/bbcpoll.html

446

Behrendt, S. and Hanelt, C.-P. (eds) (2000), *Bound to Cooperate: Europe and the Middle East*, Gütersloh, Bertelsmann.

Biezen, I. van and Hopkin, J. (2005), 'The Presidentialization of Spanish Democracy: Sources of Prime Ministerial Power in Post-Franco Spain', in T. Poguntke and P. Webb (eds), *The Presidentialization of Politics in Democratic Societies?*, Oxford, Oxford University Press, pp. 105–25.

Bilčík, V. (2001), *Can Slovakia Catch Up? The Implications of EU Accession Talks a Year after the Helsinki Summit*, Copenhagen, Danish Institute of International Affairs.

Biscop, S. (2005), *The European Security Strategy: A Global Agenda for Positive Power*, Aldershot, Ashgate.

Blair, T. (2002), 'A Clear Course for Europe', Cardiff, 28 November, www.pm.gov.uk/output/page6709.asp

Bodansky, D. (2003), 'Transatlantic Environmental Relations', in J. Peterson and M. Pollack (eds), *Europe, America, Bush: Transatlantic Relations in the Twenty-first century*, London, Routledge.

Bogdanor, V. (2004), *Joined-up Government*, Oxford, Oxford University Press.

——and Woodcock, G. (1991), 'The European Community and Sovereignty', *Parliamentary Affairs*, 44, 4, 481–92.

Bouckaert, G. (2001), 'Pride and Performance in the Public Service: Some Patterns of Analysis', *International Review of Administrative Sciences*, 67, 15–27.

Bowler, S. and Farrell, D. M. (1995), 'The Organization of the European Parliament: Committees, Specialisation and Co-ordination', *British Journal of Political Science*, 25, 219–43.

Bracher, K. D. (1963), 'Problems of Parliamentary Democracy', in S. R. Graubard (ed.), *A New Europe*, Boston MA, Beacon.

Bruneau, T. (ed.) (1997), *Political Parties and Democracy in Portugal: Organizations, Elections and Public Opinion*, Boulder CO, Westview Press.

Bulmer, S. and Wessels, W. (1987), *The European Council: Decision-making in European Politics*, London, Macmillan.

Bunce, V. (1995), 'Should Transitologists be Grounded?', *Slavic Review*, 54, 1, 111–27.

Burley, A. and Mattli, W. (1993), 'Europe before the Court', *International Organization*, 47, 41–76.

Buti, M., Eijffinger, S. and Franco, D. (2003), 'Revisiting in Stability and Growth Pact: Grand Design or Internal Adjustment?', *European Economy*, Working Paper 180, Brussels, European Commission.

Carbone, M. (2004), 'Development Policy', in N. Nugent (ed.), *European Union Enlargement*, London, Palgrave, pp. 242–52.

Carpenter, T. G. (2000), *NATO's Empty Victory*, Washington DC, Cato.

Cassese, S. (1997), *Il consiglio di Stato e la riforma costituzionale*, Milan, Giuffre.

Center for Strategic and International Studies (2004), *The Transatlantic Dialogue on Terrorism: Initial Findings*, Washington DC, August, available at www.csis.org/isp/0408_transatlanticterrorism.pdf

Cerny, P. (1997), 'Paradoxes of the Competition State: The Dynamics of Political Globalization', *Government and Opposition*, 32, 2, 251–74.

Chirac, J. (2002), Interview of President Jacques Chirac by the *New York Times*, Elysée Palace, 8 September, www.elysee.fr/elysee/anglais/speeches_and_documents/2002–2001/interview_of_president_jacques_chirac_by_the_new_york_times-elysee_palace-sunday_september_8_2002.14617.html

——(2003), Interview of President Jacques Chirac by the *New York Times*, 22 September, www.elysee.fr/elysee/elysee.fr/francais/interventions/interviews_articles_de_presse_et_interventions_televisees./2003/septembre/interview_accordee_par_m_jacques_chirac_president_de_la_republique_au_new_york_times.2767.html

Christiansen, T. (1997), 'Tensions of European Governance: Politicised Bureaucracy and Multiple Accountability in the European Commission', *Journal of European Public Policy*, 4, 1, 73–90.

——and Kirchner, E. (2000), *Committee Governance in the European Union*, Manchester, Manchester University Press.

——and Laegreid, P. (2001), *New Public Management: The Transformation of Ideas and Practice*, Aldershot, Ashgate.

Cimbalo, J. (2004), 'Saving NATO from Europe', *Foreign Affairs*, 83, 6, November/December.

Cini, M. (1997), 'Administrative Culture in the European Communities: The Cases of Competition and Environment', in N. Nugent (ed.), *At the Heart of the Union*, Basingstoke, Macmillan, pp. 71–88.

——and McGowan, L. (1998), *Competition Policy in the European Union*, London, Macmillan.

Clarke, R. (2004), *Against All Enemies: Inside America's War on Terror*, New York, Free Press.

Clark, T. and Verseckaitë, E. (2005), 'PaksasGate: Lithuania Impeaches a President', *Problems of Post-Communism*, 52, 3, 16–24.

Cogan, C. (1994), *Oldest Allies, Guarded Friends: The United States and France since 1940*, Westport CT, Praeger.

Colard, D. and Daille, G. (1992), 'Le Général de Gaulle et les Alliances', in [Institut Charles de Gaulle] (ed.), *De Gaulle en son Siècle, volume 4*, Paris, Plon.

Conant, L. (2002), *Justice Contained*, Ithaca NY, Cornell University Press.

Cooper, R. (2003), *The Breaking of Nations: Order and Chaos in the Twenty-first Century*, New York, Atlantic Monthly.

Corkill, D. (1995), 'Party Factionalism and Democratization in Portugal', in R. Gillespie, M. Waller and L. López Nieto (eds), *Factional Politics and Democratization*, special issue of *Democratization*, 2, 1, 64–76.

Costa, D. L. and Kahn, M. E. (2002), 'Civic Engagement and Community Heterogeneity: An Economist's Perspective', Paper presented at the Conference on Social Connectedness and Public Activism, Harvard University.

Cremona, M. (ed.) (2003), *The Enlargement of the European Union*, Oxford, Oxford University Press.

Curzon Price, V. (2001), 'Industrial Policy', in A. M. El Agraa (ed.), *The European Union*, London, Prentice Hall, pp. 203–30.

Daalder, H. (1966), 'The Netherlands: Opposition in a Segmented Society', in R. A. Dahl (ed.), *Political Oppositions in Western Democracies*, New Haven CT, Yale University Press, pp. 188–236.

Daalder, I. H. and Lindsay, J. M. (2003), *America Unbound: The Bush Revolution in Foreign Policy*, Washington DC, Brookings.

Dalton, R. (1988), *Citizen Politics: Public Opinion and Political Parties in Advanced Western Democracies*, Chatham, Chatham House Publishers.

Damgaard, E. (1992), 'Denmark: Experiments in Parliamentary Democracy', in E. Damgaard (ed.), *Parliamentary Change in Nordic Countries*, Oslo, Scandinavian University Press.

Dannreuther, R. and Peterson, J. (eds) (2006), *Security Strategy and Transatlantic Relations*, London, Routledge.

Dassu, M. and Menotti, R. (2005), 'Europe and America in the Age of Bush', *Survival*, 47, 1.

Deschouwer, K. (1999), 'From Consociation to Federation: How the Belgian Parties Won', in Luther and Deschouwer, pp. 74–107.

Deutsch, K. (1953), *Nationalism and Social Communication: An Inquiry into the Foundations of Nationality*, Cambridge MA, MIT Press.

De Winter, L. (2004), 'Government Declarations and Law Production', in H. Döring and M. Hallerberg (eds), *Patterns of Parliamentary Behaviour*, Aldershot, Ashgate.

Dinan, D. (2005), *Ever Closer Europe: An Introduction to European Integration*, 3rd edn, London, Palgrave Macmillan.

Dobbins, J. (2003), *America's Role in Nation-building: From Germany to Iraq*, Santa Monica CA, Rand.

Drinan, R. F. (2001), *The Mobilization of Shame: A World View of Human Rights*, New Haven CT, Yale University Press.

Duverger, M. (1980), 'A New Political System Model: Semi-presidential Government', *European Journal of Political Research*, 8, 165–87.

Dymond, W. D. and Hart, M. M. (2000), 'Post-modern Trade Policy: Reflections on the Challenges to Multilateral Trade Negotiations After Seattle', *Journal of World Trade*, 34, 3, 21–38.

Dyson, K. (2003), 'The Europeanization of German Governance', in S. Padgett, W. Paterson and G. Smith (eds), *Developments in German Politics 3*, Houndmills, Palgrave Macmillan, pp. 161–83.

Eckley, N. and Selin, H. (2004), 'All Talk, Little Action: Precaution and European Chemicals Regulation', *Journal of European Public Policy*, 11, 1, 78–105.

Edwards, G. (1996), 'National Sovereignty vs. Integration? The Council of Ministers', in J. Richardson (ed.), *European Union: Power and Policy-making*, London, Routledge, pp. 127–47.

Einhorn, E. S. and Logue J. (2003), *Modern Welfare States: Scandinavian Politics and Policy in the Global Age*, 2nd edn, Westport CT and London, Praeger.

Elgie, R. (2001), *Divided Government in Comparative Perspective*, Oxford, Oxford University Press.

Esping-Andersen, G. (1990), *The Three Worlds of Welfare Capitalism*, Cambridge, Polity Press.

—— (1999), *Social Foundations of Postindustrial Economies*, Oxford, Oxford University Press.

European Commission (2000), 'Communication from the Commission on the Precautionary Principle', Commission of the European Communities, Brussels.

—— (2004a), *The Social Situation in the European Union 2004*, Luxembourg, Office for Official Publications of the European Communities.

—— (2004b), 'Report from the Commission on the Implementation of the Directive 92/43/EEC on the Conservation of Natural Habitats and of Wild Fauna and Flora, Part I: Composite Report on Overall Progress Achieved'.

—— (2005), 'EMU after Five Years', *European Economy Special Report*, 1, February.

European Environmental Agency (2005), 'Environmental Policy Integration in Europe—State of Play and an Evaluation Framework', Technical Report, 2/2005, EEA, Copenhagen.

Eurostat (1996), *ESSPROS Manual 1996*, Luxembourg, Office for Official Publications of the European Communities.

—— (2004), *European Union Foreign Direct Investment Yearbook 2005*, Brussels, Eurostat.

Evans, P. (2003), 'Is Trade Policy Democratic? And Should It Be?', in N. Bayne and S. Woolcock (eds), *The New Economic Diplomacy: Decision-making and Negotiations in International Economic Relations*, Ashgate, pp. 147–59.

Everts, S. (2004), *Engaging Iran: A Test Case for EU Foreign Policy*, London, CER.

Falke, A. (2005), 'German Trade Policy. An Oxymoron?', in D. Kelly and W. Grant (eds), *The Politics of International Trade in the Twenty-first Century: Actors, Issues and Regional Dynamics*, London, Palgrave, pp. 252–72.

Farrell, D. and Webb, P. (2000), 'Political Parties as Campaign Organizations', in Dalton, Russell and Wattenberg (eds), *Parties without Partisans*, Oxford, Oxford University Press, pp. 102–28.

Faulenbach, B. (1980), *Ideologie des deutschen Weges. Die deutsche Geschichte in der Historiographie zwischen Kaiserreich und Nationalsozialismus*, Munich, C. H. Beck.

Featherstone, K. (1994), 'Jean Monnet and the "Democratic Deficit" in the European Union', *Journal of Common Market Studies*, 32, 2, 149–70.

Ferguson, N. (2004), *Colossus: The Price of America's Empire*, London, Penguin.

Fischermann, T. *et al.* (2005), 'Die kleinen Globalisierer. Deutsche Mittelständler investieren überall auf der Welt', *Die Zeit*, 16, 14 April, 23–4.

Follesdal, A. and Hix, S. (2005), 'Why There is a Democratic Deficit in the EU: A Reply to Majone and Moravcsik', www.connex-network.org/eurogov/pdf/egp-connex-C-05-02.pdf

Fowler, B. (2004), 'Concentrated Orange: Fidesz and the Remaking of the Hungarian Centre-Right, 1994–2002', *Journal of Communist Studies and Transition Politics*, 20, 3, 80–114.

Frankel, J. A. (1997), *Regional Trading Blocs in the World Economic System*, Washington DC, Institute for International Economics.

Friedman, T. (2005), *The World is Flat: A Brief History of the Twenty-first Century*, New York, Farrar, Straus & Giroux.

Friedrich, A., Tappe, M. and Wurzel, R. K. W. (2000), 'A New Approach to EU Environmental Policy-making? The Auto-oil I Programme', *Journal of European Public Policy*, 7, 4, 593–612.

Galenson, W. (1949), *Labor in Norway*, Cambridge MA, Harvard University Press.

Gallagher, M. Laver, M. and Mair, P. (2006), *Representative Government in Modern Europe*, 4th edn, New York, McGraw-Hill.

Garrett, G. (1992), 'International Cooperation and Institutional Choice', *International Organization*, 46, 533–60.

—— (1997), *Partisan Politics in the Global Economy*, Cambridge, Cambridge University Press.

——, Kelemen, R. and Schulz, H. (1998), 'The European Court of Justice, National Governments, and Legal Integration in the European Union', *International Organization*, 52, 149–76.

Garton Ash, T. (2004), *Free World: America, Europe and the Surprising Future of the West*, New York, Random House.

Gerber, D. (1998), *Law and Competition in Twentieth Century Europe: Protecting Prometheus*, Oxford, Clarendon Press.

German Marshall Fund of the USA (2004), *Transatlantic Trends 2004*, www.transatlantictrends.org

Geroski, P. A. (1989), 'European Industrial Policy and Industrial Policy in Europe', *Oxford Review of Economic Policy*, 5, 2.

Gibney, M. and Hansen, R. (eds) (2005), *Immigration and Asylum from 1900 to the Present*, Santa Barbara CA, ABC-CLIO.

Giddens, A. (1998), *The Third Way*, Cambridge, Polity Press.

Gillespie, R. (1989), *The Spanish Socialist Party: A History of Factionalism*, Oxford, Clarendon Press.

Gilligan, M. (2006), 'Is Enforcement Necessary for Effectiveness? A Model of the International Criminal Regime', *International Organization*.

Ginsberg, R. (2001), *The European Union in International Politics: Baptism by Fire*, Lanham MD, Rowman & Littlefield.

Gomez, R. and Peterson, J. (2001), 'The EU's Impossibly Busy Foreign Ministers: No-one is in Control', *European Foreign Affairs Review*, 6, 53–74.

Gordon, P. (1999), *The Transatlantic Allies and the Changing Middle East*, Oxford, Oxford University Press.

—— (2005), 'Trading Places: America and Europe in the Middle East', *Survival*, 47, 2.

—— and Shapiro, J. (2004), *Allies at War: America, Europe and the Crisis over Iraq*, Washington DC, Brookings.

Gough, I. (2003), 'Social Policy and Economic Policy, in P. Alcock, A. Erskine and M. May (eds), *The Student's Companion to Social Policy*, 2nd edn, Oxford, Blackwell, pp. 137–45.

Grant, C. (2003), *Transatlantic Rift: How to Bring the Two Sides Together*, London, Centre for European Reform.

Griffith, J. A. G. (1997), *The Politics of the Judiciary*, 5th edn, London, Fontana.

Gros, D., Mayer, T. and Ubide, A. (2005), *EMU at Risk*, Brussels, Centre for European Policy Studies.

Gryzma la-Busse, A. (2002), *Redeeming the Communist Past: the Regeneration of Communist Parties in East Central Europe*, Cambridge, Cambridge University Press.

Gunther, R., Sani, G. and Shabad, G. (1986), *Spain after Franco: The Making of a Competitive Party System*, Berkeley, University of California Press.

Gunther, R. and Montero, J. R. (2001), 'The Anchors of Partisanship: A Comparative Analysis of Voting Behaviour in Four Southern European Democracies', in N. Diamandouros and R. Gunther (eds), *Parties, Politics, and Democracy in the New Southern Europe*, Baltimore MD, Johns Hopkins University Press, pp. 83–152.

Gunther, R. and Hopkin, J. (2002), 'A Crisis of Institutionalization: The Collapse of the UCD in Spain', in R. Gunther, J. R. Montero and J. Linz (eds), *Political Parties: Old Concepts and New Challenges*, Oxford, Oxford University Press, pp. 191–230.

Halevy, E. and Shafeeq, G. (2003), *Winning the War; Winning the Peace: Defining Priorities for America in the Middle East*, Washington DC, Washington Institute for Near East Policy.

Hallet, M. (2004), 'Fiscal Effects of Accession in the New Member States', *European Economy Economic Papers*, 203, May, Brussels, Directorate-General for Economic and Financial Affairs, European Commission.

Hallstein, W. (1965), 'The EEC Commission: A New Factor in International Life', *International and Comparative Law Quarterly*, 14, 727–41.

Hamilton, D. (2002), 'American Views of European Security and Defence Policy', in E. Brimmer (ed.), *The EU's*

Search for a Strategic Role: ESDP and Its Strategic Implications for Transatlantic Relations, Washington DC, Center for Transatlantic Relations.

Hanley, S. (2004), 'From Neo-liberalism to National Interests: Ideology, Strategy, and Party Development in the Euroscepticism of the Czech Right', *East European Politics and Societies*, 18, 3, 513–48.

Hantrais, L. (ed.) (2000), *Gendered Policies in Europe: Reconciling Employment and Family Life*, Basingstoke, Palgrave.

—— (2004), *Family Policy Matters: Responding to Family Change in Europe*, Bristol, The Policy Press.

—— (2007), *Social Policy in the European Union*, 3rd edn, Basingstoke, Palgrave.

Haughton, T. (2001), 'HZDS: The Ideology, Organisation and Support Base of Slovakia's Most Successful Party', *Europe–Asia Studies*, 53, 5, 745–69.

—— (2005a), *Constraints and Opportunities of Leadership in Post-communist Europe*, Aldershot, Ashgate.

—— (2005b), 'Novel Appeal: Explaining Successful New Parties in Central and Eastern Europe', paper presented to VII World Congress of the International Council for Central and East European Studies, Berlin, 25–30 July.

Hay, C. (2000), 'Globalisation, Social Democracy and the Persistence of Partisan Politics: A Commentary on Garrett', *Review of International Political Economy*, 7, 1, 138–52.

—— (2004), 'Common Trajectories, Variable Paces, Divergent Outcomes? Models of European Capitalism under Conditions of Complex Economic Interdependence', *Review of International Political Economy*, 11, 2, 231–62.

—— (2006), 'What's Globalisation Got to Do With It? Economic Interdependence and the Future of European Welfare States', *Government and Opposition*, 41, 1, 1–23.

Hayward, J. E. S. and Wright, V. (2002), *Governing from the Centre: Core Executive Coordination in France*, Oxford, Oxford University Press.

Heffernan, R. (2005), 'Why the Prime Minister cannot be a President: Comparing Institutional Imperatives in Britain and America', *Parliamentary Affairs*, 58, 53–70.

Hennessy, P. (2005), 'Rulers and Servants of the State: The Blair Style of Government 1997–2004', *Parliamentary Affairs*, 58, 6–16.

Heywood, P. (1991), 'Governing a New Democracy: The Power of the Prime Minister in Spain', *West European Politics*, 14, 2, 97–115.

Hill, C. and Smith, M. (2005), *International Relations of the EU*, Oxford, Oxford University Press.

Hirschl, R. (2004), *Towards Juristocracy*, Cambridge MA, Harvard University Press.

Hirst, P. and Thompson, G. (2002), 'The Future of Globalization', *Cooperation and Conflict*, 37, 3, September, 247–65.

Hix, S. (1994), 'Approaches to the Study of the EC: The Challenge to Comparative Politics', *West European Politics*, 17, 1, 1–30.

—— (2002), 'Constitutional Agenda-setting through Discretion in Rule Interpretation: Why the European Parliament Won at Amsterdam', *British Journal of Political Science*, 32, 2, 259–80.

—— (2002), 'Linking National Politics to Europe', http://personal.lse.ac.uk/hix/Working_Papers/Hix-Linking%20National%20Politics%20to%20Europe.pdf

—— (2005), *The Political System of the European Union*, 2nd edn, Basingstoke, Palgrave.

—— and Lord, C. (1997), *Political Parties in the European Union*, London, Macmillan.

Hocking, B. (2004), 'Changing the Terms of Trade Policy Making: From the "Club" to the "Multistakeholder" Model', *World Trade Review*, 3, 1, 3–26.

Holland, M. (2004), 'Development Policy: Paradigm Shifts and the Normalization of a Privileged Partnership?', in M. G. Cowles and D. Dinan (eds), *Developments in the European Union 2*, London, Palgrave, pp. 275–95.

Holmes, P. (2005), 'British Trade Policy and the Doha Development Round', in M. Overhaus, H. W. Maull, S. Harnisch (eds), *European Trade Policy and the Doha Development Agenda: German Foreign Policy Dialogue: A Quarterly E-Newsletter on German Foreign Policy*, 15, February, www.deutsch-aussenpolitick.de, 7–12.

Hood, C. (1991), 'A Public Management for all Seasons?', *Public Administration*, 69, 3–19.

Hood, R. G. (2003), *The Death Penalty: A Worldwide Perspective*, Oxford, Oxford University Press.

Hooghe, L. (1991), *A Leap in the Dark: Nationalist Conflict and Federal Reform in Belgium*, Ithaca NY, Western Societies Program, Occasional Paper 27.

Hopkin, J. (1999), *Party Formation and Democratic Transition in Spain: The Creation and Collapse of the Union of the Democratic Centre*, London, Macmillan.

—— (2005), 'Spain: Proportional Representation with Majoritarian Outcomes', in M. Gallagher and P. Mitchell (eds), *The Politics of Electoral Systems*, Oxford, Oxford University Press, pp. 375–94.

Howorth, J. and Keeler, J. (2003), *Defending Europe: The EU, NATO and the Quest for Autonomy*, London, Palgrave.

Hull, R. (1993), 'Lobbying Brussels: A View from Within', in S. Mazey and J. Richardson (eds), *Lobbying in the European Community*, Oxford, Oxford University Press.

Hurrell, A. and Menon, A. (1994), 'Comparative Politics, International Relations and the Study of the EU', *West European Politics*, 19, 2, 386–402.

Hyde-Price, A. (1996), '"Of Dragons and Snakes": Contemporary German Security Policy', in G. Smith, W. Paterson and S. Padgett (eds), *Developments in German Politics 2*, Durham NC, Duke University Press, pp. 173–91.

Ignatieff, M. (ed.) (2005), *American Exceptionalism and Human Rights*, Princeton NJ, Princeton University Press.

Ikenberry, G. J. (ed.) (2002), *America Unrivalled: The Future of the Balance of Power*, Ithaca NY, Cornell University Press.

450

Inglehart, R. (1977), *The Silent Revolution*, Princeton NJ, Princeton University Press.

Ioakimidis, P. C. (2001), 'The Europeanisation of Greece: An Overall Assessment', in K. Featherstone and G. Kaziamas, *Europeanisation and the Southern Periphery*, London, Frank Cass, pp. 73–94.

Jacoby, W. (2004), *The Enlargement of the European Union and NATO: Ordering from the Menu in Central Europe*, Cambridge, Cambridge University Press.

James, O. (2003), *The Executive Agency Revolution in Whitehall*, Basingstoke, Palgrave.

Jensen, L. (2003), 'Aiming for Centrality: The Politico-administrative Strategies of the Danish Ministry of Finance', in J. Wanna, L. Jensen and J. de Vries, *Controlling Public Expenditure*, Cheltenham, Edward Elgar.

—— (2004), *Den Store Koordinator*, Copenhagen, Jurist og Økonomforlag.

Jessen, J. (2005), 'Fegefeuer des Marktes', *Die Zeit*, 30, 21 July, 33–4.

Johnson, M. (1998), *European Community Trade Policy and the Article 113 Committee*, London, Royal Institute of International Affairs.

—— with Rollo, J. (2001), 'Enlargement and the Making of Commercial Policy', SEI Working Paper 43, Falmer, Sussex European Institute.

Joppke, C. and Morawska, E. (2003), *Toward Assimilation and Citizenship: Immigrants in Liberal Nation-states*, Houndmills, Palgrave.

Judge, D. and Earnshaw, D. (2003), *The European Parliament*, Basingstoke, Palgrave-Macmillan.

Kagan, R. (2003), *Of Paradise and Power: America and Europe in the New World Order*, New York, Knopf.

Karlsson, G. (2000), *The History of Iceland*, Minneapolis MN, University of Minnesota

Kassim, H. and Menon, A. (2004), 'European Integration since the 1990s: Member States and the European Commission', ARENA Working Paper Series, 06/2004, Centre for European Studies, University of Oslo, Norway.

——, Menon, A., Peters, B. G. and Wright, V. (eds) (2001), *The National Coordination of EU Policy: The European Level*, Oxford, Oxford University Press.

——, Peters, B. G. and Wright, V. (eds) (2000), *The National Coordination of EU Policy: The Domestic Level*, Oxford, Oxford University Press.

Katz, R. and Mair, P. (1995), 'Changing Models of Party Organization and Party Democracy: The Emergence of the Cartel Party', *Party Politics*, 1, 1, 1–28.

Katzenstein, P. J. (2005), *A World of Regions: Asia and Europe in the American Imperium*, Ithaca NY, Cornell University Press.

Keating, M., Loughlin, J. and Deschouwer, K. (2003), *Culture, Institutions, and Economic Development: A Study of Eight European Regions*, Cheltenham and Northampton MA, Edward Elgar.

Keeler, J. T. S. (1996), 'Agricultural Power in the European Community: Explaining the Fate of CAP and GATT Negotiations', *Comparative Politics*, 28, 2, 127–49.

Kennedy, G. (1979), *Burden Sharing in NATO*, London, Duckworth.

Keleman, D. R. (2002), 'The Politics of "Eurocratic" Structure and the New European Agencies', *West European Politics*, 25, 93–118.

Kenworthy, L. (2004), *Egalitarian Capitalism; Jobs, Incomes, and Growth in Affluent Countries*, New York, Russell Sage Foundation.

Keohane, D. (2005), *The EU and Counter-terrorism*, London, CER.

Keohane, R. O., Moravcsik, M. and Slaughter, A.-M. (2000), 'Legalized Dispute Resolution: Interstate and Transnational,' *International Organization*, 54, 3, 457–88.

Kissinger, H. (1994), 'Dealing with de Gaulle', in R. O. Paxton and N. Wahl (eds), *De Gaulle and the United States: A Centennial Re-appraisal*, Oxford, Berg.

——and L. H. Summers (2004), *Renewing the Atlantic Partnership. Report of an Independent Task Force Sponsored by the Council on Foreign Relations*, Washington DC, Council on Foreign Relations, www.cfr.org/content/publications/attachments/Europe_TF.pdf

Kickert, W. J. M. (1997), 'Public Management in the United States and Europe', in W. J. M. Kickert (ed.), *Public Management and Administrative Reform in Europe and North America*, Cheltenham, Edward Elgar.

Kitschelt, H. (1988), 'Left-libertarian Parties: Explaining Innovation in Competitive Party Systems', *World Politics*, 40, 2, 194–234.

Klaus, V. (1994), *Ceska cesta*, Prague, Profile.

Kleinman, M. (2002), *A European Welfare State? European Union Social Policy in Context*, Basingstoke, Palgrave.

Kok, W. (2004), 'Facing the Challenge: The Lisbon Strategy for Growth and Employment', Report from the high-level group chaired by Wim Kok, http://ec.europa.eu/growthandjobs/pdf/2004-1866-EN-complet.pdf

Koopmans, R. (2003), 'Good Intentions Sometimes Make Bad Policy: A Comparison of Dutch and German Integration Policies', in K. A. Duffek and J. Kandel (eds), *The Challenge of Diversity: Facing Migration, Integration, and Multiculturalism*, Innsbruck, Studien Verlag.

—— (2005), 'Tradeoffs between Equality and Difference: The Failure of Dutch Multiculturalism in Cross-national Perspective', Paper presented at the Conference on 'Immigrant Political Incorporate', Radcliffe Institute for Advanced Study, Harvard University, 22–3 April.

Kreppel, A. (2002), *The European Parliament and Supranational Party System*, Cambridge, Cambridge University Press.

Kundera, M. (1984), 'The Tragedy of Central Europe', *New York Review of Books*, 26 April.

Kurzer, P. (1993), *Business and Banking*, Ithaca NY, Cornell University Press.

Langhammer, R. J. (2005), 'The EU Offer of Service Trade Liberalization in the Doha Round: Evidence of a Not-Yet-Perfect Customs Union', *JCMS*, 43, 2, 311–25.

Layton Henry, Z. (1994), 'Britain: The Would-be Zero-immigration Country', in W. Cornelius *et al.* (eds), *Controlling Immigration: A Global Perspective*, Stanford CA, Stanford University Press.

Lehmann, J.-P. (2005), 'France and the Doha Debacle', in M. Overhaus, H. W. Maull, S. Harnisch (eds), *European Trade Policy and the Doha Development Agenda: German Foreign Policy Dialogue: A Quarterly E-Newsletter on German Foreign Policy*, 15, February, www.deutsch-aussenpolitick.de, 13–19.

Leibfried, S. (2005), 'Social Policy: Left to the Judges and the Markets?', in H. Wallace, W. Wallace and M. A. Pollack (eds), *Policy-making in the European Union*, 5th edn, Oxford, Oxford University Press, pp. 243–78.

Lenschow, A. (2002), 'Greening the European Union: An Introduction', in A. Lenschow (ed.), *Environmental Policy Integration*, London, Earthscan, pp. 3–21.

Leonard, M. (2005a), *Why Europe will Run the 21st Century*, London, Fourth Estate.

Leonard, M. (2005b), *Can EU Diplomacy Stop Iran's Nuclear Programme?*, London, CER.

Levy, D., Pensky, M. and Torpey, J. (eds) (2005), *Old Europe, New Europe, Core Europe: Transatlantic Relations after the Iraq War*, London, Verso.

Lewis, J. (2003), 'Feminist Perspectives', in P. Alcock, A. Erskine and M. May (eds), *The Student's Companion to Social Policy*, 2nd edn, Oxford, Blackwell, pp. 107–12.

Lieber, R. J. (ed.) (2002), *Eagle Rules: Foreign Policy and American Primacy in the Twentieth Century*, New York, Prentice Hall.

Liefferink, D. and Andersen, M. (1998), 'Strategies of the "Green" Member States in EU Environmental Policy-making', *Journal of European Public Policy*, 5, 2, 254–70.

Lijphart, A. (1975), *The Politics of Accommodation: Pluralism and Democracy in the Netherlands*, 2nd edn, rev., Berkeley CA, University of California Press.

—— (1977), *Democracy in Plural Societies: A Comparative Exploration*, New Haven CT, Yale University Press.

—— (ed.) (1981), *Conflict and Coexistence in Belgium: The Dynamics of a Culturally Divided Society*, Berkeley CA, Institute of International Studies, University of California, Research Series 6.

—— (1984), *Democracies: Patterns of Majoritarian and Consensus Government*, New Haven CT, Yale University Press.

—— (1999), *Patterns of Democracy: Government Forms and Performance in Thirty-six Countries*, New Haven CT, Yale Press.

Lindberg, L. N. (1963), *The Political Dynamics of European Economic Integration*, Stanford CA, Stanford University Press.

Lindberg, T (ed.) (2005), *Beyond Paradise and Power: Europe, America and the Future of a Troubled Partnership*, London, Routledge.

Lindley-French, J. (2003), *Terms of Engagement: The Paradox of American Power and the Transatlantic Dilemma post-11 September*, Paris, EU-ISS.

Lindstrom, G. (2003), *Shift or Rift: Assessing US–EU Relations after Iraq*, Paris: EU-ISS, available at www.iss-eu.org/chaillot/bk2003.pdf

Linz, J. J. (1980), 'The New Spanish party System', in R. Rose (ed.), *Electoral Participation: A Comparative Analysis*, London, Sage.

Lipset, S. M. and Rokkan, S. (1967), *Party Systems and Voter Alignments*, New York, Free Press.

Long, T. (1998), 'The Environmental Lobby', in P. Lowe and S. Ward (eds), *British Environmental Policy and Europe*, London, Routledge, 105–18.

Lorwin, V. R. (1966), 'Belgium: Class and Language in National Politics', in R. A. Dahl (ed.), *Political Oppositions in Western Democracies*, New Haven CT, Yale University Press, pp. 147–87.

McCormick, J. (2001), *Environmental Policy in the European Union*, Basingstoke, Palgrave.

McEldowney, J. and McEldowney, S. (2001), *Environment Law and Regulation*, Harlow, Addison Wesley Longman.

McGowan, L. (2005), 'Europeanization Unleashed and Rebounding. Assessing the Modernisation of EU Restrictive Practices/Cartel Policy', *Journal of European Public Policy*, 12, 6, 986–1004.

McNamara, K. R. and Meunier, S. (2002), 'Between National Sovereignty and International Power: What External Voice for the Euro?', *International Affairs*, 78, 4, 849–68.

Majone, G. (2002a), 'The European Commission: The Limits of Centralization and the Perils of Parliamentarization', *Governance*, 15, 3, 375–92.

—— (2002b), 'The Precautionary Principle and Its Implications', *Journal of Common Market Studies*, 40, 1, 89–109.

—— (2005), *Dilemmas of European Integration*, Oxford, Oxford University Press.

Majone, J. M. (1998), 'Portugal: Party System Installation and Consolidation', in D. Broughton and M. Donovan (eds), *Changing Party Systems in Western Europe*, London, Cassell, pp. 232–54.

Malová, D. and Haughton T. (2002), 'Making Institutions in Central and Eastern Europe, and the Impact of Europe', *West European Politics*, 25, 2, 101–20.

Malová, D. and Haughton, T. (2006), 'Challenge from the Pace-setting Periphery: The Causes and Consequences of Slovakia's Stance on Further European Integration', in W. Sadurski (ed.), *Après Enlargement: Taking Stock of the Immediate Legal and Political Responses to the Accession of Central*

452

*and Eastern European States to the EU*, Florence, Robert Schuman Center, pp. 323–37.

Malová, D. and Ilonszki, G. (2006, forthcoming), 'Prime Ministers', in J. Blondel, F. Muller-Rommel and D. Malova, *Governing New European Democracies*, Basingstoke, Palgrave Macmillan.

Malová, D. and Rybář, M. (2003), 'The European Union's Policies towards Slovakia: The Carrots and Sticks of Political Conditionality', in J. Rupnik and J. Zielonka (eds), *The Road to the European Union volume 1: The Czech and Slovak Republics*, Manchester, Manchester University Press, pp. 98–112.

Mann, J. (2004), *Rise of the Vulcans: The History of Bush's War Cabinet*, New York, Viking-Penguin.

Marsh, D., Richards, D. and Smith, M. J. (2001), *Changing Patterns of Governance in the United Kingdom: Changing Whitehall*, Basingstoke, Palgrave.

Marshall, T. H. (1965), *Class, Citizenship, and Social Development*, New York, Anchor/Doubleday.

Massot, J. (1997), *Alternance et cohabitation sous la Ve Republique*, Paris, La documentation française.

Mattli, W. and Slaughter, A. (1998), 'Revisiting the European Court of Justice', *International Organization*, 52, 177–209.

Maurer, A. (2003), 'The Legislative Powers and Impact of the European Parliament', *Journal of Common Market Studies*, 41, 2, 227–47.

Maurer, L. (1999), 'Parliamentary Influence in a New Democracy: The Spanish Congress', *Journal of Legislative Studies*, 5, 2, 24–45.

Mavratsas, C. (1997), 'The Ideological Contest between Greek Cypriot Nationalism and Cypriotism 1974–1995', *Ethnic and Racial Studies*, 20, 4, 718–37.

May, M. (2003), 'The Role of Comparative Study', in P. Alcock, A. Erskine and M. May (eds), *The Student's Companion to Social Policy*, 2nd edn, Oxford, Blackwell, pp. 17–24.

Mearsheimer, J. (2001), *The Tragedy of Great Power Politics*, New York, Norton.

—— and Walt, S. (2006), 'The Israel Lobby', *London Review of Books*, 28, 6, 23 March, accessed at www.lrb.co.uk/v28/n06/mear01_.html

Menon, A. (2004), 'From Crisis to Catharsis: ESDP after Iraq', *International Affairs*, 80, 4, July.

—— (2007), 'The Limits of Comparative Politics: International Relations in the European Union', in A. Menon and M. Schain (eds), *Comparative Federalism: The United States and European Union*, Oxford, Oxford University Press.

—— and Weatherill, S. (2006), 'Democratic Politics in a Globalising World: Supranationalism and Legitimacy in the European Union', unpublished mimeo.

Metcalf, L. K. (2000), 'Measuring Presidential Power', *Comparative Political Studies*, 33, 660–85.

Meunier, S. (2005), *Trading Voices: The European Union in International Commercial Negotiations*, Princeton NJ, Princeton University Press.

—— and Nicolaïdis, K. (2006), 'The European Union as a Conflicted Trade Power', *Journal of European Public Policy*, 13, 6, 906–205.

Meyers, M. K. and Vorsanger, S. (2003), 'Street-level Bureaucrats and the Implementation of Public Policy', in B. G. Peters and J. Pierre (eds), *Handbook of Public Administration*, London, Sage.

Montero, J. R. (1994), 'Sobre las preferencias electorales en España: fragmentación y polarización (1977–93)', in P. del Castillo (ed.), *Comportamiento político y electoral*, Madrid, Centro de Investigaciones Sociológicas, pp. 51–124.

—— (1998), 'Stabilizing the Democratic Order: Electoral Behaviour in Spain', *West European Politics*, 21, 4, 53–79.

——, Llera, F. and Torcal, M. (1992), 'Sistemas electorales en España: una recapitulación', *Revista Española de Investigaciones Sociológicas*, 58, 7–56.

Moran, M. (2001), 'Governing European Corporate Life', in G. Thompson (ed.), *Governing the European Economy*, Sage, London.

Moravcsik, A. (2000), 'The Origins of Human Rights Regimes', *International Organization*, 54, 217–52.

—— (2002), 'Reassessing Legitimacy in the European Union', *Journal of Common Market Studies*, 4, 4, 603–24.

Morlino, L. (1995), 'Political Parties and Democratic Consolidation in Southern Europe', in R. Gunther, N. Diamandouros and H.-J. Puhle (eds), *The Politics of Democratic Consolidation: Southern Europe in Comparative Perspective*, Baltimore MD, Johns Hopkins University Press, pp. 315–88.

Mosher, J. S. and Trubek, D. M. (2003), 'Alternative Approaches to Governance In the EU: EU Social Policy and the European Employment Strategy', *Journal of Common Market Studies*, 41, 63–8.

Mowle, T. (2004), *Allies at Odds: The United States and the European Union*, London, Palgrave.

Mulgan, R. (2000), 'Accountability: An Ever Expanding Concept', *Public Administration*, 78, 555–74.

Myles, G. (ed.) (1992), *EEC Brief*, Lisbon, Locksley Press.

Newell, P. and Grant, W. (2000), 'Environmental NGOs and EU Environmental Law', in H. Somsen (ed.), *The Yearbook of European Environmental Law*, Oxford, Oxford University Press, pp. 225–52.

Nicol, D. (2001), *EC Membership and the Judicialization of British Politics*, Oxford, Oxford University Press.

NTA (1995), *The New Transatlantic Agenda, December 1995*, accessed at www.eu.int/comm/external_relations/us/new_transatlantic_agenda/text.htm

Nousiainen, J. (1996), 'Finland: Operational Cabinet Autonomy in a Party Centered System', in J. Blondel and M. Cotta (eds), *Party and Government*, Basingstoke, Macmillan.

O'Brian, R. (1992), *Global Financial Integration: The End of Geography*, New York, Council on Foreign Relations.

REFERENCES

O'Gorman, F. (2004), 'The European Union, the United States and the Middle East: A Troubled Trio?', in P. G. Xuereb (ed.), *The European Union and the Mediterranean: The Mediterranean's European Challenge, volume 5*, Malta, EDRC.

Olsen, J. P. (1997), 'European Challenges to the Nation State', in B. Steuenenberg and F. van Vught (eds), *Political Institutions and Public Policy*, Kluwer.

Padgett, S. (2003), 'Political Economy: The German Model under Stress', in S. Padgett, W. Paterson and G. Smith (eds), *Developments in German Politics 3*, Houndmills, Palgrave Macmillan, pp. 121–42.

Pagano, M. and Von Thadden, E.-L. (2004), 'The European Bond Markets under EMU', *Oxford Review of Economic Policy*, 20, 4, 532–54.

Page, E. C. and Wouters, L. (1994), 'Bureaucratic Politics and Political Leadership in Brussels', *Public Administration*, 72, 445–59.

Parsons, C. (2002), 'Showing Ideas as Causes: The Origins of the European Union', *International Organization*, 56, 1, 47–84.

Paterson, W. and Sloam, J. (2005), 'Learning from the West: Policy Transfer and Political Parties', *Journal of Communist Studies and Transition Politics*, 21, 1, 33–47.

Patten, C. (2006), *Cousins and Strangers: America, Britain and Europe in the New Century*, New York, Holt.

Pennings, P., Keman, H. and Kleinnijenhuis (1999), *Doing Research in Political Science: An Introduction to Comparative Methods and Statistics*, London, Sage.

Pereira, J. P. (1988), 'A Case of Orthodoxy: The Communist Party of Portugal', in M. Waller and M. Fennema (eds), *Communist Parties in Western Europe: Decline or Adaptation?*, Oxford, Blackwell, pp. 86–95.

Perkovich, G. (2005), *Changing Iran's Nuclear Interests*, Carnegie Endowment for International Peace, Policy Outlook.

Peters, B. G. (1997), 'Separation of Powers in Parliamentary Systems', in K. Von Mettenheim (ed.), *Presidential Institutions and Democratic Politics*, Baltimore MD, Johns Hopkins University Press.

——(2006), *The Politics of Bureaucracy*, 6th edn, London, Longman.

——, Rhodes, R. A. W. and Wright, V. (2000), *Administering the Summit*, London, Macmillan.

Peterson, J. and Bomberg, E. (1999), *Decision-making in the European Union*, Basingstoke, Macmillan.

——and Pollack, M. (eds) (2003), *Europe, America, Bush: Transatlantic Relations in the Twenty-first Century*, London, Routledge.

Pew Research Center (2004), *A Year after Iraq: Mistrust of America in Europe Ever Higher, Muslim Anger Persists*, http://people-press.org/reports/display.php3?ReportID=206

Picq, J. (1995), *L'État en France. Servir une nation ouverte au monde*, Paris, La Documentation française.

Pierre, J. (2003), 'Agencies in Sweden: Report from Utopis', in C. Pollitt and C. Talbot (eds), *Unbundled Government*, London, Routledge.

Pierson, P. (1996), 'The Path to European Integration: A Historical Institutionalist Analysis', *Comparative Political Analysis*, 29, 2, April, 123–63.

Pollack, M.A. (1996), 'The New Institutionalism and EC Governance: The Promise and Limits of Institutional Analysis', *Governance*, 9, 4, 429–58.

——(2003), *The Engines of European Integration*, Oxford, Oxford University Press.

Pollitt, C., Talbot, C., Caulfield, J. and Smullen, A. (2004), *Agencies: How Governments Do Things Through Semi-autonomous Agencies*, Basingstoke, Macmillan.

Pond, E. (2004), *Friendly Fire: The Near Death of the Transatlantic Alliance*, Washington DC, Brookings.

Posen, B. (2004), 'ESDP and the Structure of World Power', *The International Spectator*, 39, 1.

Poulton, H. (1997), *Top Hat, Grey Wolf and Crescent*, London, Hurst & Co.

Preston, P. (1986), *The Triumph of Democracy in Spain*, London, Methuen.

Pridham, G. (2002), 'EU Enlargement and Consolidating Democracy in Post-communist States—Formality and Reality', *Journal of Common Market Studies*, 40, 3, 953–73.

Prior, P. M. and Sykes, R. (2001), 'Globalization and the European Welfare States: Evaluating the Theories and Evidence', in R. Sykes, B. Palier and P. M. Prior (eds), *Globalization and European Welfare States: Challenges and Change*, Basingstoke, Palgrave, pp. 195–210.

Provine, D. M. (1997), 'Courts in the Political Process in France', in H. Jacob *et al.*, *Courts, Law and Politics in Comparative Perspective*, New Haven CT, Yale University Press, pp. 177–248.

Prützel-Thomas, M. (1993), 'The Abortion Issue and the Federal Constitutional Court', *German Politics*, 2, 467–84.

Quinlan, J. (2003), *Drifting Apart or Growing Together? The Primacy of the Transatlantic Economy*, Washington DC, Center for Transatlantic Relations.

Ramiro, L. (2000), 'Entre coalición y partido: la evolución del modelo organizativo de Izquierda Unida', *Revista Española de ciencia política*, 1, 2, 237–68.

Reichard, C. (1994), *Umdenken im Rathaus: Neue Steuerungsmodelle in der deutschen Kommunalverwaltung*, Berlin, Sigma.

Reid, T. R. (2004), *The United States of Europe: The New Superpower and the End of American Supremacy*, New York, Penguin.

Rifkin, J. (2004), *The European Dream: How Europe's Vision of the Future is Quietly Eclipsing the American Dream*, New York, Penguin.

Rittberger, B. (2005), *Building Europe's Parliament: Democratic Representation Beyond the Nation State*, Oxford, Oxford University Press.

454

Rokkan, S. (1967), 'Votes Count but Resources Decide', in R. A. Dahl (ed.), *Political Oppositions in Western Democracies*, New Haven CT, Yale University Press.

Rose, R. (1974), *The Problem of Party Government*, London, Macmillan.

Russett, B. and Oneal, J. (2001), *Triangulating Peace: Democracy, Interdependence and International* Organizations, New York, Norton.

Rustow, D. (1955), *The Politics of Compromise: A Study of Parties and Cabinet Government in Sweden*, Princeton NJ, Princeton University Press.

Sands, P. (ed.) (2003), *From Nuremberg to The Hague: The Future of International Criminal Justice*, Cambridge, Cambridge University Press.

Sanford, G. (2002), *Democratic Government in Poland: Constitutional Politics since 1989*, Basingtoke, Palgrave Macmillan.

Sapir, A., Aghion, P., Bertola, G., Hellwih, M., Pisani-Ferry, D., Rozali, J., Vinals, J. and Wallace, H. (2003), *An Agenda for a Growing Europe: Making the EU System Deliver*, President of the European Commission, Brussels, July.

Sartori, G. (1971), 'Concept Misformation in Comparative Politics', *American Political Science Review*, 64, 1033–53.

—— (1976), *Parties and Party Systems*, Cambridge, Cambridge University Press.

Sausman, C. and Locke, C. (2004), 'The United Kingdom', in B. G. Peters and J. Pierre (eds), *Politicization of the Civil Service in Comparative Perspective*, London, Routledge.

Sbragia, A. M. (2000), 'Environmental Policy', in H. Wallace and W. Wallace (eds), *Policy-making in the European Union*, 4th edn, Oxford, Oxford University Press, pp. 293–316.

Scarrow, S. (2000), 'Parties without Members? Party Organization in a Changing Electoral Environment', in R. Dalton and M. Wattenberg (eds), *Parties without Partisans*, Oxford, Oxford University Press, pp. 79–101.

Scharpf, F.W. (2002), *Governing in Europe: Effective and Democratic?*, Oxford, Oxford University Press.

Schmitter, P. C. (2000), *How to Democratize the European Union … And Why Bother?*, Lanham MD, Rowman & Littlefield.

Schout, J. A. and Jordan, A. J. (2005), 'Coordinated European Governance: Self organising or Centrally Steered?', *Public Administration*, 83, 1, 201–20.

Schröder, G. (2005), 'Auf die Kleinen ist Verlass', *Die Zeit*, 43, 20 October, 5.

Schwartz, H. (2000), *The Struggle for Constitutional Justice in Post-communist Europe*, Chicago IL, University of Chicago Press.

Scully, R. (2005), *Becoming Europeans? Attitudes, Roles and Socialization in the European Parliament*, Oxford, Oxford University Press.

Shapiro, M. (1981), *Courts: A Comparative and Political Analysis*, Chicago IL, University of Chicago Press.

Siaroff, A. (2003), 'Varieties of Parliamentarianism in Advanced Industrial Democracies', *International Political Science Review*, 24, 445–64.

Slaughter, A. (2004), *A New World Order*, Princeton NJ, Princeton University Press.

Sloan, S. R. (1999), *The US and Transatlantic Burdensharing*, Paris, IFRI-Notes 11.

—— (2005a), 'How Does Religion Affect Relations Between America and Europe', *EuroFuture*, winter.

—— (2005b), *NATO, the European Union and the Atlantic Community*, 2nd edn, Lanham MD, Rowman & Littlefield.

Smith, D. (2003), 'Minority Rights, Multiculturalism and EU Enlargement: the Case of Estonia', *Journal on Ethnopolitics and Minority Issues in Europe*, 1, posted at www.ecmi.de/jemie/download/Focus1-2003_Smith.pdf

Smith, G. (1989), 'Core Persistence: System Change and the "People's Party"', *West European Politics*, 12, 4, 157–68.

Smith, K. E. (2005), 'Engagement and Conditionality: Incompatible or Mutually Reinforcing?', in R. Youngs (ed.), *Global Europe Report 2: New Terms of Engagement*, London, Foreign Policy Centre, pp. 23–9.

Sotiropoulos, D. A (1996), *Populism and Bureaucracy: The Case of Greece under PASOK*, London, University of Notre Dame Press.

Sousa, L. de (2004), 'Political Corruption and Party Financing in Portugal', mimeo, Lisbon, ISCTE.

Spence, D. and Stevens, A. (2006), 'Staff and Personnel Policy in the Commission', in D. Spence and G. Edwards (eds), *The European Commission*, 3rd edn, London, John Harper.

St Clair Bradley, K. (2002), 'The European Court of Justice', in J. Peterson and M. Shackleton (eds), *The Institutions of the European Union*, Oxford, Oxford University Press.

Stone, A. (1992), *The Birth of Judicial Politics in France*, New York, Oxford University Press.

Stone Sweet, A. (1998), 'Constitutional Dialogues in the European Community', in A.-M. Slaughter, A. Stone Sweet and J. H. H. Weiler (eds), *The European Court and National Courts—Doctrine and Jurisprudence*, Oxford, Hart Publishing, pp. 305–30.

—— (2000), *Governing with Judges*, New York, Oxford University Press.

—— and Brunell, T. (1998), 'Constructing a Supranational Constitution', *American Political Science Review*, 92, 63–81.

Strom, K. (1990), *Minority Government and Majority Rule*, Cambridge, Cambridge University Press.

Sturm, R. (1996), 'The German Cartel in a Hostile Environment', in G. B. Doern and S. Wilks (eds), *Comparative Competition Policy: National Institutions in a Global Market*, Oxford, Clarendon Press, pp. 185–224.

Sykes, R. (2003), 'Social Policy and Globalization', in P. Alcock, A. Erskine and M. May (eds), *The Student's Companion to Social Policy*, 2nd edn, Oxford, Blackwell, pp. 160–6.

Szczerbiak, A. (2002), 'Dealing with the Communist Past or the Politics of the Present? Lustration in Post-communist Poland', *Europe–Asia Studies*, 54, 4, 553–72.

—— (2003), 'Old and New Divisions in Polish Politics: Polish Parties' Electoral Strategies and Bases of Support', *Europe–Asia Studies*, 55, 5, 729–46.

Taggart, P. and Szczerbiak, A. (eds) (2007), *Opposing Europe? The Comparative Party Politics of Euroscepticism, volumes 1 and 2*, Oxford, Oxford University Press.

Tawney, R. H. (1920), *The Acquisitive Society*, New York, Harcourt, Brace & Howe.

Thiel, S. van (2001), *Quangos: Trends, Causes and Consequences*, Aldershot, Ashgate.

Titmuss, R. M. (1974), *Social Policy: An Introduction*, ed. by B. Abel-Smith and K. Titmuss, London, George Allen & Unwin.

Tsoukalis, L. (1997), *The New European Economy Revisited*, Oxford, Oxford University Press.

Vachudova, M. (2005), *Europe Undivided: Democracy, Leverage, and Integration after Communism*, Oxford, Oxford University Press.

Verhoest, K., Verschuere, B., Peters, B. G. and Bouckaert, G. (2004), 'Controlling Autonomous Public Organizations as an Indicator of New Public Management', *Management International*, 9, 25–36.

Victor, D. (2000), *The Collapse of the Kyoto Protocol and the Struggle to Slow Global Warming*, Princeton NJ, Princeton University Press.

Villepin, D. de (2003), *Un Autre Monde*, Paris, L'Herne.

Visser, J. and Hemerijck, A. (1997), *A Dutch Miracle: Job Growth, Welfare Reform, and Corporatism in the Netherlands*, Amsterdam, Amsterdam University Press.

VROM (2004), Press release from the Dutch Ministry of Spatial Planning, Housing and the Environment, www2.vrom.nl/pagina.html?id=9190

Vogel, D. (2003), 'The Hare and the Tortoise Revisited: The New Politics of Consumer and Environmental Regulation in Europe', *British Journal of Political Science*, 33.

Wallace, H. (1991), 'Making Multilateral Negotiations Work', in W. Wallace (ed.), *The Dynamics of European Integration*, London, Royal Institute of International Affairs and Routledge & Kegan Paul.

—— (2005), 'An Institutional Anatomy and Five Policy Modes', in H. Wallace, W. Wallace and M. A. Pollack (eds), *Policy-making in the European Union*, 5th edn, Oxford, Oxford University Press, pp. 49–90.

Walt, S. (2005), *Taming American Power: The Global Response to US Primacy*, New York, Norton.

Weale, A. (1996), 'Environmental Rules and Rule-making in the European Union', *European Journal of Public Policy*, 3, 4, 594–611.

Webster, R. (2002), 'Greening Europe Together: The Collaborative Strategies of the European Environmental NGOs',
paper presented at the annual conference of the Political Studies Association, Aberdeen.

Weiler, J. H. H. with Haltern, U. R. and Mayer, F. C. (1995), 'European Democracy and Its Critique', *West European Politics*, 18, 3, 24–33.

Westlake, M. and Galloway, D. (2004), *The European Council*, 3rd edn, London, John Harper.

Whish, R. (2003), *Competition Law*, London, Butterworths.

Whitman, R. (1998), *From Civilian Power to Superpower: The International Identity of the European Union*, London, Macmillan.

Wilensky, H. and Lebeaux, C. (1958), *Industrial Society and Welfare*, New York, Free Press.

Wilks, S. (1996), 'The Prolonged Reform of United Kingdom Competition Policy', in G. B. Doern and S. Wilks (eds), *Comparative Competition Policy: National Institutions in a Global Market*, Oxford, Clarendon Press, pp. 139–84.

—— (1999), *In the Public Interest: Competition Policy and the Monopolies and Mergers Commission*, Manchester, Manchester University Press.

Williams, S. (1991), 'Sovereignty and Accountability in the European Community', in R. O. Keohane and S. Hoffman (eds), *The New European Community: Decisionmaking and Institutional Change*, Boulder CO, Westview Press.

Wincott, D. (2003), 'Beyond Social Regulation? New Instruments and/or a New Agenda for Social Policy at Lisbon', *Public Administration*, 81, 3, 533–53.

Winter, L. de, Frognier, A. P. and Rihoux, B. (1996), 'Belgium: Still the Age of Party Government', in J. Blondel and M. Cotta (eds), *Party and Government*, Basingstoke, Macmillan, pp. 153–79.

Winters, L. A. (2001), 'European Union Trade Policy: Actually or Just Nominally Liberal?', in H. Wallace (ed.), *Interlocking Dimensions of European Integration*, London, Palgrave, pp. 25–44.

Witte, E. and van Velthoven, H. (1999), *Language and Politics: The Belgian Case Study in Historical Perspective*, Brussels, VUB University Press.

Witte, E., Craeybeckx, J. and Meynen, A. (2000), *Political History of Belgium from 1830 onwards*, trans. R. Casert, Antwerp, Standarard Uitgeverij; Brussels, VUB University Press.

Wolczuk, K. and Wolzcuk, R. (2002), *Poland and Ukraine: A Strategic Partnership in a Changing Europe?*, London, Royal Institute of International Affairs.

Wolinetz, S. B. (2001), 'Modell Nederland: Social Partnership and Competitive Corporatism in the Netherlands', in N. Bermeo (ed.), *Unemployment in the New Europe*, Cambridge, Cambridge University Press, pp. 245–67.

Woolcock, S. (2005a), 'European Union Trade Policy: Domestic Institutions and Systemic Factors,' in D. Kelly and W. Grant (eds), *The Politics of International Trade in the Twenty-first Century*, London, Palgrave, pp. 234–51.

456

Woolcock, S. (2005b), 'Trade Policy: From Uruguay to Doha and Beyond', in H. Wallace, W. Wallace and M. Pollack (eds), *Policy-making in the European Union*, 5th edn, Oxford, Oxford University Press, pp. 377–99.

World Bank (2001), *World Development Report 2000/2001*, Washington, World Bank.

World Trade Organization (2002), *Trade Policy Review: European Union*, WT/TPR/S/102, 26 June, Geneva, World Trade Organization.

Wright, V. and Page, E. C. (1999), *Bureaucratic Elites in Western European Countries*, Oxford, Oxford University Press.

Young, A. R. (2002), *Extending European Cooperation: The European Union and the 'New' International Trade Agenda*, Manchester, Manchester University Press.

—— (2004), 'The Incidental Fortress: The Single European Market and World Trade', *Journal of Common Market Studies*, 42, 2, 393–414.

—— (2005), 'The Single European Market: A New Approach to Policy', in H. Wallace, W. Wallace and M. A. Pollack (eds), *Policy-making in the European Union*, 5th edn, Oxford, Oxford University Press, pp. 93–112.

——, Holmes, P. and Rollo, J. (2000), 'The EU's Multilateral Trade Agenda after Seattle', in I. Falautano and P. Guerrieri (eds), *Beyond Seattle: A New Strategic Approach in the WTO 2000*, IAI Quaderni No. 11, Istituto Affari Internazionali.

Young, S. (2000), 'New Labour and the Environment', in D. Coates and P. Lawler (eds), *New Labour in Power*, Manchester, Manchester University Press, pp. 149–68.

Youngs, R. (2001), *The European Union and the Promotion of Democracy*, Oxford, Oxford University Press.

—— (2004), 'Normative Dynamics and Strategic Interests in the EU's External Identity', *Journal of Common Market Studies*, 42, 2, 415–35.

Zaborowski, M. (2006), *Friends Again? EU–US Relations after the Crisis*, Paris, EU-ISS, available at www.iss-eu.org/books/transat06.pdf

Zürn, M. and Joerges, C. (eds) (2005), *Law and Governance in Postnational Europe*, Cambridge, Cambridge University Press.

# Index